The image on the reverse side is based on a DeMille Studios publicity photo of Sally Rand, circa 1926.

The four dust jacket images of Sally taken at the height of her career have been modified and colorized by the author.

BAREFOOT TO THE CHIN

THE FANTASTIC LIFE OF
SALLY RAND

JIM LOWE

In collaboration with Bonnie Egan

Book and jacket design by Jim and Sharon Lowe

Library of Congress Cataloging-in-Publication Data
Names: Lowe, James R., author
Title: Barefoot to the Chin: The Fantastic Life of Sally Rand
Description: Tallahassee: Sentry Press.
Includes bibliographical references and index.
Identifiers: LCCN 2018942651 ISBN 978-1-889574-45-5 (hardback)
Subjects: Rand, Sally 1904-1979—biography—20th century—performing artists
LC record available at http://lccn.loc.gov/2018942651

Manufactured in the United States of America

First Edition

For so very much,
This is for my grandfather,

James Hollis Robson

Author's Note

A word about book design. Many biographies include "notes" — small-print information that supplements, or indicates the source of, material in the main text. There was a time when such notes were commonly placed at the bottom of the page or the end of a chapter, their existence indicated by a marker or superscript number at an appropriate place in the text. Apparently, book designers found this format to be unattractive, a distraction to the reader. And so a new style emerged. Superscript numbers or markers were generally retained in the text, but the notes themselves were moved to the back of the book.

More recently, book designers have also found this approach to be indecorous. Nowadays, many if not most nonfiction authors (publishers?) prefer not only to place notes at the back of the book but also to remove all indicators from the text, thereby leaving no clue that notes even exist. The reader is left to rely upon some mysterious ability to intuit that, somewhere in the book's recesses, delightful information may silently lie in waiting.

This book is intended for those who wish to accompany Sally Rand on her life journey, immersing themselves in the evolving culture within which it took place. For this reason, I have chosen to position the quaint and curious tidbits — those items that readers like me can't get enough of — in a place where they can hardly be overlooked. Actual "source notes" are relegated to the back of the book, where they are referenced to relevant page numbers.

Also, a word about inflation. This book contains numerous references to incomes, ticket prices, lawsuit settlements, and the like. In some cases, I have clarified what these sums would be if valued in current dollars, but, rather than burden the reader with too many such references, I offer the following approximations: Using the Consumer Price Index and comparing July values, each 1933 dollar was worth about $18.70 in 2017 (making Sally's initial salary at the Chicago World's Fair of $90 per week equal to about $1,680 a week). A 1945 dollar would now be worth $13.50; a 1955 dollar – $9.00; a 1965 dollar – $7.75; and a 1975 dollar – $4.50.

CONTENTS

PART THREE: THE WAY WE WERE

PART FOUR: FROM HERE TO ETERNITY

Introduction

The word fame, to me, has always borne the connotation
of a kind of immortality, that is, having accomplished
something, or done something, or been something that
people will remember always. I don't feel that is true
with me. I don't believe that the little dance I have done
or my appearances in the theater have made a sufficient
contribution to the art of the world to immortalize me.

~ Sally Rand, December 1951

Sally Rand was once the most talked about woman in America. Now,
nearly 40 years after her passing, the telling of her story, in all its warts
and wonders, is long overdue. Remembered primarily as a "fan dancer,"
there was oh so much more to this extraordinary woman. She plowed her
way through life with an exuberance and determination matched by few.
During her later years, Sally earnestly approached the task of writing her
memoirs but, in the end, she never found the time. In 1969, she expressed
her views on the subject of celebrity autobiographies:

I can't help but feel that the average person who writes an
autobiography or a memoir is essentially a pompous son of a bitch.
For instance, I give you that Irish Catholic, Pat O'Brien, and that
dull little tome of Bette Davis. Mind you, I adore Bette; I have a
great admiration and respect for her ability and courage and I am
positively prostrate at her talent, but, oh, God, her book is dull and
Pat O'Brien's is positively vomity.

It is this type of pomposity that I will avoid if I ever write the
goddamn book!

Sally never did write that "goddamn book" and so it has fallen to others to
take up the task. We can only hope that the remarkable subject of this book
would have found this effort to be without pomposity and worthy of her
higher expectations.

Whatever else she was, Sally Rand was a talented writer. Although a manuscript of her memoirs was long rumored to exist, only a fragment was ever

actually written. Even so, a fair portion of this volume consists of Sally's own words. In a draft of her intended autobiography, she wrote:

> When I was about 13 years old … in school we had to write an essay about ourselves — really a 250 word "autobiography." How heartbroken I was. I couldn't say I had been born in a raging storm or in a ship in the middle of the Atlantic or even that my birth occurred in the middle of the night…. As I recall, most of the 250 words were devoted to the dramatic exploits of my dog and two kittens and a frog that I happened to own at the time.

> The reason I find myself recalling this long-ago incident is all too obvious to me: once again, I am in the same darn situation — I still haven't a heart-rending life story to tell.
> - I can't enthrall you with the exciting details of how I licked the dope habit….
> - I can't hold you glued to this book as I reveal the horrors I went through when I kicked that terrifying curse of alcohol….
> - I haven't fought my way back from a mental mashup….
> - I haven't been deceived by an army of men who have married me for my fame and/or fortune….
> - I haven't been betrayed by managers or agents who cheated me out of five million dollars….

> So once again I find myself just a little bit envious of those who have a "story" to tell. Between thirteen and sixty-two, it stands to reason that I should have improved my autobiographical possibilities. Not so…. But my charming publishers have asked me to write this book nevertheless….

Truth be told, Sally's was a far more interesting life than she modestly acknowledged. And, like each of us, she was inextricably bound to the fortunes and failures of her family, her culture, and her gender. The fascinating details of her life can be fully understood only in the context of her surroundings and the challenges of her time. So, in the course of these pages, we shall venture down a number of compelling byways and encounter an assortment of characters, both famous and obscure, whose own journeys enhanced, diminished, informed, or otherwise intersected with the odyssey of our subject. As the great naturalist John Muir once so elegantly observed: "When we try to pick out anything by itself we find that it is bound fast, by a thousand invisible cords that cannot be broken, to everything in the universe."

Prologue

> I had a daddy didn't I? He wasn't perfect and he
> certainly wasn't the one I'd dreamed he would have
> been, but I had one all the same. And I'd love him as
> much as I'd hated him, hadn't I? All that distance, all
> that time wasted, but the fact that he'd inspired such
> passion in me meant something in itself.
> ~ Melodie Ramone, *After Forever Ends* (2013)

The most horrible tragedy it has ever been our lot to chronicle occurred at the little village of Elkton in the south part of the county last Saturday night." So began a vivid account published on October 16, 1890, in the Hermitage, Missouri, weekly newspaper *The Index*, under the headline: "THOS. MASHBURN SHOT AND INSTANTLY KILLED BY WM. BECK."

Who was Thomas Mashburn? Or, more to the point, who was this dangerous killer William Beck? Sixteen years earlier, on Valentine's Day, February 14, 1874, in Fayette County, Illinois, William Francis Beck, grandson of George Washington Beck and son of William Henry Harrison Beck, had entered the world. At the age of six, his family had moved to Missouri. Ten years later, his life took a sudden and dramatic turn.

One day William Francis Beck would participate in the Spanish-American War with the "Rough Riders" at San Juan Hill and charge into battle with future President Theodore Roosevelt. One day, William F. Beck would become a decorated veteran of the First World War and go on to a career with the United States Post Office Department. But on this October day in 1890, standing his ground in Elkton, Missouri, the 16-year-old Will Beck would shoot and kill the town bully in the middle of the road.

The quick-tempered young William was no stranger to violence, as evidenced by his account of a previous run-in with schoolmate Joe Kelly:

> Joe and I were natural antagonists…. Once at school, Joe stole my
> McGuffey Blue Back speller and wrote his name all through it. I
> found it in his desk and took it away from him. He declared he
> would get me on the last day of school…. The last day came …

when here came Joe Kelly carrying a big rock in his hand, and declaring his intention to bust my head. He got one swing on the side of my face with that rock when I got hold of him, threw him down in the snow, took away the rock and started in to beat him to death. I remember ... [everyone] began to yell "A fight, a fight, everybody come and see the fight!"

By that time there was blood all over the snow (Joe Kelly's blood). Meanwhile some of the oldsters came running; and seeing all that blood on the snow thought there was a murder being done. My grandfather got hold of me and pulled me off Kelly, and Kelly's big brother, Bill, helped Joe up off the ground and started him off home. Ever after that whenever Joe saw me come to Elkton he would sneak off home and get a gun or a knife or a club and come back up to the store.

On August 5, 1947, recalling his shooting of the town bully, Colonel Beck set forth the details of the event in a letter to Mrs. Rosa Steward, an old school friend:

Dear Friend and Former Schoolmate:

... I [recently] read of the death of Mrs. Minnie Pitts; and that really unrolled a great volume of memories of infinite interest to me of which you doubtless still hold a vivid recollection....

Minnie married young Tom Mashburn, whom I shot and killed in the middle of the road not far from the corner of Andy Steward's drugstore in Elkton.

It all came out of a clear sky!

It was late Saturday afternoon [October 11, 1890].... Father told me to hitch up the team and go to the Post Office for the mail.... I took my grandfather's old family revolver he'd bought in Ft. Worth in the late seventies. My friend Ernie Gardner was going hunting with me that evening, so ... I met Ernie coming out of church, [and] we both started for the post office, intending to go from there directly to the hunting grounds....

Just before Ernie and I reached the post office, we were stopped by three men standing in the middle of the road, drinking out of a bottle. As Ernie and I approached ... one of them spoke up and said, "Where the hell you think you are going?" I replied that I was going to the post office. He said something like, "How the hell do you know you are?" and, grabbing me by one arm and Ernie by the other, he smashed our heads together like a couple of gourds. With a boy held in each hand, he spun us around at arm's length, threw us full force into the ditch, then picked Ernie up and threw him on top of me. He turned to his friends and said, "By God, look what a man can do." Bill Kimball said, "Tommy, you ought not to do that to a couple of kids." That was the first time I knew it was Mashburn. Tommy replied: "To hell with them and you, too! Let kids stay in kids' places...."

As I heard him say these words ... I passed from the mental state of a peaceable, inoffensive boy to one of killing fury. No person ever saw the day, before that or since, that he could manhandle me like that and get away with it. Mashburn had his sentence from that moment; and if I had not gotten him then it would have been later....

Ernie was still lying on the ground. Sick and dizzy, I staggered to my feet, head spinning and seeing stars. I told [Tom], "... don't try to do that to me again!" His answer, as he lunged at me, was, "What in hell will you do about it?" as he came charging in. My head was swimming, I kept blacking out, my eyes wouldn't focus, I could only see him dimly. Just as he got hold of me, I went backwards, he on top of me, [and] the gun went off. I had shot him! He died so quickly I had to crawl out from under him.

Mashburn's misfortune was that he had always manhandled and pushed people around. Fearing his violence and abuse, they took it. He had grown to expect them to.[1] That we were just kids and strangers, made no difference to him....

As it came out later (but never became a part of the evidence), Mashburn and Kimball came to Elkton that evening, got a pint of whiskey, and drank it. Then they went across to the Rule store ... and weighed themselves. Mashburn weighed 170 pounds.... At that time I weighed 119 pounds.

At the trial, the state had Ernie Gardner as a witness. The prosecutor asked him, "When Tommy started in to play with you that night, you did not put up any objection like this defendant, did you?" Gardner says "No." The prosecutor asked, "Why didn't you?"

---

[1] Apparently, violent incidents were fairly common in Hickory County. The account of Mashburn's killing in *The Index* noted that: "Hoodlumry has ever been the bane of this county." The paper's fascinating account of the incident, including a statement given by Beck from his jail cell, may be found at: www.newspapers.com.

Gardner replied, "I was hardly in a position to do anything lying on the ground; besides, I was so used to being kicked and beaten by him at school and everywhere, I knew it was no use to object."

The prosecutor almost threw a fit. He started in to abuse the witness until my lawyer got up and remarked, "If it please the court, I would like to state that we have just seen an extraordinary example of the state's treatment of one of its own witnesses."

In the preliminary excitement, Mashburn's shortcomings were all forgotten. He was a local young man, newly married. He was dead, and I was the killer.

The church folks were against me because the shooting had broken up their meeting; they also claimed I had brought a pistol to their church. I had not come near their church. Preacher Tatum, who was conducting the protracted meeting, was furious. He was paying off a mortgage on his farm that fall and was expecting a heavy church contribution that night. When the congregation heard the shots, scenting excitement, they got up and ran out on him before the baskets had been passed. At the next day's Sunday services, Tatum made the announcement deploring "the untimely death of that fine young man, Thomas Mashburn," and hoped that "that young desperado who had so wantonly murdered the innocent young man would be hanged higher than Haman."

Doc Steward was angered too! He came to the hotel where they had me, and said to me in the presence of many people, "Will, you have done a very bad thing; and it will reflect upon us and our business at the drugstore." Doc later became a good friend.

The trial was a farce. Besides Bill Harryman, George Mashburn employed three additional prosecutors, Graff Robertson of Buffalo, a ripping, ranting, roaring rabble rouser, Bud Hastain of Sedalia, a smooth, dressy Beau Brummel, who very successfully cried during his speech, and F. Marion Wilson of Hermitage who, with Brooks Pitts, worked up a witch's brew of false evidence. Bill Harryman was heard to say my father had refused to support him in the last election, so he would get even by hanging the boy.

That was in the days when the old Grand Army was still rampant and controlled about everything political in Hickory County. [2] George Mashburn was a Grand Army man; and wore his blue suit and brass buttons at the trial. The judge was a Grand Army man. Bill Harryman was a Grand Army man. Nine of the jury were Grand Army men or related to them. One juror was a hired man who worked for a Grand Army man. Another juror, William Edde, just out of school, thought it smart business to sit as a juror along with those older men, and try to hang a 16-year old kid.

The foreman of the jury was old man McClure, a sort of Grand Army leader in the county, who used to blow the bugle, and command the little squads of old men carrying muskets.... In the ensuing trial, he left no doubt that, not only was he of a biased opinion, but, in his capacity as foreman of the jury, he was determined to impose that opinion on the other jurors, and railroad me to the gallows, if possible.

Since several timid friends had advised my father not to get me out on bond (the bond was set at $6,000), as some of the Mashburn crowd might try to do something to me, or force me to do something to them, I remained behind bars through the winter until the spring term of Circuit court.

They brought in Alva Remington as a witness for the state. Alva and I had never gotten along too well. After his father, Dr. Remington, succumbed to a brain tumor, he grew up there in Elkton practically without control, exposed to the riffraff and the tough element that came to the drugstore for liquor.... Subsequently the family was terribly poor ... and Alva had to bring cornbread to school — which was looked upon as something of a disgrace. One day at noontime, my little brother, Jim, came to me crying; and said that Alva Remington had taken away his buttered biscuits. I got to Alva just as he was cramming down the last of the bread. Brother Jim was undersized and not quite able to hold his own; and it enraged me for a big boy like Alva to take the little fellow's food. We fought and I left him crying on the ground. Alva never forgot it.

---

[2] Founded in 1866, the "Grand Army of the Republic" was a fraternal organization made up of veterans who fought on the side of the Union in the Civil War. At one time the G.A.R. had hundreds of local posts in predominantly northern communities across the country. At the time of William Beck's trial, only 25 years after the end of the Civil War, the group boasted a membership of nearly 500,000. The last surviving member, Albert Woolson, died in 1956 at the age of 106.

A few days before the Mashburn affair, Alva saw me buying a box
of ammunition for the revolver and wanted to know all about it.
Boys have always played at games of Sheriff and horse thief,
policeman and robber; thinking of our school games, I told him I
was going to "get my man." After the Mashburn shooting, Alva
told about the cartridge incident, and Brooks Pitts heard him; so
Pitts went to Alva, and told him that if he would consent to go as a
state witness at the Beck trial, and tell the story about the cartridges
and what I had said, he (Alva) would receive witness fees of a
dollar for every day he was at Hermitage; and that he (Pitts) would
pay Alva's board at the best hotel in Hermitage. Alva did just that.
The story, the way it was told, did not do me any good.

The lawyer bungled the case. He insisted that I go on the witness
stand and say that the shooting was an accident. I was not a very
good liar. It was plain to everyone in the courtroom that the
accident story was not true. It would have been much better for
me to come right out with the facts and say I shot in self-defense.
The jury came in with a verdict of second degree murder, and
22 years in [prison][3]....

The case and its ultimate wind-up was the talk of the county for a
few days; and was then forgotten by most — [but] remembered by
some as a fitting example of what should be done to an embryo
Jesse James (quoting Marion Wilson at the preliminary hearing)
who came to church with an arsenal in his pocket.

---

[3] Written more than 55 years after the incident, Beck's account is a somewhat truncated
version of events. Based on contemporaneous accounts (mainly from *The Index* in
Hermitage, Mo.), a first trial was held in May 1891 in the Hickory County Circuit Court
where Beck was convicted of second-degree murder and sentenced to 22 years in prison.
However, because Judge Wallace had given no instruction to the jury regarding the
defense's claim that the shooting had been accidental, a motion for a new trial was
granted. The defense was also granted a change of venue. On August 27th, while being
transported from one jail to another with a group of 10 prisoners, Beck was among those
who refused to join six others in making a successful escape, although he had "every
chance to get away." In late November, a second trial was held in Lebanon, the county
seat of Laclede County. On the 10th of December, the jury returned after a lengthy
deliberation with a new sentence of 10 years.

I eventually found myself in the big-house, where one has a number instead of a name.[4] I was neither horrified nor worried by the environment. The place was filled with hardened and noted criminals, but I found it as easy to get along in there as anywhere else. My extreme youth was in my favor with the authorities. I had been shut away from the sun so long that my skin had bleached out fair and pale. Being small of size, I looked like a child. I was 17 the 14th of that February.

I was given a break when I first arrived. The warden's grown son saw me in the dressing-in room. He immediately arranged that I be assigned to the squad that worked in the State Clothing Section — where men worked at sewing machines, turning out the suits that men were given when they left the prison. They were a rather decent bunch in there (about a dozen), the guard was easy going, as was the discipline, and we could do a little talking among ourselves. I soon learned to run a sewing machine, sew up a seam and make buttonholes. The life in there never fell heavily upon me. Naturally it weighed upon my father. The prison food, while plain and simple, was not bad for one like me with a boy's appetite. About once a week, I could get a book from the library. Once a week I could write home.

A few months after I went in, there was a new state administration, a new governor and a new warden. Meanwhile my father had kept alive a movement with a public petition to get me out, or have the sentence reduced; and one of the last official acts of outgoing Governor David R. Francis was to reduce the sentence to six years.

Shortly following the advent of the new administration, a series of incidents occurred which I have always felt marked the turning point in my life.

One day, the new warden, Colonel James L. Pace, an old officer of the Confederacy, came up into the clothing shop. He looked at me running a machine. I saw him turn to the guard and ask something

---

[4]   In 1940, when Beck was retired and back in the Elkton area having his car serviced by an auto mechanic, he learned that it could have been much worse for him: "The proprietor of the garage came up to me, and greeted me with a handshake, and says, 'My father kept you from being hanged once upon a time.' I says 'How is that?' And he replied 'My father was on the jury that tried you for murder; and when some of that jury voted for the death penalty my father told them he would hang that jury to doomsday before he would consent to it.'"

about me. After Warden Pace had gone, Guard Adams called me and said I was wanted at the Warden's office.

The warden himself was waiting to see me. His first words were, "You don't look to me as if you belonged here; I want to hear your story of how you came to be here, and I want only the truth." He was keenly appraising and listened attentively while I narrated the whole affair. When I had finished, the warden sat for a long while, shaking his head from time to time. He then told me he was satisfied I had told the truth, and asked me if I would like a better assignment than the clothing shop. I told him no, that I was learning to sew and work with cloth, and that I intended to learn the trade when and if I ever got out. The warden dismissed me, and I forgot the incident.

Sometime later I caught a cold which turned into pneumonia, and spent about a week in a hospital ward. After leaving the hospital I was to convalesce in the cell, without marching out to work. Inmates who were in cells marched out to the dining hall ahead of the columns from the workshops. So, on this particular day, I had come out to the dining hall, and taken my regular place at the table. I was sitting there alone, when a party of visitors came through the hall.

At this point I pause to wonder. I wonder about destiny. Is it luck or chance? Is there a destiny that shapes our ends? Or is it a metaphysical phenomenon, wherein a forebear, gone before, becomes a guardian angel and reaches down from the great unknown realms of God's universe to guide the steps, and safeguard the well-being of earthly Man?

My frail, beautiful, little mother, seventeen when she gave me life, died when she was twenty-two. No child ever loved his mother more than I loved my "Little Ma." She was the kind of mother to whom a child with a bruised finger, a broken toy, or some childish tragedy could come, to bury his face in the folds of her gown to be comforted.

Throughout my life, in hours of extreme peril, when grave danger, even death stalked, there has seemed to be a mysterious something that fended off the great destroyer. I have wondered about that, if the guardian angel wings of "Little Ma" formed the shield of protection.

Were the series of incidents that shaped the focal point of my destiny coincidence? IF I had not been ill and in the hospital. IF my convalescence had not been under conditions that put me into the dining hall alone, at the exact time that distinguished visitors came through. IF I had been marching in line with 1,700 other men and not been seen. IF ....

My recent illness had left me rather pale, I suppose. The visiting party came to a point opposite me, where I was sitting alone. A woman in the party stopped, and said, "Governor Stone, what is this child in here for?" The Governor replied, "I do not know, Mrs. Jones; but we will soon find out." Calling a guard, the Governor directed him to ascertain why I was there.

Mrs. Jones was the wife of Colonel H. Jones, Editor of the Saint Louis Republic, largest democratic paper in the state, which had supported Colonel William J. Stone in his recent campaign for governor. The two families were old friends, and Mrs. Jones was a guest at the Executive Mansion. The guard came over and asked me what I had been sent up for, and I told him. He in turn told the Governor's party. Mrs. Jones exclaimed, "That child never murdered anyone. He is no criminal." She then asked permission to speak to me, and said, "Will you tell me the particulars of your trouble?"

I was not very well trained socially, but I did have sense enough to get on my feet. I told her briefly that while on my way to go hunting, I had met a drunken mob, and had been set upon. A drunken bully had jumped me without provocation; when he fell on me, he was shot and killed.

Mrs. Jones took my name and address, and said she was going to investigate the case, and try to get me out of there. She then rejoined the visiting party, and said to the governor who was standing with the warden, "Governor Stone, I will write you on this matter after my return to Saint Louis. If the boy is stating facts, as I fully believe he is, then a terrible wrong has been done in sending him here, and that wrong should be righted."

The next Sunday after chapel I was summoned to the warden's office and there I was met by Governor William J. Stone. Although I was an ignorant and unsophisticated boy, I did realize that not one time in a million would the governor of a great state go out of his way to make a personal visit to interview an inmate of a state prison.

I have never forgotten the personal appearance of Governor Stone. He was a typical Southerner of slight and wiry build. He had been a colonel in the Confederate Army in the War of the Rebellion. He was dressed in a black suit, of material known in that day as Clay worsted; and he wore boots of fine calfskin leather, with trousers pulled down over the tops.

Warden Pace introduced me to the Governor, who explained that the lady whom I had met in the dining hall had written him from Saint Louis asking him to go fully into my case to find if there were grounds upon which I could be taken out of a place where the surrounding influences could be anything [but good] for one of my age. The Governor directed that I give him the full and complete story.

I told how I had been called an embryo Jesse James who carried a pistol to church "to get my man," when, in fact, I had never gone near a church with the pistol, and was only carrying the revolver to shoot possums from persimmon trees at night to earn a little money for Christmas. I told him about the element of the Grand Army of the Republic — the circuit judge who presided being a member of the GAR, the prosecuting attorney being a member of the GAR, all the jurors being members of the GAR, the father of the man I had shot sitting in the court dressed in the blues, and the badges, and the brass buttons of the GAR. The Governor, being an ex-confederate and Democrat, hated the influence that that powerful organization wielded at that period in the political affairs of the country.

When I reached the end of my story, the Governor of Missouri was a very wrathful man. He thundered, "Young man, if you are telling me the truth, your case represents the most infamous travesty on justice that I have ever known throughout my long career as a lawyer." He asked me to give him the name of the prosecuting attorney, and his address where he could be reached in the mail. I did.

The Governor wrote Harryman demanding to know at once why William Beck, a mere child, had been tried and convicted for murder for defending himself against an unprovoked attack by a drunken bully twice his size. Harryman, when he received that letter from the Governor, hastened to write the Governor that the findings of the jury were all wrong, and that it was public opinion that there should have been no such conviction, ending with the recommendation that young William Beck be released at the earliest reasonable date.

The governor, utilizing his judicial prerogative, directed an unequivocal pardon, the annulment of all charges, the restoration of all rights and privileges, and that the entire proceedings be expunged from my record. Since I was a minor, he ordered the state to indemnify my father for the long months of my imprisonment.

And so I went home....[5]

I went to work on the farm as before. I went back to school, studied and learned all I could. I saw the nation approaching a war with Spain, and joined the United States Army to be ready for the emergency.

When the war came, I was privileged to have an outstanding part. My services as a sharpshooter against a Spanish battery, earned me an appointment on the field as a non-commissioned officer, and a commendation from my regimental commander.

The intervening years of a lifetime have been filled with what I hope have not been unworthy efforts and achievements. In the pursuance of my service in the military establishment, I have been in every part of the inhabited globe, achieved rank, and retired a full Colonel.

After my retirement, I returned to Hickory County and the farm.

One day, while I was in Elkton, Ort Paxton asked me out for a talk. He said, "I have received a letter from Kansas telling of Bill Kimball's death. Before he passed on, he called out for you; and wanted to tell you on his deathbed that, as prosecuting witness for the state, he swore falsely against you when he said that Tom Mashburn was only making horseplay. To right this wrong, he wanted to clear the matter, and go before his maker with an easy conscience." So that is that....

With my best regards, I am your sincere friend,

Wm. F. Beck

---

[5]   On July 3, 1893, Governor Stone wrote to Missouri's Secretary of State: "In accordance with a custom for years observed in this Department of pardoning at least two convicts from the Penitentiary on the Fourth day of July, I have this day pardoned, and do hereby pardon, William Beck, convicted before the Circuit Court of Laclede County of murder and sentenced to ten years imprisonment from December 3, 1891. I am induced to make this pardon because of the youth and good conduct of the convict. Please issue papers accordingly."

During that same visit to Elkton, Beck had also encountered Jim Kelly, the fellow whom he had once beaten with a rock in the snow. As Beck later recounted:

> The brother-in-law, Jim Kelly, had said ... [that] he would take my scalp if he ever met me. He met me after I came back, on the porch of Andy Steward's drugstore. I says "Well, if it isn't that bad man, Jim Kelly. Now, Kelly, that you have a chance to act instead of talk, do you still feel lucky?" He made no reply.

Around the turn of the 20th century, William F. Beck would meet a beautiful Quaker girl called Nettie Grove. He would woo her, marry her, hold her close and, so, join in the creation of a baby girl who would one day become famous for dancing around in the same costume she was wearing at the moment of her birth.

William Francis Beck was small of stature, but big of heart — the sort of person who was not reluctant to stand up for himself. One sultry night in the summer of 1903, this genetic legacy was passed on to his daughter, the subject of this book.

Part One

A Star Is Born

The image of preteen Helen Beck in her American Flag dress
was probably taken on May 20, 1916, in Kansas City, Missouri.

CHAPTER ONE

In the Beginning

The two most important days in your life are the day you
are born and the day you find out why.
~ Mark Twain

The clip and the clop of horses' hooves on the streets of Chicago were
once as common as the pungent odors from the city's Union
Stockyards. Old timers well remembered the resonant clatter when city
streets were paved with wooden blocks. Horse-drawn traffic was once a
part of everyday life, but, by December 9, 1932 — not so much. So, on that
very chilly late fall evening, bundled pedestrians must have been taken
aback by the sight of a seemingly naked young woman riding a horse right
down Michigan Avenue.

Frigid weather in Chicago had claimed the lives of five within the previous
24 hours. Government meteorologist J. R. Lloyd predicted the temperature
would dive close to zero degrees Fahrenheit before nightfall. It was not an
evening to be out, certainly not in the buff. Much of the Midwest was in
lockdown. Even the famous polar explorer, Admiral Richard E. Byrd, was
forced to cancel his speech to the annual American Farm Bureau convention when the snow became too much for him en route to Chicago.

Inside the comfortably heated ballroom of the Stevens Hotel, the annual
Gold Coast Beaux Arts Ball was in full swing. The famous Versailles-
inspired Grand Ballroom, with its Italianate columns and gold leaf trim-
mings, had accommodated many famous guests during the preceding five
years. Only two days after its grand opening in 1927, some 3,000 Hollywood personalities, including Cecil B. DeMille, had attended the Motion
Picture Association Ball.

Everyone who was anyone stayed at the Stevens when visiting Chicago. If
you stayed at the Stevens, you must be "somebody." Otherwise, you
wouldn't be there. Well, "somebody" was seeking entry at the front door.
Somebody riding a horse. Somebody with long blond hair. Somebody
with some *body*. She insisted she was expected, but the dumbstruck

doorman wasn't quite sure what to make of the spectacle before him. This called for a decision above his pay grade.

Decked out in colorful costumes, the guests partying within were fully aware that "Lady Godiva" was expected, as a newspaper picture had announced her appearance several days earlier. Now, with the hour at hand, it began to look as if there might be an issue. The doorman told the thinly clad young miss to wait while he summoned the manager. Discussion ensued.

The goose-pimpled rider shifted her position on the horse as clouds of chilly mist poured forth from its nostrils. After what must have seemed an eternity to the nearly frozen entourage of press hounds, late arrivers, and the stone-cold curious, the hotel manager and his would-be guest reached an accommodation. The doorman pulled the handle and bowed respectfully. A shivering vision passed through that door and into history. The world of popular entertainment, the prospects for feminism, and the ubiquity of celebrity press coverage would never be the same. Sally Rand was about to become a household name.

There would be the saving of a World's Fair — and not just one, but three. Vaudeville, legitimate theater and motion pictures — each would play a significant role in her life. So, too, would the nagging presence of repeated arrests and lawsuits. There would be big money and small stages. Multiple suitors would press their cases and marriages would ensue. There would be state fairs and county fairs and traveling tent shows. Radio, television, Las Vegas and Broadway. Even speaking appearances at Harvard — and not just one, but three. There would be accolades, and there would be derision. Millions would be made and there would be bankruptcy — and not just one.

But all this lay in the future. To fully appreciate Sally's story, we must turn back the clock to a springtime morning long before, to the bedroom of a modest farm house in the rolling Ozark country of Hickory County, Missouri.

It was Easter Sunday, April 3, 1904. Most folks in the area were attending religious services celebrating the resurrection, the dawn of a new age. But 22-year-old Annette Mary Grove Beck, a Quaker girl from Pennsylvania, was not among them. Rather, she was at home in bed suffering labor pains.

While the baby's mother-to-be had never shot and killed a town bully in the middle of the road, the details of her ancestry are no less notable than those of the baby's father. She had a heritage as well.

Gilbert du Motier de Lafayette (Marquis de Lafayette) was a French aristocrat and military officer who fought for independence in the American Revolution at the side of George Washington, and who later became a key figure in the French Revolution. He returned to visit the newly-independent nation in 1780 and again, at the behest of President James Monroe, in 1824. That year, as a gentleman of 67 years, he toured all 24 states of the union, traveling more than 6,000 miles by stagecoach, horseback, canal barge and steamboat, greeted by large enthusiastic crowds. All of her life, Sally Rand enjoyed reciting how:

> Great-grandmother Palmer kept me spellbound for many
> childhood hours telling me about when she was a little girl in
> Virginia. The time Lafayette came to this country the last time. He
> was a very old man, and she was a very little girl. He was dressed
> resplendent in full dress uniform, cocked hat, with a snowy white
> plume, riding a great dappled grey horse. She with other little girls
> dressed in sprigged muslin hoop skirts and long lacy pantaloons,
> lined the roads in Virginia, to see and pay homage, and strew
> flowers in his path. She told it so vividly, described it in such detail,
> I really thought I'd seen it.

Like Mary Frances Palmer, considered by her great-granddaughter to be a "pretty good story teller," Sally would also develop quite a reputation as a raconteur. And, just as with some of Sally's own tales repeated with conviction over many years, the only shortcoming in the story was — it never happened. Sally's great-grandmother Palmer could not have personally witnessed Lafayette passing by, as she was not born until September 3, 1828, four years after the event.

But an even more compelling (and actually true) tale involving Sally's maternal grandfather has also come down to us through her family. In 1859, Mary Frances Palmer gave birth to a daughter, Mollie Palmer, who grew up to become the second wife of a teacher and minister named James Grove. Sally's grandfather Grove was a handsome man, tall of stature and very erect, but his life had been anything but easy. He had originally brought his family to Missouri in a covered wagon from Winchester, Kentucky, eager to improve the family's prospects and hopeful that his first wife Sarah would recover from her affliction, "galloping consumption" — the disease now known as tuberculosis. Following a failed general store venture, his fortunes worsened when Sarah died, leaving him not only in financial distress but also a widower with four young children to raise.

When Sally's grandmother Mollie Palmer married James Grove, he was 41 years old and she was only 18, a young bride with four stepchildren. During their marriage the couple would have five children of their own, the eldest being Annette Mary Grove who was born on June 30, 1881. At some point, James relocated his family from Pisgah to Hickory County. Ministers were scarce in that part of Missouri and so, seizing the opportunity to supplement his income as a teacher, he accepted a position as an itinerant minister, serving and traveling between the two small Hickory County communities of Wheatland and Pittsburg.

On the last Sunday in March 1890, after conducting the morning service in Wheatland and pausing for dinner, the Reverend Grove took note of the inclement weather and began to ride to Pittsburg in order to conduct the afternoon service. He reached the Pomme de Terre River where he was accustomed to navigating a shallow crossing, but it had been raining and the river had become a small torrent. James sat for a while, staring at the churning water and thinking of the people who were awaiting his arrival.

His horse was a good swimmer so he decided to take the risk, plunging into the stream. He was halfway across when his horse lost its footing, throwing James into the water. Horse and rider were swept downstream, but finally reached the opposite bank where Grove remounted and continued on to Pittsburg. But before he could reach his destination, the temperature plummeted and his clothes were frozen to the saddle. Arriving at the church, he had to be pried from his mount by friends. He was taken inside where he could dry his clothing before the fire. After preaching his sermon, James returned home apparently none the worse for the experience. By the following Friday he was dead of pneumonia.

Annette Mary Grove was only eight years old when her father died. Although devastated by the loss of her father, his lifelong quest for knowledge inspired her to pursue her own higher education. She did so with a passion, graduating from Warrensburg Teachers College (now the University of Central Missouri). Annette, who came to be called "Nettie," grew into a long-legged and beautiful woman who, according to her daughter:

> ... grew so tall so fast that her mother and grandmother were kept busy lengthening her skirts and making her new, more grown up, dresses.

> In those days everyone in the county knew one another. They were neighbors or kinfolks. They played and went fishing together as children, dated and went to play-parties as teen-agers (not dances, heaven forbid).

It was at one of these Missouri play-parties hosted by her uncle Carlos Palmer in Elkton that Annette encountered a dashing young lieutenant on leave from service in the Philippines, an island group that had been taken from Spain in the Spanish-American War. The handsome Lt. William F. Beck was enchanted by Nettie's grace and beauty. She was flattered by the attention of a local war hero who seemed to offer decent prospects. Once he was discharged from the Army, the two secured a marriage license at the Hickory County Courthouse in Hermitage and, on May 21, 1903, they were joined together in holy matrimony.

It wasn't long before Annette found herself with child. At the time, the couple was living in Springfield, Missouri. As Sally later explained:

> It was May of 1903 and my parents, the William F. Becks, moved into "light housekeeping rooms" right in town, near the Springfield Post Office where my father worked. It was there my young and soon pregnant mother dreamed her dreams, started my baby clothes, made do with what she had, and baked her fat golden loaves of light bread in a little square oven on top of a one-burner kerosene stove.

> It was here she met her dearest friend, a beautiful girl who was always my "Aunt Lucy" .... They used to lie in the hammock and watch me grow until it came time for Mama to go back to Grandpa's farm at Elkton for me to be born.[1]

Elsewhere in Missouri, work was nearing completion for the April 30th opening of the Louisiana Purchase Exposition, a "world's fair" to be held in St. Louis in celebration of the 100th anniversary of Thomas Jefferson's acquisition of 828,000 square miles of territory from Napoleon Bonaparte of France — part or all of 14 current states — for the modest price of $15 million. In the days before radio, top tunes were determined by sheet music sales, and the music for "Meet Me in St. Louis, Louis" was racking up big sales across the land.[2] American consumers were about to be blessed with the availability of many new products introduced or popularized at the St. Louis fair, including puffed wheat cereal, the ice cream cone, and the incomparable soft drink, Dr. Pepper.

---

[1] Lucy Newton was not really an "aunt" but, rather, a lifelong friend of Sally's mother. The two were so close that Annette came to regard Lucy as a sister.

[2] Also topping the charts in 1904 were such songs as "I'm A Yankee Doodle Dandy" and "Give My Regards to Broadway" by George M. Cohan, along with a couple of little ditties called "The Goo-Goo Man" and "Won't You Fondle Me."

The 1904 fair would also host the Summer Olympic Games, at which American gymnast George Eyser would win six Olympic medals in a single day (including three gold), even though his left leg was made of wood. (He had lost his real leg following an unfortunate encounter with a steam locomotive.) Theodore Roosevelt was in the White House, having only recently designated Pelican Island in Florida as a National Wildlife Refuge — a move that presaged the decline of the feathered hat industry.

Not quite four months earlier, two bicycle mechanics named Orville and Wilbur had successfully made the first powered flight of a heavier-than-air aircraft at Kitty Hawk, North Carolina. For the preceding eight months, Dr. Ernst Pfenning of Chicago had been driving the first-ever Ford Model A "motor car." The Victorian Age was over. A new generation of "modern" people was being born.

O n April 4th at 11 o'clock in the morning just as the late-arriving parishioners were settling into the last row of pews in their Easter Sunday best, back in that farmhouse bedroom on her grandfather's farm near the tiny community of Elkton, Missouri, the infant who would someday be called "Sally Rand" entered the world. While Elkton isn't exactly square in the middle of no place, it's still a long way from most anywhere else. The county seat at Hermitage is 12 miles up the road. Springfield is some 50 miles away, Kansas City around 125. "It was so small" she once explained, "that they had to catch me to put shoes on me. And I've never really outgrown it. I'm still going barefoot — up to my chin."

The family had summoned Dr. C. V. Steward from Bolivar, Missouri, some 15 miles to the south of the Beck farm. Recalling the event 29 years later, Dr. Steward observed "but of course I couldn't tell then she was going to be famous. She just looked like any newborn babe to me."[3] The infant weighed 6½ pounds and had grey eyes. Writing of the event 62 years later, Sally revealed that, according to her mother, "when the doctor gave me the traditional slap on the back that sets a baby's little lungs to pumping, I didn't even cry. I laughed."

W hile the baby's mother may have been partial to the name Harriet, her father, retired Colonel William F. Beck, a veteran of the Spanish American War, preferred to honor one the most admired angels of that conflict, Helen Gould. She was the daughter of the notorious 19th century

---

[3] Coincidentally, Dr. Steward's wife Rosa was the "Dear Friend and Former Schoolmate" to whom William Beck wrote the letter set forth in the Prologue describing his deadly encounter with town bully Tom Mashburn and the fateful aftermath.

robber baron Jay Gould, and was regarded by many as the ethical opposite of her father. When Gould died in 1892, his daughter inherited ten million dollars. At the outbreak of the Spanish-American War, Miss Gould donated $100,000 to the government for war expenses. While her financial support was exceptional (it would be valued at millions today), it was Miss Gould's hands-on personal attention to the needs of war veterans that endeared her to Americans. She even took many injured veterans into her own home and reportedly received handwritten letters of praise from more than 3,000 soldiers and sailors.

And so it was that the newborn's names were all strung together. Harriet Helen Gould Beck had entered the world with a twinkle in her eye.[4] As she told Studs Terkel many years later, "I was born in the last naive moment America was ever to enjoy ... between the Spanish-American War and the First World War. Things were S. S. & G. — Sweet, Simple and Girlish."

On the Fourth of July 1906, the 130th anniversary of the signing of the Declaration of Independence, President Theodore Roosevelt had stepped down from his train car at Oyster Bay, Long Island, New York, and was preparing to enter his carriage with Mrs. Roosevelt, when they were suddenly approached by a photographer who shoved a black box toward the president and snapped the shutter of his camera. Acting instinctively, Secret Service Chief James B. Sloane jumped on the man, Clarence Legendre, striking him on the cheek and knocking him over. Once it was clear the President was safe and everyone had moved on, Legendre brushed himself off and filed a complaint of battery against Sloane. The village constable, a Mr. McQuade, placed Sloane under arrest and took him before Squire Franklin who released him on his own recognizance pending his appearance on July 9th to answer a charge of third degree assault.

An editorial in the *Washington Post* applauded Officer Sloane for his alert response, saying:

> We trust the law-giver of Oyster Bay will not only discharge
> Sloane, but commend him for his alertness and bravery in looking
> out for the safety of the President. There was no time to investigate
> whether the man with the box was merely a pestiferous camera
> fiend or an assassin in that disguise.... Without waiting to deter-

---

4   Sally may never have had a birth certificate. Several sources identify her as "Harriet Helen Gould Beck." In the 1910 Federal Census, the 6-year-old was listed as "Helen H." Some sources report that a social security card (SS# 349-10-00) was issued to her under the name "Harriet Helen Beck." Somewhere along the way, "Harriet" was dropped.

mine this point, the officer very properly did his duty by knocking
the camera man over. He would have been grossly negligent if he
had done otherwise. Equal watchfulness and prompt action at
Buffalo would have saved the life of President McKinley.

A compelling argument by today's standards, certainly. Yet, on that day,
Secret Service Chief Sloane entered a plea of guilty to the charge of assault
and was fined $10 (about $250 today).

By 1894, aggressive photographers had become so common that the term
"camera fiends" was coined to describe them. Today, those who ply the
trade are known as "paparazzi" (derived from an Italian term meaning the
annoying buzzing of mosquitos), but so-called camera fiends had become a
nuisance to public figures even before the turn of the 20th Century. We will
encounter them again in chapter 14.

H elen was a precocious child. At the age of two, she and her mother
went to visit her mother's dear friend Lucy Newton at St. Joseph's
hospital in Kansas City. Lucy recalled Helen's concern:

> "Oh Mummy," she said on the way, "let's take her some flowers."
>
> "I would love to dear, but I have no money."
>
> "Do you have my dime, Mummy?"
>
> "Yes, darling, but it wouldn't buy much."
>
> "Maybe it would buy a rose, Mummy."
>
> "We will try, sweetheart, when we come to a flower shop."

Helen ran into the florist's shop and presented her dime, saying, "I want a
rose for my Aunt Lucy. She's very sick in the hospital." She came out, with
the rose in her hand, beaming with joy which did not fade until her baby
hand had presented it to "Aunt Lucy," who said: "It was the most beautiful
rose that I had ever seen, because of its message to me. How could one ever
forget that sweet smiling baby face?"

Writing of her childhood in 1938, Sally recalled:

> Inasmuch as I was my father's and mother's first child I had no
> high chair and I remember sitting between my father's knees with
> my hands folded below the table level and being fed. What a temp-
> tation it was to reach above the table and just touch something!
>
> I think that was my first lesson in discipline, and my father still
> points with pride to what an obedient child I was, but he always
> forgets to tell about the time there was company for dinner and I

sat on my mother's lap and the temptation was too great and the
paternal eye was off me because of company — I waved a fork
excitedly over my head and into mother's eye. Tragedy of
tragedies! How ashamed and humiliated I was that I had not only
misbehaved at the table but that had really hurt my mother whom I
adore. Fortunately the injury recovered and my mother's eye was
undamaged.

In early 1908, Helen was joined by a baby brother, christened Harold
Lawton Beck, who from time to time would be an important figure in her
life.[5] Although overshadowed by his famous sister, he would enjoy a
moderately successful show business career of his own. As children, Helen
and Harold used to swim in a nearby river they called the "Plumly Tar."
Sally later said, "It wasn't until I saw a Missouri map as an adult that I
realized it was actually the Pomme De Terre River" — the very same river
that had played a role in her grandfather's untimely death.

Some sources report that Sally had a difficult and sickly childhood on the
farm, yet her own recollections often reflected a happier time. In a radio
interview many years later, a wistful Sally "talked as tenderly and lyrically
as any poet about the sudden pink of apple blossoms in the Missouri
spring, summer nights in the country when you can hear a rhythmical
insect chorus through the murmurous dark, the supper-time fragrance of
hickory-smoked ham and browning potatoes."

She often spoke of her early years on the farm, recalling the black walnut
barn, the corn crib, the smokehouse, and the log cabin that her grandfather
built to share with his bride while the main house was being finished. In
many ways this was an idyllic time for her, when she and her brother
Harold would play with the ducks and guinea hens that wandered through
the petunia beds near the main house. They would eat slices of hickory-
smoked ham with "red-eye" gravy and hot biscuits with butter churned on
the farm. They relished sleeping in their grandfather's walnut trundle bed
and hiding in a fallen tree trunk until the family would ring the old iron
dinner bell to bring them home.

---

[5]   As was the case with his sister, Harold's middle name was a tribute to one of their
father's admired heroes of the Spanish-American War — Major General Henry W.
Lawton. Like Colonel Beck's regiment, Lawton's division was associated with the
assault on San Juan Hill in Cuba. In 1899, while he was engaged in the Philippine
Islands campaign, Lawton became the highest ranking American officer to be killed
during the war. The city of Lawton, Oklahoma, is named for him.

While she waxed poetic in a diary entry about the farm's "untidy apple orchard [that] tumbles down the hill in tipsy abandon," and the freshwater spring that, "in hot, droughty summers, would almost dry up, and catfish would lay gasping in the small stagnant pools," she also wrote of the "poverty" of the soil and of the main house with its kitchen windows on either side of a black wood-burning stove that faced the "old McCracker place and the little cemetery where five generations of my kin lie serenely under the wild yellow roses and blackberry brambles."

Colonel Beck moved his family to Kansas City in 1910, staying at the Savoy Hotel while looking for a more permanent place to live. Sally was enrolled in Greenwood Grammar School where she began her transition from a relatively unsophisticated farm girl to the young lady who would soon develop a fascination for the wider world.

In this same year the famous Russian ballerina Anna Pavlova embarked on her first tour of the United States. Her American debut had occurred in February at the Metropolitan Opera House in New York City. By the time the company reached Kansas City, reports of her magnificent performances had reached the masses. Sally's adopted aunt, Lucy Newton, secured a pair of tickets and the previously barefoot 6-year-old soon found herself perched on a plush theater seat in Kansas City. The great Pavlova performed "the Dying Swan," the famous solo choreographed in 1907 that would serve as a signature piece for the rest of her life. The ballerina's striking costume was decorated with the feathers of real swans.

Pavlova's dancing completely captivated the little girl. As Sally later described her emotions to Studs Terkel, "I sat up and wept uncontrollably. At that moment, there was born this true knowledge: I was going to be a dancer, a ballerina."

Such an ambition had not always been considered proper for a Missouri farm girl — or any other American girl for that matter. On February 7, 1827, the Bowery Theatre, a gas-lit venue that had opened just 15 weeks earlier in lower Manhattan, played host to the first modern ballet performance ever presented in the United States. The elegantly decorated theater[6] had been built

---

6   With the biggest capacity of any theatre in the United States, the Bowery Theatre seated an audience of 3,500. Its opening on October 22, 1826, was not to the satisfaction of everyone. A publication of the Dutch Reformed Church mentioned the event — not to call attention to its availability but "to excite Christians to pray against the wide-spreading pestilence; to exhort Christian parents to keep their children from the vortex of destruction."

to serve a high-class clientele or, as New York City Mayor Philip Hone described it, "those whose standing in society enables them to control the opinions and direct the judgment of others." John Quincy Adams was in the White House, fashionably dressed patrons were in their seats, and, direct from Paris, danseuse Madame Francisque Hutin was in the wings, about to perform "La Bergère Coquette" (The Coquettish Shepherdess).

As theatre critic Joseph Ireland described it, no sooner had the graceful danseuse bounded "like a startled fawn upon the stage, her light and scanty drapery floating in the air" than the curious and expectant members of the packed house were stunned to find that Madame Hutin's "fine figure was ... not concealed in her dress of gauze." When a "bewildering pirouette" displayed "still more liberally her symmetrical proportions, a subdued expression of fear and terror escaped from the ladies present, and the cheeks of the greater portion of the audience crimsoned with shame." Alarm turned to near panic as "every lady in the lower tier of boxes rushed from the house."[7]

During the three-minute performance, Hutin had not only exposed her bare ankles but had also allowed an occasional glimpse of her bare legs. Writing in the *New York Observer*, Finley Morse, son of a Calvinist minister, excoriated the performance as smut: "The exhibition is to all intents and purposes the public exposure of a naked female."[8] Simply put, in 1827, such an outrage could not be permitted to pass without reproach. Critics in our own time might note a hint of irony in the placement of Madame Hutin's performance on the program — immediately following a pantomime of *Much Ado about Nothing*.

I was going to be a dancer, a ballerina," she had said. And it was true. Professional ballet would play an important role in her future. As Helen sat in that Kansas City theater with her Aunt Lucy, totally enchanted by the famous Pavlova, it had been 83 years since the brouhaha over Madame

---

7   Despite the scandalized reaction, the experience had been exhilarating for the ladies in the audience. In 1827, it was disputed whether women should be attending the theatre at all. According to one source, "women seemed transfixed by Hutin." The tide finally turned after Mme. Hutin responded to the uproar by covering her legs with a pair of filmy Turkish trousers. However, within weeks, she was back in her original ballet costume by popular demand. She performed at the Bowery periodically until the theatre burned down in 1828.

8   Finley Morse's critique was so well received that he started a daily paper of his own, the *Journal of Commerce*, which, he assured his audience, would not "pander to the appetites of the depraved by enticing them to scenes of licentiousness." Finley's full name was Samuel F.B. Morse. Seventeen years later he would tap out the now famous message "What hath God wrought" in Morse Code over a telegraph line between Washington, D.C., and Baltimore, Maryland.

Hutin's performance at the Bowery Theatre. By 1910, ballet was considered highbrow and perfectly acceptable for female audiences, even those who were only six years old.

And young Helen's interest extended well beyond the dance; she also loved the music. According to Lucy:

> I gave her piano lessons when she was six. When I presented her a lullaby to learn, she said, "Oh Goody. Will you play it for me, Aunt Lucy?" (A request seldom granted until the student had practiced it.) But this was my Helen. She had a way of winning. I played it carelessly, not realizing that I had a competent critic listening. It did not please Helen. No, not at all. With troubled face, she said, "Why Aunt Lucy, that would wake the baby up." I have carried that wise little girl's expression all down my teaching career.

Faith

The year 1910 was eventful not only for the young Miss Beck, but also for members of the Bacon family. In 1876, the wealthy Henry Douglas Bacon — a direct descendant of Peregrine White, the first child born to Mayflower Pilgrims in the New World — offered to donate to the fledgling University of California, Berkeley his private library of 1,410 volumes, as well as his collection of paintings and statuary, and to fund construction of a library building to house the collections.

In 1910, his grandson Frank Page Bacon, Jr., fathered an adorable baby girl named Frances Yvonne Bacon. And, one day, Broadway impresario Flo Ziegfeld would proclaim "Faith Bacon" to be the most beautiful girl in America. She will prove to be a major figure in our story.

Still warm from the afterglow of Pavlova's performance, young Helen worked out a deal with her mother, promising to practice on the "hated piano" in exchange for dancing lessons. Although family members described her as something of a shrinking violet in her early years, Helen began to blossom once the image of performing in public had been impressed on her mind.

According to Lucy, Helen had "never feared anything or anybody":

> When Helen decides to act, the world could step aside — and LOOK OUT! Three teen-aged boys had pestered her eight-year-old brother until Helen's patience had frayed. She was only eleven but she tackled all three. I'll give one guess as to who won — and for keeps.

Yet, in 1912, Helen suffered what must have been the most distressing experience of her young life. Her parents' relationship deteriorated and her father took off for parts unknown. As Sally told Lloyd Shearer in 1961:

> When I was a child of eight, my father, a colonel in the U.S. Army, in the cavalry no less, walked out on his family. He left me and Mother and a brother — it was a simple case of desertion — but to me it became more than that. It became a case of rejection. I never thought, "Father has rejected Mother." Never that. It was always, "Father has rejected me." It left me with the idea that no man would ever want me.

The exact cause of her parents' separation remains a mystery. As Sally recalled it: "From my child's eye view, I could not see any problems between my parents that might have led to this separation." Yet, from this traumatic event came a never fully satisfied hunger for the approval of men in general and her father in particular.

By 1913, the 9-year-old Helen Beck had accumulated the beginnings of what would later become a large collection of dolls. As a regular visitor at Lucy Newton's house, she had begun using colored scraps of fabric from Aunt Lucy's sewing machine drawers to create outfits for her dolls. She soon developed a genuine talent for making costumes (particularly the hats), as well as an interest in fashion generally.

That summer, a brief fad captured the attention of the country and signaled yet another evolution in fashion and morality. As described in the *Monroe News-Star* (Louisiana):

> The "good old summer time" is here and with it has come the telltale transparent dress, which when worn by a woman with the sun or an electric light between the wearer and the "audience," reveals the absence of sufficient undergarments.

> Wednesday afternoon the News-Star carried a local story to the effect that an engineer stopped his train and hastened to a point of vantage in order to gaze wistfully upon a lady going down the street in one of the diaphanous costumes. The sun was shining brightly, and he had the satisfaction of knowing he saw practically all there was to see. Very little was left to the imagination. Wednesday morning a business man while gazing at a lady going down the street in a transparent outfit, fell and hurt himself so badly that a physician was needed to dress his wounds....

This remarkable unattributed article, written more than 100 years ago, went on to say that such attire on a man would spark little interest:

> But woman was fashioned along different lines. Her lines, in fact, are all curves. There is a symmetry — a pleasing bulging here and a slight rounding there, and when she is dressed in one of these diaphanous outfits which reveal to the best advantage all these peculiarities, a man just simply cannot be blamed if he allows his eyes to rest longer on the wearer than strict etiquette calls for.

This diaphanous and transparent attire was quickly dubbed the "X-Ray Dress," and bold young ladies from coast to coast began strolling forth in them. Official reaction was close behind. Mayor Albee of Portland, Oregon, ordered Chief of Police Clarke to arrest every woman found wearing the new X-Ray dress on the streets. Objectionable attire was defined as "immodest dress," including necks cut too low, sheathed skirts too much sheathed, and slit skirts too much slit. The Mayor made clear to the police that they were not to discriminate; it didn't matter whether the offender was a "reigning social matron or belle or a woman of the streets."

Los Angeles quickly followed suit. Seventh Day Adventist Rev. I. H. Evans harrumphed that if he were a judge and if a "devotee to modern feminine dress" had brought to him a complaint against a young man, he would charge the girl herself with contributing to the delinquency of the man because, he said, women had adopted the X-Ray dress deliberately for the purpose of luring men. Another perspective was expressed by a Portland, Oregon, columnist: "It reflects seriously upon the morality and mentality of mankind when it is impossible to pass a woman on the street with an X-ray gown on her body without arousing unchaste passions."

Meanwhile, in Tucson, Arizona, Judge L. O. Cowan was hearing charges against opera singer Claire Simpson, who had been arrested for violating a city ordinance against "lewd and indecent dress." It seems she had caused such a mob of men and boys to congregate that downtown traffic was blocked on Congress Street. Following prolonged testimony, the judge declared himself to be incompetent to decide whether pink tights worn under a dress were immodest or not. In South Norwalk, Connecticut, the papers reported that the wearing of an X-Ray Dress caused the loss of a ball game when "a fetching little damsel tripped upon the field and took a point of vantage near third base, said point being directly between the setting sun and the players."

The last word on the matter seems to have come in February 1914 when the benighted community of Zion City, Illinois, adopted an ordinance strictly prohibiting the wearing of "X-Ray" and other "Peek-a-boo" attire, which, in the view of Reverend Wilbur Glenn Voliva, smacked of the works of the Devil and reeked of the flesh pots of Egypt.[9] The expansive ordinance also forbade public flirting and sitting on the lap of a member of the opposite sex in public. For good measure, penalties of up to a $200 fine or six months' imprisonment were also extended to apply to any woman so brazen as to ride upon a horse in any manner save sideways.

With the onset of winter, the siren song of the X-Ray Dress was ended . . . but the melody lingered on.

In 1915 the seasonal flu epidemic was severe enough to close the public schools in Kansas City. With no classes to attend, 10-year-old Helen Beck took what may have been her first paying job — trimming and modeling millinery in a local shop. This may also have been her first experience with the notion of using bird feathers for personal adornment.

The young Missouri girl probably wasn't aware of it, but the art of millinery has a long and storied history. The origin of the term "millinery" dates back to the 1400s when fine hats were made in Milan, Italy, a leading fashion center to this day. By the late 15th century, feathered caps had become very fashionable among the European elite, with ostrich and peacock feathers particularly in demand. Millinery was big business. In 1901, the industry employed 83,000 people — one out of every 1,000 Americans. As related by Ken Burns in his 2009 PBS documentary *The National Parks: America's Best Idea*:

> By 1900, feathers were in fashion and no woman's hat, it seemed,
> was complete without an array of plumes. Some hats even
> included entire stuffed birds. The long, white plumes of egrets had
> become more valuable than gold. To satisfy the demands of this
> latest fashion trend, more than five million birds a year were being
> slaughtered; nearly 95 percent of Florida's shore birds had been
> killed by plume hunters.

---

[9]   In this same year Reverend Voliva came to national attention as the most prominent advocate of the "flat earth" theory, offering a $5,000 prize to anyone who could prove otherwise. He later became the world's first evangelist to own a radio station, WCBD. In 1942, Voliva stepped down in disgrace, tearfully admitting that he had misappropriated church funds to support his lavish life style.

The demand for feathered hats reached its peak during the Edwardian Age — that period from 1901 to 1910 when King Edward VII sat on the British throne. As the immediate successor to the staid and long-serving Queen Victoria, her son Edward was the leader of a fashionable elite that set a style influenced by the art and fashions of continental Europe.

> A FEATHERED CAP
>
> Consider the Revolutionary War era "Yankee Doodle," a song about a young dandy who "stuck a feather in his cap and called it macaroni." This cryptic lyric, which has amused generations of school-children, has nothing to do with pasta. Rather, it refers to the continental fashion of later 18th century foppish Englishmen who came to be known as "Macaronies." As described in *The Oxford Magazine*: "There is indeed a kind of animal, neither male nor female, a thing of the neuter gender, lately started up among us. It is called a macaroni. It talks without meaning, it smiles without pleasantry, it eats without appetite, it rides without exercise, it wenches without passion."

In 1903, the Millinery Merchant's Protective Agency of New York reached an agreement with the New York Audubon Society to stop the trade in gulls, terns, grebes, hummingbirds and songbirds — a small localized step toward protecting the species from extinction. The rest is a long and fascinating story. Suffice it to say that in 1915 young Helen was getting into the trade at a time when the flamboyant feathered fashion was more or less in terminal decline.

This history aside, Sally's early exposure to millinery would lead to a lifelong passion for decorating hats and designing costumes — not just the minimal ones she designed for herself, but also those for the many dancers and chorus girls who would one day be in her employ. Being young, beautiful, and photogenic, young Helen's duties were expanded to include modeling hats as a photographer's model. This experience at the tender age of ten no doubt gave her an early perspective on the idea of presenting herself in an attractive manner for the enjoyment of others.

Faith

Well, ten certainly is a tender age but, in 1916, somewhere in Southern California, the aforementioned Francis Yvonne Bacon, whose parents had divorced two years earlier, was earning a few dollars for her mother by posing in the nude for so-called life drawing artists at the even more tender age of six. Whatever else might be said, Yvonne's experience at such an early age may have engendered a certain confidence with respect to appearing unclothed in the presence of others. Not to mention being paid for it. It was the beginning of a journey. She would one day refer to herself as "the best nude in the business."

On May 30, 1916, former President Theodore Roosevelt came to Kansas City, Missouri, to make a special Memorial Day address. A huge enthusiastic turnout estimated at more than 100,000 crushed into Union Station plaza to greet him. Police officers struggled to wedge the former president through to a waiting car. A reported 100 "motor cars" were the centerpiece of the downtown parade that escorted Mr. Roosevelt to the newly opened Hotel Muehlebach. Marching members of the American Legion and veterans of every stripe bracketed the motorcade like bookends. Standing in his car and bowing again and again, Roosevelt maintained a constant stream of conversation with those along the parade route. When his car passed by banners declaring "Votes for Women," Teddy waved his hat and shouted "Hurrah, Hurrah."

At one point, an unidentified man hurled an open jackknife toward the car. Press accounts vary, but the knife apparently grazed Roosevelt's hand, bounced off his private secretary, John McGrath, and fell onto the running board of the car without seriously injuring either man. The perpetrator, a tall man wearing brown clothes and a straw hat, retreated through the crowd and was never apprehended. When the parade reached the hotel without further incident, Roosevelt bounded up the steps to the lobby. As the former president came into view, he was greeted joyously by 100 little girls, all dressed in costumes resembling draped American flags, singing "America, I Love You."[10]

Roosevelt was noticeably touched, declaring to the children: "I would have been glad to have come all the way to Kansas City just for this reception." Placing his hands upon the shoulders of Major William Warner, chairman of the reception committee, and Colonel John B. Stone, a Confederate veteran, Mr. Roosevelt said, "I stand today by the side of a man who wore the blue in the civil war and a man who wore the gray. But now we're all Americans and nothing else."

Amid speculation that he might once again run for president in November, Roosevelt's day was packed with appearances. Before his scheduled address in Convention Hall, 5,000 seats had been reserved for both Union

---

[10] It is unclear whether young Helen Beck was one of the "100 little girls all dressed in costumes resembling draped American flags," but she may well have been. A photo-graph in her collection shows her as a young girl in an outfit that exactly matches this description. Regarding the photograph, Sally was quoted as having said: "If I wore that many clothes now, it would be news."

and Confederate veterans. Another 5,000 guests would later be squeezed into unreserved areas. While devoting the majority of his speech to the necessity of military preparedness against foreign aggression, Roosevelt also stressed that the higher purpose is to preserve a nation of equal opportunity, defined by principles and a common spirit which are actually worth defending. His remarks were words of wisdom from a leader who had a rare talent for crafting and delivering them.

But Theodore Roosevelt wasn't the only eloquent man in Kansas City that day. The famous evangelist Billy Sunday was also there, conducting a seven-week series of revival meetings. Upwards of 40,000 souls braved a driving rain to see him on the first day. Addressing the exuberant, rain-soaked throng from a specially erected platform beneath a large "Kansas City for Christ" banner, Sunday tore into his adversaries:

> Come on you traducers. Come on you triple extract of infamy.
> Come on you assassins of character. Come on you sponsors of
> harlotry. Come on you defamers of God and enemies of the
> Church. Come on you bull-necked, beetle-browed, hog-jowled,
> peanut-brained, weasel-eyed four flushers, false alarms and excess
> baggage. In the name of God, I challenge and defy you....

> The dirty, black-hearted, rotten, degenerate, whiskey bunch in
> Kansas City has been lying about me. The spawn of hell. I under-
> stand the fellow is here in this tabernacle tonight who sent those
> lying circulars out about me. Stand up, you dirty dog. Stand up till
> I cram that lie down your dirty throat.

Reading between the lines, one might have deduced that Billy Sunday would probably have opposed young Helen's desire to become a dancer. In fact, very much so. Consider this excerpt from one of his most popular sermons, "Theatre, Cards and Dance":

> The dance is simply a hugging match set to music. The dance is a
> sexual love feast. This crusade against the dance is for everybody,
> not merely for the preacher or the old man or woman who couldn't
> dance if they wanted to, but for everybody interested in morals,
> whether in the church or out of the church.

> My wife and I have been at the bedside of a girl who was dying in a
> house of ill fame. She said the reason of her downfall had been the
> dance, which she began when fifteen years old. She used to attend
> Sunday School. When we asked her if she had any message for the
> girls, she cried, "Tell the girls and warn them to let the dance alone."

Do you know that three-fourths of all the girls who are ruined owe their downfall to that very thing. You let a young man whose character would make a black mark on a piece of tar paper, who goes down the line every other night, hug and dance with your daughter, and see what happens. They are dancing the tango, the rottenest, most putrid, stinkingest dance that ever wriggled out of the pot of perdition — that's what the tango is.

I have more respect for a saloon-keeper than for a dancing teacher. I don't believe the saloons will do as much to damn the morals of young people as the dancing school.[11]

Earlier, Mr. Roosevelt had been the honored guest at a noon luncheon sponsored by 300 members of the Commercial Club in the restaurant of the Hotel Muehlebach. Escorted to his table, the former president found himself seated next to Billy Sunday. The consummate politician, Roosevelt greeted the evangelist effusively: "By George, Billy, I'm glad to see you." Teddy smiled broadly as Sunday, who had earlier described Teddy as "the greatest American alive," pressed him about once again running for the presidency: "I don't think it, I know it, and if you are nominated at Chicago you will receive the biggest vote given a candidate in the history of the country."

Roosevelt thanked the evangelist for his support and cheerfully maintained his good humor as Billy proceeded to bend his ear for 15 minutes. But it was another man that day whom the former president likely regarded as the more amiable companion — a former comrade-in-arms, retired Colonel William F. Beck. The two had served together in Cuba during the Spanish-American War some 18 years earlier, and each recalled those days as among the most intense and meaningful in his own experience.

The former president was delighted to greet his former comrade after so many years and even more "dee-lighted" to meet the charming little girl who accompanied him. Although still separated from her mother, Colonel Beck had brought along his daughter Helen, of whom he was most proud. He was eager to introduce her to the great man. Being quite small for her age, Helen looked much younger than her actual 12 years. Roosevelt promptly swept her up onto his lap.

---

[11] Billy Sunday probably knew as much about the Bible as any man of his generation, yet he seems to have been oblivious to the admonition in Ecclesiastes 3 : 1-8 that: "To every thing there is a season, and a time to every purpose under the heaven: A time to be born, and a time to die; ... A time to weep, and a time to laugh; a time to mourn, and a time to dance."

What with an early rising and all the singing and associated hoopla, it had been an exhausting morning for little Helen. So, as the animated conversation between her father and Mr. Roosevelt droned on, she snuggled more closely against his chest, closed her eyes and fell asleep.

Recalling the encounter in later years, Sally always loved to tell about the time: "I sat on Teddy's lap. I don't remember anything he said, but I remember he had on a rough tweed suit, and I remember how nice he smelled."

The eminent Mr. Roosevelt thought it was just "bully" that Colonel Beck had honored his daughter with the name of Helen Gould. And, despite the distractions of an otherwise busy day, he must have also taken note of the extraordinary charm and beauty of the enchanting Miss Beck.

He would not be the last.

CHAPTER TWO

Coming of Age

I went into first year French in high school better equipped
than the other people in my class.... English Lit, starting with
Shakespeare, sounded exciting. Gym and swimming, what the
hell, I could always dive deeper, stay under longer, and come
up drier than any of the boys I knew. So it looked like
everything was going to be just great. How little I knew.
~ Sally Rand

On July 7, 1898, only a few days after the young William Beck had taken
part in the battle for San Juan Hill in Cuba, President McKinley signed
a resolution approving the annexation of the Hawaiian Islands to become a
territory of the United States. This action laid the groundwork for expansion
of trade with the mainland, particularly after the opening of the Panama
Canal in 1914. This great realignment of shipping lanes was officially
celebrated at the 1915 Panama-Pacific International Exposition in San
Francisco — the first "World's Fair" to be held in California.

As would so often prove to be the case, one of the exposition's most popular
attractions would be neither an imposing structure nor a highbrow presentation, but rather, the appearance of unheralded performers. Indeed, the
Royal Hawaiian Quartet's rendition of "On the Beach at Waikiki" launched an
interest in Hawaiian music that would persist for another 25 years. By the
time the exposition closed, an estimated 17 million visitors had passed
through the Hawaii Pavilion, attracted not only by the catchy music but also
by a frenetic and sexually provocative dance called the "hula." Today, the
hula is performed primarily for tourists in a family-friendly manner, but in
the late 1800s and early 20th century, certain forms of the native dance were
overtly suggestive, if not outright simulations of sexual intercourse.

Commenting on a performance he witnessed in 1866 as part of the funeral
ceremonies for the Hawaiian King's sister, Helen Beck's distant cousin
Mark Twain observed:

At night they feasted and the girls danced the lascivious hula hula
dance that is said to exhibit the very perfection of educated motion

of limb and arm, hand, head and body, and the exactest uniformity
of movement and accuracy of "time." It was performed by a circle
of girls with no raiment on them to speak of, who went through an
infinite variety of motions and figures without prompting, and yet
so true was their "time," and in such perfect concert did they move
that when they were placed in a straight line, hands, arms, bodies,
limbs and heads waved, swayed, gesticulated, bowed, stooped,
whirled, squirmed, twisted and undulated as if they were part and
parcel of a single individual; and it was difficult to believe they
were not moved in a body by some exquisite piece of mechanism.

The story of the hula goes to the essence of Hawaii's past, present and
future, and it has always fascinated beholders.

Faith

Among the fascinated in 1919 was nine-year-old Frances Yvonne Bacon.
In an interview with Kaspar Monahan years later, she revealed that she had
been "peeping from the top of a Hawaiian hut at the dance orgies of natives."
The precocious Miss Bacon's familiarity with nudity and suggestive dancing
would ultimately lead to a singular development without which there would
have been little impetus for writing this book. We had best keep an eye
on her.

Mary Belle

Miss Bacon was not the only one worth watching. On May 31, 1916, the very
next day after 12-year-old Helen Beck fell asleep in the lap of former
President Theodore Roosevelt, a man named George Withrow, recently
returned from 13 years in the Yukon and Alaska, died in the home of his
daughter Mary Belle. By then she was married to Richard Vance Spencer, a
Chicago physician, and was looking to become a professional woman in her
own right. Mary Belle Spencer and young Helen were on a collision course
that would be 17 years in the making.

Between the fall of 1911 and spring of 1918, young Helen Beck attended
Greenwood Grammar School, located near an impoverished orphanage.
Classes at Greenwood were crowded, so much so that the adoption of split
sessions only brought class sizes down to forty. In 1914, the Missouri school
welcomed a first-grader named Bobby Heinlein, whose father was
employed as a cashier by the local International Harvester dealer. Bobby
loved school and he loved books. Copies of L. Frank Baum's *Sky Island* and
Roy Rockwood's *Through Space to Mars* were said to be among his most
prized possessions.

No ordinary young man, Bobby grew up to become the famous science fiction writer Robert A. Heinlein, author of *The Puppet Masters* and *Stranger in a Strange Land*. Although he was three years younger, Heinlein developed a crush on Helen that would last in some form or another for the rest of his life. (There continues to be speculation that Heinlein enjoyed an open marriage and that he and Sally had a sexual relationship at some point.)

A newspaper advertisement for the Georgia Brown Dramatic School of Kansas City, Missouri, read:

> HAVE YOU DRAMATIC TALENT? Every day thousands of young men and women are preparing for occupations which ultimately become monotonous and distasteful and bring failure. If you have a wish or desire for a successful stage career, it is only fair to yourself to prepare for it.

By the time Helen Beck graduated from Greenwood Grammar School, the 13-year-old was already pursuing her dreams at Mrs. Brown's popular school, an institution that had been training young stage aspirants for more than 15 years.

On June 18, 1917, the school presented its annual review at Kansas City's expansive Auditorium Theater. Helen's part was small — one of eight girls singing a tune called "The Bell," presented midway through the program. Although just three months earlier the Georgia Brown Players had produced a weekly series of plays in which many young male students had been featured, Helen's recital was an all-girl show. In a reversal of Shakespearean tradition, even the male parts were performed by girls. Mrs. Brown had denied permission for her male students to train for the performance because, in April of that year, the country had entered the Great War in Europe and she believed that "their talent for the stage should be abandoned for military training."

The entry of the United States into World War I also led to the departure of Helen's estranged father. It isn't clear whether William Beck resumed his military career at age 43 for patriotic or economic reasons, or whether he just needed an excuse to finally remove himself from any further relationship with his wife. In any case, he was gone, and he wasn't in France very long before he secured a divorce, met and married Mademoiselle Marie Louise Delamazure (22 years his junior), and started a second family.

Between the ages of 13 and 16, Helen Beck made a number of stage appearances at various Kansas City theaters and dance venues.

Because so many of her interviews and press releases in later years were slanted toward creating an image for herself, it is often difficult to separate fact from invention in the various biographical sketches released to the media over the years. What can be said with a degree of certainty is that she did study under several ballet teachers and did perform as a member of more than one local stock company.

Among the more suspect reports of Helen's young life is the lengthy account by another author that describes her running away from home as a 14-year-old to join a traveling carnival. Supposedly, she had been fantasizing about carnival life, had walked barefoot to the show grounds, and had impressed the carnival manager so much that he offered her a job.

Sally herself embellished her life story in a 1934 interview with James Aswell, offering an unconfirmed version of another early sojourn:

Q: Were you born in New York, Miss Rand?

A: Ah, no. I am a country girl, a farm girl.... I was thirteen and already contributing a good deal to the family support, working in a theatrical stock company. So I came to New York.

Q: At thirteen?

A: Ah, yes at thirteen.[1] I was a mere child. I obtained a job in a nightclub, but I found the atmosphere — the milieu, if you understand — warred with my sense of delicacy, my good taste. I used to weep when I told my Italian ballet master of the vulgarities of my surroundings.

Q: Then you got a job in a Broadway show, I believe?

A: Yes. But there, too, I was unhappy. I yearned for dramatic roles and only chorus positions were available at the time. I was so unhappy in the theater, Mr. Aswell, so unhappy. The patter backstage was strange to my childish ears. People jested about matters which had always been sacred to me. I rebelled. I went back home and studied dancing some more.

During the later years of her life, Sally made sporadic attempts to write her memoirs, a project she took most seriously, even exchanging

---

[1] While it seems unlikely that Helen actually went to New York by herself at such a young age, her description of events does correspond with her experiences in New York (recounted in chapter 3) when she was 18. She may have felt compelled to exaggerate her youth to James Aswell because, at the time of his 1934 interview, many believed that she was younger than her actual 30 years of age.

correspondence with a number of interested agents and publishers. Though never completed, tantalizing fragments of what might have become an autobiography have survived.

Sally devoted an extensive reminiscence to her time at Christian College in Columbia, Missouri (now Columbia College). The "college" she attended at the age of 15 — really a boarding school for girls located 140 miles to the east of Kansas City — advertised itself in local papers as "An Ideal Junior College for Women." What follows is Sally's own lively account of her sole semester there (lightly edited and condensed for clarity):

> The summer of 1919, after having spent my first year of high school at Central in Kansas City, Mama started talking to me about boarding school for my second year of high school. We looked in the magazines and sent off for brochures and literature from various girls' boarding schools in the area.
>
> Actually, I sent off to New York for brochures from the American Academy of Dramatic Arts, the Denishawn School of Dance, and various well known schools of ballet. I was dreaming of the theater and of being another Pavlova. Mother had been very patient with me as concerned these ambitions. I had seen Pavlova dance at our Convention Hall in Kansas City, at a Saturday matinee performance when I was in the fourth grade. I returned home from this matinee performance with my program clutched in my little hot hand (I still have that program), dazed, starry-eyed, enchanted, and with a fierce fixation and determination that this was to be my life, the ballet. I lived it, dreamed it, ate it, and slept it. I drove everybody up the walls, pleading for lessons.
>
> Mother finally capitulated and enrolled me at Georgia Brown's School of Drama and Dance which had a curriculum based upon the Delsarte's system of philosophy, body building, speech, gestures, etc., including basic French and posture. The final portion of these Saturday afternoon sessions was devoted to cotillions, at which time we wore white gloves and were taught how a young man asks a lady to dance and how a young lady accepts a dance and the various dance steps that were then popular, such as the waltz, Maxixe, and maybe even the tango.
>
> The 2:30 afternoon cotillion sessions really turned me off. First of all, I didn't have the white gloves, I didn't give a damn whether I danced with a boy or not, I was only interested in the ballet. So I took

the money my mother gave me every Saturday and went down the street to Professor Peri's School of the Ballet. One of the girls in my fourth grade was also a student there. When mother found out and investigated the school she was content for me to make the change.

Receiving all that literature and brochures from many, many schools, as well as from the schools of drama and ballet in New York, was very exciting. Mother let me dream about the dramatic and ballet schools but sent off for more information about some of the girls' boarding schools in our area. I was not really convinced that I was "too young" to go to New York or an eastern school of drama or ballet, but she did thoroughly convince me that I wouldn't be going to any of them that fall. So, together, for various reasons we decided upon Christian College.

I wish I had those books, catalogues, and brochures from Christian at that time. The big gate was beautiful and awesome then, even as it is now. The sweeping lawns and trees and the front doors looked very much then as they do now. The gussied-up photographs of a "typical" student's room were just as erroneous then as they are now. The "minimum clothing" list, viewed by today's standards, is pretty hysterical....[2]

Observe, please, that we wore uniforms to all classes; cotton stockings were de rigueur, while silk stockings were verboten, as were silk lingerie and high heels, even "baby French."

Parents were instructed to answer a very personal questionnaire which included marital, financial and religious status, plus the names and addresses of banker, attorney, pastor of church, plus the names of six persons to whom the school might write, if they wished, for references as to the moral, financial, and religious responsibility of said parents and daughters. An asterisk at the marital status question directed one's attention to a footnote which said, "The daughters of divorced parents are not normally welcomed at Christian College. Mitigating circumstances, however, if verified, may abrogate this rule."

This questionnaire gave Mom a few difficult moments, like, who had a banker? And who needed an attorney? Of course, the pastor of our church was no problem. As for six references as to financial,

---

[2]   The brochure's lengthy list included several "Peter Thompson dresses," and special clothes (including gloves and a "nice little suit") for Sunday church and Friday evening dinners, plus cotton underwear and night clothes, "gym bloomers," etc.

moral, and religious responsibility, there was our corner grocery store, with whom we had had an account for years. There was the publisher and the editor of the *Kansas City Post*, for whom mother worked as a reporter, and the doctors and the hospital for whom she nursed,[3] and of course we did own our own home. Well, not exactly owned it. We were paying for it in installments, so the mortgage department at the Commerce Trust Company would do for a banker. Then, there was Brother Sinclair, pastor of our Jackson Avenue Christian Church, to which we had all belonged since my brother and I had been infants in the Cradle Roll.

The marital status thing bugged Mom a little. But she felt sure all could be explained. Father was a captain in the army with Pershing's American Expeditionary Forces in Europe. Actually, he was shacking up with some glamorous broad in Paris, and had just written my mother asking her to get a divorce or he would proceed with one. This was the most shocking and traumatic experience of my Mother's life.

Mom went for spiritual support and advice to Brother Sinclair, a knowledgeable and sophisticated man, considering his profession and the time in which he lived. He advised mother that men away from home, at war in strange and new environments, sometimes lost sight of virtues. That father was just infatuated, would get over it, and would return home contrite and sorry. That mother should do nothing at this time, but await his return home, and meanwhile to pray, not to feel angry and bitter, but to pray for her own toler-ance, compassion, to give love and to know that Father would awaken from his fantasy. Prayer and the knowledge that prayers are answered — that is the answer. So Mother went forward with this presumption — faith and prayer. It never occurred to Mother that all of this would not be understood and taken into considera-tion by Christian College. After all, wasn't it "Christian" College?

---

[3] Helen's mother was not only a trained nurse, but also a reporter for the *Kansas City Post*. According to Kelly McEniry of the University of Missouri-Kansas City, the *Post* achieved remarkable success as a below-the-belt tabloid newspaper. When Annette Beck worked there, the editors encouraged every yellow journalistic method and reinforced the daily paper's allegiance to political boss Tom Pendergast. As the city's only Democratic sheet, it captured readers with elaborate photo spreads, comic strips, biting editorials and banner headlines printed in red ink. A 1979 article by Bob Thomas suggested that Helen became enamored with show business because, as a *Post* reporter, her mother was able to get free theater passes.

The brochures further listed the price of room and board. The
prices quoted for tuition included the 3R's and P.E. only.
Everything else cost extra: tuition, music, singing, dancing, art, art
materials, chemistry equipment, the use of the practice room for
piano, etc. There were also three different prices of rooms. Highest
were the big front suites, "bedroom, alcove, and sometimes bath."
Next were less desirable rooms with more roommates, and last the
inside rooms facing the court, called "tin pan alley," with
roommates according to the size of the room, one bath with four
shower stalls (no tubs), three washbowls, and two "commodes" (I
quote commodes), for all the occupants of tin pan alley.

This hall was directly across from, and so close to, the rooms where
many girls practiced on many pianos. From morning till night there
was constant, distracting sound; therefore, I guess, "tin pan alley."

To Mother, the prices quoted for tuition only (with no extras, plus
the very cheapest room) were startling, almost prohibitive....
Parents were instructed to send a cashier's check for tuition, board,
room, plus a suitable deposit for purchases made at the commissary,
laundry, and weekly allowances they wished their daughters to
have. This check was to accompany the questionnaire....

If proper credit was established, in rare cases arrangements could
be made for partial payment of tuition and room, but all extras and
the deposit for laundry, commissary and weekly allowance had to
be paid in advance. Mother had faith that such arrangements could
be made in our case, and so she sent the completed questionnaire,
plus a small down payment for tuition and the deposit for the
extras and then we waited.

And we waited, and waited.

Mother grew less and less cheerful. I had mixed feelings. I was by
turns excited about going away to school and equally depressed
when I thought of leaving all my friends and schoolmates, having
to wear a uniform, strict regimentation (to which I had never been
subjected). I had a feeling of rejection that even my own Father
didn't love me enough to feed, clothe, and shelter me and had
taken off with "that woman," and now even my Mother wanted to
send me away. So I didn't much care if we never got a letter from
Christian College. Finally it came, with many doubts and
misgivings — and if's, the's, and's, and but's — but I was finally
accepted as a student at Christian College.

I don't know how Mother felt. She probably had mixed feelings, too. As for myself, I started feeling hostile, like "Who the hell do they think they are? And what's so great about boarding school?" And so forth and so forth!

But now the die was cast and preparations were started. Mother kept enough money every week to buy the Peter Thompson dresses and we shopped for weeks to find a "nice little suit" that we could afford. It was lovely, soft brown wool (I hate brown) with a Norfolk jacket, pleated and belted. But we did find a pretty, bright coral blouse to wear with it, and my aunt in the millinery business matched it with a vagabond sailor felt hat and medium-heeled brown pumps. That was my "good suit" outfit.

Up to this time, for underwear I had been wearing panty waists, with little slots for supporters to fasten one's long stockings to. These came with drawers that fastened onto the bottom of the panty waist, but now that I was getting bumps in the right places and I was going to a school where people would see my underwear, I wanted it to be pretty and fancy. So Mama bought me some pink cotton crepe and white cotton lace. We selected a pattern that had camisole and panties, in one piece, with lace around the top and lace shoulder straps and lace around the bottom of the drawers, with a drop seat. How jazzy can you get?

I sewed well enough to make many of my dresses and so I sat down and made two pairs of cotton underthings and diligently sewed all the lace on by hand. Gosh, I thought they were just beautiful. There was enough material to make a pink cotton wraparound kimono, my very first robe. And we sewed labels on everything.

Time was getting short and we had no trunks or luggage, so we packed everything in one of Papa's old army lockers.

The brochures told how a Christian College representative, Mrs. So-and-So, would be at the Union Station, in Kansas City, Missouri, at a certain hour, on a certain day, to chaperone all the Kansas City girls from Kansas City to Columbia, Missouri, and then by bus to Christian College. By this time Mama was getting pretty nervous about money so she decided we couldn't afford the train trip. A friend of ours, who lived down that way, had a Model T. Since she was going to be in Kansas City she agreed to drive us down to Christian College on the Friday preceding the opening of school. It was the first time I had ever been on a long trip in a car. I had driven

around the city a couple of times. It really was a lovely trip, but the
closer we got to Columbia, Missouri, the more miserable and unhappy I became, until I finally arrived, sobbing my heart out on my
Mother's bosom. It was a hell of a way to arrive at my new school.

By the time we got there all the Kansas City girls had arrived very
elegantly by train, and when our little Model T showed up at the
front door with the old army locker, I began to feel a little
embarrassed. Mama and I went in to an empty reception room,
found somebody, and said who and what we were, and why. Our
obviously country friend dragged the army locker in, and there we
stood ... that stinking army locker, standing on its end, seemed to
be getting bigger and bigger and more conspicuous, and I got more
and more embarrassed ... I dried my eyes, tried to compose myself,
but that terrible, dreadful, awful army locker, sticking straight up
in the middle of that elegant reception room so humiliated me that
I wanted to hide under any convenient chair or sofa. I finally
scrunched down on an inconspicuous hassock.

Mrs. Moss, the president of the college (whom I identified by her
pictures), arose in the queen position, on the front-facing sofa. Her
hair had been perfectly coifed into marcelled washboard waves,
which was the proper style for a lady (girls who had been so bold
as to have their hair bobbed were considered the hippies of that
time). She cast a limpid eye upon the sea of fresh young teenage
faces. Her gaze finally came to rest, startled, on the goddamn foot
locker. "What," she queried imperiously, "is it, and what is it doing
here?" I shrank still further into the Brussels carpet. One of the
graduate students ... broke the hypnotic silence and hustled the
locker off into the hall.

Now that this alien and horrendous thing had been removed from
her elegant drawing room, Mrs. Moss continued. She introduced
herself as the president of Christian College, briefly sketched its
founding, history and purpose, and pointed out the high honor
bestowed upon we who were students at Christian.[4] She made arch
reference — "Ha-ha" — to "Christian girls," and in sterner tones

---

4   According to Columbia College, Luella St. Clair-Moss served three separate terms as
     president and pushed through so many initiatives that she was dubbed a "steam engine
     in petticoats." She ran for Congress in 1920, among the first women to do so. Defeating
     two men in the primary to secure the Democratic Party nomination, she lost to the
     Republican incumbent by a considerable margin in the general election. It would be
     another 32 years before Missouri would send a woman to Congress.

commented on the profound obligation of each to uphold with fervor and pride and standards and traditions of Old CC, to maintain high grade levels, sportsmanship, leadership, elegance in behavior and attitude, etc., etc.

I was too miserable and homesick and unhappy to listen, hear, or understand very much, but as she continued I finally looked up and looked around at my peers. Golly, they all looked like princesses, so beautiful, ladylike, cool, detached. "Oh, God, what the hell was I doing here?" Ugly, ungroomed, travel-worn, badly dressed, and utterly miserable. How could they like me? I could never make friends with them here. I would run away. I would just run home, that's all.

Well, I might as well wait until this is over, so I gave my attention to Mrs. Moss. From the top of her iron grey hair to the tips of her toes that you couldn't see under her dress, she was impeccable. The creamy Battenberg lace collar and yoke of her gown was held high on the neck, implacably, by invisible stays, and the same lace trimmed the full-length sleeves. The fit of her gown left one in no doubt of the invulnerability, strength, and purpose of her whalebone corset. There was not the slightest indication of the pink and white softness of anything so vulgar and unmentionable as female flesh.

I almost giggled when I thought about the time my Quaker grandmother told me her husband had never seen her without her corset and my totally unintended impertinence when I naively replied, "Yes, Grandmother, but we are here."

I paid attention again as she was introducing another beautiful lady, Mrs. Hardin, white-haired in a soft blue dress trimmed in white lace, with pink cheeks, blue eyes, and a sparkling smile. Mrs. Hardin was really the acting head of the school, and spoke to us briefly and sympathetically about how the first few days were difficult, but we would soon find our way around to a happy, constructive year, what good friends we would make, etc. She also said it was perfectly natural to be homesick when you first came away to school like this and not be ashamed of it, but to keep busy, and write home and try to adjust, and pretty soon everything would be all right. This made me warm up to her right away. Especially when she said that her office was always open and that we could come to see her at any time with any of our problems or anxieties and that whatever we said in her office was strictly confidential. All right, maybe this wasn't going to be so bad.

And then Miss Law was introduced as the principal. A spinster, her iron grey hair was drawn uncompromisingly over a high intelligent forehead into a small tight bun at the base of her neck. Her dark dress was hard to describe; maybe it was puce or bottle-green or off-black, but there was no doubt that it was devoid of ornament, style, and fashion, save only the cameo pin on its high neck. She seemed very old to me, but gosh, when you're that age your mother, who is only 20 years older than you, seems like an old lady and your grandmother, in her fifties, ready for the grave. Miss Law had things to say, but in a very gentle voice. She kept her hands clasped tightly at her waistline, over her abdomen, and reminded us that there were rules, implacable, which must be kept. That the irrevocable result of breaking the rules was punishment. And punishment was very undesirable.

We were informed that the traditional Saturday school holiday was not so at Christian — that Monday was our school holiday. Sundays were devoted to religious training and church services. After Sunday dinner, served at noon, there was the "quiet hour of contemplation," after which we might walk around the campus or visit with relatives who had first been cleared at the office for such visitations, after which there was a light early supper, vespers, study hour, and lights out.

Tomorrow, Saturday, would not start classes. The morning hours until lunch would be devoted to unpacking clothes, arranging rooms, etc. We were to present ourselves at lunch in our blue Peter Thompson school uniforms. After lunch each grade group would convene in a different place to be assigned classes, teachers, classrooms, and their hours of recitation and study.

Except for brief chaperoned shopping trips, no student was permitted outside or off the campus under any circumstances, for any reason whatsoever.... With small groups of girls leaving the campus with chaperones, no student of Christian College was permitted to speak to or stop and talk to any male under any circumstances whatsoever, unless prior permission had been given before leaving campus. Oh well, what the hell, I didn't know anybody in Columbia, Missouri, anyway (I thought) and besides, who is going shopping? No matter what I needed, I didn't have any money to go shopping.

We were finally dismissed and told to find our roommates, go to our rooms, and get ready for bed for early lights out, so we could start a busy day tomorrow. There was a great rush and exit.

And there I stood, in an agony of loneliness and embarrassment. I had never been above stairs; I didn't know where the hell I was going, where my room was, or if I even had a roommate, and, "Oh, God, what roommate?" I had never had a sister, I never roomed with another girl — this was going to be awful.

I finally stumbled out into the hall, drawn by a light shining through an open wicket, which indicated it might be an office and maybe even somebody in it. By standing on tiptoe I was able to rest my chin on the small protruding shelf, where I mumbled incoherent queries at a white shirtwaist, bending over a desk. What might have looked like a disembodied head swimming in the wicket in a dark, deserted hall must have scared the hell out of her. After the first startled yelp she scurried around with lists. There seemed to be some uncertainty about the whole thing. Maybe I wasn't even supposed to be there, I thought. But we finally wound up on the third floor, back in Tin Pan Alley, in the smallest room in school.

Sitting on the floor was a strange fat girl with the worst case of teenage acne I have ever seen, peering fixedly at the contents of several empty suitcases lying around, which she had piled up in a very untidy pile in front of her. The room was lit by a naked electric bulb, suspended on the end of a long black electric wire, directly in the center of the high-ceilinged room. The room contained two narrow, flat, springed cots covered by thin mattresses, two small golden oak chests, two straight chairs, and a frayed piece of faded green carpet. A torn green window shade hung limp and lopsided at the uncurtained window. Ugh!

The empty suitcases reminded me of the foot locker, somewhere in the hall below. I wanted to just ignore it, but I knew it was too heavy for me to carry upstairs by myself. I knew I was going to have to get ready for bed in front of this strange girl, so I would have to say something about it.

The fat girl leaped up with a greater alacrity than her bulk would have presumed.... The three of us staggered up three flights of narrow stairs with much huffing and puffing from Fatty. Tousled heads and people poked out of closed doors at our noisy passage, to remain transfixed and staring at this strange parade. Every

previously closed door on Tin Pan Alley was crowded with
onlookers to see what the hell was going on.

Meanwhile, I died a thousand deaths and finally collapsed behind
the closed door. Miss Shirtwaist made a hasty exit while Fatty and I
stared miserable and wordless at each other. Cheerfully avoiding
her own "Pike's Peak," she helped me get the foot locker under the
bare window like a kind of window seat, and stood back curiously
to watch me open it.

Oh, man, this was it. I couldn't think of any valid reason for
stalling any longer, so I opened it and started putting my things
away in the nearest golden oak dresser. Every single thing received
a rigid scrutiny by that mental inventory taker.

All my things I had once thought so pretty, and upon which I had
lavished such painstaking stitchery, suddenly seemed ugly and
cheap, even my pretty bright coral blouse and "good suit." I
wanted to hide in the bottom of the trunk. But I couldn't, I had to
hang them out because I had to wear them to church tomorrow.

Finally, when everything was hung and the last small piece put in
drawers, she asked me sort of off-handedly, "Where's your dinner
dress?"

By this time I was so unstrung and miserable that I didn't even try
to think of anything. I just blurted out, "I haven't got any. I'm just
going to wear my suit skirt and blouse." Time stopped for a
moment while this standing proclamation hung in the air. She sat
down on a cot, took off her glasses, and never looking up said, "Me
neither." It took a moment for the impact of this cogent piece of
information to penetrate my numbed brain and then we both
collapsed in helpless laughter.

We heard a timid knock at the door, immediately followed by its
bursting open and a whole crowd streaming in, asking "What in
the hell's so funny?" We finally got them out by telling them we
weren't unpacked yet and they could come back in a few minutes.

I rushed to get my new pink kimono over the foot locker window
seat, covered my bed with my white cotton crepe bedspread, put
the pictures of Mother, Brother, and Papa in his captain's uniform
on the dresser, and helped Fatty shove all her stuff under the bed,
where it could be hidden by her white bedspread. I never thought
of bringing a lampshade or curtains, I even forgot a pillow. It never

crossed my mind to bring food or candy. The only time we had candy at home was once a month when we paid the grocery bill.

But leave it to Fatty, out she came with a box of chocolates, a tin can of cookies, and a fringed leather sofa pillow with an Indian chief tastefully burned and painted on it (jazzy). Out came a pin tray made of cigar bands and another sofa pillow, made of six-inch squares of brightly patterned cotton flannel simulating miniature Indian blankets that came as prizes in Camel cigarettes (no doubt as an added inducement to start our fathers off as future cancer victims). Fatty dived under the bed and dragged out two lengths of patterned chintz, which we hastily pinned over the base window. Things were looking up. Another foray in the diminishing pile under the bed brought forth a highly colored lampshade, complete with fringe originally intended to be a "student's lamp," which Fatty's Mom had thoughtfully packed. I was impressed.

Damn! Anyone who wanted to read or write at my house used the dining room table, over which hung, suspended, a glass simulation of a morning glory flower, with globe, at a convenient height over the dining table. Any reading I did in bed was accomplished by the light of a candle I kept under my pillow and lighted under the blanket. This was strictly forbidden, of course, and I'd had my bubble butt[5] switched a hundred times for it, but I still persisted because if I had my "druthers," I'd rather bear the pain than not finish the story. It's a wonder I didn't burn the house down.

Now back to our cheerful room on Tin Pan Alley. We invited girls in, passed around the candy and cookies and indulged in our first "bull session." Giggling, whispering, and shushing until the blurry-eyed teacher who had been assigned to our hall to keep things down to a bare pandemonium finally dragged everyone out, with dire threats, and we fell down dead. I slept in my underwear; I was too tired to get on my nightgown with the lace on it or to show off my new pink underdrawers with the lace.

Suddenly bells were ringing, bright sunlight was streaming through our sleazy chintz curtains, and we leaped into the hall on a

---

[5] Most commonly understood to be a somewhat prominent, round and firm pair of buttocks which resemble a pair of bubbles, the origin of the phrase is unknown. It is not clear when Sally wrote the account of her time at Christian College so, while this may be an early usage, she probably didn't coin the term.

dead run to get to the bathroom first. We should have saved our strength; there they stood in line outside the bathroom door.

Fatty was in her "Omar the Tentmaker" cotton pink knickers and cotton vest bulges, and me in my pantywaist with the garters hanging suspended attached to nothing and my wrinkled cotton crepe drawers. Everybody else in line was very properly and tastefully attired in proper bathrobes, housecoats, and negligees. Seeing we were both a long way from the bathroom door, we slunk down the hall, put on our kimonos, and returned. We were practically the last to get into the shower stalls where we shrieked and shivered in a trickle of lukewarm water. Back to our room and into our Peter Thompson dresses. In the middle of which the breakfast bell sounded and I didn't get a chance to show off my new pink and white cotton lace underwear. Damn!

I hadn't been assigned a table yet, so I sat with Fatty at the table to which she had been assigned. We both ate like harvest hands. This was the morning we were to straighten up our rooms and unpack. Well, we'd done most of that last night. We did fasten a butcher string to the top of the chintz curtains, which we fastened to two already conveniently hammered nails. Of course it sagged a little in the center, but who cared?

This was just the time for a nice cozy chat, but both of us found ourselves curiously silent. She had seen all of my stuff, and I'd seen most of hers, so what's to talk about? We were comforted, though, by a kind of silent communion. By some curious and rapidly achieved overnight maturity we both understood the terror of stark aloneness — the misery of homesickness, the cold, sweaty, clammy discomfort of feeling different, not like the others, of not belonging, of not having things like the others had. So we paid our way with candy and cookies and disguised our lack of possessions by hastily pinned up decor, but we hadn't backed down, they even came to visit in our room, they might even like us, what the hell? Comforted by singularly quiet reflections on the events of the preceding evening, we spent a quiet morning, ate enormously at lunch, and went to the assigned classes and teachers.

I had a little going for me on this score; in this area I was pretty bright. I had discovered by accident that reading was my escape from reality. I was avidly curious and enjoyed studying to find out. I was pleasantly excited to find out about my new studies. Math was easy, an "eight ball in the side pocket." I had a little trouble with algebra the first year in high school, but having once reduced it to my grade school understanding of 1 x w = a, no sweat; it was easy and I was looking forward to the geometry which would be new that year and using all those instruments and rulers and making all those marks and figures. I was really excited about ancient history. In my grammar school years I had gone through the simplified versions of the Iliad and the Odyssey like a dose of salts, and kept finding new story books in the library on the same subject. I knew a little about Egypt from my Sunday school teaching and I figured this was going to be fun.

Because I had basic French at Georgia Brown's, I went into first year French in high school better equipped than the other people in my class. Mama, having been a school teacher, had given me good basic English grammar, without which you really can't learn a foreign language, and so second year French would be fun. English Lit, starting with Shakespeare, sounded exciting. Gym and swimming, what the hell, I could always dive deeper, stay under longer, and come up drier than any of the boys I knew. So it looked like everything was going to be just great. How little I knew.

Memory plays strange tricks. Psychiatrists tell us that the subconscious has no conscience. It stands guard at the door of consciousness and keeps you from remembering painful or unpleasant things. Maybe so. Oddly enough, I remember the names and everything about every one of my grade school teachers from kindergarten on. I vividly remember all the things I learned through kindergarten and from first to seventh grade; even my domestic science teacher. I remember all my teachers during my first year of high school, etc. I can't remember the name of a single one at Christian. I remember I liked my ancient history teacher, and I think she also doubled either in math or French. I can't remember a thing about my English teacher. I do remember our gym teacher was very pregnant, which limited our gymnastic activities somewhat, and I remember I was quite disappointed that we weren't going to do any dancing on account of her condition.

My not remembering this area of learning out of textbooks is probably because I was doing quite a bit of pretty mature emotional learning.

Notwithstanding the fact that my chubby roommate and I were getting on very well, it was not to last very long, because her sister was also going to Christian and it was decided that even though there was some disparity in their ages it probably would be better for them to room together, so they did. My new roommate's name was Charnelcie Allen, and I just adored her and still do. She was from Cape Girardeau. Her daddy was an attorney and her mother was dead. She was beautiful and still is, and a very talented artist and still is. I see her very often when I play Springfield, Illinois, as she lives close by with her husband in Taylorville. She paints beautifully and sells much of her work.

Charnelcie had more experience than I did being around girls. Actually, she was the type of person who would get along with anybody, anywhere. She was much more emotionally secure and socially integrated than I. It's very lucky for me that I had her for a roommate. I was violently homesick, terribly depressed, and very hostile to what seemed to me to be over-regimentation.

I got in trouble right away. On one of the rare trips I ever made off campus into town, just to get an ice cream soda with a chaperone and several other girls, I stopped to talk to two boys I had gone to Sunday School with ever since I'd been in the primary class. They were the sons of our Jackson Avenue Christian Church Sunday School super-intendent. Golly, I had known them all my life, and here they were enrolled at Missouri University. Like wow! I had forgotten about the rule that you were not supposed to talk to any males on the street unless you had prior permission. How could I get prior permission when I didn't even know they were there — but I got campused for it.

I got special permission, and very special, too, to go to the Missouri-Kansas football game with Lee Broer, the youngest of our Sunday school superintendent's boys. He was a freshman at MU. After the game, Lee invited me over to his older brother's fraternity house and of course I went, had a buffet dinner, went for a ride around the lake and got back to Christian after 8:00 o'clock. Horrors! I was campused again.

It was just after this that Mrs. Moss asked me into her office for a very private discussion, during which she told me how a certain girl had gone buggy riding with a boy and became pregnant. The way Mrs. Moss told it, it appeared that it was the buggy ride that caused it. I'm sure I didn't endear myself to this austere lady by asking "You mean like Mary and the Immaculate Conception?" Listen, I wasn't being impertinent; actually I was just trying to find out. From thenceforth I had the feeling that Mrs. Moss took a dim view of me.

Then there was that bit about "dressing for dinner." Frankly, we had never lived very "high on the hog," and I really didn't understand exactly what it meant — "to dress for dinner." The best I had was my suit and my coral shirtwaist, that's all I had, and so I wore it, and wore it, and wore it, Friday after Friday, until I was too embarrassed to wear it again and just didn't show up for Friday dinner. After several Friday absences Mrs. Hardin asked me into her office and asked me why. I just told her the truth — that I really didn't mind, I wasn't very hungry, and that I always took a little something from lunch, to do me. Bless her, she did understand and said that was all right, that I could have Charnelcie bring me something up from dinner, which she did.

This was my first and only time to have a crush on a "big girl." She was a junior, belonged to the Student Council, and I thought she was so elegant and so beautiful. She seemed to invite confidences, so I confided some rather personal things to her about my Father and his being in France and how badly I felt because he hadn't come home — and about a boy I thought I was very much in love with who had gone away to school. The result of this confiding was that it was all retold to the Student Council with what must have been some rather bizarre embellishments.

Being asked very pointed questions about the details of those confidences by the Student Council and both Mrs. Moss and Mrs. Hardin, in a joint session, was one of the most humiliating experiences of my life. I remember I didn't want to face anybody ever again. I just wanted to crawl off into a hole and pull it in after me. But it was also a great lesson which I have never forgotten. Never tell anyone anything you don't want everyone else in the whole world to know. I may have decided later in my life that there are exceptions to this rule, but I never used them and I still think that it's a very good rule to follow. It makes for being a loner, but what's so bad about that, actually?

The things I loved about Christian were the grassy lawns, the big beautiful trees that turned such beautiful colors, the majesty of the two big columns at the front gate, the quiet dignity of its architecture, the feeling of security behind its high fence. I loved my room in late afternoons. Before I put the light on I would sit on my contrived window seat, that hateful army trunk, and listen to all the girls practicing piano just across from me. What had once been a cacophony became melodious and beautiful and much to be desired. How I wished Mama could have afforded piano lessons for me! Then the early dusk would peep in and girls would be coming from different classrooms and different places and it was very quiet, that time just before dinner, and I liked that.

Charnelcie would come bursting in, laughing and happy, having just left some friendly group, which was one of the things I didn't seem able to manage. She turned on the light and it would be gay and fun and she'd take my hand and we would go down to dinner together. How much I appreciated this friendly, sisterly, kind way she was with me.

I also enjoyed the quiet study hours and for the first time I realized how conducive this was to getting your lessons better. In our noisy house, with a younger brother and lots of kin folks coming and going all the time, I had no special place to study or any special time. The dining room table was everybody else's. Newspapers and writing and everything else on it were all I'd ever known. I thought it was pretty wonderful, but I found I could do much better work and much more accurate with a room of my own and a place to read and write without distraction. I liked it very much.

Some Friday afternoons and some Sunday afternoons at Christian were devoted to tea parties, at which tea and cake were served. We were instructed in the proper way of meeting and serving guests, sitting, standing, and walking, and these are things I have never forgotten: how to sit with the knees together and one foot placed slightly in front of the other, erect with the back straight and the hands serenely in one's lap, not fidgeting, not tearing handkerchiefs to pieces, and not jittering, certainly never crossing the knees or winding your toes around the legs of a chair — horrors, no!

I'm not laughing at it or about it. I'm not making fun of it. It's beautiful and right; I have remembered it all these years and have never stopped practicing it. The way of introductions, younger people to adults — one asks permission to present a young friend to an adult; a younger person always stands when an older woman comes into a room and always stands to be presented; a lady adjusts her hat and all of her apparel before she leaves the front door, including her gloves. A lady wears her hat and her gloves outside the door or the very adjacent yard of her domicile, except after five, and then one does not wear a hat to dinner or thereafter. Good manners and good rules to be remembered always.

Christian did a play that year.... I remember that one of the numbers in it was "Aba Daba Daba said the Monkey to the Chimp," and another about the "Yamaha Girl." It should have been very exciting for me, since I was so stage-struck, but I had a couple of other things on my mind that were pretty distracting for a youngster.

I had received a letter from my Father in Paris, saying that he would be coming home at a certain time in late November or around the first of December, and that his boat would be coming into New Orleans. After spending a few days in New Orleans, he would then go on to Kansas City, but then he became pretty vague about what his plans were. I wrote and asked him if he couldn't come by Columbia and see me on his way up from New Orleans. I wanted to talk to him privately so desperately; and then of course I wanted to show him off in his beautiful uniform in front of all the girls.

His answer was that he didn't think there would be time, that he was still in the army and had to get back to New York to make military plans, and so forth. This answer dashed my hopes to a certain extent, but I still had plans and the more I thought of it the more determined I became — I decided to do it. I would just take the train and go down to New Orleans and meet my father's boat; that's what I would do.

Having once made the decision, now for ways and means. I ascertained that it would cost $7.00 each way to go from Columbia, Missouri, to New Orleans on the train in a chair car. At that time $14.00 was as far out of my reach as $1,400.00; still I knew there must be some way, so I wrote my Grandfather down in Elkton. I didn't tell him what I wanted it for, but I said that Mom was having a pretty hard time and that I needed a little bit of spending money and could he send me some. God bless him, he sent me two bucks.

That just about exhausted my ways and means department until I thought of a boy I'd known in high school, Frank Taylor, who was really just a friend. I hadn't even had an ice cream soda with him, let alone dated him, ... but this boy had a very good job and I knew he was saving money to go to college, so I figured if I could borrow some money from him, I could get a job during the Christmas holidays and pay him back.... He sent it to me in cash, in a letter by return mail ... and so now I was all set, almost. Now I had to find out exactly when that boat got in and at what time the train left from Columbia that would get me down to New Orleans at the right time, and all of these very important details. I finally got the whole thing together.

Getting all the details and working out the plan was very exciting, but the closer it got to putting it into action, the more scared I got. I had learned my lesson about confiding anything to anyone and so Charnelcie didn't know anything about it, although she did know that there was something awfully wrong with me and she was worried about it.

Fortunately the boat that Papa was going to come in on got in on a Tuesday afternoon. The train I could take out of Columbia left in the evening around 7:00 o'clock or so, so that made it just fine. Monday was our day off, so Sunday evening after vespers and Sunday supper, I packed my little bag and sneaked off campus down to the railroad station, bought my tickets and got on the train.

The excitement of doing all this brought my spirits up for the time being, but the minute those wheels started turning away from Columbia, Missouri, I was really almost physically ill with fear and apprehension. The faster the wheels clacked the more scared I was. First of all, how Papa would take it and just how mad he would be at me, and then how to go back to school and face Mrs. Moss and Mrs. Hardin and all those girls. Maybe I might be expelled and poor Mama would be so upset. I suppose I finally did sleep a little and when morning came I washed my face and hands and tidied up in the ladies room. Finally the train stopped in New Orleans and I got off.

I had been warned about asking strangers how to get places, so I went to the Stationmaster and explained that I had to get down to meet a certain boat. He told me what street car to take to get down to the wharf and said that there I should go ask the Wharf Master, which I did.

The boat wasn't in yet, but would be in shortly because they were out after it with the tugs, so I waited. It was very exciting being on the dock watching big cargo ships being unloaded; the very smell was strange and exciting. It was as close as I had ever been to the ocean.

Finally the little tugs started nudging the boat into its slip and my heart did a flip. My heart was pounding so fast I could hardly breathe. How would I know where he was coming off, and would I miss him? It wasn't really a big troop ship. There were quite a number of officers and military personnel aboard and so it was not difficult to see each one as they all came down the gangplank. I spotted my father before he left the deck and tried to be very inconspicuous, so he wouldn't see me. I need not have feared this because he wasn't looking for me. As he reached the end of the gangplank and stepped onto the pier, there were several other girls who had come to meet him, too, besides me; but he did notice me right away and looked utterly stunned.

He greeted his lady friends with great dignity and formality. I think he was a little surprised that three of them had shown up. He introduced me to them and then asked where he might be in touch with them later; they all wrote down things on papers and gave them to him. He then excused himself, saying that he would take his daughter out for early dinner and would be able to talk to them later, so away we went by cab to Galatoire's. Neither of us was very yacky on the way to the restaurant and he seemed utterly sad. He didn't seem to think that there was anything terribly wrong about my being there, although he was surprised, of course. But also I didn't tell him that I had run away from school, that I had borrowed money from Grandpa and a strange boy to get there, and I didn't tell him that Mama had no idea I was there. He asked me all the usual parental questions about how I was doing in school and how I liked the boarding school. He didn't mention Mama at all.

Finally I just couldn't stand it any longer. I told him how terrible it was for Mama, and how sad she had been and how she had cried and cried and cried and could never get over it, and what were brother and I going to do without a father, and would he please come home and make it like it was before.

His face grew sadder and sadder and when I finally started quietly crying he came around to my side of the table and cuddled me in his arms like he used to do. For a fleeting moment I thought that everything was going to be all right. Then he dried my eyes with his clean handkerchief and said things that parents usually do — kids just don't understand parents' problems — there are things that happen between men and women, or between a man and his wife which children could never understand — and on and on and on.

I scarcely listened. What did he think I was, an idiot? Of course I knew where babies came from and all things like that! What I didn't know was that he had a new baby in Paris and that he was torn between returning to a life that had been established with his two half-grown children and his wife of 17 years, and whatever it is a man feels about what had happened — about what was waiting for him in Paris. I didn't know this and probably wouldn't have understood it had I known it. It turned out not to be a very cheerful meal for either of us, and even the elaborate dessert with whipped cream and a maraschino cherry on the top didn't do much to raise my spirits — I couldn't even eat all of it. Now what?

Papa didn't know that I had run away from school, and probably thought that Mama had let me come, or had even sent me so that I would try to induce him to come home. He didn't seem as concerned as I thought he ought to be about what train I was going to get back, or what time I was going to leave, or anything. I guess he thought these arrangements had been made by an adult. He did take me to the train station, apparently believing that my train was going to leave quite soon. I waited long, dreary hours, more frightened and unhappy than I had ever been in my whole life.

It was a dreadful trip back to Christian, where I arrived late Tuesday evening, having been away from school all night Sunday night, all day Monday, all day Tuesday, and here it was bedtime Tuesday evening. I walked the long walk from the station up to Christian; a little more time wasn't going to make it any worse. I knew I was going to have to face the music and I knew it was going to be dreadful, and it was!

They had called Mother on the telephone and she was pretty frantic except that she knew, too, that Daddy's boat was coming in and she guessed that was where I had gone. He had called her from New Orleans and told her that I was on the train back to school, and was absolutely shocked that she had known nothing about it.

I told the whole story exactly the way it was. They even made me tell from whom I had borrowed the money, and that seemed to them to be the most shocking thing of all, not the fact that I had been out overnight and on a train and in the wicked city of New Orleans, but the fact that I had borrowed money from a man. How terrible! The fact that he was a boy whom I had known all my life and had gone to school with didn't seem to make any difference — I had taken money from a man — Wow!

I really was in very great danger of being expelled. If I had been, I don't think I could have borne it. There had been a couple of instances during that first semester where girls had been expelled. We in the lower grades had no idea what for, and all the details were kept carefully from us, but it certainly was sinister and terrible and awful! I knew it would have broken my Mother's heart, that she could never have faced it. Fortunately, everything I said, everything I told, was the truth and could be verified and was verified by Mama by telephone, and subsequently by my Father who, after he talked to Mother again, called the school to tell them.

The reprimands, while severe, were somewhat mitigated I suppose because even they could understand how terrible my need was to see my father, and how much I wanted to bring my parents back together again. I was campused from then until the Christmas holidays; I didn't even care. It seemed so trivial in comparison to the big grief I was carrying. I finally got to my room and to Charnelcie. I cried my tears and fell asleep exhausted, to get up early and make my morning classes.

I don't remember too much about what happened from there on out. I know Mama sent me money to come home for Christmas, but I knew before I left that I would never come back again.

I hadn't really made any friends excepting Charnelcie. I didn't blame anybody for it; I knew that it was really my own fault, that I hadn't made any outgoing gestures or really tried to be friends with people. I was very ingrown and very ungiving. Mine had been a completely different kind of life from that of the other girls, most of whom had been raised in families much better off economically than mine, and many of them were really very rich....

As the Christmas holidays grew closer and closer, I knew more and more surely that I wouldn't be coming back. This was a sadness because I had really come to like being there, notwithstanding everything that had happened. I really had an ambition to become one of them and to be like those other girls and have friends and be gay, but somehow I just knew it wasn't going to be that way. So when the day came to leave on the train, I found myself very sad at leaving, when I had thought I would be exuberant and happy to get home to my friends and Mom and the city.

It was just the opposite. I remember I didn't want to go back on the train with all the rest of the girls going to Kansas City, so I stalled around and got a later train by myself. Mom met me at the station and her hugs and kisses made me know that everything was going to be all right. Home was never so dear, wonderful and comfortable — home and Mom and familiar things and familiar ways and not being on edge all the time for fear you wouldn't say or do the right thing — what blessed peace!

Mama looked worn and tired. I thought it was because Daddy had been home, but they hadn't been able to make it up, and he had gone back to New York. That was only partially true. Mama had been doing twelve and sixteen-hour duties at the hospital to make enough money to pay my tuition at school. When I found this out I knew I just couldn't let her do this again, and I felt sure that I wasn't going back to Christian, that I'd look for a job.

Looking for a job sounds very simple and very brave, just saying it. But it's a very different matter when you start looking in those want-ad sections, and discover that you have no skills that anybody wants to pay for, and no education. You get very scared. Mama wanted me to go back to Central High School again, and I guess I expected to as soon as the Christmas holidays were over. But the opening of school was delayed because of a flu epidemic. I got a job briefly at the Frankel, Frank & Company wholesale millinery house and paid back the money I owed Frank Taylor and also the two dollars from Grandpa which Mama insisted I send.

When that job ended (it really didn't pay very much) I started looking at the want-ads again. I remember one particular day there were two ads to answer, one as a biscuit girl at the Nance Cafeteria, and the other as a "cigarette girl" at the Green Mill Restaurant. The job of biscuit girl at the Nance Restaurant had been filled by the time I got there, so I went up to the Green Mill Restaurant.... The Green Mill Restaurant was really a nightclub, and the start of my being in show business.

The Green Mill Café where Helen secured employment as a cigarette girl was located in "Electric Park," a popular Kansas City amusement park that featured an electric fountain water show and a wide variety of offerings, including band concerts and vaudeville shows, plus a ballroom, a carousel and other amusement rides.[6] Once a fixture in nightclubs and casinos, a "cigarette girl" was an attractive young woman in a short skirt (and commonly a pillbox hat) who roamed the club floor carrying a tray secured by a neck strap from which she dispensed cigarettes, cigars, candy, and novelty items. A cigarette girl may have been entitled to a small percentage of her sales, but her primary compensation came from tips.[7] Speaking of her experience 20 years later, Sally recalled her long blond curls and added coyly, "I was a cutie pie." She made $7 in tips the first night and $60 the first week she worked (the modern equivalent is $710 a week).

Not everything at the Green Mill Café was "merry and gay" during the holiday season. It turned out that Helen was a little too young for the job since the girls were required to "mix" with the customers. Furthermore, the Hotel and Restaurant Employees' International Alliance had been attempting to unionize waiters in Kansas City and the proprietor of the Green Mill responded by threatening to fire all the "colored" waiters and cooks. Mixing and labor issues aside, the 15-year-old's experience at the Green Mill in early 1920 had introduced her to working with the public within the confines of a large amusement park — heralding what would be waiting for her 13 years in the future.[8]

Mary Belle

On December 14, 1919, as Helen Beck was coming to the end of her time at Christian College, the 39-year-old Mrs. Mary Belle Spencer, renowned as the only female attorney in Chicago to have successfully handled a murder case, gave birth to a daughter she named Mary Belle Spencer, Jr. Two years later, a second daughter, Victoria, would follow. At the time, Mrs. Spencer achieved a measure of notoriety, finding herself at the center of a debate over whether or not a woman could successfully combine motherhood with a career. The

---

6   Electric Park also offered a shooting gallery, fortune tellers, and penny parlors, a Temple of Mirth, soda fountains and ice cream shops, as well as a scenic railway, boat tours, an alligator farm, outdoor swimming, and a horseless buggy garage. Souvenirs from the park touted it as "Kansas City's Coney Island," a venue it matched by illuminating its buildings with a display of 100,000 light bulbs. Live entertainment at the park included such vaudeville acts as Gorham's Midsummer Revue featuring Miss Rae Samuels ("The Blue Streak of Rag Time") and "The Seven Jolly Jesters."

7   In 1939, columnist Cal Tinney explained that "in case you don't know what a cigarette girl is, she's somebody who charges 15 cents for the fags and ten cents for the smile."

8   Besides her other jobs and appearances, the adolescent Miss Beck was once described as that "bathing suit girl in the *Follies* at Electric Park." The major summer attraction at Electric Park, the *Follies* was an annual extravaganza featuring a live orchestra, singers, dancers, and the sort of performers commonly featured in big vaudeville houses.

answer, at least in her case, would one day rise to the level of national interest.

In 1893, the City of Chicago had hosted its first World's Fair — the Columbian Exposition. Among the hundreds of workers who had helped to build the so-called White City was a carpenter named Elias Charles Disney. Elias remained in Chicago until 1906 when he moved his family (including his four-year old son Walter) to Marceline, Missouri, some 150 miles north of where two-year-old Helen Beck was running barefoot on her grandfather's farm. William Beck moved his family to Kansas City in 1910, and in 1911 Elias Disney did the same.

As a nine-year-old boy living in Kansas City, Walter was a regular visitor to Electric Park. His visits provided early inspiration for a family-oriented theme park he would design and develop decades later in Anaheim, California, naming it "Disneyland" after himself.[9] It was also in Kansas City that young Walt Disney developed an interest in animation. While working at the Laugh-O-Gram studio, he is said to have kept some pet mice, one of which became a favorite. The little mouse seemed insignificant at the time, but would become consequential once Walt had relocated to Hollywood. Speaking of his little Kansas City pets, the elder Mr. Disney once told an interviewer:

> They used to fight for crumbs in my wastebasket when I worked alone late at night. I lifted them out and kept them in wire cages on my desk. I grew particularly fond of one brown house mouse. He was a timid little guy. By tapping him on the nose with my pencil, I trained him to run inside a black circle I drew on my drawing board. When I left Kansas to try my luck at Hollywood, I hated to leave him behind. So I carefully carried him to a backyard, making sure it was a nice neighborhood, and the tame little fellow scampered to freedom.

In January 1920, Walt Disney and his fellow aspiring animator, Ub Iwerks, formed a company called "Iwerks-Disney Commercial Artists." The venture proved a financial challenge and the two soon found themselves employed by the Kansas City Slide Company, where they produced advertising slides for silent movie houses and also dabbled in the rudiments of animation.

---

[9]   Disney later incorporated many features of the Kansas City Electric Park into Disneyland (including a train whose track ringed the park grounds, as well as the daily fireworks at closing time). Unlike other amusement parks of the time, the grounds of Electric Park were meticulously maintained with landscaping designed to accentuate the park's rides and other attractions — another feature that Disney repeated.

One day the work schedule called for them to shoot a commercial for a "hornless" record player made by the Victor Talking Machine Company. A 15-year-old local model was to be featured in the commercial. And who should walk in the door but a pint-sized teenager named Helen Beck, just back from Christian College and working at the Green Mill. Did Walt say: "Hey, I know you — you're the cigarette girl from out at Electric Park"? We'll never know, but he could have.[10] The modeling session led to Helen's first film appearance. She later speculated that it was probably one of the earliest filmed commercials to be shown in movie houses.

Disney labored in Kansas City for another three years, experiencing both success and failure. Ultimately, he left Kansas City, financially embarrassed and with uncertain prospects. In early August 1923, he arrived in Hollywood. Iwerks soon joined him and the two proceeded to their rendezvous with everlasting fame.[11] Meanwhile, young Helen had collected her modest modeling fee, exited the Kansas City Slide Company, and stepped into the cool winter sunshine, little suspecting that fame in Hollywood was awaiting her as well.

Home from Christian College and resuming her quest to make something of herself as a dancer, Helen joined the stock company of Al and Loie Bridge, formed by Alan Morton Bridge after he returned from service in World War I. Among other engagements, the company performed as the "High Jinks Musical Comedy Co." at the Empress Theatre — "The Popular Priced Musical Comedy House, catering especially to women and children."

As a novice, Helen started at the bottom — her first stage experience consisting of little more than passing a spear to a bit player who then carried it onstage. Soon her looks, charm, and dance training earned her a place in the Hi Jinks Beauty Chorus — "All pretty girls, every one a talented singer and dancer." Her irrepressible personality caught the eye of *Kansas City Journal* drama critic Goodman Ace, who wrote in what may have been her first press notice: "Unless I am very much mistaken, the new

---

10 According to biographer Neal Gabler, Disney had "surprisingly little interest in women....
    In Kansas City, even as a young man on his own, he concentrated on animation and on
    Laugh-O-Gram rather than on romance, though he occasionally dated Dorothy Wendt ...
    taking her to the Alamo Theatre or the dance pavilion at the Electric Park."

11 In mid-May 1928, a silent animated short film created and directed by Walt Disney and
    Ub Iwerks, *Plane Crazy*, was given a test screening in Hollywood. The cartoon featured
    the first screen appearance of Mickey Mouse.

girl in Loie-Bridges chorus has the makings of a star and we'll hear more about her in the future."[12]

That future reportedly began in the summer of 1920 when Helen — now performing as "Billie Beck" — hit the road with Adolph Bolm's Chicago Ballet Company.[13] The company toured the Midwestern states "bringing culture to the masses," as Sally later told Studs Terkel. So it was that young Helen/Billie Beck began to build a resume as a professional dancer. But, as a still insecure 16-year-old young lady, she wasn't quite ready to leave the nest. Other opportunities were awaiting her back in her comfort zone — Kansas City.

In those days it was a very big deal when the circus came to town. As one local paper described the typical experience:

> A crowd of several thousand persons gathered yesterday afternoon at the circus grounds, Sixteenth Street and Indiana Avenue, to watch the unloading of the first of four trains of the Ringling Brothers and Barnum and Bailey Circus. The first train arrived at 2:30 o'clock and the work of erecting tents and clearing grounds began immediately.... A street parade will be given at 10 o'clock this morning.

In the absence of talking movies, television or the Internet, what could have been more thrilling than watching a trainload of exotic animals and circus equipment being unloaded? What public spectacle could have matched the sight of elephants, lions, clowns, and pretty girls high-stepping down

---

12 Two years later in his *Kansas City Journal-Post* column, Goodman Ace reminisced: "In the chorus was a neat little blonde, doing her bit in a sincere and pleasing fashion. I learned her name and mentioned her thereafter. Perhaps in the season at least half a dozen times.... Her name was Billie Beck.... I didn't make her ... but the mere mentioning had something to do with the making of Billie. It was the iron you find in raisins. It was the stimulant that gave Billie the confidence so necessary in the line. I'm not asking a booker's commission. But please don't take away the privilege of stroking my venerable beard and smiling in satisfaction." Ace and his wife Jane later achieved their own showbiz success as stars of the popular *Easy Aces* network radio show from 1930 to 1945.

13 Having trained at the Imperial Ballet School in St. Petersburg, Bolm was a highly regarded member of the Russian émigré generation in 1903 when, at 19, he emerged as the principal dancer at the Mariinsky Theatre, often partnering with star ballerina Anna Pavlova. After touring with the Metropolitan Opera Company and settling in New York in 1917, he relocated to Chicago in 1919 where he became a major figure on the ballet scene. His accomplishments included the creation of *Krazy Kat: A Jazz Pantomime*, a stage production based on the popular comic strip. Bolm was in the 1922 silent film *Danse Macabre*, one of the earliest ballet performances captured on film and he was hired in 1933 as the first director and ballet master of the San Francisco Opera Ballet, now considered the oldest professional ballet company in America.

Grand Boulevard to the beat of a marching band? Helen "Billie" Beck was among those eager to see the arrival of the Greatest Show on Earth, but not only as a spectator. She had a more ambitious notion — to become a circus performer herself.

By one account, Billie joined the Ringling Brothers Circus "when it came to Kansas City in 1920." Supposedly, she "finished the season as a flyer with the Famous 'Flying Wards' Trapeze act." This may have been a bit of press puffery, but in later years Sally did confirm her circus association in a rather odd context — that of female breast enhancement. Describing advice she intended to offer young women in *Here's How,* a handbook she hoped to publish, Sally explained:

> I go through the whole bit on boobs, honestly and frankly, like if you're under 30, to exercise the pectorals, which hold up the mammary glands. I did it accidentally, by doing a trapeze act with the Ringling Circus when I was 16, but it won't do you much good after you're 30. I think there is much too much focus on them in our time, but then, I've never had the problem of not having any.

However brief her association with the circus may have been, it represented yet another step toward celebrity for the former hat model, cigarette girl, and aspiring ballerina.

A very wise man once said, "There comes a time in every man's life, and I've had plenty of them." It is a little known fact that *that* wise man — Charles Dillon "Casey" Stengel — the most famous major league baseball manager in the history of the game, came by his nickname because he was originally from Kansas City ("K.C.").

Long before Stengel became a household name, he had aspired to a quite different career. Always athletic, he had played all three major sports even in grade school. In high school, he had been a star athlete. By 1910, the 20-year-old found himself playing minor league baseball and saving his money in order to enroll at Western Dental College in the off-season. However, there was a problem. Although left-handers are highly sought after as baseball players, there is little demand for them as dentists. In those days at least, most dental instruments were designed for the right hand. So, when he was drafted by the Brooklyn Dodgers in 1912, Casey quickly saw that the prospect of pulling teeth couldn't match the appeal of pulling baseballs over the right field fence.

In later years, Sally often recalled the days when she and Casey Stengel had attended the same high school in Kansas City. "Of course, he was ahead of me," she was careful to point out, "but after World War I he came back for some time to go to dental school, and I dated him."[14]

So, is it true that, as a teenager, Helen Beck once dated the twice-her-age Mr. Stengel? Well, Casey never denied it and an Internet search does reveal numerous references to the event. As Stengel himself was fond of saying: "You could look it up!"

At the 1920 Olympic Games in Antwerp, Belgium, the acclaimed American swimmer Ethelda Bleibtrey won a fistful of Olympic medals, several golds among them, setting world records in the process. But she had received less welcome national attention the year before when, as a 17-year-old girl, she had removed the stockings from her bathing costume and, as a consequence, had been arrested at Manhattan Beach for "nude" swimming. Apparently she had violated a local ordinance that banned the baring of "the lower female extremities for public bathing." Supporters of the famous Miss Bleibtrey raised such a stink over her arrest that New York bluenose officials lost their enthusiasm for further enforcement. The end result was that the modern bathing suit would become a more and more common sight on public beaches.

The notion of dancing around in the buff was still a dozen years in the future for Billie, but for another winsome gal the future was now. Accompanied by "a Coterie of Cute Girls Waiting to Celebrate Their 20th Birthday — Absolutely the Greatest Collection of Feminine Beauty Ever Assembled," Mademoiselle Yvonne Vallal, the "Famous French Bellerina," was making her first American tour direct from the *Folies Bergère* in Paris. By the autumn of 1919, Mlle. Vallal had become a featured dancer in *Oh! Baby!* — a "smart revue deluxe" featuring a vivacious song and dance group known as "the Famous Marcus Peaches." The show played to enthusiastic audiences from coast to coast. Seeing that the bright and breezy *Oh! Baby!* was coming to town, an Oregon columnist noted the introduction of what he called: "The stockingless fad."

During a 40-week season in 1919, *Oh! Baby!* toured the United States and Canada. It was a huge success, taking in more than $500,000 (about $6 million today), at a time when tickets sold for as little as fifty cents apiece.

---

14 Actually, by 1918 Stengel had already left dental school behind. He *did* enlist in the Navy and spent much of his wartime service coaching the Brooklyn Navy Yard's base-ball team. Why did he enlist? Although he enjoyed a major league career at the time, Casey was tired of fighting contract disputes, and, to add insult to injury, he had recently been traded to the Pittsburgh Pirates by Brooklyn Dodgers' owner, Charles Ebbets.

But, you may ask, how did it play in Peoria? Under the headline "Cops Didn't Know Art" an uncredited columnist for the *Iowa City Press-Citizen* provided this answer:

> Mlle. Vallal is an aesthete. She is regarded as the leading exponent of the back to the soil variety of dancing ... sans shoes, stockings and other things. Mam'zelle loves her work on the stage but in order to keep in trim she loves to get close to nature [and] craves to disport herself amid the flowers and birds....

> When *Oh! Baby!* played Peoria, Mlle. Vallal betook herself to Al Fresco Park. There she assumed herself to be free from the gaze of prying mortals. But alack and alas! A square-toed copper appeared on the scene and, despite bitter protestation that she was communing with nature and must not be disturbed, carted her off to the lock up.... Only the timely intervention of several prominent club women who knew what real artistic dancing is saved Mlle. Vallal from a very trying predicament.

> "Oh such — what you call ett — ett us ze bone head. Oh, la, la, la" is her comment according to the solemn assertion of the propaganda inciter.

In a May 1920 syndicated column headlined "How We Should Live," Mlle. Vallal expanded on her outlook:

> Who can say that man-made vestments are more healthful or more modest than Nature's raiment? I predict a return of reason. I believe that the time will come when society as a whole will say: "What is convention? What does it mean? If it is better that we should do thus and so, let us by all means do it. Custom does not necessarily mean right...."

> Even in Paris we have prudes, but they are not so drastic or active as they are in this country.... In Paris before I left, women of fashion were appearing on the boulevard sans stockings.

> When I produced the ballets *The Artist's Model* and *Danse D'Eve* at the Folies Bergere last spring, no one made objections to several nude figures. In fact the critics were of one accord in pronouncing the spectacles at once artistic and chaste....

> While I do not suppose you would say that either my coryphees or myself are overly dressed in our ballets in *Oh! Baby!*, nevertheless it is more than we employed in Paris. I assure you this is true.

Donning bathing suits without stockings? Dancing on stage as Mother Nature intended? Disporting oneself "au naturel" amid the flowers and birds? Those who resisted such changes must have suffered dearly from the pangs of culture shock, musing to themselves: "The next thing you know, they'll be sponsoring contests where young girls compete with each other to determine who is the most beautiful." Outrageous!

CHAPTER THREE

Ladies and Gents: Miss Billie Beck

> Our family had always been one of those delightfully improvident ones.... As the only really practical member, I thought that things were now up to me.
> ~ Sally Rand

Where did we turn for entertainment in the days before modern electronic devices? Today we are distracted and consumed by motion pictures, talk radio, DVDs, CDs, the Internet, big-screen-high-definition TVs, video games, and smart phones. It is easy to forget there was a time, little more than 100 years ago, when virtually all entertainment was live. With a musical instrument or two, some training, and a bit of imagination, you could make your own amusement, or for the small price of admission you could simply go to your local theater to see a live show.

Opera houses and philharmonic societies provided highbrow entertainment, of course, but foremost among the live shows tailored for the masses, especially between 1881 and 1932, was the theatrical genre known as vaudeville. A classic vaudeville show was more upscale than an old-time medicine show, "Wild West" trick-riding spectacle, saloon show, or minstrel act, yet less grand than a big-budget Broadway revue. It was a highly entertaining, traveling variety show commonly made up of a dozen or more acts — musicians and singers, dancers, comedy acts, scenes or sketches, impersonators, ventriloquists, magicians, jugglers, plate-spinners, acrobats, trained animal acts, and even lecturers. Shows generally ran no more than a couple of hours (or even less in later years when a live show typically shared the program with a movie screening).

A long list of big names got their start in vaudeville — Milton Berle, George Burns and Gracie Allen, Jack Benny, Red Skelton, Danny Kaye, Bob Hope, Abbott and Costello, Judy Garland, James Cagney, Cary Grant, and Will Rogers, to name a few. Even Mae West appeared at age 14 under the name "Baby Mae," wearing blackface makeup and performing as a minstrel-style singer (or "coon shouter" — the derogatory term used at the time). Many highly successful black entertainers like Jackie "Moms" Mabley, Bill

Robinson, the Nicholas Brothers, Eubie Blake, the Mills Brothers, and Sammy Davis, Jr., also got their start in vaudeville.

While the history and development of live theater in the form of minstrel shows, traveling medicine shows and vaudeville is well beyond the scope of this book, it is fair to say that by the time the Victorian age had passed and Helen Gould Beck was born, every town of any size had a vaudeville theater where touring groups of performers were eagerly welcomed by ordinary citizens seeking a night on the town.

Having achieved popularity on the local stage, favorable press notices brought the teenaged Billie Beck to the attention of the Dubinsky Brothers, who, after many years of managing a number of traveling tent shows throughout the Midwest, had recently purchased the Regent Theater in Kansas City, Missouri. Billie[1] landed a chorus line job in the Dubinsky Brothers Stock Company at $35 a week (about $500 today). More importantly, during her brief tenure there, she caught the attention of someone who could offer a much brighter future.

Gus Edwards, whose touring vaudeville company made regular stops at the Orpheum Theater in Kansas City, recognized the petite Miss Beck's appeal right away. The 41-year-old Edwards had been staging and appearing in vaudeville shows since the turn of the century. As a successful impresario, Edwards was well-known for developing young talent and is credited with launching the successful careers of many "kid actors," among them: Groucho Marx, George Jessel, Eddie Cantor, Ray Bolger, and Phil Silvers.[2]

After a tryout with other local youngsters at the Orpheum in Kansas City, Billie was offered an opportunity to join Edwards' *School Days Revue* and perform a ballet act. She was quick to accept:

> My father was an army officer in France. We received word that he
> had met with a very serious accident. We did not realize until a
> little later how very serious it really was. Our family had always
> been one of those delightfully improvident ones so often found
> among army people. As the only really practical member, I thought
> that things were now up to me.

---

[1]   Helen Beck's early stage name was variously spelled Billy or Billie, sometimes even Billye. For consistency, except in quoted material, she is referred to herein as "Billie."

[2]   Gus Edwards was also an accomplished songwriter, best known for "School Days" ("... good old golden rule days") and "By the Light of the Silvery Moon." He was portrayed by Bing Crosby in the 1939 film *The Star Maker*, a dramatized account of his life.

An early interviewer, Hal Wells, wrote of Billie's development: "With the pluck and calm courage of a little thoroughbred, [she] assumed the unfamiliar burden of wage earner." At age 17, Billie Beck hit the road in search of, if not a fortune, at least enough to help support her mother and little brother back home. Gus Edwards' wife and her sister chaperoned the mostly underage members of the company. Even so, for a young girl in a challenging situation, there were many adjustments to be made: "At that age I was a perfect technician, but I had no creative ability." Still, she soon "discovered the world wasn't too big an apple to bite into."

Chaperoned she may have been, but no one can keep track of a large group of youngsters 24 hours a day. If Sally's own recollections can be believed, the Gus Edwards' *School Days* stop in Madison, Wisconsin, was the site of an important event in the life of any young woman.

In a 1935 interview during a return engagement to Madison, Sally confessed that the first love affair of her life occurred on the campus of the University of Wisconsin when she visited there as a teenager with the Gus Edwards vaudeville show:

> I came to Madison for a three day engagement.... I met the student the first day I was here. He was a student at the university, big tall, handsome, with long eyelashes. It was the thrill of a lifetime. We went canoe riding on the lake back of the fraternity houses. It was very delightful. Then we took an automobile ride through a long lane that led to some woods. I can still remember those woods. They were beautiful.
>
> It was an experience that you read about in books. He was like a knight-errant out of a story book. I have always been grateful to fate that my first date should be under such auspices. It was the most beautiful scenery I can remember in my life. It was fall. The harvest was in. The leaves were turning brown.
>
> His name was Duke Duchme. I wonder where he is now.[3]

Things went well enough until the company reached New York City where, after a short run, the troupe disbanded and Billie found herself — a small town girl— alone and facing the perils of the metropolis. According to an

---

[3] This story is suspect, not least because, when asked about her age, Sally responded: "I was 14 — a well-developed 14. I was almost as big then as I am now." (She would actually have been 17 when traveling with the Gus Edwards show.) An Internet search returns no results for anyone named Duke Duchme. No such name appeared on the university's registration lists.

NEA wire services story, she was a little alarmed by the overtures made to her by men offering her somewhat questionable contracts. In a 1933 interview with Kathleen Nichols, Sally reported: "With my immature experience and lack of knowledge of New York, I found the going very difficult. It was my first taste of bitter disappointment."

In any case, Billie made her way back to Kansas City where she could pursue her dreams under more secure circumstances. It turned out that Goodman Ace was not the only local reporter enchanted by the diminutive Miss Beck. Her millinery modeling career reached a high point on August 1, 1921, when she appeared as one of "twelve Kansas City girls peacocked in hats of velvet and ostrich" modeling at the weeklong fall millinery show at Electric Park.

As the *Kansas City Star* described the event:

> Eighteen times each model descended the wide staircase, wearing at every entrance a different hat — wearing it superbly….
>
> When the smallest model, Billie Beck, made her first appearance … she wove an intricate pattern of Pavlova motions against the staircase. The audience, stirred to a steadily rising wave of enthusiasm at each radiant figure, lost all sense of reserve when the piquant Billie appeared with her exaggerated steps. Peacock Alley, Petticoat Lane, the Rue de la Paix, not to speak of Broadway and the latest New York revue, could offer nothing to eclipse Billie Beck's equipment for a fashion show. She was a success going upstairs as well as coming down.

According to the September 1921 issue of *The Millinery Trade Review*, 3,000 milliners from the South and West attended the show during the course of its six evening performances. Five hundred seats were reserved for milliners and another 500 were left open for the general public. The show was so popular that standing-room-only tickets were sold each night.

Just as this *Kansas City Star* columnist was gushing about Billie, the competing *Kansas City Journal-Post* was sponsoring a beauty contest to discover the most beautiful girl in the city. The papers encouraged readers to submit pictures of themselves or their candidates. Submissions flooded in over a period of weeks and the judges ultimately reviewed more than 2,000 photographs of the city's "fairest daughters." The field was narrowed to 100 girls who were to appear in person before the judges. As the deadline approached, several of the frontrunners were showcased in the paper under the headline: "Six Beauties Selected to Take Part in Big Pageant Tomorrow."

Of the six featured Kansas City finalists, only one ("charming Billie Beck") stands out at first, but movie trivia buffs would recognize another standout: Lucille LeSueur. A lifelong chum of Sally Rand, Miss LeSueur gained fame under the stage name she adopted when she signed a Hollywood film contract — a name selected by fans voting in a movie magazine contest — "Joan Crawford."

In 1917, President Woodrow Wilson went back on his word to keep the nation out of the war in Europe. The Democrat had been reelected to a second term in 1916 with the campaign slogan "He kept us out of war," yet barely four weeks into Wilson's second term circumstances would lead him to call a special joint session of Congress to request a declaration of war on Germany — to make "the world safe for democracy." For this and other perceived failures, Warren G. Harding, the Republican candidate for president in 1920, defeated his Democratic opponent in a landslide, carrying 37 states including, for the first time, Oklahoma.

Among those swept into Congress by the Republican surge was an unheralded candidate from Oklahoma, Manuel Herrick, who would soon become better known for his peculiarities than for his political acumen. It seems that the gentleman took a rather dim view of beauty contests. In fact, he steadfastly opposed them as an exploitation of otherwise virtuous young women.

Herrick's election to Congress had been something of a fluke. The popular incumbent had died shortly before the election — too late for anyone else to qualify. Other than being a Republican, Herrick's main credentials seemed to be that as a teenager he had attempted to rob a Santa Fe train near Black Bear Creek and thereafter spent more than a year in a mental institution. Oh, and also that his mother believed him to be the second coming of Christ.

Herrick's odd behavior soon caught the attention of the Washington press corps, which seemed to delight in reporting his latest antics. Once, while aboard a Navy vessel to conduct an inspection of naval operations, Herrick made an official tour of the bridge. At one point, squinting through the wrong end of a telescope, the congressman turned away in disgust, declaring: "Here is a sample of the way the Navy wastes millions of dollars on useless equipment."

But it was with the introduction of his first piece of major legislation that the newly installed congressman would thrust himself onto the national stage — a bill to outlaw newspaper-sponsored beauty contests and to provide that any newspaper editor attempting to conduct such a contest would face a jail sentence. Representative Herrick had reportedly complained that women were thinking more of their looks than their homes. In response to criticism of his proposal to criminalize beauty contests, the congressman mounted a competition of his own — a "love contest" in which he boldly promised his hand in marriage to the lucky winner of a beauty contest being sponsored by the *Washington Herald*. To get the ball rolling, he sent a rambling form letter to the 49 finalists, inviting them to enter his personal "contest":

Dear Miss:

You have entered into one prize contest. You are now entering the second prize contest in which you may win. Do you wish to enter a third prize contest, the contest for the greatest prize on earth that any woman could ever win — the contest for the whole heart and soul love, and hand in marriage of one of the 15 men who is now living on the earth who can look God and all humanity square in the eye and say: "Against my body and against my soul there rests no moral stain, for I have kept my soul and my body free from all moral stain in order that I may look my virgin bride in the eye without guilt and shame in my heart."

The girl who is the winner of this contest will have won the love of a man whose love will be so great that if that was the one and only price that would purchase your soul salvation, he would ransom your soul out of hell with price of his own, and if you should enter this contest and be the winner, it would go a long way toward assuring you of being the winner in the contest to become Miss Washington, for this man now holds one of the highest offices in the Nation and will at a time not to exceed eight years hold the highest, and the girl who wins his love can rest assured that he will exert every atom of his powerful influence to have his sweetheart selected to be Miss Washington.

You, quite naturally, want to know something about the man who invites you to enter a contest for his love, so here is a description: Age, 31; height, 6 ft; weight, 184 pounds; chestnut brown hair, brown eyes, and as far as masculine beauty taking 100 as perfection, would grade about as follows: Face, 89 percent; body, 98 percent....

Owing to my high position, it is necessary that this contest be carried on secretly, in order not to bring notoriety or ridicule upon my high position by my political enemies; and any young lady to whom this invitation may come and who shall decline to enter this contest will have taken a far-reaching step toward eliminating herself from being selected as Miss Washington.

And now a few words in closing: I am the last scion of a noble family who lost their political power during the overrunning of Europe by Napoleon I, and whose family has now become extinct, except for myself.

Left practically an orphan in infancy, I faced a cold and cruel world penniless and alone, and after overcoming superhuman obstacles have fought my way to wealth and power, and am now seeking a bride worthy of my love.

No young lady should hesitate to enter this contest because she may think herself too young to become a wife, for if any such enter the contest and be the winner, the marriage would be cheerfully deferred until she should have attained sufficient age; and any young lady to whom this invitation may come, whether the same is sent to you by mail or is brought to you by my personal ambassador, will please indorse the same with your name and address and the notation "Accepted" or "Rejected" and return in order that the process of selecting a winner may proceed.

Immediately upon the acceptance by any young lady of this invitation to enter this contest a meeting between myself and the young lady will be arranged by my ambassador.

By Herrick's fervent account, all but one of the 49 finalists in the Miss Washington, D.C., contest responded to his unsolicited mailing. Thus encouraged, he arranged for several home visits where he would speak not only to the presumably willing young ladies but also to their mothers. Eventually, at least one of the contestants turned his letter over to postal inspectors.

When Herrick was called in to explain, the story was leaked to the press, producing widespread ridicule. The publically embarrassed congressman protested that the true purpose of his letter had been to obtain evidence to submit to the House Judiciary Committee (which was considering his bill). He claimed he had hoped to show just how susceptible pretty girls could be to invitations from strangers who get their names and addresses from newspaper beauty contest columns.

While the postal inspectors accepted his dubious claim, an angry father and an irate husband and were having none of it. Wanting Herrick indicted, they accused him of forging the names of two of the young women in bogus letters that allegedly apologized to him for turning over "decoy love letters" to postal authorities. The two aggrieved men even cornered Herrick in his congressional office in an effort to force a retraction. After a spirited scuffle, the slippery congressman escaped into the corridor, yelling for help from the Capitol police. "Let the slur writers rave," Herrick complained of his perceived enemies, adding that "social Hyenas, Moral Reprobates and Moral Lepers" were out to get him. Speaking of himself in the third person, he declared:

> He has never been guilty of an act of Moral turpitude in His whole
> life so he is willing for the Morally Unclean to Howl as long and as
> loud as they like. It disturbs Him Not and He will go right on
> trying to Make this world a better and cleaner place to live in.

Two months later, still seeking the last word, Herrick announced that he was starting a weekly newspaper to be called *Retribution*, the mission of which would be to respond to his critics.[4] He predicted the paper would be a "hot baby" and said he was now spending most of his time working on libel suits against newspapers.

The congressman's proposal to outlaw beauty contests met a predictable fate, succinctly expressed by the headline: "HERRICK'S ANTI-BEAUTY CONTEST BILL LAUGHED OUT OF CONGRESS." A *Pittsburgh Post-Gazette* editorial addressed the matter more subtly: "… it must be said for the Oklahoman that he is a rare specimen…. The [biographical] sketch, which is furnished by the subject himself, also notes that he had few educational advantages. As much might be suspected."

About that same time, at a little get-together in Atlantic City, New Jersey, more than 100,000 spectators had come to the boardwalk to witness the crowning of the first "Miss America." Within 35 years, television viewers both young and old would be tuning in to hear Bert Parks melodiously croon: "Ther-r-re she is …" and, along with millions of others, would consider it a really big deal.

Who won the competition to become the first "Miss America"? It was 16-year old charmer Margaret "Margee" Gorman, a young contestant who had come to Atlantic City as "Miss Washington, DC" — winner of the beauty contest sponsored by . . . wait for it . . . the *Washington Herald*. We don't know whether Miss Gorman was one of the 49 girls personally approached by Congressman Herrick, but chances are good that she was.

---

4   Research has failed to confirm that any such newspaper was ever published.

As happens every day in the world of news media, the beauty contest hubbub was soon eclipsed by the next big story. On the very same day that young Miss Gorman donned her crown in Atlantic City, a fateful three-day bash was underway nearly 3,000 miles away in a suite of rooms at the St. Francis Hotel in San Francisco. When the party was over, a beautiful young actress named Virginia Rappe would be dead and comedy film star Roscoe "Fatty" Arbuckle would be blamed for her rape and murder. Beauty contest stories were moved to the back pages.

Margaret Gorman, the first "Miss America," would enter the contest again in both 1922 and 1923 without success. One-term congressman Manuel Herrick would move on to take his place as a footnote in the history of the United States Congress. And, though she had fallen short in her quest to become Miss Kansas City and advance to Atlantic City in 1921, the ambitious Miss Beck would triumph in other areas in years to come.

A t some point, Billie accepted an offer to go to Chicago and perform as a dancer in Ernie Young's *Frolics* at the Marigold Garden nightclub. (Young was a popular impresario and orchestra leader known by some as the "Ziegfeld of Chicago.") A relatively safe environment for a young dancer, the Marigold was among the large Chicago ballrooms that had reached an understanding with Chicago's Juvenile Protection Association (JPA) to offer the public a "carefully engineered and sanitized musical and dance experience."[5]

> **THE FIRST "MISS AMERICA"**
>
> At only 5'1" tall, Miss Gorman remains the most petite Miss America ever crowned. In 1925 "Margee" married Victor Cahill, a real estate broker. Over the years Mrs. Cahill avoided publicity and, in a 1956 interview, quoted her husband as saying that he regarded the hoopla surrounding the Miss America contest to be "a lot of foolishness" that "should be forgotten." She added: "It's a wife's duty to bow to her husband's wishes." In 1960, three years after her husband died, she returned to Atlantic City to participate in a reunion of Miss Americas. She crowned that year's winner and was grand marshal of the parade, but registered her displeasure when pageant officials declined to reimburse her for $1,500 in travel expenses. Margaret Gorman Cahill died on October 1, 1995, at the age of 90.

---

5   A popular entertainment complex, Marigold Gardens had a German-style outdoor beer garden with the biggest outdoor dance floor in Chicago, plus a large concert hall and cabaret.

As told by William Howland Kinney in *Chicago Jazz*:

> Ballroom managers had agreed to hire JPA observers ("hostesses")
> to supervise [the] social behavior of the dancers.... Cooperation
> between dance hall entrepreneurs and urban reformers shaped the
> commercialization of the dance craze and created a demand for fast
> paced "peppy," but morally sanitary, jazz age social dance music.

While dancing at the Marigold Garden occupied Billie's evening hours, her
mornings and afternoons were open and she was able to pick up a little extra
cash posing as a life study model for students at the famous Art Institute of
Chicago. As Sally later recalled:

> This was a fine opportunity because I had a chance to study
> dancing with the Pavley Oukrainsky Dancing School,[6] and my
> contacts and associates at the Art Institute gave me the desire to
> learn more about art, color and form.... The entire institute was at
> my disposal and the criticisms and lectures were absorbed by me
> as avidly as they were by the students.

In words that still resonate more than 80 years later, Sally continued:

> I mention this especially, because I think it is one of the most
> important extras that the schools should provide, and at this time
> when school appropriations are being cut to the limit and many
> of the so-called extras are being taken out of the school programs,
> I think the adult people should pause and consider how empty
> the lives of people are when they are without appreciation and
> understanding of art, form, color and music, which can appeal to
> the poorest person.

Ten years later, Chicago would provide the launching pad for a life-changing
experience, but for the moment Billie made her way back to Kansas City and
in 1922 undertook a second tour with the Gus Edwards revue. Oddly, the
result was the same as before — the tour disbanded and Billie again found
herself out of work in New York City with few dollars to her name. She
managed to find a place to stay, a small windowless bedroom. She reportedly

---

6   Andreas Pavley and Serge Oukrainskey were associates of Billie's childhood idol
     Anna Pavlova. Leaving Pavlova's company in 1915, the two handsome young men
     settled in the Chicago area and established a connection with the Chicago Grand
     Opera. They were much talked about in society circles, and not only for their dancing
     prowess. When Oukrainskey formed his own troupe and began touring South
     America, Pavley fell on hard times. In 1931, unwilling to appease a blackmailer who
     threatened to expose his sexual orientation, the 36-year-old Pavley leapt to his death
     from a 16th story window of Chicago's Hotel McCormick.

had to walk "fifty long blocks twice a day to save car fare" while "shiveringly trying to make light summer clothing suffice in winter snow storms." As she remembered it:

> Although I found many unscrupulous men in my path, I had a
> more mature viewpoint and could meet situations with more intel-
> ligence and sophistication. I did go broke, but I didn't care; I did go
> hungry and I didn't mind; I was put out of my little $4-a-week
> room and had to sleep in Central Park, but it didn't matter.

Billie finally caught a break when, together with a dancing partner, she scored a two-week booking at the Palace Theatre, the flagship venue of the Keith-Albee circuit and the most prestigious vaudeville house in America. Beyond that, as she later recalled:

> I kept on making the rounds until I finally got a chance ... with Lew
> Leslie. He was doing a café show and I went into it as one the
> minor principals. He had a great idea — an interpretation of the
> story of Aphrodite to the music of the *Scheherazade* suite.[7]

The show was *The Cabinet of Terpsichore* and Leslie was having trouble with his leading lady who "hadn't caught the mood of the thing." The temple scene was not coming off as anything near what it should have been.

During a morning rehearsal, Leslie was leaning on the music stand when he was approached by a young "slip of a chorine" who casually remarked: "Did you know that a flute solo is missing in this Aphrodite score?" Startled, Leslie asked: "You know the music?" "Very well," said Billie. "I worked over it for months at school." Not only did she know the music, but, with nowhere else to go and reportedly still sleeping in the park, she had been arriving early each morning and interpreting the temple scene for her own amusement. She performed it for Leslie and, by the time the sun went down that evening, Billie Beck was hanging up her clothes in the star's dressing room.

As Sally recollected:

> Believe me, I was grateful then for my accidentally acquired
> knowledge of the arts.... I had learned the story [of Aphrodite] at
> the Art Institute, looking over the displays of the old fragments of
> Grecian art and I had heard the music at the morning symphony
> concerts which had the score described in the program. During the

---

7   Lew Leslie (1886-1953) was a white man best known for staging shows featuring
     black performers, notably his famous 13-year series of musical revues that began with
     Blackbirds of 1926 and ended with Blackbirds of 1939.

rehearsal ... the principals who were selected were entirely
unacquainted with the idea the producers had in mind. After
discussion with Mr. Leslie ... he gave me the lead in the show,
which was the greatest proof I ever had that everything you learn,
no matter how far-fetched it seems from your profession, will
eventually prove valuable.

With the closing of the Leslie show, and with diminishing prospects and a
bank balance to match, 18-year-old Billie decided to return home to Kansas
City where she could be more of a big fish in a little pond. She resumed
performing in the Electric Park *Follies* and, during a three-month period,
was featured in local papers once again for participating in a Kansas City
beauty pageant and modeling in at least two fashion shows sponsored by
local businessmen. Under a provocative, hands-on-hips photograph, published in connection with her appearance at the Isis Theatre,[8] the *South
Kansas City Press* declared that Miss Billie Beck was "considered by many to
be the most beautiful girl in Kansas City."

L ittle is known of Billie's endeavors in the next few months, but she did
    return to New York where she scraped by on whatever opportunities
presented themselves. As paying engagements were few and far between,
she was open to most anything that might keep her in the public eye.

When the Kiwanis Club of Asbury Park, New Jersey, staged a benefit show
at the Lyric Theatre in June of 1923, Billie approached theatrical producer
Nils Granlund and volunteered her services.[9] The show included such big
names as the wisecracking actress and night club personality, Texas Guinan,
and Will Morrissey, a comedian (popular for working from the audience)
who had been a sensation at similar affairs all over the country. Reflecting
on the meeting four years later, Granlund wrote that, although it was
summer, Billie "had only an old warm suit." He bought her "a little white
silk dress, white shoes, and a white hat ... all for $30." Reluctant to accept

---

8   Isis was an ancient Egyptian goddess. At one time, there were quite a few theaters
     around the country that carried that name. Oddly enough, several were still in
     operation in 2017. As recently as November of 2015, it was announced that the Isis
     Theater in Aspen, Colorado, in operation for more than 100 years, had no intention of
     changing its name despite the notoriety of the terrorist group bearing the same name.

9   Although nearly forgotten today, Nils T. Granlund (1882-1957) was a famous show
     business entrepreneur and creator of the modern night club, credited with making the
     first movie preview, filming the first commercial, and being the first to broadcast a
     live sports event. As a popular radio personality, "Granny" introduced the Jazz Age to
     America via his broadcasts from the Cotton Club in Harlem.

Granlund's generosity as an outright gift, Billie had offered to "work three clubs to pay for it."

With her professional future as much in doubt as ever it had been, Billie was on the lookout for a more secure position, something that might offer more reliable income over a longer term.

Enter William Seabury.

While Gus Edwards' *School Days Revue* was largely a showcase for "kid" talent, William Seabury's *Frivolics* presented a full blown adult vaudeville program. Seabury, who was holding auditions for a new tour, knew a talented dancer when he saw one. He himself had often been described as an "eccentric dancer" and "one of the greatest of today's creators and exponents of terpsichore." To be selected to join his dance troupe was no small achievement. Several hundred girls wanted in, so to make the selection: "Every girl was made to remove her shoes and stockings." With the "touch of the fortune teller," Seabury "chose the ones who had the most artistic feet." Apparently, he had "found by long experience that the long narrow foot is the artistic one." Only five girls were chosen.

Billie was one of the "quintet of fascinating femininity" featured in Seabury's 1923 *Frivolics*, the second edition. The revue toured the country in Orpheum circuit theaters with a program that included dancers, singers, acrobats and comedians.[10] It was described by one critic as "an entrancing exposition of grace" and by another as a well-produced revue with "all the elements of a big musical show boiled down to less than half an hour." At this abbreviated length, the show could share the bill with a major motion picture and still be performed several times a day.

One critic offered an intriguing description of the show during its stint at the Hamilton Theatre in New York City:

> The second edition of the *Frivolics* which Seabury is now doing in vaudeville, is about the best big act he has as yet done in that field. Seabury has five girls with him ... and a prettier looking quintet would be difficult to find....
>
> The opening scene ... [takes place in] a doctor's office with the girls coming in to find out what's wrong with their dancing. In all the numbers, none of the girls wear stockings, and it may not be out of

---

10 To facilitate the booking of traveling shows and maximize profits, wealthy entrepreneurs bought up local theaters, turning them into circuits. The Orpheum circuit was among the most prominent, with 45 theaters coast to coast.

place to say here that a ... shapelier set of limbs couldn't be found
in the *Follies* or the *Scandals*....

Perhaps the best bit in the act, and one of the most effective, is the
"slow-motion" dance scene, done behind a scrim by four of the
girls, attired in tights and long wigs, a la Lady Godiva. The
spotlight is revolved, leaving the stage alternately light and dark
every other second, and giving a wonderful slow motion effect to
the dancing.[11]

Seabury's famous "cane dance" routine follows this, and then the
girls appear as a jazz band, all playing different instruments. The
instruments appear to be real but are played as one plays a
"kazoo," by humming the tune into it.

The humor in *Frivolics* was not appreciated by everyone. Commenting on a
performance that took place after Billie had left the show, a critic for the
Kansas City Star was not amused:

Worst of all, in almost everyone's opinion, was the curtain call ...
when Mr. Seabury ... ended by rubbing his hand over a girl's
highly-powdered bare leg, tasting the hand, and saying, "That's
baking powder you have on! I'll bet when you perspire you
break all out into little biscuits." Gentlemen of the Orpheum
circuit, oh, gentlemen of the Orpheum circuit! Do you call that
vaudeville?

Pretty young girls performing onstage without the benefit of stockings?
Could it get any worse? Back in New York City the Shubert Brothers were
already testing the limits of what an audience and the police would
tolerate, with the August 20, 1923, opening of their *Artists and Models*
revue at the famous Shubert Theatre.

Yet, *New York Daily News* theater critic Burns Mantle seemed to be happy
enough:

Most of the excitement last week was caused by the introduction of
a parade of models in a revue called "Artists and Models".... They
came from the back, these young women, presumably from the
darkened recesses of a painter's studio....

As they approached the center of the stage in single file they wheeled
suddenly into a circle of light and the audience gasped. At least a

---

[11]   This "wonderful slow motion effect" was created by a clever, anonymous, lighting
technician some eight years before the invention of the strobe light.

part of it gasped and another part giggled. Because the models were wearing no more than their studio clothes, and those, in effect, were their birthday clothes. For the first time in the history of American revues its show girls were on display sans brassiere and, so far as we could see, sans shame.

We are essentially, as you know, a clean minded people. We are even a little censorious. Particularly in New York. But we are also a thrifty people and like to feel that we are getting as much for our money as the next fellow.... Consequently, immediately after the closing of the performance of "Artists and Models" on Monday night our people began making arrangements to get into as close contact with the show as possible before the police arrived.

After noting the long lines forming daily at the Schubert's box office windows, Mantle continued, tongue firmly in cheek:

The investigation is continuing as I write. And though it threatens to demoralize traffic conditions in Forty-fourth street, the chances are good that before the Anti-Vice society can act a large number of curious men and women will have satisfied themselves that, in all important particulars, the Lord is still making females according to the same pattern that he used when Eve was picking her frocks from the vine. A pattern, we may add, that has long proved most satisfactory."

Crossing the country from New York City, the Seabury revue reached California by mid-Autumn 1923. Of the five principal girls in the show, Billie was getting the most press. In what was most likely a puff piece, an unknown writer claimed to "explain" why Billie hadn't stayed in New York and joined the *Ziegfeld Follies*:

The reason "Billy" left Broadway, she says, is that she had to go on the road to get a job. Ziegfeld and all the other managers who are continually looking for pretty girls to sing and dance did not over-look Billy Beck. No, they wanted her, but they couldn't afford to take a chance.

Every time that Billy Beck took her place in the row of a chorus the other girls walked off. Billy says they couldn't stand up under the test. She has been measured and modeled from the tip of her top to her little pink ear and the artists say she's the perfect type of chorus girl. Not a Venus nor a Psyche, but just a "perfect little darling of a chorus girl."

In November of 1923, while Billie was performing with the Seabury troupe at the Orpheum in Los Angeles, her picture began to appear in the *Los Angeles Times* on a regular basis, a phenomenon that would continue for decades to come. On November 13th, the *Times* showed her on the beach with four other girls from the show rolling a pair of oversized dice in what was described as a game of "Jungle Billiards." On another day, the same girls were pictured on the same beach "introducing feminine football to America" — with Billie as the quarterback.

On November 19th, the front page of Section 2 of the *Times* depicted Billie on a racing bike declaring that: "Bicycle riding, like swimming is one of the few forms of exercise which makes every muscle in the body work. I believe there is nothing better, especially for reducing." The associated article declared: "Miss Beck recently was in a bicycle race with six comely young women, and proved that practice makes perfect by winning the race." Then, as if beach games, football and bike racing weren't enough, the following day's *Times* featured a picture of "Orpheum dancer and amateur boxer" Billie Beck dressed in full boxing attire and high heels! The photo's caption claimed she had gone "several rounds" with featherweight boxer Dandy Dillon just a short time before his defeat of Frankie Brown at Legion Stadium in Hollywood. Stressing the benefits of this workout, Billie declared:

> Boxing not only keeps one in perfect physical condition, and
> without an ounce of excess flesh, but ... a girl who keeps in trim by
> boxing will never need to fear lung trouble or blood pressure.... If
> one knows the rudiments of boxing, she can quickly rid herself of
> any obnoxious pests ... she may encounter. We had an experience
> of this sort in a northern city where we were playing a few weeks
> ago. The poor fellow is probably still wondering what hit him.

In short, Billie Beck was becoming a press agent's dream.

To round out her California publicity campaign, Billie and Marion Hart were pictured in the press as "aviation fannettes" who were supposedly flying "their own planes" every day. The syndicated photo shows the two girls posing in leather helmets and aviation goggles, sitting in the cockpit of a small plane. Was this merely a publicity stunt or did they actually own an aircraft? And did they use it to travel from one venue to another as some sources suggested? The answers are lost to us but, whatever the details,

Billie wasn't just fooling around. She actually did become a licensed pilot and for many years would pursue her serious passion for flight.[12]

In the early 1920s, flying was more than just a sport or novelty for aficionados and barnstorming stunt pilots. The Wright Brothers had made their first powered flight in late 1903 and, as always, commercial exploitation of the new technology wasn't far behind. The first transcontinental air service was completed on September 11, 1920, when airplane No. 151 of the U.S. Aerial Mail Service, carrying six bags of mail and piloted by E.E. Mouton, landed at San Francisco's Marina Field, having covered the last 250 miles of the trip from Reno, Nevada, in one hour and fifty-eight minutes, breaking all previous records for the same distance. Nearly 19 years later, Mouton would be on board when another small plane, piloted by an enterprising young woman, would attempt to break that record time. Perhaps you can guess who she was.

Mary Belle

With the 1920 adoption of the 19th amendment to the United States Constitution, women not only gained the right to vote but also the opportunity to run for office. So it was that Mary Belle Spencer, prominent Chicago attorney and mother of two small daughters, tossed her hat into the political ring in March of 1922, seeking the nomination to complete the term of the late Congressman William E. Mason.

As to the propriety of a woman with small children running for public office, Mrs. Spencer declared:

> The woman's place is in the home just as long as it is necessary to
> attend to the welfare of her children. After that, a woman's place is
> in the office, politics, the legislature or wherever she may be of
> public service. Simply because she is a mother she need not limit
> herself to the occupation of housewife.

A press release declared: "She ... is opposed to obnoxious paid tax reformers who wish to saddle their rule upon our nation!" In the end, Mary Belle's pioneering effort was in vain, as she lost to Congressman Mason's daughter in the Republican primary.

Remarking on the outcome of the 1922 general election (in which every female candidate was defeated), Miss Alice Paul, a prominent suffragette,

---

[12]   While not, of course, the first female aviator, Billie was certainly an early adopter. Just weeks before William Seabury kicked off the second edition of his *Frivolics* tour in 1923, famed aviatrix Amelia Earhart became the 16th woman to be issued a pilot's license.

women's rights activist, and early feminist, urged women to wake up, have more self-respect, and cast their votes for other women:

> Women remain a subject class because they have no sense of sex solidarity. Unless they desire in the future as the past to be governed by men, they must rouse themselves and prepare themselves to take part in government to which as citizens and voters they are entitled.

> In this women must help each other. Men will not help women to get anything they want themselves and men do want seats in the senate and house, which mean power. Therefore, though they will take all they can get in the way of service and money from women, men will not, if they can avoid it, vote for a woman.

Somewhat surprisingly, the always outspoken Mary Belle Spencer took umbrage at Miss Paul's remarks, declaring:

> This woman says women do not deserve success, because they do not vote for women [or] take their legal and physical ills to women lawyers and doctors. She's wrong. What makes me furious is that any woman should imply that women use their sex as a weapon in the political contest with men. In the primaries last year I received 73,678 votes and I'd die of shame if I thought I got one of them simply because I am a woman.

Mary Belle Spencer was a force to be reckoned with. In little more than a decade, Sally Rand would have occasion to reckon with her.

As a featured dancer in Seabury's *Frivolics*, Billie Beck was getting glowing press notices and, though only 19 years old, she was settling in as an experienced trouper. It was not to last.

During a performance at the Clunie-Orpheum Theater in Sacramento, Billie began experiencing sharp abdominal pains in her lower right side. Rushed to the hospital, she was diagnosed with a ruptured appendix. Surgery and a sufficient period of recovery were required. William Seabury had no choice but to leave her behind while the show moved on.

For the third time, her tenure with a vaudeville troupe had been aborted. Billie was again abandoned, this time in unfamiliar territory 1,700 miles from home. Sometimes misfortune leads to fortune. Fortunately, this would be one of those times.

CHAPTER FOUR

Making a Splash in Hollywood

An extra in Hollywood is like a man on a raft in mid-
ocean. If you're not noticed — you're sunk!
~ Sally Rand

A lert the press! Bostonians are agog! A girl in a one-piece bathing suit
has been charged with indecent exposure.

The year was 1907. The venue was Boston's Revere Beach, opened only 11
years earlier as "America's first public beach." The beach attracted large
crowds in the summer months, not only because of its proximity to downtown Boston, but also because of the original "Wonderland" — a sort of
forerunner to Disneyland — that offered daily parades, a beautiful lagoon
with its Shoot-the-Chute water slide, thrilling roller coaster rides, and the
fabulous Hippodrome carousel. It was considered by some to be America's
foremost amusement park.

At the height of the summer, temperatures at the beach might soar to
90 degrees. But in the view of the local fashion police, even the heat of
hellfire itself would not justify public display of the female figure, let alone
exposure of bare arms and legs. The culprit in the case was 20-year-old
Annette Kellerman, the record-setting swimmer from Australia, whose tour
of the United States as an underwater ballerina had recently arrived in
Boston after playing to critical acclaim in more tolerant Chicago.

Boston was leading the charge in keeping a lid on such matters. Founded in
1878, The New England Watch and Ward Society had been keeping watch
and warding off these evils for quite some time. At the height of the
society's power, the Boston Public Library responded by keeping its
"objectionable" books in a locked room, while publishers and booksellers
trod lightly lest the society's influence with prosecutors and judges lead to
strict censorship, if not outright bans. Throughout much of the 20th
Century, the phrase "Banned in Boston" served as a successful marketing
slogan. Meanwhile, running barefoot on her grandfather's farm, Helen

Beck had just turned three. Little did she know that forces already in motion would steer her future course.

Mary Belle

More than 10 years later, a careful reader of the June 20, 1918, edition of the *Chicago Heights Star* might have noticed a small item on page 2 under the heading "professional cards." A young barrister named Mary Belle Spencer was announcing that she would be conducting business from an office in the Unity Building at 1602 Otto Boulevard in Chicago. The newly minted lawyer had just graduated from Northwestern University School of Law. Within six weeks, the 36-year-old Mrs. Spencer, well known for her many years of social and civic welfare work, would be appointed by Illinois Governor Lowden as the Cook County Public Guardian. Mary Belle quickly achieved great success, both in public and private practice.

On November 2, 1923, at a site just an hour's drive from where a recuperating Billie Beck was about to embark upon a promising new career, Undersheriff Walker of Ventura County, California, was examining the body of special agricultural investigator S. T. Kahlly, found lying in an alfalfa field about 75 feet from the highway. His head had been smashed to a pulp and a four of diamonds playing card lay on his body as though carefully placed there. The bloodstained handle of a broken hammer, as well as a large blood-covered rock and a bloody tree trunk, were located nearby. The time of death was later established by showing that maggots found in the victim's wounds would have taken 24 hours to develop.

Described as an "educated Hindoo" with many friends, Kahlly had served four years as a chaplain in the British army under Lord Kitchener before coming to California from India in 1912 to study agriculture. According to his close friend, Mrs. Clara Cooley, "He was unusual in his dealings. He always assumed that everyone with whom he dealt was honest, that they would not lie and that they would deal scrupulously with him. Hence, he lost everything he had."

The murder investigation dragged on for eight months until June 20, 1924, when the "notorious bandit and bad man" Jesse Mendoza was arrested and charged with the killing. Mendoza and his cohort Willy Vegas had apparently attempted to "borrow" Kahlly's Oldsmobile and were resisted. Upon questioning, Mendoza made a complete confession. But, as so often happens, it wouldn't be that simple. Mendoza later claimed the confession had been beaten out of him: "I told them Willie Vegas killed Kahlly."

Meanwhile, practicing law more than 2,000 miles away in Chicago Heights, Mary Belle Spencer was handed an important request. As she later explained:

> One day I received a telegram.... It asked me to defend Jesse
> Mendoza. I did not know him or his people.... Perhaps I was
> chosen by these boys' parents because several years ago I acquitted
> a Mexican boy accused of murder.

Despite the fact that the murder had been described as "one of the most fiendish in the history of the county," and even though she could not very well leave Chicago without arranging for the care of her two little daughters, ages four and two, Mary Belle agreed to represent the unsympathetic Mendoza. She packed her bags and headed for California.

During the trial, Mrs. Spencer stamped her foot dramatically, pounding the court reporter's desk and interrupting the testimony of former Undersheriff R. N. Haydon (who had been present during Mendoza's confession). She accused Haydon of threatening the defendant with: "You'd better talk, and if you don't then the blood will come out of your nose."

Haydon denied saying any such thing. Judge Rogers admonished Mrs. Spencer: "There is no occasion to be vehement. Your statement of what happened, Mrs. Spencer, is not evidence. There are limits to which counsel may go and you will conduct this case in an orderly manner."[1]

Despite a vigorous defense, Mendoza was found guilty and sentenced to life imprisonment at San Quentin. Mary Belle declined to appeal, choosing instead to resume her professional and parental duties back in Chicago. Meanwhile, the feisty Mrs. Spencer and young Billie Beck were headed in each other's direction. It would be another nine years before the collision.

Billie Beck had been released from the Sacramento hospital after surgery and was now at loose ends. She was lucky to get a proper diagnosis. In those days appendicitis was no small concern. When accompanied by peritonitis, it was commonly a matter of life or death.

---

[1]   Obstinacy would become a hallmark of Mrs. Spencer's character. In April of 1925, she was charged with contempt of court and fined $50 for openly accusing a county judge in Chicago of unfair treatment. She would then be jailed for late payment after insisting on paying the fine with a check (a request the judge denied when he learned she intended to frame the check for display in her office). To retaliate, Mary Belle called in the press to take her picture behind bars and announced, "I'm pleased to go to jail. This fine will give me a thousand dollars' worth of publicity."

Now you might think a healthy 19-year-old would be an unlikely candidate for an appendectomy, but you would be wrong. In fact, most cases of appendicitis occur in children and young adults between 10 and 30 years of age. Healthy young people tend to disregard symptoms like abdominal pain and mild fever. Since the appendix can burst or rupture within two or three days after symptoms appear, it was truly fortunate that Billie felt ill enough to abandon the stage and seek medical care.

An extended stay in a hospital bed tends to atrophy the muscles of even the fittest athlete. And so, in critical need of physical rehabilitation, Billie borrowed $10 from a sympathetic doctor and made her way from Sacramento to Hollywood, where she embarked on a rigorous exercise regimen. William Seabury's vaudeville troupe had long since moved on, leaving Billie high and dry. Well, not exactly dry. As an aspiring ballerina, she had long understood the importance of daily attention to keeping her "equipment" in top form. Accordingly, as part of her recovery, Billie included swimming and diving in her daily workout.

She had been in the Los Angeles area only a short time when she was invited to a get-together at the Harry Carey Ranch in the Santa Clarita Valley. The valley was becoming known as a location for the booming western movie business, and the buildings on the ranch offered a perfect setting for shooting western movies. Harry Carey himself was a popular western silent film actor who had already appeared in about 200 films. His ranch had become a magnet for any number of major stars, attracting the likes of John Wayne, William S. Hart, and Gary Cooper. During the course of her visit, Billie had signed the guest book: "Someday you will see my name in electric lights!" That day would come sooner than she knew.

I n those early days in Hollywood, Billie had kept body and soul together by working as an artist's model. One such artist, a sculptor, allowed her to stay in a small room in the back of his studio. Her comfort was short-lived, as he soon asked a girlfriend working at the Mack Sennett Studios to see if there might be a job there for Billie. As Sally later recalled:

> I think he got me the job to get rid of me. I was in the way of his amorous pursuits. I mean, with a young innocent girl living in the studio, he could hardly bring girls in at all hours for little else than modeling. I guess I played hell with his sex life.

Although Billie was new in town, the enterprising Mack Sennett had been making his mark in Hollywood for more than a decade. After creating Keystone Studios in 1912, Sennett had made it big with his "Keystone

Kops" slapstick comedy shorts. In 1916, he signed 17-year-old Gloria May Josephine Svensson (soon to become Gloria Swanson) to appear in his less raucous comedies. Along the way, he also introduced his "Splash Girls," the original so-called bathing beauties.

There was a time when a bathing suit or swimsuit was just that — a suit or costume you were expected to wear when going for a swim. The notion that a young girl might parade around in a bathing suit for the sole purpose of public exhibition had not occurred to anyone. Then, along came Mack Sennett. To absolutely no one's surprise, movie fans rather enjoyed seeing pretty girls prancing around in swimming attire.

The origin of the swimsuit or "tank suit" goes back to antiquity and is so wrapped up in the development of diverse cultures as to merit a book of its own. For our purposes, the story begins in 1907 when the aforementioned Australian swimmer Annette Kellerman caused such a fuss in Boston with her "indecent" one-piece bathing suit. The next year, after conducting a study of 3,000 women, physical fitness pioneer Dr. Dudley Sargent of Harvard proclaimed her to be "the most beautifully formed woman of modern times."

Kellerman was among the first to parlay the finer aspects of her anatomy into a significant flow of cash. Posters for her personal appearances touted her as "The Perfect Woman." She was able to profit from her notoriety in 1914 by starring in a big-budget silent feature, *Neptune's Daughter*, billed as "the film masterpiece of the world."[2] The film's poster featured a chart of her measurements, which were touted to "almost surpass belief." Besides disclosing her perfect "33-26-32," the chart detailed nine other measurements (including head, thigh, and ankle) along with comparisons to those of Venus de Milo and Diana the Huntress.

In 1916, Kellerman starred in *A Daughter of the Gods*. Shot in Jamaica on a reported budget of more than a million dollars (over $22 million today), the now lost film is best remembered for its tasteful nude scenes in which her seemingly naked form would have been fully exposed but for the strategic placement of her long hair. She also created and marketed a popular line of modern bathing suits that women could actually swim in without the impediment of skirts and pantaloons. As she told the press: "I can't swim wearing more stuff than you hang on a clothesline." Her films and personal appearances created such a stir that for many years her one-piece bathing suit was referred to as a "Kellerman."

---

[2] Excerpts from *Neptune's Daughter* can be seen on YouTube. Annette Kellerman was portrayed by Esther Williams in the 1952 biopic *Million Dollar Mermaid*.

M ack Sennett was always on the lookout for new talent. He could easily have turned to Kellerman for the idea he had in mind, but by 1923, she was 36 years old and Sennett had an eye for younger girls.

Steered in his direction, Billie Beck recalled:

> I crashed Mack Sennett's private office and told him Ziegfeld
> wanted him to give me a job. I went broke in Sacramento when I
> got sick ... [and] when I got to Hollywood, $7.50 a day as an extra
> girl in a bathing suit for Sennett looked good to me. I boosted that
> to $15 by doing high dives.

A slightly different account suggests that while making his rounds one day Sennett encountered a "vision of loveliness" — a girl who moved with such grace that he could hardly fail to notice her. Years later, relating this version, Sally explained that "plain luck" had led to her success in the movie business:

> I was on the two-a-day vaudeville circuit when I was taken ill. I
> went to Southern California to swim my way back to health. Mack
> Sennett saw me doing some stunts off a diving board at the beach.
> During a chat I let him know that I could swim. He promptly
> engaged me to do a 30-foot dive for which I was to receive $15, my
> first check for an appearance in a motion picture. I needed the
> money and I wanted a chance in pictures. So I agreed to the stunt
> and was placed up on the trapeze. That dive might be called my
> plunge into screen work.

The so-called tank act — where the performer dives from a high board or trapeze into a tank of water — was one of the more popular stunts of the time. Resourceful performers had devised variations that included ice in the tank or even performing seals. As early as 1902, Annette Kellerman herself had incorporated the exploit into a popular aquatic show that featured high dives as well as swimming with fish in a large glass tank. So it was that the nubile Billie Beck, bare armed and bare legged in a Kellerman bathing suit, dove not only into a tank of water, but into a whole new way of life.

Billie's first silent film experiences took place at Sennett's Keystone studios and, while it's possible she once portrayed one of his bathing beauties, if she did, the titles and details are unknown. Her first appearance on the big screen was in a two-reel comedy that began filming in December of 1923 under the working title *The Lady Barber*. Released as *Flickering Youth* on April 27, 1924, it starred Harry Langdon, who, along with Charlie Chaplin,

Buster Keaton and Harold Lloyd, was considered one of the top comedy actors of the day.

According to one report:

> Another feature of *The Lady Barber* will be a specialty dance number by Miss Billie Beck, one of the most widely known artists of Terpsichore in the country. Miss Beck dances a humorous dance number in one of the big scenes of this comedy…. This will mark Miss Beck's first appearance on the screen.

Billie's brief tenure with Mack Sennett came to an end when, following in the footsteps of Harold Lloyd and Will Rogers, she accepted an offer to work at the Hal Roach studios in Culver City.[3] Roach was one busy man, producing more than 90 short comedies in 1924 alone. An October 1924 movie magazine shows "Billye Beck" ("a former vaudeville dancer") posing with a full-grown male lion for one of those productions. She was said to have brought to the Roach Studios "new variations to the technique of the comedy vamp."[4] Billie stayed with Roach for eight months, appearing in an unknown number of his short films.

Parting ways with Roach, Billie wrapped up her two-reeler comedy career with a four-month stint at the Christie Film Company, run by brothers Al and Charles Christie out of facilities on Sunset Boulevard in Hollywood.[5] In contrast to the riotous, more theatrical comedies being produced at the time, Christie Studios emphasized relatable situational comedies that encouraged the audience to laugh *with* the characters, not at them.[6]

---

[3] Best remembered today as the producer of the *Our Gang* comedies and his baker's dozen classic feature films starring Stan Laurel and Oliver Hardy, in the silent film era, Roach was Sennett's biggest competitor.

[4] In one of Sally's earliest scrapbooks, an unidentified movie magazine clipping "Why Men Leave Home – in comedies" defines a comedy vamp as a girl with a talent for "luring men from the safe and too sane fireside." She might be a girl with "spit curls and a wiggle … whose sole duty is to tempt them from the straight and narrow."

[5] With one notable exception, it appears that none of Billie Beck's early short films have survived the years. The one exception is *Court Plaster*, released by Christie on September 28, 1924.

[6] Canadian born Al Christie was something of a visionary. In 1929, he hired African-American Spencer Williams as a sound technician but soon recognized his other talents and engaged him as a script writer to create the dialogue for a series of two-reel comedy films featuring all-black casts. More than 20 years later, Williams assumed the role of Andrew H. Brown in the wildly popular *Amos & Andy* television show. When Williams accepted the part, he returned to a familiar location: the CBS television studios had been built on the former site of the Christie Studios.

Sometimes featuring showgirls wearing scanty costumes, their films had such titles as *Tootsie Wootsie, Beauty ala Mud* and *Campus Cuties*.

Why Billie left Mack Sennett to make films for Hal Roach and why she then moved on to work with Al Christie is not clear. It may have been the money. It may have been a man, either to follow or to run from. Much like today, a great many pretty girls were in Hollywood hoping for fame. Lots of opportunities and many a tale of heartbreak.

Her motivation aside, on August 25, 1924, Billie signed an Actor's Equity contract to return to the stage as a soubrette[7] in *Harry Carroll's Pickings*, a musical comedy to be presented at the Orange Grove Theatre in Los Angeles. The musical was a big hit — showcasing such popular tunes as "Hay Foot, Straw Foot," "Chop Sticks," "Charleston Time," and "I'm a Pickford Nobody Picked." [8] It was still running on the day when Billie was inspired to pursue a meeting with a certain 43-year-old film producer who was rumored to be starting his own movie studio.

So it was that, in the fall of 1924, Billie Beck came to the attention of Cecil B. DeMille just as he was wrapping up a decade-long association with film producer Jesse L. Lasky. With visions of striking out on his own, DeMille was looking for new talent. Sally's somewhat dubious account of their initial meeting is a bit melodramatic:

> I learned the ropes and crashed Cecil B. DeMille's office, pushing
> his secretary out of the way. I got by his desk spotlight without
> tripping over his trick rug, and showed him my stills, all kinds of
> poses. He said "Okay" and I got bits right away.

However it happened, DeMille's first encounter with Billie Beck occurred while he was directing *The Golden Bed* — described by its trailer as "a juicy melodrama, featuring sin, opulence, peril and intrigue, and featuring the stunning 'Candy Ball' sequence."[9] Sources differ as to whether Billie had a

---

7   In theater, a "soubrette" is a comedic female character, often a maid, who is saucy and girlish, mischievous, lighthearted, and coquettish, and who displays a flirtatious or even sexually aggressive nature. Sounds like pretty smart casting.

8   A drummer in the show was pressed into service to entertain the audience during intermission — an aspiring singer named Harry Lillis Crosby, Jr. — later known to the world as "Bing."

9   They just don't make 'em like this anymore. The famous "Candy Ball" scene (with costumes by Edith Head) culminates when the real candy bars on the ladies' gowns are enthusiastically devoured by their gentleman suitors. A color tinted print of the film exists.

bit part. Indeed, she may have been on the set but not in the film. As she once explained: "I would have been in *The Golden Bed* if smoking a cigarette hadn't brought tears to my eyes and run the mascara all over my face." In any case, this would be the last film DeMille would produce and direct for Famous Players-Lasky Corporation before securing the funds to set up his own studio.

Cecil B. DeMille aspired to be his own boss. He had originated the "stock company" idea in his early days with Lasky, nurturing such stars-to-be as Mary Pickford and Gloria Swanson. Now he was determined to duplicate that model in a shop all his own. Initially, he was interested in assembling a group of 20 to 30 talented individuals, without regard to whether they were well known. "There is no other industry," he said, "in which true ability may be so easily recognized and rewarded." Those lucky enough to be put under contract with him may have been paid as little as $50 a week, but they were assured of a steady income.

The nucleus of first hires at DeMille's new studio consisted of some 15 members, among them Leatrice Joy, Vera Reynolds, Rod LaRoque, William Boyd (later known as Hopalong Cassidy) and one other — the fresh-faced subject of this biography. As the youngest of the group, DeMille took her under his wing, directing her to stay with him constantly, or as Sally later put it: "... from the moment we came on the lot in the morning until he left at night. I spent half my time outside men's rooms."

Billie Beck's introduction to Cecil B. DeMille led to the most transformative event in her career. Accounts differ, but the essentials are these. DeMille was so taken by Miss Beck that he foresaw her future as America's sweetheart. At 20 years of age, Billie was as bright and shiny as a newly minted gold piece, but for whatever reason DeMille felt she needed a new professional name. According to one source, a conversation between the two, which probably occurred during the filming of *The Golden Bed*, went something like this:

> Learning that her name was Billie Beck, Mr. DeMille reacted, "I see you as 'Sally.'"

> "Sally Beck?" she inquired.

> DeMille reportedly spotted a road atlas on his desk and proclaimed: "That's it!"

> "My god," she said, "not Sally McNally!"

The great man's famous scowl[10] slowly became a rare smile: "No, goose — Sally Rand."

Thus was "Sally Rand" born. Repeated countless times over the years, some version or other of this story became standard narrative in her press releases.

An interesting variation of this story comes from a 1976 interview where Sally was quoted as saying: "One day I was in his office ... and Mr. DeMille said he thought Billie Beck was too girly-girly. 'You're going to be doing more dignified parts now and I think you ought to have a new name,' he told me.

There was a Rand-McNally atlas on his desk, and I said 'What about Rand?' And that's how it came about. The 'Sally' is diminutive for Sarah, one of my grandmother's names. So we drank a glass of champagne and that was my christening."

Later in life, Sally told her son Sean that, while DeMille had indeed chosen "Rand" from the road atlas, he left it up to her to choose a first name. Imagining how the name would look "in lights," she had chosen "Sally" simply because she thought the upper and lower case appearance of all the letters "had a good flow to it."

So, the little girl named Helen Beck who became Billie Beck had now become Sally Rand. DeMille was happy with the name, "Sally" was satisfied, and her family would come to be as well.

Her father soon weighed in, writing:

> I forgot to answer your question as to how I liked your show name. I like it fine. It is all right. "Billye Beck" was fine, and I was mighty well satisfied with that, but evidently you had good reasons for taking the other, and it's perfectly all right.

---

[10] The DeMille scowl was legendary. He was a stern taskmaster and never predictable. An oft-told story describes the famous director on a movie set one day, about to film an important scene. While giving complicated instructions to a huge crowd of extras, DeMille suddenly noticed one extra talking to another. Enraged, he shouted, "Will you kindly tell everyone here what you are talking about that is so important?!" She replied, "I was just saying to my friend, 'I wonder when that bald-headed son of a bitch is going to call lunch.'" DeMille glared at her for a moment, and then yelled, "Lunch!"

S ally Rand is the most beautiful girl in America," DeMille proclaimed after signing the eager young actress to a long-term contract. "She is young, piquant, athletic and intelligent — possessed of a trim type of film fascination which should make her a star of the first magnitude."

DeMille was not the only one to notice Sally's special appeal. Apparently, she was quite a party girl:

> Though diminutive, provocative with youth and naive, she seems rather individually certain of her right to the spotlight. That quality caused her to stand out pointedly among the comedy girls, and at parties she manages, by sheer personality, to be the focus of the youngsters' attention.

With a major boost from DeMille, Sally got a leg up on thousands of other aspiring young actresses in Hollywood. Still, she was keenly aware of her competition, explaining:

> People with serious screen hopes must realize that they are competing with hundreds of other players with just as much excuse for being present as themselves. The casting directors are used to seeing pretty girls by droves and swarms, and mere good looks and modish clothes don't make much of an impression — not in Hollywood they don't! Competition in Hollywood is faster than a horse race. A horse has only to run, but a girl trying to break into pictures has to think of everything.[11]

> For instance, I think the Charleston helped me a lot. I learned it in New York, and when the craze hit Hollywood I knew how to step it when most people were just learning. Taking advantage of the opportunity I entered Charleston contests, and won half a dozen cups at the Cocoanut Grove.[12]

---

[11] An anonymous columnist made this same point in a clipping taken from Sally's scrapbooks: "Behind Sally Rand's blonde petiteness and constantly smiling lips there is an amazing strength and an iron will to succeed which ... [are] so incompatible with her dainty, almost childish exterior.... Hollywood is full of beautiful girls. You can buy beauty by the carload. But the girls who lift themselves out of mediocrity are those who have the personality, the intelligence, but more than anything else the courage to stand years of disappointment."

[12] As one paper put it: "Twice in three weeks, dainty Sally Rand, a member of Cecil B. DeMille's cinema stock company, has won a silver loving cup at the famous Cocoanut Grove for excellence in dancing the 'Charleston.'" Sally's Kansas City childhood buddy Lucille LeSueur (Joan Crawford) was also known for winning quite a few Charleston contests at the Cocoanut Grove.

Sally's growing reputation as a leading exponent of the Charleston opened yet another avenue of opportunity. On July 12, 1925, a news item headlined "THAT SWAYING, SWINGING CHARLESTON DANCE! HERE'S HOW YOU DO IT" declared Sally Rand to be "one of the first dancers to do the Charleston on the New York stage."

An adjacent article over the byline "By Sally Rand" was possibly the first published piece credited to the lady herself:

> You have to be happy to do the Charleston. It is a dance that is full of the joy of living. The Negroes in the South have been doing it for years and it is only lately that we learned it from them. Broadway, New York, has gone crazy over it.

> Never has any other craze so completely conquered New York. Everybody is dancing Charleston. Scarcely a music show is without a Charleston chorus. The roofs are doing it.[13] The street organs begin to play over on the East Side and the kiddies do it. And their mothers and fathers and aunts and uncles and grandfathers. And if we had not given it a name suggestive of modern jazz, how much like its African brother would it be! Charleston is quite primitive, but altogether fascinating. But how is it done?

> The first and most important thing is the tempo. The accented counts come on the first and a little after the third count of 4-4 time. You really have to hear the music and figure it out for yourself, but if you follow the simple rule of accenting the counts as I have suggested, you will have something to start with.

There followed a lengthy step-by-step description of exactly what to do, concluding with:

> When you get this step perfected, it is time to attempt the famous "knee wiggle," which means the moving of the knees from left to right while you travel, moving hands in a circular motion from the front of one knee to the other, continuing to move toes and heels to the right and left alternately as in the other movement.

> I have told you about but three of the steps. The number and variations are unlimited and may even be improvised at will, so long as the keynote is kept — the rhythm, the barbaric, primitive, happy dancing, guaranteed to drive your blues away.

---

[13] "The roofs" refers to shows presented at such venues as the Madison Square roof garden in New York City.

Sally was all about self-promotion and DeMille did his part to keep it going. The article concluded with a notice that: "Miss Rand will give several public exhibitions of the Charleston…. Watch for the announcement of her first appearance through the courtesy of Cecil B. DeMille."

S ally appeared in up to half a dozen films produced by DeMille's studio in 1925 alone, the publicity machine humming all the while to make sure her name and image were prominently and repeatedly displayed. The first of these puff pieces appeared in newspapers across the country on February 3, 1925, above the caption: "If you think that Sally Rand isn't one of the most beautiful women in the world you can get an argument out of Cecil B. DeMille, who declares she is." Just a few weeks later, an article showing Sally wearing "a paper curl bob" hairdo[14] extoled her features: "Her golden head, blue eyes, laughing lips and short, straight nose have been immortalized on many canvases, as she was a model at the Chicago Art Institute before she came to Hollywood."

DeMille's designation of Sally as the "most beautiful girl in America" was part of a larger publicity campaign organized by Paramount Pictures and producer Jesse Lasky to identify the 14 most beautiful girls in the world, each of whom was to be featured in the upcoming film *The Dressmaker from Paris*. In the film's early planning stages, Lasky cautioned director Paul Bern that, in the search for beautiful girls: "Each one must be of striking type, not one who is 'good enough,' but the best."

It was first thought that these girls could be found in the Los Angeles area — in department stores, art schools, and elsewhere. However, after an unsuccessful local search, Bern reported back to Lasky, who then declared: "All right, we will postpone production of the picture and choose our girls from everywhere." In their quest, they solicited the services of the "greatest connoisseurs of beauty," among them Broadway showman Florenz Ziegfeld, famed illustrator Coles Phillips, French fashion and perfume designer Jean Patou, and, of course, film director Cecil B. DeMille.

For his part, the great DeMille instructed his casting office to bring together for his personal inspection a score of the most attractive girls available. From those paraded before him, DeMille narrowed the field to four girls,

---

[14]   It's not clear what the term "paper curl bob" denotes, as this term seems to have been fashioned for the article. Sally's illustrated bob was full and just-past-earlobe length, with soft, loose curls. Plugging the short hairstyle, the article advised readers that "Hollywood says bobbed hair is here to stay." Besides Sally's trendy cut, the half-page article touted the "shingle bob," the "marcel bob," and the "Dutch bob."

Sally not among them. Actually, she wasn't even in the room, as in the eyes of the casting director she didn't seem to be anything special. When DeMille finally did have occasion to observe her, the 19-year-old Sally quickly rose to the top of his list.

According to a contemporary press report:

> Sally answers the description given by Ziegfeld of the girl of tomorrow who, he says, supplants the flapper of today. She has a boyish figure, is just a shade over 5 feet tall, weighs 115 pounds, has blue eyes and ash blond hair.

On March 15, 1925, one week before release of *The Dressmaker from Paris*, newspapers ran a full-page promotion headlined "BEAUTY SECRETS BY SOME OF THE NEW BEAUTY STARS" featuring Sally and the film's other stars. Each girl was described as the epitome of such characteristics as "complexion, figure, hair, and poise." Sally was presented as the essence of "feminine grace." And, as she would do in years to come, Sally extolled the benefits of exercise:

> "I'd like all girls to know how happy it makes you to exercise," she says, in her lovely little-girl way. "Everybody wants to be happy. And this is so simple!"

> "A girl should do her daily dozen not to get muscle, but in order to become supple. It is command over every muscle that you want. The old-fashioned exercise of touching the floor is one of the best beauty exercises I know; then touch it at the sides — do the windmill movement — deep breathing — bending from the waist."

> "To keep down the little pad of flesh on the back of the neck, bend your neck back and forth — nodding movement — whenever you think of it — you can't do it too often."

> "For a beautiful back ... turn from the waist from side to side, keeping the lower part of the body still. You will feel the muscles as you move."

> "But remember that the value of any exercise is regularity."

The Roaring Twenties were about more than illegal booze, silent movie stars, flappers dancing the Charleston, and an expanding economy. The era also saw a significant escalation in female exposure. The apple pie variety of this trend was represented by the debut of the Miss America Pageant in Atlantic City. Although the contest winner was not called "Miss

America" until the following year — when, incidentally, Norman Rockwell would be among the celebrity judges — this iconic beauty competition actually originated on September 7, 1921, and, as we have learned, Margaret Gorman, a 16-year-old from Washington, D.C., was the victor.

These new opportunities for gawking were quite popular but, of course, there was also a vocal chorus of disapproval. One newspaper endorsed the efforts of the Young Women's Christian Association under the headline "YWCA OPENS WAR ON BEAUTY CONTESTS":

> The shocking costumes which such contests encourage certainly call for protests from organizations interested in girl welfare.... It was noticed by competent observers that the outlook on life of girls who participated was completely changed. Before the competition they were splendid examples of innocent and pure womanhood. Afterward their heads were filled with vicious ideas.

Three days later, an editorial in the same paper argued that the idea of wearing bathing suits for any purpose other than swimming — the very basis of a beauty contest — was detestable, even a bit evil:

> ... the effect of these rivalries on the contestants is deplorable. They may be good girls when they enter, but whether they win or lose the coveted prizes, they have deteriorated after judgment has been passed. They have learned to mistake notoriety for fame, their estimate of relative values has been utterly destroyed....

> A more reprehensible way to advertise Atlantic City or any other town could not be devised by the devil himself.

But for any number of young women in the 1920s the whole point of going to a beach was to show off their figures. They fervently sought, in the Mack Sennett inspired parlance of the day, to be bathing beauties.

Mack Sennett wasn't the only one taken with the notion of presenting young ladies in a state of partial undress. A major mover in this revolution of epidermal expression was Earl Carroll, a showman sometimes called the "Picker of Pulchritude," who was himself a judge at the 1924 Miss America contest.

For more than 25 years, the annual *Ziegfeld Follies* was one of the hottest attractions on Broadway. Inspired by the shows at the Folies Bergère in Paris, Florenz Ziegfeld's lavish revues originated in 1907 and soon grew into what can fairly be called elaborate high class vaudeville variety revues. These annual revues featured both known and unknown entertainers, along with lots and lots of pretty girls. Ziegfeld's productions were so successful that they inevitably gave rise to more than one competitor. Foremost among the rivals was *Earl Carroll's Vanities*, which began in 1923. Within a short time, Carroll's approach of pushing the nudity envelope posed a serious challenge to the dominance of the *Follies*. Someone once quipped that while Ziegfeld had the best-dressed showgirls, Carroll made sure that he had the best undressed. A critic in the *Brooklyn Eagle* was particularly harsh, writing that "Carroll's showmanship consisted in selling gutter humor and naked female flesh to morons."

Carroll's biographer reported that, in the opening number of his 1924 *Vanities* featuring the lovely Kathryn Ray swinging "nude" on a giant clock pendulum, vice squad officers watching from the wings on the night of September 11th felt the call of duty and rushed onto the stage. One over-zealous officer pulled the offender from her upside-down position and tried to wrap her in a blanket. Miss Ray managed to wriggle free and take off running. The ensuing chase produced a scene reminiscent of Mack Sennett's Keystone Kops. Mistaking the whole affair for part of the show, the audience roared with delight and leapt to their feet in applause.

Carroll escaped prosecution for a time, but he landed in the Court of Special Sessions on November 10, 1924, for displaying obscene posters in the theater lobby. At his trial Carroll called attention to the nude marble statues on the facade of the New York Public Library and, in his defense, read from a prepared statement:

> A vast amount of words have been spoken and written on the subject of censorship, most of it, on both sides, in bitterness. I have nothing to say against the censor individually, but I will point out clearly, I hope, and without rancor, how reactionary and out of date the Board of Censors is. It is a commonplace to everyone who has given any attention to the origin and history of ethics, that what is prohibited in one age is apt to be orthodox and quite correct in the next....

> Infinitely better than concentrating the power of censorship in one individual's hands ... [it] is my sincere belief that such standards can be safely left to the people. Only then can we have regulation without strangulation.

Upon retiring to deliberate, the three judge panel announced that its ruling would be founded solely on a question of fact: Were the images immoral? The verdict was brief: "We have examined the exhibits that are specimens of nudity and find they are not sufficient to hold the defendant. We find the defendant should be acquitted." And so the show went on, albeit treading a fine line between titillation and indecency.

But Carroll was incorrigible. He ended up in hot water once again in 1926, following an event he hosted on February 22nd. According to the party invitation, the revelry would last from "midnight to unconscious." His guests were given a further clue that the night might be a wild one when, upon arrival, each was required to sign a form releasing Carroll from responsibility for any claims arising out of "injury or death that may occur to me by reason of said revel."

Carroll's guest list included many dignitaries, both foreign and domestic. Among those in attendance were Walter Winchell, Condé Nast, and the columnist and future television variety show impresario, Ed Sullivan. To make a long story short, a certain Joyce Hawley was convinced to disrobe and step into a bathtub filled with sparkling champagne, from which she proceeded to ladle out drinks to the assemblage, before sinking deeper into the bubbly and passing out. An orgy reportedly ensued. For his efforts, the ever-genial host was subsequently convicted of violating prohibition laws and ended up serving a stretch in the federal penitentiary in Atlanta. This inconvenient incarceration aside, we have not heard the last of Mr. Carroll.

No sooner had DeMille signed Sally Rand to a contract than his publicity department arranged for her first movie magazine interview, a lengthy piece entitled "Sally Dove into the Movies" by Hal K. Wells.[15] Not quite five years older than Sally, Wells was duly impressed:

> Yesterday morning, in her tiny dressing room at the DeMille studio, Sally gave her first interview for any motion picture magazine, and she handled the affair with the cool poise and quiet confidence that are innate traits of this very personable young player. Incidentally, she also gave me the surprise of my life before our interview was over.

> I knew that Sally was very young, and very attractive to the eye. I also knew that she had been a star dancer on the Orpheum circuit, and that she was famous in Hollywood for her ability to add new and even more weird contortions to that alleged dancing exhibition known as the Charleston. Putting these bits of knowledge together, I anticipated a chat that, while pleasant, would probably be about as solid as the interior section of a cream puff.

---

[15] Mr. Wells would gain a modicum of fame in years to come writing science fiction stories for pulp magazines like *Weird Tales*, *Astounding Stories* and *Thrilling Wonder Stories*, bearing such intriguing titles as "Flame Worms of Yokku," "Black Pool for Hell Maidens," and (we kid you not) "Give a Man a Chair He Can Lick."

Instead, before I fairly had time to catch my breath, I found myself involved in a discussion of psycho-analysis that left me feeling about as intelligent as a Fiji Islander who had unwittingly opened a book on differential calculus. Sally Rand has an eight-cylinder brain, and she knows exceptionally well how to use it.

It is Sally's amazing youth and beauty that are so misleading on first acquaintance. One does not expect Venus to speak with the intellectual brilliance of Minerva.

Barely out of her teens when her first interview was published, Sally was already startling supposedly well-educated men with the breadth of her curiosity and abilities. Mr. Wells was only the first in what would be a long line of journalists, businessmen and professors who would be moved to look past her physical attributes and marvel at her sophistication.

W ithin months of joining the DeMille stock company, Sally already had a few film credits under her belt. Her semi-estranged but very proud father, now working for the post office and living with his French wife, Marie, and their children in New York City, wrote a long letter to Sally on June 30, 1925, commenting on the state of their relationship:

I wonder where you are, and how you are! I have been thinking about you so much of late, and wondering if it be tragedy or good fortune that besets your pathway, and if the gulf of affection is as wide between us as the material gulf that separates us at this time.

On your part that may be true, but to me you are the same baby Helen that I once cuddled in my arms and loved with all the daddy love that one man could hold within his heart for his first-born....

Your picture, the one that you sent to me at Elkton last Winter, hangs framed upon the wall of my home. Not that I can say that I altogether like it. While it is a gorgeous picture with costume of the Louis XV vogue, yet the portrait in its likeness is not MY HELEN. What I would like, and as Marie was saying a couple of evenings ago as we sat here looking at the picture, is a real picture of Helen as she was and is to us.

William Beck didn't think much of the film industry, but affection for his daughter trumped his reservations:

Of course I know that all that you need is a fighting chance to make good, and you will win. It is a hard old game, and a heart-breaking one, played with a crowd more heartless, more unprincipled, and more unfeeling than any class of employer that ever walked the face of the Earth.

If you win, it will be YOU WHO WON, and no credit to anyone else. Just as I told those bush folks down at Elkton when they looked rather askance at the idea of a girl going in for stage and film work, I said "My girl has chosen that career because it is an outlet for her talent, and promised greater, and higher things for her than she could attain by following in the sordid and menial footsteps of the average girl such as you have here in this community."

Sally's divorced parents were not on good terms — no surprise when one considers their history. Her father's letter from New York grants us entry to his point of view:

I returned here in January.... I rather wanted to get away from New York, and settle down in or near the old home belt, but several things finally determined me on returning here, one of them being that your mother had engaged a lawyer to annoy and harass me with threatening letters relative to payments of alimony that she felt that I should be paying....

Of course I know ... that at a tender age both of you children were led to believe that your father was a very bad man, and you both grew up with that theme stamped upon your plastic mentality, and so it seems just natural that it should be that way. Sometime you will both know differently. Time clarifies all things....

You have two of the finest brothers here that any girl ever had.... Both of the babies are the best dispositioned little ones that I ever saw, not excepting Harold. As for you, you know that you were always an imp of mischief. We are all very happy and contented here together. Marie with her shy and retiring French disposition is very sweet. She often speaks of you and, although she lays a lot of her past worries and troubles to certain acts of your mother, she certainly does not hold that against you, and I know that down in her heart she has a lot of regard for you. In fact she has always loved you as much as you would allow her, seeing that you and she have never had the opportunity for intimate association.

Back at the beach in California, an unexpected chink began to appear in the armor of moral indignation when controversial Christian evangelist Aimee Semple McPherson agreed to officiate at the wedding of an Ocean

Beach lifeguard to a young woman whom he had once rescued from the salty depths. The happy couple was attended by twenty bridesmaids attired in bathing suits and twenty groomsmen wearing their lifeguard uniforms. Describing the stunt as "cheap and nauseating," the influential Methodist minister, Robert P. "Fighting Bob" Shuler, Sr., took Miss McPherson to task, declaring that she was holding "wedlock on a level with a leg show at a bathing beach." He proclaimed that this was a disappointment to God, who did not "place his approval upon the administration of the holy ordinance of marriage to the tune of 20 pairs of nude legs displayed by female attendants." When Sister Aimee later appeared before the cameras in an "abbreviated bathing suit," the senior Shuler could hardly contain his fury.[16]

In years to come, Sally would have countless run-ins with the moral guardians of the community, but what may have been the very first of these took place on January 4, 1926. The 21-year-old aspiring film actress had agreed to appear at a special meeting of the Santa Ana Chamber of Commerce, where it was announced that she would "offer several arrangements of the Charleston step" — a dance she was credited with having introduced to Southern California — in a "costume especially designed for the occasion." Expecting a large crowd, the organizers moved the event from Ketner's Cafe to St. Ann's Inn (an imposing first-class hotel), and the price of dinner was bumped from the usual 75 cents to $1.00 a plate.

Mason Yould, chairman of the entertainment committee, engaged the services of Joe Sanford's Snappy Five to provide the music, announcing: "We want to start the New Year off with a bang. We want to show the Santa Ana Chamber of Commerce what kind of meetings we hold. We want ... to make Santa Ana bigger and better for all concerned."

According to a local press report, members seemed to enjoy themselves well enough, but:

> Sally Rand, petite film star and dancer was scored roundly today
> by Santa Ana churchmen, who claim she "compromised the moral
> standing" of Santa Ana business men by dancing before them in an
> "abbreviated costume."

Outraged, the congregation of the First Methodist Episcopal Church of Santa Ana sent a resolution of protest to the Chamber of Commerce

---

[16]   Yes, he was the father of Robert P. Shuler, Jr., whose *Hour of Power* television
      broadcasts from the Crystal Cathedral in Garden Grove, California, mesmerized
      millions of followers around the globe before financial woes brought the ministry low.

declaring: "The dance was particularly inimical to the best interests of the youths of the city." Sally stood her ground. She indignantly denied that there was anything immoral in her routine, maintaining:

> I gave them a relatively tame version of the Hollywood Charleston. There is nothing "sexy" or risqué in any of my dance stuff. I do the real southern hoe-down Charleston, and there is more skill than sex in that dance. As for my costume, it is modeled after the bathing suit I wore for Mack Sennett when I was making films for him.

"More skill than sex." This self-assessment would become Sally's standard defense and explanation of her act over the next 50 years.

In January of 1926, the country at large welcomed in a new year and, as for members of the Santa Ana Chamber of Commerce and the good people of the local Methodist church, well, they were present at the very beginning.

Sally would appear in more than 20 silent films between 1925 and 1928, mostly as a member of the DeMille stock company. Even though the majority of these films are now lost, some of Sally's roles and her exploits in connection with their filming are worthy of mention.[17]

The first silent feature in which she had any significant part was *The Dressmaker from Paris*, released on March 30, 1925. The story concerns a World War I Air Force officer who becomes captivated by a dressmaker's apprentice while on leave in Paris. The centerpiece of the film is an elaborate fashion show featuring the 14 beautiful "models" selected after the international search orchestrated by Lasky and Bern. Although no print of the film is known to exist, still photographs of Sally survive in private collections and can be seen online.

The subject matter of *Dressmaker* was tailor-made (*ouch*) for local promotional tie-ins. Across the country, theaters promoted film showings by staging Style Prologues in which live models — "On Promenade" — would present "the very latest style creations in millinery, costumes and footwear," much like a modern-day runway fashion show.

Shortly after the film's release, Sally traveled to San Jose to begin a four-day appearance at the Liberty Theatre in connection with a special prologue to

---

[17] To describe each film is beyond the scope of this book. An Internet search will reveal their titles, as well as indicate which films are known or believed to still exist. Several can be viewed at www.free-classic-movies.com.

the film in which she would model "the actual gown worn by her in the fashion revue of the glamorous production."[18] At a session with members of the press, Sally described her own charming gown:

> All the gowns worn in the picture have enchanting names. Mine is called "The First Kiss." Paul Bern ... sent for a very marvelous designer from Paris. We collaborated on my gown. I always wear my hair in Nell Brinkley curls, and my gown was being built on that idea. It's pink tulle, layer upon layer, ruffle upon ruffle, embroidered in silver and edged with white swan's-down — a fluffy-fluffy, powdery thing — lovelier in reality than in the picture. With it I carry a little parasol bordered in pink roses.

When asked by a *San Jose Mercury-Herald* columnist if she had a hobby, Sally "smiled radiantly and became, if possible, more witching than ever," replying:

> I collect dolls. I've some really lovely ones. Several Russian and Belgian dolls will be used in the boudoir scene in which I appear at the Liberty theatre.... Several friends have given me those fuzzy-haired French dolls that have had such a vogue because they think they look like me.

> My newest doll is as big as a small child. It looks so much like a real little boy that it almost defies detection. When I had it with me on the New York subway, and on sleeper jumps during a recent Orpheum tour, people commented on how cruel it was to take a child out in winter so lightly dressed.

This Cecil B. DeMille production, written by Howard Hawks and released by Paramount Pictures, remains of interest today primarily because it was directed by Paul Bern. At the time, the 35-year-old Bern was an up-and-coming screenwriter and director, known in some circles as a ladies' man, if not a womanizer. Oddly, in some other circles he was suspected of being something of a lady himself.

Writing of her several relationships during her days with the DeMille studio, Sally recalled that she and Bern had enjoyed a cozy relationship:

> Paul ... was my steady cerebral date. He had a position at MGM as an assistant to Irving Thalberg. This gave me great status. He was a

---

[18]   On these same four days, "Ziegfeld Follies Beauty" Sally would also appear twice a day at M. Blum & Company "in our Fountain Street Windows wearing original model gowns from the screen production."

very rich man and took me to the nicest places and the most glamourous parties, adored me, and gave me beautiful presents. And I
helped him with script reading and I adored him.

It is safe to say that Paul Bern was smitten with Sally Rand. A letter from
boyfriend Carl Schlaet, written to her in the fall of 1926, confirms as much:

> Your friend Mr. Bern must have thought it was Christmas from the
> list of presents he gave you. They sound as tho his interest must be
> considerably more than friendly. However, since I can't see how any
> man could help but fall in love with you, I can't blame him much.

And just what were these "presents"? Sally's son Sean still has at least one
of them: "I actually have a little pink monkey — the top of the head comes
off and it's lipstick. Also, the chest cavity opens up and it's a compact with
powder and a mirror inside." Sean continued: "She told me that Paul Bern
had given it to her on the Queen Mary," adding that she had been on board
the ship with him sailing to England.[19]

While Bern did enjoy notable success as a director and film writer, he is best
remembered for his involvement with blond bombshell Jean Harlow. On
July 2, 1932, the 42-year-old MGM executive married the 21-year-old star of
such films as *Hell's Angels* and *Platinum Blonde*. Barely two months later on
September 5th, he was found dead in the newlyweds' Beverly Hills home
from a gunshot wound to the head. A suicide note was found near the body.

Rumors soon circulated that Bern had killed himself because he was
impotent — unable to perform as the husband of one of the most desirable
women in the country. The controversy over his death continues to this day.
Some believed the rumors that Bern had tiny malformed genitals and that
he had attempted suicide several times in the past (awkwardly on one
occasion when he supposedly got his head stuck in a toilet seat and a
plumber had to be summoned to extract him). Bern's supporters dismissed
this chatter, contending that it was mostly gossip based on unfounded
charges made by novelist and journalist Adela Rogers St. Johns, who had
leaked the coroner's observation of Bern's underdeveloped genitals and

---

[19] This anecdote is from Bonnie Egan's 2014 interview of Sally's son Sean. The RMS
Queen Mary has been permanently moored in Long Beach, California, as a tourist
attraction since 1968. Sean said he had once offered to take his mother for a tour but
she had declined, explaining: "Because it would make me sad. I traveled that ship
when it was out on the seas. I have no interest in seeing it docked." At the very least,
Sally had dramatically embellished the tale she told her son, since the RMS Queen
Mary's maiden voyage did not take place until May 27, 1936, several years after Paul
Bern's death on September 5, 1932.

then embellished the story of his so-called deformity, including a statement attributed to actress Leatrice Joy — who accidentally saw him naked — that his penis was "smaller than my pinkie."

There is no doubt that Sally Rand and Paul Bern had a sexual relationship during the filming of *Dressmaker*; she freely admitted as much. In an interview many years after the fact with Chicago media personality Irv Kupcinet, Sally confidently stated: "I can speak from experience. I know firsthand and can vouch for it, Paul Bern was not impotent."

When asked in a 1972 interview about Irving Shulman's intimate biography of Harlow, Sally warmed to the subject:

> Shulman is full of it. For instance he kept saying that Paul Bern was
> impotent and that is why he killed himself. Well let me tell you, he
> was NOT impotent. There was nothing wrong with him at all;
> Shulman lied and never even talked to me! Paul Bern was
> murdered, a lot of people knew that but who is gonna put their
> number one star in a bad light? Harlow did not kill him, of course;
> it was some woman he was married to years before.[20]

While Sally apparently did have true affection for Bern, relations between film executives and their employees were not always sweet and innocent. Indeed, Hollywood in the 1910s and 1920s was infamous for the "casting couch" system for advancement of pretty young starlets.

It is a long-held notion that show business is full of disreputable characters. Even in the time of Shakespeare, the guardians of public morality considered plays to be profane and actors to be irresponsible and immoral people. Taverns and other shady enterprises were commonly located in theater districts and church leaders regularly complained that theaters themselves were little more than public gathering places for spreading disease.

Traveling vaudeville shows and silent film studios had a similar reputation in more conservative circles. Even clergyman Charles C. Selecman, the forward thinking pastor of Trinity Methodist Church in Los Angeles, characterized the situation in Los Angeles as "appalling."[21] He was responding to a 1915 grand jury inquiry into charges by young girls that "liberties had been

---

[20] The woman referred to is Dorothy Millette, characterized by some as Bern's mentally
       deranged common-law wife, who had lately emerged after 10 years in a sanitarium.

[21] Did we say forward thinking? Reverend Selecman anticipated the mega-churches of
       today by many decades, having just opened a nine-story church building that included
       a hotel for men, a room for motion pictures, a barber shop and cafeteria, as well as a
       roof garden, smoking room, nursery, hospital, and bowling alley.

taken" by film directors and that it was next to impossible for a pure girl to remain so if she chose to continue her career. The minister demanded a thorough inquiry into the alleged wrongdoing.

The rise of the casting couch culture in the film industry was truly appalling. According to one article from a weekly paper published by Henry Ford in December 1921, practices at the comedy studios were particularly egregious:

> A college girl who had done some newspaper work before coming to Hollywood and going into the movies, told the writer about a certain well-known comedy company where the brother of the producer ... hired the girls used in the pictures. Before a girl was given employment she took a walk with this man and [her engagement depended] on her acceptance or rejection of his advances....[22]

> It takes a girl of exceptionally strong character to emerge unscathed from the temptations presented at the studios, and all honor should be given to those who do.... Small wonder that so few of them hold out. The blame does not rest on them, but on the whole rotten system, a system that will endure until the public has convinced the producers that there are some things more precious than the dollar.

In the December 1921 issue of *Shadowland* magazine, influential novelist Theodore Dreiser addressed the subject in his article "Hollywood: Its Morals and Manners." Finding the practice of treating adolescent girls as sexual prey inexcusable, Dreiser's legendary sense of social justice shined through:

> The general assumption on the part of many directors, assistant-directors and even stage carpenters and electricians is that, somehow, because these hundreds and even thousands of girls are compelled to or, at any rate, are desirous of making their living or their way in this field, and have all too little, financially, wherewith to do that, therefore they are, and of right ought to be, the sexual prey of these men.

Vaudeville? A movie studio? Off a wooded lane near the University of Wisconsin? It is not known where, when or with whom Helen Beck/Sally Rand lost her virginity. That, as a 20-year old girl, she was attractive almost beyond compare is not disputed. (A *Chicago Daily News* article claimed that even the great DeMille himself propositioned her.) The

---

[22]   Of the three "well-known" comedy producers — Mack Sennett, Hal Roach, and Al Christie — only the latter had a brother (Charles) who was in charge of the business side of the operation.

details of her dalliances and the question of her consent or coercion aside, Sally is reputed to have shared her favors somewhat liberally during this period. In addition to Paul Bern and other suitors we shall meet in chapter 6, Sally recalled that: "There was Erwin Gelsey,[23] that brilliant young red headed assistant to Walter Wanger, just coming on the scene and fun to be with. And Abe Lipsey, my oldest boyfriend in L.A. and a darling, going to USC and slated to be Hollywood's largest seller of mink coats."[24]

Asked in May 1925, "What sort of man appeals to you?" Sally described her ideal prince charming: "I'd like a Pan boy," she said, "slim and brown with long, slim, brown fingers — creative fingers. Hands mean such a lot. The kind of man who appeals to me would produce because he is a creative man and so I suppose he'd make money." Did Sally know that the mythological Greek god Pan was famous for his sexual prowess? The reader is free to speculate.[25]

Faith

On the very day that *Dressmaker of Paris* was released in New York City, the comely young "Yvonne Bacon"[26] was on stage as a member of the ensemble in the closing performance of *Bringing Up Father in Ireland* at the Lyric Theatre on 42nd Street. Based on the popular comic strip by George McManus featuring the fractious family life of "Maggie and Jiggs," the show closed after only 24 performances. It had fared much better in previews on the road. For example, in Lebanon, Pennsylvania, the local press had reported: "... the only complaint the theatre managers have ... is that they haven't enough seats to hold the crowds."

Yvonne was out of work, but not for long. Within a few weeks, she was back on Broadway strutting her not inconsiderable stuff in *Artists and Models* at the remodeled Winter Garden Theatre. The show was "the third and most daring of all *Artists and Models* productions" — the "new Paris Edition." The Shubert brothers' production promised the "Greatest Revue Cast Ever Assembled,"

---

[23] Four years older than Sally, Erwin Gelsey did become a screenwriter on more than two dozen films produced between 1932 and 1950, including *Flying Down to Rio* with Ginger Rogers and Fred Astaire and *Cover Girl* with Rita Hayworth and Gene Kelly.

[24] As Sally predicted, Abe Lipsey would amass a fortune as the celebrated "Furrier to the Stars" in Beverly Hills. Neighbors to Frank Sinatra in Palm Springs, Lipsey and his wife would become renowned for their philanthropy.

[25] In the late 19th century, Pan became an increasingly common figure in literature and art. Some say the Greek god is even alluded to in J. M. Barrie's character Peter Pan.

[26] The 14-year-old performer Frances Yvonne Bacon had not yet adopted the stage name "Faith Bacon."

featuring "the Incomparable 18 Gertrude Hoffman Girls direct from the Moulin Rouge in Paris," as well as many other beautiful singers and dancers. The exquisite Miss Bacon was one of the "models" appearing in such scenes as "The Magic Garden of Love." She was also featured as a lavaliere (one of the "Jewel Girls") in Scene 7, entitled "Cellini's Dream."

As the critic for the *New York Evening Post* observed:

> If the artists are not there the models are, and the posing is most artistic, far and away better than anything of the kind ever shown in the Winter Garden, particularly beautiful being "Cellini's Dream" and "The Rotisserie" with the trussed chickens on the spit and waiting their turn.[27]

Erte and Georges Barbier of Paris designed costumes for the show. And what costumes they were! Details are elusive, but they were likely no less revealing than those featured in the original 1923 edition of *Artists and Models* — characterized by *Variety* magazine as the "smartest, fastest, dirtiest revue in American history." Remarking that "the Shubert exhibits an entire chorus with unveiled bosoms," the editors wondered why the police didn't stop it.

Critics and local police were not the only authority figures concerned about so-called indecent performances. Many church congregations felt obliged to weigh in as well. Among them were members of the Jehovah's Witnesses, a movement which began in the late 1870s with Charles Taze Russell's co-founding of "Zion's Watch Tower Tract Society."

When Russell died in 1916 he was succeeded by the controversial Joseph Franklin Rutherford, who proceeded to run the organization with an autocratic hand. In 1922, he initiated the practice of requiring adherents to distribute literature via door-to-door preaching (now you know who to blame) and, somewhere along the way, he allowed himself to be referred to as Judge Rutherford.

Jehovah's Witnesses are known to be quite conservative, even admonishing members not to use any sort of foul language on the grounds that it is expressly forbidden in the Bible. So you would not imagine that many in the movement would be attending shows like the *Follies* or the *Vanities*. But Rutherford was a flawed messenger.[28] On April 27, 1926, George H. Fisher,

---

[27] At the time "chicken" was slang for a young woman.

[28] Known to use vulgar language, Rutherford was also reputed to be an alcoholic. During World War I, he was charged with crimes under the 1917 Espionage Act and sentenced to 20 years imprisonment. However, he was released on appeal and resumed his mission.

a trusted colleague, wrote a letter accusing Rutherford of attending the Winter Garden Theatre in New York City to see the Paris Edition of *Artists and Models* accompanied by a young woman, presumably not his wife. Rutherford's supporters dismissed Fisher's accusation as "the Devil's malicious charges." And, besides, Rutherford was said to be too busy engaging in the Lord's work to be bothered with replying to such grossly false and libelous criticism.

These denials (if they even *were* denials) were not taken seriously by those in the know who had long heard rumors about Rutherford — that he frequently attended nude or girlie-type shows, particularly when traveling abroad. He surely had the opportunity, as he was known to have apartments in New York, London, and Magdeburg, Germany, separate from the well-appointed apartments in those same cities provided for him courtesy of the Watch Tower Society.

It is not known whether Miss Bacon performed topless in *Artists and Models,* but whatever the extent of her coverage, there is little doubt that any costume she sported would have been of a seductive, abbreviated and diaphanous nature. However exposed she may have been, what the falsely pious Judge Rutherford — and presumably other members of the audience — didn't know was that the provocative Miss Bacon was a minor — just 15 years of age.[29]

Only 11 days after *Artists and Models* closed, the Winter Garden Theatre opened its doors to a new extravaganza, *The Great Temptations*, a revue in two acts which, like *Artists and Models,* was a Shubert Brothers production. Due to the popularity of its predecessor, the show opened to "a multitude which filled every seat in the house and stood four rows deep wherever there was standing room." It ran for nearly 6 months (223 performances).

The famous New York drama critic George Jean Nathan gave the show a mixed review, noting:

> At the Winter Garden, Mr. J. J. Shubert has mounted a spectacular dancing show that, if it lacks humor, yet has many points to recommend it. In the first place, it moves swiftly and easily; in the second place, it is attractively costumed; in the third place, it discloses an exceptionally well-trained dancing ensemble; in the

---

[29] The show enjoyed a long run of 416 performances between June 24, 1925, and May 7, 1926, (during which time Yvonne turned 15). No doubt, the production's success was due in part to the comforting assurance that the theatre was "sanitized by means of the Perfumed Aerzonator Air Purifying Blocs."

fourth place, it has called upon certain Parisian revues for some of their more beguiling features....

So far as comedy goes, the one outstanding number is a dialogue of a *Gentlemen Prefer Blondes* order between a Miss Dorothy McNulty, who handles her end superbly, and a competent feeder named Jack Benny. This is funny stuff; Ernest Boyd and I almost swallowed our Cremo Coronas laughing at it.

This show marked the Broadway debut of Jack Benny, who somehow managed to bear the indignity of having to share the stage with a bevy of beautiful girls in an atmosphere of crudity and nudity for a weekly wage of $600 (or some $8,300 in 2017). The dancing Duell Sisters were also in the cast. (In years to come, Dorothy Duell would become Sally Rand's best friend and closest confidant.)[30] And the still-too-young Yvonne Bacon was among the *Great Temptations* performers listed in the opening night cast.

According to Eleanor Duell, Dorothy's sister and dance partner, the show included more than its share of exposed flesh:

We were anxiously anticipating seeing the Guy Sisters perform-ance.[31] Their number couldn't actually be called a dance — their costumes consisted of such tremendous plumed headdresses and long plumed trains that they could hardly maneuver, let alone dance. The hats and trains were all they wore!

It also offered dancing partners Roseray and Capella, performing "a very fancy dance with very few clothes and lots of thrills." (He wore a loincloth "open at the sides to allow for a great flesh display" and she sported "some beads on a headdress" and a well-placed "rhinestone thingamajig.")

Besides the Guy Sisters and Roseray and Capella, from 15 to 20 members of the *Great Temptations* cast appeared onstage in a state of near nudity. While the nature of Yvonne Bacon's performance or just how much of her 15-year-old epidermis was on display is not clear, an issue of *Art Studies Magazine* published a picture of her from the show, veiled only by a whiff of trans-parent material. This lithe young girl — who could have been arrested if authorities had known she was a minor — was beginning to attract attention.

---

[30] Dorothy would later marry Henry "Heinz" Scott Rubel, a former Episcopalian minister and gag writer for radio comedians, and move to Glendora, California, where Sally Rand would also make her home.

[31] The Guy sisters were known for their classic all-but-nude performances in the music halls of Paris.

By the summer of 1925, Sally's star was clearly on the rise, and DeMille's publicity machine had seen to it that her picture was prominently placed in newspapers and magazines — as many as possible, as often as possible. As she pursued all manner of physical activity, assorted publications followed Sally's every move. When she went to the ice rink, they breathlessly reported that the "dainty DeMille actress has become enthusiastic over ice-skating, and can now do all the fancy steps on the ice with which she made such an excellent reputation when dancing ... in vaudeville." In July, as Sally motored via Lincoln sedan to the California Yacht Club where she boarded a 32-foot cruiser bound for Catalina Island, reporters tagged along. During the outing she was photographed in her bathing suit "aquaplaning" behind the cruiser on a surfboard. According to the *Los Angeles Evening Express*, she fell off "only once."

A letter from her father, dated October 19th, plainly displayed his pride in her emerging fame:

Dearest Helen:

... I wonder if you know that the New York papers have been printing pictures of you doing your toe-writing. The picture has appeared in two of the dailies. A neighbor of ours ... came in the other morning. She looked at your picture on the wall, and read the name, and exclaimed: "Why, I saw that girl's picture in the paper this morning. What is she to you?" Marie replied that she was her husband's daughter. ... The girls at the office were all on the qui vive[32] about it and passed the picture around. You know how excited a bunch of girls will get over a thing like that, and the fact that they work in the same office with a fellow who has a daughter in the movies with one of the great producers, and with her picture in the papers.

I was all "het up" about it myself, as it was the first time that I had seen you in the New York papers ... and it showed that the press agent — who is a mighty important functionary to successful publicity — was busy even this far East. Just keep going girl-o-mine, and we will see your name in electric lights on Broadway before very long. You will be the greatest Beck of the whole crowd yet. I am not very proud of the Beck line. None of them ever did anything very big. With a poor environment, no high education, and small initiative, they were inclined to meander within a small circle, and never get very far.

---

[32] "On the qui vive" is based on a 16th century French martial term meaning "on the alert" or "on the lookout," but in this context it could translate to "all psyched up" or "all aquiver."

In another letter written a few months later, he added: "None of them ever ... owned any palaces or railroads. Conversely, none of them ever was hanged, died in the poor-house, or went insane."

"Toe writing"? Well, yes. A photograph syndicated to papers around the country showed Sally, sitting on a stool, writing with a pen held between the toes of her right foot. Under the headline "DANCER WRITES CHECKS WITH HER FEET," the copy improbably asserted:

> Sally Rand, Los Angeles film star and dancer, has trained her shell pink toes to answer her correspondence. She has developed toe penmanship to a point where more than one of her ardent fans treasure a letter written by Sally in this novel fashion. She also signs checks with a special pen made to fit her toes.

An inset photo displays a highly legible "Greetings" over the signature "Sally Rand," her toe pen apparently having just been lifted from the page.

In a letter dated December 29, 1925, Sally's father thanked her effusively for the many Christmas packages that she had sent to him and his family:

> My Dear Girl:
>
> ... I will say that Marie was thrown into transports of delight at the sight of the wonderful dainty things that were in those boxes. You know her heart is set on dainty things that way....
>
> Now, that dressing gown is mighty fine for your daddy. I have not as yet worn it, but believe me I intend to — when things are a little different. In this flat with some of the children always trying to climb up my leg, it would hardly be the best policy to try to wear a fine article like that.
>
> I am sorry that I could not have anything to send you but a card, but that card bears a love message from all of us....
>
> Darling, I do not have any idea how much money you are earning, but I do want to ask you to save every bit that you can. Put it in a bank and let it grow. I want to see you a grand lady, and live in a castle like some of those other movie girls are at present. Learn something about business, so that you will know how to handle your money wisely, and invest it properly....
>
> Your loving Daddy

As you might expect, "the most beautiful girl in America" was getting quite a lot of attention from the opposite sex. In a letter written to her mother on January 22, 1926, Sally hinted at her improved financial condition (which would soon make it possible for her mother to leave Missouri and join her in California), at the same time raising tantalizing questions about her current beau:[33]

I have really been having some very lovely trips lately while making "Braveheart."[34] I spent a most delightful week at Lake Arrowhead. The Lake Arrowhead Lodge there is one of the most beautiful rustic places I have ever seen, facing a large lake with boats and canoes and horseback riding in the months when there is no snow, and skiing and ice skating and winter sports around Christmas time. We were there just before Thanksgiving when I think it is the most beautiful time of the year. Johnny came up to spend the weekend, too, and we had lots of fun.

Thanksgiving I cooked dinner at Johnny's house, with turkey and all the things we used to have for Thanksgiving dinner. I cooked my turkey in a paper bag, too. The day after Thanksgiving, Johnny and I went up with Aunt Joe and Uncle Howard to Lake Arrowhead again to be the guests of some friends of theirs who have a wonderful cabin in the mountains, which overlooks the valley and one can count fourteen lighted towns at night.

About three weeks ago we took our last yachting trip to Catalina on the Molly-Lou, the sail boat which we often told you about. We had a little excitement in the night — it blew up quite a little storm and we had to pull out of the unsheltered harbor in which we were moored and dash for a little fisherman's cove, which is safe in any kind of storm. We had lots of fun watching the battle from our safe anchorage.

---

33   This letter was typed on Sally's personal typewriter in the distinctive type that resembles the old Olivetti Lettera 22 with a slanting typeface. Hereafter, the content from Sally's letters is set forth in an approximation of that typeface.

34   Not to be confused with the 1995 film about William Wallace, the 13th century Scottish warrior who led the Scots in a war for independence against the King of England, the 1925 *Braveheart* is a very different movie. It concerns an American Indian football player who goes to law school to gain the skills he needs to fight for the property rights of his people. The film still exists and is available on DVD. Sally has a minor role, but she can be glimpsed standing in the bleachers, waving a pennant and eagerly cheering on the team.

The skipper of the Molly-Lou, Mr. Hesselberger, is entering his boat in the California-Honolulu race, June 12, and Johnny is going with him, and I hope I may also. If there is room, I will by all means. It will be a wonderful trip, with very little or no expenses.[35]

Two weeks ago, Johnny and I went to San Diego. We had a wonderful trip. It was the first time I had ever been to Tijuana. I think the first time I have ever seen a real bar, and gambling and that sort of thing. It is the first time I ever saw a horse race, too, and I had lots of fun betting. I came out even, altho I was quite lucky the first of the race. I also attended to some very urgent business which you know about, and it turned out very happily for me.

The mention of the "very urgent business" that Sally had attended to in Tijuana may explain why she was never able to bear a child of her own.[36] So, just who was this "Johnny" who had shown Sally such a good time and accompanied her to Tijuana? Years later, when recalling her boyfriends from the 1920s in surviving fragments of her hoped-for but ultimately unpublished autobiography, she described their relationship:

There was Johnny Maschio, for whom I had wangled a position of Asst. to Mitch Leisen, DeMille's head designer and set dresser. [37] We did a lot of sailing together and a lot of happy lovemaking and went to Friday night dances at the Ambassador, and ... Saturday afternoon tea dances at the Cocoanut Grove and had a wonderful time.

---

[35] Sally didn't make the trip, although Mrs. Hesselberger did, one of only two women in the entire field of boats. The "Mollilou" (the yawl's actual name) failed to finish the race.

[36] There is little doubt that Sally had an abortion while in Tijuana. Seven months after her visit there, in a letter from her boyfriend Carl Schlaet, he advised her "to get more details from Dr. Hart" concerning "the question of whether any part of the tubes were left."

[37] Maschio was no doubt appreciative of Sally's help at the DeMille studios, as he parlayed his association with future director Mitchell Leison into a successful career as an actors' agent, ultimately becoming the most prominent "agent to the stars" in Hollywood. His list of clients would include Humphrey Bogart, Henry Fonda, Jean Harlow, Gregory Peck, John Wayne, Kim Novak, and Marilyn Monroe, among many others.

All the "happy lovemaking" aside, Johnny Maschio was only one of several suitors competing for her attention.[38] Ultimately, Sally and Johnny parted ways — but not because it was his idea.

Sally had made a big enough splash in Hollywood that she was soon swimming in much fancier pools. In this same letter to her mother she described one such occasion:

> *I want to tell you about Mary Pickford's farewell party....*
> *There were many notables there, among whom were Mr. and*
> *Mrs. Charlie Chaplin, Joseph Hergesheimer, Donald Ogden*
> *Stuart, Mary Pickford and Douglas Fairbanks, Jack Gilbert,*
> *King Vidor, Madam Elinor Glynn, Eileen Pringle, Sam*
> *Goldwyn, Jesse Lasky, Joseph Schenck, Marcus Loew, Eleanor*
> *Boardman and many others.[39] All the people whom I have*
> *mentioned sat at one table and all gave very marvelous and*
> *witty speeches. I don't think I have ever been in a more*
> *celebrated, witty and intelligent company than that. Mary*
> *Pickford was charming and so sweet. I am very thrilled*
> *because it was the first time I had ever seen either she or*
> *Douglas Fairbanks, and I was not disappointed at all.*

Sally's newfound success in Hollywood led to a significant bump in her disposable income. So why not splurge a little and let everyone know you have arrived? Little more than a chat with the amiable and unusually attentive salesman at Walter M. Murphy Motors, plus signing her name a few times, put Sally behind the wheel of an automobile worthy of being seen in. She would now be motoring in style in a brand new Essex.

As reported in a Valentine's Day puff piece:

> ... the other day, when she drove into the service department for an oil
> change at the end of the first 500 miles, the famous little dancer-actress

---

[38] Carl Schlaet was aware of his competition, not only from Paul Bern, but also from Johnny Maschio. Responding to a letter from Sally that had cheerfully brought him up to date with respect to each of her other lovers, Carl wrote: "Since I didn't know that Johnny even had a 'cookie-duster,' it's hard for me to get excited about its removal. I imagine he'd look better without it. Wish I could have taken his place on your visit to Diamond Bar." [That's a small city east of Los Angeles. And "cookie duster"? It's a bushy full mustache!]

[39] Although Sally misspelled some of the names, her list was a veritable "who's who" of Hollywood's most influential movers and shakers, including stage and film stars, studio heads, and celebrated writers.

expressed the highest regard for the car's performance. "See," she exclaimed, lifting her skirts and shaking her tiny feet in a nifty Charleston step, "I even had the car's initials embroidered on my hose."

Sure enough — there they were: the initials "S-X" which, as the motoring world knows, stand for the only car on the market which can boast a pair of initials.[40]

An adjacent photograph captioned "AND IT'S A NICE CAR, TOO" shows Sally standing next to her car, beaming broadly and hiking up her skirt to reveal an 'S' on one thigh and an 'X' on the other "just above her dimpled patella."[41]

This was just one of the many publicity stunts that the DeMille Studios either arranged or permitted in 1926 to promote their popular little honey. On May 15th, to demonstrate the "frugal characteristics of MacMillan gasoline," the MacMillan Petroleum Products Company sponsored a 25-mile drive starting at Long Beach City Hall and ending at the auto salon tent of the California Valencia Orange Show at Anaheim. The automobile had been painted for the event in a vibrant plaid pattern. Just before the engine started, a "big Scottish bagpiper" stepped into the car. The starting gun was fired, accompanied by the "shrill notes of a Scottish bagpipe." The piper continued to play "wild Gaelic tunes all along the route" as a squad of motorcycle police escorted the vehicle to Anaheim. And who was behind the wheel? None other than Sally Rand, "garbed in full Highland regalia — bonnet, plaidie and kiltie."

Apparently, it was within Sally's skill set to operate virtually any form of transport. When the local newspaper reported the exciting news that a trainload of marvelous new Maytag washing machines would be passing through Riverside on its way to Los Angeles for distribution in Southern California, mention was made that "Sally Rand, DeMille Studios moving picture star, will drive the train into the yards."

Ten years before Jack LaLanne opened what is generally regarded to be the first modern health club, Sally Rand was a serious and vocal advocate of proper diet and exercise. Newspapers and movie magazines

---

[40] At least this is the version that DeMille's publicity people offered to the press. Writing of her financial condition at the time, Sally mentioned that she was making "the car payment on my Star Coupe," presumably a Durant, not an Essex.

[41] Like every other decade, the Twenties had its share of fads and follies. Among them, a short-lived fad caught Sally's attention: "I noticed a newspaper story in which it stated that some actresses out in Hollywood are having their sweetheart's initials embroidered on their hose. So since I'm really in love with my Essex, I decided to start a Culver City fad."

regularly ran pictures of her performing her daily dozen, stretching and smiling in a silk bathing suit or gym suit, with captions touting the benefits of regular workouts:

> It hasn't been difficult to maintain "training rules" since Mr. Cecil B. DeMille placed me under contract in his studio.... Before I entered pictures I was a dancer in New York — and a professional dancer must always keep in the finest physical form.
>
> By twists and turns does beauty come. But not just any twists and turns. I have always maintained that exercises not scientifically planned to achieve certain results are little better than no exercise at all. They merely fag you without taking off a single ounce of overweight or stretching a single muscle that needs it.

As if writing with one's foot, operating a locomotive and posing for cheesecake exercise shots were not enough, DeMille's publicity director Barrett C. Kiesling had also arranged for a wide variety of other photo ops — Sally at the Santa Monica Security Bank sitting atop a huge display of scrapbooks holding $40,000,000 worth of forged documents, Sally posing with Babe Ruth at the Los Angeles train depot with six other aspiring starlets,[42] and Sally wielding a paint brush while suspended in a boatswain's chair over the side of the *SS Belgenland*, a luxury cruise ship. (Once back on deck, she gave Captain Thomas Howell a few pointers on dancing the Charleston.)

And so it went.

While most of Sally's early film roles were quite small, she did appear with notable stars in a number of silent films, among them *The Night of Love* (1927) with Ronald Coleman and *The Last Frontier* (1926) with William Boyd. In *Galloping Fury* (1927), she was cast as the female lead opposite western star Hoot Gibson in a plot built around the discovery of "beauty mud" on the ranch.[43]

It is a great shame that so many silent films no longer exist. What fun it would be to watch Sally in *Heroes in Blue* (1927) playing the motherless

---

[42] In the photograph, Sally looks up at the Bambino adoringly, while the other girls look directly at the camera. The event at Union Station publicized Ruth's arrival in Los Angeles to begin filming *Babe Comes Home* (released in May 1927). This was also the year when Ruth hit a record 60 home runs for the New York Yankees. (While the film is considered lost, a brief behind-the-scenes excerpt can be seen on YouTube.)

[43] A short clip from *Galloping Fury* may be viewed on YouTube. The excerpt is a bit jittery, as it is displayed on a vintage Mutoscope movie machine, but it is possible to glimpse the youthful Sally as Dorothy Shelton.

daughter of a fire chief. Shot on location at a real fire station, the film made her a big favorite with all the firemen. In one scene, she got to sit behind the wheel of one of the biggest fire trucks of the Los Angeles Fire Department, maneuvering the massive vehicle through the streets of the city. At the time Sally said she enjoyed her work in *Heroes in Blue* more than any earlier film, despite the scene where she was called upon to jump from the window of a burning building. She later said the flames leaping up at the window got so hot that it felt more like reality than a movie scene. She lost no time diving into the net held by her co-starring firemen four floors below.[44]

We are also the poorer for the loss of *Nameless Men* (1928), a silent movie in which Sally was featured in a "brilliant cabaret scene" with Stepin Fetchit.[45] In the words of an uncredited reviewer present at the filming:

> In this scene Sally Rand, dressed in a cute little black satin costume trimmed with rhinestones with gorgeous blazing red slippers embroidered with gold, appears as an entertainer. The music droned and banged while Sally stepped forth with intricate dance steps that once again proved her vaudeville experiences came in handy. So inspired was she with the music and her part that she was loathe to leave the set and begged Director Christy Cabanne to continue the scene a little longer.

Faith

The *Ziegfeld Follies, Earl Carroll's Vanities,* and similar shows all drew inspiration from French music hall productions that had for many years featured sexually provocative performances. Indeed, the history of such shows can be traced as far back as 1779. By 1894, the actors, singers, dancers and jugglers in such venues as the Folies Bergère were being overshadowed by sensational displays of female nudity.

Fresh from her Broadway stint at the Winter Garden Theatre and seeking to expand on her experience performing in daring Broadway revues, the now-16-year-old Yvonne Bacon was ready for new ventures. Accompanied by her mother Charmion Bacon-Morris (posing as her sister), the

---

[44] *Heroes in Blue* was also said to contain an "inside" gag where the characters played by Sally Rand and her co-star John Bowers attend a movie starring — who else? — Sally Rand and John Bowers!

[45] The first black actor to achieve a screen credit and the first to become a millionaire, comedian and film actor Lincoln Theodore Monroe Andrew Perry gained fame under the stage name "Stepin Fetchit."

striking and talented girl headed to Europe, hoping to gain even greater exposure.

In the music halls of France, Yvonne reportedly performed with famed French entertainer Maurice Chevalier in one of his revues, possibly in a somewhat minimal and provocative costume. Chevalier had a legendary eye for the girls and, while the extent of his contact with Miss Bacon is unknown, there is evidence to suggest that some sort of physical relationship existed between the two, however brief.

Yvonne turned 17 during the summer of 1927 while appearing at the famous Casino de Paris. On the same program in the revue *Paris - New York* with the Dolly Sisters and many others, she had a featured part in "The French Garden," one of six segments in a tableau called *Les plus beaux Jardins du Monde* (The most beautiful gardens of the World).

Yvonne and her mother left France on October 29, 1927, traveling from the Paris suburbs to London and from there to New York aboard the Atlantic Transport Line's *SS Minnekahda*. Yvonne would soon change her stage name to Faith Bacon and in time would play a pivotal role in the fortunes of the woman whose image appears on the cover of this book.

D o blondes really have more fun? Maybe, maybe not. In an interview with Hollywood columnist Dan Thomas in November of 1926, Sally expressed her view:

> No. There are plenty of reasons why I would rather be a brunette. First of all, I believe I am better looking with dark hair. It suits my features better. Then too, it is much more fun to be a brunette. Men have blondes labeled as all being alike, and all men treat all blondes just the same. They think we are frivolous and unthinking. It is difficult for a blonde not to show her thoughts and emotions in her eyes. That's another disadvantage.
>
> But brunettes — oh, they're all so different! You never can tell what a brunette will do and men know it. That is what makes it possible for dark-haired girls to enjoy themselves more.

Hypothetical disadvantages aside, Sally did not let her hair go brown. And, within days after her remarks were published, the 22-year old Miss Rand's profile (blond hair and all) was elevated considerably by her selection to an elite group — The WAMPAS Baby Stars of 1927.

First staged five years earlier, by 1927 the Frolic had become a must-be-there occasion. On February 17th of that year, the event was held at the famous Ambassador Hotel on Wilshire Boulevard.[46] According to columnist Dan Campbell:

> The sixth annual frolic and ball drew the elite of the artistic and social world to the Ambassador hotel where for hours before the stars began to arrive, thousands of curious screen fans lined the corridors, waiting for a glimpse of some favorite player.

> Preceded by a program that presented some of the most famous personages of the stage and screen, the baby stars of 1927 were presented to the vast audience of more than 3,000, in a dazzling array of stunning gowns in a brilliant setting.

One girl stood out from the rest. As the syndicated columnist Dan Thomas put it:

> The Wampas frolic — huge glaring searchlights illuminating the Ambassador Hotel grounds as celluloid notables and ordinary actors arrive — hundreds of outsiders defying threatening skies so that they can return to Iowa and say that they saw Douglas Fairbanks and Mary Pickford.

> Inside the huge auditorium ... [there were] many dull acts and then the presentation of the thirteen Wampas Baby Stars.... [The] most

---

WAMPAS BABY STARS

Before the birth of Oscar and the ballyhooed arrival of stars on the red carpet at the annual Academy Awards, Hollywood moguls employed other means to promote their emerging young stars. Foremost among them was the annual "WAMPAS Frolic," a gala sponsored by the Western Association of Motion Picture Advertisers. Each year, association officials would convene to consider the relative merits of "junior" or "baby" actresses — ingénues nominated by the various movie studios as most likely to attain stardom in the year ahead. Thirteen young women would be designated as WAMPAS Baby Stars for the coming year and would receive front page coverage across the country. The 13 ingénues would then be formally presented at an annual ball or frolic. Among the "baby stars" selected at the WAMPAS meeting on November 15, 1926, was a young woman who was reportedly "growing more and more popular on the Cecil B. DeMille lot" — Sally Rand.

---

[46] Site of six Academy Award ceremonies from 1930 to 1943, the Ambassador Hotel was also home to the Cocoanut Grove nightclub where Sally had won so many Charleston dance contests. Sadly, on June 5, 1968, the hotel became more infamous than famous when Sen. Robert F. Kennedy was killed in the hotel kitchen by Palestinian immigrant Sirhan Sirhan. In January 2006, the landmark structure was demolished despite the efforts of preservationists.

exquisite of all, Sally Rand, is awarded a beautiful baby blue evening wrap for selling more tickets than any of her sister stars. She is a bit overdressed, too much unnecessary fluffiness.... The highlight of the program [is] a dance by Sally Rand. She ... is strikingly beautiful.

Also cheering Sally on from afar was her ardent admirer Carl Schlaet, then laboring in the oil fields of Tampico, Mexico:

You can't realize how much I appreciate your writing. Only I want to know — what are you worried about? I anticipated that you'd be tired. It's your nature to work your blooming head off at the slightest excuse.... But please don't overdo it, as I know you're inclined to.

I wrote my mother and asked her to get your Wampas Ball flowers as I wasn't sure that I'd be in the US in time to attend to it myself, and you can't wire flowers from Mexico....

One of several adoring suitors who were bewitched and frustrated by Sally in equal measure, Carl wrote to her the week after the WAMPAS Frolic:

Sweetheart —

Got in here at midnight last night ... [and] what a disappointment it was to find a stack of mail without a single word from you! Of course I know how busy you've been and you know that I don't want to interfere with your work until I take you away from it altogether. Still dear, it only takes five minutes every two days to scribble me a line. Surely you can spare me that.

My mother writes lots of nice things about you and the Wampas Ball. How I wish I could have been there! What was the matter with the flowers — didn't they go well with your dress? I'm proud of you, but not at all surprised that you got the prize for selling the most tickets....

Don't overwork honey. I know how ambitious and energetic you are, but please remember that your health is worth more than anything, and life is too short to risk it.

I love you more every day Brat, even if you do make me mad and worried in turn by not writing.... Kisses and things for you, and if I don't see you soon I'm going to swell up and BUST!

'Night darlin,

Carl

Despite extensive media coverage, public interest waned and the baby stars event was ended after the 1934 ceremonies.[47] Truth be told, the prize and all the attendant publicity didn't do that much to boost Sally's movie career. She had played in quite a few films before the event and would be cast in many more thereafter, but her Hollywood profile was not much higher than it had been. She did, however, prominently employ the title when publicizing her return to the vaudeville circuit the following year.

In a draft of what was intended as a chapter in her autobiography, Sally provided an insider's look at life at the DeMille Studios. She had just completed work on *The Road to Yesterday*, a fantasy about quarreling newlyweds involved in a train wreck who find themselves thrust back in time to another world in which they had been lovers.[48] As Sally recalled:

> Up to this point all the pictures I had ever done for Mr. DeMille had been great fun, pleasure, excitement, and I had loved it. But this one made me nervous. Jeanie MacPherson was Mr. DeMille's brilliant scriptwriter and had been with him for years and was once maybe his girlfriend (no one was ever sure). But now Jeanie had big eyes for Joseph Schildkraut.

> At that time he was a handsome young leading man…. He really was a spectacular looking young man and very bright. He realized that Mr. DeMille listened to Jeanie, had his ear, and he was going to use her or anyone else to strengthen his position at the studio…. With this in mind, he led Jeanie down the primrose path.

> Jeanie was a very plain, middle-aged spinster, devoted to her mother, madly in love with Mr. DeMille, though she realized that any further involvement in that area would come to no fruition. Whatever she'd had, she'd had it, and he was permanently enamored of his beautiful mistress….

---

[47] Disagreements between movie studios and advertisers over which young actresses should be promoted ended the "baby stars" program. Although few are remembered today, along with Sally Rand, several went on to become big names, among them: Clara Bow (1924), Jean Arthur and Loretta Young (1929), Joan Blondell (1931) and Ginger Rogers (1932). The year 1926 was something of a banner year, as Mary Astor, Joan Crawford, Delores Del Rio, Janet Gaynor, and Fay Wray were all WAMPAS starlets.

[48] To see DeMille's 1925 silent film *The Road to Yesterday*, go to: www.dailymotion.com. The starring roles were played by Joseph Schildkraut, Jetta Goudal, William Boyd, and Vera Reynolds. Sally had a very small part as a party guest in this time-shifting film.

Truth to tell, Joseph was a cocksman who made love to anybody who would listen or hold still. He had a dozen little shoddy affairs going but Jeanie was really the focus of his attention. Jeanie wasn't a very pretty lady, she spent jillions of dollars on clothes, all of which looked tacky, but Joseph wined and dined her and gave her his full attention.

I loved and admired Jeanie very much. I learned from her. She was very generous with me, she gave me many beautiful, priceless couture dresses which I made over to look very spectacular on me. She invited me to many fantastic Hollywood parties which were elegant and gave me status. So I had much for which to be grateful to her.

She called me into her office one day and, with the greatest secrecy, real cloak and dagger stuff, assigned me to spy on Joseph and his various peccadillos.... So I was in big trouble.

Jeanie MacPherson's demands had placed Sally in a ticklish situation, potentially even jeopardizing her position at the studio:

I certainly wasn't going to start spying on Joseph Schildkraut for Jeanie, no matter what.

For the first time in the four or five years I had been with DeMille, Jeanie used to appear on the set rather surreptitiously looking at me to see if I had anything to tell her and I always looked totally innocent. She thought I knew more than I did. Actually, I didn't know anything 'cause I was too busy minding my own business.... It was all I could do to keep my own little affairs running smoothly.

As a player in DeMille's stock company, Sally was often in a sort of holding pattern, waiting to be assigned to a particular picture. As a consequence, she found time to take parts in films that were being shot at other studios, sometimes for "a lot more money than I got from my own studio." Among them were *Galloping Fury* at Universal Studios, *A Girl in Every Port* as directed by Howard Hawks at Fox, and *Getting Gertie's Garter*[49] at Metropolitan Pictures (the "Metro" of Metro-Goldwyn-Mayer — MGM).

---

[49] *Getting Gertie's Garter* is available on DVD, as well as at YouTube and elsewhere online. But, before you invest your time, be forewarned that, in a 1921 review of the play on which it was based, O. L. Hall, critic for the *Chicago Daily Journal*, described the production thus: "It reveals the delicate touch of the pile driver, the nimble wit of the porcupine, and the inventive genius of the missing link. It is a farrago of vulgar nonsense."

Sally made her last film appearance under DeMille's direction in his crowning achievement of the silent era, *The King of Kings*. Released in 1927, the film presented the "Greatest Story Ever Told" as only DeMille could, portraying the last weeks of the life of Jesus Christ leading up to his crucifixion and resurrection. Supported by one of the biggest budgets in the silent film era, the production featured a cast of thousands and text drawn directly from the Bible. The film was both a critical and box office success. While most of it was shot in black and white, audiences were particularly moved by the resurrection scene, which was presented in Technicolor, a rarity in the silent film era.

To preserve the film's spiritual nature, DeMille reportedly made his stars sign contracts with clauses demanding exemplary conduct on and off the set. Restricted activities were said to include attending ball games, playing cards, frequenting night clubs, swimming, and riding in convertibles. In addition, DeMille distributed copies of the Bible to cast and crew and "had an organ installed in the studio to play inspirational hymns for the actors." He even required the actor playing the lead role of Jesus Christ to "eat and sleep in solitude, ride in a curtained limousine, and wear a veil over his head while walking to and from the studio."

J. B. Warner had originally been cast in the starring role. However, when he unexpectedly died of tuberculosis at age 29, the part of the Messiah was given to the veteran English actor H. B. Warner (no relation), who had worked for DeMille as early as 1914. In spite of the contractual restrictions, or maybe because the long hours of solitude had revived an old drinking problem, Warner soon became involved with an extra on the film set. Who she was will come as no surprise.

With a cast of thousands, countless "pretty young things" were out walking around the set. Among them, appearing in a small part as Mary Magdalene's slave girl, was our Sally. She was 22 years old and 5 feet tall, while the lead actor Warner was 51 and 6 feet tall — so naturally they were drawn to one another.

According to one writer:

> While H. B. Warner was playing the role of Christ, he started an intimate off-screen relationship with actress Sally Rand.... One day, the real-world lovers arrived late on the set, which greatly angered the punctilious DeMille, and so he thundered from on

high: "Miss Rand, leave my Jesus Christ alone! If you must screw someone, screw Pontius Pilate!"[50]

Improbably, another Miss Rand was on the set of *The King of Kings* — another whose birth name hadn't been "Rand." Born in St. Petersburg, Russia, on February 2, 1905, Alisa Rosenbaum got permission in late 1925 to leave Soviet Russia in order to visit relatives in the United States. She arrived in New York City in February of 1926, but within six months she had headed for Hollywood with aspirations of becoming a screenwriter.

The story goes that, on her second day in Tinseltown, Miss Rosenbaum was making her way to the DeMille studios only to find herself denied entry at the gate. As she contemplated her next move, Cecil B. DeMille, returning from lunch, pulled up in his car. Noticing her standing on the curb, he offered her a ride to the set. DeMille subsequently offered the young immigrant a job and she ended up as a spear-carrying extra in this legendary silent film.

Before arriving on our shores, Miss Rosenbaum had adopted the professional name Ayn Rand. Under her nom-de-plume, this other Miss Rand did, in fact, achieve a measure of Hollywood success as a screenwriter before publishing her first novel, the semi-autobiographical *We the Living*, in 1936.

Did Ayn and Sally ever meet? Probably. They were within nine months of being the same age; both were petite, chain-smoking, ambitious young women; and both temporarily enjoyed the indulgence of Cecil B. DeMille. If they did encounter each other, neither seems to have left an account of it. We do know for certain that Ayn Rand met *another* extra on the set of *The King of Kings* — the actor Frank O'Connor — whom she married in 1929. They pursued the same political path and remained together until his death 50 years later. Of course, it is Ayn Rand's hugely popular novels,

---

[50] Despite DeMille's displeasure, Warner's career survived the incident. Though he is now largely forgotten, the actor appeared in more than two dozen films before *The King of Kings* and went on to enjoy another 30 years in the business, playing character roles in more than 100 other films. His last credited role, oddly enough, was a small part in DeMille's 1956 remake of *The Ten Commandments* with Charlton Heston. Warner also appeared in several beloved favorites directed by Frank Capra. And here's a bit of trivia you can use to impress your friends — the actor who once played Jesus Christ in the silent blockbuster *The King of Kings* is the very same man who later played Mr. Gower, the despondent druggist that young George Bailey saved from committing a lethal medication error in the Capra classic *It's a Wonderful Life*.

The Fountainhead and *Atlas Shrugged,* and the resulting objectivist political philosophy for which she is known and in some quarters idolized today.[51]

The year 1927 was a watershed in American history and popular culture. Charles Lindbergh completed the first solo transatlantic flight, the last Model T Ford rolled off the assembly line, Babe Ruth hit 60 home runs for the New York Yankees, the Harlem Globetrotters played their first basketball game, the Cyclone roller coaster opened on Coney Island, and the first official transatlantic telephone call was made from New York City to London. The Grand Ole Opry made its first radio broadcast and Philo Farnsworth demonstrated the earliest transmission of what he called "electronic television." In the Black Hills of South Dakota, sculptor Gutzon Borglum, at the age of 60, began drilling and dynamiting his way into a 5,700-foot mountain to create the granite monument that 14 years later would be known as the Mount Rushmore National Memorial. And, in Hollywood, California, Grauman's Chinese Theater opened on May 18th with the premiere showing of *The King of Kings.*

With a running time of 155 minutes, DeMille's spectacular production was truly an epic film. The movie's two Technicolor sequences heralded the future of the industry; fans flocked to the box office and critics were effusive in their praise. Yet, scarcely weeks after its release, Hollywood buzz had already turned to a new and exciting production said to be underway at Warner Bros. Big budgets were fine, color footage — yes. But, as popular as silent pictures had become, the absence of integrated sound — and the lack of nuance that personal dialogue could convey — continued to impede truly intimate engagement with the audience.

The Jazz Singer, generally regarded as the first feature-length "talking picture," was released by Warner Bros. Studios on October 6, 1927. Starring Al Jolson (perhaps the most popular entertainer of the time), the landmark film was a box office smash, earning over $2.6 million in the United States and abroad, almost a million dollars more than the previous record for a Warner Bros. film.

---

[51] While negatively reviewed at first, Ayn Rand's books have never gone out of print and together have sold about 30 million copies. In recent decades, she has become an icon of the political right. As one of the fiercest opponents of federal insurance programs, critics of the social safety net commonly invoke her philosophy. They may not be aware that Ayn Rand herself collected Social Security. Federal records confirm that, from age 70 until her death in March 1982, Rand collected $11,002 in monthly Social Security payments. Her husband Frank also received $2,943 in benefits in the last six years of his life.

The advent of talking pictures led not only to a dramatic paradigm shift in Hollywood, but also to the end of Sally Rand's aspirations to establish herself as a big-time star in the movies — she was said to have had a lisp. Her prospects, both short and long term, were cast in doubt.

The resourceful Miss Rand needn't have worried. Her future was fully foretold by that prophetic line uttered by Al Jolson — "You ain't heard nothin' yet."[52]

---

[52] According to Al Jolson's biographer, Michael Freeland, that one sentence, voiced onscreen, effectively killed off silent movies. In 1877, Thomas Edison had invented the phonograph or "gramophone" — the first mechanism to reproduce recorded sound — but he had been unable to find a way to bring sound to films, although he tried for many years. It was nearly 50 years after the invention of the gramophone before Sam Warner linked up with Western Electric to synchronize recorded sound with projected images and amplify these sounds for the audience to hear.

CHAPTER FIVE

The Vaudeville Years

Now I ask you very confidentially,
Ain't she sweet?
~ Jack Yellen (1927)

Talking pictures may have become all the rage, but vaudeville was far from dead. A larger than life actor speaking from the silver screen was an amazing novelty, but a live performance featuring human beings right there in front of your face was still something special. Sally had played plenty of vaudeville venues in the years before she landed in Hollywood. So, if her film career was mostly over, it should be no surprise that she responded to the call of vaudeville once again.

Many top vaudeville stars who had also tried to make a go of it in Hollywood were now back on the boards, banjo-eyed Eddie Cantor among them.[1] Cantor had been in vaudeville since 1907 and, like Sally, had once performed with Gus Edwards' Kid Kabaret (even though he was 20 years old at the time). He was still going strong in 1927 when a bright new tune came to his attention. The still familiar "Ain't She Sweet?" soon became a staple in Cantor's repertoire. Appearing at the Orpheum Theatre in Los Angeles, Cantor was delivering the lyric "Ain't she nice? Look her over once or twice," when a beautiful little blonde — none other than Sally Rand — strode across the stage, to the delight of the cheering audience. Sally was back in business.

At just 23 years of age, Sally had become prosperous enough by 1927 to pay for her single mother Annette and her 19-year-old brother Harold to leave Kansas City and join her in California. Tall, talented and good-looking, Harold was eager to move to the west coast, enchanted by the prospect of following his sister into show business.

---

[1] Eddie Cantor (born Edward Israel Iskowitz) was a singer and songwriter. It is a little known fact that he was one of the composers credited with writing the theme for the Warner Bros. *Merrie Melodies* cartoon series.

Sally encouraged his ambitions by enrolling him in a local acting school. After several months had passed, she visited the school to inquire about the schedule for graduation. A school official replied: "You mean Harold Beck? He dropped out after week two!" Taken aback, Sally blurted: "Week two? I've been paying here all along. You guys have been taking my checks!"

The next day, when Harold left the house on his way to "school," Sally trailed him from a safe distance. She found him at the tennis courts giving lessons to a couple of young beauties. (Harold had been a championship-level player back in Missouri.) As he went back and forth from one side of the net to the other, Sally watched from the bushes while her brother instructed first one girl and then the other. When the session was over, Harold jumped over the net, took his racket, and playfully swatted one of the girls on the butt. At that moment, Sally flew out of the shrubberies yelling and screaming at him. "Both of the girls took off," she laughed, "thinking I was his wife."

H aving been so well received by the Eddie Cantor audience at the Orpheum Theatre, Sally wasted no time in mounting her own show, *Sally from Hollywood*. A Fanchon and Marco "musical extravaganza," the show opened at the T&D Theatre in Oakland, California, in early June 1928.[2] While details are scarce, surviving evidence indicates that it would have provided a very memorable night on the town. Along with her dance numbers, Sally also sang a tune or two and may have appeared in comedy skits as well. Her dance partners included Harvey Karels and ardent suitor, Jack Crosby. The show also featured the "banjo wizard," Eddie Peabody, whose "own program alone was almost a show in itself."[3] A July 29th review of the performance in Ogden, Utah, raved that:

> Sally Rand, with her wonderful personality and gorgeous costumes, won the heart of Paramount theatre-goers.... Sally brought along a splendid group of boyfriends, who are also clever dancers.... The California producers have not sent a better show to Ogden in many months.... The 10 fellows would be excellent as a theatrical

---

[2]   In the 1920s and '30s, the popular sister-and-brother ballroom dance team of Fanchon Simon and Marco Wolff was a major producer of vaudeville tours, performed in the nation's grander movie theaters.

[3]   To see why a reviewer might say such a thing about Eddie Peabody, check out the remarkable *YouTube* video of Eddie with the Hal Kemp band in 1928. For a later, even more animated Eddie (as he might have appeared in Sally's show), look for videos of him on *The Lawrence Welk Show*, where he was a frequent guest (his performance in 1962 is a particular delight).

attraction anyway, but with Sally they just have to take lesser places.... In her appearance here she does a toe dance, an adagio "fantasie" ... and "The Wobbly Walk."[4]

Live shows of this sort were only part of the evening's entertainment, as a feature film was also on the bill. Or, as the advertisement for the T&D Theatre in Oakland explained: "People of discrimination prefer a West Coast theatre where the best of motion pictures and stage divertissement are the rule; always different and distinctive." The feature film that accompanied Sally's show in Oakland was a 90-minute silent MGM offering entitled *The Enemy*, starring Lillian Gish. This arrangement of the program, together with an intermission, gave the performers a chance to catch their breath before repeating the live show. A vaudeville troupe would commonly perform three times a day — a matinee and two evening shows. Tickets might be as little as 25 cents for a matinee balcony seat ($3.45 today).

As *Sally from Hollywood* moved east, Harvey Karels and Jack Crosby traveled with the show, but the other supporting acts varied from city to city. At some point the title was changed to *Sally and her Boys*. By the time it reached Milwaukee, the show was well practiced and humming along. One local music critic observed:

> In a first class program ... the outstanding and coruscating figure is Miss Sally Rand, one-time "Wampas baby." She is petite, with a figger that is all a figger ought to be and rarely is. She is likewise radiantly blond, and not in the least content to rest her fame on her good looks.

The Milwaukee supporting cast included Roy Cummings, an eccentric dancer whose antics sometimes included backing up toward the footlights and falling into the orchestra pit. "Al Katz and his Kittens" provided the orchestral accompaniment.

By September, *Sally and her Boys* had reached the east coast and was playing at the Palace Theatre in New York City. Twenty-four-year-old Sally was supporting not only herself and her mother, Annette, but also her 18-year-old brother, Harold, both of whom were traveling with the show. Annette Beck had been divorced from Sally's father for many years and was being courted at the time by Ernest Kisling, who was living back in the family's home base of Glendora, California. On September 28, 1928, in a letter

---

4   We can only imagine how wonderfully entertaining Sally's song and dance numbers must have been. For a more contemporary music hall rendition of "They All Walk the Wibbly Wobbly Walk," or to hear the original gramophone recording made famous by Bert Courtney, search for "wibbly wobbly walk" on *YouTube*.

written to him on Hotel Somerset stationery, Sally's mother shared her impressions of the big city:

> I can't say that I like NY so far. I haven't had a single thrill since I came here; not even when I shook hands with my ex — ha. The two "Kids" had dinner with their father one evening and they later brought him up to the Hotel to see me.

> Sally said "it burnt him up when he saw how young and beautiful I was." He is bald and what little hair he has is white; he has four little boys under six years of age and is living in this city on a P.O. clerk's salary; 'nuff said. I expect to get a thrill when I gaze upon the Statue of Liberty and go up to the top of the Woolworth Building, sixty stories high.

> [We] attended the most spectacular "hot" show two nights ago I ever expect to see. It's called "Blackbirds" and the entire cast is colored people; although there was one red-headed blonde in line; they were all wonderful performers and the best looking bunch you ever saw.[5]

> I say regretfully (on account of <u>Race</u>) it was the best show I ever saw. They gave a midnight performance for the benefit of theatrical folks.

The first week of October saw Sally and company moving from the somewhat neglected Palace in Manhattan to a truly palatial site that had cost $3.5 million to build in 1923 ($50 million today) — the ornate E. F. Albee Theatre in Brooklyn — plushly seating an audience of 3,100. Sally shared top billing there with legendary blues and jazz singer Ethel Waters, described by the *Brooklyn Daily Eagle* as "the greatest artist of her race and generation."

Greatly appreciating the change of venue, Sally's mother wrote to Ernest on October 5, 1928:

> The Albee Theatre is the most beautiful I have ever seen; when one opens the <u>backstage</u> door it looks like the lobby of the Ambassador Hotel; a gorgeously furnished reception room; dressing rooms with white tile bath and vanity dressers; ice water faucet for drinking. The front corridor and theatre is indescribable in beauty and quite a con-trast to the old "Palace" of last week. But of course the Palace is the center of all theatricals which makes it important as every producer,

---

[5]   A huge hit, Lew Leslie's *Blackbirds of 1928* ran for 518 performances at the Liberty Theater, introducing the hit songs "Diga, Diga, Do" and "I Can't Give You Anything But Love." The cast included Adelaide Hall, Bill "Bojangles" Robinson, and Tim Moore who would later play George "Kingfish" Stevens in the *Amos 'n' Andy* television show.

agent and writer attends the shows there. So far as I am concerned it's only a rat-hole with no accommodations and a fight for everything one has to use, such as lights, a place to make quick changes on stage, etc....

The vaudeville tour had its ups and downs but, on the whole, Sally's mother thoroughly enjoyed the experience. In a letter to Ernest dated November 15, 1928, she provided a glimpse into her daily experiences:

Well Baby we have had a pleasant engagement here in Wilmington. The Chrysler auto people had a parade for us Tuesday at noon; five new Chryslers took the company out around the city with big advertisements on the cars like this: "Sally Rand Official Car."

Sally, Jack [Crosby] and I rode in the first car with a driver. Then yesterday the whole company went for an airplane ride over the city and back at noon. Sally gave a luncheon here at the hotel for two newspaper women including she and I and today she gave a talk in one of the stores on make-up; also how to dress well. She had a big crowd and made a nice talk. After the store affair we were guests at "Reynolds" for lunch then hurried to the theatre for an afternoon show; and so the days go by. This has all been a very nice trip for me. We stop at the best hotels and it's all very nice and I appreciate being able to come along. Sally has been wonderful to me and has done so many nice things to make me happy.

On November 28th, Sally's mother wrote to Anna Kisling, her future sister-in-law, offering insight into life in the city and the daily routine of the tour:

It is now 12:30 and we have just arrived at home after our first day at Jamaica, L.I. It's very nice over there and I like it. In fact I like any place on earth better than NY City. It is a wonderful place to visit and shop if one has plenty of money but I wouldn't live here under any circumstances. Too many gloomy, morbid-looking people. Everybody is for himself and the devil for Sunday. Please excuse the rude way of expressing it. But I wouldn't live in a place that would make me hard and cold and selfish like this place does. It has a rather depressing effect upon me as soon as I get here.

But on the other hand I wouldn't have missed seeing this place for anything. Nothing else like it in the world; marvelous buildings (beautiful skyline) and wonderful sights at night. The people live it up all night, to attend midnight shows, to dance and dine....

You see we live in NY proper and it's so far to go and come, we never get home before one to one thirty AM. Last night we gave a benefit performance for the firemen and did not get home until two o'clock. By the time we get proper rest it's time to get ready and start to work again.... I am beginning to feel very tired of trooping about but I would surely like to see the "Kids" <u>set</u> before I leave them.

One agent is looking up bookings for them in Europe, France and Germany. Sally has been offered a number of things for herself but to keep the Company of so many intact is another thing....

I believe she will stay here and study for a while. It seems to be the thing she wants most to do. They have been very fortunate to keep at work continuously as so many good people in Vaudeville have been out of work....

I often wish that Ernest would kidnap me and drag me bodily <u>some-where;</u> then the whole plan that seems so hard to formulate would be over. (This is confidential.) I know I don't lack anything in my feeling and love for Ernest but it just seems so hard to make definite plans.

If the Kids go overseas I know they will all insist upon me going, but don't think I could go without Ernest.

She would not be without him for much longer. Exactly when Annette returned to California is unclear, but she had written to Ernest in late November: "Are you going to hang up your stocking and how would you like for Santa Claus to bring you a Big Blond Dolly from N.Y. City?" Little more than three months later, on March 10, 1929, "Annette Rand Beck" and "Ernest Gordon Kisling" were married in Glendora.[6]

A lthough four years had passed since Paul Bern directed Sally in *The Dressmaker from Paris*, the two had kept in touch. In a July 20, 1929, letter to Sally on Metro-Goldwyn-Mayer Studio letterhead, he expressed his continuing admiration:

My dear sweet child:

(When I had finished dictating that line, Miss Harrison interrupted me. What she said was, to quote verbatim, "Of all your girls, I like Miss Rand best," and this I suppose is, if not exactly the proper,

---

6   Sally's brother Harold had adopted "Harold Rand" as his stage name. Not to be outdone by "the Kids," Sally's mother followed suit, even having custom stationery made for herself with the name "Annette Rand" at the top. On the marriage license, Ernest was recorded as being 42, which was probably correct. Annette was shown as being 40. Actually, she was 47.

still an intriguing opening for my letter.) So I suppose I shall have to start all over. Well, here goes:

Dear sweet child, you have no idea how happy I was when I saw your cunning, funny handwriting on the envelope I found at the hotel when I came in at 10:45 last night. I had been at the station, seeing Irving [Thalberg] and Norma [Shearer]. They are going to New York for a few days…. I was dead tired, as usual, but such is the amazing stimulation of emotion, the fatigue vanished entirely and instantly.

You write of many interesting, and in a way tremendous, incidents in connection with yourself, achievements which, to me, seem almost heroic, for I know at what expense of will power, determination and physical energy they were achieved. As always when I think of you, I have the most profound respect for what you accomplish.

Of course I am not particularly surprised at what you write concerning your ambitions. You always had a great hunger for education and knowledge, and always took advantage of every person and every situation to satisfy your hunger in this respect.

Sally was, in fact, seeking to continue her education. Within a few months after reading Bern's letter, she was in the classroom, having applied to and been accepted by Columbia University in New York City. A 1934 article in the *Columbia Spectator* described her as taking a number of extension courses in the fall of 1929 (including journalism, modern languages and a secretarial course), observing: "Despite the notoriety that she has achieved, Miss Rand is … a cultured lady who holds advanced opinions on modern higher education."

Speaking in a low, quiet voice, Sally had given the interviewer her impressions of Columbia:

I had the feeling of being in a tremendous organization, composed of many unconnected units. The students were going there to learn what they wanted to know. Sports and social life were not the chief reason for going. I liked that. The students seemed sincere in their effort to assimilate the work given them. All the men in my class studied hard…. I was only there for a few months and then the banks began to close. I found I couldn't keep up my studies and continue my dancing, so I had to leave Columbia. But in the time I was there I got the impression that a greater percentage of the students were going there to learn something than in the average American college.

And college football? Well, Miss Rand's opinion would still resonate in some quarters more than 80 years later: "When only twenty-two men play football with a student body of several thousand, you must realize that it gets more attention than it deserves."

Although her time there was abbreviated, the young lady from the Ozark region of Missouri, arriving via Hollywood and the vaudeville stage, had been duly impressed with the Ivy League halls of Columbia:

> College is a fine melting pot — a pot in which to rub shoulders
> with the great multitude and learn to oil the machinery of living. It
> is because Columbia does draw from so many different and varied
> groups that it is the finest place in the world to learn how to adjust
> yourself to society.

"WALL ST. IN PANIC AS STOCKS CRASH" — so read the headline on "Black Thursday" in the October 24, 1929, edition of the *Brooklyn Daily Eagle*. After several days of severe volatility, the market had lost 11 percent of its total value by the opening bell. On the following Monday, market losses cascaded. The *Santa Ana Register* disclosed the scope of the fallout: "BILLIONS LOST AS STOCKS CRASH." Soon, banks would begin to fail, workers would be laid off, and a "Great Depression" would drag on for a decade, taking its toll on the American spirit.

In the meantime, Sally's mother returned to Glendora to marry Ernest Kisling. After the crash, times had turned tough for those still looking to scrape by in vaudeville. In a lengthy letter written on December 30, 1929, Sally offered insight into her situation:

> *Mother dearest,*
>
> *Well we did a 10 o'clock show this morning and between now
> and the time we do the one o'clock I will write. The work here is
> so hard and so confining. We have a nine o'clock rehearsal
> every morning, 8:15 Fridays. We rehearse until half hour before
> show time, do a show and rehearsal is 15 min after finale,
> rehearsal till next show, one hour and 15 min for dinner,
> another show, another rehearsal, another show. When I get
> home I am so exhausted and sleepy I can't take a bath, just fall
> in bed and take a bath at dinner hour at the theater and run
> across the street for something to eat real quick, and all for $50
> a week. As you can see I have no time to take lessons so I do not
> think I will stay after this week. I am trying to get a job in a
> show as I will have only 7 performances a week, in the chorus of*

course, under another name as I am doing here. My name here is Norma Lee. If I can't get a job in a show, I will take a job as a waitress in a nice restaurant, just anything so I can take my voice lessons.[7]

Mrs. Wills came down and straightened up the Apt for me at 203 West 13th. I am going under my own name down there of course. I only sleep there and go to the toilet and wash my teeth. A lovely girl about my own age ... has moved down to live with me and share expenses. She too is studying and is old enough to be sensible and is very sweet & quiet. I think I told you about little Sally Munger who has been living with me.... So we will be 3 nice girls all studying and playing & singing. Sally Munger will do the house work in the mornings as part of her share of the expenses.

I spent a very miserable Xmas, just the same work and rehearsal and no one here I know....

Whoopee!!!! — Father just came by the theater and brought my Xmas box. And I leave my robe on and my dolly on the dressing table. I adore them. Just think you got the dolly way last summer. I love the little papoose and the robe will be grand for the apartment.

I feel so ashamed of my two little measly sachets with this nice big one you sent. I was almost beside myself over Xmas presents for you. I was put to such an expense for moving and paying rent in advance. And with no one to take me to dinner food is high and I just couldn't get caught up for Xmas. Just didn't buy one single thing. As soon as I can get a little ahead I will make it up.... Harvey [Karels] has been awfully good to me — loaned me money when I was so bad off and helped me get my job here and helped me with my toe work and [has] just been a peach....

Jack [Crosby] sent me a lovely Cloisonné vanity. Carl [Schlaet] gave me $20. I sent Brother a telegram and he sent one in return and that's all the Xmas there was.

I went out to Dad's Xmas eve & helped them trim the tree but it was so late when I got there and it all seemed so strange &

---

[7]   Sally did, in fact, work in the chorus at the Capitol Theater and for a short time as a waitress at the popular Alp's Restaurant on 58th Street. She also took a job making hats in a wholesale house.

unreal. I felt so terribly blue & had such bad luck before I got there & locked the keys to the Apt in the Apt & had to climb through snow and slush & over back fences to get in. I got the little kids some crayons at the 10¢ store & cut some pictures out of magazines for them to color. Father is not well at all. Just nearly dies with asthma, can't breathe and gets so sick at his stomach. Did you get my Xmas wish?

Honey I don't think I have written about the lovely gift from you & Ernest of $20. It was so grand & came at such a time that I needed it. I was just trying to get moved and it would have been a life saver, but I took it to the theater to cash it and someone stole it not realizing they could not cash it….

Well tomorrow is New Year's Eve and we do 5 shows. Again 10 shows in 2 days, together with rehearsals. How well I remember last year & what fun we had. And last Xmas — didn't we have fun? God I wish it was back again. Ah well the only thing is we must try to make better ones in the future…. Please give Ernest best love & tell him I will find something nice for him now for Xmas. All my love to the one I love best.

How could Sally's circumstances have fallen so low in such a short time? How could she have been reduced from a highly paid, coast-to-coast headliner to taking second jobs under an assumed name? There may have been contractual restrictions affecting her ability to work, or she may have lacked a cabaret license. Or it may have been as simple as this — changing times and changing tastes can overtake the best of us. The looming Great Depression surely had an impact. Vaudeville producers Fanchon and Marco were shifting focus from their elaborate productions — staged in grand movie palaces — to other endeavors, including the creation of musical dance numbers for the emerging "talkie" motion picture industry.

Had Sally accepted offers to tour in Europe, her fortunes might have taken a different turn. As it was, she chose to stay in New York, hoping to grow as an artist by studying voice and acting. She may have been a little down, but she certainly wasn't out. Just as with the changing of the seasons, when one field of stars dips below the horizon, another comes into view.

Sally was not performing in a vacuum. Indeed, her vaudeville show was relatively modest compared to other entertainment available to those seeking a night on the town in greater New York City. Not only was she competing with shows similar to her own, but also with elaborate revues like the *Ziegfeld Follies* that played to large audiences for months on end. Ziegfeld himself faced formidable competition from other large-scale productions, foremost among them George White's *Scandals*, and the controversial *Vanities*, both notable for pushing the sexually explicit envelope.

Earl Carroll, producer of the annual *Vanities* Broadway revue, had been involved in a number of scandals, notably the "girl in the bathtub" incident at a 1926 party that ended up with the producer spending 6 months in the federal penitentiary in Atlanta. Carroll was a complex character, both hated and admired. Comedian Milton Berle summed up the situation:

> The first time I met Earl Carroll, I didn't like him. He was chilly and he was cold. But when I got to work with him, learned more about him, I realized he was all business and was strictly thinking of what was to come theatrically.

> I think Carroll has taken a lot of bum raps. I've heard him dismissed as a guy who sold gals and giggles, tits and titters, cunts and comedy, but he was more than that — much more. Some people even intimated that because his handshake was like shaking hands with a flounder — a wet fish — it made him a homo. I never knew whether he was AC or DC, and I don't give a damn, but his coolness, his suavity, his mannerisms, his sophistication were unusual in show business. Earl Carroll was a gentleman.

Bottom line — Carroll paid higher salaries for his "most beautiful" show girls than anyone else, but he was extremely particular in choosing them. His requirements were actually reduced to a science:

> He has ten requirements. They are beauty of features, skin, general coloring, eyes, teeth, hair, hands, feet, personality, and age, a ratio deterioration being allowed for each year…. He has a perfect standard as to measurements, which are, height, five feet, six inches; weight, 121 pounds, neck 12¾ inches; bust 33¾ inches; waist 26½ inches; hips 36 inches; thigh 21 inches; calf 12½ inches; ankle 9 inches; forearm 9 inches and wrist 6 inches. Variations are allowed for different proportions in measurement, but an applicant must pass the ten cardinal requirements at nearly 100 percent.

Carroll's biographer provided a more provocative example of his interest in flawless femininity:

> He was determined that only fresh, animated faces, with the pristine bloom of youth and typical of the wholesome, clean-cut American girl, would smile across the footlights, and he planned to display them like goodies, temptingly laid out in a show window — meant

to be looked at, not touched — except, of course, by Carroll's
personal barber, who had the enviable job of shaving all the hair off
the girls' bodies, not excluding the most private places. When you
consider that Carroll interviewed between 1,000 and 2,000 prospective beauties for his new show — that's a helluva lot of lather!

A tiresome task to be sure, but dedicated service often requires sacrifice.

Faith

Thousands of young women were interviewed for parts in Carroll's show in
the summer of 1928. Among the hopefuls was Yvonne Bacon, a remarkably
lithesome beauty just barely 18 years of age and fresh from her turn at the
Casino de Paris. The 1928 *Vanities* opened on August 6th at the Earl Carroll
Theater in New York City, with Miss Bacon among those who made the cut.

The star of the 1928 *Vanities* was a 48-year-old gentleman, born William
Claude Dukenfield, but known professionally as "W. C. Fields." At the time
Bill Fields was a successful star of vaudeville and silent films on the verge of
breaking out as a major comedy star in talking films. He wrote or was
featured in seven *Vanities* "scenes." The show's musical numbers were staged
by none other than Busby Berkeley, who would soon be riding his genius for
over-the-top, elaborately choreographed production numbers to great fame
in talking (and singing and dancing) films.[8]

Featured performer Dorothy Knapp was proclaimed by Earl Carroll to be
"the most beautiful girl in the world." She was in fact quite a looker, but his
assessment was due in no small part to her also being Carroll's main squeeze.
Yvonne Bacon may not have been front and center (that would come later),
but she *was* one of the thirteen "Yellow Roses" surrounding Neil Golden in
Scene 3 as he sang a tune entitled "Pretty Girl." Nine of the thirteen were
certified beauty queens, among them "Miss Denmark," "Miss Bronx," and
"Miss Universe."[9]

The *Vanities of 1928* ran for 6 months (200 performances). A good time was
had by all. Yvonne Bacon remained under contract to Earl Carroll and went
on to appear in his 1929 musical comedy production *Fioretta*, as well as his
1929 show *Earl Carroll's Sketch Book*, which played to full houses for nearly
a year before closing after 392 performances and then going on the road.

---

[8]   One of the greatest stage and film choreographers of all time, Busby Berkeley
      apparently never had a dancing lesson.

[9]   No, not the modern Miss Universe. The original "Miss Universe" was crowned at the
      "International Pageant of Pulchritude," an event held in one form or another from
      1926 to 1935.

Her appearance in each of these revues was mere preamble. Having adopted the stage name "Faith Bacon," she was on the threshold of notoriety, about to embark on a path that, for the next 27 years, would make her a person of interest to us.

By 1930, Miss Bacon's fortunes were about to take a turn for the better. Earl Carroll was always looking for a way to feature more nudity in his shows without running afoul of the authorities. In New York State it was permissible for a stage show to include nudity so long as the performers remained perfectly still, representing a statue for instance, or perhaps posing as a member of a "tableaux" with stationary nudes of the sort found in the music halls of France. However, Carroll was of a mind to do something a little more exciting than "still life art."

During a rehearsal for the 1930 show, just as Carroll was expressing his frustration over the legal impediments, "... a chorine stepped out of line and offered a suggestion." The chorus girl was, of course, Faith Bacon, figuring that this was just the time to approach the boss with her new idea. "Mr. Carroll," she said, "why can't we do a number where I'm covered when I move, and undraped when I stop? For example, let's say the orchestra plays a waltz. I dance around, but on every third note, the music stops and I stand still and uncover!" Intrigued, Carroll stepped closer and asked her what she might use to cover herself during the waltzing interludes. Faith suggested that ostrich feather fans would do the trick ... and the rest, as they say, is history.[10]

On Tuesday evening, July 1, 1930, the eighth edition of *Earl Carroll's Vanities* — "the world's greatest revue, a super-spectacular of 68 scenes" — opened at the New Amsterdam Theatre on 42nd Street in Times Square. In Act One, Scene 5, the audience was introduced to the lovely Faith Bacon performing her "Heart of the Daisies" fan dance. And, just as she had described, Faith glided around the stage, teasing and twirling, bending the ostrich feathers to her will, all to the obvious delight of an appreciative audience.

Miss Bacon was also featured as "Neptune" in a tribute to the "celestial bodies," and as "Neptune's Daughter" in the mermaid production "From Out of the Sea." The evening was rounded out with an appearance by the 36-year-old comedian Jack Benny.[11]

---

[10] Faith was once quoted as saying: "Mr. Carroll and I conceived the idea of me using fans of daisies. Later we decided ostrich feather fans would be better."

[11] Jack Benny (who would only admit to aging another three years over the course of the next four decades) appeared with Faith in a sketch entitled "Where There's A Will." Jack played a lawyer and Faith played "Yvonne" (her actual middle name). Among Benny's other contributions was a reading of Lincoln's *Gettysburg Address*. Within two

According to Earl Carroll's biography, Faith got off to a rather rocky start:

> On opening night, an unfortunate mishap occurred during Miss
> Bacon's pelvic gyrations. The top part of the "pastie" covering her
> most strategic area came loose, and a long piece of tape dangled
> between her legs, causing the audience to gasp and leading them to
> wonder if it were indeed the real Faith Bacon or simply a careless
> female impersonator.

It seems Carroll had introduced the self-styled "Carroll's chastity belt" — a thin strip covering a showgirl's privates — at least six years earlier, but since no technological advance is ever perfect, a "wardrobe malfunction" could be expected to happen from time to time.

The remaining 63 scenes went on more or less without a hitch, but despite Carroll's legendary attention to detail and the declaration that his shows represented "sophisticated entertainment," the authorities were not looking the other way. On July 9th, a squad of policemen raided the theater. They arrested Faith for her "obscene, indecent, immoral and impure" performance and, along with seven other showgirls and the diminutive comedian Jimmy Savo, hauled her to the Jefferson Market Police Court in Greenwich Village. Jack Benny, who hadn't been arrested, quipped: "The police did not recognize me with my clothes on." When a search of the theater revealed that Earl Carroll was not present, a warrant was issued for his arrest.

The police had become agitated not only by Faith Bacon's nudity, but also by a skit entitled "Modes – A Window At Merl's" in which Jimmy Savo, playing a window dresser, dressed and undressed five live "mannequins," including the reigning Miss America, Irene Ahlberg, in an allegedly "obscene manner." (Yes, things were different back then.)

A preliminary hearing was held to determine whether the case should go to trial. Surveying the crowded courtroom, Magistrate Maurice H. Gotlieb remarked: "I see here a lot of young men and boys who would be better off either at work or looking for jobs." He then ordered that a space in front of the railing be cleared to make room for the defendants to be seated. In the words of a *New York Times* reporter: "The eight *Vanities* girls, in their silk stockings, furs, Panama hats and colorful dresses were comfortably seated in a row."

In support of the charge that segments of Carroll's show constituted an indecent performance, Assistant District Attorney Louis Wasser presented the testimony of acting police captain James J. Coy. "The task could have

---

years, he would be on his way to becoming a comedy legend with his weekly radio show, *The Jack Benny Program.*

been done with less immoral effect, much less immoral effect," Coy contended. Captain Coy also claimed that he was able to see Faith Bacon in the nude. He stated that he had seen rows of girls all lying flat on their backs, waving white fans, when:

> Suddenly Faith Bacon came down a long ensemble of girls with
> two white fans and made various movements. Then she turned, I
> could see her nude body, and when she went off stage I could see
> her nude body.

As she danced, he reported, she kept drawing one fan after the other down in front of her, but "she was in an absolutely nude condition, so that the public could fully observe the entire naked condition of the defendant."

Magistrate Maurice H. Gotlieb asked, "Was she completely nude?"

"Yes sir, absolutely nude," answered Coy.

Turning his attention to the row of eight young women, the judge then asked which one was Miss Bacon. Faith rose. According to the *Times*, "She stood up rather timidly, and tucked a bit of blond hair beneath her hat. Captain Coy said there could be no mistake, that she was the girl."

Earl Carroll's attorney, Louis Vorhaus, handled the initial cross-examination. Officer Coy's testimony suggests he was an enthusiastic witness:

> Coy: If I had two fans, I'd show you just how it was done.

> Vorhaus: Does the title you bear, that of "acting Captain," signify a
> rank in the police department or a connection with the stage? In
> other words, are you a dramatic critic or an actor?

> Coy: No.

> Vorhaus: Were you ever an actor?

> Coy: Well, yes and no. I used to get 50 cents a day in a circus for
> washing the elephants. They let me play the part of the Maharajah
> of Baluchistan in one of the circus pageants. I don't know whether
> you would call that acting or not.

> Vorhaus: Isn't it true that Miss Bacon was covered at all times by
> one of two large fans?

> Coy: The fans were about four feet long and one foot wide at the
> widest. But when she turned, I could see her profile. As far as I am
> concerned, it was an indecent performance.

The prosecutor established that, although Coy had previously testified to sitting in the 10th row, he was actually seated in the 12th row; and he further established that, during the fan dance, a gauze curtain was stretched between the performers and the audience.

The questions continued:

> Vorhaus: Viewing the performance through a curtain from your vantage point in the 12th row could you tell whether or not Miss Bacon was wearing dancer's tights?
>
> Coy: Well, it is a matter of vision. My eyes are pretty good.

At this point, cross-examination was taken over by Benjamin J. Rabin, representing Miss Bacon:

> Rabin: In all your experience attending the theater, have you ever watched interpretive dancing? Have you ever seen Isadora Duncan or Pavlova?
>
> Coy: I have seen Pavlova. I don't know that I would consider what Miss Bacon was doing as interpretive dancing. I never saw a dance like that before in my long experience around Broadway.

Magistrate Gotlieb agreed that Coy had made a good case against the show and suggested that, unless something was presented that would convince him otherwise, the case should be presented to the grand jury, observing: "No matter how liberal we are here in New York, a nude dance is lewd."

Ultimately, the fan dance matter went before a jury of 12 men good and true, each of whom leaned forward with focused anticipation when Miss Bacon began to testify:

> I did not dance completely nude as the police censor said. I wouldn't unless I knew everyone in the audience was an artist who would see only the esthetic beauty of such a dance. People ask me if I'm not embarrassed to appear with so few clothes on. I'm not, because ever since I was a little girl I have been posing for artists. To me it is just a part of the job of art. I was reared in a convent you know. But I really am a Presbyterian.

A spokesman for Earl Carroll stated that Faith Bacon wasn't really naked under the fans, insisting that she wore some sort of "chiffon arrangement."

The case dragged on for a month. On August 12th, the grand jury accepted Coy's offer to demonstrate what he had seen. The press reported that, despite his best attempts at "twisting, writhing and squirming to demonstrate to the grand jury how Faith Bacon apparently did the fan dance in the nude," the police captain failed to persuade the panel that *Earl Carroll's Vanities* was indecent.[12] The grand jury needed only five minutes of deliberation; the charges were dismissed.

Reminiscing 33 years later about the memorable evening and "Faith Bacon, a beautiful fan dancer," Jack Benny recalled:

> I must tell you that in that show Carroll really did out-Ziegfeld Flo Ziegfeld and his "Follies." He was always trying to do that. There were never so many gorgeous girls in one show as in that "Vanities." Audiences cheered the sight of them. It was a really beautiful production.... I was supposed to have played the window dresser. When I found out what the sketch was like, I told Carroll I wouldn't do it. He threatened me with breach of contract charges and I said that if Actors' Equity ruled that I had to do the scene, I'd quit show business. He gave in and had Jimmy Savo play it.

The *Vanities of 1930* did not disappoint. Much like earlier editions (and despite the harsh economy), the show ran for six months, 215 performances. When theater doors opened after each night's performance, those pouring onto the sidewalk and not yet ready to call it a night could take a 15-minute taxi ride to the Cotton Club in Harlem and extend the evening's revels with *The Blackberries of 1930*, featuring a cast of 50 in the popular "brown sugar, but unrefined" show. And, they could dance into the wee hours to the sweet tones of "Duke Ellington and his famous Cotton Club Orchestra." How fabulous would that have been?

B y spring, the reality of the economic downturn that would come to be known as the Great Depression was beginning to influence consumer purchasing. Those in the entertainment business were becoming concerned.

Paul Bern's letter to Sally on March 10th hints of her changing circumstances:

> Dear Sally:
>
> I have had your last couple of notes, and intended writing you a long letter some time ago, but I have been really terribly busy and

---

[12] Captain Coy was no novice at this sort of thing. A bare four months earlier he had led a raid and was the prosecution's chief witness in a case involving a Mae West production entitled *The Pleasure Man* that featured a number of transvestites. When asked to imitate their gestures, Coy eagerly obliged, prancing around the courtroom, hands on hips, much to the delight of spectators. Miss West protested: "I have some lady impersonators in the play. In fact, I have five of them. But what of it?"

didn't want to write you just a superficial note. How are you feeling? What is new with you? . . .

I am starting two new pictures this morning, ROMANCE with Greta Garbo and LET US BE GAY with Norma Shearer, so I haven't really as much time as I would like. I will write you again shortly at more length. In the meantime, I am enclosing a check which I hope you will be able to cash somewhere where the ill-repute of my name has not reached.

My love and best wishes, Always, [signed] Paul

Apart from his film duties, Bern was so "terribly busy" due to his growing attachment to the blond bombshell Jean Harlow, whom he had met some months earlier. The couple would come to the attention of the public at large within a few weeks when they would appear arm-in-arm for the premiere of *Hell's Angels* at Grauman's Chinese Theater. Two years later, they would become man and wife.

In September 1930, as Faith Bacon was fanning her way to fame at the New Amsterdam Theatre, Sally Rand was appearing at Hammerstein's Theater, some 11 blocks to the North.[13] The show was *Luana*, a musical comedy set in Hawaii and produced by Arthur Hammerstein, son of the original Oscar Hammerstein and uncle of the better known Oscar Hammerstein II.[14] Sally and her brother Harold had both secured roles in the "ensemble," mostly as a means of keeping food on the table during hard times. Unfortunately, *Luana* flopped, opening on September 17, 1930, and closing on October 4th after only 21 performances.

In fact, colorful court proceedings prompted by a surprising on-stage melee actually ran longer than the production itself. During a late-July rehearsal more than a month before opening day, the show's dance director, Jack Haskell, had a run-in with chorus dancer Harold Rand and told him he was fired. A heated discussion followed, producer Arthur Hammerstein intervened, and according to press reports a brawl ensued during which both Rand and Hammerstein "broke their fists" while punching poor Haskell.

---

[13] Both venues exist today. The New Amsterdam is booking shows, while Hammerstein's, now the Ed Sullivan Theater, is the home of *The Late Show with Stephen Colbert*.

[14] The musical *Luana* involved an island princess in love with a young American doctor. Although the show failed, it may well have inspired Hammerstein's nephew to, years later, produce a wildly successful wartime musical with a similar plot and subplot — *South Pacific*.

Ever the loyal sister, Sally had supposedly joined the fray and had even gotten in a few licks of her own.

As the most seriously injured participant, Haskell pressed charges, leading to an August 1st appearance by Haskell, Sally, Harold, and Hammerstein before Magistrate George W. Simpson in the famed Tombs Court. According to *Variety* magazine, the courtroom "looked like a field hospital. Haskell's left optic was swollen and copiously bandaged. Hammerstein, in a blue ensemble, had his left mitt in splints." Harold also sported splints on his right hand and forearm. The aggrieved plaintiff, Jack Haskell, presented no witnesses on his behalf, saying that cast members couldn't afford to be present since their jobs were at stake.

Haskell testified that he had fired Harold for disrupting the rehearsal with his loud and intrusive behind-the-scenes tap dancing, ignoring instructions to sit down and be quiet. Describing the situation for the judge, Haskell said he had then marched into producer Hammerstein's office to advise him of the firing and, when he returned to the stage, Harold had threatened him, saying: "When I get you outside, I'll tear you to bits for this." According to Haskell, Harold was punching him without provocation and calling him names so obscene he would only whisper them to the judge. A heavy signet ring on Harold's hand had torn the skin over his eye, Haskell claimed.

When Sally intervened, Haskell also fired her on the spot. As the fracas escalated to a three-way brawl, Hammerstein had emerged from his office, sized up the situation, and, after questioning several eyewitnesses, reinstated the Rands. According to Haskell, Hammerstein had then commenced thrashing him as well. Claiming self-defense, the producer said that he had simply beaten Haskell to the punch. Both Harold Rand and Arthur Hammerstein had ostensibly sustained fractures to their hands, the producer quipping that: "Mr. Haskell ran into my hand and broke my wrist. His eye hit my fist."

In his own defense, Harold testified that he had been upset over being unfairly fired: "I told him it was a low down trick. Haskell blew smoke in my face and made an attempt to strike me. I warded off the blow and he knocked some of the skin from my elbow. I then punched him in self-defense."

Joseph Macaulay, one of seven witnesses who appeared on Harold's behalf, affirmed that it had been the quick-tempered dance director who was to blame: "Mr. Haskell is naturally emotional like most directors. He called Rand a pest and Sally a nuisance." Sally and five other "comely chorus girls" also appeared in support of Harold's version of events.

In the courtroom, attorneys and actors were shouting and mocking each other to such an extent that Magistrate Simpson had difficulty preserving order. The proceedings took a curious turn when one of the attorneys asked Haskell about the visit of a certain "Mr. Sinnott." According to *Variety*, Haskell almost leaped out of the witness chair, shouting "Yes, and I can tell about the bar in Mr. Hammerstein's office and also about the orgies." This line of questioning was quickly shut down, and even the best efforts of the tabloid press could not dredge up the details.

To rebut Harold's many witnesses, New York City prosecuting attorney Ferdinand Pecora asserted that most of the testimony was manufactured, rehearsed perjury. Seeking to clarify the issue, Magistrate Simpson observed: "The question is, does the blowing of smoke into the face justify this strong, young athletic man striking this elderly and apparently weak dancing director?" (The elderly Mr. Haskell was 44 years old.) Ignoring his own question, Magistrate Simpson declared that the question of guilt was an issue for judges of another court to settle.

More than a month later on September 19th, Hammerstein and the Rands were ordered to stand trial for assaulting Haskell. On October 9th, by which time tempers had cooled down, the show had closed, and everyone was in a more convivial mood, assault charges were dismissed against all of the principals. Afterward, the grinning parties posed amicably for photographers.

Faith

In the fall of 1930, Faith Bacon and Sally Rand were both appearing in New York City — a circumstance that would have given Sally the opportunity to observe Faith performing the fan dance. But, did she? Did Sally Rand actually see Faith Bacon dancing with ostrich feather fans, say to herself "Hmmm," and file the idea away for future reference? It certainly could have happened. (Look for Miss Bacon's account of events in chapter 14.)

Faith Bacon's star was on the rise. She was clearly a favorite in the practiced eye of Earl Carroll. When Florenz Ziegfeld, Earl Carroll, and George White were asked to name the most beautiful showgirls of 1931, Carroll had selected Faith Bacon as the beauty "who represents his highest standards." As flattering as it must have been for Faith, barely out of her teens, to be chosen by Carroll and to have her picture syndicated in the papers as one of the "Big Three" in the theatrical world of beauties, it still wasn't enough to keep her in the Earl Carroll fold. On opening night of the *Ziegfeld Follies of 1931*, it was none other than Miss Bacon who was the featured performer in the opening number, "The Spirit of the Follies."

Flo Ziegfeld boasted: "My theatre is the only legitimate theatre equipped with a frigid air cooling system." No doubt patrons of the *Ziegfeld Follies of 1931* were appreciative. It was a hot July night when the show's first performance was staged. Much of the country was in the grip of a record heat wave, with temperatures reaching the mid-90s in upstate New York. The pavement was sizzling outside the Ziegfeld Theatre and the show on stage was plenty hot as well.[15]

S ally soldiered on. Once the Rand siblings' legal skirmish in New York City had concluded amicably, she was back on the vaudeville circuit, playing in revues presented under the auspices of several producers, including RKO and Paramount. Even in a depressed economy, Sally did her best to provide employment for those closest to her. One of the "Boys" in her Binghamton, New York, engagement on March 16, 1931, was her brother Harold and another was Charles Mayon, her beau at the time.

Among those sharing the stage with the "beautiful and bewitching" Miss Rand were "The Great Johnson, one of the most remarkable contortionists ever," and "Doran, West, and Doran" — billed as "Three American Beauties not glorified by Ziegfeld" (no doubt overlooked by Ziegfeld because they were, in fact, popular female impersonators).[16] The comic trio closed the show "sending everyone home weak from laughter."

Interviewed by the local press, Sally exhibited her lifelong facility for gab. Outfitted in a "blue polo shirt and white sailor trousers" and inhaling deeply as she smoked a cigarette in her dressing room, she remarked:

> Children are women's reason for being. What else is all this striving
> for, if not to be able to bear children and give them all you have
> missed in life? Every woman who is honest with herself admits
> that children are the meaning of life.

Sally mentioned that her "domestic tendencies began with cooking" when she and Joan Crawford were both "little fat-legged girls" in Kansas City. "Cooking is a delight," she declared. "As a girl, I baked bread and exhibited it at the county fairs where I won several medals."

---

[15] Besides appearing in the opening number, Faith was also featured as a dancer in the "Tom Tom Dance" segment of the jungle scene "Legend of the Islands" and as the "whisk broom" in "Clinching the Sale."

[16] Some three months earlier, the trio had appeared at the Pansy Club on 48th and Broadway (Times Square), in a show billed as *Pansies on Parade*.

While "brushing and braiding her long, blond hair," Sally discussed the relative merits of Greta Garbo, Marlene Dietrich, and Clara Bow, and challenged the notion that Hollywood is a lawless place:

> I think it is a myth. During the four years I was there I found no more wrongdoing than in any other community. Because it is in the public eye, Hollywood has become a target for scandal lovers.

She also offered her opinion on women's fashion trends:

> The Victorian trend in women's clothes — long skirts, high waists — is here only because it is the last possible backward swing from the other extreme, the flapper model of short skirts and severe lines. I think the new styles are very graceful and becoming for evening wear. But for daytime wear the American woman will never adopt a style that hinders her freedom of movement.

And, long before anorexia and bulimia became public concerns, Sally was asked whether she thought there could be some risk in the Hollywood "craze for slimness." Her response would be generally accepted today. As she scrutinized the slender figure mirrored before her, she declared emphatically:

> No. Dieting is necessary. It is pathetic to see a young girl eating herself into a bad figure. But dieting requires the advice of a physician. The important thing is to maintain a balanced diet and to get enough rest. For breakfast, black coffee, fruit juice or tomato juice, one egg. Luncheon, a raw vegetable salad. Dinner, lean roast beef or lamb chops, vegetables, without cream sauces and salad. Sweets? Never.

For an engagement at the Dewitt Theater in Syracuse, New York, in September 1931, Sally shared top billing with "Sunshine Sammy," the "negro juvenile" formerly with Hal Roach's *Our Gang* (a series of short black and white comedy films also popularly known as *The Little Rascals*).[17] According to local critic Chester B. Bahn:

> Both screen veterans stress dancing in their stage turns. Sammy borrows from the Bill Robinson school [of dance] for his *pièce de résistance*, a tap number which brings in, of course, a stairs routine. Miss Rand's most striking effort is the primitive rumba.

---

17 As an infant, Ernest Fredric "Ernie" Morrison entered show business, where he acquired the stage name "Sunshine Sammy." He is reported to have been the first child picked to play in the *Our Gang* series.

The 1927 Wampas baby star, whose blond beauty won the admiration of Cecil B. DeMille, makes her entrance to the strains of "I Wonder What Happened to Sally." And dressed in a figure-clinging black gown and ermine wrap, an effective entrance it is.

Between dances, there's a brief cinematic intermission: you see Sally in the arms of Hoot Gibson, Rod La Roque, Douglas Fairbanks, Jr., and, would you believe it, that former Syracuse stock idol Harrison Ford.[18]

The following summer Sally accepted an offer to star on the Chicago stage as a ballet dancer on a ghost ship in a play called *The World Between* by Chicago playwright Fritz Blocki. The 1932 production, Sally's first legitimate stage appearance as a professional, offered the 28-year-old an opportunity not only to resume her career as a ballet dancer, but also to establish herself as someone who could have a future on the stage.

The play chronicles the grotesque tale of a derelict ship in the Sargasso Sea. All but two of the surreal characters are a motley collection of ghosts. The two humans are transatlantic aviators, a young man and woman, who survive a plane crash only to slowly starve to death under the watchful gaze of the ghosts. Playing the wraith of a British Barrister, the star of the production was DeWolf Hopper, a veteran performer whose credits dated back to the days of Gilbert and Sullivan.[19]

The World Between opened at Chicago's Adelphi Theatre on September 17, 1932, and, artistic merits aside, closed after only four weeks.

While Sally was performing her demi-pointes and pirouettes at the Adelphi, an affair unofficially called a "Fête Charrette" was being staged just 8 miles south at the Drake Hotel to raise money for 1,200 out-of-work architects. The event foreshadowed the sort of "entertainment" that would soon be extracting hard-earned dollars from patrons of the Chicago "Century of Progress Exposition," scheduled to open only eight months later.

---

[18] No relation to the modern-day actor, *this* Harrison Ford was a stage and film star in the silent era.

[19] The six-foot-five, 230-pound Hopper was 74 years old. He had enjoyed a long career on the stage, but was best known for his dramatic recitation of "Casey at the Bat." His fifth wife (of six) was Hedda Hopper, the famous Hollywood gossip columnist. Their son DeWolf, Jr., (known as William) is remembered today for his role as private investigator "Paul Drake" on the old *Perry Mason* television show.

As one report described the scene at the benefit:

> In a small room off the mezzanine floor of Chicago's Drake Hotel
> one evening last week sat a nude young woman of considerable
> charm, safe behind a barrier of chicken wire. For $1 anyone could go
> in, sit behind a drawing board for ten minutes and try or pretend to
> sketch her. Elsewhere in the Drake that evening were peep shows,
> slot machines, bars, roulette tables, smart shops, fortune-telling
> booths, a gangplank and reproduction of one side of the *Ile de France*.
> Milling around in costumes that tried earnestly to look bohemian
> were 2,500 Chicago socialites and celebrities. Fresh from welcoming
> Governor Roosevelt to town, Mayor Anton Joseph Cermak arrived in
> an orange beret, stayed late.

With the closing of *The World Between*, Sally once again joined the ranks of the
unemployed, a group that included a great many others. The young dancer
and the Chicago architects were not the only ones suffering. By one account:

> The Great Depression was particularly severe in Chicago because
> of the city's reliance on manufacturing, the hardest hit sector
> nationally. Only 50 percent of the Chicagoans who had worked in
> the manufacturing sector in 1927 were still working there in 1933.
> African Americans and Mexicans were particularly hurt. By 1932,
> 40 to 50 percent of black workers in Chicago were unemployed.

While ordinary working people were hardest hit, at least one very famous
casualty was about to be given *his* pink slip. By 1932, millions of voters across
the country had become disillusioned with President Herbert Hoover and the
Republican Party. Despite the fact that Hoover had carried 40 of the 48 states
in the election of 1928 (apparently persuading voters with the campaign
slogan "a chicken in every pot and a car in every garage"), four years later the
nation experienced a complete reversal of political allegiance. When Franklin
Delano Roosevelt became President-elect, he carried 42 states and ushered
into Congress a new Democratic majority.

Only in retrospect do we acknowledge the ending of an era. After three
years of suffering through the Depression, it had become clear that the
Roaring Twenties were over. But, could better times be just around the
corner? Optimistic over the election results, giddy Democrats were finding
themselves hopeful that "happy days are here again."

CHAPTER SIX

The Suitors

One can find women who have never had a love affair,
but it is rare indeed to find any who have had only one.
~ Francois de La Rochefoucauld (1613-1680)

Before the Great Depression, the economy had been booming; fashion-able attire and relaxed inhibitions were the order of the day. Young women had begun to assert their independence. In the midst of postwar optimism, Sally Rand had been something of a social networking pioneer. A Cecil B. DeMille starlet and featured guest at any number of parties and receptions, she enjoyed meeting people and people certainly enjoyed meeting her. Declared by DeMille to be the fairest of them all, she had become one of the most desirable young women in all the land.

As a 1927 Wampas "Baby Star," teenagers clipped her pictures from movie magazines. Eligible young men turned giddy at the very sight of her, and those who managed to actually encounter her in the flesh became helpless victims under her spell.

Still deeply insecure from the impression that she wasn't worthy of her father's love, Sally did little to discourage those who seriously pursued her. Several of her more earnest admirers imagined themselves becoming her life partner. A most ardent four actually did their best to make it true. And, at a time when handwritten correspondence was still very much in vogue, these suitors expressed their unbound passion in a flood of love letters.

A surprising number of these letters have survived.[1] Their content bears honest witness to the nature of each relationship. The dates in brackets after each man's name suggest the period during which he pursued her. You will notice the overlap.

---

[1] In an August 2012 interview, Sally's son Sean told Bonnie Egan that he had found an envelope of pictures she had labeled "The Men I Should Have Married" and another labeled "The Sons of Bitches I Did Marry."

Carl Schlaet [1926-1929]

In 1901, the largest oil gusher the world had ever known indicated the presence of significant oil reserves at a site called "Spindletop" near Beaumont, Texas. The oil field soon lured hundreds of would-be tycoons into the area, including oil man Joseph S. "Buckskin Joe" Cullinan. Seizing the opportunity, Cullinan quickly partnered with a group of investors headed by New York investment manager Arnold Schlaet to establish The Texas Fuel Company (a.k.a. The Texas Company), which after many mergers and acquisitions eventually became known as Texaco.

In 1920, Arnold Schlaet, by then chairman of the board, opened an office in Tampico, Mexico, to scout out potential oil fields in that area, putting his 25-year-old son Carl in charge.[2] This was no cushy assignment, as became alarmingly clear in late June of 1922 when Mexican rebels attacked the Tampico facilities of the Cortez Oil Corporation, capturing 40 American oil workers and demanding a ransom for their release. (Two days later, federal troops routed the rebels and freed the hostages.)

At the time, Cortez Oil was under the supervision of general manager W. P. Taylor, an executive whom young Carl Schlaet had come to know quite well. Americans in Tampico tended to socialize among themselves, so it wasn't long before Carl encountered and became enamored of Taylor's daughter Dorothy. Apparently the feeling was mutual, as the two were married in March of 1922 (just a few months before the Cortez attack). Sadly, it wasn't long before the magic began to fade.

By 1926, Carl, whether legally available or not, had begun a relationship with a comely Hollywood silent movie starlet. How they came to meet is unclear, but young Carl was soon beguiled by the famous Sally Rand charisma. In a letter written to her on May 14, 1926, he lamented:

> Here I've been east three whole days, without a word from you! That's my idea of neglect! ...
>
> Saw Neville Penrose today — he who has the ranch near Tampico.... Neville raved over the snapshot of you.... He said —

---

2   Born April 15, 1895, Carl Vail Schlaet was almost nine years Sally's senior. As a student at Yale (where he captained the university swim team for the 1915-16 season), "Whitie" Schlaet's team broke college and world records for the 200-yard relay at the Yale-Columbia meet and won the 400-yard relay in the intercollegiate relay swimming championship of America in Chicago. He was named as a member of the all-star swimming team for 1916. Schlaet's competitors on the annual western trip included Hawaiian swimming legend, Duke Kahanamoku (look for his statue on the beach at Waikiki).

"Does she know anyone who looks like her in New York?" I said
"There isn't anyone who looks like her, but she offered me letters to
various girlfriends in NY, which I refused." He said — "You damn
fool!" I said — "You can wire her if you want to and she might
send 'em to you."[3]

As an accomplished Yale man, Schlaet felt a certain duty to hasten Sally's
refinement, an edifying tendency that would persist over the course of their
relationship:

> I got you Phelps' book on Browning today, but won't send it for a
> week or so, as I want to mark and note it, and try to emphasize
> Phelps' remarkable personality as much as possible. Have you read
> Carlyle's "Sartor Resartus" or "Past and Present"? I want very
> much to read those — and Browning — with you. A real under-
> standing of them (which is not easy to get) is worth fourteen of the
> book list you showed me.
>
> I'm so lonesome for you dear — it seems years since you waved
> adios from the station platform. I'm just hungry for you —
> mentally and physically....
>
> Be my good Brat. Write to me soon and often, and don't forget to love
>
> Me

Carl eventually obtained a Mexican divorce from Dorothy Taylor, yet his
marital status in the states remained a concern to Sally. In a postscript to a
letter dated April 27, 1927, he tried to put her mind at ease:

> My attorney says it is not necessary to have my Mexican divorce
> papers approved by any US court, that they are valid anywhere in
> the US without further action.

Just coming of age, Sally's brother Harold was more interested in striking
out on his own than in pursuing higher education. In short, he was at loose
ends and his mother was most concerned. Carl Schlaet came to the rescue,
offering to take the 18-year-old with him to Tampico for a few months.
Their trip from San Antonio to Tampico in Carl's airplane (which he called
"Sally") proved to be the most exciting adventure of young Harold's life.

---

[3]   Neville Penrose was also a Texas oil man. Twenty-seven years later in 1953, he
urged repeal of the Texas poll tax and passage of a state anti-lynching law as a way
to disassociate Texas from a lot of "unwarranted criticism." He argued such
changes would hasten the day when a Southerner, even a Texan, could be elected
President of the United States.

While en route, Carl described the pair's harrowing flight in a letter to Sally, written from the Miller Hotel in Brownsville, Texas, on August 4, 1926:

> We lit out from San Antonio Monday afternoon. It was HOT, very bumpy, and as soon as we got high enough to cool off we were in a forty-mile headwind. After fighting this for an hour we saw black "twisters" — most of them with lightning — coming from all directions, and decided to sit down and wait for them to pass.
>
> We did — in what turned out to be Governor "Ma" Ferguson's cotton field — near a little town called George West.[4]
>
> After an hour the air cleared and we took off. Before we were 500 feet up the radiator thermometer was over 212°, so we sat down again … in a plowed field, and dug a bale or so of cotton out of the radiator. She cooled off then, but when we tried to take off old Sally swerved to the right — we stopped just short of the fence — and as the wheels didn't seem to run true, we decided the axle was bent.
>
> By this time it was getting darkish, so we lugged our baggage to a Mexican's shack and walked a mile or so to a ranch house from which we borrowed a flivver ride into town. Next morning we took a blacksmith out to the ship, but found that swapping the wheels seemed to fix our trouble so we didn't take the axle out....
>
> Happening to look thru a San Antonio paper I discovered that we were lost, so we sent flocks of telegrams (including one to your mother) to keep people from worrying. I didn't send you any because I don't think the L.A. papers will get it, and if they did they wouldn't have sense enough to put it in the funnies, so you wouldn't see it.
>
> That is that! Harold is getting an interesting trip, a big kick out of Matamoros (where he was vaccinated today) and is a good traveling companion and a lot of help. Gosh! How glad I am that you and I didn't start for Tampico. We'll be here until we get the necessary permits. Maybe tomorrow, maybe in a week or two.
>
> In spite of all this, life is very empty without you Brat. Even Griffith Park would seem like heaven!

---

4   The first female Governor of Texas (and the second in the United States), Miriam Amanda "Ma" Ferguson was elected in 1924. Her husband, James Edward "Pa" Ferguson, had been governor from 1915 to 1917, when he was impeached, convicted by the Texas Senate, and removed from office. Because he couldn't get his name on the ballot in 1924, his wife ran instead, offering to provide Texans "two governors for the price of one." She served two nonconsecutive terms, 1925-1927 and 1933-1935.

Safely in Tampico, Harold was becoming noticed as the handsome young newcomer in town. It wasn't long before the locals deduced who he was:

> Tampico has something to talk about now. I have been introducing Harold as the son of a friend and cautioned him that it would be best not to mention you, to avoid misunderstanding. It worked for one day. Then someone mentioned something about one of DeMille's pictures that you were in and Harold piped up "Sister is in that!"

One girl soon figured it out: "Carl is crazy about your sister, isn't he?"

In what he saw as his duty to foster Sally's self-improvement, Carl couldn't resist the urge to admonish her, calling attention to 15 errors he found in her letters to him. Among them:

> Ambassador — you spelled with an "e" on the end. Don't do it.
> Pieces — not peices
> Never start a sentence with "because," or "well."
> Truly — not truely
> Mimsy — not mimesy
> Mome raths — not momraiths

> One of your letters showed considerable improvement in the writing. The others didn't. Keep at it darlin'. [I] would much rather receive the worst kind of a scrawl from you than no letter at all....

> I miss you heaps, and love you more every day. Do take care of your health. That's the main thing. Without it you have nothing. As for the rest, I know you'll continue to develop the best there is in you in every way. Please know that I have every trust and confidence in you.

Carl was nothing if not determined. He was playing every angle for all it was worth. Not only did he take Sally's brother Harold under his wing, but he also acquired a prizewinning 17-month-old German shepherd imported from Munich named Pierrot — "His pedigree is splendid" — and began training him with the idea of turning him over to Sally. Apparently, the pooch took to Carl right away, as he wrote to Sally on January 31, 1927:[5]

> Your pup is a perfect peach. I'm getting acquainted with him and more fond of him in the process. His affectionate disposition is somewhat disconcerting at times, as he runs at me about forty miles

---

[5]   About six months later, one of Sally's most popular films, *His Dog*, was released. The film was based on the best-selling book by Albert Payson Terhune. Junior screenwriter Alisa Rosenbaum (Ayn Rand) contributed to the film adaptation.

an hour, puts his paws (about the size of hams) on my shoulders and lets fly at my face with a yard or so of very wet tongue.

The bond was such that Carl ended up keeping the dog in Tampico. A postscript to a letter written 18 months later reads: "Pierrot sends wags and licks."

Carl often expressed his frustration with Sally's infrequent letters and urged her to abandon show business as a waste of time:

> Why won't you write to me? I try to be patient and trust in your love, but it does seem as tho' you could spare me a half hour every few days. Aside from my loneliness and repeated disappointment at not hearing from you, it makes correspondence so awfully one-sided that it's hard to write....

> Darlin' I want to see you so! I've dreamed about you twice in the last week, and you seem so very far and so disgustingly attached to your damned Merry-go-round. Shake it dear, it isn't worth the best years of your life. Probably I'm not either, but I love you so much and I can't bear to know you're wasting your life trying to please a bunch of directors, most of whom wouldn't care if you died tomorrow provided they could collect your insurance. Forgive this outburst honey; I'm just so damn lonesome and hungry for you.

By early 1927, Sally had apparently agreed to marry Carl and had even sent him a sketch for a custom designed ring. Although elated to get one of Sally's rare letters, Carl couldn't resist the urge to nag:

> The frog footman finally arrived again — bless him! — and brought your letter. It worries me, because I know you're up to your old trick of over-working. Darling, must you get seriously ill before you'll realize that even such a cast-iron constitution as yours will only stand just so much? I'm proud of you and your work, but if you continue to abuse your health you just won't have any.

> Are you seriously planning to go to New York? If so, when, and why, and for how long, and what about your contract with DeMille? ...

> Thank you for sending the ring design. It would be foolish to have a ring sent to me here — doubt if it could be insured in transit at any premium. That leaves two alternatives. I can either send the design to Cartier and have him send the ring direct to you, or I can take it with me — go to N.Y. before coming out to see you — and bring it with me. Which would you rather I did? ...

> Can't you be happy dear, without being on the theatrical jump
> continually, day and night? It's not worth the price honey, really!
> If you truly love me, I know I can make you happy. Won't you
> give me a chance?

Around this same time, and seemingly content that things were now going
his way, Carl revealed a potential snag in their wedding plans — the little
matter of an unresolved legal entanglement:

> It was so sweet to get your letter this morning. You don't know how
> hearing from you makes the sun come out! Please keep it out. Also,
> you can't know how happy it makes me to get down to actual dates.
> It brings our relationship from a delightful dream to an even more
> delightful reality....
>
> Meanwhile, we have several important things to consider. Most
> important of all is your divorce. That, of course, must be definitely
> completed, and you must have the final papers before we can
> marry. Please look into it, and let me know exactly how it stands....
> I think you'll agree that it would be best for us to get the license in
> your real name — Helen Beck.
>
> If you are quite certain that the fact of your former marriage will
> never come out, I can see no reason for its being mentioned —
> even to my mother and Dad.[6] Of course, your father and mother
> know it, Harold too, I presume — your ex and his and your
> friends of that time.... Think over the possibilities, and we'll
> decide what's best. Perhaps it would be better for my parents to
> know all about it.... Their knowledge would go no further you
> may be sure of that.

Carl was well aware of the reason Sally felt compelled to work so hard —
she was also supporting both her younger brother and her single mother:

> Then comes the question of your mother and Harold's support. The
> only solution ... is for me to make them as much of a regular

---

[6] The identity (or even existence) of Sally's first husband remains a mystery. Several
online sources suggest that she had first married Clarence Aaron "Tod" Robbins,
writer and director of the 1932 cult classic film *Freaks*, but this is demonstrably
incorrect. (Robbins was married to at least four and possibly as many as six different
women, but nary a one of them was named Helen Beck or Sally Rand.) In 1938,
Sally reportedly made a standing offer of $1,000 to anyone who could prove that she
had ever been married. Columnist Walter Winchell suggested in 1941 that the
shadowy figure was someone named Cassey Gay, but research into the matter has
reached a dead end.

allowance as I can reasonably afford. The amount of course … will be sufficient for their comfort at least.

I plan to write my father and mother of our definite engagement as soon as you let me have your views on the desirability of telling them of your former marriage. The more I think of it the more I feel it would be best to tell them….

He closed with a cryptic postscript:

P.S. Better burn this. Remember Printouts' curiosity and your former experience.

Several weeks passed with limited communication between them. Carl was mostly on the receiving end of the silent treatment. From the Daniels Hotel in Cisco, Texas, on March 8th, he conveyed his exasperation in a letter dispatched to his "Brat":

Got your wire in Brownwood yesterday and telegraphed you $200. Hope it was enough to cover your needs. If you want more, let me know….

It's now been twenty-six days since I've had a letter from you, and my thoughts on the subject are nobody's business! Still, honey, I'm counting on you until you tell me otherwise. If you don't write both soon and often, I'm going to drop everything and come out there.

Really dear, how can I explain your not writing (after all your promises) except on the assumption that you think more of your work than you do of me? If this is so, please tell me. I dreamed the other night that I saw you — you were most chilly and distant. I asked if you didn't care for me anymore, and you said "I guess that's it." I woke up in a cold sweat.

Write and tell me the whole truth darling. Do you love me enough to marry me in July and feel sure of happiness with me? Or not. You know you have all my love.

Carl Schlaet had played every card in the deck, courting not only Sally but also her mother and her brother (even going so far as to find and care for a dog he chose just for her). July 1927 came and went without a wedding ceremony. Indeed, July 1928 also came and went, with Carl still writing and hoping.[7] On October 8, 1928, the two spent the day at his family's estate, but by then other eager suitors had entered the competition.

Jack Crosby [1928-1930]

Seven months older than Sally, the tall and handsome Mr. Crosby seems to have been consumed by all things masculine. He was a champion rifle shot in his high school ROTC unit in 1921 and 1922. His favorite sport was deep sea fishing — with a bow and arrow. As a youth he had also worked as a railroad fireman, a cowpuncher, a miner and a prizefighter before turning his attention to, of all things — dance. Together with his younger brother Bob, the two boys from Ogden, Utah (unrelated to Bing and *his* brother Bob), formed an act that led to prominent roles in several musical comedies, including the 1926 Gershwin production *Oh, Kay*, which debuted the hit standard "Someone to Watch Over Me." Along the way, Jack's path crossed that of Sally Rand. And, like so many others before and after, he was smitten.

In a letter written on February 3, 1928, from the Hotel Senator in Sacramento, Jack opened his heart to the 23-year-old girl of his dreams, his "Dear Sweet Sally":

> I looked into a pair of wonderful eyes when I was with you and honey girl I caught a glimpse of paradise. You can make this a heaven on earth for me. When I think of those too few hours I spent with you dear one I long for you. The memory of your soft sweet lips, a tender kiss, your arms about me, and the beating of your heart, all comes back to me. Your pictures are before me and to me you seem like a beautiful fairy princess from a book. I want to be a prince charming and to have the wonderful princess love me. Little girl you are always "Sunny" to me and I love you and your dear sweet ways. Your smile, your eyes, your hair and everything about you is perfect to me and I want to hold you close to me once more to whisper I love you....
>
> Honey, I do adore you and something tells me that the love you & I have for each other would make this old world a beautiful place.

---

[7] Carl was not the only one still hoping. Sally's mother, traveling with Sally's show, wrote to her beau Ernest Kisling in Glendora on November 6, 1928: "There is so much uncertainty about the show business.... I would give worlds if Sally would decide to marry Old Sweet Carl and get out of it.... While in NY he asked her to go to Europe with him ... but as she would not consent he went back to Mexico to make more money." This same letter, written on Election Day, began: "I would sure like to be in L.A. today to vote for Hoover."

We could have a "blue heaven" too sweetheart. Tell me darling that you love me. I love you.

Just two days later, in San Francisco for the opening of *Sunny* at the Columbia Theatre, Jack composed another letter to his "Wonderful One."

Clearly, at some point in the recent past, Sally had been intimate with him:

> I am listening to some wonderful music dear, and every beautiful strain brings to me wonderful memories of you. Sad beautiful music that tugs at my heart. Never before dear one have I felt this way. It is because of you. Those three days and the night of nights that I spent with you were the happiest of my life. Ah, Sally I can't bear to be away from you ... and I'll never be really happy again till I feel your sweet lips on mine. Oh I want to crush you to me, to forget the world, everything but love. Tell me dear one that you love me.
>
> When I think of you there comes over me a wonderful feeling of tenderness — a beautiful golden warmth it seems, that makes me feel like nothing ever did before. Sally it's because I love you.... Sweet Sally I have memories of you that nothing can outlast. You are mine and I'll never let anyone else have you Sally. I adore you sweetheart of mine. I've thought of nothing else but you, since I left you. When the train pulled out from Los Angeles I stood out on the observation car and watched the lights recede. I realized then that I was leaving the most wonderful thing that ever came into my life.

And this is but one small part of a 6-page missive.

Barely another 48 hours had passed before, on February 7th, Crosby was moved once again to pledge his love to his "Dear Little Princess":

> You are my princess now you know. You know of course that a princess is all that is pure and good. Whoever heard of a princess that wasn't sweet and beautiful? You are all these and more. You were so gentle and lovable. I can see your sweet face as it was that night, in the dim light. Your sweet smile, your eyes and your soft white arms. It all comes back to me and leaves me wondering if there was ever anyone so wonderful as you. Do you always want to be my princess?
>
> You would make such a jolly little pal to always run around with. You are just the type darling and I'm crazy about you. Honest I am. No one else means anything to me now. All the girls have lost their charm for me now.... I didn't receive a letter today from you and I

was disappointed but there really hasn't been time for you to write I guess. I hope I shall hear tomorrow....

Honey you have the keenest pair of legs in the world. Pardon me for being so outspoken but that's my story and I'm proud of those darling feet and legs of yours.

Three more days went by and, with still no response from his beloved "jolly little pal," Jack was getting concerned:

I'm feeling awfully blue just now. I wonder a great deal about you Sally. Is it possible that you were only "playing" when you and I were together? Perhaps I was unwise to write like I did. I couldn't ever express how I felt anyway so I guess I was foolish to try. You aren't the first girl I ever liked, but Sally you are the only girl that I would have done anything for. If I could only know that your caresses were all for me. That your lips were mine alone, then I'd throw cares away....

Did you forget your promise to write to me from the mountains. Have you been stepping out on me? I've always tried to be above anything else a square shooter. I really have been a good boy so far and gee, I'm not sorry because you mean so much to me. I think it only fair that you should be the same, so if you do not care to answer this letter I'll know that you don't really care and then I'll try to stop worrying about you.

When *Sunny* closed in San Francisco, Jack boarded a train for Phoenix, Arizona. Hoping for even the briefest encounter, he sent a telegram to Los Angeles on February 26th:

DEAREST SALLY WILL BE AT THE 5TH AND CENTRAL DEPOT BETWEEN 745 & 830 ON MY WAY TO PHOENIX CAN YOU COME TO SEE ME LOVE = JACK CROSBY

Jack dealt with unrequited love the best he could. Though disappointed and frustrated by Sally's lack of serious interest, he wrangled a spot as her dance partner in *Sally from Hollywood*, the Fanchon and Marco vaudeville revue that opened in Oakland, California, in June 1928. Positioning himself as close to Sally as he could manage, Jack continued to hope for the best. Their dance act must have been something to see. (At 6 foot 2, Jack was more than a foot taller than Sally, no doubt making her appear even more petite than she was.)

Sally was fully aware of Crosby's prowess as a sharpshooter. Addressing the press upon her arrival in Oakland, she spoke of her support for the military:

> I hoped that Mr. Crosby and I could visit the schools and talk to the young people about the value of military training for everyone. I know what I am talking about, for my father was a lieutenant colonel in the Army, a veteran of the Spanish-American and the World war and he taught me the value of discipline of mind and body, of order in life.

Crosby could hardly have been more proud of Sally as she demonstrated, at barely 24 years of age, the ability to speak with authority on a wide range of subjects. He must, however, have been somewhat less enchanted as she addressed the topic of marriage:

> I think that so many stage marriages end in divorce because in constantly moving about there is no chance to build up a stock of common interests and activities outside of one's work.

> When I marry it will be outside the profession. But the man must be one who will realize that having led a very busy life I must continue to be busy. I believe in real partnership between married people — a partnership business as well as personal. The man I marry must be willing to have me, after proper study, take an active part in his affairs. I believe that is the one inevitable solution nowadays when women have become so used to steering their own lives. For that reason, I am trying to learn to be intelligent about as many things as possible outside my own work — aviation for instance....

> The time will come in a very few years when it will be no more a distinction for a woman to pilot a plane than for her to be a good chauffeur. But the commercial aspects of aviation, the designing and manufacturing of planes, is the thing that interests me and that I am studying hard. That is the sort of business project I should like to go into when I marry. But meanwhile, I'm very glad indeed of the chance to be a dancer and a "baby star."

Around the same time, Sally had described her conception of the perfect mate in a magazine interview:

> My ideal man? Well, I do like a sophisticated man and one who is just a little bit reserved. He must be well-read, suave and a gentleman. And, of course, he's got to be tall and athletic and good looking! ... I thought once I had found my ideal.... It was at a party of some sort. I was admiring a certain young man who seemed so

reserved and quiet. Then all of a sudden he jumped up and commenced to do the Charleston! Now what do you think of that?

Thinking Sally would soon join him in Atlantic City, Jack imagined in a letter written on July 18, 1929, that "you are there beside me":

> I see your cute little baby mouth that I love so well. Your pretty hair and your beautiful eyes into which I have looked so many times. How I long to "scramp" my Mousie and to hold her and to feel her little nose snuggling behind my ear. No fooling, you are my little wench and I knew some day you'd wish for me to "maul" you and scramp you and to tenderly kiss you, to pet you and to love you forever.[8]

Sally didn't really want an exclusive relationship with Jack, but she gave him just enough encouragement to keep his hopes alive. Once she reached Atlantic City, the two were apparently intimate again, revitalizing Crosby's romantic zeal. Some eight months later, on February 25, 1930, having been on the road with another show for an extended period, his pining for his "Dearest Sally" ramped up:

> I am somewhere in Kansas now and it is six o'clock at night.... I hope my future will be as rosy as this beautiful sunset. My very heart seems to thrill of the things ahead. Still at times as I look back along the long winding rails and I realize I am leaving you further and further behind I am very sad ....

> You know I thought perhaps that the eight months I was away with the show would help to make me forget you but on the contrary it makes me more lonesome for you as the days go by. I know how useless it is to ask you to write to me....

In a way-too-long letter of undetermined date, Jack, obviously despondent, offered some insight into the history of his feelings for Sally:

> At this moment I am at one of the most terrible moments in my whole life. I have never before felt as I do now. Please don't think I am looking for sympathy for I'm not. Something inside me seems to be wrong. I can't control my present emotion or rather this lot of mixed emotions that are driving me nearly mad. I suppose that it

---

8   While the term is now archaic, there is little doubt what Jack meant by "scramp." Used as a verb, one definition of the word in the online *Urban Dictionary* is "to have sexual intercourse without using a condom." When used as a noun, another less delicate definition is "A beautiful, bangin' chick, whom you would bone on the spot."

may be that I am disillusioned to the extent that nothing is worthwhile. It seems that I can never talk to you in a manner that you understand. I must get this out of my system or I feel that I shall perish in its flames. It's a long story I have to tell and I want to start at the beginning.

Several years ago in a beautiful gilded palace where there was beautiful music and laughing crowds I saw a beautiful creature dancing on a floor mirror like and surrounded by an eager pressing crowd. The rhythmic music the lights were there and into it danced one of God's most beautiful creatures. At first she seemed fairy like and unreal but I was fascinated by her beauty, as tho' touched by a wand the rest of the surroundings disappeared. I was left alone watching this girl dance and something seemed to say to me that she was meant for me alone. The music finally stopped, the dance was over, and back to earth I came.

Several years later as tho' the Gods had willed it I was in a show and I heard that my fairy princess was to be the star. (My guiding star.) 'Till now she didn't know I existed. Then one day we met only for a brief instant. "The way to the office?" "This way I'll take you there." It was over that soon but I had spoken to the girl that had haunted my memory. To me she was almost ethereal. An angel in my mind. How I adored her. I was happy because she was to be near. I had determined to know her to somehow make her love me. High ambitions for an ordinary boy of 24, to try to make an angel fall in love with him.

One day came news that tumbled my dreams once again. She wasn't going to do the show. It is quite useless to try to explain my feelings. In order to exist I had to go with the show and leave behind the girl whom I loved but was unconscious of it all. It was those thoughts that brought to me despair that faintly resembles that which is now mine.

At last the gods being kind to me thru' some circumstances that I had nothing to do with, I was asked to dance with this girl in a picture.

In my memory are many pictures that to me are priceless and sometimes I turn them over in my mind like leaves in an old album. This one I see now. The girl and myself meet once more and finally I sit talking with her alone in her dressing room. A beautiful radiant creature and myself left alone to talk. The realization sweeping over me that my love for her was real and that it was with my whole heart that I loved her. I determined then that my whole heart mind and body were hers forever. I don't know what it was but I knew she fell in love with me.

That night I spent with my darling. Never in this world will anything approach that night I spent with her. God above, how I adored and worshiped that girl.

Then came parting time when I had to go on the road. We promised to write, to phone and to love each other during the time we were apart. I hated to leave but I was happy in the thought that she loved me.

Soon, too soon, came the first little thing that hurt. I promised to call her at a certain hour. I called and found she had gone with boyfriends to the mountains. It seemed as tho' someone had slapped me when I wasn't looking. I had a sort of funny little feeling which I tried to laugh off. But still it hurt. That one time was only a forerunner of many more times. The hurts became more real. In reality they were nothing but to me who had given, at our first night together, all of my heart and soul, it seemed cruel.

Then the return and happier days together. (I find myself brightening even now when I look back over the vistas of the happy months.) Our act, the rehearsals and Loews and then the road.

San Diego, the cottage on the ocean front, the swimming, the sail boats. All the dainty wonderful morsels my "Momsy" made for me. The laughter and the fun. Gee, it was a beautiful world.

Then the sailors came and with it the realization that maybe my idol had feet of clay. I had those terrible slaps given to me again. Imagine a girl being able to hurt me. Me, the once upon a time Romeo, who had given all his love to this girl.

Then came to me the knowledge that I had hurt my Momsy too. Was it my fault, did I do it intentionally to try to get her to see what she was doing to me? Then more weeks of happiness, more quarrels, more disillusions and, God help me, finally downright unhappiness.

The story is long, it is the same over and over again until finally the girl, the angel told me that no longer did she love me as she did. I was then for the first time in my life completely crushed. I can't get it out of my mind. My life is ruined if it is the truth. I still love her as I did at first. The hurts, the wounds, I disregard. They even help me to know how much I do love her. As God is in heaven I love her as I did when she was the little dancing fairy of my dreams.

There is much I haven't told and much that is still in my heart, but I want you to have this before you go. Sally, please forgive me for all the things I've done as I've forgiven you. Let's go back to the first night we were together. Let's start over and profit by all our mistakes.

(The rest of the letter is missing.)

Another five months passed. On July 21, 1930, Jack opened his heart once again:

When you receive this letter nearly a year will have passed since I saw you last. A year all but a day or two since I last held you in my arms and kissed your baby mouth. It has been an eternity to me. Time the great healer, hasn't meant a thing to me. I still feel your arms about me. I can feel your little body close to mine.

I sat by the sea today, alone thinking, thinking, listening to the rush of the waves on the shore. The blue of your eyes was in the sky, your hair in the flying foam. You are always everywhere Sally. I can't seem to escape you somehow. It has been a year and still I can't rid myself of that longing for you. I wonder how long it will be before I don't care anymore. At night you always come to me and kiss me…. Life for me without you hasn't meant much. I don't suppose it ever will.

Five more pages followed in which Jack recounted his recent experiences and how he had struggled with the decision whether to accept a role with a traveling production or continue his budding career as a choreographer with the movie studios. Finally, he closed:

I'd better not write another page because I feel like romancing again and I have no doubt but what it bores you. I'll end this letter, and I don't know of a better way than to say, I love you more than ever.

Three months later, Sally was in New York City, possibly observing Faith Bacon's performance of the fan dance in Earl Carrol's *Vanities*. Meanwhile, Jack Crosby was stoically facing up to the reality of his prospects. On October 29th, he wrote a rambling 16-page letter to his "dear little Wench," finally opening his hand and allowing his long-held dream to fly away:

I received your letter just 1 day before I left home. I was so glad to get it. I must admit that I haven't written to you for a long long time but somehow I didn't think it would matter so very much. One can do a lot of thinking in 12 or 14 months.

It has always seemed sort of impossible for me to write to you without trying to show how much I loved you. In the year that has passed I think that at last I have realized how you feel and I think that at last I've come to realize how foolish I was. It used to hurt me terribly when I didn't hear from you or when I thought you didn't love me. But that has all passed now. I am at last free from the actual torment. I'm glad that it is all over. I am happier than I have been for several years. I shall never forget you or the wonderful times we had together. It is all very dear to me and nothing shall ever displace it in my heart or my memory.

The bulk of Jack's farewell letter recounted details of his current show and criticized those in the film industry who had "gone Hollywood." He closed with this advice "From Fuzzy Pops":

How is Harold and his virgin? I'll bet that is all off months ago.... [H]e's my pal and I got one terrific kick out of the paper one night when I read about his socking of the pan of a certain dance director — Whoops. Atta boy Hal....

Sally dear I'm sorry the breaks have been so tough, but it can't last forever. I'm sure you will get a break soon. I'm pulling for you so hard. You are the only girl that has ever mattered to me and I do want you to succeed. You know some lives are smooth and uneventful, others stormy and rocky and the going is tough. But when the game of life has been conquered and when we have attained the goal we have set, we can all look back and to the ones who have traveled the rough road, the glory is greater and we then realize life was all the better and more interesting.

It reminds me of a football game. The kick-off. The man receives the ball and starts for the goal line. By good fortune his opponents all break their legs and he runs on unhindered to a touchdown. At another stadium another game goes on. The kick-off. Man receives the ball and starts for his goal line. A few steps and he is smacked by a big tackle, down he goes rolls over gets up and starts to run. A few more steps then he dodges, twists, straight arms, he gets a jolt that makes his head swim; but on he goes finally to cross the line with two or three tackles hanging on to him. What an ovation from the stands and the world at large. He has done something more won-derful than the other runner, because thru thick and thin, over obstacles and thru them, he has won. The tougher the game the better he likes it.

You must be like that Sally. You sure have been tackled hard and you've straight armed a few. Look at the old goal posts and smash right on regardless.

I don't know how this will all sound as I haven't read it yet but anyhow it is my idea of life and people and of what you must do....

How can we account for the depth and endurance of Jack Crosby's feelings? It is really quite simple. When a man encounters "the most beautiful girl in America," when he regards this newly discovered object of his affection as the embodiment of all his previous fantasies, and when his actual physical experience with that person meets, indeed exceeds, all his expectations, then he remains a hopeful fool, even when harsh reality intrudes. Jack's reflective analysis of his experience with Sally clearly illustrates the distinction between love and infatuation. Some have said that "love makes the world go round," but, as was articulated in the little-known opera, *The Second Mrs. Kong*: "It is not love that moves the world from night to morning; it is not love that makes the new day dawn.... No. It is the longing for what cannot be."

John "Jimmie" Thach [1927 - 1929]

In 1928, the U.S. Aircraft Squadrons, Battle Fleet, operated out of San Diego, California. The large convoy included a class of ships of relatively recent origin — the aircraft carrier. Among those seeking to be trained as a carrier pilot was 23-year-old Arkansan John S. "Jimmie" Thach, a 1927 graduate of the U.S. Naval Academy (494th in a class of 579). Somehow the path of the newly minted naval airman crossed that of a certain Hollywood starlet and young Thach fell under the same spell that had mesmerized so many others.

While serving on the USS Mississippi, and little knowing that Jack Crosby and Carl Schlaet were engaged in a similar effort, Ensign Thach took pen in hand on January 19, 1928, in pursuit of his own "Sally dearest":

Turned in for about two hours yesterday afternoon and dreamed of you! Do you know Sally my mind is so filled with you that I can think of nothing else and whenever I close my eyes I can see your face close to mine and hear you whispering in my ear.

Sally please can I see you next Sunday.... Please, Please!

I love you, Sally.

The two did manage to see each other at an officers' club on weekend breaks between fleet exercises.[9] And, on March 19, 1928, Thach risked expressing his emotions without reserve:

> Since I saw you at the club Sunday I haven't been able to control my heart beats. Honey do you know seeing you just those few precious minutes made me want to give myself up and really cry instead of just doing it inside of me.
>
> Sweetheart it was like having for a few moments something you have dreamed of and lived for all your life. And angel those few moments went so quickly. Oh God! Why can't I tell you how much I really worship you? Sally I know it will always be this way. I want you for my own. I know I'm selfish, but precious, if you love me and can continue to love me then it won't be selfishness it will be happiness....

Not long afterward, aware that he was facing a long absence from his "Angel precious," Jimmie wrote:

> There have been disappointments in my life but never have I felt quite so keenly the hurt that this one gave me. Honey you can imagine how I felt only after you know how eagerly I have been looking forward to seeing you once more before a long wait of indefiniteness. I told most everyone that you would be here for dinner Sunday and we planned big things.
>
> Sweetheart it helped me so much just to talk to you, I could almost see your angel eyes looking at me with little fires in 'em (you know how I mean).
>
> Honey I got that staff job. When I arrived on board the West Virginia Monday morning to see about it I wasn't so sure I would get it for there were four others over there to see the Flag Secretary about it....
>
> Darling I love you, I can always picture you so close to me on one of those beautiful soft cool summer nights and you are forever looking up at the moon. Someday I will go up and get it for you.
>
> Good night Sally. Please write to me.

---

[9] Sally later wrote: "I had just met Jimmy Thach, fresh out of the Naval Academy, one of the young J.G.'s on the battleship Mississippi, anchored at San Pedro Harbor. Having dinner on the Missy in the Officers mess was really glamourous, and I loved it."

The passage of a year or two did little to cool Jimmie's ardor, as this fragment from a letter written during the early months of the Depression indicates:

> A terrible thing just happened at home; 148 banks have closed in
> Arkansas and my Dad's insurance company has gone on the
> rocks. I don't know what he is going to do. He is pretty old to
> be starting all over again, but he is disgustingly healthy, thank
> God … !

He closed with a proposal:

> Sweetheart, I love you, there is no one else, and I want to marry
> you as soon as possible, if you still love me???

Clearly, Sally could have an enormous impact on a young man's mental balance. An oil man's son,[10] a fellow vaudevillian, a Navy fighter pilot — all attractive, all seemingly pleasant, articulate, and substantial men — each pled his case to an ultimately unresponsive ear and was emotionally shattered. What became of these men? All will be revealed in the Epilogue.

Oh, and there was yet one more — an outgoing fellow who would cleverly gain the inside track on all the others.

Charles "Chissie" Mayon [1929 - 1935]

According to Sally, Charles Mayon was "tall, and slim, and redheaded and freckled." The son of "a wealthy tobacco merchant," he nonetheless sought a career in the entertainment business.

Sally probably met Mayon through her brother Harold. By early 1931, Charles Mayon, Harold Rand, and a man named Eddie Gall were appearing together in a vaudeville act they called "Three Life Boys." Known as "Chissie" (pronounced and sometimes spelled "Chizzy"), Mayon was six months younger than Sally. His surviving letters, while undated, appear to have been written later than those from the other men in her life.

---

10   Many years later, recalling her suitors, Sally would write: "Then there was darling
     Carl Schlaet whose father ... had founded the Texas Oil Co. and owned 51% of the
     stock. Carl had two airplanes, his parents wintered in Pasadena at the elegant Vista
     Del Arroyo Hotel. With Carl the sky was the limit. We did wonderful things, he
     taught me to fly, gave me an airplane, money was no object.

As Sally struggled to make a go of it in Florida (apparently in the winter of 1930-31), Chissie wrote to her from New York, lamenting about his own hard times. His letter began warmly with "Hello Sweetheart":

> Just going to write a couple of lines so you will know that I am thinking of you every day, all day and nite long....
>
> Gee, honey, isn't it lousy being down there without money and things. I know how it is and I feel terrible to think that I can't help you right now, but what to do? It's the curse of being poor I guess, at least poor as far as money goes, and that has a lot to do with so many things, hasn't it.... You know honey, in a way I'm glad you're in Florida now where it's at least nice and warm and all because up here it's been so cold the past couple of days and when it isn't cold, it rains most of the time . . . Oh nitsy baby, I do miss you so and I am so much in love with you, you sweet, lovely, delicious little sonofabitch, I could eat you alive right now....
>
> I love you

While she was "on vacation" in Hollywood, Mayon wrote to Sally expressing similar sentiments:

> How's your vacation doing by you? Do you feel any better by now? ... [Vaudeville promoters] will work us if we will work cheap enough, and we will, you can bet on that. [Fanchon and Marco] just sent another notice to all units of a 25% cut in salary so that means you have to pay them to let you work.... I hope I'm not scaring you too much with my news of the way conditions are now, but you might as well know sooner as later. Never mind sweets we'll get by somehow and break your butt doing it, or shall we break mine for a change ... ?
>
> I need a new suit bad but I'm afraid to get one until I'm sure how much longer we work with Van. Hurry up home sweets so I can really relax and have just one real nites sleep all snuggled up close to you. I can't ever again get used to being alone and I have to sleep alone unless you're with me. No one else could ever do. You're just the loveliest person in the world.
>
> All my love my sweet

Once upon a time, at least four presumably stable and promising young men found themselves captive to an irresistible longing — hopelessly unable to abandon the fantasy of spending a lifetime with Sally Rand in marital bliss. How much head-to-head competition there may have been is unclear, but Jack Crosby, at least, was acquainted with the other three. In a letter written on October 28, 1929, he told Sally: "You once said that if you married Jimmie, life would be smooth. I can't promise you that, but at least it would be exciting and fun, and thrilling."

What could have spurred these young men not only to pour out their hearts to her, but to nurture their romantic obsessions for years? Surviving photographs of Sally from that time are mostly studio portraits or publicity poses that don't really do justice to her remarkable personal appeal. Fortunately, there is a 1929 amateur movie film that reveals Sally as the sort of playful vixen who might well have inspired ardent suitors to address her as "brat" or "little wench." Roughly half of the two-minute film features a girlish and mischievous 25-year-old Sally with long blond hair and a form-fitting bathing suit, frolicking on the beach at Atlantic City with fellow vaudeville performer George Mann. The cameraman may well have been our own eager suitor, Jack Crosby.[11] These few seconds of exposure leave little doubt that the Sally Rand of that era was as cute and cuddly and downright flirtatious as any heartbreaker could ever be.

Carl Schlaet, Jack Crosby, and Jimmie Thach, each a sort of All-American guy, gave it their very best. But it was "Chissie" Mayon who, at least part of the time, was actually living with Sally. He would advance closer to his goal than any of the others, as we shall see.

---

[11] On July 18, 1929, while performing in an Atlantic City show, Jack wrote to Sally from the St. Charles hotel: "George Mann came down for the opening and he is now staying here for a week or so. We are having lots of fun swimming and taking pictures. It's almost like a vacation. We have one show at night and all day long to stay on the beach.... I have all my movie equipment here and I can show you the flying films and we can take a lot more also." George Mann's diary of July 25th confirms that he spent most of the day swimming and sharing the company of Sally, her brother Harold, and Jack Crosby. Years later, Mann became an acclaimed photographer. You can view this delightful 16 millimeter film at: www.thegeorgemannarchive.com. (Pause it at the 20-second mark and you can see the handsome Jack Crosby, in tank top and swimsuit, on the left side of the frame.)

CHAPTER SEVEN

The Nighttime Ride of Sally Rand

Life isn't about finding yourself. Life is about creating yourself.

~ George Bernard Shaw

W ith the closing of *The World Between*, Sally once again found herself among the unemployed. Times were tough. In 1932, "Brother Can You Spare a Dime" was a popular refrain. Sally badly needed a boost, perhaps some sort of press coverage and, as was so often the case with her, a certain amount of *uncoverage* would be an ingredient in the mix.

Lake Michigan is a large and chilly body of water. The swimming season for sane bathers is mostly limited to July and August. But members of the Chicago Polar Bear Club will brave the waters during any season — the annual New Year's Day plunge regularly drawing hundreds of participants. So it was that Sally Rand, having previously arranged for press photographers to be present, chose the coldest October day in Chicago since 1906 to become a member of the Polar Bear Club. On October 18, only a few days after the shuttering of *The World Between*, newspapers across the country published a photograph of a smiling Sally "Braving Icy Waters of Lake Michigan" in a one-piece swimsuit.[1]

While she had no visible means of support, Sally had the advantage of being a known performer, if not quite a big star. Having performed in Chicago in the 1920s, she still had valuable contacts all over town. As she told columnist John Wheeler in 1972: "It was during the Depression and I was touched by the poor selling apples and other trifles, to try to get enough to eat."

---

[1]   With water temperatures typically between 50 and 60 degrees Fahrenheit in October, a dip in Lake Michigan, the fifth largest lake in the world, would have been frigid indeed.

Thanks to a certain notoriety and despite long unemployment lines, Sally was confident that she could find a way to keep the wolves from the door. As she later recalled:

> It was the worst of the Depression. I had thought that if things got tough I'd just pick up my toe slippers and go back into the ballet. But there wasn't a working ballet company in America. No theaters had openings because of the Depression. There were no nightclubs because of Prohibition. Getting laid was easier than getting drunk. There were more whorehouses than speakeasies. So what does a ballerina do? You do the best you can with what you've got — and I did.

Jobs were hard to come by and Sally was not the only struggling young woman looking to improve her fortunes. In 1932, the national unemployment rate was 23.6 percent, heading toward the depression era peak in 1933 of nearly 25 percent. More than 200 Chicago banks had failed in 1931, another 200 or more in 1932. In December 1932, the repeal of Prohibition was still a year away. Anyone in Chicago looking for a cozy place to have a drink and enjoy a little live entertainment had as many as 10,000 "speakeasy" clubs to choose from.[2]

There are competing accounts of how Sally secured employment at the Paramount Club. Some sources say she took advantage of shady connections to "convince" the club manager to put her on stage. She later told Studs Terkel that one of the boys she knew from a previous show advised her: "All my uncles are stagehands and the rest of 'em are bootleggers. Pick out a nightclub you want to work, we'll work." Sally said she landed at the Paramount Club, reportedly at $75 a week, "only because Tony's uncles were delivering alky to Frankie the owner."

At any rate, in late October 1932 Sally once again had a confirmed engagement and could breathe a little easier. This time there would be no top billing, no name in lights; indeed, she was a solo act — one among several. But, unlike so many other desperate performers, Sally Rand was employed. She was told to report at 10:00 pm.

---

2   Alcohol was supplied to these clubs through a network of criminal enterprises. The competition was fierce — not unlike clashes between drug cartels in our day. The term "speakeasy" comes from the practice of speaking softly within or near these illegal establishments, so as not to arouse suspicion. (A speakeasy was also sometimes called a "blind pig" or "blind tiger." Why? This question is worthy of an Internet search.)

But what sort of act did she plan to perform? Sally had evidently been thinking of doing something like the "fan dance" for quite a while. Over the years, she had often said that the dance had been inspired by her childhood recollections of herons flying in the moonlight,[3] but, if she had actually observed Faith Bacon performing *her* version of the fan dance a mere two years earlier — well, that could hardly have faded from her memory. In a 1933 interview, Sally explained:

> I became inspired to do my fan dance while I was modeling for an artist here [in New York]. Every day as I sat on the model's platform I looked at a lovely picture of Leda and the swan. I wanted to do a dance to interpret it.
>
> So first I tried it with two huge wings fastened to my arms and I wore a little costume of feathers. But it wasn't what I wanted. I tried all kinds of costumes and then I realized that the only correct one is what I wear now — just nothing.

Sally told and retold the details of how her fan dance originated so many times, and with such variation, that it is now impossible to divine the absolute truth. Could her dance be traced to a serendipitous encounter? Being an excellent seamstress, she was commonly looking for materials from which to fashion a costume. While browsing the aisles of a secondhand shop, might Sally have spotted a pair of neglected fans in a dusty corner?

Memory fades. Distinct past events merge into one. Suspect accounts gain credence through repetition. But, after considering the most plausible elements from several accounts, the truth may be pretty close to the version Sally related to Studs Terkel in 1969:

> I went down to Maybelle Shearer's costume shop. She had a lot of old fans laying on the counter. I'd been wanting to do "White Birds Fly in the Moonlight" for a long time. I used to see these white herons come down on my grandfather's farm. I'm harking back to Pavlova and her bird dance, "The Swan." As a youngster, I tied wings on my shoulders. I'm glad I had the good taste even then to know this wasn't it. Then I saw pictures of Isadora Duncan. I may

---

[3]   Walter A. Schroeder and Howard Wight Marshall's *Missouri: The WPA Guide to the "Show Me" State*, Missouri History Museum Press (1998) describes Sally's Ozark region of Missouri as "a wild fragrant region where night falls swiftly and white herons rest in willow thickets."

have been a fine dancer, but I wasn't ready to create. So, necessity being the mother of invention....

I picked up a pair of these feathered fans that prima donnas used to hit the high note with. Anytime any female puts a fan in her hand, she instantly becomes a *femme fatale*. A coquette. I've seen this happen down in the Ozarks at Baptist revival meetings. The lady in a poke bonnet and calico picks up a palmy fan and instantly becomes the Queen of Sheba. So I picked up the fans and looked in the mirror. I immediately tried my inscrutable smile and the whole thing. Suddenly I saw the fans did exactly what I wanted.

I ordered a beautiful pair from New York. The fans came C.O.D. and I couldn't spring them, having no money whatsoever. Ollie, a girl I know who was running a floating crap game, said, "Don't worry about a thing. Petey's coming in from Canada with a load. He'll be loaded." When Petey came back, the rear end of his Buick looked like a sieve. He'd been hijacked and no money to spring the fans. But he hocked his rings, and they sprung the fans for me.

As to just exactly how Sally chose a "costume" with which to present her fan dance at the Paramount, we also have apocryphal versions of the story and then, as always, there is the truth. In this case it may not be possible to separate them. Did Sally intend all along to dance without a costume? Was this master seamstress somehow unable to finish her costume before being suddenly called up as the first act of the night? Various sources suggest as much.

Many years later, Sally offered this version:

I finally convinced one club owner that if my costume was small enough and the fans big enough, the audience would love it. I spent most of the afternoon putting blue gels into all the spot- lights, to give a moonlight effect, and rehearsing the pianist for the right tempo for the Moonlight Sonata. Suddenly it was time to go on and I didn't have time to go back to the hotel to get the little nightgown I was going to cut down and use for a costume. I knew if I didn't go on I would miss my only chance. So I reasoned that if I kept the fans moving fast enough no one would know if I had on a costume or not.

Portrait of Helen at age four, with her father

Helen and her brother Harold, circa 1911

Helen and Harold
with their parents —

Sally's notation reads:
"About 1913"

Christmas 1912 —

Sally was eight
and her brother
Harold was four.
Sally's notation:
"Miss Doll is
wearing a hat,
fur neck piece and
muff from Paris"

The 15-year-old Helen Beck when she was a student at Christian College in 1918

Congressman
Manuel Herrick

Helen Beck as a Kansas City
hat model in 1919

Helen Beck, dance student, circa 1920

Mrs. Mary Belle Spencer ("Mother of two babies"), as a candidate for Congress, 1922

Billie Beck in the "Follies" at Electric Park in Kansas City, August 1922

BILLY THE BATHER

As described in the June 10, 1923, *Kansas City Journal-Post:* "Winsome Billy Beck, a favorite with Kansas City musical comedy lovers, now one of the 'shining lights' in Gus Edwards' revue, poses a la the bathing beach."

Billie Beck and Marion Hart take an exercise break from their 1923 tour with the Gus Edwards Vaudeville troupe

"Mashers Be Warned, Orpheum Dancer Takes Up 'Manly' Art of Self-Defense" read the headline of the November 20, 1923, edition of the *Los Angeles Daily Times* over the picture of Billie Beck and Dandy Dillon in the boxing ring.

"Billye Beck" in an unknown Hal Roach comedy

Sally demonstrates the
"Charleston," circa 1925

Sally in *The Dressmaker from Paris,* 1925

Sally as a Gypsy dancer in 1927 film *One Night of Love*

A 1925 publicity photo of Sally taken for an unknown film

Yvonne Bacon in a promotional photo for *Artists and Models (Paris Edition)*, the 1925 revue. Producers may have been unaware that she was only 15 years old.

Sally with Franklin Pangborn in *Getting Gertie's Garter* (1927) —
(this silent film still exists and may be seen on YouTube)

The Wampas Baby Stars of 1927

Inset at right: Sally proudly poses,
looking straight at the cameraman

Sally with her glamorous mother
and handsome brother in 1926

Ballet dancer Sally in her revue *Sally from Hollywood* (1928)

Sally with the
Magand Brothers,
a Latin combo, at the
New York Hippodrome
(circa 1931)

Faith Bacon — the
"original" fan dancer —
at the second year of
the Chicago World's
Fair (1934)

Carl Schlaet —
(Autographed: "To Sally
with all my love, Carl")

Jack Crosby — Atlantic City Beach, 1929

Jimmie Thach —
The inscription on
the mat reads:
"For Sally, the
sweetest little
'Cardinal' of all"

Charles "Chissie" Mayon —
Sally's beau and fiancé from
the early 1930s to 1935,
later employed as Sally's
technical director

Rehearsing at the Granada Café
for her nighttime ride as Lady Godiva
(December 1932)

Sally performs "barefoot to the chin"
at the Paramount Club, Chicago, 1933

It worked. Maybe too well. I've never been quite sure if the audience was stunned by the beauty of the dance or by the uneasy feeling that they had just seen a naked lady dancing before them for five minutes.

Working with spotlights and rehearsing the pianist were typical of Sally's meticulous approach to preparing her act. While she commonly employed both Beethoven's "Moonlight Sonata" and Frédéric Chopin's "Waltz in C Sharp Minor," the signature accompaniment for her fan dance over the years would be Claude Debussy's 1890 composition "Clair de Lune" — literally "the light of the moon" in French.[4]

And so, on an auspicious night in late October 1932, Sally stepped onstage and performed her fan dance for the very first time. When asked if maybe she had planned to be naked all along, Sally merely smiled and said:

Now, you know that nude dancing was strictly against the law in those days. Do I look like I would deliberately break the law? Somehow, I knew the act would sell and I wanted to showcase it at the World's Fair. Getting into that place was harder than getting a real cup of tea in a speakeasy. I had to get some flashy publicity.

Even without a big stage and a big production, Sally was still Sally — irrepressible, irresistible. Word got around. In early December she shared top billing in an "all-star show" at the Café Granada at 6800 Cottage Grove. Newspaper ads described her as a "Wampas Star." The other headliner was Mildred Harris Chaplin, who had acted in dozens of silent films, but whose main claims to fame were her short-lived marriage to Charlie Chaplin and her subsequent fling with the Prince of Wales before he abdicated the throne of England in order to be with Wallace Simpson — "the woman I love."[5]

---

4   Sally's choice of "Clair de Lune" was certainly apropos of her "herons in the moonlight" vision. Also written in 1890, Paul Verlaine's poem "Clair de Lune" includes the lines: "The melancholy moonlight, sweet and lone, that makes to dream the birds upon the tree."

5   Also on the Café Granada bill that week were Bud and Betty, "Dance Team Extraordinaire." This particular "Bud" was almost certainly Bud Abbott who worked the vaudeville circuit with his wife Betty before teaming up with Lou Costello. The newspaper ad was headlined "All the Ginger Ale You Can Drink — $1 per person." With Prohibition still in force, the club furnished the ginger ale and the clientele took it from there.

While her club gigs more or less paid for the groceries, Sally's future prospects were far from settled. No stranger to self-promotion, she was always on the lookout for new and creative ways to advance her career. Learning that an always well-attended annual costume ball celebrating art and architecture was coming up, Sally began to consider how she might use the event to raise her profile and maybe even do a little something for the less fortunate: "I got an idea that I would appear as Lady Godiva and raise money for the undernourished."

The Beaux Arts Ball in Chicago was an annual affair in which wildly costumed students of the arts partied into the night and, incidentally, sought to raise funds for a worthy cause.[6] By 1927, the ball had established itself as a much anticipated date on Chicago's social calendar. The theme that year was an exploration of what the art world might be like in the year 2000.

In planning the event, quite a controversy developed in the Arts Ball Committee over one of the proposed feature attractions. Fearing the annual occasion had become somewhat stale, two committee members, architects Benjamin Marshall and Andrew Rebori, agreed that the masked ball needed something new and exciting to pump up ticket sales. Chairman Rebori proposed that the highlight of the affair should be an appearance by "Lady Godiva," complete with her horse, but otherwise lacking any cover beyond her own golden mane.

Marshall supported the idea, but favored an even more audacious option:

> Certainly we should have a Lady Godiva. The legend about her is beautiful. Her appearance on a horse, provided it isn't too cold, will be an artistic achievement such as Chicago has seldom seen.

> Originally it was Rebori's idea to have just one Godiva. But I am going to give him help by bringing in six more. I have an artistic picture frame 2,000 years old which I purchased in Italy. I propose to bring this frame, which is twelve feet long and nine feet high, to the ball and pose in it the six Godivas on foot.

---

6   Originating in Paris at the National School of Fine Arts in 1892, the Mardi-Gras-like affair known as "Bal des Quat'z'Arts" was an annual event celebrating architecture, painting, sculpture and engraving. This annual costume party inspired architectural societies in the U.S. to do likewise and in 1914 the Society of Beaux-Arts Architects in New York City held the first ball in America. This and those that came after were extremely popular occasions for high society.

As to the fate of "Peeping Tom," Marshall went on to explain:

> Those who fear to lose any eyesight by looking on a whole collection of Godivas[7] will be cared for. Smoked glasses will be issued at the door and oculists will be in waiting.

Objecting to the whole idea, Marian Gheen, the 54-year-old leader of the committee's conservative wing, noted:

> The basic idea for the pageant is a conception of art in 2000 A.D. Surely Lady Godiva is not connected to that era. Then too, I do object on moral grounds. A nude may have its place in art, but its place is not in such a temporary setting as will be provided by the ball. It would be positively indecent under such circumstances. It would be neither artistic nor moral to have a show that the police might interpret as a stag.

After a spirited argument, the committee voted to support the multiple-Godiva plan but, in the fortnight between the vote and the event's scheduled occurrence on November 25th, committee members had second thoughts. Anticipating possible traffic problems and acknowledging the impropriety of presenting nude women at an arts benefit, they decided to drop the horse and otherwise scale back the whole presentation.

> ### LADY GODIVA
>
> The story of the legendary Lady Godiva dates to at least the 13th Century. In its most elementary form, it concerns a young lady taking pity on the townspeople of Coventry, England, who were suffering under the burden of taxes imposed by His Eminence, Lord Godiva. She begged her husband's indulgence. He consented to grant them relief, but only on the condition that his wife would ride naked through the streets of the town clad simply in her long golden hair. This she agreed to do, with the understanding that all the townspeople would remain behind locked doors and windows, taking no notice of her passage. The iconic image of this tale has been memorialized ever since in paintings and statuary, as well as in reenactments.

Meanwhile, architect Rebori had arranged for 20-something Rosalind Hightower (a former "Miss Detroit") to fly to Chicago and play the role of Lady Godiva "because of her wonderful golden hair and all-around

---

[7]   Among many variants of the legend, one dating to the 11th Century relates the adventures of seven naked Godiva sisters, the inspiration no doubt for architect Marshall's proposal for the 1927 ball. Students of the subject may enjoy *The Seven Lady Godivas: The True Facts Concerning History's Barest Family*, a 1939 picture book written and illustrated by none other than Dr. Seuss.

pulchritude." As she descended the stairway from her flight, she was asked by reporters what she intended to "appear in." She responded: "In the moonlight," adding that it would be "implausible" to ride in on a horse "for fear that a dowager or two might get trampled." To queries about her golden locks being her only costume, she replied:

> Immodest? Not as I see it. To me, a short fat woman in an abbre-
> viated skirt is vulgar. But the human body is a thing of beauty
> when its mass is well proportioned. A nude to me is nothing more
> than a cow is to others.

On the night of the event, some 3,000 guests gathered in the grand ball-room of the newly opened Stevens Hotel in rapt anticipation of eyeballing whatever the committee had chosen to present. Their patience was not well rewarded. Around 1:30 in the morning, those who remained were presented with a stationary "Lady Godiva" (in a large gilt frame), together with an eerily life-like wax facsimile. Sadly, this scaled-back unveiling was so botched by the curtain operator that even those in the front row with brand new prescription lenses could observe little, if any, actual epidermis.[8]

As the *Chicago Daily Tribune* put it (under the headline "GODIVA GOES TO ARTS BALL AND ALL SURVIVE IT"):

> Those whose ... temperature remained normal broke into a babel of
> discussion as to what they had seen and whether they had seen
> what they thought they had or, whether anything but a wax figure
> had been there; whether they had been hoaxed or coaxed; teased or
> pleased; whether there was a Lady Godiva or a Santa Claus.

Leap forward five years to December 1932. Stung by the onset of the Depression, Andrew Rebori had fewer assignments as an architect, but was still very much involved in seeking to entertain Chicago's 400 with cocktail parties, novel dances, and the upcoming Beaux Arts Ball, to be held once again at the Stevens Hotel.

---

[8]   The revelers had advance notice that Lady Godiva would be posing unclad in a gilt
      frame (without her horse). But when the curtains were first parted, the assemblage
      was greeted by a wax replica of Miss Hightower. The curtains were then closed and
      opened again, whereupon Miss Hightower was supposed to step from her gilt frame
      and move to the front of the stage. But the stagehand got his cues mixed and dropped
      the curtains before she could take a step, thus denying the audience the sight of
      Godiva in motion.

According to one observer, writing a few days before the ball, a "little but hefty blonde girl" named Sally Rand approached Mr. Rebori, saying that she "would do anything for publicity" and proposing that he permit her to appear at his ball as Lady Godiva, riding a white horse and clothed in nothing but her golden tresses.

Perhaps recalling his aborted effort in 1927, Rebori replied: "It's all right with me. It may help you in what you're aiming at. All I can give you is a pass." That was OK with Sally and Rebori gave her a handwritten pass. Any qualms he may have had were tempered by the prospects embodied in Sally's smiling face. This time there would be no wax replica, no gilded picture frame, no bungling stagehand — just a straight-ahead All American girl, piquant, delightful and genuinely in the buff. The more he thought about the idea, the better he liked it.[9]

And so it was that Sally secured an invitation to appear as Lady Godiva at the annual Beaux Arts Ball to be held on December 9, 1932, at the elegant Stevens Hotel. Only five years old, the hotel already had a checkered history. When it opened on May 2, 1927, the Stevens was the largest hotel in the world and may have been the most grandly appointed.[10] Situated near the center of Chicago and facing Lake Michigan, it was 28 stories high and featured some 3,000 rooms, each with a private bath.

Designed in a style reflective of Beaux-Arts architecture and built at a cost of $30 million ($410 million today), the massive edifice had been developed by the Stevens family, who also owned Chicago's 22-story LaSalle Hotel. Unfortunately, the huge upscale Stevens Hotel had opened during that falsely flush period just before the stock market crash of 1929 and the dawn of the Great Depression.

Like so many others, the hotel was soon in financial distress and conditions for the Stevens family would only get worse. In 1933, hotelier Ernest Stevens was charged with attempting to divert cash from the family's life insurance business to make bond payments on the insolvent hotel. Ernest's brother, Raymond, and their father, James, were charged as co-conspirators.

---

[9]   An alternate and possibly more accurate version of how Sally managed to be invited to the Beaux Arts Ball (involving press agent Lou Fink, Alderman Charley Weber, and event director Cati Mount) was published in the August 29, 1960, edition of the *Chicago Tribune*. You pays your money and you takes your choice.

[10] Promoted as effectively containing a "city within a city," the hotel complex included a movie theater, barbershop, ice cream parlor, drugstore, bowling alley, and even a rooftop miniature golf course.

(Shortly after his arrest, Raymond Stevens committed suicide and James suffered a stroke.)

Acting on an impulse for self-preservation, Ernest obtained European passports for himself, his children and his wife. Alerted to the family's possible intention to flee the country, the state's attorney quickly obtained a warrant and Ernest was arrested at his home, while his son John, then 13, listened furtively from the top of the stairs. Mr. Stevens was fully exonerated by the Illinois Supreme Court in 1934, but by then the once fabulously wealthy hotelier had been reduced to running a food concession in the English Village at the Century of Progress World's Fair. His teenaged son spent the summer in period costume "as a strolling vendor of Banbury tarts" outside a replica of the Red Lion Inn in Colchester, England.

Whether or not young John Stevens ever met Sally Rand remains open to speculation, but many years later he would meet with a success unexpected in common hours.[11]

Faith

As the winter of 1932 settled in, original fan dancer Faith Bacon found herself a central figure in a rather odd situation. An item in the *New York Daily News* noted that Wall Street broker Jack Stanley Morris was seeking an annulment of his week-old marriage to nightclub entertainer Jean Coventry on the grounds that "her body was constantly exposed to the gaze of the public." Besides, declared Morris (an apparent stranger to irony), the woman he really wanted to marry was Faith Bacon.

The details were these. Jack Morris was a Wall Street broker, yes, but he was also a gentleman with a reputation as a playboy, and he had witnessed Faith Bacon waving her ostrich feather fans at Nils Granlund's Hollywood Restaurant on Broadway. He had been so instantly smitten that he vowed to make her his wife. Despite his best efforts at wining and dining her, Miss Bacon managed to resist his charms.

---

[11] On December 17, 1975, by a vote of 98-0, John Paul Stevens was confirmed by the United States Senate as an associate justice of the United States Supreme Court, where he served until his retirement on June 29, 2010.

As one report put it:

> Faith, at this point, read Jack a kindly but frigid lecture on the
> Nude in Love and Art. She explained that her body was a work of
> design, created to give pure esthetic delight (whenever the fans
> parted) to connoisseurs in Row A and at the ringside. Her person
> was, therefore, far too precious to be scuffed ever so slightly by
> the shackles of matrimony.

In other words, "Thanks, but no thanks." Morris persevered at first, but
was persuaded to abandon his quest for Faith when, back at the Hollywood
Restaurant, Nils Granlund suggested that he turn his attention to one Jean
Coventry, a young woman who had recently been jilted by lightweight
boxing champion Jackie "Kid" Berg.

Jack Morris liked what he saw in Miss Coventry. Both were on the re-
bound, and each seemed to feel that the other was a suitable alternative.
An impetuous wedding followed, but, no sooner had the honeymoon
started than they found reasons to seek an annulment. Jack claimed Jean
made herself physically unavailable, apparently considering her form
"too sacred to touch." How could she be so cavalier, he thought, about
displaying her charms in public for the enjoyment of a club full of
drunken revelers and yet deny them to her husband in the privacy of
their honeymoon suite? In her rejoinder, Jean contended that Jack had
lied about his financial condition, had married her just to spite the
equally icy Faith Bacon, and had declined to participate in a religious
ceremony after promising to do so.

The annulment was granted, and the judge ordered Jack to pay Jean $50 a
week in alimony. But Miss Coventry never collected a cent, as Jack went on
the lam, leaving poor Jean to continue earning her way through the skillful
titillation of the Hollywood Restaurant clientele.

Jack Morris was of a mind to resume his pursuit of Faith Bacon, but she
was not around. By early 1933, she was touring the country with the road
show version of *Ziegfeld Follies of 1931* in the company of Harry Richman,
Hal Le Roy, Dorothy Dell and Gladys Glad, lately called by Flo Ziegfeld
"the most beautiful girl in the world."[12] This must have come as sobering

---

[12] Gladys Glad (her real name) had indeed been singled out by Ziegfeld, but any awareness
of her today would have more to do with her marriage. In 1929, she married Mark
Hellinger a young columnist for the *New York Daily News*. Hellinger suffered a fatal
coronary attack at 44, but in his brief, prolific life the journalist authored many plays,
articles, and short stories, some of which became Hollywood films.

news to Faith, as it hadn't been that long since the scrupulous impresario had bestowed this very same appellation upon *her*.

S ally couldn't very well attend a grand ball nude on a horse without due preparation. Still appearing at the Café Granada, she discussed her plans with owner Al Quodbach, a shady character who had "connections" all over town.

Quodbach was a tall, intimidating character with a penchant for diamond cuff links and shirt studs. His Café Granada featured an upstairs casino and a downstairs shooting range. Four years earlier, "Stubby" McGovern and "Gunner" McFadden, two gangsters and labor racketeers, had been shot and killed at his café. George Maloney, a member of Bugs Moran's gang, had gunned down the two Al Capone "goons" in retaliation for their teasing him about an incident a few nights earlier when Maloney had been pushed off the stage by band leader Guy Lombardo, right in front of Al Jolson. The shooting was aired live over Chicago's WBBM, as the orchestra was in the midst of a remote live broadcast.[13]

His dubious character aside, Quodbach happily arranged for a horse to be brought to the club and Sally made sure an Acme News photographer was on hand to record her rehearsal. As she recalled:

> I hired a white horse for $50, which was a lot of money for me in
> those days. The horse was not all white, so to cover some dark
> spots we put a white shawl over him.

As the date of the 1932 Beaux Arts Ball approached, NEA news service distributed a picture captioned "Portrait of a Lady with a Fan," which was printed in papers all across the country. The photo showed Sally sitting astride a horse, holding an ostrich feather fan, seemingly in the buff.[14]

---

[13]   Less than two years after Sally's appearance there, the Café Granada club was destroyed by a fire of mysterious origin. Despite a lifestyle of catering to the whims of competing mobsters, Quodbach somehow survived for many years, dying in Las Vegas in 1978 at the age of 89.

[14]   *The Daily News* of Huntingdon, Pennsylvania, ran Sally's picture just above a photograph of film stars Colleen Moore and Norma Shearer under the heading "Muffs Make Movie Debuts." The text under the pictures reads: "Muffs, big, little or medium, are the thing for winter, and the movie stars have been quick to seize the new vogue. At the left is Colleen Moore, who likes her muff small. At the right is Norma Shearer, who goes for a large one. And there were lots of medium-sized ones at the Los Angeles premiere they attended."

During the week leading up to the big event, the Chicago winter had turned nasty — some would say *very* nasty. Sally was not deterred, insisting she intended to attend the ball as Lady Godiva "even if the mercury falls to zero."

The evening of the grand ball on December 9th, costumed attendees were totally oblivious to the hotel owners' financial dilemma. Nor were their minds on the weather. They had heard the buzz. They had seen the picture of Sally and her horse in the paper. They were in the mood to party and anticipation of a good time was running high.

As the appointed hour approached, trailed by members of the press, Sally dutifully appeared at the hotel entrance astride her rented steed, covered by little more than a long blond wig. The doorman, rattled by the sight that greeted him, quickly recognized the limits of his authority and called for the manager. Although well aware of the affair in progress, he wasn't comfortable with granting admission to the shivering twosome. And so, Sally was left cooling her heels at the lobby door, as if they weren't quite cool enough already.

Finally, after giving the matter sufficient consideration, the hotel manager decided that he couldn't risk damaging the ballroom floor. Further negotiation ensued, but Sally was not of a mind to be turned away. Guests inside the ballroom began checking their watches. It was beginning to look as if the nighttime ride of Sally Rand might not happen after all. Years later, Sally recalled: "I tried to take the horse into the Stevens Hotel, but they would not let me in because he did not have on rubber shoes."

The impasse was ultimately resolved by leaving the horse behind. The director of the occasion, Miss Cati Mount, had previously joked that Sally would certainly be welcome to attend, but "the horse would need its own ticket."[15]

Eventually, Sally was ceremoniously carried into the hotel "riding" a kitchen table hoisted aloft by steadfast volunteers said to be dressed as "Egyptians." Any pretense of ceremony was soon abandoned, as the four

---

[15] As you might imagine, Cati Mount has a story of her own. Described by *Time* magazine as the "brash *enfante terrible* of Chicago's art world," the 24-year-old graduate of the Chicago Art Institute ran the Little Gallery in the stately old Auditorium Building. She came to the attention of the public in 1932 as the organizer of an art show in Grant Park which drew such large crowds that park commissioners had to enlist the police to move them out. According to *Time*, the nonplused Miss Mount "snappily ran the show" while sitting under a yellow umbrella, "showing red toenails through her pointed sandals."

slightly inebriated art students rushed her into the ballroom in a jovial and careless manner, swaying and rocking the table from side to side, seemingly intent on throwing her into the assembled partygoers. In all the excitement, someone lost his grip, the table collapsed, and whatever small degree of dignity Sally may have previously enjoyed was momentarily lost in the tumble. After a brief spell of embarrassment, she bounced up and managed to regain her composure.

In essence, a mighty group of costumed heroes had arrived to save the day and the once prim and proper Missouri farm girl had grown more comfortable with the notion of being bare naked in the midst of supportive fans.

Sally's appearance as Lady Godiva may not have gone exactly as planned, but the reaction of the press and the squeals of delight from the Beaux Arts crowd did not pass without notice. The girl on the horse was the talk of the town. Business picked up for her club appearances and the Godiva stunt was filed away in her memory bank. It wouldn't lie dormant for long.

CHAPTER EIGHT

Crashing the Party

People are always blaming their circumstances for what
they are. I don't believe in circumstances. The people
who get on in this world are the people who get up and
look for the circumstances they want, and, if they can't
find them, make them.

~ George Bernard Shaw, *Mrs. Warren's Profession*

S ally Rand wasn't the first to use a dramatic publicity stunt to gain the
attention of the nation. She wasn't even the first woman to do so. That
distinction may belong to Annie Edson Taylor, a former dance instructor
who, on her 63rd birthday in 1901, became the first person to go over
Niagara Falls in a barrel. After surviving her ordeal, Annie told the press:

If it was with my dying breath, I would caution anyone against
attempting the feat.... I would sooner walk up to the mouth of a
cannon, knowing it was going to blow me to pieces, than make
another trip over the Falls.

Sally wasn't about to go over the Falls. Even the prospect of repeating her
plunge into the icy waters of Lake Michigan had little appeal, but the notion
of taking her show on the road — well, that was another matter. Escaping the
wintery chill of the Windy City in 1932, she headed for Miami, a seasonal
retreat that offered not only warmth and comfort but also a chance to cash in
on her recent "Lady Godiva" notoriety and present her newly developed
ostrich feather dance to a new audience. Since Sally was chiefly known as a
film actress and vaudeville dancer, her new "fan dance" came as something
of a shock to patrons of Miami's large Olympia Theater, and dozens of the
"pure at heart" were moved to write indignant letters of protest.

She soon relocated to a smaller Miami venue where she received top billing
as a "Star of Stage and Screen Offering Her Eye-Filling Fan Dance." Other

performers on the bill at the Frolics "Two Bits" Club[1] included Etta Reed, the "Empress of Harmony Lane," Bee Jackson, a "World Famous Charleston Dancer",[2] Kay Erickson, the roller skating "Cyclone of Pep," and Anderson & Allen, circus acrobats known as the "Barons of Balance."

In March, Miami columnist Edgar Hay interviewed Sally between shows and, as with so many other unsuspecting journalists meeting Sally for the first time, he was impressed:

> I was frankly amazed at my tête-à-tête conversationalist — maybe I was bulging my eyes a trifle and getting an adenoidal droop to my jaw — because this was not the sort of talk I expected from her.
>
> It was Sally Rand — she of the voluptuous curves, she who has fascinated thousands at the Frolics with her startling fan dance, ... she who — unlike the majority of mankind — is perfectly at home in her body — Sally Rand, a nightclub performer.

As was her habit, the 28-year old Sally waxed eloquent on a wide range of topics:

> Work, and accomplishment in your work, that's the best happiness you can get out of life. I don't care whether your work is just winding string on a spool or whether you're one of those poor little housewives in bare feet you see along the railroad tracks out through the middle West, or whether you're a dancer in a night club or a movie star or an eminent scientist trying to discover a cure for some malignant disease. Idle persons are the unhappy ones. But they who have work to do and are busy at it, occupying their minds and hands and bodies with it, filling their lives with the joy of accomplishing something, they're the ones who get the most out of life. They know what a good place this earth is.

Hay also noted that, while he and Sally chatted with a group between shows:

> The rest of 'em were talking races or show business or something. Sally, in a modest evening frock, with the mascara and rouge still on her face, and I, still with amazement on mine, were in a private huddle to ourselves — not a newspaper man and a theatrical star

---

[1]   With Prohibition still in force, "two bits" referred to the 25-cent cover charge for setups and ice provided for patrons who came prepared to imbibe. Otherwise, the club charged no admission, imposed no minimum, and offered a full program of entertainment.

[2]   Like Sally, Bee did not invent the Charleston, but she may have been its best-known American practitioner. Although the term "bee's knees" actually predated her fame, it was believed by many to refer to her.

in the self-conscious attitude of a formal interview, but just as a couple of human beings discovering they speak the same language....

There is that wholesome quality about this unusual young woman. She stems from the good, clean soil. From the earth she learns her wisdom, from books her amazing knowledge.

Sally continued with her thoughts on the meaning of it all:

I'm not afraid of death. And I don't have any wish to endure in con-sciousness after death. I have no fear of anything, I believe. Of course I've been frightened suddenly. But it has been a reflex, physical reaction. Just as soon as my reason functions, I know that I am not afraid. People may hurt me or maim me or even kill me, but as long as I have my reason I know that I am me. They cannot harm this vital thing that is me. Fear is the most horrible curse in the world. Do you know that a mother nursing a baby can poison it to death by fear? Fear is the greatest enemy to life. Our whole structure of social living, from the days of the cave men, has been built to eradicate fear from human minds. The home, the church, social attitudes, polite-ness, conventions — all are a mantle of protection against fear.[3]

"You've read your philosophers," Hay observed. Sally continued:

No. I haven't read much philosophy. Once I had a need for Schopenhauer. I was in Hollywood. I was quite young and successful — too young to appreciate my success rightly. I was commencing to "Go Hollywood" — thinking that I was the center of the universe the most important actress in the world. Schopenhauer enabled me, with his pessimism, to get outside myself and look objectively at the silly little girl I was. There was a fine intelligence — Schopenhauer's — that wallowed in misery and gloated over the muckiness and cruelty in mankind.

Hay then tentatively suggested the "mens sana in corpore sano" principal (suggesting that a healthy body supports a healthy mind) which Sally more or less dismissed:

No. I've known plenty of ill people, men and women, who had marvelously brilliant minds. But I don't see why people scorn the

---

[3]   Edgar Hay's column quoting Sally was published exactly two weeks after President Franklin D. Roosevelt's first inaugural address in which he famously declared: "The only thing we have to fear is fear itself."

physical phases of life as vulgar. Just taking a good deep breath of
fresh air is a perfect joy — or eating a good dinner — or becoming
tired from physical exercise — or falling off to sleep — those are
facts than can be a continual delight to a person.

And do you know, today I spent one of the most pleasant days I've
ever had here. Know why? Because I cooked, all by myself, a
chicken dinner — fried chicken, mashed potatoes, corn on the cob
and a lemon meringue pie — for eight people. That was the most
fun I've had in a long while.

Turning to the subject of dance, Hay asked Sally if she had ever seen a "real
rhumba dance." She responded:

No. That rhumba I did at the Olympia was just my American idea
of the dance. But the "hula" I do here is the real dance. You know
it's a ceremonial dance, glorifying the queen who is supposed to be
the incarnate spirit of the great Pele volcano.

And so it went, Edgar Hay concluding:

And there we were off again on strange topics, so incongruous in a
night club. It was a swell adventure. And Sally made it so with the
sparkle of her mind, as well as the sparkle of her eyes.

She left us. In another quarter hour she was out there on the floor,
in a blue spotlight, doing her almost-nude fan dance.

Always open to self-improvement, Sally found in Miami not only a cozy
haven in winter but also an opportunity to get in top physical condition, the better to tackle the job market. In the past, Sally's small stature and
so-called overdeveloped legs had impeded her advancement. Indeed, one
critic had described the situation with the uncharitable assessment that there
was "too much on the gal."

In Miami, Sally sought the services of Doc Field, a well-known masseur
and trainer of famous boxers, who ran a gymnasium in Miami Beach.
During the winter season each year, Doc operated in a solarium atop an
upscale beach hotel where he helped affluent ladies shed their excess heft.
He told a reporter: "That's what the little gal from Hollywood wanted."

"If you can beat twenty pounds off my fanny," Sally explained, "I can get a
hell of a summer job in Chicago." Reportedly, Doc looked her over critically
and decided it would be even better if she took off 25 pounds. He advised
Sally on what to eat, exercised her until she could barely move, and

massaged her until she howled for mercy. The result? She got back down to fighting trim and was ready to take on the world.

Faith

"HELLO AMERICA! IT'S HERE! NEW YORK'S NEWEST MOST SENSATIONAL CABARET RESTAURANT" — So screamed newspaper ads in February 1933, touting the Monte Carlo Casino on 48th Street, west of Broadway in New York City. Here a couple out on the town could savor a "deluxe dinner" and delight in the performances of "40 — Gorgeous Girls — 40." Anticipating the speed-dating craze by some 65 years, the Monte Carlo featured numbered tables with a special telephone installed on each one. An eager swain prepared to part with 50 cents[4] during the Depression could patch through to the switchboard and ring up the attractive (and presumably eligible) young woman across the room. As Broadway columnist Paul Harrison wrote: "The whole thing makes for fun and informality, and not as many quarrels as you'd expect."

Among the "40 Gorgeous Girls" at the Monte Carlo was Faith Bacon, "hiding behind a few beads now, instead of ostrich plumes." As Harrison observed:

> Miss Bacon says calmly that she's "the best nude in the business." It seems that the technique of such theatrical exhibitions is very difficult, the less a girl wears the more cleverly must she impart an impression of aloofness and propriety.

While Miss Bacon danced the night away in New York and Miss Rand teased and tormented her audiences in Miami, construction of the Century of Progress International Exposition in Chicago continued apace. The attraction would loom large in the future of these two and would soon enough bring them face to face. Each would skillfully wave her ostrich feathers to the delight of her respective followers, and the course of their fortunes would be forever altered.

Traveling north from Miami, Sally stopped off in Louisville, Kentucky, on May 6, 1933, to attend a little annual event at Churchill Downs — the 1.25-mile stakes race for thoroughbred three-year-olds known as the Kentucky Derby. Forty years after the event, she accurately remembered that a horse called Broker's Tip had been declared the winner, explaining: "I was there,

---

[4] This was not as inexpensive as it sounds. Adjusted for inflation, a single call across the room at that rate would cost from $9.00 to $10.00 today.

but more interested in the jockey I was dating. That's the year two winning jocks whipped each other all the way to the finish line, in bib overalls."[5]

Back in Chicago, Sally resumed her engagement at the Paramount Club, but the buzz around town was all about the upcoming World's Fair — the "Century of Progress" — scheduled to open on May 27th. Here was an opportunity for several solid months of employment. But with the sponsors of the exposition determined to focus on the more uplifting aspects of our culture and commerce, to the exclusion of tawdry, morally questionable forms of entertainment, how was a young lady with little to offer beyond a curvy body and a pair of ostrich feather fans going to wrangle her way onto the premises?

Sally first sought assistance from Chicago Alderman Charlie Weber, self-styled "boss" of the 45th Ward, who held a beer concession at the Streets of Paris. She implored him to help her get a job as a dancer at one of the clubs he was servicing. The Streets of Paris was among the fair's most ambitious exhibit areas, featuring replicas of Paris Streets, strolling French entertainers, and sidewalk cafes. However, reliance on Weber and other influential contacts, shady or otherwise, proved to be of little help. Despite her relative fame and her best efforts to secure a spot at the fairgrounds, Sally was stymied at every turn.

As she told Studs Terkel many years later:

> Now I'm harassing Charlie Weber for that job at the World's Fair, and he's not coming up with it. Because the Streets of Paris was sponsored by the high and mighty of this town, the social set. It was all French entertainment. Mr. Weber just didn't swing it big enough to get a job for me there. He suggested I crash the preview, the night before it opens. Mrs. Hearst was giving one of her famous Milk Fund dinners: "You'll get your foot in the door."

---

[5] Well, maybe not in bib overalls, but Sally was essentially correct. The lead jockeys did violently flog each other as they approached the finish line. Jockey Don Meade rode Broker's Tip — the only racehorse in history whose sole win was the Kentucky Derby— and was awarded the win by a nose. The "Fighting Finish" occurred before the existence of reliable photo-finish equipment, and the actual winner is still disputed by old-timers. A video of the race can be seen on YouTube. And which of the jockeys was Sally dating? It was 9th-place finisher Duke Bellizzi. Their relationship was cut short when, little more than a year later, Bellizzi, leading the Youthful Stakes at the Jamaica Race Course in New York, fell from his mount and was trampled by several following horses. He died a few days later.

Millicent Hearst, wife of the famous newspaper magnate William Randolph Hearst, had founded the "Free Milk Fund for Babies" in 1921 and had been engaged ever since in fundraising activities in support of a variety of causes, not only for poverty stricken babies, but also for crippled children, unemployed girls, and the Democratic National Committee.

On this grand occasion, Mrs. Hearst had invited all of Chicago's elite, including the fair organizers and local officials, to attend a fundraising dinner in the Streets of Paris on the evening before the formal opening of the Century of Progress exposition. As many as 3,000 notables were in attendance. The money raised was to be donated to the Illinois Children's Home and Aid Society. Invitees were issued "passports" and escorted to the gala on a flotilla of yachts anchored on the shores of Lake Michigan. According to reports from local papers:

> The cream of Chicago glided through the party in formal evening clothes or in clever costumes that sometimes aped their social inferiors — cavemen, Native Americans, peasants, and French maids. Costumed fair workers drifted among them, portraying artists' models, soldiers, top-hatted gentlemen, and flower vendors.

> "One even wore a dress made out of thousand dollar bills," Sally later remarked, "which annoyed me, thinking of the poor selling apples and other trifles, to try to get enough to eat."

As long as she was going to crash Mrs. Hearst's fundraiser, Sally figured she might as well do it up right. In this case, that meant dusting off her Lady Godiva act that had been so successful only five months before. As she later told Studs Terkel:

> I hired the horse again, but the gates of the Fair were closed.... [W]e go up to the Wrigley docks. The Streets of Paris had a yacht landing there.... So I paid $8 for the tickets to the boat. He said: "Who's going with you?" I said, "Just a friend." So I brought the horse on the boat, and the man demurred. I said: "What do you care if it's a horse or a human?" At the yacht landing of the Streets of Paris, there was this little Frenchman who spoke no English. He figured that a broad that arrives in a boat with a horse is *supposed* to be there. So he opened the gate. The master of ceremonies, poor soul, figured: "God, here's a woman with a horse and nobody told me about it."

Up to this time, the party'd been pretty dull. They had two
bands.... The fanfare sounded and the MC announced: "Now,
Lady Godiva will take her famous ride." Music played. Every
photographer in the business, especially the Hearst ones, were
there. Flashlights went off and the music played, and everybody
was happy. They said: "Do it again." So I did it again.

Some of the bigwigs at the Milk Fund Dinner were appalled, but most were
elated. No one knew for sure if Lady Godiva was part of the planned entertainment or if they had all been punked by a mysterious intruder. As Sally
would say many years later: "Let's face it, that was the most exciting thing
that had happened to those phonies in weeks. Until my entry, they were
just sitting around staring at each other, comparing jewelry and furs."

The risky caper had become a major coup. The girl on the horse was once
again the talk of the town. Thousands, learning about Lady Godiva's crashing of the Hearst affair, had a common query: "Who was that girl? Where
can I see her?"

In later years, Sally enjoyed telling about the next morning, the opening
day of the Fair, when she went down to the Streets of Paris to once again
seek employment. This time the welcome mat was out. Management was
more than eager to see her: "They hired me at $90 a week.[6] I had to go
home immediately and get the fans. They had no piano, just a xylophone.
That's how we got started."

The Lady Godiva stunt was far more than just how Sally "got started." It
may be a cliché to say it, but, in a most profound way, it was the first day of
the rest of her life.

---

[6]   This was a more than decent paycheck for a young woman just "getting started" —
over $1,600 per week today.

Part Two

My Fair Lady

This image of a youthful Sally wrapped in her fans is a publicity photo taken during the 1933 Century of Progress Exhibition in Chicago.

CHAPTER NINE

The Nude Deal

The truth is, as everyone knows, that the great artists of
the world are never Puritans, and seldom even ordinarily
respectable.

~ H. L. Mencken, 1919

T he whooping and hollering could hardly have been misunderstood.
Someone was having a good time. The enthusiasm generated by
Sally's crashing of the Milk Fund Dinner created a wave that she was
determined to ride. No longer persona non grata at the fair, she would soon
be writing her own ticket. A starting salary of $90 a week quickly jumped to
$125. As word spread and crowds built, her compensation increased
dramatically, reportedly reaching thousands per week.

While a comprehensive treatment of the expanse and impact of the Chicago
Fair is beyond the scope of these pages, one thing is clear: In their search
for a signature emblem, the fair's planners could not have foreseen the
surprising emergence of a certain 115-pound creature of the female gender.
Whatever else might be said, few could have predicted that a diminutive
young lady not that far removed from wondering where her next meal
might be found would end up being the star of the whole shebang.

A grand celebration marking the centennial of the founding of the City
of Chicago had been proposed as early as 1923, but it wasn't until
January 5, 1928, that a nonprofit corporation was formed for the purpose of
"the holding of a World's Fair in Chicago in the year 1933." The U.S.
Congress followed suit, passing a joint resolution authorizing the President
to invite the nations of the world to participate.

At a time when it was little more than a village, home to some 350 settlers,
the City of Chicago was originally incorporated as a town in 1833. Its actual
settlement — by white people, that is — dates back another half century to
1803 when Captain John Whistler was ordered to lead his men to the
mouth of the Chicago River, there to construct a fort to guard the northwest
frontier. A detailed replica of Fort Dearborn was one of the main exhibits at

the 1933 Fair. Oddly, Captain Whistler's grandson was responsible for supplying the only other female attraction at the fair who could honestly claim to be drawing as much attention as Miss Rand.

The Chicago of the late 1920s had come a long way since its founding. Indeed, it was one of the largest municipalities in the world. The city's leading citizens were determined to burnish its image and make Chicago known for something other than its cows or its mobsters. When construction for the fair began, Chicagoans shared the general enthusiasm abroad in the land. A stock market collapse and resulting depression were the furthest things from their minds.

On June 27, 1932, less than a year before the fair's scheduled opening on the Chicago lakeshore, the Democratic Convention had convened in nearby Chicago Stadium. New York Governor Franklin Delano Roosevelt had secured the presidential nomination on the fourth ballot and, breaking with tradition, had flown to Chicago to accept the nomination in person. On July 2nd, after decrying the effects of the Depression on working people and outlining his program for recovery, FDR concluded his acceptance speech with the now famous statement: "I pledge myself to a new deal for the American people." In the national election held on Tuesday, November 8, 1932, he had carried all but six states, defeating Republican candidate Herbert Hoover, the sitting president, in a landslide.

Returning from a fishing trip on February 15, 1933 (a little over two weeks before his inauguration), President-elect Roosevelt and his motorcade drove through Downtown Miami, Florida, to stop off at a political rally in Bayfront Park. Among the throng of supporters waiting there to greet him, Chicago mayor and avid World's Fair booster Anton "Tony" Cermak was seated with a group of party big shots. After addressing the crowd, Roosevelt motioned Cermak over to his open car.

Not far away, Giuseppe Zangara, just five feet tall, stood unsteadily on a shaky metal folding chair, trying to see over the mob. As Mayor Cermak approached, Zangara suddenly produced a .32 caliber pistol and wildly fired off five shots before he could be subdued. Missing the President-elect, he hit five other people, wounding two badly, including Cermak. Transported to the hospital in Roosevelt's car, the mayor reportedly whispered "I'm glad it was me and not you, Mr. President" — words now inscribed on a plaque in Miami's Bayfront Park.

Though Cermak's injury was serious (the bullet had pierced his lung and lodged near his spine), his treatment appeared at first to be successful. From his hospital bed three days later, he reportedly said: "Tell Chicago I'll pull through.... This is a tough old body of mine and a mere bullet isn't going to pull me down. I was elected to be World's Fair mayor and that's what I'm going to be." Sadly, it was wishful thinking.

Roosevelt was sworn into office as the 32nd President of the United States on March 4th —17 days after the failed assassination attempt and not quite three months before the opening of the fair. After suffering for weeks with spiking fevers, pneumonia, delirium, gangrene, and other grave complications, Mayor Anton Cermak died two days later on March 6th.

In those days, criminal matters could be settled in short order. Zangara was charged within hours of the shooting. He pleaded guilty to murder and was sentenced to death.[1] He was seated in Florida's "Old Sparky" and executed on March 20th, a mere two weeks after Cermak died. At the time of the shooting and its aftermath, Sally Rand was appearing just a mile up the road at the Frolics Club in Miami. It must have crossed her mind that taking a break from Chicago and its mobsters had not delivered any real respite from random gunfire.

As FDR began his mission to pull the country out of the Depression, and Sally endeavored to make the most of her assets, the economy continued spiraling downward. The banking system was headed toward a complete nationwide shutdown as President Hoover's term came to an end. And therein lay the problem for the Century of Progress Fair. When first proposed, the American economy was riding the wave of the Roaring Twenties, but as opening day of the fair drew near, the financial prospects of the entire enterprise were seriously in doubt.

The gates of "A Century of Progress International Exposition" officially swung open at 10:00 a.m. on May 27, 1933. Following the model of the 1893 Fair, the 1933 Exposition featured elaborate exhibits from the nations of the world, as well as displays sponsored by major commercial, scientific and industrial enterprises.

While there were several entrances, most visitors entered the fairgrounds at the northern gate and strolled down the Avenue of Flags. This approach brought them to the Hall of Science, a very impressive structure designed by Paul Cret, whose other commissions would include the Federal Reserve Bank of Philadelphia, the Bethesda Naval Hospital and the Duke Ellington Bridge in Washington, D.C. Here, at the entrance to the Hall of Science, a visitor was

---

[1]   On the charge of attempted murder, Zangara insisted on entering a guilty plea, saying: "No point living. Give me electric chair." Sentenced to four separate terms of 20 years, he told the judge, "Don't be stingy, give me hundred." When Mayor Cermak died, Zangara's sentence was changed to death.

introduced not only to the scientific theme of the fair but also to its most impressive display of nudity — John Storrs' formidable sculpture *Knowledge Combating Ignorance*. The sculpture, rendered in white against a brilliant blue background, featured a huge man and a snake, once described as "a giant Promethean, [a] boldly nude and well-endowed figure ready to strike the serpent coiling around his right leg." A modern viewer might well perceive this epitome of masculinity, with his head turned toward his cocked-arm and shoulder, legs spread wide in full frontal exposure, as somewhat homoerotic.

But, however the figure was regarded at the time, those who stood before it were certainly put on notice that their day at the fair might well include an eye-opener or two.

The Century of Progress Exposition had something for everyone. Not interested in the Art Institute? Perhaps the "Midget Village" would be more to your taste. (Where else could you get a haircut in a midget barbershop?) If the Midget Village didn't appeal, you could check out the Sinclair Oil Dinosaur, General Motors' fully functional assembly line, Admiral Byrd's South Polar Flagship, or the 218-foot-tall Havoline Thermometer. Or maybe take a ride in the sky.

After the Paris planners built the iconic Eiffel Tower as an entrance arch for the 1889 Exposition Universelle, and Chicago had followed up by constructing the original "Ferris Wheel" for the 1893 World's Columbian Exposition, people had come to expect that every subsequent World's Fair would also have a signature structure. Designed to fill this role, the massive "Sky-Ride" — an aerial ferry system that transported people across the manmade lagoon at the center of the fair — was the 1933 Chicago Fair's most dominant structure.

THE OTHER WOMAN

And just who was that "other woman" attracting so much attention at the fair? Well, you could find her at the nearby Art Institute. An impressive collection of famous paintings had been assembled for the exhibit, but the most popular among them was an oversized oil simply titled *Arrangement in Grey and Black No.1*, on loan from a museum in Paris. The artist was the grandson of Captain John Whistler, and his famous painting with the rather generic title became more commonly known as *Whistler's Mother*. Despite critical acclaim, the work hadn't drawn much attention when first displayed in 1872. In fact, when other potential buyers showed little interest, the French government picked it up in 1891 for a mere $800 (the equivalent of about $15,000 today). Fifty years later, fairgoers were awed to learn that the picture had been insured for half a million dollars. The painting, also known as *Portrait of the Artist's Mother*, was valued in 2009 at about $30 million. It hangs today in the Musee D'Orsay in Paris.

Passengers would ride in large rocket-shaped, double-decker cabin cars suspended about 215 feet above the ground between two towers 628 feet high and 1,850 feet apart.[2] From their lofty vantage point, those paying the ride's 40-cent fare (25 cents for children) could enjoy a bird's-eye view of the entire fairgrounds and downtown Chicago.[3] For another 40 cents, visitors could take an elevator to the observation decks atop the towers to see parts of four states.

In addition to all the imposing structures and exhibits, the 1933 Chicago World's Fair introduced many consumer products, not least of which was the famous Ingersoll Mickey Mouse wrist watch. Tourists with nothing better to do could visit the Kraft Mayonnaise Kitchen to observe a new salad dressing being prepared in the exclusive Kraft Miracle Whip mixing machine. Visitors could travel through time by way of such exhibits as The World a Million Years Ago and the House of Tomorrow. They might even watch a demonstration of pancakes prepared and served up by Quaker Oats employee Anna Robinson dressed in stereotypical "Mammy" garb as "Aunt Jemima."

In short, there was plenty to see at the Century of Progress. Anyone seeking to be enlightened and educated by the latest advances of the day could spend hour after hour in sublime edification. And, for those of us lowbrows from the sticks who just wanted to be titillated and otherwise entertained, well — there was the Midway.

At the popular Ripley's *Believe It or Not* "Odditorium" you could gawk at Freda Pushnik, the "Little Half Girl" who was born without arms or legs. Or, if she wasn't odd enough for you, you could take a peek at Leonard "Popeye" Perry demonstrating the uncanny ability to pop his eyes out of their sockets, either one at a time, or both at once. Of course, not everything at the Odditorium was so disturbing. Some attractions actually were just "odd." Among these was Lydia McPherson, said to have the longest red hair in the world. Photos depict her with hair touching the floor, even as she stood on a footstool.

---

[2] According to one of the fair's chroniclers, "The two Sky-Ride towers were nicknamed 'Amos' and 'Andy' after the popular radio series, which had begun on station WMAQ in Chicago. Each of the rocket cars was named after a character from the show, including Amos, Andy, Battle Axe, Kingfish, Madame Queen, and Brother Crawford. The series stars, Freeman Gosden (Amos) and Charles Correll (Andy), opened the ride by breaking a bottle of champagne against the Brother Crawford car."

[3] The Sky-Ride transported over 4.5 million people during the fair. It undoubtedly afforded its riders an exciting view, even if somewhat less impressive than the view offered by the original Ferris Wheel at 264 feet.

But the sensation of the day, the most talked about attraction on the Midway
— the inimitable Sally Rand — was holding forth within the cozy confines of
the "Streets of Paris."

Following his success with the Beaux Arts Ball, architect Andrew Rebori
attracted funding from a number of wealthy investors who put him in
charge of designing the Streets of Paris, perhaps the most popular venue at
the fair. Located in the heart of the Midway, the exterior to the Streets of
Paris concession was cleverly designed to resemble the gangway entrance
to a luxury cruise liner. Large lettering proclaimed: "Here's where you'll
get your REAL FRENCH ATMOSPHERE." Fairgoers paid 25 cents for admission
to the complex. As the official guidebook to the fair portrayed it, the Streets
of Paris concession was:

> … Paris moved over to America, for entertainment. Here, in
> narrow stone paved streets, are gendarmes, sidewalk cafes, quaint
> shops, chestnut vendors, strolling artists, milkmaids and
> musicians. There is music and dancing, wax works, and an atelier.
> There is a beauty revue, and clowns, peep shows, a chamber of
> horrors. The streets are named as in Paris, the buildings faithful
> reproductions. There are even some of the famous Parisian
> restaurants.

The Café de la Paix with its colorful striped awnings was the largest of
these restaurants. Much of its seating was outside, as you might imagine.
Its bandstand would become one of the most famous in the land.

Some venues in the concession sported classy French names. Among these
was the Colonie Nudiste, the name of which, while quite straightforward,
was not exactly accurate. Those who offered their coins for an opportunity
to "meet the nudists face to face" ended up feeling pretty silly since peering
through a keyhole revealed nothing more than a mirror image of their own
head resting on a painted naked body.

The enclave encompassing the Streets of Paris attraction[4] covered only about
three acres — not even one percent of the 424 acres occupied by the fair. In

---

[4]   The venue was a major operation, staffed by more than 1,300 employees serving in
       67 distinct attractions. Unlike the Moroccan Village and other nationally sponsored
       exhibits, the Streets of Paris had no official connection to the Nation of France.
       Rather, it was created by a group of Chicago investors who fronted some $300,000 for
       the enterprise. The area's reputation was such that the French ambassador is said to
       have protested the display of a French flag, lest the honor of his noble nation be
       sullied in the eyes of some hayseed from the hinterlands.

the Century of Progress official guidebook, the description of the exhibit consists of only seven lines in a book of 176 pages. Yet, when all the huge exhibits, scientific wonders of the age, and even the "Towering Sky-Ride" had mostly been forgotten, the performances by a fan-dancing young woman in the Streets of Paris would persist in the memory and survive as an iconic symbol of the entire enterprise.

While solid citizens by the thousands were roaming the aisles of the international, industrial, and technology exhibits, more than a few curious gentlemen became inexplicably lost in the crowd, returning to rejoin their families only after a mysterious interlude. "Oh, well," a sheepish husband might have offered, "I was just checking out the baby incubators." Such a man, fresh from a clandestine viewing of Sally's show, might even have managed to sell that explanation. Dr. Martin Couney's baby incubator exhibit, featuring real live premature babies on loan from local hospitals, actually was adjacent to the Streets of Paris. Indeed, after one of her many run-ins with the law, Miss Rand is said to have observed: "those babies are exposing more flesh than I am, but no one is making a fuss about it."

Times being what they were, by 1933, bandleaders like Joe Kayser were taking any job they could find. And so it was that, following successful engagements at such famous Chicago sites as the Aragon Ballroom, Kayser's band accepted a booking to back up a pretty young fan dancer named Sally Rand at the Century of Progress. Hey, it was a living. And, as Joe and his boys soon came to appreciate, the band members had the best seats in the house, with a largely uninterrupted view of Miss Rand's exposed posterior.

Since her fan dance lasted only a few minutes, Sally could perform it as often as 16 times a day. The act seldom varied from an established format. She would make her entrance descending a small flight of stairs wearing a wispy, barely opaque gown. So attired, she would wave large fans overhead and twirl them at her sides. After a few turns around the stage, she would step into the wings and momentarily disappear behind the curtain. When she emerged, her gown would be gone and the fans would be positioned, front and back, in such a way as to make a sort of sandwich of her body.

These ostrich-feather fans were quite large and, fully extended, seemed equal in span to Sally's height.[5] At this point, apparently nude, she would cover the front of her body with one fan while deftly twirling the other above her head. She would then, all in one motion, lift the fan in front and replace it with the other, denying the audience more than a glimpse of her actual flesh. In a twist on the traditional patter of a stage magician, Sally always liked to quip: "The Rand is quicker than the eye."

While most of us enjoy being teased, as a savvy businesswoman Sally understood that paying customers also expect to eventually see the goods. With this in mind, she would usually conclude her dance by facing the audience and raising both fans above her head just as the stage lights were dimming. There, if only for a fleeting moment, the lovely nude body of this charming young woman was fully revealed for all to see.

Or was it? There has been much discussion over the years — did Sally Rand truly perform her act in the nude? The conclusive answer can hardly be left to the recollection of eyewitnesses. After all, the whole point of Sally's performance was to create and preserve a certain air of mystery. "Now you see it, now you don't." But did you really "see it" even when you saw it?

Photographs suggest, and some firsthand accounts assert, that Sally used a thick white body makeup; other accounts say she sometimes wore a sheer body stocking. Lorie Barnes O'Brien, who worked with Sally in 1947-48, says she was nude. Hilda Vincent, a comedienne who worked with her in 1973, said that Sally ordered milliner's silk from New York to make her G-strings. More on all this later.

Fortunately, a 1933 version of Sally's famous fan dance at the Café de la Paix has been preserved in a short, black and white silent film.[6] Regrettably, the sequence featuring Miss Rand lasts no more than 50 seconds. Even so, there she is, in the great outdoors, at the dawn of her fan dancing career — blond hair, high-heeled shoes, big smile, and lithe body— adroitly making the fluid motions of an irrepressible babe in all her glory. She is a total

---

5   Sally's fans were not only large and broad, but also quite heavy (about 7 pounds each). Wind resistance could sometimes be an issue. In the beginning, Sally found that her wrists would become painfully swollen from manipulating them.

6   *Streets of Paris* is one of a set of films about the Century of Progress Exhibition produced by Burton Holmes. A pioneer documentary filmmaker, he coined the term "travelogue" as early as 1897. Available from several online sources, the film is also posted on YouTube (search for "1933 streets of paris"). Sally's fan dance appears in the latter third of the video.

delight and many thanks are owed to the documentary filmmaker for preserving these delightful images.[7]

An eyewitness account, while helpful, still leaves the exact setting of Sally's indoor performances unclear:

> Each night at about 11, Miss Rand walks down a carpeted runway
> to a sunken floor around which sit the customers, most of them
> sipping beer. With only two large fans to hide her nudity, Sally
> dances. The sunken floor, incidentally, is always crowded at
> 11 p.m. On windy nights the crowds are larger and many nights
> are windy there because the floor is about 50 feet from Lake
> Michigan.

Sally's exploits at the fair were getting plenty of press coverage and she was determined to keep it that way. Entertainment reporter Ben Kaufman revealed that she had put a standing reservation for newspapermen on one of the tables at the Café de la Paix for which she and the house paid all the bills.

Once it became clear that Sally was generating big money at the Streets of Paris, others rushed to get in on the act. It wasn't long before "indecent" shows were popping up all over the Midway. As chatter about these performances spread, the community's moral antennae soon detected the threat posed by all the gaiety. Sally had hardly cashed her first paycheck before the squad leaders of indignation were on the case.

Mary Belle

Years before, when Mary Belle Withrow's father left his family behind to seek his fortune in the Klondike Gold Rush, her mother had moved the 12-year-old girl and her three sisters from Wisconsin to Chicago, where the girls attended public school. At age 27, Mary Belle married prominent physician Richard Vance Spencer. Not inclined to settle for a life of quiet domesticity, she chose to continue her education, earning a Bachelor of Laws degree from Northwestern University, Class of 1918, five days shy of her 36th birthday.

---

[7] It remains unclear how Sally's daily performances were staged. While the Café de la Paix had both indoor and outdoor seating, the dance preserved in this video may not represent the norm. Indeed, it may have been staged solely for the benefit of the filmmaker since lighting conditions would have been less than optimal for interior filming. And the proprietors could not very well have charged a fee for an outdoor performance visible to all passersby. (Notice the absence of a backing band, with accompaniment furnished simply by accordion and violin.)

That same year, at a time when women in Illinois had not yet secured the right to vote, Governor Frank Lowden appointed Mary Belle Spencer to the office of Public Guardian of Cook County. A year later, she gave birth to her first daughter. A second followed in 1921. (Mary Belle, Jr. and Victoria would make news of their own in years to come.) Mrs. Spencer resolutely pursued her legal career despite public discussion as to whether a mother of two young girls could successfully combine motherhood with a career.

By 1933, at 50 years of age Mary Belle had become well known for her crusades on behalf of public morality. By this time, the actions of another strong-minded, self-made, and uninhibited woman had come to her attention, and she was not amused. Where was the public outrage? Where were the police? If no one else was willing to bear the burden, she would take it upon herself. Determined to clean up the Century of Progress International Exposition, Mary Belle rushed a telegram to her congressman demanding that Washington investigate the questionable "entertainment" being presented on the Midway.

A handsome and stylish ex-boxer, Congressman Fred A. Britten, Republican from Chicago, already had a full plate wrestling with FDR's ambitious new agenda. On June 7th, he wired a reply to Mrs. Spencer:

> I have every confidence that A Century of Progress officials are making the fair attractive to people of every walk of life. If the Streets of Paris depicts life in its most artistic phases, it will certainly open the eyes of Kansas and Oklahoma. The adoption of a resolution for the congressional investigation at this time would seriously interfere with the President's legislative program for early adjournment of the congress.

Rebuffed, but undeterred, Mary Belle Spencer was just getting started. Having struck out with her appeal to Congress, she turned to the Superior Court of Cook County, filing a petition seeking a court order to enjoin "lewd and lascivious dances and exhibitions" at the Streets of Paris. She was particularly offended by two attractions: Sally's act at the Café de la Paix and appearances by model Dorothy Kibbee at the popular "life class" for artists — an artist being anyone willing to pay 25 cents to be ushered in the door, issued a sketch pad and pencil, and seated inside the so-called class.

Mrs. Spencer didn't mince words. Her petition alleged that the nude exhibitions were "a cesspool of iniquity, a condition of depravity and total disregard of purity and display of the most disgraceful lewdness and abandon ever publicly shown in any institution of the character such as this Century of Progress purports to represent." Moreover, she added, this "licentious and libidinous assortment of carnal shame" would negatively impact the reputation of Illinois at large. Whatever else you might say about her, the lady had a way with words.[8]

Mary Belle convinced the court to issue subpoenas to appear and took it upon herself to serve the papers personally. On the night of July 17th, when she arrived at the entrance to the life class, she found Miss Kibbee engaged in a posing session, so she gave the subpoena to Roy Hall, general manager of the Streets of Paris, who promised to see that it was properly served. But Mary Belle *was* able to confront Sally Rand in her dressing room backstage at the Café de la Paix and present the summons face to face.

If Mrs. Spencer had a poor opinion of Sally, the feeling was certainly mutual. In a 1973 letter to James Quinlan, Sally characterized the state of affairs between them:

> *The day the Century of Progress opened, Madam Spencer set out as a committee of one to censor fair exhibits. She cited the following:*
>
> *The Hall of Science: The transparent man that showed "in living color" the respiratory, digestive and nervous systems. He was complete with genitals. It was the latter to which she objected.*
>
> *The East Indian Exhibit: An ancient golden statue of the god Siva — with 8 arms. One hand rested on the right thigh near the groin. Mary Belle claimed masturbation.*
>
> *The Historic Chicago Indian Massacre: A wax replica of an Indian scalping a white woman showed "cleavage," and his prone position atop the female indicated "pogery"![9]*

---

[8]   It has been suggested that the whole thing was a setup. Supposedly, backers of the exposition had brought in publicist Ben Serkowitch to engineer a boost in the fair's financial well-being. After checking out the dancers in various venues, he had settled on Sally as "an experienced trouper — one to be depended on in any contingency." Posing as an aggrieved citizen, Serkowitch then placed a call to attorney Mary Belle Spencer ("known for her strict ideas on morals and public behavior") and "chided her [for] standing by and permitting a nude woman to flaunt her nakedness daily in public." Another report claimed that Mary Belle was "not one bit suspicious that she was but a cog in a tremendous wheel of publicity."

[9]   If you can find a definition of this term, you may have a future as a paid researcher. Perhaps Sally meant to say "buggery" (which you are welcome to look up for yourself).

The Ford Exhibit: An internal combustion Ford motor, cut away to show how gasoline converted from liquid to vapor, mixed with oxygen, expanded, thereby lifting the sleeve of pistons, etc. "All those things going up and down like that." Pornographic.

And of course . . . Me, Sally Rand, at the Streets of Paris.

The next morning, Tuesday, July 18th, the courtroom of Superior Judge Joseph B. David was called to order with a crowd of interested parties in attendance. Attorney Jay J. McCarthy represented petitioner Mary Belle Spencer and attorney J. B. Martineau represented Streets of Paris, Inc. An attorney representing A Century of Progress, Thomas H. Slusser, challenged the legal sufficiency of Mrs. Spencer's claim.

Judge David had a reputation as a no-nonsense jurist, not to mention being somewhat fiery on occasion. Two years earlier, he had heard and disposed of 35 cases in a two-hour period, successfully cutting down on the population of the Cook County jail.

Getting the proceedings underway, Mary Belle's attorney, Jay McCarthy, expounded:

> ... this is an action to abate a nuisance which is corrupting public morals by lewd and lascivious exhibitions. We will show that one woman dances with nothing but a pair of fans about her and that in other exhibits women twist and turn about without wearing even a fig leaf. It's disgraceful.

Citing a variant of the well-known phrase "beauty is in the eye of the beholder," Judge David interrupted McCarthy to observe: "Honi soit qui mal y pense." McCarthy, who apparently knew his French ("evil to him who evil thinks"), responded by inviting the judge to witness the shows for himself, seemingly confident that the judge would recognize evil when he saw it.

Various press accounts reported that the ensuing colloquy went something like this:

> Judge David: I've never been there and I don't want to go. The Streets of Paris could starve to death for all I care. When I go to the fair, I go to see the exhibits and perhaps to enjoy a good glass of beer.

> Attorney McCarthy: But your honor. There is a blond lady who comes out naked in the Streets of Paris with nothing more than two

ostrich feather fans to distinguish her from Mother Eve! She dances
before everybody — paying customers I mean.

Judge David: You don't say. Is she pretty? Is the dance pretty?

Attorney McCarthy: Why, yes, she's pretty, but she gyrates
around without any clothes. It isn't right!

Judge David: Why not?

Attorney McCarthy: The girl is nude, your honor. Sally Rand is
nude as a pair of tongs, except for two fans. And when the wind
blows off the lake they don't count for much.

Judge David: What if the wind does blow? Is nudity a crime?
They've been dancing in the nude for years. Take for example, the
wood nymphs. They prance about without a stitch and no one
pays any attention to it. If nudity is such a crime, why doesn't
somebody put pants on them? In Canada we have the Doukhobor
nudist colonies.[10] In Japan, there is nothing unusual about entire
families bathing together in the nude. The court holds no brief for
the prurient and the ignorant. Let them walk out if they wish.
Fifty years ago, they tried to arrest Dr. Mary Walker for wearing
pants. Now women believe they are not in style unless they *do*
wear them. Whether they wear them or whether they don't is all
right with me. And if this Sally Rand wants to go without them,
that's all right with me too.

Attorney McCarthy: But your honor, consider the influence of
such lewdness on our youth!

Judge David: As far as lewdness is concerned, I have my own
opinions, but I don't have to state them here. I could, but I won't.
Some people would like to put pants on a horse. I hear that even
some in this community are concerned that the cherubs on the
roof of the county building aren't wearing diapers. Someday
someone is likely to climb up there and drape them.

---

[10] Originally a group of Russian immigrants who fled religious persecution in the late
1890s and ended up in Canada, the Doukhobors gained notoriety by parading in the
nude as a form of protest against materialism. Radical pacifists, they held that human
skin, a creation of God, was more perfect than clothing, which was nothing but the
imperfect work of human hands. The group was fresh in the judge's mind as, just in
the past year, the police of British Columbia had confronted hundreds of Doukhobors,
employed "itch powder" against their bare skin, and herded them into trucks. The
adults were incarcerated and the children were placed in foster homes and orphanages.

Attorney McCarthy: But your honor, the models in some of these so-called art classes are presenting themselves without benefit of coverage.

Judge David: There is no harm in exposing the human body. It is a beautiful work of nature. Artist's models can't get a dime from me. But if someone else wants to pay, that's their business. If the officials of A Century of Progress want to encourage art or if a woman wiggles about with a fan, it is not the business of this court. Despite your being offended, the other side responds "What of it?" I agree. Thousands of art students come here to pursue their endeavors. Why deprive them of the opportunity? The statute under which you act is purely of a criminal nature designed to afford a way of action against houses of assignation. If you wish to end what you term lewdness, the proper procedure is to go to the state's attorney and have the officials of the concession and of the fair arrested.

Attorney McCarthy: Your honor, the fan dancer Sally Rand and one of the nude models Dorothy Kibbee were both subpoenaed last night by my client Mrs. Spencer. Would you care to hear their testimony?

Judge David: I've said all I have to say.

Attorney McCarthy (making one last attempt): But judge, surely you must consider the impact of these exhibitions on the thousands of visitors to the fair. It is shocking!

Judge David: Shocking? I was watching an exhibit in the Hall of Science a short time ago. It showed the evolution of the human race. There were a few old ladies around who remarked that it was terrible, shocking. That goes to show how some people can be shocked. As for people who pay to see these dancers and models, if you ask me, they are just a lot of boobs who come to see a woman wiggle with a fan or pose without fig leaves. So we have a certain number of boobs and while we have them they will be catered to. Patrons come to the Streets of Paris to see what they never saw before. If they are shocked, they can go home. If you think this court is going to reform the world, you are badly mistaken. People were nude, I suppose, millions of years ago. As far as I am concerned, all these charges are just a lot of old stuff. Case dismissed for want of equity.

Judge David's "pants on a horse" quip was featured in newspaper accounts of the trial across the country, many on the front page. In later years Sally was fond of saying: "This profound opinion was rendered on a slow news day, a day when the Pope hadn't raped the Queen."

Chicago newspapers responded to Judge David's remarks with cleverly arranged pictures of horses wearing pants, of roof statuary adorned with trousers, and of "September Morn" in a bathing suit.

Rather than feeling intimidated, Sally's competitors on the Midway were quite envious:

> The rest of the girls who dance more or less nude at the Century of Progress Exposition pouted today because Sally Rand has been getting all the attention. "Why don't they arrest me too?" queried Miss Jean, a dancer at the Folies Bergere. ... Dorothy Wahl, who appears in the Oriental Village show ... also joined the protest. "What makes those reformers think I'm so respectable?" she asked. "Is it because my hair is so long it falls down around my knees? If that's it, believe me, I'll get a bob tomorrow."

With disposable cash in short supply, competition at the fair was intense. Many attractions posted a "barker" outside who, through a constant stream of enthusiastic patter, did his best to entice wavering patrons to part with their hard-earned coins. Barkers were often quite clever:

> From the top of her shapely head to the soles of her dainty feet, every muscle, every tissue, every fiber of her beautiful body vibrates and quivers in a poetry of motion that is beautiful to behold.

This accolade was not about Sally.[11] No, this spiel was the handiwork of Pat Delaney, the fellow who claimed first prize in a contest to select the best barker on the Midway at the 1933 Fair. His award-winning ballyhoo was delivered at the Oriental Village in support of a young lady who called herself "Little Egypt" and danced in little more than a filmy veil that had a way of sliding to the floor whenever Delaney wished to emphasize a point. Elsewhere on the Midway, still another dancer, 21-year-old Zeanes Ali "of Alexandria, Egypt" was also calling herself "Little Egypt" and undulating

---

[11] Seventeen-year-old Claude Kirchner filled this role for Sally Rand. Few fairgoers would remember the tall skinny kid imploring onlookers to enter the Café de la Paix, but years later he built quite a following as the ringmaster on *Super Circus*, a big hit in the early days of television. (Fun fact: As a young man, longtime newscaster Mike Wallace also appeared on this show dressed as a carnival barker and hawking Peter Pan peanut butter.)

to the delight of an audience of greybeards, each with a supposed academic interest in "oriental" dance.

Somewhere on the South Side of Chicago, a matronly housewife got wind of the Midway action and must have thought to herself: "Hey, wait a minute. What's going on here? I'm the original Little Egypt." This housewife's name was Farida Mazar Spyropoulos and she had a costume in the back of her closet that she would soon be dusting off.

Just as the 1933 Fair had its Italian Village and Streets of Paris, the Columbian Exposition of 1893 (also in Chicago) had the Algerian Village and A Street in Cairo. Those who know about the original Little Egypt may also "know" that she was the Middle Eastern belly dancer who caused a sensation at the 1893 Exposition. As the star of the Midway, she supposedly drew such big crowds that the fair's shaky financial prospects were turned around solely due to her performances.

Surprisingly, careful research has revealed no dancer at the 1893 Columbian Exposition known as "Little Egypt." This is not to say there weren't popular "oriental" dancers at the fair. Indeed, quite a few were performing in such concessions as the Algerian Village, the Turkish Village, and A Street in Cairo. It's just that nary a one of them was billed as "Little Egypt." Many of these ladies performed the "danse du ventre" or belly dance — the well-known Middle Eastern dance that features undulations of the torso that were quite shocking to proper society at the time. (It is from these performances that the "Hoochie Koochie" was born.)

The impression that there was an actual living, breathing individual called "Little Egypt" at the Columbian Exhibition arose barely three years after the event closed in 1894. This was in large part due to an enterprising young girl named Ashea Wabe who, using the name Little Egypt, performed a provocative dance at a private dinner party held at Sherry's, a chic restaurant on Fifth Avenue in New York City. Authorities were tipped off that a shameless young woman would be dancing in the nude. Police raided the premises and the sordid details were splashed across the front pages of New York papers.

The episode exploded into the headlines as the infamous "Awful Seely's Dinner" affair, the principals landed in court, and the public followed the proceedings with drool cups firmly attached to their chins. Consider this comment from the *New York World* of January 9, 1897:

> It is expected that the nature of the testimony will become very much more disgusting than even yesterday, [as] "Little Egypt,"

Minnie Renwood and other women who have made confessions
to Capt. Chapman of the disgraceful scenes enacted at the dinner
will testify.

In all likelihood, the scandalous Ashea Wabe never set foot on the grounds
of the Chicago fair, or on the banks of the Nile for that matter, but she
continued to cash in on her image as best she could.[12] Although Miss Wabe
garnered the lion's share of press coverage, another claimant to the name
actually *was* in a group of dancers performing at A Street in Cairo. She was
Farida Mazar, and after a period of years she too began billing herself as
"Little Egypt." Mazar temporarily gave up her belly dancing career in 1905
when she married restaurant owner Gus Spyropoulos and contented
herself with her role as a housewife. Until 1933, that is.

Learning that Sally Rand and a couple of faux "Little Egypt" dancers were
raking in big bucks at the World's Fair, Farida figured that maybe she
could manage to put together a few Depression-era greenbacks for herself.
Sure enough, Farida Mazar Spyropoulos retrieved her costume from the
back of the closet, made a few phone calls, and soon found herself onstage
again, performing as "the original Little Egypt" in the Oriental Village. At
age 62, Mazar may have had a few grey hairs but, as United Press
reported, she could still "toss off a shimmy and a graceful pirouette
between puffs on a cigarette."

Questioned about the absence of attire on so many other dancers at the fair,
Farida indicated she had no interest in performing in the nude herself,
gruffly telling a reporter: "I have never lowered myself to vulgarity. I'd
never go before an audience like that. You see what I wear, seven different
pieces of apparel — count 'em."

So, if no one can successfully claim to have been the original Little Egypt, or
if indeed there never was such a person, where did the name come from in
the first place? If no one performed at the 1893 Columbian Exposition as
"Little Egypt," why would Ashea Wabe and Farida Mazar, among others
choose to adopt the moniker? Why would it be meaningful to persuade
potential audiences that you were the original of a person who never existed?

Well, we have a theory. Just because there was no such person doesn't mean
people didn't think there was. Before radio, television, or newspapers with
national circulation, a lot of information was passed by word of mouth. The

---

[12] Ashea Wabe ultimately passed into obscurity, but not before topping the bill at
Chicago's Clark Street Dime Museum, sharing the stage with Cora Beckwith and her
act — "World's Champion Woman Swimmer and Her Funny School of Fat Girl
Bathers." Gee, we'd have paid to see that.

section of the 1893 Fair known as A Street in Cairo could easily have come to be known as "Little Egypt" in the same way that ethnic neighborhoods in major cities are called Germantown, Little Italy, and the like. It's no great leap to imagine that fairgoers, impressed by the sensual dancers, may have remarked to friends and relatives: "Hey, Charlie, if you're going to the fair, be sure to see Little Egypt." It wouldn't take many repetitions for the venue's nickname to become conflated with the dancers themselves.

S ally had been building a loyal following since day one. Invited to speak to the Chicago Junior Chamber of Commerce as a luncheon guest, she offered some perspective on her career:

> I haven't been out of a day's work since I took my clothes off.
> Heretofore, as a ballet dancer, I wasn't so hot. Engagements were
> fewer and the money wasn't much. Now I'm earning an excellent
> living as a fan dancer with more offers of jobs than I know what to
> do with. I look better, feel better and act better without clothes than
> in them. Why wear them?

Sally had interpreted Judge David's ruling as license to do as she pleased; but her reprieve proved to be short-lived. Fair organizers had contrived a "three-point" coverage decree to shield the public from female breasts and the pubic area, but these guidelines were honored more in breach than in observance. Bowing to persistent protests, Mayor Edward J. Kelly finally agreed to look into the matter.

On the evening of July 31st, less than two weeks after Judge David's pronouncements, the mayor set off on a personal inspection tour to judge the "indecent" performances for himself. A 57-year-old Roman Catholic who had previously worked for 30 years in Chicago's Sanitary Department, Kelly surveyed the situation at length and applied his own sense of propriety. Declaring that he was "shocked and amazed," Kelly was particularly offended by three attractions — Ernie Young's rhumba and nude show at the Manhattan Gardens, "Lady Godiva" riding a camel, and the fan dance of an apparently unclad young woman at the Streets of Paris.

"Clothes or close!" became the order of the day. Mayor Kelly immediately ordered the proprietors of these "indecent" shows to either clean up their acts or be shut down. His appraisal was markedly ungenerous:

> They are rotten, and if the showmen continue to put on these lewd
> and vulgar demonstrations, they will be closed. At the old fair
> there were hootchy kootchy dancers, but they at least had some
> clothes on. We will not permit these dances by naked women.

"Nude dancing at A Century of Progress is at an end," declared the daily papers on August 2nd. Detectives closed three of the livelier shows at the Oriental Village — one of which, "Theater Comique," featured flamboyant female impersonators. Most of the shows made at least a token effort to behave, but compliance was reluctant at best. Hot-Cha-San at the Old Mexico concession donned a coat of gilt paint, while Sally Rand acquiesced with a wisp of gauze.

As the issue escalated, supporters and detractors began weighing in. The fair became Exhibit A in the ongoing struggle between those of a more puritanical bent and those who considered themselves more sophisticated. When Mayor Kelly supposedly turned "bashful pink" at seeing female dancers clad in "purely hypothetical costumes," the Italian Village's manager offered this acerbic assessment: "I doubt the mayor is a reliable weathervane when it comes to art and morality."

While Sally Rand surely wasn't the only provocation, the urge to go nude was spreading like wildfire. In late July it was reported that "the 'raw-raw' boys of Philip Yarrow's Illinois Vigilance Committee are busy these sunny days collecting the naked facts on Chicago's ultra-modernistic craze for nudism. For Chicago suddenly has become 'nude conscious.'"[13] Having visited the fair's concessions "in various disguises ... night after night," Reverend Yarrow's critique of Sally was none too charitable:

> I have never seen such a disgusting display of nakedness in my life. Every night at 10:30 o'clock a girl named Sally Rand comes out with nothing on to cover her but two fans and dances before men, women and children. It is evident that she is nude. It's absolutely rotten.

The whole uproar brings to mind words reminiscent of H. L. Mencken's description of Puritanism — it is the haunting fear that someone, somewhere, may be enjoying himself.

---

[13]   Rev. Philip Yarrow, the white-haired President of the Illinois Vigilance Association, had been laboring at this sort of thing for quite a while. In 1921, Yarrow had denounced jazz music as the reason that girls go wrong: "From the dance palaces of Chicago, from the dance rooms in country towns come girls whose entrance into the life of moral subnormality was accompanied by the music of the jazz orchestra." He had alleged that in the prior year his association had traced the downfall of 1,000 girls to the music's influence, leading him to conclude that "feeble-minded morality is the first result of the weird, neurotic strains of the so-called jazz orchestra."

Perhaps public sentiment was best expressed by Chicagoan James Thomas when he was moved to dash off a letter to the editor of the *Chicago Tribune*, published on August 5th:

> So King Kelly and Sheriff Meyering are going to safeguard our morals by making the skin dancers put on some clothes? It is to laugh. What are they trying to do, ruin the fair? Don't they know that all the people from out in the sticks where they still call them "leg shows" are saving their corn money to come up to Chicago and see if the fan dancers really don't wear nothing nohow? First it was Belle (Don't Forget to Use My Name) Spencer ... that [was] trying to make the fair a 9 o'clock show in a 1 o'clock town. Now it's King Kelly and our sleepy sheriff that are trying to get a few headlines in the papers by cleaning up the fair.... Why begrudge the yokels this pitiful glory in their hometown sessions at the ice cream parlor or the horseshoe lot?

Sally's extraordinary success had come about so suddenly and in such an unconventional manner that her family back in Glendora must have been both astonished and ambivalent. Her Aunt Lucy's assessment probably summed up their reaction best: "I winced when informed of her dance, loving her as I did; but when I saw it under an electric moonlight, a white statue wafting the great white fans in the dreamy dance, I was enthralled by its beauty."

While Millicent Hearst may have been taken aback by the disruptive appearance of "Lady Godiva" at her charitable gala the night before the exposition's grand opening, her husband William Randolph Hearst had a different take on the matter. With a small financial interest in the fair, the newspaper mogul was on hand that summer to sign the large gold guestbook in which the autographs of important visiting dignitaries were recorded. The president of the exposition had given Hearst "the A-1 treatment," escorting him to the guestbook and turning the page to the next available spot. Momentarily rattled by what he saw, he had hurriedly skipped forward a few pages before passing the book to Hearst. It seems Sally had signed the book only a short time before, writing: "Sally Rand, I'm the little gal who made this damn fair famous." Observing his host's sleight of hand, the curious Mr. Hearst flipped back the pages to see for himself. Just under Sally's signature, he added: "William Randolph Hearst, one of her fans."

W ith the fair drawing thousands of out-of-town visitors to Chicago, downtown theaters and hotels had beefed up their entertainment programs to attract the growing after-hours clientele. Sophie Tucker, who in later years would be billed as the "Last of the Red Hot Mammas," was heading up a show at the 225 Club; only blocks away, Evelyn Nesbit Thaw, who gained notoriety as "the girl in the red velvet swing" and became the centerpiece of the famous Stanford White murder trial, was singing at Club Alabam; just a mile up the street Ted Weems and his Orchestra were holding forth at The Blackhawk; and bandleaders Guy Lombardo and Ted ("Is everybody happy?") Lewis were hosting big shows at The Dells Road-house,[14] 20 miles northwest of Chicago in Morton Grove.

And at the fairgrounds themselves? As one promotional sheet declared: "Suddenly hundreds of Fan Dancers joined the race — the tall, the lean, the short and the fat regardless of figure or size, they proclaimed themselves, Fan Dancers for 'Art's' sake, for nickels and dimes and what have you."

Faith

With all the skin action taking place in the Second City, some may have wondered what had happened to the "original" fan dancer, Faith Bacon. Actually, the 23-year-old was still commanding the attention of many an eyeball at the Monte Carlo Casino in Manhattan. Although things were going very well in New York, when word of the clamor in Chicago came to her attention, Faith was curious about the goings on, knowing in her heart that *she* was the one who had originally created the fan dance. If Sally was packing them in for several shows a day, Faith saw no reason why she couldn't do the same. Sure, she was doing okay at the Monte Carlo, but the Depression was just as real in Gotham as anywhere else. And, so, assuming a risk that only the most confident among us are willing to take, the alluring Miss Bacon took a deep breath, picked herself up, and headed for the Windy City.

D uring the first week of August 1933, in the heart of the Loop, the Chicago Theatre featured an all-star bill that included the rotund "ton of fun" Johnny Perkins and a group of popular singing and dancing

---

[14] One of several roadhouses in the Chicago area reportedly under the control of Al Capone's crime syndicate, The Dells was the infamous site of the hoax abduction of con man and swindler John "Jake the Barber" Factor. Chief investigator on the case was Capt. Daniel "Tubbo" Gilbert. The ensuing trial vied with the fair for daily headlines.

midgets. Moreover, those who attended the theater on Friday, August 4th, were in for a special treat, not to mention quite a commotion.

With Mayor Kelly's crackdown at the fair threatening her livelihood, Sally had contracted for a one-week engagement, joining the star-studded show at the Chicago Theater. Her first appearance was at 1:30 in the afternoon. But, no sooner had she stepped into the wings after her dance than Sergeant Harry Costello and Policewoman Bessie McShane approached. As the policewoman raised one of Sally's fans to take a look, Sally screamed. Sally's brother Harold attempted to explain: "You have nothing on her," he asserted. "You mean *she* has nothing on her," countered Costello. Johnny Perkins then interposed his considerable girth between them and Sally retreated to her dressing room. Persistent policewoman McShane followed.

As Sally related to Studs Turkel many years later:

> This enormous policewoman, a giantess, came crashing through the scrim curtain. I thought she was a sex maniac. Here I am locked in my dressing room with a tiny little reporter trying to get a story. The police sirens are going, and the whole detective squad is out there.

Finally emerging in white silk pajamas, Sally was sufficiently attired to submit to arrest. Claiming she had been assisted by others in making her brief escape, the officers corralled a carload of theater people who were also taken to the station. The group included Sally, her brother Harold, her African-American maid Mattie Wheeler, and her theater production manager Louis Lipstone. Sally and Lipstone were charged with staging an indecent exhibition, the others with disorderly conduct. All were released on personal bonds.

The entire assembly, including officers Costello and McShane, returned to the Chicago Theater where Sally was scheduled to perform again at 3:30 that afternoon. Officer McShane produced a supply of gauze, safety pins and adhesive tape, saying: "Either you put on some of this or you go to the station house." "OK," Sally parried, "but it is not very artistic."

"Maybe not," McShane countered, "but it covers the law."

Sally proceeded to perform her fan dance, wearing her usual greasepaint and a little gauze in strategic places. Still, despite her best intentions or perhaps in response to encouragement from the audience, the gauze somehow "slipped off" during the act, so that it ended up covering neither the law nor anything else.

The constabulary was on the case. Bursting onstage through the curtain, Sergeant Costello laid hands on Sally's shoulders. At first she managed to slip away. After all, grabbing an agile young woman in greasepaint is not unlike chasing down a greased pig. "I couldn't help it," she protested to McShane, "it dropped off." The explanation fell on deaf ears. Sally was arrested once again.

This time, however, she was in no mood to be transported in the "nasty" patrol wagon. She insisted that unless she was allowed to dress and go to court in a taxi she was prepared to go "as is." Costello and McShane relented, and Sally went to court in her silk pajamas, where she was once again charged with indecent exposure. Theater manager Lipstone was also charged and both were released on bond of $400 each (collectively about $15,000 today).

Word spread. An expectant early evening crowd filed into the Chicago Theater. At 6:30 p.m. Sally repeated her performance, and so did the police. At the station, a pint-sized policewoman advised her: "Honey, don't worry about it. It wouldn't make a difference if you were wrapped up in the backdrop. They'd still arrest you."

Just as with Miss Rand's epidermis, there was more to all of this than met the eye. Mayor Kelly, who had inherited the office just five months earlier following the shooting death of Mayor Cermak, had himself been a target of ongoing unfavorable press exposing his involvement in several tax scandals.[15] The mayor was perfectly happy to have someone else's travails hog the headlines for a while. Nor were Sally's promoters necessarily unhappy about all the publicity she was getting. A cynic might even suggest that they had advised her to perform in a way that would assure an arrest worthy of press coverage.

That night at the 8:20 show, Sally tried a diversionary move by donning a costume, but the police decided to hang around and, when she performed the fan dance yet again, she was arrested for the fourth time in the same day. This final arrest was "technical" in nature, so a fourth trip to the station was averted. Instead, Sally was permitted to return to the Streets of Paris to carry out her regular engagement at the fair. Policewoman McShane tagged along.

---

[15]   Mayor Kelly's scandals included not only allegations that he had mismanaged local property taxes but also charges that he had misreported personal income to the IRS. Also, back in 1930, he had been indicted for bribery and conspiracy to defraud taxpayers out of $5,000,000 (an indictment that was quashed in 1931).

In all fairness, Sally had been warned that a policeman would be attending her show that day with pad and pencil, taking notes on the state of her attire. "He can leave his pencil at home and throw his pad away," Sally reportedly said. "He will have no notes to take."

Notes or not, it had been a long day and would be a short night. Sally was scheduled for arraignment on Saturday morning and would end up pleading her case that day before two judges in two separate court rooms. Faced with possible fines or imprisonment, the whole entourage just hoped that the matter might be settled once and for all.

It was not to be.

CHAPTER TEN

The Most Famous Woman in America

> How idiotic civilization is. Why be given a body if you
> have to keep it shut up in a case like a rare, rare fiddle?
> ~ Katherine Mansfield, *Bliss and Other Stories*

Perfectly beautiful. These are the words that greeted readers on Saturday, August 5th, in the *Chicago Tribune* review of Sally's fan dance. While the front page of that same edition featured a detailed account of her arrests — four times the previous day — for putting on an "indecent exhibition," Sally's performances at the Chicago Theatre had delighted the paper's theater critic "Mae Tinee":[1]

> Perfectly beautiful — as presented and lighted. Airy, exquisite,
> artistic! So adept is Miss Rand with her fans, so cunning the hand
> at the colored light switch, that you're good if you can tell where
> body starts and fans stop. The lady and her huge softly waving
> plumes seem one.... If there's anything indecent about the fan
> dance I couldn't see it.

Bolstered by conflicting assessments of her dance, Sally's attorney, Nat Ruvell (a former assistant state's attorney), proceeded to seek a court order to restrain the police from further interfering with "her physical expression of the arts." And so it was that, bright and early on Saturday morning, Chicago's most notorious dancer found herself on the docket in two separate Cook County courtrooms.

Sally's first appearance was before Judge Charles A. Williams — the magistrate from whom she was seeking the injunction. Her attorney declared that being arrested four times in the same day on trumped up charges was just

---

[1] Between 1915 and 1966, "Mae Tinee" was the nom de plume used by a number of movie critics writing for the *Chicago Tribune*. In 1924, the job was filled by Maurine Dallas Watkins, the same person who in 1926 wrote the play that would later be adapted into the award-winning musical *Chicago*. In 1969, the *Tribune* movie critic chores were assigned to a 23-year-old newcomer — Gene Siskel.

too much, saying: "The police are harassing her. One arrest was enough to test the matter."

Enough was enough. But Ruvell's most urgent pleas fell on deaf ears. The elderly Judge Williams was unpersuaded, saying that he could see no particular reason for protecting Sally from the police.

Sally then headed to the Women's Court to face charges of engaging in an indecent performance. On the way, she was confronted by four girls in white dresses, each carrying a copy of the Bible. Identifying themselves as evangelists, they advised her that she was "not on the righteous road." Speaking for the group, Miss Ethel Ruby Willitts of Lafayette, Indiana, addressed Sally directly, piously declaring her intention to "save you from yourself. Any of us girls could have gone the same way as you have, but we saw the light in time. We have been praying for you and we hope to convert you to mending your ways." Urged by Miss Willitts to attend one of her nightly tent meetings, Sally brushed by the young woman, saying: "I'll think about it."

According to press reports, the evangelists and their press agent remained in the courtroom all day hoping for an opportunity to burst into song. It never came, but Willitts approached Sally once again during a lull in the proceedings, to advise her that "The Bible says it is not nice to pose in the nude." Sally countered: "God has given me a beautiful body. Why shouldn't I share that beauty with others?" Miss Willitts' sober reply: "God has also given you a beautiful soul. Why not save it?" [2]

A heady consideration, to be sure, but for the moment Sally was consumed with the matter at hand. Judge Erwin J. Hasten had asked Sally whether she tried to keep herself covered at all times while onstage. "I do," she declared, "with the exception that at the finish I lean the fans on my shoulder. I hold that pose through four bars of music. I cover myself in whitewash in order to give the appearance of a statue. It is all very artistic." The judge then declined Sally's offer to demonstrate that her dance was all for art's sake, saying that he might find time over the weekend to see her show. The case was then continued until Monday.

---

[2]   Miss Willitts held a series of revival and healing meetings during a 17-week period coincident with the Chicago Fair. According to the website www.healingandrevival.com, she was a highly controversial revivalist and her style was quite flamboyant. Her meetings featured large choirs with as many as 300 members, as well as a full orchestra. ("She had little education and she was as much an entertainer as a preacher.") Willitts elicited a strong response from those who heard her, some claiming miraculous healings, others denouncing her as a fraud.

The judge did, in fact, attend a performance that very evening. And, over that same weekend, police detective Dennis H. Parkerson also found time to take in the show. When the hearing resumed on Monday, the veteran police officer appeared as the state's star witness, testifying that, at one point during her performance, "Miss Rand's entire body from her head to her foot was revealed nude"— adding that, despite his long experience inspecting burlesque shows, for him to be abashed by a dance was a new experience.

Taking the witness stand, Sally claimed the reason she performed without clothing was that "the feathers of my fans would catch in the clothes, and I wouldn't [have been] able to use my fans the way that is necessary for the dance." Momentarily charmed by the presence before him, Judge Hasten leaned down from the bench to tell Sally that he had seen her show on Saturday night and that she was a "beautiful artistic dancer." Admiration aside, he nevertheless fined her $25, saying: "The only human being that should be allowed to appear nude in public is a baby." He further advised Sally that, in the future, she should arrange to cover herself in some manner.

Sally went back to work, more or less ignoring the judge's admonition and continuing to draw big crowds. Her detractors returned to their efforts as well, not of a mind to let the matter rest.

Throughout August and September of 1933, as lawyers continued to wrangle, legal briefs were filed, and court appearances were postponed, Sally maintained an amazing schedule. On top of her daily shows at the World's Fair, she remained at the Chicago Theatre performing in the "brilliant Million Dollar Fur Fashion Show," where she was held over from week to week, sharing the bill with such popular personalities as Cab Calloway, Amos 'n' Andy, and George Burns and Gracie Allen. She also continued her appearances at the Paramount Club, along with *Ziegfeld Follies'* songstress Frances White (she of "I'd Like to be a Monkey in the Zoo" fame).

Years later, George Burns recalled:

> I remember playing the Chicago World's Fair in the 1930s. I was on the same bill with Sally Rand. She did her famous fan dance, and it was supposed to be very, very naughty. But it was nothing.
>
> She came out on the stage wearing flesh colored leotards, and the lights on the stage were dark blue — you could hardly see her. And when she did her fan dance, her fans were so big, they covered her completely. That was it. She got sick one night, so I took her place and nobody knew the difference.

George and Gracie and Sally were not the only young performers at the Chicago Theatre whose stars were on the rise. British born Leslie Townes Hope was also on the threshold of success. By age 4 he had immigrated to the United States and settled in Cleveland, Ohio, where, as a child, he won a talent contest by impersonating Charlie Chaplin. In 1925, young Leslie was booked by Fatty Arbuckle into a show called *Hurley's Jolly Follies*. The following year he formed the "Dancemedians," a most unusual dance and comedy act featuring the Hilton Sisters (conjoined twins who gained renown by thrilling their audiences with a clever tap dancing routine).

Soon enough, Leslie would be on the radio and in time would become the most popular entertainer in the world. Years later, he would send a telegram to the hospital on the day that Sally died. But back then, in the third week of August 1933, performing as "Bob Hope & His Company," he merited only third billing to Sally, just between then-popular radio comedians, Stoopnagle and Budd, and Alex Morrison, "The Trick Shot Golf Ace."

Despite or possibly because of her troubles with the law, Sally remained the biggest attraction at the fair. Columnist W.A.S. Douglas observed that, while Sally was "packing them in" at the Streets of Paris, "forty men could toss a medicine ball around in the Hall of Science and never bother the customers ... and, at the Adler planetarium where you can see the progress of the stars since the beginning of time, the attendants are growing fat from having nothing to do."

The stress of Sally's legal scrapes, together with the frenetic pace of her schedule, had taken its toll. Soon after facing two judges, suffering from exhaustion, she was rushed to St. Luke's hospital after collapsing in her dressing room. Attending physicians concluded that the strain of recurrent court appearances had brought her to a state of extreme nervousness. Complicating all of this, a salary dispute developed with the managers of the Streets of Paris.

On August 18th, having endured more than enough aggravation, Sally abruptly declared she was withdrawing from the fair and would henceforth concentrate on her stage and screen career. She was hot and in no mood to calm down. Leaving the fairgrounds around midnight, she headed downtown to fulfill her regular late-night engagement. But, as a wise man might once have said: "Just because things are bad doesn't mean they can't get worse."

To get from the fairgrounds to her engagement at the Chicago Theatre, Sally commonly traveled by rickshaw to the dock and then by speedboat for just over three miles on Lake Michigan and the Chicago River. Ordinarily, this transit combination[3] was a smart choice. It not only avoided traffic and saved time, but also gave her a chance for reflection as the vessel bounced along from dock to dock. On this particular evening, however, Sally's mind was racing.

As she casually stood up in the late-summer breeze, the pilot made a sudden sharp turn near the mouth of the Chicago River, at which point Sally lost her footing on the slippery deck and was abruptly tossed overboard. Luckily, 26-year-old coast guardsman George Arnold heard her screams, dove into the chilly water, and swam 100 feet from Navy Pier to reach her. Taken to a nearby Coast Guard station, Sally was soon chatting cheerfully with her rescuer, ready to face her challenges with a refreshed perspective.

Given this chance to literally cool down, Sally backed off her threat to leave Chicago. Instead, she merely folded her fans in the Streets of Paris and accepted an offer to relocate her show to Ernie Young's Old Manhattan Garden in the Italian Village at a reported salary of $950 a week ($17,000 today). One reporter noted that she was "no longer attempting to conceal the rear view of her naked body."[4] This was not long after Mayor Kelly himself had toured the fairgrounds and threatened to shut down a number of so-called "nude" shows, in particular, Ernie Young's "rhumba" dance which he had found especially objectionable.

Despite deciding to stay in Chicago, Sally did have opportunities awaiting in Hollywood. Paramount studio head, Adolph Zukor, had recently passed through Chicago on his way west, met with Sally, and signed her to a one-picture deal, with an option for others to follow. On September 9th, *The Hollywood Reporter* magazine stated that Paramount was planning to "brave possible criticism and sign Sally Rand, Chicago's fan girl," to appear in *Search for Beauty* opposite Buster Crabbe and Ida Lupino. Gossip columnist Louella Parsons announced that it was a done deal. It never happened.[5]

---

[3] Transportation services at the fairgrounds were limited, so attendees and employees had to walk, ride a shuttle bus, or be pulled about in a rickshaw. Many of the rickshaws were manned by college students who took the job during the summer to pay for tuition and expenses.

[4] The unnamed journalist, while admitting that he had at first been disappointed with Sally's "graceful pirouetting to waltz time," ultimately confessed: "The next day the music keeps running through your mind and you see the fans gracefully moving, half concealing, half revealing and you decide that, after all, this is a scene you'll never forget."

[5] While not in the movie, Sally did "appear" with Buster Crabbe and Ida Lupino on the date of the film's release when she hosted the "Borden Friday Frolic" on radio station KMJ in Fresno, California. (*Search for Beauty* was notable for the display of Buster Crabbe's bare buttocks. See for yourself online at the very interesting www.pre-code.com.)

Faith

By Labor Day, the fair had been operating for more than three months with only two months to go. Better late than never, Faith Bacon hustled to Chicago from New York City and started an engagement at the "Hollywood" concession. By this time, Sally Rand's remarkable success had already spawned a number of imitators and competitors working throughout the fairgrounds. Most noteworthy among them was Rosalie who, along with a supporting cadre of eight assistant fan dancers, was packing them in at Old Mexico, literally right next door to the spot where Faith was hoping to do the same. The Hollywood venue attempted to distinguish itself from the competition with a large placard above the box office reading: "FAITH BACON — THE ORIGINATOR OF THE FAN DANCE — APPEARING NIGHTLY — GLORIFYING THE ART OF NUDITY."

Offering fairgoers a look at the latest in entertainment media production techniques, a sign above the entrance to the Hollywood concession proclaimed: "Sound Motion Pictures in the Making." In addition to a demonstration of radio broadcasting, the venue offered an eatery and, of course, a live floor show.

Faith played to a full house on opening night (an audience that reportedly included the conflicted Chicago Mayor Edward J. Kelly). Late in the evening, a jovial group headed by Sally Rand entered the room and made their way to a table in the front. According to a press report, Sally had "applauded loudly when Miss Bacon completed her graceful dance."

The enthusiastic reception for Faith's act was just the spur that Sally needed. Returning to the Paramount Club for her regular late-night engagement, Sally put on a 12-minute specialty number, employing her fans a bit less conservatively than usual and turning up the stage lights a little brighter. With Sally, Faith, Rosalie, and the others each giving it her all, newspaper headlines expressed the essence of the situation: "FAN DANCERS WAR — BATTLE OF BELLES BEING STAGED TO SEE WHO CAN WEAR THE LEAST."

And the battles weren't limited to the stage. On Monday morning, September 18th, Sally waltzed into the Chicago Avenue Police Station sporting a newly acquired black eye and filed charges against Sam Balkin, manager of the Paramount Club. The police accompanied her back to the club where Balkin readily admitted his part in the affair, but showed the officers a set of teeth marks on his wrist, which he said were put there by Sally. Unhappy with the state of affairs ("Look, she bites the hand that feeds her!"), he filed countercharges. The parties each signed a disorderly conduct complaint against the other and posted a $25 cash bond.

Claiming her black eye was evidence that Balkin had "clouted" her with his fist and that she had only bitten him in self-defense, Sally offered her version of events:

> I told Mr. Balkin I was going to resign. I started there at $150 a week. The position was a life-saver, and I have remained there out of gratitude, after getting other work elsewhere.
>
> My pay envelope contained $75, instead of $150, and I asked why. Mr. Balkin said that he had deducted the difference because of the times I had been absent from the club. Then the trouble started. Now, it all seems unimportant. I did bite Mr. Balkin, but only after he had socked me in the eye. Oh, I hope the eye doesn't turn completely black. You can't cover up a black eye with grease paint. I've seen it tried.

At Balkin's request, the case was delayed for several days. Leaving the courtroom, Sally said "when a man hits a woman for nothing, he ought to be punished." By September 29th, both pugilists had cooled down and agreed to drop their complaints, but, in the meantime, Sally's other legal situation had taken a very serious turn.

On September 24th, the page one headline of the *Chicago Sunday Tribune* screamed "YEAR IN JAIL FOR SALLY RAND." The moment had been building for more than a month. Virginia Gardner reported that Sally:

> ... was found guilty last evening of willfully performing an obscene and indecent dance in a public place by a jury of twelve men, most of them young. She was sentenced by Municipal Judge Joseph H. McGarry, before whom the jury returned its verdict in the South State street court.

The prosecution's chief witness had been our old friend Officer Harry M. Costello, described by Miss Gardner as "an aging lieutenant from the vice squad who of course knew the legal definition of obscenity." Assistant State's Attorney Patrick F. Daniher, who prosecuted the case, asked Costello what he had seen. The witness squirmed: "I seen her butticks."

"And how did this affect you?" Daniher probed.

According to Gardner, the aging detective's leathery countenance had remained impassive. "It aroused my passions," he said.[6]

On the stand, responding to questioning by Defense Attorney Samuel Berke, Sally had testified that she always performed coated with white theatrical cream with a piece of net tied around her hips. "As I wave my fans around, the net slips down and I step out of it." She then described how she ended her act by climbing a flight of steps and standing with one knee raised and her fans held over her head for the final bars of music.

As Sally was concluding her testimony, Defense Attorney Berke produced two "huge feather fans" and asked her to execute the eight steps of her dance for the jury. Gardner reported that Sally then stepped down from the stand, took the fans and demonstrated her routine:

> At the finale she raised one knee showing a tiny line of bare leg above a rolled stocking. The jury sat forward, gaping and grinning. A small gray haired juror with a melancholy face smiled a thin lipped smile, while his eyes behind thick lenses grew moist. A young juror giggled and punched his neighbor, a ponderous man who sat with open mouth....

> Only one member of the jury, a neatly dressed young man who later was pointed out by his fellow jurors as the one who was hard to convince that Sally was guilty of indecency, appeared unconcerned and sat back with a bored expression during her dance.

The orchestra conductor at the Chicago Theatre, Joseph Cherniavsky, well known for his Yiddish American Jazz Band, had testified that there was nothing indecent or seductive in Sally's dance: "There couldn't be, as it is danced to slow, dreamy music. There can't be anything such as is called 'hotcha' danced to slow music. No one can dance suggestively to 'adagio' time."

The last defense witness was a staff surgeon at Michael Reese Hospital who testified that "it would be a physical impossibility for Sally to reveal in a dance all that the policemen said they saw."

In his closing argument, Defense Attorney Berke emphasized that, while four police officers testified that their "passions were aroused" by Sally's dance,

---

6   Called to the editor's desk, Virginia Gardner was asked if she thought the story should appear on the paper's front page. She *did* think so, saying that, in addition to being amusing, "the aging detective's testimony revealed a lot about the virtue, or lack of it, in arresting Rand." Gardner would later become a writer for the communist *Daily Worker* and the biographer of Julius and Ethyl Rosenberg.

several musicians in the orchestra had testified to the contrary, despite repeatedly observing the lady at close range. "It's asinine for the law to permit us to view the life-size statue of a nude man in the Art Institute — and experts agree that a man is more ugly in the nude than a woman — and yet bring a criminal charge against a woman for dancing with her body covered with thick white cream," Berke concluded.

Assistant State's Attorney John Jarecki, whose "passion" had also been elevated, presented the closing argument for the prosecution. As described by Gardner:

> His long, lean figure swaying, he begged the jury in a voice that shook with emotion to consider the effect of their verdict on countless mothers.

> "Are you gentlemen, whether married or single, to permit the stamp of approval to be put on such a nude and indecent performance?" he cried.... If you do ... you will return us to paganism.

> He urged the jurors, who sat forward with solemn faces as he spoke, not "to crucify decency on a cross of gold — the commercialization of a woman who would show her body in the nude to crowds in a theater."

> "On the other hand, gentlemen," he said, "future generations of mothers will rise up and call you blessed if you return a verdict of guilty."

The jury deliberated for an hour and 15 minutes while Sally rushed back to the Chicago Theatre to give one of her scheduled performances. Judge McGarry waited for her return before accepting the verdict from the jury foreman and pronouncing sentence.

The jurors' solemn demeanor as they filed back into the jury box was in stark contrast to their previously jovial mood. Upon reading the verdict — "guilty" — and without further ado, Judge McGarry imposed the maximum sentence possible — one year in county jail and a fine of $200.

Declaring that his jury instructions had clearly favored the defendant, Judge McGarry dismissed the defense's motion for a new trial. Even so, he did agree to a 60-day stay, which gave Berke ample opportunity to file a bill of exceptions. Sally was released from custody on cash bond of $2,000. Many regarded the sentence as too harsh at a time when bootlegging and various other crimes spawned by organized criminal activity in Chicago were proceeding unchecked.

In Virginia Gardner's account:

> While her bond was being arranged the fan dancer pointed out that she had received a sentence twice as long as that ordinarily given public enemies convicted under the new criminal reputation law.

> "If the jury is right, and the dance I do actually is indecent, and the court is right in sentencing me to a year in jail," she said, "all I can say is that everyone who is engaged in sculpture, painting, music or dancing ought to quit." Then she stepped into Judge McGarry's chambers and thanked him "for a fair trial."

The classic Henry Fonda film *12 Angry Men* tells the story of a jury that, although initially inclined to convict, ultimately finds a young defendant not guilty after the persistent appeals of a lone holdout. Here, the scenario was reversed as "Eight Agitated Men" ultimately persuaded the holdouts to convict. According to Gardner:

> William M. Gaston, foreman of the jury, said that three ballots were taken. On the first, eight jurors voted for a guilty verdict, three voted not guilty and one did not vote. Twenty minutes later a second ballot showed that the vote was eleven to one for guilty.

> "From then on," Gaston said, "it was a matter of our convincing this one fellow. He was young. We all took a hand in talking to him. He maintained that he knew she was nude all right, but that didn't make the dance indecent."

> "But we finally convinced him," Gaston went on, wiping the perspiration from his rather fleshy face, "that it wasn't a question of indecency, but of nudeness."

> "You mean that any woman who appears in the nude is indecent under any circumstances?" Gaston was asked.

> "Yes, if it's in public that way," he said.

> Other members of the jury stood around the courtroom talking and laughing after the trial. They grew serious, however, when asked if there was much disagreement among them.

> "The only man who held out any length of time was young, and he wasn't married," one juror said. "He didn't know no better."

> Several remarked that the sentence was more severe than they had expected.

Within two days of sentencing, Policewoman Bessie McShane decided to come clean. She had participated in Sally's four arrests on August 4th and had testified against her before Judge McGarry, but she had also often observed Sally putting a thick coat of cream on herself in her dressing room. As McShane described the situation:

> The fact is that Sally pays $42 a week for the pants she wears. I know she wears a new pair for every performance. They are made of maline, which is a net. They are sewed on tight and pasted down. Over her breasts she wears similar material, pasted on so that no strap shall show when she turns around. She spends more time dressing for the stage than she does in dancing. It hurts when she takes off her costume because it's stuck to her.

> We didn't have anything really against Sally, except that if we didn't keep her under control there would be thousands of Sally Rands bursting into spotlights all over town — and we couldn't stand that. Even as it is, we have our eye on nine imitation Sally Rands. They've got to be good. That's all. As for the people who stand in line to see such shows, they're suckers.

And so the wheels of justice turn.

While Officer McShane may have been willing to cut Sally some slack, certain members of the clergy remained steadfast in their unqualified disapproval. An eccentric 82-year-old Omaha pastor, Rev. Charles W. Savidge, left no ambiguity in his stern assessment:

> When the judgment day comes and Sally appears before the bar of judgment in her two fans, it is my belief she will feel like 30 cents. God is likely to tell Sally: "You go to hell for that Chicago business." I would give more for the chances of a $3-a-week servant girl with clothes on at the last judgment than for Sally with her $2,000 a week.[7]

Sally Rand the fan dancer was all the rage, but Sally Rand the person was also beginning to attract the attention of the press.

---

[7] Said to have officiated at 6,663 marriage ceremonies in his career, Rev. Savidge died less than 16 months later. After his death, he was described as an "Omaha institution" whose "frock coat, black hat, stiff collar and black tie were a familiar sight in downtown Omaha." His unique physical features (including a wildly oversized mustache) combined with "his courtly manners, his vast store of homespun humor ... and his frank utterances" to make him "a distinctive figure." It is unknown whether these utterances ever included an explanation of Matthew 7:1 — "Judge not lest ye be judged."

One journalist offered a mixed assessment:

> She's a nice-looking person dressed up, but so are thousands of other
> girls in Chicago. Without her clothes she's the fan dancer who has
> received as much publicity as the World Fair where she does her act.
> Dressed, or undressed, she is 5 feet tall. Dressed, she weighs 109
> pounds. She has enough black grease around her eyes to polish a
> kitchen stove, reads Thorne Smith and Tiffany Thayer; smokes
> mentholated cigarettes; could cook an omelet if she had to; talks like
> a manicurist who has read 12 of the 1,200 pages of *Anthony Adverse*;
> knows law from having been in police court so often; uses straw-
> berry lipstick and saves on laundry bills by wearing little more than
> a white enamel coating as her stage costume.

As if judicial skirmishes and censure from moralists weren't enough to bear, Sally was soon the subject of criticism from a completely unexpected quarter — nudists! The Midway at the Chicago Fair wasn't the only public place folks were cavorting in their birthday suits. "Nudism," a new physical culture movement confined mostly to the idyllic forests of Germany, was beginning to stir in the United States.[8] It was on the minds of the avant-garde in Chicago, as well.[9]

Alois Knapp, Chicago attorney and founder of the Zoro Nature League nudist camp across the state line in Indiana, offered his two cents on the topic of the day:

> If all the world was naked, Sally Rand wouldn't have a chance.
> Intelligent nudism would destroy the market for fan dancers.
> Nobody would want to see them because nudism eliminates morbid
> sex impulses. Nudity is just another word for naturalness. Nudism is
> good for the health and good for the morals. Everybody knows that
> sunlight is the best thing for the body.

Extolling the physical and psychological virtues of nudism, Knapp declared:

> Many times I have seen many men peeking through windows to
> see women undress. If the world practiced nudism that would be

---

[8] The American League for Physical Culture, America's first nudist organization, was
     founded in 1930 and the first American nudist magazines were becoming available
     behind newsstand counters at about the same time as curious, but otherwise dignified,
     gentlemen were beginning to make a beeline for the Streets of Paris.

[9] For example, *This Nude World*, a 62-minute documentary film, opened at the Castle
     Theatre in Chicago on July 3, 1933, after several failed attempts to show the film in
     other cities.

ended quickly.... Our camp has been operating for just three months and already there [are] a rapidly growing number of people who come here. Many people work in Chicago during the week and come out here to spend the weekend in the nude. They are healthy and their minds have been purged of a lot of silly ideas.

One thing is certain. Sally didn't appreciate being dragged into the debate, and her observations on the subject were none too charitable:

Nudism? Phooey! I think it's not only immoral but ridiculous. Of course this is only my opinion, but I can't see any benefits in this nudist fad that couldn't be obtained more satisfactorily and more comfortably in private. My principal objection to the idea of a nudist colony is the utter needlessness of enduring actual discomforts to get a backyard sun bath.

My moral objection to nudism isn't the mere point of nudity. As I said, lewdness is primarily mental. Any artistically inclined person can gaze at a beautiful body without the shadow of an improper thought. But when people will tread rocks barefooted and get themselves all scratched up by brush at some nudist camp just to be in on a mass display of nudity — well, what's your answer? Don't you think at least some of them must have something on their minds besides health and beauty?

If you must know it, one of the foremost leaders of the nudist movement in this country came to me the other day and offered me $5,000 if I would endorse nudism. I refused.

On October 4th, the court agreed to give Sally a rehearing largely on the strength of an affidavit from the young bachelor on the jury who had wanted to find her not guilty but said he had been overwhelmed by the other jurors' arguments. He claimed he was suffering from a headache so severe that he had been given aspirin and put to bed in the stuffy jury room. In addition, he claimed to have been assured that Miss Rand would not go to jail, but would only be fined.

On November 2nd the court reduced Sally's one-year sentence to just ten days in jail, plus a $200 fine.[10] Still not satisfied, her attorney announced

---

[10] On this same day, popular bandleader Cab Calloway recorded "The Lady with the Fan." (Search for a video of this delightful number on YouTube, with Calloway, resplendent in white shoes, white tie and tails, cavorting with a bevy of beautiful girls kept relatively modest only by their cleverly manipulated ostrich feather fans.)

that he would pursue yet another appeal. Ultimately, the Chicago jail cell would remain vacant and Sally would be free to pursue a backlog of tempting opportunities. Speaking to columnist Dorothy Goulet about her legal situation, Sally pulled no punches:

> The mayor felt the need of convincing the voters that he was a moral man. So he picked on a girl like me who is simply trying to make a living and dragged my art in the mud, showering me with undesirable publicity and plenty of legal headaches, which are taking all my hard-earned savings to fight. The sentence, a year in jail and a $250 fine, passed on me, was one of the most unjust decisions ever handed down from any bench, especially coming from a Chicago court, in which city it is common knowledge that murderers and gangsters are allowed to roam the streets unmolested on suspended sentences. At least 500 girls here in Chicago are trying to cash in on my publicity.... Not one of them has been bothered. I have been a pawn in this political game.

Goulet noted that Sally's attorneys were seeking permission from the court for her to leave Chicago for a week's engagement at the Paramount Theatre in New York. Looking forward to getting out of town, Sally also had some parting shots for the "Chicago Machine":

> They have hurt, more than helped, themselves by picking on me. Hundreds who have seen my dance realize that they have no ground for their charges and more hundreds who will see it in New York will recognize at once that I have been used as a stooge for the would-be sanctimoniousness of Chicago's mayor.

Sally kept pulling in big crowds for her appearances outside the fair. In early October, with Duke Ellington's band at the Chicago Theatre, her show grossed $47,000 for the week. And when Judge McGarry granted her leave to travel, Sally proceeded to fulfill her contract in New York,[11] where she would share top billing with Milton Berle.

---

11 Different versions of how Sally came to leave Chicago for New York have been reported elsewhere. In *Sally Rand, From Film to Fans*, Holly Knox said Vito Genovese leaned on Sally to come to work at his Chicago club and claimed that someone named "Big Ed Callahan," supposed manager of the Paramount Club, was bumped off by the mob. (Extensive research failed to support this story or even confirm that anyone named "Callahan" was ever associated with the club. Sam Balkin was manager when Sally allegedly put the bite on him.) Sally did sometimes tell family members that she left for New York to distance herself from Al Capone. There is little doubt that Chicago entertainment venues did operate under mob influence, if not control, and these unsavory arrangements could well have impacted Sally's

The Paramount Theatre represented the "big time" for any performer. The lavishly decorated venue, located at 1501 Broadway on Times Square, had opened just seven years earlier. Its lobby was modeled after the Paris Opera House and the auditorium could seat more than 3,600 patrons. The theater's Wurlitzer organ was considered to be a masterpiece. Sally's debut there generated plenty of press coverage — with one columnist noting that "her shapely chassis [was] sheathed in just about enough gauze to bind a wounded finger until the doctor comes ... a costume she could mail at the postage rate for a one-ounce letter."

A reporter in Bridgeport, Connecticut, disclosed information that today would call for a "spoiler alert":

> Here's the inside, *HERALD* buyers: A half hour before Sally Rand's due to go on, she covers her body, which is entirely shaved, with the white powder most flesh revealing professionals use. After that comes a tissue-thin transparent adhesive, placed, quite strategically, there and there and there! The top layer's cold cream and plenty of it. After this, which takes 30 minutes, Sally goes on, a Godiva of Terpsichore, hiding behind the fan and coming out from hiding, with a climax in the apparent altogether.

Sally was not the only controversial young woman in the Big Apple seeking to generate some cash on Broadway in the fall of 1933. As reported by columnist Paul Harrison, the marquee of the Capitol Theatre displayed the towering figure of a white-robed woman, arms upraised in exhortation — like a huge detour sign "attempting to divert Gotham's Gay Way to the paths of righteousness." Illustrated posters declared:

AIMEE SEMPLE MCPHERSON IN PERSON —
HER FIRST APPEARANCE ON ANY STAGE.

The controversial Christian evangelist, whom we last encountered officiating at a bathing beach wedding eight years before, was now engaged in several legal actions, including a divorce initiated by her third husband. She was also still dealing with repercussions from her so-called kidnapping in 1926. With all this in mind, Miss McPherson decided that the Broadway stage might offer an answer to her various predicaments. Indeed, she had been encouraged to believe she could earn thousands for her appearances.

---

performance contracts during the 1930s. Details are unknown, but, since Capone was in federal prison from 1932 to 1939, he could not very well have had direct personal contact with her. A story yet to be told.

Aimee approached the opportunity with reflective modesty:

> Of course, I'm not an actress. Oh dear me, I don't know the least
> thing about the stage. I've never even been in a dressing room
> before.... I'm not the least nervous, even though I know I'm not an
> actress. I remain serene because I know that 70,000 people are on
> their knees at this very moment, praying that I may have the
> courage and inspiration to say the right words.

While many of her followers questioned the wisdom of appearing on the
vaudeville stage and potentially sullying the reputation of the church,
Aimee assured them: "We are carrying the war right into enemy country,
carrying the Gospel into the Babylon of Broadway." Besides, she said: "I
am merely heeding my Master's command," explaining that her sojourn
to Broadway was supported by the scriptural command: "Go ye into the
streets, the lanes and the broad ways and compel them to come in, that
My house may be filled"— a passage that has eluded the best efforts of
biblical scholars to identify.

Some accounts place Sister McPherson's presentation at the end of the
program, following "two acrobats and a midget." Others say her lecture
was sandwiched between the harmonies of the "Radio Aces" and a troupe
of Cuban fan dancers. To say that Aimee's appearance was in stark contrast
to other parts of the program would be an understatement.

As one columnist described it, the evangelist had emerged from the
parting curtains into a spotlight, wearing a snow-white satin gown that
fell "from her shoulders to the tips of [her] white satin shoes." Telling the
audience she stood before them in "humility and reverence," Aimee had
then told the story of how she came to be a woman of faith and the many
burdens she had borne.

A columnist for The New Yorker expressed the audience's frustration: "We
were hearing about Aimee McPherson, not about God. And even then, it is
the sad truth that in the end she let us down. She didn't get around to the
divorces.... [I]t was difficult to look at her for a single moment without
thinking of the five thousand dollars [$95,000 today] she will receive for her
week's work." Then, while the band played "Onward, Christian Soldiers,"
Aimee was ushered off the stage as the Cuban fan dancers rushed on.

Despite a few positive reviews, the truth was that typical Broadway
theatergoers weren't that interested in paying good money for what turned
out to be reminiscences and admonitions from an emissary of the Lord, no
matter how well attired and attractive she might be — especially if she
wasn't going to talk about her many romances and rumored scandals. The

show closed as audiences shrank. What had been announced as a six-week engagement lasted only one. Her next scheduled appearance at Loew's Theatre in Washington, DC, was cancelled. *Variety* magazine delivered the unkindest cut of all, calling her performance probably "the poorest freak draw yet found."

B ack at the Paramount, eager fans had lined up two abreast extending around the corner from the box office to catch the opening of Sally's show. She could hardly have been more pleased:

> I am tickled to death about it, because that Aimee McPherson laid an egg on Broadway. They tell me she was a total flop. And after what she said about me!

> She was supposed to play on the same bill with me in Chicago. So she comes around and says she won't be on the same bill with any fan dancer. I said I would get off the bill, but the management said I was a better draw than her. And here they are paying me $5,000 a week on Broadway — the same thing they paid her — and me drawing the crowds.

If Sally's compensation sounds like a lot of money for the time, it was. Her show grossed $52,000 for the week ending October 12th. That's nearly a million dollars nowadays. And the take might well have been more if the city license commissioner, Sidney S. Levine, had not ordered her to put on more clothes the day before the engagement closed.

Appointed to his position only a couple of days before, Levine charged that his predecessor had allowed obscene shows to continue running in New York City for no other reason than to embarrass Mayor John P. O'Brien. Levine was determined to impress his new boss by stamping out indecent theatrical performances in burlesque, vaudeville, and motion picture houses. His motto: "This is a city for decent people." He decided to kick off his cleanup campaign with a high profile target. In an official letter to management of the Paramount Cabaret Restaurant, Levine advised:

> Inasmuch as the exhibition of Sally Rand is so repulsive to common decency, and being immediately dangerous to public morals, I am compelled to inform you that I cannot permit another performance of this act by this actress unless properly clad in opaque raiment. Unless you immediately comply with this demand, I shall forth-with revoke your theatre license at the said address.

Pressed on the matter, Levine proclaimed:

> Whether the signs outside advertise burlesque or the Metropolitan
> Opera means nothing. It's what is inside that counts and I am
> determined that it shall be clean. We cannot permit our city to be
> the receptacle for the cast-off filth of other cities.[12]

Sally had a ready response. For the 7:15 show on her final night, she appeared
that night in long flannel underwear:

> ... manipulating her fans with such dexterity that no one in the
> audience knew she was wearing anything.... Then, with dramatic
> suddenness, she stood before the audience and brought the fans
> away from her body with a swish. The audience gasped, sat
> stupefied, then burst into roars of laughter.

Another report claimed that Sally had "tripped about the stage of the
Paramount Theatre ... in a pair of bloomers that were white and lacy,"
noting that "The audience did not clap with its usual fervor."

Commissioner Levine's reaction to Sally's New York engagement established a
pattern. Catholic bishops, chiefs of police, and assorted other local officials
and self-appointed moralists would, for the rest of her life, disparage what she
considered an art form. At only 29 years of age, after years on the vaudeville
circuit dealing with the kinds of problems to be expected when you organize
and maintain a successful road show, Sally now had to deal with a whole new
world of concerns — bail bondsmen, attorneys, judges and juries — all due to
the relentless scrutiny of people who seemingly had a whole lot of time to
attend to someone else's business.

Sally would have to sell even more tickets in order to cover her legal costs,
pay expenses, and continue to make any kind of living for herself. And she
would soon come to appreciate this observation by George Sand:

> It is always the same fight ... against the same enemies, prejudice
> and narrow-mindedness.

Just when she could really use it, Sally got an endorsement from a most
surprising source — a Christian minister from the rural heartland.
Reverend Fred Smith, a pastor from Newton, Kansas, shared his impressions

---

[12] One can only wonder if the Jewish Mr. Levine recognized the irony when his actions
were reported on the front pages of newspapers adjacent to a story relating how
Germany had banned "Negro jazz" music: "A spokesman in the ministry of propa-
ganda told the press that the ragtime airs were under official ban, as being un-German."

after seeing Sally perform at the Chicago Theatre. The entire text is well
worth reading, but here is an abbreviated version:

> I had not expected to see her dance when I went up to Chicago to
> The Century of Progress World's Fair. The simple reason was that I
> was not even aware of the existence of anyone by the name of Sally
> Rand.... True, my knowledge, [of modern dance] such as it is, is
> rather bookish. How could it be otherwise when one lives in
> central Kansas? ....
>
> Then came the chance ... to see Sally Rand dance.... At last I had a
> chance to see an outstanding dancer.... The purity organizations
> were up in arms against her. Evidently something had gone wrong
> for her, but not for the theatre. It was packed to the doors. I wiggled,
> advanced by sporadic runs, from row to row until I settled,
> victorious, on the end seat of the third row on the middle aisle.
> That was near enough for me. The front row was a paradise taboo
> to such as I....
>
> I recall an announcer.... He was announcing, as one who brings on
> an appetizing hot turkey, the epiphany of Sally Rand. He became
> discursive. Sally was a little late. She had been detained. "Of course
> you all know the trouble she is having in appearing before the
> public." Then a pause. A knowing look. Then, as mellifluously as a
> megaphone can achieve mellifluousness, came the modulated
> announcement: "Ladies and gentlemen: Sally Rand!"
>
> The curtain swung back. A dozen dancing girls appeared, clothed
> in black sateen.... It was good stuff. Then they subsided artistically
> on a staircase fixed centrally on the stage. A pause. The curtains
> parted and.... There she was — Sally — a vision of loveliness. I saw
> two large fans held as cover for a human form and for a face
> looking out from above them. I thought it revealed sadness. But the
> orchestra was playing on and Sally Rand was coming down. At
> least the fans were. How gracefully she could do it. A long
> diaphanous veil trailed behind her. Then the dance.
>
> I have never seen Pavlova or Duncan, or any of the later outstand-
> ing dancers. One cannot live in central Kansas and see such things.
> But I saw Sally Rand dance and was satisfied. Her fans were
> geometry come alive. It was a study of two triangles as related to
> curvature. She swung to the stage side and, guarded by her fans,
> someone unloosed the long flowing veil....

The dance was ended. Slowly she ascended the stairs and at last I saw
Sally Rand, but it was as Moses saw God, from the cleft of the rock....

A week later a friend told me they were after Sally Rand. Her case
was to come up in court. I said, enigmatically, "I thought as much...."
Yet, with regard to Sally Rand, I had *not* seen too much. I had gone to
see her dance. I saw the dance. I again repeat: I saw Sally Rand
dance but I did not see Sally Rand, except as Moses saw God on that
already mentioned occasion....

And now I am back in Kansas, back where none know of Sally
Rand and her kind, save those who went up to Chicago. She and
her fans are not a problem for us. Kansas has its own problems.

Sally carried copies of this article in her traveling trunk for many years,
pointing out on various occasions that, in the face of the unending criticism
heaped upon her from many a pious pulpit, she also had the considered
support of at least one respected gentleman of the cloth.

Faith

No sooner had the Chicago Fair closed than Faith Bacon became the victim of
a potentially career-ending hit-and-run accident. On November 6th, she
suffered severe bruises, a badly sprained back, and possible internal injuries
when the car in which she was riding was sideswiped by a vehicle that sped
from the scene without stopping. A brush with death? Perhaps. And there
would be others.

With her show closing in New York and a Hollywood contract in her
pocket, Sally headed west, stopping off for a triumphant return to the
scene of the crime — an engagement at the Chicago Theatre. She accepted
the Chicago booking unaware that she would be pinch-hitting for Aimee
Semple McPherson (this being another of the venues where McPherson's
show had been cancelled). "Mercy, no," said Sally, as she stepped from the
train, "I didn't know Aimee had anything to do with it. I won't be any more
evangelical than usual though." Columnist John T. Thompson had interviewed Sally in the railroad terminal dining room where, as he put it, she had
"crossed her silken-clad knees and sipped a tomato-juice cocktail." Mentioning her upcoming return to filmdom, Sally had boasted: "It's bigger game for
me now. I have met Chicago, New York and Indianapolis and they are mine.
It's Hollywood next. Of course, I'll only have a small part at first but that was
all Mae West had at first. I'm going to follow in West's hip-steps."

Cheers of Broadway audiences were still ringing in her ears when, temporarily free from the specter of incarceration, Sally returned to Hollywood in early November under contract with Paramount Pictures, hoping to turn her sudden national fame into a big payday. Paramount had secured the rights from French composer Maurice Ravel to use the title of his 1928 composition *Boléro* for a film featuring rising stars George Raft and Carole Lombard. To pump up interest in the film, the notorious Sally Rand had been added to the cast for the benefit of those who had read about her scandalous "fan dance" in the papers but hadn't seen her in Chicago. Announcing a possible shift in her career path, Sally told a Hollywood magazine interviewer:

> I'm placing my faith in the future now on my ability to emote a bit for the cameras. I know I'm going to have a difficult time convincing them out there that I have a single acting bone in my body. All I am going to hear is "fan dance." But, from here on, I want to carry on with acting as my principal qualification....

> My act has class. It's art with a big A. That's the difference between me and those cooch dancers in burlesque.

Sally was accompanied by Stella Onizuka, her "quaint Japanese maid," of whom, in the manner of the time, it was reported: "The little Nipponese always wears her native kimono, sandals, and socks."

No sooner had Sally set foot on the movie lot than misunderstandings led to controversy between the film's principals. She had it in her mind that the picture would serve as her springboard to a long-term acting career. Paramount had seen it as a way to cash in on her notoriety and create extra buzz for a film that already featured a pair of big names. The studio proposed to give her a few lines of dialogue, but otherwise her appearance in the film would be strictly subordinate.

Sally was frustrated. After enduring the exhaustion of putting on several shows a day in Chicago and suffering both the wrath of Mary Belle Spencer and the heavy hand of the judicial system, she had hoped to toss her fans aside, settle into a more secure situation, and resume a career in Hollywood that, only four years before, had been disrupted by the stock market crash and the advent of talking pictures. It didn't help that her fan dance would be "trimmed" to satisfy certain "powers that be." Deeply disappointed, Sally threatened to pack up her fans and walk away.

And who were these "powers that be"? A bunch of film industry censors operating as the Motion Picture Producers and Distributors of America — a group formed ten years earlier to rehabilitate the image of the film industry after the "Fatty" Arbuckle scandal involving the alleged rape and murder of model and actress Virginia Rappe. The studios also wanted to quell the objections of certain religious groups calling for federal censorship of the movies. Appointed by the industry itself in an effort to avoid government regulation, the MPPDA was headed by William Harrison Hays, Sr. What came to be called the "Hays Code" served as a significant brake on the studios' tendency to test the limits of prurient interest in their product.

John Hammell, Paramount's contact man with the Hays Office, had the unenviable assignment of smoothing Sally's ruffled feathers, while at the same time ensuring that her dance scene would not jeopardize release of the film. The gentleman proved up to the task. As Sally saw it: "For film purposes, the dance had been cut to the point where I feared it would appear incoherent and would harm my reputation as a dancer. But the studio has been very considerate of my viewpoint, and other difficulties have all been ironed out." The bruises on Sally's ego managed to fade soon enough. After all, it's not every day that a young dancer collects $20,000 for one or two days' work on a sound stage.

On the first day of filming, Sally's dance was scheduled to be shot on a closed set. Despite security measures, 73 low-level executives claiming to be assistant directors had tried to get by the doorman. Sally's co-star George Raft was quoted as quipping that: "If all the mugs trying to get on this set were laid end to end — it would serve them right."

Several film stars, including Fredric March, ventured in from other sound stages to witness the goings-on. Even Marlene Dietrich reportedly took a break from shooting *The Scarlet Empress* to watch the proceedings from the sidelines in her "Catherine the Great" costume, later remarking: "It's indecent. Indecent."

Bolero remains watchable today. The story opens shortly before the outbreak of World War I. The George Raft character, "Raoul De Baere," is a dancer from New York City with visions of becoming king of the European night-club circuit. He tries to persuade "Annette" (Sally's character) to be his dancing partner, but she refuses. He then devises an extremely athletic routine to be performed to the accompaniment of Ravel's "Boléro"[13] and recruits "Helen Hathaway" (Lombard's character) to dance with him. After a few plot twists (and the introduction of Ray Milland as "Lord Robert Coray"), poor Annette misses another career opportunity by turning up drunk. Raoul then overdoes his dance routine, collapses, and dies.

---

[13] This is actually an interesting anachronism, as Ravel's composition was not written until 1928, 10 years after the end of World War I.

O n November 15th, Sally arrived in San Francisco where she was met by
Mayor Angelo Rossi and a gaggle of press photographers.[14] Although
best known for being undressed, Sally was always smartly dressed in public
and eager to greet the press. But, when asked to pose in a provocative
manner "with her legs crossed," she was in no mood to comply, reacting:
"Why, it would be immodest." When the photographer persisted, Sally lit
into him: "Say you! Every dame that gets off a liner, a train, an airplane, a
bicycle, or has a baby, or shoots her husband has to pose for pictures with her
legs crossed. I'm not going to and that's final."

Sally had a local theater engagement that day, but she first made her way to a
Bay Area hotel room where she was to promote *Bolero* by giving a private
demonstration of her fan dance for members of the press. Journalist Roger
Wagoner described the situation: "The lame and the halt and all but the blind
of journalism were there." Somehow the heavyweight boxer Max Baer was
also in the room. At this point in his career, Baer didn't yet hold a title, but he
was a contender. While no one seemed to know why he was there, not one
among the slight newspapermen volunteered to give him the toss.

The handsome and popular boxer was currently making his own splash
in Hollywood playing opposite Myrna Loy in the just released *The
Prizefighter and the Lady*, a film that also featured reigning heavyweight
champ Primo Carnera and former champ Jack Dempsey. As Max was
known to have an eye for the ladies, the opportunity to cozy up to Sally
Rand must have been irresistible.[15]

Despite the private and unambiguous nature of the occasion, Baer couldn't
resist his natural impulse to make himself the center of attention. Oblivious to
protocol, he engaged whoever was near enough to listen, talking in low tones
about Hollywood in general and his recent film in particular. When talk
turned to the recent marriage of Johnny "Tarzan" Weissmuller and Lupe "the
Mexican Spitfire" Velez, Baer exclaimed: "Who cares about that? Nobody! Did
it rate the front page? But in a couple of months you'll see somebody make the
front page and that certain party isn't far away. Guess who?"

---

[14] The *Stanford Daily* university newspaper was quite critical of Mayor Rossi for wasting
his valuable time to personally greet Sally, questioning how many free tickets he had
received to her show and sarcastically suggesting he may as well have welcomed a
mob racketeer.

[15] Baer was still trying to live down the controversy surrounding his severe beating of
Frankie Campbell (who had died the day after Max had pummeled him for five
rounds). Brain specialist Dr. Tilton E. Tillman declared that Campbell's "death had
been caused by a succession of blows on the jaw" and that his brain had been
"knocked completely loose from his skull" by Baer's punches.

Turning their attention completely away from Sally, several reporters followed Max from the room as he excused himself, saying he had a date to call upon Estelle Taylor, former wife of Jack Dempsey. Well, Sally had heard quite enough. She proceeded to address what was left of her audience with pointed comments about the gentleman's lack of manners. A few minutes later the telephone rang: "This is Max. Tell Sally I was standing right outside the door and heard everything she said. Tell her I'm still a pretty poor parlor man, anyway." To which Miss Rand replied: "Pooh! Who's afraid of the big bad Baer?"

Extending her California stay through the end of the year, Sally had a chance to spend the holidays with her mother. While there, she hosted a holiday party for all the boys who had appeared in her vaudeville shows over the years, including her brother Harold, the smitten Jack Crosby, and her early dance partner Harvey Karels. It was during this trip that Sally reportedly invested "most of the proceeds from her Chicago fan dancing in a fifteen-acre orange orchard in Glendora, California" and presented the deed to her mother on Christmas day.

Back east, even with Sally out of town, the New York City fan dancing craze continued apace. As described by syndicated columnist Don O'Malley:

> ... every nightclub in town, it seems, features a chorus routine with fans. Every motion picture house prologue has another Sally Rand on the bill.... Every fan dancer in Manhattan — and they are legion — is hoping and praying that she will be honored with a polite raiding party, but John Law doesn't seem interested.

Faith

The World's Fair was over, but that didn't stop a number of the fair's performers from trying to cash in on whatever fame they may have achieved there. By January, having bounced back from her auto accident, Faith Bacon began a five-month tour with the so-called *Century of Progress Revue*, said to be the finest of several stage revues assembled after the Chicago Fair closed. She regularly enjoyed top billing as the revue played from coast to coast,[16] making stops in Pittsburgh, Columbus, Indianapolis, Cleveland, Oakland, and Los Angeles, among many others.

---

[16] In some venues, "in person" appearances by characters from Robert Ripley's *Believe It Or Not* Odditorium gave Faith a run for her money as the revue's most popular attraction.

The revue also featured a dozen or more "Parisienne models direct from the Streets of Paris," as well as the notorious rhumba dancers, Alfredo and Delores. The show's staging replicated the Chicago Fair Midway. An actual Midway barker (former hog caller Bob Robinson) served as master of ceremonies. When the show reached the Roosevelt Theatre in Los Angeles, Renee Villon was brought up from her engagement across the border at the Agua Caliente in Mexico to do her own version of the fan dance with "illuminated fans." Still, Faith was the main attraction. As one L.A. critic put it, she was: "A graceful sylph, and her fan dance is the height of coquetry. She dances in a semi-dark stage so that it is hard to tell whether she wears even gauze undies."

An obsession with fan dancing was loose in the land. Demand for instruction in the art rose to such a level that even the prestigious New York School of Music added a fan dancing class to its curriculum.

Legitimate performers from the Chicago Fair weren't the only ones seeking to cash in on the popularity of its most notorious attraction. Within weeks of the fair's closing, imitators and imposters were popping up like daisies. At the Ritz Theatre in Blytheville, Arkansas, "Sally Randall" was packing them in for her "Famous Fan Dance ... Direct from World's Fair." At the Miller Theater in Jefferson City, Missouri, "Sally De Rand" executed *her* version of the "famed fan dance exactly as presented in the 'Streets of Paris' at the World's Fair in Chicago." The Wildey Theatre in Edwardsville, Illinois, offered *Streets of Paris* — a "one day only" musical revue — featuring "the Sensational Fan Dance exactly as presented by Sally Rand." And then there was "Sally Rend," billed as "The Dance Sensation of 1933," who got a two-month jump on everyone else, performing her "novelty fan dance" at the Mississippi Valley fairgrounds in Davenport, Iowa, on Labor Day.

Several other would-be "Sally Rands" developed a significant fan base of their own. Miss Flo Ash, the dancer whose diminutive stature and personality most resembled Sally's, was arrested in San Antonio in February 1934 and charged with indecent exposure after a nightclub appearance. Details of Flo's adventures and those of several other fairly successful fan dancers from the period await you in chapter 16. Among them were performers of every size, shape, and race. And, since the Chicago Fair featured fan dancers in one venue and midgets in another, was there also a "midget Sally Rand"? Why not?

Sally's experience with the filming of *Bolero* had proven to be a disappointment. She had fought (and mostly lost) a battle to secure a more substantial dramatic role and her announced casting in a second picture, *Search for Beauty*, had fallen through. Reporters captured her reaction:

> I left Hollywood several years ago because I was just an ingénue,
> playing roles of silly little girls. I couldn't convince anyone that I
> could do better things. So I went on the stage and made a lot of
> money — which I lost when a bank closed. I had intended to come
> back to Hollywood and live on that money. I intended to make a
> big splurge, live in a big house and make the movies really want
> me. I had a definite campaign plan, and I think it would have
> worked. But so many things happened that I had to find some
> other way of getting back to the movies.
>
> The fan dance was a very deliberate, carefully planned and well
> executed move to get me back to Hollywood. And here I am,
> without the things I wanted. So I'm going back into vaudeville for
> forty weeks. By next fall I'll have saved enough money to allow me
> to live comfortably for a long, long time.

On January 29, 1934, front page headlines across the country explained why Sally had extended her stay in Southern California for several weeks beyond the Christmas holidays: "SALLY RAND'S FIANCÉ IS CRITICALLY ILL." Various wire services reported that Charles ("Chissie"/"Chizzy") Mayon was at "death's door" in his room at Cedars of Lebanon Hospital, having undergone two operations and several blood transfusions due to amoebic dysentery. His condition was considered critical. Sally was described as living in an adjoining hospital room for the previous five weeks, serving as his nurse. She had also phoned his mother in New York and arranged for her to fly out to be by his side.

Wait a minute! What was that "fiancé" part again? Yes, as Sally told the press, the two had been secretly engaged:

> We have been engaged for four years, although there never was any
> such thing as a formal announcement to that effect. We expected even-
> tually to get married, although we had never set any definite date.
>
> Chizzy was taken sick five weeks ago.... His illness is a complication
> following an attack of amoebic dysentery contracted during the fair
> in Chicago. He is critically ill, I know, but today the doctors said his
> condition was slightly improved, and I have renewed hope.

Within a week, Chissie's doctors pronounced him well enough to leave the hospital. Sally arranged for him to stay at her mother's home under the care of a trained nurse. Asked when the two were to be married, Sally replied: "I don't think we should consider that while Mr. Mayon is still an invalid do you?" When the reporter suggested that "perhaps married life might speed his recovery," Sally quipped: "Perhaps he'd have a relapse too." With Chissie on her mind, Sally departed with her *World Fair Revue* on what, at the time, was to be a 30-week, coast-to-coast tour.

T he World's most famous girl — In Person and on the screen in the WORLD PREMIERE OF "BOLERO" — Biggest theatrical event in Omaha History!" So trumpeted display ads in the *Omaha World-Herald*. Sally was scheduled to open a week's engagement at the Paramount Theater in Omaha, appearing both on stage and on screen in the just released, big-budget film. But first she had to get there.

The date was February 22, 1934. St. Louis was braced against a bitter chill, and Sally was expected to perform in neighboring Nebraska the following afternoon. Faced with the challenge of driving some 500 miles to Omaha in dead-of-winter weather, she opted instead to arrange for a charter flight. Being a pilot herself, Sally knew a thing or two about flying. So it was that she engaged the services of Forrest O'Brine.

The City of St. Louis and the history of manned flight are inextricably linked. It was the citizens of St. Louis who had bankrolled the building of *The Spirit of St. Louis* for then-resident aviator Charles A. Lindbergh. But, after his world famous solo flight across the Atlantic in 1927, Lindbergh had other interests to pursue, and so, by 1934, O'Brine was the best known pilot in town. A few years before, in August 1930, he and his co-pilot Dale "Red" Jackson, had established an endurance record by flying their *Greater St. Louis* over the city for a record-breaking 647 hours, 28 minutes and 30 seconds, without ever touching the ground.[17]

David Lipton, Sally's publicist, was already in Omaha when she phoned him with instructions to meet her at the airport.[18] With arrangements in place, she and her entourage looked forward to a pleasant flight above the weather. In addition to Sally and O'Brine, the party included Sally's personal assistant Ralph Hobart, her Japanese maid Stella Onizuka, and her two Pekinese dogs, Snootie and China Boy. The journey was expected to be uneventful.

---

[17] More than 27 days aloft?! How was it possible? O'Brine and Jackson were able to circle Lambert-St. Louis Field for nearly four weeks thanks to a refueling team servicing them from another aircraft. Engine trouble ended their endurance attempt.

[18] Sally's publicist from 1934 to 1938, Lipton later became publicity director for Universal Studios and ultimately vice president of advertising and publicity for its parent company, MCA Inc.

In a warm and cozy farmhouse, 20 miles east of Council Bluffs, Iowa, William Schieder and his family were holed up against the elements. They too were expecting an uneventful day on this, the 202nd anniversary of the birth of President George Washington. The area was in the grip of winter; the forecast high for the day — well below freezing.

Mr. Schieder may have filled his time reading the *Omaha World-Herald*, perhaps even scanning the front page remarks of War Secretary (and Nebraska native) George Dern praising President Roosevelt for recognizing that the nation must be prepared for war. Whatever his midday activities may have been, they were suddenly interrupted by an insistent banging on the door. Rising from his chair, Schieder must have approached the knocking with a mix of curiosity and concern. Could a neighbor be at his threshold in need of assistance?

Opening the door barely more than a crack against the chilling wind, when what to his wondering eyes should appear, but a quaking ensemble with an oil-soaked veneer. A more unlikely assortment could hardly have been imagined. Standing before him was a petite and beautiful young woman tightly clutching her mink coat, a Japanese lady dressed in a kimono, a slight young man literally shivering in his boots, and a leather-helmeted airplane pilot. The farmer's mind was racing. Was this a winter hallucination?

Heeding the pleas of the four disheveled refugees, Schieder ushered them into his home to stand before the fire. Only then did he notice the four sparkling eyes of little Snootie and China Boy peeking out from the folds of Sally's mink. His wife and son stood by in rapt disbelief. The question was so obvious that, without waiting for her host to speak, Sally blurted out: "I'm sure you must be wondering who we are."

Meanwhile, Sally's publicist, patiently waiting at the Omaha airport with the press in tow, once again checked his wristwatch. Reminiscing with Lipton 40 years later, Sally recalled:

> We had to charter a plane. The dead of winter, me in my mink, Stella in her kimono, Ralphie and the Pekes. How would we know there was no heat in the plane? We were numb with cold and miserable. Just as we got over Council Bluffs, in sight of Omaha, the oil line broke and we made a forced landing in a meadow, straight into a haystack! Covered with black oil and hay, the minks, the kimonos, the Pekes. We struggled up the country road looking for a phone.
>
> You had preceded us to Omaha and were waiting at the airport with all the news media and photographers. We went to a farmer's house to phone you. The farmer, his wife, and his son didn't believe

their eyes or their ears. Sally Rand? Japanese maid? Forced landing? Phooey, neither did the news media.

The farmer drove us into Omaha and to the theater. No interviews, no photographers, they just didn't believe that B.S. My feet were frostbitten and so were Ralphie's ears. We were never able to get the black oil off my mink coat or Stella's kimono. We could have been killed, burned to death, but not one word ever hit the newspapers. Just goes to show you.

Never mind that the tale of Sally and the haystack hadn't come to the attention of readers around the country. The Iowa farmer and his family had a story to tell for the rest of their days.

This is not to say Sally's Omaha engagement failed to get *any* press coverage. To the contrary, the much ballyhooed appearance of the famous Miss Rand on both stage and screen had the whole town talking. Predictably, not everyone appreciated the art of the dance.

Bishop Joseph Francis Rummel of the Diocese of Omaha was none too pleased to learn that Sally was coming to town and he wasn't going to take the affront to his community sitting down. In a pastoral letter penned on the Wednesday before her show opened, the bishop proclaimed that Catholics in the Omaha diocese were forbidden to attend "under pain of grievous sin":

> It is imperative that we warn our Catholic people against the contemptible performance which is to be presented in the Paramount Theater beginning Friday of this week. The individual featured in this performance became notorious last summer in connection with the Century of Progress exposition in Chicago. Evidently she is now exploiting the publicity she received by appearing "in person and on the screen" wherever she finds civil moral standards low enough to give her a welcome.

> Unfortunately it seems that the city of Omaha comes within this classification, since we have had recently a series of objectionable presentations in our theaters, some of which are not tolerated in many other communities. Judging from the filthy advertisements which have appeared in our daily papers ... it is evident that Omaha is considered "wide open" in this regard.

Bishop Rummel also wrote to Mayor Roy Towl, just in case the threat had escaped his attention:

> The reputation of this individual is sufficiently well known. If her show is in line with this reputation, its presentation here will

certainly not add to the moral tone of our city. I bring this matter to
your attention in the hope that you may ... have this show blocked
or a guarantee given that it will carry no demoralizing features.

Although the celebrated Miss Rand's appearance was eagerly anticipated,
the bishop was not without his supporters. Area Protestant ministers had
recently formed a committee to investigate offensive theatric performances
and Mayor Towl had received many written objections, including one from
104 students of a local high school. Reacting to the controversy, a local
businessmen's club had cancelled Sally's scheduled talk on "advertising."
Dr. Charles Durden, pastor of the First Baptist Church, called Sally's appearance "an affront to womanhood," something that was "not the kind of thing
we ought to introduce to our boys and girls in Omaha."

Ward S. Calvert expressed another view in a letter to the editor:

Why the furor at this late date about Sally Rand? Her act was stolen
and displayed in Omaha several months ago and did not even get a
raise at that time. The girl that copied the original was clever and
showed all that was possible.... From all that I can learn, Sally
"almosts" but still is smart enough to leave a lot to the imagination.
People should enjoy it, without moral degeneration.

We see beautiful statues in stone and we call it art. Is it obscene if
we who are alive see the statue living and it might possibly have a
living smile?

The bishop was a strong-willed man, but Sally was no shrinking violet. In a
Thursday night telegram from St. Louis to the *Omaha World-Herald*, she
insisted her dance was sweet, pure art alone, and added: "I respectfully
appeal to your sense of fairness to withhold your condemnation and judgment of my dance until you or your delegates have had an opportunity
to see it." Defending her honor, Sally also pointed out that she was a
member of a Christian Science Church in Los Angeles and counted many
Catholic priests among her friends.

All the same, after Mayor Towl and his police commissioner discussed the
matter, Chief of Police George Allen announced: "If Sally appears nude, she
will be arrested and so will the management. There will be an officer at
every performance to see that there are no slips."

At 1:30 Friday afternoon, the curtain went up for the first of four daily shows.
Admittance could be had for as little as 25 cents. Among those attending were
Police Chief Allen and a number of "inspectors" seated in the auditorium in
such a way as to provide each one a good look at Sally from a different

vantage point. None of the officials had a view from the wings, as it was built into Sally's contract that nobody, not even a stagehand, was permitted to watch from the wings while she danced. Bishop Rummel received a special invitation from theater manager Ralph Goldberg, but sent his regrets.

A good number of Nebraskans were undaunted by the bishop's edicts. Taking their chances with perdition at the theater, they proceeded to enjoy themselves very much indeed. And why not? It was a special day. In addition to being enchanted by the fan dance queen herself, the audience was entertained by Sally's 12-girl "Bevy of Beauties," several other talented performers, and a 25-piece "Symphonic Orchestra." No other theater on earth was presenting the fabulous Miss Rand, in the flesh, together with the world premiere of her most recent film, *Bolero*.

In the afterglow of the premiere program, the Omaha movie critic could hardly have been more effusive:

> That so-much-talked-about Sally Rand is worth seeing. Even the
> grossness of the kind of front page notoriety that first came to her in
> Chicago will not spoil for some of us the charm of her rhythmic
> motion, the billowy foam-flutter of plumes used for her raimenting,
> nor the feline suppleness and fluent lithesomeness of her delicate
> graces.... One of its most attractive elements is that entrance ...
> down the flight of dark steps. [Her] feet go over those steps as
> lightly as the movement of a summer cloud.

Police Chief Allen admitted that he had seen nothing suggestive about the show. He said he considered Sally's fan dance to be "artistic" and added that if anyone had expected something else they would have found her performance pretty "tame."[19]

Headlined "SALLY AND CENSORSHIP," a *World-Herald* editorial observed:

> It is entirely likely that the publicity man for Sally Rand has been
> busily shaking hands with himself, and that theater managers
> locally are thinking what swell publicity the fan dancer got. Surely,
> they may have reflected, the opposition and criticism of the clergy
> heralding her advent would insure great crowds.
>
> Possibly it is true that all the preliminary fanfare merely meant that
> a gullible public, acting on a sly hope to see something ordinarily
> forbidden would fill the theater for a week.

---

[19] Less than 5 months later, Chief Allen submitted a letter of "retirement" under conditions that suggest he was forced out at the age of 52.

While editors for the local papers declared censorship to be "repugnant to the average American," at the same time they lamented that "blatant build-ups for borderline entertainments are encouraged ... for the sake of some quick and ready cash."

Bishop Rummel was unmoved:

> The absolution by the police and welfare departments ... and the plaudits of the theatrical critics do not surprise me. Neither do they affect the moral issues involved in a theatrical exhibition, which is highly publicized through an appeal to morbid curiosity. The promotion of a performance through such an appeal is morally reprehensible, whether the curiosity is actually satisfied or not. The public exhibition of nudity, whether it be real or feigned or cellophaned, continuous or intermittent, under the white glare of the klieg reflector or in the gloaming of cleverly manipulated stage lights, is a violation of objective moral standards. Such exhibitions are helping to destroy the sense of modesty in our American youth. They cannot be condoned by the pretext of artistry.[20]

And so the Earth continued to revolve. Forrest O'Brine arranged for the oil line on his aircraft to be repaired, Bishop Rummel conducted Sunday Mass, the Omaha constabulary went back to arresting drunk drivers, and "The Gateway to the West" went back to sleep. And Sally? Instead of having her ticket punched to Hades, she was on her way to Paradise — the Paradise Cabaret in New York City, that is.

---

[20] His animosity toward Sally aside, Bishop Rummel was not a totally rigid conservative. In later years, as Archbishop of New Orleans, he played a leading role in the desegregation of churches and schools, even in the period before the 1954 Supreme Court decision in *Brown v. Board of Education*.

CHAPTER ELEVEN

The Second Time Around

I think on-stage nudity is disgusting, shameful and damaging to all things American. But if I were 22 with a great body, it would be artistic, tasteful, patriotic and a progressive religious experience.

~ Shelley Winters

Fresh from her success at the 1933 Chicago Fair, Sally Rand could hardly help but notice that imitators were popping up like mushrooms. Every burg in the country seemed to have a fan dancer of its own. To distinguish herself from the pack, she needed something new. Fortunately, the outlines of something special had already begun to percolate in her mind. Meanwhile, a lucrative engagement would suit her very well.

The year before, on December 23, 1932, despite the Depression's continuing drag on the economy, legendary impresario Nils Thor Granlund (affectionately known as "Granny") had opened the Paradise Cabaret Restaurant on the second floor of the Brill Building at 49th Street and Broadway. In preparing for its grand opening, Granlund had gone for broke. Having previously announced that he would cater to an upscale clientele and would offer "stupendous and extravagant revues" of unparalleled quality, he made every effort to fulfill his pledge.

With an eye for beauty that put him in the same league as Earl Carroll and with Busby Berkley as his talent scout, Granlund had arranged to have a planeload of would-be showgirls flown in from Hollywood to audition for six-month contracts paying $100 per week (over $1,800 today). To put the girls at ease, he had asked his friend, the platinum blonde movie star Jean Harlow, to sit in on the auditions. Vouching for his character, Harlow had reassured the girls that "if any of you take this job and find that Granny has broken his promise, I'll personally make good on it."

Opening night had drawn a packed house. The Paradise was a roaring success.

When Sally arrived at the venue 14 months later, local officials were fully aware of her record of obscenity arrests in Chicago. But Granlund and Rand were ready for them. According to a syndicated columnist: "It is true that Miss Rand does her dance in the same costume, or lack of it, she wore at the exposition, but the lights have been so dimmed that it is almost impossible to see the other members of your party, much less Miss Rand." For the few critics who did manage to see something, Sally observed: "The human body is God's creation. It is beautiful and only the minds of men are ugly."

Sally's sojourn in Paradise proceeded without incident. Before wrapping up her engagement, she wrote John McMahon, co-owner of the Streets of Paris concession, offering to return as "the feature attraction" at the 1934 edition of the Chicago Fair. McMahon brushed aside Sally's offer, declaring: "The Streets of Paris is to be clean this year. It will be a place where any young man would not be ashamed to bring his mother, his sweetheart or his sister."

Sally shrugged off the snub, declaring that McMahon was making a big mistake. If Chicago didn't want her, well, plenty of other places did. Departing New York, she began a new tour with an all-star revue featuring "15 of the World's Fairest Girls" — making stops in Pennsylvania, Ohio, and Iowa.

The "bigger, better, more refined" Century of Progress Exposition opened on May 26, 1934, with considerable fanfare, but without the services of its most celebrated entertainer. Word on the street was that Sally, still on tour, was commanding weekly compensation of up to $8,500, a sum that even the most optimistic bean counters at the fair were reluctant to offer.

Organizers were refreshed, renewed, and ready to offer fairgoers a new, shiny, uplifting experience. New attractions included Henry Ford's 11-acre complex. The controversial Midway was relocated to a less prominent spot, as fair promoters continued to imagine that the public would surely be more interested in high-toned cultural and industrial attractions than in shows of a less refined nature. One report predicted: "It will display more of the meritorious and less of the meretricious. It will give ampler room to things worth seeing and clutter itself less with the trivial.... It will remain startling, but avoid the shocking."

In other words, exhibition sponsors couldn't bring themselves to acknowledge the contribution that Sally Rand had made to their financial well-being.

As one syndicated columnist put it, "Some people said the World Fair made Miss Sally Rand, but it would be more like it to say that she made the World Fair ... [as] the only prosperous attraction in the entire effort."

Remarking on the "many lesser ladies in little booths and cubicles along the midway," he went on to refer rather indelicately to Sally's exposed skin as "a pelt which, in the long run, has proved much more valuable than any garment of chinchilla or Russian sable ever manufactured."

Despite solemn promises of decency from the sponsors of the 1934 Fair, its managers soon came to understand which side their bread was buttered on. It didn't take long. On June 1st, only a few days after the fair's opening, the Streets of Paris concession was ordered closed because of two "indecent shows." As Bruce Grant's syndicated column remarked: "There are ... goings-on and comings-off in practically every café, beer garden or racy concession at the fair."

Sally Rand may not have been present in the Streets of Paris, but Miss Mona Leslie, the lovely 18-year-old "Diving Venus," certainly *was* there, and something about her performance was seducing more than a few fairgoers to take a look. That "something" was her attire — a combination of makeup and gilt paint.

Informed that Miss Leslie was performing "au naturelle," officials ordered her to desist immediately, going so far as to threaten closure of the entire Streets of Paris venue if the ban was ignored.

Concession operators had a more flexible take on the matter. After all, Miss Leslie was bringing in the big bucks. Besides, they argued, no one was being knocked over the head and dragged into the shows. And, if "The Diving Venus"[1] wasn't exactly your cup of tea, there were plenty of other attractions that would accept your money.

Sally was the most talked about woman in America. If some other female had a credible claim to that title in 1934, she was not a contemporary entertainer, politician or world figure. Rather, the challenge to Sally's standing would come from a very unlikely place indeed — a small farm near the Canadian village of Corbeil, Ontario.

At this remote spot, two days after the Chicago Fair reopened, a young woman named Mrs. Elzire Dionne had given birth two months prematurely

---

[1] Mona Leslie was well known for her aquatic talents. In April 1938, a husky coast guardsman rescued Mona from icy Lake Michigan when she suffered cramps and nearly drowned while performing a publicity stunt.

to five little girls. In the days and years to come, the "Dionne Quintuplets" would become world famous — the first such quintette ever to have survived infancy. Dr. Allan Roy Dafoe, who had delivered the five with the help of two midwives, would become the most famous physician in North America and Sally Rand would slip from first to sixth on the list of the nation's most talked about girls.

W ith community morality in mind, the Most Reverend John Aloysius Duffy, Bishop of Syracuse, selflessly volunteered to monitor the content of motion pictures and theatrical productions seeking an audience in his fair city. His offer was in line with the mission of the recently established "Legion of Decency."[2] Getting wind of the scheduled appearance of Miss Rand in June 1934, and probably aware of the frustrated efforts of his counterpart in Omaha, Bishop Duffy warned:

> I must regard the presence of the Rand woman on the stage of
> Loew's Theater as an act of public defiance of the moral sentiments
> of the Catholic people of Syracuse. This dancer has been an object of
> criticism in many cities of the United States. Her act, by all
> accounts, has nothing to recommend it but its appeal to the senses.
> I want every Catholic to know that attendance at her performance
> is an act for which they are morally responsible.

A local journalist offered another, more worldly perspective: "... now after seeing scores of imitators, Syracuse will see the original version of the dance which proved such a boom to the ostrich fan industry."

Scores of imitators? The truth is, the fan dance wasn't anything new to Syracuse. Just three months earlier, the RKO Keith's Theatre had staged Faith Bacon's "Century of Progress Revue." As derided by one critic:

> Not even in the days when the old Savoy was playing tag with the
> police censor did Syracuse see the equivalent of the display of near
> nudity featured on the Keith stage yesterday. The artist was, I take
> it, Faith Bacon, styled as the originator of the fan dance. True, Miss
> Bacon had one or two fans in her support at times, but ... [it] was
> the closest thing to a stag show "specialty" that a major Syracuse
> theater has offered in my time.

---

2   The National Legion of Decency was organized by the Catholic Church in 1933 to
monitor movies for content considered offensive from the church's perspective. All
Hollywood films first needed to secure approval under the movie industry's own
secular production code, before being submitted to the Legion for review. Disapproval
meant over 20 million Catholics were theoretically forbidden from seeing the picture.

Bishop Duffy must have been otherwise engaged on that occasion. But in the present instant he plowed straight ahead, raising such a stink and rallying support from so many other churches and religious organizations that Loew's State Theatre acceded to the protests and announced the cancellation of Sally's show.

From her dressing room in Rochester, New York, where she was wrapping up a one-week engagement, Sally played the "you can't fire me, I quit" card: "So Syracuse doesn't want me. Well, they're a little too late. I'd already cancelled my engagement there before the city fathers, or whoever they are, got up in arms."

She then displayed a telegram from Joseph Imburgio, impresario of the Italian Village concession at the Chicago Fair: "Cancel all engagements. We must have you here by Monday." Taking issue with Bishop Duffy's assessment of Sally's show, Imburgio offered: "It is quite artistic. In fact it's a wow."

O n her way to Chicago, Sally stopped for a night at the Park Central Hotel in New York City. No sooner did she sit down for an interview with H. Allen Smith than the telephone rang. It was Max Baer, the celebrated boxer who, a week earlier at the outdoor Madison Square Garden Bowl on Long Island, had knocked out the 275-pound Primo Carnera to become Heavyweight Champion of the World. Also staying at the hotel, Max was hoping to join Sally in her room. In his mind they were chums. After all, only seven months earlier, the two had appeared in a photo together peeking above Sally's fans and smiling at newspaper readers across the land.

In truth, Max regarded himself as more of a ladies' man than the ladies themselves did. Clearly annoyed by the champ's solicitation, Sally gave him an earful. As Smith overheard just before she slammed down the receiver: "Listen, you bum, I heard enough of your blab out on the coast. Go chase yourself around Central Park and when you get back don't try to chime in on my game." Then, turning to her guest, Sally continued:

> If that guy comes up here, I am going to smack him with a hairbrush.
> He's a nuisance. He tried to crash in on me at Chicago and again in
> Frisco. I find it necessary to give him the ice. A constant noise in my
> ear is very upsetting. And anyway, I'm engaged.

Having once again contracted to appear at the Century of Progress International Exposition, Sally left for Chicago with the secure knowledge that she had another four months of prosperity in hand.

Mary Belle

A mere four days before Sally's heralded return, young Mr. Samuel Wallace, Jr., and Miss Gertrude Boone Schubeck had managed to grab some national headlines of their own by holding their wedding rites on the grounds of the Chicago Fair, under the watchful eyes of life-size dinosaurs in an exhibit called "Down the Lost River to the World a Million Years Ago."

The ceremony would have been unremarkable but for the adventurous young couple's intention to lend authenticity to the "Garden of Eden" location. Under the headline "NUDISTS WED IN CAVEMAN FASHION," syndicated articles reported that: "The unblushing bride wore a suit given her on her birthday twenty-three years ago, but she hid a going away outfit behind a stuffed brontosaurus in the bushes. The bridegroom wore a smile."

While the wedding party had apparently begun their river tour fully clothed, they had surreptitiously slipped out of the boat at a concealed location, doffed their garments, and quickly staged the secluded ritual at 10:30 in the morning. "Since it was private," said the concession manager, "we felt that the fair officials would not object."

Well, not exactly private. In addition to the wedding party of nine plus two official witnesses (including Alois Knapp of the Zoro Nature League nudist camp), the bold young couple had invited a small press contingent to document the ceremony. This proved to be a mistake. The concession manager may not have personally objected, but he was not the sole arbiter of such matters. With Sally Rand prepping for her return to the fairgrounds, another of the previous year's cast of characters predictably came out of the woodwork.

Within 48 hours of their marriage, the newlyweds were arrested on a charge of "participating in an indecent and obscene exhibition." The arrest had been arranged by none other than our old friend Mary Belle Spencer (who had yet to succeed in her attempts to escort Sally Rand to the Big House). Mrs. Spencer had somehow learned of the couple's intentions and had dispatched a divinity student, Joseph Patterson, to attend their nuptials posing as a press photographer. Arrest warrants were sworn out in the name of her "client," the "high minded" young Patterson, and served on the happy couple as they were eating a honeymoon breakfast.

A hearing was scheduled for Monday, July 2nd, but when both Patterson and Spencer failed to appear, the case was continued to the following Friday. Adjusting his large horn-rimmed glasses, Municipal Judge Francis Borelli was heard to remark: "That woman gets under my skin." He was no more charitable regarding the whole event: "A Century of Progress!

What kind of progress is this — going back to worse than Adam and Eve. At least *they* wore fig leaves. It seems like anything without clothes is a big sensation over at the fair."

Addressing the press, the ardent young husband tried to explain: "We wanted to be married in prehistoric surroundings and we thought it was going to be a private affair. We never would have been there if we had known what was going to happen."[3] The couple was released on bonds of $1,000 each.

In court on Friday, all the players were present and accounted for. The "nudelyweds" offered a spirited defense, proclaiming the purity of their intentions and asserting that nudism is a "health movement," a call of nature that stirs the soul. Their attorney, Sydney R. Drebin, argued that the unorthodox ceremony had been performed to demonstrate the sincerity of his clients and that he knew of no law which prohibits the "exposure of sincerity." Characterized as the complainant's "mannishly attired attorney," Mary Belle Spencer countered that the defendant's own statements proved that the naked ceremony had been "nothing but a sacrilegious burlesque show — getting married without clothes on." She declared: "They are corrupting public morals."

In preparing her case, Mary Belle had subpoenaed several psychiatrists, including Dr. Harry Hoffman of the Cook County Behavior Clinic, to testify that nude weddings were a true menace to the nation's morals. Several photographers and newsreel cameramen were in line to get subpoenas, as well. "We're going to show movies of that disgraceful affair when we get into court," the stern Mrs. Spencer promised.

However, by the time the case did come before a judge, not everyone was still on board. Reportedly harassed and threatened by unnamed parties, divinity student Patterson had experienced a change of heart. Telling the court that he regretted signing a complaint against the couple, he added: "The surroundings were beautiful. It was a wonderful and impressive ceremony, I thought. I've repented now and I don't think the affair was obscene."

In the end, pleas for tolerance fell on deaf ears. Judge Borelli's disposition was more in tune with that of Paramount News cameraman Martin Barnett, who testified that he felt the wedding was "a very disgusting affair." Citing the fall of Rome and the decadence of the Israelites during

---

3   This plea of purity by the groom is somewhat suspect as he failed to mention that the couple had actually repeated the nude ceremony for the benefit of photographers who weren't able to focus their cameras the first time around.

the absence of Moses, Judge Borelli declared that "nudism has no place in any civilized country" and pronounced the couple guilty of an indecent exhibition. (It's a good thing Sally was tried before Judge David last year, rather than this guy!)

The prosecution recommended leniency, and sentencing was delayed for several days. When the court reconvened, Judge Borelli asked the newly-weds: "Will you stay away from nudist colonies?" After the chastened pair nodded their agreement, the judge decreed: "All right. I'll sentence you to one year in jail on the grounds of indecent exposure, but I'll hold up the sentence and put you on probation. Put nudism behind you. Sacrifice your unusual ideas for the sake of your parents and for the nation at large."

The case was closed and everybody was relatively happy. Well, maybe not *everybody*. Moral crusader Mary Belle Spencer was indignant at the leniency shown the young couple. "They should have gone to jail," she said.

As the parties and onlookers emerged from the Cook County Courthouse into the light of a sunny July day, hundreds of other spectators across town at the Century of Progress fairgrounds were lining up to catch the new and improved act of the year's most talked about performer. Popular show-man Ernie Young had been engaged to produce a revue at the Italian Village and, even without Sally's return, his show had been an immediate hit. Additional tables had been squeezed in to accommodate the overflow crowds cheering a line of chorus girls as they strutted their stuff through such numbers as a military drill that concluded in a blaze of neon fire (guns carried by the girls illuminated to spell "Italy").[4]

It was icing on the cake for the Italian Village when Sally was installed on July 3rd as the featured performer in *Ernie Young's 1934 World's Fair Revue*. The celebrated dancer had returned triumphant. Despite national saturation and overexposure of the fan dancing craze, the "original" fan dance was still a big draw. And there was also talk of an exciting new dance — something about a giant bubble! Regarding her return, Sally observed: "I was so scared I wasn't going to get to play it a second year. I guess Branfield really got it done with the Mafia."

---

[4] Meanwhile, at an *actual* Italian villa, German Chancellor Adolf Hitler and Italian
     dictator Benito Mussolini were meeting face to face for the first time. Two weeks later
     Hitler would order a purge of his "enemies" both within and without the Nazi party, in
     what would come to be called the "Night of the Long Knives."

The Mafia? Well, Ernie Young's revue was, after all, presented at the Ristorante San Carlo in the Italian Village, a locale reputed to be a favorite of Al Capone's associates. Joseph Imburgio, manager at the Italian Village, also held office as President of the Unione Siciliana and was regarded by many as a "mouthpiece" for the Chicago Mafia. In short, he was a man accustomed to getting his way. Sally may have been absent during the revue's first month of operation, but if Imburgio wanted her back at the fair, he had connections that could make it happen.

Sally wasn't the only noteworthy gal working at the restaurant. Eighteen-year-old mob "moll" Virginia Hill was also at the San Carlo, where she did a little dancing and worked as a waitress, although for such low wages that she was reputed to be earning more on her back than on her feet. She soon became a trusted confidant and cash courier for the mob, helping to launder suitcases full of dirty money.[5]

Little is known about any connection there may have been between Sally and the Chicago mob, although Louie Greenberg (financial advisor to Al Capone) once claimed that the people he represented "owned Sally Rand." The man who represented Benny Goodman and many other top dance bands, Jules Stein, President of the Music Corporation of America (MCA), is known to have accommodated certain shady but influential figures in order to secure bookings in Chicago venues controlled by Capone.[6]

For several months Sally had felt confident that she would eventually return to the fair. The novelty of fan dancing may have been on the wane, but Sally had something new up her sleeve: "I knew I'd be back, so while I toured the country, I worked on my 'encore.'" The encore was to be the "bubble dance," a number in which she would appear to be naked, by turns concealed and revealed behind a huge translucent bubble, complete with lighting and choreography set to Beethoven's *Moonlight Sonata*, Brahms' *Waltz*, and Debussy's *Claire de Lune*.

All that remained was to somehow come up with a supply of five-foot, semitransparent balloons. Ordering ostrich feather fans had become a

---

[5]   Miss Hill was the girlfriend of mobster "Bugsy" Siegel, who was assassinated in her California home in 1947, just four days after she had departed for Paris. The couple's lives were portrayed in the 1991 film *Bugsy*, starring Annette Bening and Warren Beatty.

[6]   Al Capone wasn't the only Chicago mobster making news in 1934. Some of the biggest names in crime were grabbing headlines. On July 22nd, John Dillinger ("Public Enemy No. 1") was shot and killed by FBI agents outside Chicago's Biograph Theater. And, on November 27th, George "Baby Face" Nelson, after hiding out in the Chicago area, was gunned down in a shootout that also took the lives of two FBI agents.

routine matter, but finding a balloon big enough, transparent enough, and yet tough enough to resist bursting was a tall order. Did such a thing even exist? And, if not, could it be created?

Toward that end, Sally contacted several major companies that produced balloons and other rubber products, but none could provide a giant bubble with the characteristics she required. The cost of manufacture would be prohibitive. As Sally described it:

> I found that the balloon I required, sixty inches in diameter (which is my height), of a translucent, transparent quality, had never been manufactured by any rubber company, and that no equipment existed to manufacture one. The largest balloon then being made was for government use. It was of a heavy red rubber, thirty inches in diameter, and was used for target practice by the War Department. I would have to provide expensive equipment, and funds for experimentation to obtain a light balloon with the ethereal quality I believed necessary to make my new dance effective.
>
> The estimate ... was so great that I had to be sure of a large return to warrant such an investment. How to measure the possibility of such a return? Only the faith and confidence one has in oneself, and in the merchandise to be sold, could justify such an expenditure.

Undaunted, Sally approached the Oak Rubber Company of Ravenna, Ohio, a firm that had been turning out millions of special purpose balloons since 1916. To jumpstart the project, she offered to personally finance the creation of a new aluminum mold of the type required to manufacture her special balloon. After a few false starts, while Sally was investing $11,000 to bring the project to completion, a suitable balloon was finally produced — one that could be replicated at about $25 a pop.[7]

As she continued touring in the spring of 1934 (with the new "equipment" secretly in hand), Sally practiced her new dance in any space she could find that offered the necessary 25 feet of headroom. By the time she arrived at the Italian Village, her new routine had been pretty much perfected.

While an air of mystery cloaked the actual details, Sally's press agent leaked enough advance information to raise expectations. Fair officials were con-

---

[7] Several sources indicate that Sally owned the patent either on the balloons' design or on the machine that made them. The Navy reportedly used the balloons for target practice, paying Sally a $25 royalty for each one (or about $450 per balloon today). The federal government may have also used them as weather balloons. It's not clear whether there was any truth to these claims, beyond the imaginings of a press agent.

cerned enough to demand a preview. Sally demurred, confident that no one
could legally stop a show that hadn't yet been seen. "I can get an injunction
to prove it," she said. It was known only that Miss Rand planned to appear in
a low light setting, either enclosed or hidden by a "great transparent bubble."
The dance was said to consist of soft music and slow weaving steps. And
then, the luminous sphere would "slowly float upward, leaving Sally. And
not much else."

Visitors to the second edition of the fair could hardly turn around
without bumping into a fan dancer. But on July 3rd Sally strode forth
with something specifically designed to separate herself from the flock. The
bubble dance itself is somewhat difficult to describe. It involved a lot of
turning, tossing, and tip-toeing, as Sally negotiated the translucent balloon
around the stage wearing a sort of see-through mini-toga that she coyly
snatched away as the lights dimmed and the audience leaned forward. An
eyewitness described it:

> To the strains of soft music, the central back draperies parted and
> there ... stood the fair, famous Sally Rand. In the semi-darkness,
> you could see that her exquisitely proportioned and apparently
> absolutely nude little body was painted white. A blue spotlight
> played upon the shining and iridescent balloon which she held
> before her. The contrast between the blue balloon and her white
> statue-like body was truly artistic. With all the grace of a woodland
> nymph, she toyed and danced around and played with and tossed
> into the air her transparent soap bubble. Somehow, one felt as
> though secretly watching some little woodland creature at play in
> the moonlight. The audience seemed hardly to breathe! In a few
> moments, there was an orchestral climax and Sally and her bubble
> vanished into the folds of stage draperies.

The new dance was received with enthusiasm. Indeed, it was so popular
that Ernie Young was forced to schedule extra performances — as many as
13 shows a day. Sally recalled: "I had to have two sets of actors, singers,
and dancers. Otherwise the schedule would have killed them all."[8]

---

[8] According to a *Chicago Daily News* article by Clark Rodenbach, acts that preceded
Sally's appearance included "the Radions, a handsome and graceful team of ballroom
dancers; Paul Gordon, a bicyclist as much at home on wheels as on his feet; Carita, a
lady with a voice; Lazaar, a dancer with a 'drunk' specialty [act], and the Novelle
Brothers, nut violinists, who work with a pretty girl stooge and an educated dog."
Another "highly entertaining" act in the show was "Black Midnight," in which twenty
shapely girls danced while "tastefully adorned in ebony paint and plumes in their hair."

All the rehearsal time had been well spent and the bubble dance went without a hitch — well, at least for the first couple of days. Early in the first week, managers of the Italian Village nixed the act, having determined that strong air currents off Lake Michigan would interfere with Sally's ability to properly maneuver the large inflatable. Rather than disappoint the paying customers, Sally agreed to perform her fan dance instead, even though appeals of her obscenity trial had still not run their course.

Despite a few mishaps like the bubble suddenly bursting or simply floating away, the new routine was a resounding success. Her fan dance was still well received, of course, and there was even a third dance — the little remembered "gorilla" dance. Teamed up with dancer Bill Raisch, who wore a gorilla suit, Sally allowed herself to be flung "around ruthlessly in a wild adagio."[9]

Oddly, Sally appeared to be more "nude" doing her 1934 bubble dance than she ever did when performing the 1933 fan dance. So, why wasn't she being arrested? The intervening court cases, the money that the fair was raking in, and, frankly, a change in public opinion — all played a role. "Nudity" and "Art" had become matters of public debate.

Chicago columnist Hob Steely described critics as bewailing:

> If they would at least don brassieres and panties, they might be
> forgiven. But when it comes right down to their birthday clothes,
> it's a disgrace. The may call it art, but to us this nudity is nothing
> short of barbaric paganism and exploitation of the form divine.
> Heaven deliver us from a naked nation.

When Steely asked Sally about her many arrests in the previous year, she cheerfully replied:

> Last year when those fans kept my body covered, I was
> persecuted. That was because the people had not become fully
> educated. This year, I wear absolutely nothing and depend upon
> a transparent bubble as my only adornment, and I am hailed as a
> genius. Figure that out.

9
  Once an adagio dancer in the *Ziegfeld Follies*, Bill Raisch had also appeared in the
  stage musical *Whoopee* with Eddie Cantor. He lost his right arm from above the
  elbow in World War II, putting an end to his adagio dancing days. Nevertheless, he
  made his way to Hollywood in 1944 and over the next two decades appeared in
  around 20 films, all in uncredited roles. In 1963, he landed the role of the mysterious
  "one-armed man" in the popular television series *The Fugitive*, starring David Janssen.
  The first episode in which he appeared was titled "The Girl from Little Egypt."

Since I was six years old, I have studied dancing. And I learned almost from the beginning that nudity is essential to dancing just like it is to the portrait painter. It's art and nothing else.

When I started the fan dance my father, a staid, old fashioned army officer, was shocked. No girl of his was going to peel off her clothes and gyrate in front of the public. But after he saw me dance, his opinion was changed completely. So was my mother's view altered. So you see, this nudism certainly should not offend even our grandmothers. It's just one way of forcefully expressing our dance. The painter requires nudity, so why not the stage?

B eginning around 1915, the "Great Black Migration," brought tens of thousands of African Americans from the southern states to Chicago, gradually turning the character of the city from one influenced almost exclusively by European immigrants to a much more culturally diverse society. Eventually the Chicago melting pot would bring to prominence such disparate characters as author Studs Terkel, blues great Muddy Waters, mob boss Alphonse "Scarface" Capone, *Ebony* magazine publisher John Johnson, and the controversial Mayor Richard J. Daley (not to mention a mixed-race young gentleman who would ascend to the presidency of the United States).

In the midst of this migration came the "Century of Progress" World's Fair, an enterprise that needed to appeal to all comers in order to be financially successful. Chicago was an integrated community, one in which all residents expected equal treatment. But, as we know, expectations don't always match up with reality. Rufus C. Dawes, president of the exposition, had assured black civic leaders that discrimination would not be tolerated and his good intentions were seemingly being realized, at least at first.

In 1933, the opening day parade down Michigan Avenue featured "a color guard of Negro policemen." The replica of a log cabin built in 1779 by Jean Baptiste due Sable, a man of color and Chicago's first settler, was also a point of pride for black visitors. But, at "Darkest Africa," while the ceremonial dances may have been educational on some level, many considered the gyrations of the dancers in their animal skins and ostrich feathers to be offensive. At the Midway's blatantly racist "African Dip," fairgoers tossed balls at a target, seeking to dunk a seated black man from his platform into a tank of water. The participants commonly taunted each other.

Black patrons visited the fair in large numbers despite many reports of discrimination, including accounts of restaurants where they were refused service or were otherwise insulted. Court actions were initiated against such venues as the Pabst Blue Ribbon Casino and the Old Mexico concession.

With jobs scarce during the Depression, black leaders were encouraged to believe that the fair would provide their people opportunities for decent paying employment. When black entrepreneur Sam Hunter was awarded the washroom concession, hopes were raised. According to the *Chicago Defender*, this was both:

> ... the beginning and the end of the Race employment at the first installment of the fair. Of course members of the Race[10] crept in at various places, but so few and far between were [there] any employees who happened not to be connected with washrooms that they constituted a negligible minority on the staff of fair employees.

By the time the fair reopened in 1934, conditions had markedly improved for African Americans. From a mere 75 black employees working on the fairgrounds in 1933, the figure had risen to around 300 for the 1934 fair. Fewer cases of discrimination were reported and black patrons were generally met with a more receptive attitude. A notable exception, reported by the *Defender*, involved the Orange Crush concession where black patrons were served drinks in paper cups, while the popular beverage was served to white customers in standard glasses. In short, the racial justice situation was uneven at best, as would be the case for many decades to come.

A few years earlier on March 25, 1931, nine black teenage boys were pulled off a train at Paint Rock, Alabama, by a local sheriff and his deputized posse. The nine were arrested and ultimately charged with raping two white girls. The case was first heard in Scottsboro, Alabama, where the boys received little competent representation. All but one were hurriedly convicted and sentenced to death. The resulting outrage and ensuing series of appeals brought the "Scottsboro Boys" to the nation's attention. By October 1932, the case had reached the U.S. Supreme Court. Finding none of the defendants had received a fair trial, seven of the nine Justices voted to send the case back to the Alabama court system for retrial — the first time a state criminal conviction had been reversed for a violation of the U.S. Bill of Rights.

The seemingly endless series of appeals, together with the continuing influence of the Ku Klux Klan and rising tensions due in part to the impact of the Great Depression, motivated the National Association for the

---

10 As used here, "the Race" dates back to the 1930s. As one writer explained: "... some terms that blacks used for themselves were so common they escaped notice and debate, most notably *the Race*, with the word *Race* usually capitalized.... Black newspapers were 'Race papers'.... The phrases 'our group' and 'our people' were equally common."

Advancement of Colored People (NAACP) to create a National Defense Fund devoted to offsetting the expense of fighting civil rights court cases.[11] To assist in filling its coffers, the NAACP scheduled a major fundraiser at the Regal Theater in the heart of Chicago's "Bronzeville," to be held at midnight, Saturday, August 4, 1934. Dozens of performers well known in the African American community had agreed to appear, but event sponsors were still hoping to secure one or two big names to further assure a successful event.

Between her Tuesday evening shows at the Italian Village, Sally met with a prominent pair of African American visitors — famous orchestra leader and songwriter, Noble Sissle (best known for his collaboration with Eubie Blake and their hit song "I'm Just Wild About Harry" from the 1921 Broadway musical *Shuffle Along*), and his companion Wilson Lovett, a local banker, insurance executive, and chairman of the NAACP benefit committee. The pair sought the meeting to explain the group's efforts to promote justice for African Americans and to invite Sally to perform at the special midnight benefit four nights later. Her response to their presentation, as reported by the *Chicago Defender* newspaper, was quite warm and enthusiastic:

> This is a wonderful, marvelous work. What you are asking me to do might seem like a small matter to you, but it isn't. I have hundreds of calls to do the same thing for worthy causes. I cannot agree to all of them.... But I am coming to your benefit.[12] You may tell your people that I'll be there and bring my show. I am going to make your benefit the occasion of my only appearance outside the fairgrounds this season. I am coming because I want to and desire to help. Not only on the night of the affair, but from now on you may count on me to help in any way I can.

The feeling was mutual. A local press report about the event exulted:

> "Sally and her Fan!" "Sally and her Fan!" "SALLY AND HER FAN!" Everybody's sayin' it. Young and old, the sophisticates, the aristocrats, the dreamers and the doers, all of them are talking about Sally Rand and her Fan.

---

[11] The NAACP Legal Defense Fund went on to play a major role in the civil rights movement. It's most famous advocate, Thurgood Marshall, successfully argued the 1954 landmark school desegregation case *Brown v. Board of Education*. He later became the first black justice of the United States Supreme Court.

[12] This was the capper to a most successful day for Sissle and Lovett, who just a few hours earlier had persuaded big game hunter Frank "Bring 'em Back Alive" Buck to also take the stage at the benefit and describe his many and varied experiences with wild animals.

As the day of the big show drew closer, more and more entertainers wanted in on the action. The African American opera star Kenneth Spencer offered to come all the way from San Francisco: "Let me know immediately if you will use my services." Sunshine Sammy and his orchestra from the Shim Sham Shimmy Club joined the show. Faith Bacon called six times to offer her services, but there was little demand for a second fan dancer so the sponsors wired their regrets. As one journalist put it, "Unfortunately, only so many persons can be used in a four-hour show."

One fine summer morning in a posh Chicago hotel, as Sally was preparing for her groundbreaking appearance at the Regal Theater, nine well-dressed professional men and women were sitting down for a six-course breakfast. They were seated at a corner table, surrounded by paneled walls and facing a starched white tablecloth arrayed with fine china, polished silverware, and fancy water pitchers. Everyone was in good spirits; everyone that is except for the tenth guest, positioned at the head of the table. There was something a little odd about *him*.

Oddities were the order of the day. After all, Robert Ripley's "Odditorium" was one of the fair's most successful attractions. One might come upon most anything at the World's Fair — fan dancers, hucksters, incubator babies, midgets — even famed aviator Amelia Earhart being pulled around in a rickshaw. Into the mix, one might encounter pickpockets, predators, prudes, prevaricators, prostitutes, psychopaths and, yes, even naprapaths.

Wait a minute. What was that last one again? Let's return to that special breakfast meeting at Chicago's famous Palmer House Hotel. This was no ordinary breakfast. It was the first meeting of the so-called Post Mortem Club, held in conjunction with the 25th annual convention of practitioners of Naprapathy. The founder of the Chicago College of Naprapathy, Dr. Oakley Smith, had arranged for and presided over the meal, but the guest of honor was a certain Mr. J. M. McAdou, just in from Florida. Well, sort of, anyway. Since McAdou had died the previous year, the gentleman was present only in skeletal form, having arrived in Chicago the day before in a large crate delivered c/o Dr. Oakley Smith.

Mr. McAdou had been a patient of Dr. Smith seven years before when he had promised to bequeath his skeleton to Smith for further study of his incurable case of advanced paralysis. In any case, what remained of the good doctor's former patient was now wired together, propped up on a couple of thick Chicago phone books and seated at the head of the table with Dr. Smith at his left. From this vantage point, with a cigarette casually placed between his jaws, the former J. M. McAdou seemed to be enjoying the occasion as best he could in the company of Smith and the eight other naprapaths.

Dr. Smith, a bald-headed 54 year old, smartly attired in gold-rimmed glasses and winged collar, patted McAdou's smooth skull affectionately and explained: "He told me he had an object d'art which he would deliver to me in person one of these days. Yesterday it arrived in a packing case. I instantly recognized my old friend from his spinal curves."

Informed of the situation, the other breakfast guests cheerfully pledged to Dr. Oakley that, in the interest of the advancement of Naprapathy, each would, at an appropriate time of course, also dedicate his or her skeleton to the cause. Dr. Smith graciously accepted their generous offers, assuring the Post Mortem Club members that each skeleton would be feted as the honored guest at a similar breakfast table in the future.

Such macabre doings may seem outrageous if not disturbing to the modern reader, but we are talking about a time of more spare and simple entertainment. Diversions like television, video games, and smart phones were almost unimaginable. This was a time when the infamous quack Dr. John R. Brinkley promoted transplanting goat testicles into human males as a cure for impotency and Dr. Wilhelm Reich promoted sexual liberation, proclaiming that certain mental disorders have their origins in a person's sexual and socio-economic experience, and stem from an insufficiency of what the controversial doctor called "orgastic potency."[13] Even phrenology still had its adherents.

Yes, yes, you may say, this is all very diverting, but what exactly is Naprapathy? OK. Here it is. Naprapathy, simply defined, is a drug-free healing system based on the theory that disease or illness is caused by strained ligaments and other connective tissue disorders. Treatment consists of manipulation of muscles, joints, and ligaments to stimulate the natural healing process. Or, as Dr. Smith put it in a 1933 Iowa court case: "This is not only a method of treatment of human ailments but I have cured horses. It is not limited to human ailments. It is limited to anything that has a spinal column and joints and ligaments. It is a healing art."

[13] Believing a healthy orgasm to be the cure for all ills, Reich invented the "Orgone Box" — a wooden cupboard about the size of a telephone booth intended to prevent "severe biopathic disturbances" — and influenced a surprising number of literary and political figures to adopt his unorthodox practices in the 1940s and 50s.

Serious assertions of its founder aside, in Dr. Smith's day, Naprapathy was seen as little more than a somewhat questionable offshoot of Chiropractic.[14] Indeed, one magazine item charged: "There was not a regular doctor in Chicago, in Illinois or in the U.S. last week who had anything but supreme contempt for the medical theories of 'Dr.' Oakley Smith."

Apparently, not everyone is capable of recognizing true genius when they see it. With this in mind, Dr. Smith decided that the practice of Naprapathy could benefit from a dash of upbeat publicity, something that didn't involve the display of a former patient's remains. So, he prevailed upon a certain "bubble dancer" from the World's Fair to make an appearance at his convention and undergo a Naprapathy exam. And since she seldom passed up the chance to have her picture in the paper, Sally cheerfully assented.

With her hair pulled up and wearing a sporty white hat, in preparation for her examination, Sally lowered the top of her polka-dot dress to present her upper back, sans brassiere, for Dr. Smith's professional scrutiny. Arranging his "multitherm" apparatus in such a way as to apply gentle pressure to various points on her bare back, Dr. Smith demonstrated his technique for recording the temperature of tissue and locating suspicious nerve bundles around the area of her spine. The stated goal was to reveal the presence of any "ligatights" that might be the cause of undiagnosed pressure on specific nerves. Finding none, he declared Miss Rand to be a perfectly healthy specimen, something quite apparent to anyone who had observed her walking into the room.

The press was on hand, of course, and the resulting photo appeared in newspapers across the land, even in the *Syracuse Herald* where Bishop Duffy could easily clip it out and paste it in his scrapbook.

Faith

Sally was making the cash registers chime but, of course, she was not alone. Her chief rival had returned to Chicago for a second year as well. As a press report urged readers:

> One of the best shows on the Northerly Island is that which graces
> the dance floor at the Hollywood-at-the Fair. Here the shapely
> Faith Bacon, real originator of the dance of the fans and once
> chosen by Flo Ziegfeld as the "Most Beautiful Girl in America,"
> does her stuff in several nightly revues.

---

[14] The Chicago College of Naprapathic Medicine continues in operation to this day. If you are a young person trying to figure out what to do with the rest of your life, you might want to visit its web page at www.naprapathicmedicine.edu.

Just as Sally brought something new to the fair, Faith did as well. In her "Gardenia Dance," Faith would traipse around the stage wearing only a girdle of gardenia blossoms, thoughtfully discarding them as she went along, much to the disappointment (as one commentator quipped) of customers who had hoped she would appear with only one gardenia and then discard the petals. Faith described her dance:

> I come out with nothing on but gardenias. I begin to toss them away. Then I climb to the top of a fountain with only one gardenia on and, as the music reaches a crescendo, I pull that off, kiss it and toss it into the audience. Nice huh!

What with Sally packing them in at the Italian Village and Faith turning heads at the Hollywood concession, operators of the Streets of Paris were somewhat out in the cold, looking for a way to reclaim the top dog position the venue had enjoyed in 1933.

Enter Avrom Hirsch Goldbogen, the youngest of nine children of Polish immigrants who had settled in Chicago after the First World War. A budding producer at the age of 25, he had come up with an idea for a dance based on the allegory of the moth and the flame. It wasn't long before dancer Shannon Dean, dressed in a gauzy winged moth costume, took to the stage in the Streets of Paris with "The Flame Dance." The idea was for the dancer to flutter around the stage, coming closer and closer to a huge candle powered by a gas flame controlled by a mechanism under the stage. At the climax of the dance, the below-stage operator would turn up the gas, whereupon Miss Dean's costume would catch fire and fall away, leaving the dancer apparently nude as she hurriedly exited the stage. It was a tricky bit of business. The young producer later quipped: "I burned up four girls before I got it right."[15]

On August 4, 1934, a year to the day after her famous "arrested-four-times-in-the-same-day" adventure, the notorious fan dancer from the Century of Progress Fair emerged from behind a velvet curtain at 1:00 o'clock

---

[15] Avrom Goldbogen, whose family nickname had been "Toat" or "Toad," legally changed his name to Michael Todd at age 19. Despite any blunders in the Streets of Paris, he went on to fame as a theatrical impresario and Hollywood producer, marrying his third wife, cinema icon Elizabeth Taylor, in 1957. That same year his movie *Around the World in Eighty Days* won the Academy Award for Best Picture. Little more than a year after the marriage, while on his way to New York to accept the "Showman of the Year" award, Mike Todd was killed in the crash of his private plane near Grants, New Mexico.

in the morning and set her foot upon the stage of the lavishly decorated, six-year-old Regal Theater in Chicago, one of the country's finest entertainment venues catering to an essentially exclusive black clientele. The audience was delighted, but, artistry and the merits of the cause aside, not everyone was comfortable with the notion that a young white lady was prepared to parade around the stage in minimal attire for the entertainment of a predominantly African American audience.

"SALLY RAND STEALS SHOW AT NAACP BENEFIT" — So trumpeted the outsized headline on page 8 of the *Chicago Defender*. The midnight extravaganza at the Regal Theater kicked off to the rhythms of Claude Hopkins and his big band, followed by master of ceremonies, Leonard Reed. A 27-year-old light-skinned gentleman of black, white, and Choctaw ancestry, Reed was a popular tap dancer, known in black vaudeville and clubs as the "Shim Sham Shimmy" man.[16] According to the *Defender*, his "wisecracks kept the place gay throughout the evening. Leonard is one of the finest emcees in the business and the crowd generally finds him as interesting as the show itself."[17]

Several other bands and stage performers from local nightclubs entertained the audience of an estimated 2,000 enthusiastic donors well into the wee hours. True to her word, Sally was on hand, complete with her 20-person revue and the Art Frasik Band from the Italian Village. As reported by the *Defender*, she was very well received:

> The midnight benefit given at the Regal Theater last Saturday
> under the auspices of the NAACP scored a tremendous hit with
> local theatergoers. The galaxy of stars appearing brought round
> after round of applause with their fine dance and song numbers as
> some of the country's leading bands played. The big feature of the
> evening, of course, was Sally Rand, fan dancer, who stepped about
> the stage to a trio of encores costumed in two large white fans. Miss
> Rand brought along her own band and show which likewise
> proved popular with the patrons.

---

[16] A tap dance routine often called the "national anthem of tap," the Shim Sham (or Shim Sham Shimmy) began as a dance called the "Goofus," performed to "Turkey in the Straw." Created by Leonard Reed and Willie Bryant in the early 1930s, the dance became so popular that many Harlem club performances closed with the show's musicians, singers, and dancers (and even waiters and audience members) assembling to perform the routine onstage, down the aisle, and even out the doors and up and down the avenue.

[17] Reed later managed the famous Apollo Theater in New York City where he served as master of ceremonies for 20 years. At the age of 93, he received a Lifetime Achievement Award from the American Music Awards in 2000.

A good time was had by all. The next day, Sally was back at the fair and the Defense Fund's coffers had been at least somewhat recharged. Total collections were reported at $1,775, but, even though Sally and the other performers had all volunteered their services, the sponsors reported itemized expenses of $1,371 (including a payment of $36 for police guards and protection for Mayor Kelly, Sally Rand and the box office, as well as $20 to Sally's assistant Ralph Hobart for "transportation, etc.").[18]

After a short night's rest, Sally returned to the Italian Village where the cash registers were still humming along. So much so that Sally's contract was renewed in August for an additional six weeks at a reported sum of $2,500 per.

Mary Belle

On August 31st Mary Belle Spencer, Chicago attorney and Sally Rand nemesis, sat for an interview with correspondent Everett R. Holles. The exchange took place just as Mrs. Spencer was about to embark on another Midway inspection tour in search of "bad girls" — the beginning of a four-month effort during which she would be in the headlines more often than Sally herself. It seems that the afternoon editions of a local paper had published a "fetching photograph" of her 14-year-old daughter, Mary Belle, Jr., wearing a scanty bathing suit and holding a contest trophy.

As tactfully as possible, Holles asked the celebrated attorney if it weren't true that she herself had condemned fan dancing, bubble dancing and other such displays as "revolting." Mary Belle agreed: "Yes," she said. "I even called it sinful, sordid exhibitionism."

Holles rejoined: "Then you don't approve of your daughter's appearing in a bathing beauty contest?" Mary Belle sidestepped: "Well, that was a very exclusive contest. It was a very exclusive country club and they didn't receive any money for it." When the reporter pointed out that her other daughter, 12-year-old Victoria, had also entered the contest, Mrs. Spencer took umbrage: "See here, young man! Don't get the idea that my daughters are going to be fan dancers or nudists just because you saw a picture of them in bathing suits."

---

[18] Valued today, from a gross collection of about $30,000 in ticket sales, the event netted a little over $7,000. A detailed expense report was prompted by the arrest earlier in the week of Pittsburgh promoter Maurice Dancer on charges of embezzling benefit funds raised in connection with his promotion of similar NAACP "midnight shows" in New York, Philadelphia and elsewhere.

At this point, Mary Belle proceeded to lay out her rather unorthodox concept of motherhood, disclosing that never in all their lives had she ever told her daughters that they must behave:

> My girls must never be repressed. Their minds must not be filled with other people's ideas. Neither of them has ever been to school. They are self-educated and they know everything. I don't know how they learned to read.

> When they were babies, instead of reading nursery rhymes, I read the advance sheets of the Supreme Court to them. They liked blood and thunder, so I read them the record of criminal trials.

Both girls had carried guns since they were youngsters, she added, and were expert marksmen. Asked if she had ever reprimanded them, she said: "Oh, my no. But once, when they threw the Christmas tree through the front window when the weather was near zero, it was hard not to say anything. But I didn't even turn my head."

Publically admitting that her daughters had never in their lives attended a day of school proved to be a blunder. On October 18th, Mrs. Spencer found herself back in court, but this time not as a prosecutor. Rather, her husband had been charged with violating the compulsory education law by failing to send his daughters to school. When asked why the girls were not present in court, Mrs. Spencer explained: "Why, they wouldn't think of coming here. They might get in contact with a germ and become contaminated. Doubtless they are out in the open somewhere breathing God's pure air."

When truant officer Emma Di Peso testified that the Spencer children had never attended school, Mrs. Spencer argued: "Is that so? Well, first I demand that you prove the Spencer children exist." This novel and confounding ploy achieved only a temporary delay. Six days later, the court brushed aside Mrs. Spencer's 14-page brief and two-hour oration. Dr. R. V. Spencer was convicted of the charge and fined $5.00. Undeterred, Mary Belle declared compulsory school attendance to be tantamount to "slavery" and announced that she would seek relief on appeal.

Ultimately the case went before a jury, which, surprisingly, found Dr. Spencer not guilty of violating the state compulsory education law. Commenting on the outcome, Mary Belle was unrestrained in demonstrating her contempt for public education:

> I wouldn't let my daughters draw one breath in a public school if I were to be electrocuted for it…. My first impression of a public

school occurred when I was five years old. My four sisters and myself had caught the measles in school. One of my sisters died and I shall never forget the horror I experienced when I opened my eyes from unconsciousness to find the bed next to me empty. Later they brought her to me in a box so that I could see her for the last time....

The only way to develop the mind is to associate with people of superior intelligence. Development of the mind is far more important than learning that two and two is four. The brain must be used to think, not as a receptacle for the debris of the ages.

Somewhere along the line Sally became interested in investing in, or possibly developing, a birth control method or device. The IUD had been around a few years, but approval of "the pill" was still more than 20 years in the future. A letter Sally wrote on October 4, 1934, to friends in California gives tantalizing insight into her thoughts on the matter:

About the contraceptive, I have given it up as a commercial enterprise, feeling that I had not the time to give it to make it really successful, but I absolutely believe in it as a safe and sure contraceptive.... I feel that the safe period theory is im-practical for two reasons. First, that even after the period has been ascertained, which takes some time in each individual, it has been definitely proven that that period is not always "safe." Also, human nature, being what it is, you and I both know people are not going to wait for it because "when you gotta go, you gotta go."

As to her publicized engagement, Sally explained: "The boy to whom I am engaged has been with me here at the fair all summer. He is a boy I have known and gone with for five years." The "boy," of course, was 30-year-old Charles "Chissie" Mayon. He had maintained a relatively low profile since his release from a Los Angeles hospital back in January, but talk of marriage had started up again in September. With the second year of the fair winding down, Mayon, acting as emcee for Sally's show at the Italian Village, had presented her with a diamond engagement ring. Sally gushed to the press:

After the end of the season, we will go to Florida and be married. Maybe we'll even get married before then. And put this in the records, the Charles Mayons are to be married for years. This is my first and last engagement. I want to live a quiet life, raise babies, cook and see that hubby wears the right necktie when he goes to work.

No doubt Sally was speaking from the heart, but other prospects would move her marriage plans to the back burner. There they would simmer for a little while — until the flame went out.

A s the fair's closing date approached, it was generally acknowledged that whatever financial gain the enterprise had achieved was largely due to the dancing of one effervescent 5-foot-tall young woman. In recognition of Sally's impact, the Executives' Club of Chicago, a networking group for the city's leading business executives, invited her to attend their regular Friday meeting on October 5th to speak about the secret of her success.

At the meeting, Sally was introduced by special guest Italian Count Ernesto Russo, a popular speaker in his own right, who proclaimed her to be "as near an angel as a girl of this world could be" and "the lady who has made the Century of Progress a great success."[19]

H aving little else to do on a rainy afternoon in Granby, Missouri, a group of young fellows were discussing issues of the day while seeking refuge at Adkins Hardware Store. Overhearing their conversation, Dr. L. E. Rollins told the boys about a piece he had seen in the *Joplin Globe*. It seems that the general manager of the Century of Progress World's Fair had announced that, upon the closing of the exposition, all "movable objects" would be sold to the highest bidder.

Discussion ensued. Before long, styling themselves as the "Young Men's Business Club of Granby, Mo.," the group had composed the following telegram to "The President of the Century of Progress": "As per advertisement in today's paper regarding sale of all moveable parts of A Century of Progress after November 15, please quote price on Sally Rand."

It's not clear whether the "Young Men's Business Club" ever actually received a formal reply, but the next day the same Joplin newspaper carried a response to the "club":

> It's a bit hard to explain, we're sorry and all that, but you can't buy Sally Rand.... We tried to get an option on Sally, fans and bubbles included. We didn't get much satisfaction. The world's fair managers just shrug their shoulders and say Sally isn't a "movable part" of the fair.

---

[19] Addressing the Milwaukee Traffic Club in 1932 on his impressions of America, Count Russo had quipped: "In America I find 50 percent passing the buck and the other 50 percent passing the hat."

Though disappointed, the Granby fellows concluded it was just as well: "Imagine going home to friend wife and saying, 'You'll have to clean up the guest room. I've just bought Sally Rand.'"

The Century of Progress Exposition, 1934 edition, came to a close on October 31st, but not without drama. The last day of the fair had been a big success. To bid goodbye to the exposition, schools were closed by proclamation of Mayor Kelly, as were stores and offices. Large throngs lingered until midnight in anticipation of a fireworks display to mark the fair's final moments. But when the switch was thrown that would darken the fairgrounds, things turned ugly.

According to press reports, a "roaring horde of last-nighters" plundered the fairgrounds until well past midnight. Crowds damaged exhibits, tore down signs, threw chairs and benches into the lagoon and, when police guards protested, they were tossed into the drink as well. Hurling bottles, chairs, and table legs, brawlers in the Streets of Paris were dispersed only by turning a fire hose on them. Revelers masked as witches wrecked the Italian Village after Sally announced she would not appear because, at around 40 degrees, it was "too cold" to perform her bubble dance.

The fairgrounds were left in shambles — a metaphor, perhaps, for the national economy. Some said it was just as well. Demolition crews got a head start on the estimated million dollar cost of tearing down the fair. Trucks and trailers would soon begin to haul away, piece by piece, what someone described as "an undertaking erected in the blackest days of the Depression, but one that paid its way despite the times."

In midterm elections the following week, Democrats would gain another nine seats in Congress, giving President Franklin D. Roosevelt a super-majority in the Senate. He would use it to full advantage. The new Congress would pass the Social Security Act of 1935 by margins of more than ten to one in each house. By year's end, events in Germany, Italy, and Russia would hint at the horror yet to come. And Sally? She would be on the road again, about to become more truly free than she had been in a long time.

Sally had been living in a sustained state of heightened anxiety for nearly 14 months when a three-judge appellate court in Chicago reversed her lower court conviction for "willfully performing an obscene and indecent dance in a public place." In addition to other arguments, defense attorney Samuel Berke presented convincing medical testimony that persons with normal eyesight could not have seen what the state claimed had been seen.

This welcome decision came despite the fact that she had been found guilty by a 12-man jury.

The appellate court found that "where the evidence is so unreasonable, improbable or unsatisfactory as to justify a reasonable doubt of the defendant's guilt, this court should reverse judgment." Sally was relieved ("Thank God"), but not beyond words, quipping: "It was ducky of the judges. You see I always was a good woman — even before the judges said so."

Within a few days, a rejuvenated Sally Rand was back in circulation and looking for stability, both emotional and financial. Nils T. Granlund had a similar goal in mind. And, who better to put bodies in the seats at his Paradise Cabaret than Sally? So, seeking once again to turn her notoriety into hard cash, she returned to Manhattan and accepted Granlund's invitation to resume her role as a featured attraction at the Paradise.[20]

Sally had become more sophisticated in matters of stagecraft since her prior engagement with Granny. Besides correcting what the audience regarded as frustratingly dim lighting, other adjustments had proved necessary. For one thing, Sally had a transparent screen installed between herself and the audience to thwart the few rowdy or inebriated customers who couldn't seem to resist tossing lit cigarettes in the direction of her bubble. The balloons for the bubble dance cost $27 apiece — more than $450 today — so it is little wonder that Sally took measures to protect them. She also used her own electrician to operate the spotlight. In addition, she reportedly expanded her retinue at the Paradise to include a harpist, a pair of maids, and a secretary. She could well afford the embellishments, as she was commanding $2,000 a week for her show — a whopping $34,000 nowadays.

One columnist noted that, despite hard times, New York City was enjoying an influx of Saturday night merrymakers, saying: "I saw a mob descend upon Miss Sally Rand and her bubble dance at the Paradise the other night that would have discomposed a subway guard." Sally herself observed with a straight face that the Paradise had her name displayed immediately above a sign announcing: "No Cover Charge."

---

[20] En route to New York, Sally stopped in Kansas City to visit her father. On Armistice Day he escorted his daughter (the "in person" attraction) to the V.F.W. Charity Military Ball held at the sumptuous Pla-Mor Ballroom. Two thousand others were in attendance, with the proceeds going to the V.F.W. Home for Widows and Orphans. Mingling with the crowd was a local judge who, only six days earlier, had been elected to the United States Senate. World War II would intervene but, in little more than ten years, that man, Harry S. Truman, would find himself being sworn in as the 33rd President of the United States.

And, she was packing them in:

> The success of Sally Rand, with her peekaboo fans, can be
> explained by the cynical with a shrug of the shoulder or a quirked
> eyebrow. Yet, Sally … is unquestionably the biggest draw on
> Broadway at the moment.

Although raunchier entertainment was available up the street, apparently running into one's peers at Sally Rand's show did not carry the stigma that being spotted coming out of Minsky's Burlesque might have.

D r. Allan Roy Dafoe, who little more than six months earlier had delivered the famous Dionne Quintuplets, arrived in New York City on December 10th, leaving the care of his famous babies to others for the first time since their birth. After addressing an audience of more than 3,000 at Carnegie Hall, the good doctor, a sightseer from the backwoods of Canada, expressed an interest in seeing one of most intriguing sights in town. Word soon got around that one of the great man's chief desires was to meet the famous Sally Rand (and he was on his way to the Paradise to do just that).

Photographers and reporters were cautioned not to bother Dr. Dafoe at his table, but when Sally came out before the show, "swathed to the eyebrows in ermine" — well, some stimuli are simply irresistible. The two chatted cordially for several minutes. The newsmen leaned in as best they could and highlights of the conversation were prominently displayed in the next day's papers.

To make the good doctor more comfortable, Sally offered that:

> We've had doctors on both sides of our family for three generations.
> Country doctors, down in the Ozarks in Missouri and Arkansas. My
> mother is a trained nurse…. I've got a prescription blank here, too. I
> thought it would be nice to get your autograph on it. Maybe you
> could write a prescription telling me how to have quintuplets.

The doctor blushed and told Sally she would have to come up to the healthy environs of the Canadian North Woods for that. After she had excused herself and headed for the dressing room, Dafoe inquired: "These pretty girls, how much do they get?" "About $35 a week," someone replied. "Well, well. My, my, thirty-five dollars! But maybe they earn it. They work hard these little girls." He then inquired: "How much does Miss Rand get? I suppose she gets a neat salary." "More like $2,000 a week," he was told. "Fancy that," observed the astonished doctor, who himself was reportedly paid only about $200 a month, despite having to rise at all hours and tend to the medical needs of patients throughout a wide area of chilly Ontario.[21]

When Sally floated out to perform her bubble dance, coyly hidden from view by the dim lights and an oversized translucent balloon, Dr. Dafoe focused like an eager schoolboy. Just as he was adjusting his spectacles . . . BANG . . . Sally's huge balloon burst and fell limply to the stage — providing an unexpected treat for the startled doctor's baby blues. Sally hastily retreated offstage only to appear moments later with a replacement. She remained composed and smiling, but it was no laughing matter.

As one popular gossip columnist seated at the doctor's table would recall:

> On came Sally and her silly fans. She did the familiar "strip" slow
> walk (accompanied by pashy soft music) around the ringside. As
> she passed Dafoe, I whispered, "Doc, she's really a nice girl."
> Without turning his head, he mumbled, "Nice ass, too."

Before departing for the nation's capital the following day, Dafoe made a short tour of the Museum of Natural History and, returning to the propriety expected from a man of his stature, proclaimed: "It's the most interesting place I've ever been in."

Mary Belle

Things were definitely looking up for Sally. But, for her nemesis Mary Belle Spencer? Not so much. On December 23rd, prosecutors in the Lindbergh baby kidnapping case were asserting that a "deliberate and malicious effort" had been made to tamper with the jury pool on behalf of Bruno Richard Hauptmann, the defendant. The 34-year-old German immigrant carpenter had been arrested on September 19th and charged with the "Crime of the Century" — the kidnapping of the 20-month-old son of world famous aviator Charles A. Lindbergh.

What possible connection could this have to our Chicago attorney, Mrs. Spencer? Well, actually quite a strong one. Prosecutor Anthony H. Hauck charged that a 48-page booklet entitled "No. 2310, Criminal File, Exposed!

---

[21] Comparing these paychecks to their modern-day equivalents, the showgirls would have been making about $620 per week (almost $2,800 a month) and the doctor would have been earning about $3,500 a month, while Sally was pulling in what today would be about $35,000 per week (or $160,000 for one month's work at the Paradise).

Aviators' Baby Was Never Kidnaped or Murdered"[22] had been mailed to each of the 150 prospective jurors in the trial. The salient contention of the so-called exposé was that, instead of being kidnapped and murdered, the Lindbergh child had simply wandered off into the woods, gotten lost, and been killed (and partially eaten) by wild animals. The bizarre booklet was copyrighted by Mary Belle Spencer and distributed by "a confidential news syndicate at 155 North Clark Street" in Chicago — which just happened to be the address of Mrs. Spencer's very own law office. Although Mary Belle admitted she was the author, she claimed to have "no idea" how copies ended up in the hands of prospective Lindbergh jurors.

Mailed to New Jersey where the trial was to take place, the document described a fictitious case closely paralleling the kidnapping of Lindbergh's son. (In the narrative, a "John Doe" is accused of abducting the son of "Charles A. Limberg, famous aviator.") In the glare of the resulting publicity, Mrs. Spencer scrambled to laugh off the whole affair, claiming that it was a satire, written two years before Hauptmann's arrest:

> I just took a bunch of fictional background from a dozen cases and wove them into something I thought was funny to expose the complete dumbness of the whole legal system. The whole thing was a satire, written and dictated by me for my own amusement merely to poke fun at the asininity of our police and court system as a whole. It was entirely fictional, all the characters and incidents, and was intended merely to be funny.

Funny or not, 26,000 copies had been circulated, and, by some means or another, 150 of them had found their way through the postal service into the mailboxes of every member of the Hauptmann trial jury pool. A "warning notice" on page one advised each recipient not to reveal its contents because "news of this trial has been suppressed by order of the court."

The Department of Justice reportedly began an investigation. In the end, the booklet turned out to be of no consequence. A jury was selected little more than a week after the brouhaha. And, while most veniremen acknowledged having read Mary Belle's treatise, none would say that it had anything to do with the forming of an opinion.

---

[22] The author's personal copy of this booklet has the word "Aviator's" printed on a bright pink slip of paper, pasted over a key word in the title. According to online copyright information, the underlying word is "Limberg's."

It had been quite a year. Finally free from her legal entanglements, Sally was riding high and getting ready for special year-end festivities. And special they were. Couples who wished to rub elbows with the big shots attending the 1934 New Year's Eve party at the Paradise Cabaret Restaurant could expect to pay as much as $25 (more than $400 these days), depending on the location of their table. A stiff charge, to be sure, although Granlund was bringing in 50 extra girls to ease the pain. Sally's half-brother, Eugene Beck, was in town to help her celebrate. A stone's throw away, tens of thousands of revelers had gathered in Times Square to participate in the traditional countdown, watch the illuminated ball drop, and greet the New Year, a practice that had begun when Sally was only three years old.

It had been quite a year for Mary Belle Spencer as well and, although the two would never actually cross paths again, Mrs. Spencer had not heard the last of the indomitable Miss Rand.

CHAPTER TWELVE

Sally Sallies Forth

If God had meant for us to be naked, we'd have been
born that way.

~ Mark Twain

As the new year dawned Sally remained the feature attraction in Nils
T. Granlund's show at the Paradise Cabaret Restaurant.[1] To gin up
business, her press agent announced that she would ride a "fan dancing
elephant" through the streets of New York City on January 4th. The day
arrived with more than the usual chill in the air but, always the trouper, she
did in fact ride "Fanny the Fan Dancer" up University Place in Manhattan.
Braving a temperature of 13 degrees above zero, Sally observed: "I just love
animals, but it was damned cold."

While it *was* clearly cold outside, Sally was still a hot property. With
two years of the Chicago Fair behind her, she was now steering her
own ship — straight into the troubled waters of the continuing economic
depression. Once again, she needed something new. And that something
turned out to be . . . public speaking.

Sally's earlier talk before the Executives' Club of Chicago was not her first
public speaking experience, but the high profile success of that event convinced her that similar appearances and the publicity they could generate
would only enhance her bottom line.

Thus, on February 11, 1935, two hundred members of the Sales Executives
Club of New York gathered in the Hendrik Hudson Room of the Hotel
Roosevelt to receive a message from a most unlikely messenger — fan and
bubble dancer, Sally Rand. Her opening remarks are lost to us, but they

---

[1]   Sally performed both her bubble dance and fan dance at a spot on the program
immediately following a set piece entitled "Praying in Rhythm" in which eight female
"preachers" confronted sixteen dancing "sinners." A bevy of young lovelies portrayed
such characters as "Love," "Money," "Happiness," "Passion," "Purity" and, of course,
"the Devil."

may well have resembled the following anecdote that became one of her standards:

> Y'know, as I stand here before you, I'm reminded of a girlfriend of mine down in the Ozarks. This kid was all of 14 when she got married — practically an old maid as things go down there. She and her husband were getting along pretty well together, and one day he had to go down to Fort Smith on business. This left her by herself at home. She was doing the housework and all the other things a young wife does when she is all alone, when her brother-in-law wandered in.
>
> They had known each other for some time, even before she was married, and they were both feeling kind of lonesome. Well, one thing led to another, and the first thing you know they were in each other's arms.
>
> As their moment of ecstasy approached, the brother-in-law said to my girlfriend, "Kiss me, darling, kiss me."
>
> "Kiss you Hell," she replied, "I shouldn't even be doing *this!*"
>
> Now, I'm something like that girl. I shouldn't be up here doing this. My forte is dancing, not talking, as my fans can tell you.

Once the chuckling died down, Sally began her extemporaneous address to the all-male room, standing at the podium wearing a navy blue tailored business suit, shirt and tie, and "snap-brim gray felt hat." What followed was a dignified business talk in which she discussed percentages, sales methods, advertising, organization building, business charts and business equipment. Fragments of her remarks have survived:

> Nudity is not new, as you may see by looking at decorative art. It is not new for a woman to use her figure and her body. So in selling nudity I did not have a new piece of merchandise to sell. All I could hope for was some new method of merchandising.
>
> I started out on a sales campaign based on advertising. I noticed that advertising was just a matter of display. I noticed that in advertising it is necessary to dress white space. If you have seen my dance, you know that I dress white space. I observed that advertising depends a great deal on leg art. I decided I might as well go the whole way. I use a lot of leg art in my merchandising.
>
> I realized … that 90 percent of the merchandise that is sold in this country is sold to women; that sales talks, for that reason, must be directed at women. In my case, that fact presented obvious difficulties.

Still, I believed I had something salable. All I needed was a new scheme for merchandising it. I recalled the business axiom that the quickest way to get a head start in any industry is to present the product before the largest possible number of persons. Therefore, I decided to go to the World's Fair in Chicago.

Well, I knew I had something to sell and I had decided on the place where I would find the most potential buyers. I made certain connections in Chicago — I'll go so far as to admit they were political connections — and got my chance. When the World's Fair was nearing its end, I was faced with the unpleasant prospect of falling back into obscurity. I didn't want that. So I did what any merchant would have done. I extended my organization. I started hiring other people. I bought specialized training — a publicity man, an orchestra, a chorus. And I let the ones who knew their specialty perform it without interference, while I worked on my own specialty. That is the secret of a good executive. It worked out that way for me in my industry. I know it's strange to speak of fan dancing and bubble dancing as an industry, but to me it is just that; an industry with a large income.

I have been successful and I am grateful for my success. I have had some experiences that I wish I had never had, but that would be true in any business. I cannot say sincerely that I would have chosen just this road to fortune. Perhaps I might have wished for another way. But I took the opportunity that came to me.

For the audience, what had begun as prurient curiosity about a novelty speaker gradually turned to studied interest and ultimately to a hearty ovation. As Sally stepped away from the platform, the luncheon guests crowded around to congratulate her as one businessperson to another. Many lingered for up to an hour, chatting about their business problems and exchanging views on the evils of the income tax.

She had spoken to groups like this before and was always well received. But this occasion was covered by the *New York Times* and syndicated to papers across the land. Sally was no longer just a "fan dancer." She was a bona fide businesswoman. Quick on the uptake too. Appearances like this would soon become a staple of her self-promotion blitz and would continue to serve her well for the next 40 years.

If the attentive business executives had hoped for something of a more frivolous nature, perhaps they should have been at the Paradise Cabaret 10 days earlier. Shall we digress?

The fabled figure Aphrodite Kallipygos has come down to us in the form of various bronze and marble statues of the "Callipygian Venus" (or "Venus Callipyge"), the best known of which, a copy of the Greek original, has been on display in the National Archaeological Museum in Naples, Italy, since 1802.

Not to be outdone by the ancient Greeks, in late 1933 or thereabouts, the urbane press agent Max Elser approached the pioneer advertising firm of J. Walter Thompson with the idea of resurrecting the word "callipygian," familiar at the time only to crossword puzzle fans and Greek proofreaders. He proposed planting a "news" story containing the word, followed by an advertising campaign for the American corset industry. Mr. Elser enjoyed mixed success with the idea. While the "more anatomically-minded papers" published the item — "a clarion call for more shapely buttocks" — the rest "could find no legitimate excuse for it."

In any case, the word did come into vogue, thanks in part to the efforts of sculptor Bryant Baker, who made a minor splash in the press with claims that the ideal woman's beauty must be "judged from the back." A published photo shows the "eminent sculptor" in his New York studio measuring a model said to conform to the Greek callipygian ideal standard of perfection. In harmony with the slender, more straight-lined style preferences of the time, Baker contended: "The back of the thighs should be at least in the same vertical plane with the shoulder blades."

The term soon began to appear in advertisements for ladies' garments. An entertaining example appeared in a Syracuse, New York, ad for a "step-in" girdle called "Sensation" by Nemo-Flex:

> "Being a secretary is a sitting down job. My hips began to spread. I tried a Sensation. Now I'm Callipygian all the time."

> Sensations Double-Knit Back persuades spreading contours into sleek lines. Unrestricted as your own skin, yet they take no "back talk" from unwanted curves. At corset shop or department store, $2.50 to $15.00.

With advertisements suggesting that "most women have nightmare rear profiles" and offering them the opportunity to "flatten out" their bottoms, a Wisconsin advertisement providing shopping tips from "Arlene" told it like it was:

> Just in case you've been wandering around with closed ears and eyes lately, the word means "beautiful rear profile." Take a quick look at yourself in a full-length mirror — from the side. Do you "jut out" back there? You're not Callipygian if you do. And there's only one thing to do about it. Step into Burdick and Murray's on the square and have them flatten and round you out. It's really a simple process. Miss Bongey and Miss Nelson in the corset department will fit you out with a Pouff, which is the world's largest-selling girdle.... Pouff is actually so tiny it can be easily held in your tiny fist. But because of its two-way stretch it stretches until it hugs every one of your curves and bulges and puts them in their place.

Other ads proclaimed: "Today the classical 'Callipygian' Contour is essential because the exactly fitting gowns with their trim, smooth lines call for absolute flatness at the back." A certain "Miss Cooper" from the Royal

Worcester Corset Company in Massachusetts traveled as far as Melbourne, Australia, to make promotional appearances for the "Callipygian" corset. [2]

The debate over what constituted perfection in this area became so intense that, on the evening of November 13, 1934, a committee of so-called experts sponsored by a New York corset concern convened to resolve the matter. The aforementioned sculptor, Bryant Baker, was there, as were the famous art deco illustrator, Russell Patterson, the photographer, Ralph Reese, and several other lucky fellows. Following some semiserious discussion, the committee decided to stage a contest and offer a prize to the young lady who could step forward with a "perfect callipygian."

Now you might think that a random panel of normal, red-blooded men could choose a winner in such a contest by employing nothing more than simple eyeball evaluation. But you would be wrong. As Baker explained:

> It is a question of art. What might to the layman's eye seem to be a
> perfect callipygian may be imperfect to the artist. Venus did not
> have a perfect callipygian. Few of the plump models of the masters
> had one. A perfect callipygian must be slim, erect. There must be
> nothing humpy about it. Mere attractiveness is not sufficient. An
> inexperienced observer may be led astray by usual judgment. A
> perfect callipygian is a mathematical certainty.

And so it was that, during the afternoon of the first day in February at the Paradise Cabaret, sixteen showgirls offered to turn around for the studied estimation of a judging panel of three "well-known artists and fashion experts." Only one contestant was from the Paradise chorus, but Sally Rand was on hand, serving in the role of hostess. Unlike the contestants, who appeared in one-piece bathing suits, Sally was decked out in what she described as "14 pounds of clothes" that included five petticoats, pants that fastened below the knees, and an 1890's-style gown that reached the floor and included a trailing tail. Her waist had been constricted to a mere 22 inches by a steel-staved corset.

First came the prolonged drudgery of precisely measuring and otherwise evaluating the posterior aspect of each contestant (standard measuring tape was employed rather than some sort of specialty calipers). The field was eventually narrowed to three: Miss Eleanor Sheridan, Miss Jackie Daley, and the 18-year-old Miss Margery Gayle Hoffman — a comely lass from Ames,

---

[2]   Oddly, these ads completely invert the original meaning of the term as it is commonly
       understood today. In the proper reading of "callipygian," so called "perfection" lies
       not in the flattening, but rather in the pronouncement, of a woman's natural curves.
       Think Jennifer Lopez or Jessica Biel. Or Sally Rand.

Iowa, who had been appearing with Rudy Vallee in the *Hollywood Revels of 1934* at the nearby Hollywood Restaurant. After further examination and discussion, the judges declared Miss Hoffman the winner. She had measured 25½ inches at the waist and 35¼ inches at the hips, a presentation that was deemed to be "almost perfect."[3]

Sally was happy to announce the victor but, being no slouch in the rear-view department herself, she also indicated a willingness to disrobe in order to allow the judges to determine just how well *she* measured up. As reported by correspondent Theon Wright (who had apparently won the coin toss to cover the event), Sally had stripped down to her corset when a critical string snapped. "Oh, my God!" she exclaimed. Red of face and short of breath, Sally twisted, turned, grunted and strained — all to no avail. A couple of stagehands and a press agent leapt to her assistance and began tugging. The corset wouldn't budge. "I'm afraid I can't get it off," Sally gasped.

To her great frustration, Sally's efforts to disrobe were halted at a point where she was neither dressed nor undressed, the corset clasping her torso in an iron embrace. With fluffy doo-dads stringing out below and a bit of lace above, Sally retreated to her dressing room where extra hands were called in to assist. In the end, the judges took their leave without ever having compiled a record of Sally's vital measurements.

Nobody understood the enduring appeal of the female backside better than Sally, but her views on the subject of actual nudity were a bit more complicated. On the very same day of the contest, an interview conducted by a "Broadway" correspondent declared that "Sally Rand, who runs Lady Godiva a close second for being the world's most famous nude, doesn't know a thing about nudism. She never has been to a nudist camp ... and doesn't think she ever will." Indeed, in Sally's view, "the only persons who have any moral right to move around in the nude are babies." Pressed on the subject, Sally explained:

> Nudity only can be decorative if it is idealized, and of course it
> must be decorative if it is to be a part of the art of the theater....
> Nudity, if it is decorative, contributes to the spectacle of the theater.
> The theater is for the purpose of entertainment and amusement.
> Spectacle does both of these things.

---

[3] Daily papers published syndicated pictures of Miss Hoffman being measured by Sally and proudly wearing a "Miss Callipygian" banner draped across her torso.

> If one is to be mobile while in the nude, it must be in a series of
> flowing movements, so that if the body turned to stone at any
> moment, the figure would be beautiful. Sculpture, after all, is frozen
> music and dancing by the same token is living music.

While Sally had never thought much of actual, in the raw, nudists, she once told a reporter in Canada: "I will say, though, that I'm congenitally a dis-believer in cults of all sorts." Soon enough, she would be confronted by a group of the selfsame enthusiasts.

Ralph

The public's hunger for news about Sally was so great that even stories about those around her were of national interest. Ralph Hobart had been a friend since childhood and a special assistant since her vaudeville days. A picture of Ralph applying makeup to Sally's body was published in papers across the country, along with a story in which he was characterized as her "male maid." But Sally knew he was much more than that:

> Oh, I couldn't get along without Ralph. He's my Major-Domo. Making
> up for my bubble dance is quite difficult. I don't really use powder.
> It's a sort of plaster of Paris covering and it takes a man with
> strength to apply it. Furthermore, Ralph takes care of all my prop-
> erties and keeps the act going. Why, he's not a maid, he's indispensable.

Hobart added:

> Sally and I went to school together in Kansas City and we've been
> friends ever since. There have been times when we didn't have
> enough to eat, but if I was working I helped and if Sally was
> working she helped.

> I remember a day, a year or two ago, when things weren't going so
> well for Sally. I called on her; we pooled our assets and made a meal
> out of 11 cents worth of vegetables. But those days are gone forever, I
> hope, and I'm glad to be of service to Sally now, as in less prosperous
> times. Besides being an artist, she's a real human being who doesn't
> forget her rainy-day friends when the sun comes out.

Hobart knew Sally at close range, perhaps in a way matched by no other. If she had a mole somewhere, he knew where it was.

S he had been on the stage or in the entertainment business in one form or another for 20 years, and during all that time Sally continued to think of herself as a serious, professional dancer. In an article entitled "Dancing Is An Art!" written for the Canadian magazine *City Lights,* she demonstrated her knowledge of history and in the process provided subtext that spoke to the dilemma of her time as well as our own:

> Nudity is not new! The great Greek sculptor Praxiteles made use of it as a motif for his heroic figures; we acclaim Rodin's masterpieces; and ... adorning the portals of our civic buildings we find the nude immortalized....

> As to the dance itself, I stand on the premise that dancing is an art and that the ballet is the foundation for all dance forms.... During the Dark Ages when all that was beautiful and sensitive and fine was crushed under the blood and the dark cloak of fanaticism, this delicate art was obscured and well-nigh perished, except in the spirit of those indomitable souls whose instinct for joy and the expression of it in the dance could not be crushed.

> During the Renaissance, the normal instinct for man to express himself, through himself, and his joy at being alive, again brought the dance to light....

> Upon the efforts of these first 14th and 15th Century dancing masters ... has the ballet progressed until it reached its zenith in the Imperial Russian Ballet School. Here it was brought to a high point of perfection and the artists it developed have become immortal, among them being Nijinsky, Pavlova, Fokine, Petipa, Legat, Lopokova and Kschessinskaya. Other countries followed suit and produced fine ballet masters also, until today we have the finest points of each method compiled, created and named after Maestro Enrico Cecchetti, an Italian ballet master who died only a few years ago. He was the Maître de Ballet of Diaghilev, the entrepreneur who presented the ballet in all its brilliancy for the first time to the world in general as a great art.

In March, having decided that she too could be instrumental in presenting the ballet in all its brilliancy, Sally announced that she would be sponsoring a dance recital at the Guild Theater in New York City by an exotic modern dancer named Kohana. "It's a philanthropic gesture," Sally explained, "encouraging this dancer."

Interviewed in her dressing room, she continued:

> My fan dance and my bubble dance are for the great public. They
> are commercial, salable. But somebody must foot the bills for the
> really advanced dancer, the ripened artist for whom the public is
> not ripe. No matter what role life had cast me in, the dance would
> have been my avocation. I glory in the opportunity to advance the
> art of the dance.

Turning to the "new" dance *she* might have in mind, Sally demurred:

> About next season, I don't want you to think I'm snooting you or
> anything if I don't reveal my new creation. There are so many
> copyists. I was favored in having the second Chicago fair for my
> bubble dance. If the fair had run only one year, I would have been
> thought a flash in the pan. Should I say a flash in the fan?

> But with fame, even of possible spurious legitimacy, responsibili-
> ties toward one's public accumulate. The public expects more of its
> favorite every year? How can I show them more?

When someone in the dressing room suggested "an X-Ray dance," Sally
responded with a pretty moue: "No, that would be too macabre."

Kohana, once described as "a small, dark-haired beauty with large, heavily
penciled eyes, long black hair, very white skin, and a lovely body," had first
met Sally in 1929 when the two appeared together in a Miami floor show.
At that time the object of Sally's generosity was a star pupil of the great
Japanese dancer, teacher and choreographer, Michio Ito.

On the night of her New York debut, assisted by her sister Paula, Kohana
performed a series of modern dances to the music of Szymanowski, Debussy,
Ravel, Bach, Stravinsky and Prokofiev, among others. The well-known music
critic W. J. Henderson gave the recital a generally favorable review:

> A fairly large audience witnessed the performance of the evening
> and was liberal with its applause…. The dancing in its totality was
> very good and sometimes reached high levels of suggestion and
> creative appearance. Kohana was remarkably successful in her
> treatment of the contrasting moods of the Bach preludes; and in the
> gaiety and liberality of "La Puerta del Vino" to music of Debussy.

Sally was among those in the audience who were liberal with their applause.
When the program had finished, she ran backstage to congratulate her
friend, then dashed back to the Paradise for her own midnight performance.

Everyone was happy. The experience had given a boost to Kohana's career and Sally had garnered publicity for something other than being arrested.

Times were still tough, but Sally was feeling flush. Happily, she was in a position to be generous both with her money and her time. When the American Federation of Actors held its annual Actors Ball on March 30th, she was one of 11 celebrities serving as judges for the Ballroom Dancing Contest — Rudy Vallee, Sophie Tucker and Bert Lahr were among the others. And, when she completed her engagement at the Paradise Cabaret, Walter Winchell reported that she had "spent her entire last week's wages on gifts for everybody there."

That two people can "observe" the same thing yet "see" something entirely different is undeniable. Although Sally was a constant target of church groups that objected to her show, it wasn't uncommon for her to receive letters like this one from Rev. Michael J. Konwinski, pastor of St. John the Baptist Polish Church in Campbell, Ohio, written to her on May 14, 1935:

> I am exceedingly grateful for your generous offering. I am sure you will never regret it. God always rewards good deeds.
>
> I have communicated the good news to the Young Ladies Sodality. A committee and quite a number of the members went to see you perform at the Palace Theater, and they were very much elated over your act. They told me that your show is entirely different than what they anticipated. They said it was clean and very decent, and Miss Rand I am very glad to hear it.
>
> I am sure that your performance can dispel some of the perverted ideas that some people have today. The beautiful can only be seen and admired when it is decent and clean, like your act.
>
> May God bless you and keep you; we shall pray that He remember you.

Sally had a collection of such laudatory letters that she carted with her from town to town. And she quite enjoyed pulling them out now and then to wave under a judge's nose or that of an inquiring reporter.

Sally's 1935 summer tour included the usual highlights and lowlights. On June 29th she visited the Illinois State Legislature at the State Capitol in Springfield and, to the accompaniment of exploding firecrackers, caused such a commotion that private detectives were summoned to preserve order.

The following week in Sheboygan, Wisconsin, Sally found herself in court, on the defensive once again. But, this time, it was not for any personal exposure, but rather as a consequence of the posters displayed at the Sheboygan Theater. This time it was her advance man, Raymond Roger, who was in the hot seat. Posters depicting Sally in the buff had been placed outside the theater and a number of passersby had complained that the images were obscene. Police Chief Walter H. Wagner and one of his officers visited the venue and took down the life-sized images. Although in custody, Mr. Roger was soon released when Sally strode into the police station, plunking down $200 for his bond. "She is smart, she is," one officer observed. "She has had more than one run-in with the law and she knows how to handle things all right."

A jury trial was hastily arranged in municipal court and the posters were brought in as exhibits one and two. The defense introduced into evidence three locally purchased nudist magazines to demonstrate that "artistic" material of this sort was already considered acceptable in the community. On the stand, Sally maintained that the posters had been placed in front of the theater at the request of management. Moreover, she said, while the same placards had been displayed before 40 other theaters, "never have we had any trouble." According to various reports, the key testimony went something like this. First, District Attorney, Jacob A. Fessler, challenged Sally:

> Fessler: Isn't it true that in many of those places a banner had been placed across the upper part of the body?
>
> Sally: Yes.
>
> Fessler: Do you know what that banner said?
>
> Sally: I assume the banner said "Now Showing."
>
> Fessler: And truly now, just why do you suppose that banner hid the bust in the picture?
>
> Sally: To assuage the delicate feelings of such people as have made the complaints in this case.

Fessler attempted to drive his point home in a closing argument:

> I might expect to see something resembling these pictures in an art gallery, but to call this art is an audacity. What would you say if persons from a nudist colony paraded down Eighth Street? Would they be allowed to go unmolested? Supposing one of your young sons brought one of these magazines displaying these nude bodies

into your home. Would you say that he was doing so with the idea of enhancing his appreciation of art? You would not!

Sally's attorney, G. R. Dougherty of Milwaukee, countered: "There is nothing hideous about the human body. We see legs every day and especially on bright, sunny days when sheer dresses reveal the limbs of many girls." Taking a cut at the City of Sheboygan, he added: "In other cities, they probably have an artistic sense of the beautiful."

In rebuttal, the district attorney admonished: "In other cities they put a banner across those parts of the body that should be covered, but here they thought they could get away with something. Are you going to allow them to do so?"

The answer to that one turned out to be, well . . . "Yes." Retiring before lunchtime, the six-man jury hadn't been out long before asking for the posters and nudist magazines to be brought to the jury room where they could be inspected more carefully. In the meantime, smoking one cigarette after another, Sally carried on an animated conversation with both attorneys regarding what *was* and what was *not* "art." After barely half an hour, the jury filed back into the courtroom and delivered a verdict of "not guilty."

A local columnist summarized the outcome with tongue in cheek:

> Six Sheboygan connoisseurs of art decided in municipal court this morning that the pictures of Sally Rand in the nude, displayed in front of the Sheboygan Theatre on Friday, were truly works of art, and not lewd and lascivious as maintained by the state.

> Before a packed municipal courtroom of art lovers and others, Raymond Roger, an employee of Sally's, was discharged by the jury of six when it decided that the pictures were pleasing to the eye and soothing in that artistic yearning that can only be satiated by contemplating a work of art.

The publicity was a boon, of course. When the *Sally Rand Revue* came to the Capitol Theatre in Manitowoc, Wisconsin, a few days later, "attendance records which [had] stood almost since the start of talking pictures" were broken that day as several thousand eager fans attended the four performances of the show. (The matinee audience even included eight members of the Manitowoc Bridge Club, fresh from their chicken dinner and party at a local resort.)

Since 1897, Cheyenne, Wyoming has celebrated its Old West roots with "Cheyenne Frontier Days," an annual festival still touted as the world's largest outdoor rodeo. The 1935 show opened on July 24th. To boost attendance during lean times, the organizing committee had invited Sally

Rand to add her own sort of "bare back" to the bareback riding show. Not only would she perform her regular show "with her ballet of 15 beautiful girls," but she would also ride a white pony in the annual parade and otherwise participate in "the daddy of all Wild West shows." Sally's leather riding costume, consisting of a white split skirt and vest trimmed in fringe, a satin blouse, and silver conches, was such a hit at the parade that it was adopted as the official costume for "Miss Frontier" the following year.[4]

Local clergy registered their reservations, led by Bishop Patrick A. McGovern of Cheyenne, who maintained that including Miss Rand amounted to "cheapening a western institution." But, in the end, the prospect of local cash registers ringing out a prosperous tune prevailed over any misgivings.

The annual event also featured a cowpoke named Thurkel "Turk" Greenough, of Red Lodge, Montana — described in the papers as "a red-haired, long-legged bronc peeler" who revealed that "the only secret to riding outlaw horses is to 'go up when they do and come down when they do.' " On opening day, he turned in the best bronco riding performance and went on to win the saddle bronc competition, the second of three times he would do so.

Fine-looking, if a bit bashful, Turk was a favorite with the local cowgirls who happily gathered around whenever there was a chance to get a closer look. As he was signing autographs for a long line of fresh faces, he barely noticed the chipper little blonde who gave him such a big smile in exchange for his signature. As she walked away, one of his pals asked: "Do you know who *that* was?" Turk did know of the girl, but apparently hadn't recognized her. In times to come, he would have the opportunity for a much closer examination.

D espite ongoing censure from the clergy, Sally was riding high — not just on parade ponies, but in the eyes of the general public, women included. Yet she admitted to a certain loneliness:

> Do you know what's been hard? I've never had a girl friend. A real, lasting relationship. All the time when other girls were going to school, forming friendships, learning all the sweet, good things about life, I was knocking about, making trains, one night stands in small towns, seeing a girl I liked for a week, maybe, and then never again meeting her. Now, I'm a little afraid of women. I guess that's the only thing I am afraid of. They seem so secure, so regular in their routine lives, so different.

---

4   Basically the same costume has been worn by each successive "Miss Frontier" to this day. (Search Google Images for "Miss Frontier" to check out the pictures posted online.)

And as for men? Ten years earlier, Sally had described her ideal man as a "Pan boy," someone "slim and brown with long, slim, brown fingers — creative fingers," a man who would make money. Now, she saw things in a somewhat different light:

> Someday I shall turn my ambition towards marriage.... Meanwhile, I am thankful for the companionship of many men, for the stimulus they give me, and for their understanding. I am proud that they accept me as one of themselves in argument, in discussion, in debate....
>
> The man I fall for isn't going to be any smooth gigolo kind of person. He's going to be fine, and clean, and intelligent. He'll have had all the education I never had the opportunity for. And I hope he'll feel with me that there are too many things in the world to learn to ever stop studying. I've spent every available minute of my time taking courses. There's so much to know.

Born on a farm, Sally believed that she knew how to distinguish the wheat from the chaff. She had developed a mature vision of the sort of man who would be best for her and she was disinclined to settle for anything less.

On Sunday, July 28th, the day after Frontier Days closed, Sally boarded a United Airlines flight bound for Chicago, where she would take up residence in the elegant Seneca Hotel and get ready for her return to the Chicago Theatre. She had come up with a "new daring dance" in January and had been researching, preparing and rehearsing it for a good part of the summer.

According to Greek mythology, the supreme god Zeus had a hankering for the daughter of the Aetolian King Thestius, a beautiful young gal named Leda. The all-powerful Greek god could do pretty much as he pleased and get away with it. And so, being something of an enigmatic fellow, when the opportunity arose, Zeus assumed the form of a large white swan, wormed his way into Leda's private quarters, and seduced and raped the unsuspecting damsel. Awkwardly, it turns out that Leda had also slept with her husband Tyndareus on that very same night. Some nine months later, when she gave birth to a beautiful little girl who grew up to become "Helen of Troy," serious discussion arose concerning little Helen's paternity.

These days, if a woman gave birth to a human being after having intercourse with both her husband and a member of the animal kingdom, there would be little doubt as to the infant's paternity, but, seeing as how the gods move in mysterious ways and the omnipotent Zeus had accumulated a lot of street cred for any number of other amazing accomplishments, the question has remained open for thousands of years.

Popular interest in the erotic tale of Leda and the Swan persisted through the centuries and by 1500 was beginning to pop up in works of art executed by top-tier artists. Many paintings, sculptures, and other depictions of the unlikely pair are still popular exhibits in major museums today. Nor has the controversy completely subsided. In April 2010, a photograph depicting a sculpture of a naked woman and a swan was taken down in a London art gallery in Mayfair after a police officer complained that the artwork appeared to "condone bestiality."[5]

All this is overture to the fact that, on August 2, 1935, Sally Rand ("Helen of Elkton") would debut her "Leda and the Swan" dance at the Chicago Theatre. Though her fan and bubble dances were still quite popular, Sally intended to stay ahead of the curve and, if a new wave of controversy was the result, so much the better. Or, as the press release put it, "Miss Rand believes that dances, like fashions and automobiles, should be changed every year to keep public interest alive."

Displaying her wicked sense of humor, Sally chose the name "Peter" for her swan. No mere oversized puppet, Peter was exceptionally lifelike, and with good reason. He was the creation of three talented artists: a taxidermist, Sally herself, and a gentleman experienced in sewing feathers on costumes. Just how much was attributable to the skills of the taxidermist — how "real" Peter may have been — is unknown.

We do know she had problems with the apparatus from the get-go. For one thing, according to Sally, poor Peter had been "completely worn to pieces during the strenuous months of rehearsal" and was "in a disgraceful state, what with missing feathers, drooping wings and so forth." After a rejuvenation session in New York, he arrived in Chicago "looking nice and neat, every feather unruffled." Even so, Sally felt that Peter was still a bit out of shape. The effect she was getting wasn't quite "streamlined" enough, so she had to arrange for a further remodeling effort on short notice.

In the dance, Sally and the swan were intimately intertwined, its body attached to her midriff, groin to groin, in such a way as to conceal her torso, at least from the front, while her head, arms and legs were fully exposed. Two wings, each several feet long, extended from her hips, while the swan's

---

5   Owned by Tyrone and Jamie Wood (sons of Rolling Stones' guitarist Ronnie Wood), Scream is a London art gallery specializing in leading and emerging print artists in the pop and urban aesthetic. Before it was taken down, the "Leda and the Swan" piece had been exhibited for a month with no complaints from the public.

flexible neck and head also extended a couple of feet or more from her left shoulder. Several "Maurice Seymour" photographs of Sally in this costume are readily found online.[6]

No film footage of Sally's Leda dance is known to exist. Even so, it is clear that Sally could manipulate the position of the swan's neck and head, if not the wings. As it turned out, the swan costume was better as a prop for remarkable photographs than as a dancing costume. After only a few days at the Chicago Theatre, Sally realized her mistake, gave up on the dance (which the press had described as "way over the heads of the Chicago Theatre audiences" anyway), and reverted to her fans and bubbles.

In 1921, renowned British playwright, novelist, and storyteller W. Somerset Maugham penned one of his most enduring works, the short story "Rain." The plot chronicles the course of five travelers — two married couples (a pair of fervent missionaries and a mild-mannered doctor and his wife) plus a boisterous young woman of questionable background — forced to interrupt their sea voyage when a cholera outbreak strands and quarantines them in an island hotel. The story focuses on the efforts of Alfred Davidson, a Christian missionary in the South Seas, to chasten and convert the young woman — an exotic prostitute named Sadie Thompson. Much of the action takes place during a torrential downpour. In the end, the arresting Sadie is more successful in "converting" poor Alfred than the other way around.

This tale of morality and lust in Pago Pago was an instant hit. Within a year, the play was dramatized on the Broadway stage with former Ziegfeld *Follies* girl Jeanne Eagels as Sadie. The production ran for 648 performances. It was adapted for the screen in the 1928 silent film *Sadie Thompson*, starring Gloria Swanson and Lionel Barrymore. Four years later, it was remade as *Rain*, a talking picture with Joan Crawford and Walter Huston in the principal roles.[7] Tallulah Bankhead starred in a Broadway revival in 1935.

In August of that year the play was also running in summer stock at the prestigious Lakewood Theatre on the western shore of Lake Wesserunsett near Skowhegan, Maine — a major tryout venue for productions seeking to

---

[6] The Seymour studio in Chicago was the source of many pictures of Sally with her fans and bubbles. There was no actual "Maurice Seymour." Two brothers, Maurice and Seymour Zeldman, Russian expatriates, formed the Maurice Seymour photographic studio in 1929. Later, oddly, both brothers legally changed their names to "Maurice Seymour."

[7] In 1953, the story was filmed again as *Miss Sadie Thompson*, a 3D version with Rita Hayworth and Jose Ferrer.

advance to Broadway. The summer stock cast included actors more or less known at the time, but the two players of greatest interest were our own Sally Rand as the temptress Sadie Thompson and, playing the good-natured Dr. McPhail, a young man who had only recently leapt from relative obscurity to his first star turn on Broadway — Humphrey Bogart.[8]

Aside from her stage performances as a teenager in Kansas City and her brief run in *The World Between* in 1932, this was Sally's first attempt at serious drama. She understood exactly what she was getting into: "When I try my luck at acting, I want to play a trollop. That's what everyone thinks I am, anyway." The subject matter no doubt appealed to her, as she had more than enough personal experience with finger-wagging clergy.

Did Sally show promise as a serious stage actress or should she have stuck to her day job? Although critics recognized her rawness, they also saw her "natural ability," and many of the play's reviews were surprisingly positive. This excerpt from a *Newsweek* magazine review was particularly effusive:

> In *Rain* Sally and Sadie took Skowhegan as few towns have been
> taken since Grant rode into Richmond. At the Lakewood, the
> country's oldest summer theatre, they faced the most exacting kind
> of audience: half curiosity seekers hoping for a laugh; half actors —
> always hard to play to — who make the colony their summer
> home. Sally's Sadie convinced them completely. Verdict: Those fans
> and bubbles have been hiding an actress as well as a dancer.

The director of Skowhegan's production of *Rain*, A. H. Van Buren, was equally impressed:

> She is the most indefatigable person I've ever encountered in the
> theater. She would work hour after hour without stopping…. To
> accomplish what Miss Rand has done with one week of rehearsal is
> an amazing feat. The part of Sadie is difficult enough for an exper-
> ienced actress. For a dancer to learn it and play it as well as she had
> done in five short rehearsals shows she has inherent dramatic talent.

---

8   Bogart had appeared on the stage since 1922 and had played at the Lakewood Theatre
     as early as 1928 in *The Dawn of Tomorrow*. Getting his big break on Broadway in
     early 1935, he was cast as Duke Mantee in Robert Sherwood's *The Petrified Forest*, a
     taut drama about a band of gangsters who hole up in a gas station and terrorize a
     group of victims caught up in the situation. The play was a big hit, critic Paul Harrison
     observing that it would "make a fine movie." And so it did. Within a couple of weeks
     of his Lakewood appearance with Sally, Bogart was offered the role of Duke Mantee
     in the Warner Brothers film. Over the next six years, he would star in another
     36 films, including *The Maltese Falcon* and *Casablanca*. Of course, you know all this.
     After all, it's Bogie!

Sally had her own take:

> I have always wanted to be a dramatic actress and I feel playing
> Sadie is a step in the right direction. There's only one thing I want
> more than I wanted this — someday I must play "Mary of Scotland."
> I know everyone will exclaim: Sally Rand playing "Mary of
> Scotland" — why, it's as absurd as Helen Hayes doing a fan dance.

She must have had quite a bit of pull with the Lakewood producers, as two of
the minor roles went to "Chissie" (her former fiancé) and Ralph (her assistant).
As with many such summer productions, the engagement was for one week
only. "My appearance in *Rain* was an experiment ... a happy experiment."
Happy experiment or not, Sally couldn't pass up the big bucks:

> Dramatic acting is a luxury I can't afford right now. No one who is
> making the money I am has any right to commit economic suicide
> by indulging a lifelong ambition to become an actress. That will
> come later, when everybody has seen the fan dance or doesn't give
> a hoot about seeing it.

Sally acted in summer stock off and on for several more years. In 1938 she
reprised her role in *Rain*[9] and, in *Susan and God*, was cast in the title role —
"Susan," that is.

Reviews for her summer stock performances were mixed, but they were commonly more positive than not. She had been especially well received at her
return to Lakewood in 1937, with one critic quoting an admirer, who gushed:

> You could have knocked me over with a feather. Sally Rand gave
> one of the swellest performances we've ever seen in the theater as
> Amy in *They Knew What They Wanted*. It really was an exciting
> experience.... She was terrific. Our snooty dowagers climbed down
> from their high horses, had a good cry, and not only applauded
> their hands to the blisters but stood up and yelled "Bravo."

---

9   At least part of one of Sally's performances in *Rain* was captured on film. A short
     newsreel video that is available online includes a scene where Sadie is struggling with
     her costar. At the clip's conclusion, Sadie declares: "Hah, you make me laugh, you
     mealy mouthed hymn hound [*spits in Davidson's face*]. That's what I think of your
     bunk!" [Search for "Sally Rand" (include quote marks) at www.historicfilms.com and
     scroll down to VM-1471. Click on the second scene and then play the clip.] This is
     probably from her reprise of the play which she performed in 1938 at both the
     Lakewood Theatre and the Country Playhouse in Westport, Connecticut, and again in
     1941 at the newly established Woodstock Playhouse in New York. In the New York
     audience, the great caricaturist Al Hirschfeld was so impressed that he illustrated a
     scene from the play, placing Sally front and center. A print exists in a signed limited
     edition of 100 copies.

Perhaps the most withering (and personal) criticism of Sally as a stage actress was served up by actor Karl Malden in his 1997 memoir *When Do I Start?* Grousing about having to share the stage in 1941 with an "ex-stripper," Malden wrote:

> Her burlesque days were written all over her, especially in her hygiene habits.... [She] just kept dousing herself with perfume and shoveling on the makeup, layer upon layer, until it began to cake and separate so that you could see the dirt buildup in the creases around her neck....
>
> I was playing the oldest brother, Ben, in *Little Foxes*. She showed up for the first two days of rehearsals, then disappeared....
>
> Come final dress rehearsal, Miss Rand appeared. Predictably, she didn't know a word.... After we broke, I noticed her walking around on stage with her assistant later in the day. I figured she was finally learning the part. Not until the last rehearsal did I discover that she was, in fact, spending that afternoon pinning her lines all over the place, on every article of clothing and piece of furniture she could get her hands on.... I kept thinking, "There's no way she's going to know her lines by opening night. What am I going to do when she goes up?"
>
> Opening night came and there we were, Sally Rand and I, on stage together.... Suddenly, I stared at her and she stared at me. And who should go up? Who else? Yours truly. Absolutely dry.... If it hadn't been for one of the other actors making his entrance two pages early, I'd probably still be standing there.

After her initial summer stock appearance in *Rain*, Nils T. Granlund arranged for Sally to make her radio network debut as a guest on his September 10, 1935, show to be aired from the studios of WJZ, the NBC flagship station in New York City. She had been on the radio before, of course, but not in a dramatic presentation. It had been announced that, on this particular night, Sally would "do a specially prepared monologue." But when it came time for the broadcast, she was nowhere to be found. Granlund was feeling ill and it wasn't helping that Sally was apparently standing him up. The program went ahead as planned, but without its guest star.

No sooner had the live broadcast concluded than Granlund collapsed at the microphone. He was rushed to the Medical Arts Sanitarium, having suffered an attack of gastroenteritis, a condition found not to be serious. Sources at the WJZ studio later revealed that Sally had backed out because she had wanted

to perform a "torrid scene" from *Rain,* and had been told by the censors that
they simply wouldn't allow it.

S ally wasn't the only one dealing with censors. At about this same time,
Chicago Mayor Edward J. Kelly was still on the prowl. On October 21st
he had directed the Selwyn Theatre to close the popular Erskine Caldwell
play *Tobacco Road,* even though it had been running for seven weeks. After
seeing the play the night before, Mayor Kelly had declared it to be "... a
mass of outrageous obscenity," adding: "Chicago has always been a liberal
city ... but liberalism does not condone filth. There is no so-called artistic
merit to this production."

Since Sally had once been the intense focus of Mayor Kelly's attention, mem -
bers of the press naturally wanted her reaction to the play's closure. Cornered
by reporters in Providence, Rhode Island, she was quoted as responding:

> Congratulations to Chicago for owning so fearless a mayor. The
> language and actions in "Tobacco Road" are indecent and obscene,
> and its plot is inartistic. The play sickened me with its filth when I
> first saw it early in its New York run, and it has continued to sicken
> me every time I have seen it since then.

Not everyone has an ear for sarcasm, however, so Sally felt compelled to
clarify herself in a letter to gossip columnist Walter Winchell:

> *I never said that to any Rhode Island reporter or anybody!*
> *I really liked the play. I did go see it several times, though,*
> *because when I was at the Paradise, I would rush to catch*
> *what I could — and I always missed the beginning and last*
> *act. I finally got to see all of it. I want the public to know,*
> *please, that the criticism leveled at that play has been both*
> *vicious and bigoted, and I should not like my voice to be among*
> *that chorus.*

Even so, as much as four years later, columnists were still quoting Sally's
"opinion" on the matter as being among those who had objected to the play
and supported Mayor Kelly.[10]

---

[10]   The theater ultimately took the matter to federal court and, within a few days, Judge
William Holly cleared the way for *Tobacco Road* to resume, holding that the mayor
did not have the authority to close the show "at his own pleasure" solely on the
ground that he didn't believe it to be fit for public view. The original play ran on
Broadway for a total of 3,182 performances, becoming at the time the longest-
running play in history.

As the most controversial young woman in America, it was perfectly natural that reporters would seek Sally's opinion on matters, both large and small. It sold papers. But, like every public figure, she had family members who knew and observed her from a more private perspective.

We can reconstruct a celebrity's show business career from the public record, but it is only from more personal sources that we learn the details of that person's private trials, tribulations, biases, and family concerns. With this in mind, we offer, without comment, excerpts from a letter Sally's father wrote to her brother Harold on October 30, 1935. After 14 years in New York City, he had moved his new family back to Kansas City:

> In a letter some time ago to Helen, I mentioned you and wondered how things were with you.... She replied that you were somewhat in the slough of despond due to employment matters, and further aggravated by recent domestic troubles. I had hoped, and still hope, that the recent domestic affair is water over the dam — so far behind you by this time that it amounts now to zero, and I further hope that there will be no more entanglements of that character, and that the next venture that you may make along that line will be with one of our own race — good, one hundred percent American who will be a real pal, and go along with you in anything that may come to you in life's fortune or misfortune.
>
> From what you tell me it would appear that the music writing looks very good for you.... As I understand about that business it is like the stage business in one way, inasmuch as it has to be GOOD in order to get anywhere, as the competition is so great. Since Irving Berlin went to writing his exotic productions in Tin Pan Alley, and married into millions of a gentile family, it seemed like every kike around New York that was not engaged in some other racket broke out with the song writing itch.
>
> We hear from Helen once in a great while — received a letter about two weeks ago. She had not been having things so good. That damned New England crowd, you know. She was booked with her show for Providence, the contract was all set. She brought her people all to Providence for a week's engagement, and a catholic priest went to the city administration and made a protest — I do not know whether against the show or against Sally Rand.... Anyway the city administration got scared of catholic influence in politics, and embargoed the theatre against the show, and Helen and her people were a week on expenses

before the next engagement, with no recourse, as the contract did not provide for a contingency of that kind....[11]

I do not know anything about her financial affairs, but I believe that she had to borrow money on an insurance policy to finance this show of hers.

Be sure and never mention the above to Helen, as she would know that I told you, no one else knowing anything about it, but she wired me to go to her safe deposit box here, and get her insurance policy and send it to her by air mail, and she wired the bank to OK my getting into the vault. Now what did she want with that policy but to borrow on it? With all the thousands that she earned the two seasons in Chicago, and then have to go and borrow money in that way to finance her show — it sounds funny to me.... Of course I know that Helen has poured out money to other people like water out of a rain barrel, but I did hope that she would hang on to the bulk of it, so that she would never be in a jam again for funds....

You can never tell which way she will jump — at you, or away from you, as she jumps according to her feelings at the time. She did me that way about a year ago, and it took something out of me that has never returned. But she has been fine at times since then, and at other times crabby. Helen did a fine thing by the boys — sending them all away to a boy's camp in Minnesota for ten weeks during the summer. It cost her about a thousand dollars. I did not feel that she could afford it, and I would have felt better about it if some cheaper vacation method could have been used for them. That was a fine camp up there, but extremely high-priced. But one cannot tell her what to do. She gets a kick out of spending money, and I am afraid that it is not always spent wisely. Tell her nothing that I write to you....

Hope you will not wait so long to write next time. There is hardly a day that Marie does not talk of you.

Back in December 1934, the famous Dionne Quintuplets' doctor, Allan Roy Dafoe had advised Sally that if she wanted his professional advice on how to have quintuplets, she would have to come to the healthy environs of the Canadian North Woods. Now, nearly a year later, Sally did just that

---

[11] Sally and her company were banned in Providence after Rev. Thomas J. McKitchen, pastor of St. Peter and Paul's Church, demanded that police refuse to grant her show a permit.

and, although she would never give birth to quintuplets (or to anyone else for that matter), she did provoke quite a commotion.

She was just beginning a four-day stint at the Capitol Theatre in Ottawa on Friday, November 8, 1935. As usual, she had also arranged to take part in community events, having accepted an invitation to speak at a Kiwanis Club luncheon. After club president W. R. Low welcomed the "brilliant and completely charming Sally Rand" to the podium, she rose to speak.

Remarking on how readily she had been recognized when she entered the room, she delivered the well-practiced line: "It always gratifies me when anybody recognizes me . . . with my clothes on." She then proceeded to give a 20-minute address focused primarily on why, even in hard times, it is important to educate young people in the arts:

> Give them a background of appreciation and understanding. It is a fine thing, when opportunities are limited, if you can find comfort in art, music, and literature.... Show the young people that art is not an abstract thing they cannot understand. Love of art is compensation to those without wealth.

Sally had something in store for the capital city's ladies, as well. She had been engaged to make an appearance at the Freiman's Department Store, the most successful retail business in Ottawa. After performing her dances on closing night, She went across town to present an evening fashion show at the store, with her girls serving as models.

Sparing no expense, the store manager had placed a near-full-page ad in the local paper and engaged a locally popular orchestra to provide musical accompaniment. "Hundreds of women" were reportedly on hand for the event, most of them "shoving to get a bargain-counter look at glamourous Sally." Police were summoned to manage the crowd. As one witness recalled:

> There was a very large group of people at the front door ... when the doors opened for the fashion show. Everyone pushed forward, nearly suffocating ... and one of the large plate glass windows of the store was broken in the rush. Sally appeared as hostess of the show, wearing a pale blue dress, with a little round collar, most discreet and very becoming. [It] was nice to see her under such circumstances. [12]

It appears Sally was popular with almost everyone. Some preferred her with her clothes on; others, as Tweedledee might say, "Contrariwise."

---

[12]   After the event, a local high school student named Rose Carr sued the store for damages, claiming she had suffered "painful injuries to her head" and had missed nine weeks of school as a result of the accident.

Sally's Canadian tour led to speculation that she might entertain other offers from outside the USA. To this point, she had set all such bids aside, having all the work she could manage on the home front. (Indeed, she reportedly set a record with 93 weeks of continuous engagements, interrupted only by a single week of rest on the family farm in Missouri.) Offers from abroad included a potential contract with a group of South American promoters to appear for eight weeks in principal Latin American cities. A group of theater men in Asia also expressed interest in putting together a tour of Japan, China, the Philippines and other Southeast Asia destinations. Australia was also said to be interested. Ultimately, Sally chose to pass on all these overseas opportunities, as she would continue to do for the rest of her life.

On October 3, 1935, several years before Hitler's Nazi forces began invading and annexing their neighbors in Europe, Mussolini's Fascist troops had invaded Ethiopia, the only independent black nation in Africa. Responding to Emperor Haile Selassie's pleas for help, the League of Nations condemned the Italian military action and voted to impose economic sanctions on the aggressor. The situation was complicated by the fact that both Great Britain and France had colonies bordering Ethiopia and it was feared that Mussolini might react to any pressure by forming an alliance with Hitler. Thus, the League of Nations' efforts to respond were essentially ineffective. All of this registered only modest concern in the United States, although many Americans were becoming alarmed by the emergent Nazi war machine in Europe.

The subject was of sufficient interest that the Exchange Club of Reading, Pennsylvania, had invited Dr. Milton W. Hamilton, head of the history department at Albright College, to speak on the "Italian-Ethiopian situation" at its next meeting. Pleased that the local civic club recognized his expertise on such a serious matter, the good professor was happy to oblige.

With several weeks' notice and plenty of time to prepare his remarks, Dr. Hamilton little suspected that another, more controversial, speaker might be announced as a late addition to the program. As the meeting date approached, club organizers noted that Sally Rand's upcoming engagement at the Astor Theatre meant that she too would be in town that day. Moreover, she had already accepted an invitation to address the local Rotary Club. Not to be outdone by their Rotarian brothers, the Exchange Club extended her a last-minute invitation. Sally happily accepted, and the club marked her down to address its members on "The Story Behind the Fan, and Making Business of Bubbles."

The day before his scheduled address on Wednesday, November 20th, Dr. Hamilton was feeling pretty good about himself and his planned observations on the African conflict. However, when he learned that he would be sharing the stage with Sally Rand — a woman whose reputation was, shall we say, at odds with his own — well, that just wouldn't do. Indeed, the affront to his dignity was so severe that Hamilton told the Exchange Club he would not be appearing after all. What's more, he expected an apology as he hadn't been informed that Miss Rand had been added to the program.

The professor's graceless withdrawal left the Exchange Club in something of a lurch. Luncheon attendees were expecting a lecture on one of the more pressing foreign policy issues of the day, and now it was looking as if that wasn't going to happen. When Sally was told of the situation, she took measure of the matter and, with little hesitation, volunteered to fill the breech: "I'll talk on any subject the professor has decided not to talk about."

And that's exactly what she did. With less than 24 hours to prepare (not to mention her intervening performances at the Astor Theatre) Sally quickly reviewed the available reference material, boned up on the Italo-Ethiopian situation as best she could and, in the words of local columnist Jerry Kobrin, "promptly proceeded to flabbergast the Exchange Club members with a learned dissertation on the subject."

At the outset, Sally referred to the "regrettable absence of my learned colleague" and stated that she welcomed the opportunity to do "a little fanning about Il Duce and Negus Negusti, or King of Kings." Dismissing the notion that colonization and exploitation of raw materials were Italy's chief objectives in invading Ethiopia, rather, she characterized the invasion as Mussolini's "first step toward the creation of a new Roman empire."

Smartly dressed in a dark suit and a fur-trimmed toque, Sally presented an insightful analysis of the complex situation, questioning whether Great Britain's interest was truly "as serious as they pretend, or whether it was to frighten the English populace and assure the reelection of a conservative government." She expressed hope that the League of Nations' sanctions would prove successful in ending the war, adding that failure would mean "that we haven't progressed very far in the last 20 years." She further advanced the opinion that the way to permanent peace would be "to take the profits out of war." With the sort of knowing smile that those who knew her well had come to expect, she observed in conclusion that failure of the European democracies to act would "prick forever the bubble of world peace." She then stepped away from the lectern and took her seat to prolonged rounds of applause.

There is an interesting footnote to this little story and, while the salient facts are known to be true, the accounts are at odds concerning one detail. We'll leave it to the reader to decide which is the most believable:

Version 1: Despite assurances that Miss Rand would serve as an able substitute for the professor and could speak with authority on the advertised topic, his withdrawal left a last-minute hole in the program. Faced with finding a replacement on short notice, club organizers scrambled around to come up with something. After pondering their options, they quickly made a few phone calls and managed to engage a trained dog act to take the professor's place.

Version 2: The animal act was on the program all along. If so, it was Sally, not Dr. Hamilton, who was entitled to be offended. What was she supposed to think when the esteemed professor haughtily objected to occupying the stage with *her*, but was perfectly comfortable to be sharing the program with a trained dog?

Faith

Born in 1878 in Calabria, Italy — the toe of the boot — and coming to America by steamship in 1891 as a young teen, James "Big Jim" Colosimo started out as a Chicago street sweeper. Organizing the other sweepers into a union, he soon became a union boss, using his considerable personal appeal and business acumen to parlay himself into a supporting role in shady local politics. He found his calling in July of 1902 when he married Victoria Moresco, a local madam who ran a cheap brothel in a ramshackle area of town known as "Bed Bug Row." Within a very few years, Big Jim was dominating the flesh trade, running more than 100 brothels.

In 1910, Colosimo opened a restaurant at 2126 South Wabash Avenue, naming it after himself. Before long, Colosimo's Café became a Chicago institution — the watering hole of Chicago's rich and famous. Now hailed as "Diamond Jim" for his gaudy wardrobe and flashy bling, Colosimo thrived until the Volstead Act ushered in Prohibition, after which his fortunes took a more ominous turn.

By decade's end, Diamond Jim's marriage had soured; Colosimo divorced Victoria and married the much younger and prettier café songbird, Dale Winter. Accounts differ as to what happened next. We do know that Colosimo, just back from his honeymoon, had gone to the café late in the afternoon perhaps to await delivery of some bootleg liquor. When it didn't arrive, he started to leave. As he approached the door, a gunman emerged from behind, possibly from the cloakroom, and shot him dead. Several likely perpetrators were considered, but interrogations were futile, no case was made, and the actual killer was never found.

After his untimely demise, Colosimo's popular café and nightspot came under the control of his former bouncer — now gang boss — Al Capone. The nitery was still going strong in 1936 when it presented a revue of entertainers featuring eight "lovely ladies" and starring a beauty billed as the "Creator of the Fan Dance" — Faith Bacon.

Like Sally, Faith saw that if she wanted to continue working in the clubs in Chicago, she would have to accommodate the shady characters who were running the show. Interviewed at Colosimo's by a cub reporter from *The Spotlight* magazine, Faith confided: "I love all outdoor sports, although there are some pretty good sports in here some nights."

M aybe it was just a slow news day or maybe the event really was regarded as a big attraction, but on March 1, 1936, the Sunday edition of the *Daytona Beach News-Journal* announced at the very top of the front page, in huge red letters: SALLY RAND OPENS GOLF MEET TOMORROW. The story continued: "Miss Sally Rand, who usually waves fans in order to conceal her undraped body, will wave a golf club tomorrow to open the ... second annual senior golf tournament." A picture of Sally in her "Leda and the Swan" costume accompanied the article, with a caption helpfully clarifying that, at the golf tournament, "she'll be in civilian clothes, of course."

Sure enough, at 9:30 on Monday morning with cameras snapping and whirring to record the event, after some preliminary instructions from the local golf pro, Sally stepped up to the first tee at the Daytona Beach Golf and Country Club to drive the first ball in the tournament. The *News-Journal* reported: "She confessed it was the first time she had ever hit a golf ball, adding: 'I was scared to death I'd miss the thing completely.'" The item went on:

> Displaying perfect form, Sally Rand discarded her fans and
> bubbles this morning, donned sports clothes and opened the ... golf
> tournament with a booming drive of at least 60 yards.... [The ball]
> went high, sliced over to the rough to the right of the course, but it
> wasn't a bad first shot.

Wrapping up her four-week swing through Florida in Tallahassee, Sally spoke at a Lion's Club luncheon attended by Governor Sholtz and performed at the State Theater. A local columnist wondered if the mayor might present her with the key to the city. One man quipped that he'd prefer giving her the key to his apartment.

O n Valentine's Day 1936, Sally's father celebrated his 62nd birthday as he once again wrote a long letter to her brother Harold, who was in Glendora attending to the family orange groves. Commenting on the severe winter weather, he reported on the health of his family and praised Sally for arranging for a specialist to treat her half-brother Eugene's asthma ("It was fine of Helen to take Gene in hand that way").

Shifting topics, he wrote about the family farm in Hickory County, expressing his views on Sally's success, or lack of it, and grousing about the state of the national economy, still struggling through the Great Depression:

> As you know there is a lot of talent unaccountably suppressed both in the show business and the arts.... Every time I attend a picture show I see women on the screen in stellar roles who are not as good as I know Helen to be; and I leave that show wondering <u>why</u> so many mediocre "stars" are getting the breaks while our Helen, able, talented, well and favorably known all over the land, <u>never gets a chance</u>....

> I may say that the price of oranges ... is very high here at this time. I suppose that is due to those who chisel in between the producer and the ultimate consumer. As you say, the grower is the first fall-guy, and the consumer the second and last. The middle men constitute the sinister element in prostituting values, and no one seems to have the answer to that problem. The New Deal has failed so far to find a solution. Bolstering the situation with billions of dollars for relief has kept a lot of people from actual want, but seems to have accomplished little to lift a national industrial depression from the shoulders of the American people....

> Of course the depression will pass, as all things must pass.... No party or politics will have anything to do with bringing that about. An abnormal industrial condition due to world-war economics caused the depression, which was made possible by the ignorance, cupidity and greed of humanity which failed to see that after a flood of exaggerated values, prices and wages, there must come a deluge of reaction.

> As I see it no national government has any business trying to revolutionize its people or laws because of a depression that is international in scope. And I am utterly opposed to any move to exercise federal control over the individuals of a nation to the extent of telling [a man] what he shall plant or not plant, or how much of his product he shall sell or not sell, and the price that he shall receive for it. People who want such a condition should allow their whiskers to grow, and should take no more baths — as in bloody Bolshevik Russia.

Inspired by the relative success of the World's Fair in Chicago, community leaders in San Diego decided to mount the California Pacific Exposition, incorporating to some degree the same or similar attractions that drew enthusiastic crowds to the Windy City, including the "villages of the world" concept. Exhibits were to be housed in a number of "palaces" — the "Palace of Education," the "Palace of Science," and even the "Palace of Food and Beverages." The Midway would include a Ripley's *Believe It Or Not* attraction plus a midget city that would offer not only 100 or more "little people," but also an assortment of "midget" farm animals.

The San Diego Exposition opened on May 29, 1935, with all these attractions and more. Of course, those patrons seeking titillation were not neglected. Zoro Gardens — "Home of the Nudists" — featured a group of topless young women along with a number of bearded males in loin cloths who, according to the brochure, were "healthy young men and women, indulging in the freedom of outdoor living in which they so devoutly believe." So that fairgoers could better understand the "advantages of natural outdoor life," the noble nudists had presumably agreed to open their colony "to the friendly, curious gaze of the public."

For the price of admission, customers could observe naturists reading books, sunbathing, playing volleyball, and participating in pseudo-religious rituals to the Sun God. Those without sufficient funds (25 cents) could still peep through knotholes in a picket fence surrounding the garden.[13]

Both the San Diego Council of Catholic Women and the Women's Civic Center registered protests — even the San Diego Braille Club found reason to be offended by the nudists. But it was all to no avail. The attraction operated continually throughout both years of the exposition. As "Queen Zorine" (22-year-old Yvonne Stacey) put it, since Genesis 1:27 reads "So God created man in his own image," the image of God could never be indecent.

Like the Chicago Fair, the exposition was carried over for a second year, opening again on February 12, 1936. The first year had been a success of sorts, but still not what promoters were hoping for. Something was missing. But what? The exposition had midgets, it had Ripley's freak show, it even had nudists. Finally someone pointed out that what the exposition didn't have was a certain popular fan dancer. The expo's second edition would run for nearly two months before this oversight would be corrected. Organizers offered Sally the option of appearing as a free attraction, performing only

---

13   The area is now Zoro Butterfly Garden in San Diego's Balboa Park. Despite contemporaneous press accounts, it has since been acknowledged that the colony members posing for the elucidation of the public were hired actors, not actual "nudists."

during hours that she found agreeable. She would dance two shows daily in the Palace of Entertainment and two evening shows in the Plaza del Pacifico. In addition, she would make ad hoc appearances at the Café of the World. With little hesitation, she happily accepted the booking.

When she arrived in San Diego on April 9th, Sally received an invitation from Tanya, "Queen of the Nudists," to meet with her for tea. She declined the offer, saying: "The nude is my business suit. I never appear socially in it. Besides, I am opposed to nudism."[14] In light of Sally's past disparaging remarks about nudists, this snub didn't sit well with the Zoro Gardens group. Led by raven-haired Mary Pomeroy, they vowed to give Sally a battle she would never forget. Poised on a tree stump, Pomeroy expounded:

> It might be excusable in other circumstances, but we are well
> aware that last year in the east Miss Rand launched a bitter attack
> against us. She has had plenty of opportunity to acquaint herself
> with nudism's high principles, but the truth is that she doesn't
> want to. She probably figures that nudism will sound the death-
> knell of sensationalism, such as she practices.

The aggrieved Miss Pomeroy rallied her nudist comrades to mount a protest demonstration at Sally's show. Wearing sandwich boards declaring "Sally Rand Unfair to Nudism" and carrying signs they had transformed from "Welcome Sally Rand" to read "Down with Sally Rand," the group proceeded to disrupt one of her performances.

Sally was not amused, responding through her publicist, David Lipton:

> An indecent performance of this nature should not be tolerated.
> Flaunting of nakedness under the guise of nudism is not in accord
> with her principles. If this shocking event is repeated, she intends
> to resort to such legal action as may be necessary to prevent
> disruption of her performances and maintain the high character of
> dignity and beauty with which they have always been associated.

Newspapers reported that "the nudist pickets were herded back into their Zoro gardens, and a guard was set up to keep them away from Sally's exhibi-

---

14 Faith Bacon shared this view. In a 1935 letter to columnist Ashton Stevens, she
    remarked that: "I have received many offers to become "queen" of various nudist
    camps. But it always occurs to me that these people have no excuse for their stupidity,
    except, perhaps, an exhibitionist complex." She added: "If these people were sincere
    they would realize that nudism ... can have no true future.... For certainly men and
    women who have been taught by their parents that they have something to hide can
    never suddenly strip to the skin without experiencing dangerous self-consciousness."

tion." The whole dust-up made for excellent copy and reporters ate it up. In fact, this may have been the whole point of the incident. The great Sally-Rand-Versus-the-Nudists "controversy" was perhaps little more than a publicity stunt staged to separate wavering patrons from their hard-earned cash.[15]

When Sally's booking at the Pacific Exhibition was first announced, local fan dancers in the western states decided to hold a convention in San Diego on April 11th in honor of their idol. They also hoped their conference would elevate "the ethical standards" of their art and increase its "prestige with the beauty-loving public." Led by Joy Williams of San Diego, the "Western Federation of Fan Dancers" consisted of girls from San Francisco, Los Angeles, Phoenix and other western cities. While this was all well and good, it turned out that a similar group, the "United Fan, Bubble and Specialty Dancers of America," headed by Rosita Carmen of Hollywood, also demanded to be included.

Each claimed that her organization was the only official association of its type in the country. Miss Williams of San Diego felt that Miss Carmen of Hollywood was trying to horn in on the action. Miss Carmen rejoined: "Either we'll be in on that meeting or there won't be any meeting.... How can there be a convention without *our* group?"

Among other concerns, the groups disagreed on the proper length of the plumes. Miss Williams' group had apparently refused to accept a pact among the other fan dancers to use 25-inch fans, holding out for the 35-inch size. Miss Carmen called Miss Williams a "troublemaker," complaining none-too-charitably: "If she's ashamed of her figure, she ought to dance in a cape." In time, cooler heads prevailed and the two groups merged as the "United Specialty Dancers of America," with 47 delegates from 14 states and Hawaii.

Oddly, although a declared purpose for the fan dancers' convention was to welcome and honor Miss Rand, once Sally arrived, she was largely dismissive of the newly formed organization. This left its delegates to attend to other agenda items — opposition to the employment of female impersonators or male fan dancers and consideration of a proposed resolution that fan dancers should remain single (rejected). While they also voted to hold

---

[15]   Speaking of nudity and publicity, perhaps the most explicit surviving film of Sally dancing sans attire was taken during her appearance at the San Diego Exposition in 1936. In the film, we see her dancing in an outdoor fountain, topless if not completely nude, both with and without her bubble. See for yourself by searching online for "Sally Rand" and "critical past" at YouTube.

the 1937 convention in San Francisco, there is no indication that such an event was ever held. The 1936 convention adjourned on April 22nd, after pronouncing 18-year-old Barbara Brent of Miami, Florida, to be "the most perfect fan dancer."[16]

As usual, problems seemed to dog Sally at every turn. Nudist Queen Tanya, the militant Miss Pomeroy, and the other fan dancers weren't her only adversaries in San Diego. Small boys, hiding behind trees with sling-shots, proved adept at puncturing Sally's expensive bubble and otherwise peppering her with small pebbles — some not so small.[17] One eager fan got so close that he almost burned Sally's behind with a cigarette. Management agreed to post guards around her stage in the future.

Added to these aggravations were the everyday hazards of the natural world. When a swarm of bees took up residence in the shrubbery next to the plaza pool where she performed her dance each day, Sally, as always, was the perfect professional: "Bees or no bees, my dance will go on. I was stung yesterday, but not seriously. Being a former farm girl, I know how to act when bees are around." Maybe so. However, according to press reports, spectators couldn't help but notice that "several new and somewhat erratic movements had been added to the dance."

Meanwhile, Rosita Royce ("The Girl Who Shocked the World with Her Grace and Gorgeous Figure") was fulfilling an extended engagement in Salt Lake City, allowing herself to be billed as the "Originator of the Famous Bubble Dance."[18]

On April 27th, still keeping an eye out for mischievous boys and aggressive bees, Sally learned that her old boss, film director Cecil B. DeMille, was planning a film based on the life of Wild Bill Hickok, with the famous gunslinger to be played by Gary Cooper. Two days later, she read that DeMille wanted to cast *her* opposite Cooper in the part of Calamity Jane, the "tobacco-chewing, poker-playing, gunfighting Lady Hellion of the Old West." If true, the role in a big-budget film tentatively

---

[16] Chosen for her "new and vastly different fan dance," Miss Brent's dance involved electrically lighted fans that helped spectators in the back rows see the performer.

[17] Newspapers reported that Sally suffered bruises from pebbles slung at her during an outdoor performance: "Bleeding at the cheek from an injury under her eye, she reappeared upon the stage after a brief retirement, with her fans replacing her bubble."

[18] Miss Royce claimed to have a "copyright" for the bubble dance, but she admitted to reporters that she was "too shy" to seek an injunction against Sally.

titled *This Breed of Men* might well have changed the course of Sally's career in a major way.

To confirm the truth of the press report, Sally decided to pay DeMille a visit at Paramount Studios, making the three-hour drive to Hollywood between performances in San Diego. According to the publicity department, she ran into the producer as he was returning from lunch. After she smiled at him and he vaguely smiled back, Sally chirped: "What's the matter? Don't you know me with my clothes on?" Within minutes she was in his office, legs curled beneath her on a leather perch, babbling winsomely:

> I hear you're looking for a girl to play Calamity Jane in your new
> Gary Cooper picture ... and she is supposed to be the toughest,
> most glamorous, most beautiful woman in the West. Have you
> thought about me, C.B? I could play that role.

As she beamed the fetching smile that had so captivated the thousands who had seen her dance, DeMille turned the idea over in his mind. According to the press release, after thoughtfully considering Sally's appearance, her career, her talent and her potential at the box office, he stated his conclusion: "You're the best possibility for the role yet."

It never happened. While DeMille may have been serious, more likely he was simply being cordial. In any event, within weeks it was announced that Calamity Jane would be played by Jean Arthur, a proven box office star whose previous film with Cooper, *Mr. Deeds Goes to Town*, had been released only a few days before Sally's visit.[19]

So, Sally missed out on portraying one of the most colorful characters in the history of the Old West. Still, the intriguing notion of appearing in a cowgirl outfit had been implanted in her consciousness. Maybe she could still make something of the idea.

---

[19] The "Hickok" film, retitled *The Plainsman*, opened in the United States on
November 16, 1936. In the ensuing decades, it played in at least 16 countries under
alternate titles.

CHAPTER THIRTEEN

The Nude Ranch and Beyond

I haven't been out of work since the day I took my
pants off.

~ Sally Rand

In 1836, the Republic of Texas formally declared its independence from
Mexico. It was only fitting that, 100 years later, the State of Texas would
celebrate its centennial by staging a world's fair — The Texas Centennial
Exposition[1]. Dallas got the nod to be the host city (over competitors
Houston and San Antonio) largely because it had offered the biggest cash
commitment, not to mention the availability of the facilities and grounds of
the State Fair of Texas.

Amon G. Carter, publisher of the *Fort Worth Star-Telegram* and a member of
the selection committee, was taken aback when a board of Texas historians
rejected his recommendation that a portion of the funding be devoted to the
role of West Texas in the development of the state. To Carter's great chagrin,
the historians had concluded that the western part of Texas had "no history
to commemorate." The larger-than-life Amon Carter was infuriated. While he
passively agreed to the selection of Dallas as host of the "official" centennial
exposition, that didn't stop him from helping Big D's little brother horn in on
the action. With the support of wealthy friends and political connections
extending into the White House, he set about putting together an "outlaw"
exposition 35 miles to the west in Fort Worth that would demonstrate to the
State of Texas and, in particular, to the City of Dallas, that a man of his
stature could not be so easily dismissed.

On June 6, 1936, the Texas Centennial Exposition opened in Dallas as planned.
Sponsors had determined that commercial, industrial, and cultural attractions
were to be the order of the day. Even so, along with all the refined culture,
Dallas also offered the sort of attractions that had come to be associated with

---

[1]   The idea for the centennial celebration was born in a speech given by James Stephen
    Hogg in 1900. Planning for the event began as early as 1923, but the permanent Texas
    Centennial Commission wasn't established until June 1934, just two years before the
    exposition opened.

such events — premature babies in incubators, animated dinosaurs, and, of course, plenty of pretty girls. Besides demonstrations of prototype television and an amazing new breakthrough called "air conditioning," a delicious new salty snack was introduced under the name "Fritos." The grounds also included the "Hall of Negro Life" — the first time American black culture was recognized at a world's fair.

HALL OF NEGRO LIFE

Federally funded at the urging of the Dallas Negro Chamber of Commerce and other black groups, the hall was formally dedicated on June 19, 1936 (coinciding with "Juneteenth," the oldest known commemoration of the end of slavery in America). The entrance was distinguished by a large seal depicting a black male, with arms raised overhead, breaking the manacles from his wrists. Four Texas-oriented black history murals filled the lobby. Thirty-two states and the District of Columbia contributed exhibits in education, medical progress, agriculture, mechanics, business and industry, and art. Music and drama was presented daily by African American performers in a 2,000-seat outdoor amphitheater. Food and entertainment were available at a "Little Harlem" concession. Nearly a half million visitors, mostly white, attended. Regrettably, like most fair structures, the hall was eventually demolished. (See the Texas State Historical Association website at: https://tshaonline.org.)

As for the rogue exposition in Fort Worth, planning for the event had initially been placed in the hands of local women whose idea of a respectable exposition involved such attractions as the city symphony orchestra, homemade jelly and baking competitions, boy scouts painted up to portray savage frontier Indians, and an amphitheater where church choirs could perform. Not exactly what Amon Carter had in mind.

Carter sought advice from former Fort Worth resident, Rufus LeMaire, a casting director for MGM studios in Hollywood. Their conversation ultimately led to the hiring of three personalities who would take the Texas Frontier Centennial in a whole new direction. Acting on LeMaire's recommendation, Carter contracted with the first — Billy Rose — installing him as producer of entertainment.

Born William Samuel Rosenberg, Billy Rose was an up-and-coming Broadway producer, impresario of an extravaganza called "Jumbo." A small man, he was barely two inches taller than Sally Rand. Married at the time to stage, screen, and radio star Fannie Brice (who dwarfed him both in star power and stature), he was sometimes called "Mr. Brice" behind his back.

Rose's plan for Fort Worth was to go big or not go at all. To compete with the Dallas Exposition, he proposed not only to transport his entire *Jumbo* production to Fort Worth, but also to oversee construction of a grand-scale outdoor cabaret boasting the world's largest revolving stage. The outsized production would eclipse anything his competition might come up with. It wouldn't be cheap, but going big was just exactly what West Texas booster Amon Carter had in mind.[2]

Next, Billy Rose convinced the second celebrity, "King of Jazz" Paul Whiteman, to bring his hugely popular dance band to Fort Worth and hold forth for the duration of the season.

The third personality almost wasn't hired at all. At Rose's first press conference, given on horseback in Fort. Worth, he announced the details of his ambitious proposal. Although he clearly expected to

> ### CASA MAÑANA
>
> Described as the "Largest Cafe-Theatre Ever Constructed," the venue provided "tables and chairs for 4,500 amusement lovers," and claimed to have the world's largest revolving and reciprocating stage. It was more than triple the size of the stage at Radio City Music Hall and weighed 17,000 tons. Supported on metal tracks in a tank of water 130 feet in diameter and nine feet deep, the stage appeared to float above a moat as it revolved, advanced, or receded. The mechanisms to operate the stage required two motors, 450 horsepower each. It took a full minute and 45 seconds for the enormous stage to revolve. In the outdoor amphitheater, there was no physical curtain to signal the end of a scene; rather, change of scene was indicated by a "water curtain" consisting of many water jets bordering the moat. Colored spotlights projected on the glistening screen of water enhanced the curtain-like effect.

"put on a show the likes of which [had] never been seen by the human eye," Rose claimed his production would permit "neither nudity nor smut," saying: "Only once has the public responded to smut. We don't need any fans or bubble dances at the Texas Frontier Centennial and we won't have them."

Amon Carter then inquired about the one time when smut actually *was* popular, leading to the following exchange with Rose:

"At the Century of Progress in Chicago — Sally Rand had a nude act."

"Pulled 'em in, did she?"

---

2   A big man in a big state, Amon Carter's *Fort Worth Star-Telegram* was bold and freewheeling, but no more so than his smaller competitor, the *Fort Worth Press*. When a police car accidentally struck and killed a deer (later butchered and barbequed for a police picnic), it turned out the deer was actually a child's escaped pet. Seizing the opportunity for a great headline, the *Press* ran the story under: "POLICE EAT KID'S PET."

"By the thousands!"

"Let's get her."

The question remained — could Rose persuade Sally to spend her summer in Texas? Absolutely. After dealing with the rigors of the road for most of the previous year, Sally would find the chance to spend a few months in one spot (not to mention the inducement of $1,000 a week) to be irresistible. Besides, she had never stopped thinking about that charming bronco buster from the rodeo in Cheyenne. And going to Fort Worth would give her another chance to dress up as a cowgirl. So Sally was definitely on board. And, with little else to do beyond her dancing, she began to consider the prospects of making a few bucks on the side.

The night before the opening of the Frontier Centennial, Billy Rose offered an advance look at his revue on the big revolving stage, presented for a crowd of newspaper people from around the country. Almost without exception, the reviews that followed were euphoric.

Local critiques were positive, of course, but even those from the papers in competing Dallas overflowed with praise. John Rosenfield of the *Dallas Morning News* wrote: "The show beggars description.... We doubt that anything else so large or sumptuous has risen from the pavements of the world's capitals, let alone the Texas prairie." Robert Garland of the *New York World* called the production: "... a stage show glorified out of all knowing. I can't tell you the half of it. Casa Mañana is as big as Texas." The critic from the staid *New York Times* joined the choir: "Mr. Rose presents a spectacle that has no parallel in our curdled world." Even author and journalist Damon Runyon proclaimed: "There you will find Broadway and the Wild West jointly producing what probably is the biggest and most unique show ever seen in these United States."

Apparently, it was a pretty good show. The program began with three acts or "scenes" paying homage to the three most notable previous world fairs — St. Louis (1904), Paris (1925), and Chicago (1933-34) and was capped by a grand finale honoring the State of Texas. As you might imagine, Sally's "Ballet Divertissement" (led by The Californians singing "You're like a Toy Balloon") was the highlight of the scene celebrating the "Chicago Century of Progress."

The Dallas Expo had opened on June 6th, and sponsors of the Fort Worth celebration had intended to do the same but, because planning and construction had gotten such a late start, the Fort Worth opening was delayed for several weeks.

To make up for lost time, Billy Rose made a brazen pitch in an effort to draw visitors away from the Dallas expo, erecting a huge blinking neon sign, directly across from the main entrance to the Dallas fairgrounds, featuring an animated bucking bronco and declaring: "WILD & WHOO-PEE 45 MINUTES WEST." In smaller glowing text, the sign also called attention to Sally Rand and Paul Whiteman. Hundreds of billboards featuring scantily clad cowgirls were erected along Texas roadways, extending for miles around and into several neighboring states. Every motorist in the southwest was put on notice that something pretty special was happening in Fort Worth.

Although sponsors of the Dallas fair had hoped to maintain a high class profile, Miss Rand's presence could not go unanswered. In a bold attempt to keep the throngs from heading west, Dallas authorities reportedly countered by issuing health cards to over 2,000 prostitutes operating in the vicinity of the fairgrounds. The story of the rivalry between the two expos is worthy of a book of its own, but for our purposes the situation can be summed up in the words of Billy Rose, himself: "Go to Dallas for education. Come to Fort Worth for entertainment."[3]

A large crowd was pressing at the gate when the Frontier Centennial opened in Fort Worth on Saturday, July 18, 1936. The press reported that, of all the concession shows, the "Beauty and the Beast" show and Sally Rand's Nude Ranch "were the heavy drawing cards." One reporter wrongly conflated the two attractions, asserting that "Miss Rand, as a slant-eyed beauty, dances semi-nude in a cage of lions."[4]

While Sally's opinion of "nudists" in San Diego's Zoro Gardens had been quite negative, they obviously struck a chord with the public. Realizing that curious men and women would pay to watch "nudists" at leisure and at play, she got the idea to adapt the Zoro Gardens theme to a form more suitable to the expo's cowboy and western motif. Thus was born the idea for "Sally Rand's Nude Ranch," which proved to be one of the most profitable attractions at the fair.

---

[3] By the time the two expos closed, Sally Rand's magnetism aside, Dallas had outdrawn Fort Worth by 6,345,385 visitors to 986,128. Sponsors in both cities were disappointed.

[4] The "beauty" dancing bare breasted with the lions was Miss Laurene NeVell of Chicago. On one occasion three monkeys escaped from the Monkey Mountain attraction and pounced on the poor old lions, giving them such a scare it was several days before they got over it.

Sally mounted the show on short notice, running a display ad in local papers:

> SALLY RAND can use a few attractive young girls at her NUDE
> RANCH in Fort Worth. Can be any height. Perfect figure necessary.
> Highest salaries paid. Interviews Thursday, between 11 a.m. and
> 2 p.m., room 220 Adolphus Hotel. Girls must be ready to leave for
> Fort Worth at 4 o'clock same day.

Eighteen "cowgirls" were chosen to work at Sally's ranch, the feature attraction on the Sunset Trail Midway.[5] The front entrance was bounded by four columns — outsized red-haired, bare-breasted caryatids, two on either side of the box office — supporting the overhanging roof with outstretched arms. Above the pillars, large rustic letters on the roof spelled out "SALLY RANDS DUDE RANCH," with a slash mark through the capital "D" and an "N" mounted above. Adult admission was 25¢ (about $4.15 today).

Once inside, a ticketholder could expect to see a variety of cheeky cowgirls tossing horseshoes or beach balls, playing basketball, shooting arrows at a target, striking poses astride horses, and generally lounging around. Attired in cowboy boots and 10-gallon hats, the "ranch hands" were mostly "nude," even if they benefitted from flesh-colored string bikini thongs and strategically placed bandanas and holsters. Although not evident in surviving pictures, each young "heifer" was also said to have an "SR" brand rubber-stamped on her thigh.

To protect against unwelcome encounters, a wire screen separated the girls from their visitors, who were expected to pass through the building at a respectable pace and then exit the "ranch." This expectation was not always met, as more than one gentleman with a robust interest in anatomy was observed spending the better part of a day examining the exhibits. And why not? The attraction had actually been billed as "the only educational show" at the Frontier Centennial. Sally herself was not part of the attraction, although she was occasionally on hand as a sort of Walmart-style greeter.

Curious youngsters, of course, were barred from ogling the cowgirls. But that didn't stop everyone. George Lester, ten years old at the time, shared his childhood experience in the online magazine *Texas Escapes*:

> My dad and my adult brother decided to see the Billy Rose
> production called Sally Rand's Nude Ranch.... My brother Sam
> was only a year older than me, so our dad gave us money for the
> rides while they went to see the show.

---

5   Among the girls chosen for the Nude Ranch were three coeds who, when recognized, were informed by their college that they would not be welcome to return for the fall semester.

We chose to start with the Ferris wheel. On our first ascent we
discovered something the producers of the event had overlooked.
From high above we could look down onto the roofless show
below and see all the scantily clad ladies. We kept riding until we
ran out of money. I don't think we ever told our dad why we liked
the Ferris wheel so much.

As usual, local clerics were none too thrilled that Sally had come to town.
The fact that she was reportedly netting $1,000 a week from the Nude Ranch
provoked both envy and outrage from the clergy. Jealous of the crowds
flowing to the exposition, a Fort Worth minister confessed: "If I had the
money, I would rent a concession stand and preach, morning, noon and
night, and distribute religious material out there." The Reverend Joe
Scheumack of the Berry Street Baptist Church called the ranch "a contami-
nation of the centennial ... I think they're about as low as they can get." The
good reverend's opinion was based not on an actual inspection of the ranch's
activities, but rather on his distaste for the racy statues at the entrance, calling
them "an open violation of the law in themselves."

Still, Sally managed to ingratiate herself with much of the community
before her stay was over. To disarm her more conservative critics, she
engaged in a self-promotional blitz, speaking to civic groups and hosting a
tea for society women. (In town to participate in the festivities, her mother
and grandmother were among those sipping the tea.) Sally threw out the
first pitch at a softball game, posed for a photograph with the world's
largest steer (3,861 pounds), and addressed the opening session of the
Democratic State Convention. On one occasion, she donned her cowgirl
outfit and directed traffic on horseback at a Fort Worth intersection. She
even gave a pep talk to the Texas Christian University football team.

One columnist recalled: "Miss Rand ... became so prominent that one local
has complained, 'If they opened a new sewer, Sally Rand would step out.
She's everywhere.'" The contrast between her reputation as a brazen stripper
and her reality as a substantial woman was also duly noted: "She was not
only beautiful and sexy, but her knowledge was beyond belief. She was an
intellectual. She could sit down and hold her own in any conversation —
an amazingly brilliant woman."

Besides charming the locals in Fort Worth, Sally made promotional trips to
surrounding cities, including Waco, Wichita Falls and Austin. When Braniff
Airlines inaugurated air service to Corpus Christi on August 15th, company
officials arranged for Sally to serve as a "hostess" on the flight, wearing a
costume of her own design. During her one-day stay in Corpus Christi,
newspaper ads publicized her imminent "parade" through town in a

custom-built Packard convertible, after which she would host a "Special Sally Rand Banquet" on the deck of the Plaza hotel. Beyond the endorsements of Braniff, Packard, and the Plaza, Sally was also featured in newspaper ads for Hotpoint electric water heaters, the Garden Food Market, and the Cyrus-Marshall Company, a local provider of "superior cleaning, pressing, and moth proofing." She was indefatigable.

When a young couple in Sweetwater, Texas, named their baby after her, Sally sent an engraved cup to the baby, along with a telegram declaring:

> I am honored and delighted that your parents have given you my name. May you always be as beautiful as a Texas sunrise, as true blue as a Texas bluebonnet, as broadminded as your father and mother. May you always have fun when you blow bubbles and may enthusiasm never cease to fan your ambition.

One of the more remarkable episodes of Sally's sojourn in Fort Worth occurred not in front of an adoring audience but in the confines of her dressing room with the 26th governor of Florida. The details came to light only when Billy Rose himself chose to disclose them 11 years later in a syndicated newspaper column under his byline:

> One night, Governor Dave Sholtz of Florida paid us a visit. I stopped by his table to give him the big hello and to ask him if he'd mind being introduced from the stage just before the show. I explained it was our custom to have visiting celebrities take a bow. Sholtz was a friendly fellow and said he'd be honored. As I started to walk away, he asked if Miss Rand was around.... I told him Sally was probably in her dressing room and asked him if he'd like to go back and say howdy. He said, "Sure," and I took him backstage.

> I knocked on Miss Rand's dressing-room door and she yelled, "Come in." When the Governor and I entered, Sally was flat on the floor, wrapped in something pink, her chin propped up on her hands.

> She was reading the Bible.... After Sally and the Governor had swapped hellos, he picked up the Good Book and said, "Let me read you a short passage which has always been a source of comfort to me when I have the miseries." He turned to a page in the Book of Psalms and began reading quietly. I heard Whiteman's orchestra tuning up and slipped out of the room.

> A few moments later I was at the center microphone on the stage, addressing the huge Casa Mañana audience. Someone in Sholtz's

party stood up and hollered, "Introduce the Governor of Florida." "I'm sorry," I lied, "The Governor's talking long distance to Tallahassee…." I wasn't going to tell those 4,000 people that the Governor of Florida couldn't appear because he was reading the Bible in Sally Rand's dressing room![6]

Originally scheduled to close on October 31st, the Frontier Centennial was extended to November 14th in an attempt to further recoup expenses. Inconveniently, Sally had other contractual obligations. This led to a falling out with Billy Rose, who was none too happy that Sally intended to abscond with ten of his more appealing dancers to tour the state in *Sally Rand and her Texas All-Star Revue*. Rose was furious, but Sally felt justified since she had contracted with the girls when everyone had assumed the fair would close on the previously announced date. The breach would have repercussions for their relationship in years to come.

Sally may have come to town under a cloud, but unsurprisingly she charmed not only the gals under contract to perform at her Nude Ranch but also the good citizens of "Cowtown." In recognition of her "graciousness and consummate artistry," the City of Fort Worth declared November 6, 1936, as "Sally Rand Day" and presented her with a large gold key to the county — the first of its kind ever manufactured. On that day, county courts were closed for more than three hours in tribute to Sally for bringing "culture and progress" to the community.

Faith

Sally was at the top of her game, but Faith Bacon was also cruising along at what may have been the peak of her career. In a 1936 magazine article attributed to her, Faith explained how she could be so comfortable in the nude:

> Twice nightly I walk across a nightclub or theatre stage without a stitch of clothes. I am as nude as the day I was born. And yet, for some strange reason, I never feel the slightest symptoms of embarrassment. I guess I was always that way. As far back as I can remember it meant nothing to me to show my body in public.
>
> I have been told by psychologists that women who constantly display their bodies nude in show business develop, or originally

---

6   In a similar incident, a reporter had been assigned to write an in-depth story on Sally. After entering her dressing room, he too found Sally lying on her stomach reading the Bible. She was naked. Sally is said to have stretched, rolled over, and shyly covered her *mons veneris* with Psalms 35:17 (Lord, how long wilt thou look on?).

are born with, psychological defenses that permit this type of exhibition. I suppose at heart I'm a bit of an exhibitionist. But then all people in show business are. You wouldn't get out on a stage and show off if you weren't an exhibitionist.

I have another theory to account for professional exhibitionism on the stage. You see, I am very nearsighted.... The audience is nothing but a blur to me. I don't see other people distinctly, and so probably I imagine they don't see my form sharply.

I've been in Broadway shows since I was a young girl ... and all these years I've been a professional nude of one sort or another.

Faith also addressed rumors that she was cool to members of the opposite sex:

I know quite a legend has grown up about my alleged aversion to men.... I suppose I'm a bit less interested in the opposite sex than the average woman.... Some years ago a story was circulated in which I was quoted as saying, "I will never marry. I do not want my beauty marred by a man's vulgar hands." That, of course, was a publicity story....

It is true that I do not often go with men. As I have said before, I am not particularly interested in men or love or romance. That's why I am able to parade nude in front of males without a feeling of shame.

My main interest is my career. I love to dance. I love beauty.... Of course I think my body is beautiful, and try hard to keep it so, but it is not a fetish with me. I am a very normal person.... I am considered beautiful. I get paid big money to exhibit my beauty. So you can imagine that I was quite a pretty child. I was brought up in Paris, and Paris, you may have heard, is quite a wicked city.

Even as a growing girl I was constantly the object of men's attentions, and so, long before I came to Broadway, I began to loathe most males. I thought that every man was a wolf. And on Broadway it was worse. Backstage there was much to contend with. Girls in show business are constantly subject to improper advances. And because I did a nude, every man thought I was "loose" morally. I began to hate men. They disgusted me. I figured that the best way to ward off their annoying advances was to forsake them completely; to hide in my own little shell.

That action has had some advantages. Men no longer bother me because they know I'm not going to be too sociable. But it also has disadvantages. I miss much of life. I miss companionship. And now as I see the other kids I worked with in shows marry and have

happy homes, I begin to wonder if I haven't missed too much. After
all there must be some nice men. Every other woman can't be wrong.

If Tullah Hanley's accounts are to be believed, there was yet another reason
for Faith Bacon's aversion to men, confirming rumors that had followed her
over the years. Writing of her experiences with Faith, apparently in the
early 1940s, Tullah claimed that Faith was hooked on barbiturates and that
she: "... had Lesbian lovers wherever [she] traveled."[7]

Although Sally may have been the Toast of Chicago with her fan dancing,
Faith Bacon was also in demand in the Windy City. In December 1936, she
headlined *Temptations*, a revue at the State Theatre, sharing the bill with a
cabaret singer, a couple of comedy teams, and "Buddy" — a trained seal.

While "professional dancer" would not ordinarily qualify as a hazardous occupation, on December 5th, as she was performing her new "Bird of Paradise"
dance, Faith crashed through a plate glass box that was supporting her as she
posed in the nude for the finale. She sustained several cuts severe enough to be
treated at Henrotin Hospital. The resulting scars motivated her to seek
$100,000 in damages from the venue's owner, Lake Theater Corporation.
Specifically, her court papers alleged that she had suffered "deep and ugly
scars" on both legs and on the "inner aspect" of her right thigh.

The harrowing details were related by Faith and syndicated nationwide:

> I was taking a pose in the finale. The show was called "Temptations"
> and all the girls were supposed to be temptations, you know tempta-
> tions of man. One was power, another was wine, and another was
> pearls and so on. I was beauty. I was told to stand on a glass box and
> the last part of the number came when they parted the curtains and
> showed me there in the nude. I was wearing a special spray, which
> brings out the better points of the body, and there were lights shining
> on me up through the top of the glass box.

> Well, the curtains parted and I crashed through the box. All the
> girls started screaming for a doctor and running around the stage,
> but somehow I climbed out of all the broken glass and danced. If
> you're not in the show business, you won't understand. There's

---

7   According to Tullah, "Faith had flawless beauty, body, and complexion. She was
     obsessed by her own beauty and watched with anxiety as lines and crow's feet crept
     up to mar that perfection." Tullah felt that "Faith was a Lesbian by convenience and
     preference, not because nature created her so. She wanted delicate flower treatment,
     and, for her taste, men were too rough. Women were softer, and she had no patience
     to wait for a gentle male; neither could she teach one to be tender to her, she was too
     timid."

something about being in front of an audience, it numbs the senses. They didn't ring down the curtain and I finished the number. Then, just as the curtain was going down, I fell. Someone picked me up, covered my eyes, and warned me not to look down.

After undergoing 90 minutes of surgery (26 stitches) without anesthesia, Faith spent an extended period in the hospital. "It was two months before I could dance again," she said, "and I still can't toe dance. I even had to learn to walk." She said she was suing for disability, but chiefly for disfigurement. As Faith explained: "My beauty is my livelihood.... Now that beauty is marred. I have used it to support myself and my invalid sister Charmion."

The $100,000 lawsuit was ultimately settled out of court for $5,000 (about $85,000 today). Faith then bought a 10-carat diamond with the proceeds.[8] It is unclear just how this purchase aided in the support of her "invalid sister Charmion" — who, as you may recall, was actually her mother.

After the Fort Worth Exposition closed, Sally spent the next several weeks touring Texas with her "All-Star" show. Along the way she found time to teach a cooking class at the Texas State College for Women in Denton. In San Antonio, she participated in the annual firemen's Christmas toy drive for poor children and sat for an interview on KTSA radio with Fire Chief J. G. Sarran. She also spoke at a Rotary Club luncheon in Harlingen where attendees were "bowled over" by her wide knowledge of the citrus industry, watching in awe as she described in detail the steps necessary to produce and market citrus fruit.

Sally was something of a perfectionist. She expected things to be a certain way. And, if they weren't — watch out! The Texas tour was pretty much winding down when her troupe reached the Plaza Theatre in El Paso on Saturday, December 12th. When the midnight stage show was over, the chief lighting technician was taken aback as Sally stormed into the lighting booth, berating him and claiming "in loud and belligerent tones" that he had flashed the wrong light on her during the bubble dance. She was furious that he had "purposely revealed her nakedness with a bright spot light instead of the dark blue beam of light" she had instructed him to use.

She then proceeded to break into pieces the carbon used in the spotlights and slap the operators' faces, all the while stridently rebuking them. Clad

---

8   If Faith Bacon really did buy a 10-carat diamond with her proceeds, it would definitely have been a wise purchase, since the average wholesale price today for a 10-carat diamond, as certified by the Gemological Institute of America, ranges between $167,200 and $2,245,100, depending on shape, size, and quality.

only in a green negligee, she had waited until the stage show was over and the movie was playing before charging the operator's booth. Hearing the uproar, the astonished theater manager rushed to the booth, where Sally flatly informed him: "If these men are here Sunday afternoon, my show does not appear." Spectators in the balcony were said to be "astounded by the scope of Miss Rand's vocabulary."

With the Texas fair and tour behind her, Sally managed to catch a break, spending the Christmas holidays with her grandmother, Mollie Grove, near Clovis, New Mexico, where she predictably took charge of decorating the tree. Once the holidays were over, she was back to the grind, spending virtually all of 1937 touring the eastern half of the country, playing short engagements from Massachusetts to Pennsylvania to Florida to Tennessee, Indiana, Ohio, and points between. And, of course, there were many opportunities for controversy, unexpected adventures, and run-ins with local authorities.

Just how big a draw Sally was at this time is indicated by her January 7, 1937, opening at the Orpheum Theatre in Memphis, Tennessee. An ad in the local paper touted that "12,000 persons yesterday acclaimed" the appearance of Sally Rand and her "all-star stage revue" featuring "50 great stars" and "20 beautiful girls." (These audience numbers may not be exaggerated, as the Orpheum seated 2,500 and the show was performed several times a day.)

"Leaving Sally aside," Jack Bryan of the *Memphis Press-Scimitar* had found the show to be "genuinely entertaining ... a well-rounded, handsomely presented stageful of entertainment." Reflecting southern sensibilities and the ambivalence of the time, he continued:

> But you can't, of course, leave Sally aside. Not when she stands there before you stark naked. At any rate, if Sally is clothed, it is purely an academic question. A blue light partially shrouded her figure while she swung her fans and bounced her bubble, but at the end of each number, the lights went up and gave the audience an ample vista of Sally's natural charm. Whether it was from admiration, shock, disappointment or awe, the audience, packing the house, received Sally's performance in silence.
>
> Undoubtedly there will be wide difference of opinion between the city fathers and the city sons as to the propriety and desirability of such an exhibition as Sally's. To pretend that it is a triumph of art is blah. At the same time, it is by no means vulgar. Sally does her numbers with dignity and, while I would scarcely call what she does

"dancing," her work has sufficient grace and beauty to make its appeal far cleaner and more acceptable than many less frankly nude but more suggestively contrived performances.

It is possible to enjoy Sally's dances for reasons apart from what she calls her "lack of costume." The sensational buildup ... by which Sally's business thrives, is more to be censured than the act itself. And for exploiting her nakedness in this manner, Sally must carry the blame for the plague of imitators, less artful and wise than she, who have made of her work the burlesque show that it really is at heart.

After several days of performing with her "Texas Fair Follies" at the Palace Theatre[9] in Cleveland, Sally suddenly popped up in an open car, riding in the St. Patrick's Day Parade, drawing the disapprobation of the local clergy. Bishop Joseph Schrembs, the fifth Bishop of Cleveland, expressed his reaction in the March issue of the *Catholic Universe Bulletin*:

I am deeply humiliated and ashamed that a parade to honor the patron saint of Ireland should have included the internationally-known fan dancer whose performances on the stage have been so offensive to Catholics....

That she rode in an open carriage next to a float decorated to honor the blessed mother of God has shocked me greatly. I am certain that her inclusion does not represent the mind of the great Irish people in my diocese.[10]

The good bishop inquired of the parade marshal, without satisfaction, just exactly how had Sally gained entry into the parade in the first place? *Time* magazine reported that she had appeared at the invitation of the president of the local school board. Unfortunately for the staunch bishop's blood pressure, Cleveland hadn't seen the last of the fan dancers. Within a matter of months, the "original fan dancer" herself, Miss Faith Bacon, would be setting up shop for an extended run in "The Metropolis of the Western Reserve."

---

[9] Designed in French Renaissance style, Keith's Palace Theatre seated 3,100 patrons. Lit by 154 crystal chandeliers, the main lobby boasted immense columns, a grand central staircase, and walls of Carrara marble. According to the Cleveland Historical Team, the theater was "... one of the most lavish in the land. The sign on top of the building was the largest electrical sign in the world, while the lobby housed a million dollar art collection and the world's largest woven-in-one-piece carpet." For details, see: www.clevelandhistorical.org.

[10] Bishop Schrembs was born in 1866, the youngest of 16 children. He later helped to lower the family average by not fathering any children of his own.

Mary Belle

On February 26, 1937, the Oriental Theatre in Chicago presented *The King's Scandals*, a new show from Broadway producer Harry Gourfain featuring a cast of 40, including "18 King's Scandalous Ladies." One of the highlights of the evening was promoted as "This year's newest and most startling innovation 'The Dance of the Mystic Fans.'" Gourfain's traveling show was on a tight budget, so it was his practice to hire local girls to fill a few spots in the show, particularly in the chorus. Among those chosen for the Chicago performances was 15-year-old Victoria Spencer, the younger of attorney Mary Belle Spencer's "do as I darn please" daughters.

Mrs. Spencer saw the first show and was so upset that Victoria had been relegated to the chorus that she confronted the producer, protesting that her talented daughter should be given a place of prominence as a "specialty dancer." A heated row followed, culminating with Mary Belle punching Harry Gourfain in the nose. He signed a disorderly conduct complaint against her, and the theater's publicity agent ended up having to post a $25 bond for her release.

Even before this incident, young Victoria Spencer's on-set antics had proven to be a pain in the ass. In rehearsal, she had repeatedly disregarded the orchestra's tempo, demanded a private dressing room, and back-talked to the line captain. Gourfain wasn't sure what to do. The girl was incorrigible, but her mother was a prominent figure in Chicago and he didn't need an angry stage mother with a law practice bad-mouthing his show. Ultimately, he came up with a diabolical compromise. If this rebellious young girl wanted a specialty dance, well, that's exactly what he would give her.

With a "truth is stranger than fiction" ironic justice, Gourfain bowed to Victoria's confidential request that she be permitted to perform the fan dance. Satisfied that her daughter was once again a happy camper, but unaware of the details, Mary Belle was taken by surprise to see her fledgling baby girl step upon the stage and begin waving a pair of ostrich feather fans. Initially dumbstruck, Mrs. Spencer caught her breath and began shouting from the wings: "I won't have my baby exposing herself like that!"

After an off-stage scuffle, Mary Belle was forcibly ejected from the theater. Upon gaining her composure, she soon managed to return by buying a ticket. Reentering the theater, she could hardly fail to notice the joyous atmosphere. Her daughter's obvious pleasure in emulating Sally Rand and the audience's enthusiastic response prompted a change of heart. The proud mama later declared: "There is nothing so flattering as ostrich feathers, and the way Victoria does the dance, it's modest." Not only did the precocious Victoria realize her ambition to follow in Sally's footsteps, but her photograph, complete with bare legs and ostrich feather fans, was syndicated to newspapers across the country.

The crisis had passed. Mrs. Spencer was at ease. Even so, Gourfain directed the doorkeeper to bar her from ever entering again. "This is the screwiest show I have had anything to do with in 30 years," he declared.

D uring the first week of April, purely by coincidence, Sally and Gypsy Rose Lee were each appearing in Indianapolis. Indeed, the stage doors of the Lyric (where Sally had her own show) and the English (where Gypsy was appearing in the touring *Ziegfeld Follies*) actually faced each other across a narrow alley. Sally was seven years the elder and, although both women had been around awhile, the two had never met.

The local press was lobbying for the pair — described as "America's two leading merchants of feminine pulchritude" — to meet. Sally was willing: "I've often wanted to meet Miss Lee. Couldn't we arrange it before I put on my makeup? You see, I do want to look my best. I really don't want to be placed at a disadvantage if the photographers should be around." Gypsy replied: "I'd be happy to meet Miss Rand," and suggested she might drop in to see Sally's performance.

The date for a meeting was arranged and a phalanx of photographers was all set to attend, when Ben Atwell, the publicity agent for the *Follies*, abruptly nixed the deal. Miss Lee was about to leave for Hollywood to begin filming of her first movie, *You Can't Have Everything*. If Gypsy's picture was going to be in the paper, Atwell wanted it to be in connection with that career move, not for what might happen in an unscripted episode of repartee with Sally Rand. He did offer Sally the chance to pose with Gypsy's understudy in the *Follies* — an offer she politely declined.

Another opportunity Sally tactfully declined at this time was presented by Henri Marchand, New York agent for the forthcoming Exposition Internationale des Arts et Techniques dans la Vie Moderne. This global fair dedicated to modern art and technology was to be held in Paris, France, from May through November of 1937. Playing to Sally's ego, Marchand's cable urged:

> The plan contemplates an outdoor pageant of feminine grace,
> rhythm and beauty on a huge stage in the form of a gigantic world
> globe slowly turning with 500 dancers of 44 nations exhibiting at
> the fair. You would be the sole star and climax. Demand for you in
> France is tremendous, as well as from Americans. Ten thousand

American Legionnaires will attend in September. Your assistance at the American Legion in Chicago three years ago in Chicago caused thousands to request the Paris fair to engage you.

Sending her regrets, Sally cited conflicts with scheduled bookings, but the unsettled political situation in Europe may also have been of concern to her.[11] It's a shame she didn't go. She would have added another world's fair to her resume and trod another road not taken.

S ally just couldn't seem to catch a break with the Catholic Church. When an early May engagement in Elmira, New York, was announced, local priests and representatives of the Knights of Columbus mobilized to lodge a protest with the city manager. Monsignor John J. Lee didn't mince any words, decreeing that: "Anyone who attends such a performance is a sexual pervert. No one with a sense of decency would witness a show of this kind."[12] In a hastily arranged meeting of city officials and theater represen-tatives, participants concluded that they had no authority to ban the show unless and until a city ordinance providing that "no person shall appear nude in any public street or building" had actually been violated.

Though indignant at the defamation, Sally chose the high road, agreeing to allow two members of the Elmira Police Department to be posted backstage before each performance to observe both her mode of dress and the act itself. In an appearance before the Elmira Lions Club, she recounted her experience in support of the Lions' longstanding efforts in support of the blind: "While at the Texas Centennial, I had the privilege of personally delivering several of the talking books in a little town in the southern extreme of the United States." Concluding her remarks, she autographed programs and also made a personal donation to the Blind Fund of the Elmira Club.

---

[11] At first, Adolph Hitler was also inclined to skip the event, perhaps because planners had placed the German and Soviet pavilions directly across from each other. His architect Albert Speer, having an advance look at the plans for the Soviet pavilion, persuaded Hitler to go forward with the German pavilion, rather than risk being upstaged by the Communists.

[12] Concern of this sort was not limited to upstate Elmira. In furtherance of New York City Mayor La Guardia's campaign against the growing threat of nude entertainment, John Sumner's New York Society for the Suppression of Vice proclaimed that: "This type of underworld exhibition ... may give temporary entertainment to morons and perverts ... but there is no demand for it by the public in general."

Faith

Combining a world's fair and super amusement park, the successful Great Lakes Exposition in Cleveland, Ohio, was held over for a second year, reopening on May 29, 1937. The centerpiece of the fair was a floating stage where Billy Rose had set up his spectacular "Aquacade" — a water, music, and dance attraction.

The notion that a world's fair or major exposition could prosper based solely on the desire of its patrons to examine the latest advances in farm equipment, or to contemplate the higher aspirations of the scientific mind, just wouldn't die. Indeed, the exposition's sponsors had convinced themselves they could do that very thing. Even though girlie shows like the *Folies de Nuit*, featuring the fabulous Toto in her "Dance of the Tresses,"[13] had added handsomely to the expo's coffers in its first year, city fathers still saw no need to resort to "vulgar entertainment" to attract visitors to the 1937 edition. An editorial cartoon in the *Cleveland Plain Dealer* depicted a despondent fan dancer watching a workman erect a sign declaring: "Fan Dancers and Nudists Not Wanted."

The exposition's amusement director, Almon Shaffer, had promised the press: "There will be no nudity at this year's fair. For months I've been guarding the Midway's purity." (Reportedly, he had turned down numerous concession operators' requests to bring in striptease acts, peep shows, and the like.) Yet, just as reliably as night follows the day, committee members examined their cash flow, weighed their options, and discovered reasons to reconsider their earlier decision. Fairgoers suddenly had no difficulty locating exotic dancers, circus freaks, and other attractions considered beneath the notice of proper society. While those of a higher mind may have protested, the numbers crunchers were relieved that their balance sheets no longer depended on the appeal of industrial displays like "The Romance of Iron and Steel."

In early August, local supper club owner and major fair exhibitor Herman Pirchner chose to ignore the committee's misgivings and spice up the event even more by hiring Faith Bacon to appear on his chartered showboat, the S.S. Moses Cleaveland,[14] and promising that the "originator of the fan dance"

---

[13]   Instead of a fan or a bubble, Toto employed a strip of tulle fabric that, at the outset, was wound around her body. As the dance proceeded, the strip of fine netting gradually dropped away until it became a mere accessory to her dance rather than a covering.

[14]   Named for the City of Cleveland's founding father, the "million dollar Show Boat" was a featured expo attraction, with the exclusive Admiralty Club on the top deck and a spacious nightclub occupying the lower deck.

would be performing nude. In an interview seventy years later, asked why he had hired Miss Bacon, the 99-year-old Pirchner smiled mischievously and replied: "She was colorful. She entertained."[15]

The *Great Lakes Exposition Revue* had a company of 35 entertainers, starring the "Glamorous! Daring! Dazzling! Gorgeous! Faith Bacon in her newest startlingly beautiful creations." Newspaper ads trumpeted: "See why she was the last girl chosen by the late Florenz Ziegfeld as the most beautiful girl in the world."

Did she dance in the nude? It's hard to say. Faith's body was painted in such a way that reporters couldn't tell if she was really nude or not. In any case, she was bare enough to provoke the usual reaction from the usual characters. In protest, the steadfast Knights of Columbus cancelled their August 15th celebration of "Catholic Day" at the fair, while the "Improved Benevolent Protective Order of Elks of the World" (IBPOEW), a black fraternal organization, faithfully showed up on August 25th for Elks Day.

The arrival of the Faith Bacon revue in Cleveland, happening concurrently with a bathing beauty contest and the Miss Ohio pageant, prompted a local reporter to declare August of 1937 as "Curves Month" at the Great Lakes Expo. Almon Shaffer and Lincoln Dickey, who served as amusement director and general manager of the exposition, remained disgruntled, complaining to reporters that business still hadn't picked up. Nudity doesn't pay, they declared.

Also in August, Florida Governor Fred P. Cone, outfitted in top hat, cutaway coat and striped trousers, arrived in Cleveland to celebrate "Florida Week" at the exposition. The Old South theme of the Florida Exhibit, with its palm and citrus trees, was quite popular at that time. An official guidebook described the display: "In a real orange grove, negroes sing and dance as in typical plantation life."

Ohio Governor Martin L. Davey served as both host and escort for the grounds. On Saturday, August 21st, after dinner and a stage and water show at Billy Rose's Aquacade, Governor Davey suggested that their

---

[15] As a young man in Austria, Herman Pirchner held many jobs — aerialist, clown, circus strongman, pretzel-maker and busboy, among others. He immigrated to the U.S. in 1927, ending up in Cleveland. In 1933, Pirchner, wearing his typical Bavarian lederhosen and Tirolean cap, gained national recognition for performing his well-loved stunt of balancing up to 55 steins of beer while running toward a patron's table and sliding in like a baseball player . . . without spilling a drop. He died on February 15, 2009, at the age of 101.

group make a stop at the showboat where Faith Bacon was said to be entertaining "tired business men" with a dance that, if it weren't so pleasantly artistic, might be termed naughty. Governor Cone reportedly rose from his chair, hitched up his trousers, pushed his top hat to the back of his head, and declared: "Sure thing!" He did not, however, throw caution completely to the winds coming off Lake Erie. Perhaps remembering the incident in Fort Worth involving Sally Rand and Governor Dave Sholtz (his immediate predecessor in the Tallahassee state house), Cone resisted making a dressing room visit.

Like Miss Rand, Miss Bacon portrayed herself as an artist whose act should not be confused with "stripping." When interviewed in Cleveland, she stated that she required a "strictly ethereal atmosphere" for her performances. She claimed to be very happy with the efforts of solid citizens to clean up burlesque and similar shows. In her opinion, the public was growing "cleaner minded." Evaluating her audience, Faith said that "When they first came to see the female form, they came out of curiosity. Now they're more interested in the artistic side of it."

On the subject of nudism, Faith shared Sally's poor opinion of the practice: "It isn't natural. If they were serious, they would segregate the sexes or raise their children together so there would be no curiosity about it." Really? Was Faith being knowingly disingenuous or was she simply naive about the motives of those who paid to see her? By 1937, she had to know better than this. It all smacks of press agentry. Yet, when reporters elected to put this sort of straitlaced spin on the attraction, it may have helped to pacify members of the sponsoring committee.

The Great Lakes Exposition closed on September 27, 1937.[16] Faith Bacon and her complete revue went on tour for the next month or so, playing in such places as Cumberland, Maryland, and Zanesville, Ohio. Newspaper advertisements billed "Ziegfeld's Famous Beauty" as "gorgeous" and "intoxicating" — "you'll never forget her."

---

[16] During the two years of its run, the Great Lakes Exposition drew over seven million visitors from around the Midwest and beyond. In addition to Faith Bacon and her obvious assets, the lakefront industrial fair offered a "Streets of the World" international shopping and dining exhibit, a Hall of Progress, a Marine Theater, and a variety of specialty gardens. A portion of the former grounds now houses the Rock and Roll Hall of Fame.

Meanwhile, the City of Cleveland ordered that most of the exposition structures be torn down, and, within a year, nearly all were gone. Construction debris formed a giant pile at the foot of East Ninth Street, dubbed the "Lakeshore Dump." In the summer of 1938, the serial killer known as the "Torso Murderer" left the bodies of two of his decapitated victims there.

Sally's 1937 traveling "all-star revue" was no small enterprise. The company consisted of 50 American and European entertainers moving from place to place in a 70-foot baggage car filled with thousands of dollars' worth of special scenery, costumes and electrical effects. Promotional material claimed that "Miss Rand staged the

THE TORSO MURDERS

In Cleveland between 1935 and 1938, at least 12 and possibly more victims were serially beheaded and sometimes dismembered; their usually unidentified bodies were dumped in the area known as Kingsbury Run. While Sally wasn't part of the Great Lakes Exposition, she *was* appearing at the nearby Elberta Beach Dance Hall in Vermilion, Ohio, in August of 1937. Jack Wilson, a local butcher and alcoholic with a rap sheet for robbery, sodomy, and lewd behavior (who has gone down in history as a prime suspect in these grisly murders), reportedly saw Sally perform in Vermilion. He was later quoted as saying that he had "jacked off" in his pants while watching her dance. These heinous crimes were never solved.

show, designed the costumes, ordered the scenery, booked the acts, selected the girls and prepared the dance routines." [17]

Moving from town to town, the show required considerable planning and coordination to ensure that box office receipts would cover expenses. Sally's touring company was made up of performers, stage hands, and managers — many disparate personalities — and each had to be accommodated. To describe each engagement on the tour would be tedious and repetitive, yet every venue presented unique challenges. Even when everything went according to plan, Sally's days tended to consist of a whirlwind of activity enlivened by an element of unpredictability. While crucial, the shows themselves filled only a fleeting part of each day.

---

[17] Supporting acts varied throughout the length of the tour but, in addition to the "20 beautiful girls" — sometimes billed as the "Bluebonnet Belles" and sometimes as the lovely "Texas Rangerettes" — they commonly included red-headed comedienne Nell Kelly (The "Broadway Madcap") who had appeared in many two-reel comedies. The troupe also featured The Thrillers (a novelty roller skating team) and "La Cucarachita" (better known in Latin America as recording artist Eva Garza). Those of you with time to look them up on YouTube will be rewarded.

Sally had long realized how important public relations were to her bottom line. Aside from early efforts by publicists to promote circuses and other traveling shows, the practice of press agentry had emerged as a profession only a short time before Sally Rand came to prominence.[18] Her notoriety at the Chicago World's Fairs in 1933 and 1934 was so great that she hardly needed any publicity other than what she garnered for free from reporters and photographers. Like other entertainers, she employed managers, agents, and other assistants to help keep her affairs in order. Still, for most of her career she exercised significant control over her own publicity, commonly coming up with creative stunts and gimmicks to keep herself in the public eye. There is no better way to say it — Sally Rand was a publicity generating machine.

A single example illustrates how she had mastered the art of promotion — tying in her scheduled show dates with endorsements and personal appearances. On June 14 and 15, 1937, Sally was performing at the State Theatre in a small city of some 20,000 residents located 50 miles southeast of Pittsburgh — Uniontown, Pennsylvania. Over the two-day period, the two local papers ran four articles about Sally, plus 36 separate ads for her show, many with market tie-ins affecting 15 separate businesses and at least 11 distinct associated products. These were not modest ads. Many were eye-catching, including a few quarter- and half-page ads and one that took up nearly a full page.

To appreciate what this barrage of publicity must have looked like to a typical resident, let's dig in a bit. On page 10 of the Monday issue of the *News Standard*, the headline "FAMOUS SALLY RAND STARTS A TWO-DAY ENGAGEMENT AT STATE TODAY" topped a feature story with a photo captioned "Queen of Fan Dancers" — both of which Sally probably supplied in advance. An ad for Sally's "In Person" show at the "Cooled for Comfort" State Theatre ran on the same page. A variety of ads for Sally's show on pages 1, 2, 3, 5, 6, 7, and 9 included affiliations with local businesses. On page 14, a reader couldn't miss the three good-sized advertisements, each one promoting Sally's endorsement:

> SANITONE — Here's What Sally Says: "Wherever I go, I have my clothes cleaned by the 'Sanitone' method, the most effective. My advice to every young girl who wishes to look smart at all times is to go to the French Dyers & Cleaners, your local licensed Sanitone dealer, and have them do the cleaning of all your clothes."

> RED CROSS SHOES — Sally Rand says: "Be happy down to your toes in these famous Red Cross Shoes."

---

[18] In 1920, the New York State Legislature passed a law to restrict the activities of publicists after one of them faked the suicide of an actress in order to promote her film.

CARTER'S DAIRY PRODUCTS — Sally Rand says: "I've found that dairy products keep me in the best of condition. Milk keeps up my vitality. I suggest that you try a light nourishing dairy break-fast. Use CARTER'S milk or cream over your favorite cereal ... You'll find as I do that you'll feel better, sleep better these sticky, sultry days and nights...."

Each advertisement included a boxed inset advising potential customers to see Sally Rand in person with her All Star Revue at the State Theatre.

Clearly, the *News Standard* ran an impressive publicity blitz for Sally, but so did the other daily paper. The *Morning Herald* carried a different picture and promotional piece that Monday under the heading "SALLY RAND HERE IN PERSON," along with a theater ad touting "SALLY RAND IN PERSON, WITH HER OWN ALL STAR STAGE REVUE." Two large display ads on page 4 included tie-ins to Sally and her show. One promoted Liggett's Rexall Drug Store, while simultaneously marketing a foundation make-up called "Cara Nome," with Sally pictured saying: "... I have to be so particular in choosing my cosmetics. That is why I have chosen CARA NOME. Another reason for my choice ... is the fact that wherever I go there are REXALL stores, which always makes it handy." The adjacent ad proudly announced that the Turner Automobile Company was inviting members of the community "... to meet Sally Rand in Person, Monday, June 14th, 12 to 12:30 p.m." to "Hear her discuss the beautiful Packard. Have her autograph your sales slips." Page 7 carried a three-quarter-page display ad inviting the public to meet Sally in person at the refrigerator department of Sears, Roebuck and Co., on the same day between 1:00 and 1:30 p.m., to "Hear Her Discuss Sears COLDSPOT, America's Most Famous Refrigerator."[19] The ad further claimed that, at $159.50: "No other electric refrigerator ever gave so much for so little."

A very busy gal, all of these appearances were in addition to her 2:00 and 4:00 o'clock Monday matinees at the State Theatre. And she was just getting started.

Page 9 of the morning paper featured two more big ads. The first had Sally plugging a beverage for the local Nehi Bottling Works, saying that after a strenuous performance: "A bottle of Nehi refreshes me no end." The other — a half-page display ad for the G. C. Murphy Company headed "SALLY RAND, THE MOST WIDELY KNOWN WOMAN IN THE WORLD TODAY" — announced that Sally would be in the store on Tuesday, June 15th, from 1:00 to 1:30 p.m., to "Tell You Why She Always Prefers CAROLINA MOON HOSIERY" — on sale

---

19 Oddly, Sally had endorsed a Norge refrigerator just a week or so earlier in Cumberland, Maryland, but, as we know, a girl is always entitled to change her mind.

at 69 cents a pair. (Murphy's even offered readers a chance to consult with their "Sally Rand corset expert.")

The same paper carried an ad for Sally Rand ("World Famous Fan Dancer") recommending French Dyers & Cleaners and, just for good measure, yet another ad (with yet another picture) in which she endorsed a drugstore diner: "Traveling about, as I do, I have to be most particular as to what I eat and where I eat. That's why I recommend Liggett's Blue Ridge Grill for their fine foods, variety in menu, and splendid service."

On top of all the hoopla, Sally managed to make time for an interview with a local reporter in her dressing room. The resulting column, which appeared the next day in both Uniontown papers under slightly different headlines, began: "I am not an exhibitionist." To support her contention, Sally pointed out that, despite the flood of publicity that followed her from coast to coast, none of it was ever based on her private life, her family, her love affairs or her domestic background. Moreover, she declared: "I never grow tired of the footlights or the crowds. I love people. I like my job better than anything else in the world."

As if all this publicity weren't enough, there could always be more. In addition to duplicates of some of the ads from the day before, Tuesday's papers carried display ads from five more local establishments: Hunt's Jewelry Store ("Sally Rand wears a Lady Bulova from Hunt's Jewelry Store"); Penn-State Beauty Salon ("Sally Rand Says: 'I think the Penn State Beauty Salon is one of the finest I've ever seen'"); Rosenbaum. Inc. ("Sally Rand says: 'Uniontown women are extremely fortunate in being able to purchase such fine clothes as Fashion Firsts in so splendid an establishment as Rosenbaum's'"); Bill Saxon's Restaurant and Tavern ("Sally Rand says: 'Saxon's is a fine place to stop for refreshments'"); and Hibner's Gulf Stations ("Sally Rand says: 'I use Gulf Gas and Oil because it's better'"). This last one included what has to be a classic hook: "'Elmer,' you know, is the service man at these 3 fine stations. I've met Elmer and take my word for it — HE'S OK! He'll dunk your Austin Free of Charge."[20]

Whew! After her third and final personal appearance — this one at G. C. Murphy's (where it was claimed that "Miss Rand's entire company of 30 beautiful girls all wear and heartily recommend Murphy's Carolina Moon Hosiery") — plus two matinee performances at the State Theatre, Sally and her troupe closed out their stay on Tuesday evening with two more shows.

---

[20] "Dunk your Austin?" Well, no one could quibble about the price, but what does that even mean? A possible reference to a free car wash? (The Austin automobile was last produced 16 years earlier). Your guess is as good as ours.

You might think they would mark the end of a long two days by quietly retiring for the night. Think again.

Sally had given her all to make this stop on the tour a triumph, and Uniontown certainly seemed to have appreciated it. But even the most talented entertainer can't make everybody happy. No sooner had the curtain descended on her last show than Sally had a couple of less-than-welcome visitors. Despite her wall-to-wall personal appearances, her ever-present endorsements, and her boundless celebrity, Sally could never quite dodge the attention of John Law. That night, state troopers P. A. Rittleman and H. E. Harrison confronted Sally in her dressing room, and placed her under arrest for disorderly conduct and staging "an indecent dance."

True, this was not an unfamiliar situation for Sally, but this town? This night? *Really*? The Uniontown engagement was over. Sally was not amused. She and her company had people to see, places to go. Under the circumstances, she demanded resolution of the matter then and there. A theater representative suggested she could give a private performance. A call was placed to Alderman Frank R. Foster and a hearing was hastily arranged. Behind closed doors and drawn shades, a group of five, including Sally's manager, convened in Foster's office around midnight.

A gaggle of show people, reporters, and other concerned onlookers milled around, holding vigil on behalf on the good people of Uniontown. The state troopers claimed they had seen Sally disrobe on stage in violation of state laws against indecent exposure. Sally, determined to demonstrate yet again that her fan dance was artistic, performed for Alderman Foster, who, presumably, got a much closer look than anyone in the audience at the State. Once the dance was over and the point was advanced that a troupe of some 50 performers was anxious to move on to their next engagement, Foster reportedly decided that the two state troopers "must have been mistaken about Sally Rand's conduct and attire (or the lack of it)." As his office door was flung open and the group emerged smiling from the hearing room, Alderman Foster announced to the assembled curious: "Charges dismissed for lack of evidence."

And so the Uniontown foray finally reached its end. Sleep crept over Sally Rand at the end of another long day. The sun would come up in only a short time and the beat would go on.

Just three days later on June 18th, during a Friday appearance at the Capitol Theatre in Steubenville, Ohio, Sally spotted someone in the front row snapping pictures of her — a 16-year-old named Mac Erwin, attending the show with several friends. Acting on Sally's instructions, three male members of her show (later characterized by the press as "bouncers" and "muscle men") roughly removed the teenager from his seat, advising him that he "would get in trouble" unless he agreed to surrender his film — all in accord with Sally's policy of discouraging the taking of candid photos that she feared might be circulated as unflattering, if not obscene, images.

The camera's proud owner was not happy. Losing his film was one thing, but humiliation in front of his friends and the entire theater audience . . . well, he wasn't going to just let it go. Young Erwin took his complaint to the mayor's office and the next day Sally and the theater manager were called on the carpet and compelled to apologize. Erwin was reimbursed in the amount of 85 cents (about $14 today) for the roll of film that was ripped from his camera.

Coverage of this incident was apparently confined to local Steubenville press reports, but, in little more than a year, a similar contretemps with an amateur photographer would propel Sally onto front pages nationwide. The resulting charges and trial would become a matter of continuing public fascination for the better part of a year.

With summer comes summer stock theater. In July, columnist George Ross had reported that Sally "manages to get in a few hours daily with her dramatic coach, whom she carries around as a member of her troupe." Her interest in the stage grew out of her childhood feelings of rejection. Ever since her father had abandoned the family, Sally had craved attention. In later years, she admitted that the instant gratification she got from the applause of a live audience far outweighed any satisfaction she had ever derived from her film career. In July and August of 1937, Sally got the attention she desired as the featured actress in several New England theaters.

She played a lead role in *They Knew What They Wanted*, a Pulitzer-Prize-winning drama by Sidney Howard. The play tells the "Beauty and the Beast"-themed story of a wealthy vineyard owner in Napa Valley — a good natured, 60-year-old Italian immigrant named "Tony" — who travels to San Francisco and becomes smitten with "Amy," an attractive but impoverished young waitress (Sally's role). Back home, Tony is painfully aware that he is not getting any younger. Dreaming of Amy, he decides to propose marriage in a letter, inviting her to pay him a visit. But, fearing her outright rejection, he encloses the photograph of his handsome young hired hand, Joe. When Amy comes to the vineyard, predictable entanglements and problems ensue. Carole Lombard and Charles Laughton starred in the 1940 film version.

Sally also took a turn playing opposite Vincent Price[21] in *The Passing of the Third Floor Back*. Based on a short story by Jerome K. Jerome, the play is a kind of parable. The plot concerns the goings-on at a shabby-chic boarding house in Bloomsbury Square, London, that is home to an assortment of characters representing various human failings. Among them is the mistreated maid "Stasia," a rehabilitated juvenile delinquent (the role Sally played). A mysterious sad-eyed, gentle stranger enters the group, taking the room referenced by the play's title, and changes their lives for the better.

And finally, at the Wharf Theatre in Provincetown, Massachusetts, during the week of August 9-14, Sally performed in *White Cargo*, a tale of intrigue and sensuality set in a bungalow on the west coast of Africa. (Our old friend Earl Carroll had first produced the play on the New York stage in 1923.) In the 1930s, the play's interracial subject matter was considered quite edgy and controversial, even more so than the fan dance. Wearing a brunette wig and Max Factor No. 9 dark liquid makeup, Sally played the role of "Tondeleyo," a beguiling African femme fatale who contributes to the downfall of the white men who are inexorably drawn to her.

The play, written by Leon Gordon, was based on a scandalous-for-its-time novel written in 1912 by Ida Vera Simonton, titled *Hell's Playground*. Several attempts to produce a film version were aborted by censors who objected to the portrayal of a black woman intimately involved with a white man. When a 1929 British film version of *White Cargo* was shown on a limited basis in the United States, the Virginia Board of Censors noted in a lengthy critique that the movie contained many "sordid scenes which show the Negress putting forth her meretricious efforts to 'vamp' the white man."

The Academy-Award-winning actress Teresa Wright, who at age 19 was working as a scholarship apprentice at the Wharf Theater, had a close-up look at Sally's performance:

> That first summer I met wonderful professionals [like] Sally Rand.... Sally did *White Cargo*.... She would come in with little sparklers on her face and in her sarongs and say (deep voice) "I am Tondeleyo!" [22]

---

[21] Sally kept in touch with Vincent Price for the rest of her life. In 1975 he recommended her for a spot on the television game show *Hollywood Squares*. The shortsighted producers chose to pass on the opportunity.

[22] Eventually, an American film version of *White Cargo* was released by MGM in 1942, starring Hedy Lamarr as "Tondeleyo." The spelling of the name was slightly changed and the script was tailored to make it clear that the character was of mixed Egyptian and Arab ancestry. Technically, despite appearances, no actual miscegenation was depicted. For a time, "I am Tondeleyo!" became a "faddish catch phrase that served a generation of female impersonators."

But the funny thing is that she was very intent on doing away with
that image. So she did this play, but for her curtain call they had to
wait until she got into this long blue gown and a big picture hat.... It
was like she wanted everyone to know that she was really a lady.

Sally was a credible stage actress and she knew it. The program for her
stage appearance states: "It is Miss Rand's ambition to be identified with
the theatre as a star of good plays and she looks forward to the day when
the Fan Dance will be but a pleasant memory." Or, as Sally put it: "Dancing
is only a visual means of expressing oneself. It's too limited. I want to hold
an audience through the inflection in my voice, through dramatic and
intelligent portrayals of characters drawn from life."

One critic was optimistic about her chances on Broadway:

Believe it or not, Miss Rand's Tondelayo was an unusually accurate
description of Leon Gordon's African tiger rag. The young lady is
serious about invading the legitimate stage; she realizes her shortcomings and plans a serious course of study to correct them, and that
combination of determination and natural ability should see her
through. Miss Rand isn't worried about money. She's put away a neat
little nest egg and, while her fans and bubbles can still account for
$5,000 or more a week, a career on Broadway in the theater even at one-
fifth that is Sally's aim at the moment.... Broadway is due for a pleasant
surprise when Miss Rand gets around to play-acting in a year or so.

Contemplating these summer stock roles, Sally quipped:

They are going to make a loose woman out of me if it kills me. It
seems that I'm destined to be a slattern or a hussy whether I like it
or not. Lord! How I'd love to play Mary of Scotland!

As for her future path, Sally remained of two minds. Greener grass may
have beckoned, but greater legitimacy as a stage actress proved to be a
resistible calling. The fan and bubble money was just too good to give up.

L ife on the road was grueling. With little time for personal relationships
  or even an inclination toward romance, in a September interview, Sally
extemporized on the men in her life:

A man is so biological he doesn't interest me. He is a sort of hobby
that some people enjoy instead of stamp collecting or building
miniature boat models. That may be all right for those who don't
enjoy what they are doing, but I do. I'm perfectly satisfied to dance
or act 24 hours a day.

When asked if she was worried by her "exposure," she warmed to the subject:

No ... it's just a case of showing the right thing at the right time.
A knack I've mastered fairly well, if you will excuse my being
brash.... There isn't an actress alive who has taken better care of her
morals than I have. You never heard of a husband or children crop-
ping up to embarrass me, have you? Nor heard my name bandied
around in alienation-of-affection suits, nor of me caught driving
while drunk? No, sir, I've been decorous all the time, off the stage....

So, you see men just aren't necessary. I'm not looking around for
male prospects, because I don't need a hobby. I don't want ghosts or
skeletons clattering along behind me to hurt my perfect reputation.

Faith

On November 17th, news readers around the country were greeted with the
sort of headline that one simply doesn't encounter every day: "STRIP DANCER
SEES BANDITS STRIP PALS." While engaged to perform at a local theater in
Memphis, Tennessee, Faith and two comedians from her show were strolling
down a highway in the "outskirts of the city" when the three were accosted
by two "brigands." After helping themselves to $25 from each gentleman's
pocket and $50 from Miss Bacon's purse, the thieves had forced her two
companions to remove their pants.

To add insult to injury, the "two armed white men" (who seemed to relish
the act of relieving her escorts of their trousers) had been aggressively
intolerant of Faith's chosen profession, bitterly rebuking her for disrobing on
stage. "They called me a naked she-male," she complained. "It was a terrible
experience. One of the bandits slapped me so hard my head still aches."

Miss Bacon managed to survive the trauma and within a month had
opened in *Spices of 1938,* a new show featuring a new dance, the "Congo."
Her only costume was "an array of silver pheasant feathers." The clever
dancing trio of Dick, Dot and Dinah were also on the bill.

Documenting the life of a celebrity typically involves a quest to
separate fact from fiction — somehow sorting out the person's real
life from the version preserved in press puffery. In Sally's case, a rich
example involves the question of just exactly where she lived when not
on the road with her show. In January 1938, a Walter Winchell column
reported that, while Sally had "a lovely home in Westport," she did "most
of her sleeping at her West 49th Street Office!"

Columnist George Ross offered an even more fanciful view:

> In New York, Sally Rand lives at an expensive midtown hotel,
> a domicile that, for some reason or another, she keeps extremely
> secret. Besides her estate in Westport, she also owns a country
> home on Long Island.

A very different account of her circumstances is exposed in a letter Sally
wrote to her mother just a few weeks earlier on December 7, 1937:

> *I hate to write a blue letter, and this really is not a blue letter*
> *— it is a statement of the way things are. There is just not a*
> *speck of money to be had and no jobs at this moment, and I am*
> *broke, which of course always makes me feel very badly. I*
> *cannot afford to go to a hotel, and so I am living in this awful*
> *little place at 152 West 49th Street, which is Ralph's apart-*
> *ment and full of trunks and files and costumes and all the*
> *junk which it seems I have to carry around with me....*
>
> *I do not tell anybody that I am living here because it would be*
> *very bad prestige for me to stay in a neighborhood like this, and*
> *so for the sake of appearances we say that I am staying up at*
> *Westport, Connecticut with friends and that this is an office....*
>
> *I am in hopes that something very nice will break in a few*
> *days and I am sure it will.*[23]

Something very nice did break for Sally as she soon signed with Billy
Rose for a three-month engagement at the recently opened Billy Rose's
Diamond Horseshoe, a Times Square nightclub in the basement of the
Paramount Hotel. For his first production, Rose mounted *Let's Play Fair* —
a version of the Casa Mañana show that had been such a hit 18 months
earlier in Fort Worth. This was Rose's extravagant attempt to convince
organizers of the upcoming 1939 World's Fair in New York that he was
just the man to put together a large-scale revue for the exposition.

The pitch was fairly obvious. The show's theme involved the efforts of a
group of fair organizers to find the sort of talent that would attract a flood
of visitors. The cast of *Let's Play Fair* even had a character based on the
real-life Grover Whalen, who happened to be President of New York
World's Fair Corporation. And, since she had already proven to be the

---

[23] Let this be a lesson to the reader of any biography (including this one). Unless the
"facts" are based on unimpeachable primary source material, some of what you read is
likely to be incomplete or exaggerated, if not outright false. As Sally herself once
observed: "I write all my own press releases. That's how I know not to believe them."

one performer most closely associated with successful world expositions, Rose had engaged the formidable Sally Rand.

In a paid advertisement, he promised to deliver a spectacular show, even pledging that patrons would not have to tip the waiter for a front-row table. Nor would they be "railroaded into buying cigarettes, programs and flowers from the seductive sales girls." Rose further promised that the food would not be served so cold that it might as well have been brought in from Alaska.

The prologue of *Let's Play Fair* was set in the "executive office," featuring "Grover Whalen," his secretary, and a "Professor of Anatomy" — plus our Sally. There followed 11 scenes with a huge cast of singers, dancers, comedians, actors and musicians. The production was elaborate, to say the least. Dinner customers could even carve their steaks while savoring the sight of Captain Proske's snarling tigers pacing around onstage in their iron cage.

Billy Rose made good on his promises of quality food and service. A review in the Columbia College student newspaper found that: "The drinks are as good as you can get anywhere and the food is excellent.... The food prices are quite steep but the dishes are grade 'A' in quality and well prepared." The same reviewer was quite taken with Sally, writing:

> Sally Rand is a center of attraction with her balloon dance interpre-
> tation of "butterfly love." Although she has become slightly more
> plump in one or more of the posterior regions since her appearance
> at the Chicago World's Fair, she still has a good figure which she knows
> how to use to her good advantage and to the audience's delight.

Besides her regular nightly performances in two complete shows, Billy Rose designated Sally as the venue's "Mistress of Conversation." In this role, she chatted with customers between shows in the Palm Beach Bar on the second floor. One evening in mid-March, *New York Post* journalist Michel Mok sat at her table, engaging in a conversation that continued into her dressing room. Describing her as "a surprisingly small woman in her ripe thirties," Mok ordered a drink and inquired: "Have you read any good books lately?" "Yes," she replied. "I've read Plato's *Republic* and the *Comedies of Aristophanes* and *The Quest for Certainty* by John Dewey, and Stanislavsky's *An Actor Prepares.*" Asked how she liked Plato, Sally replied:

> Fine. He's working toward a theoretical ideal that cannot ever be
> accomplished. He propounds a utopian state which he calls his
> Republic. I tell you, it's a beautiful setup. Plato leaves you with one
> thing that's unforgettable. He wrote it in dialogue, you see, and

there's one place where they ask him when all these things will come
to pass and he says when a king or son of a king becomes a
philosopher. In my opinion, that's just about tops.

The conversation continued, touching on the distinction between a philosopher and an "emotionalist." Mok noted that Sally's dressing room was
full of books and flowers: "Books and vases of flowers on the dressing
shelf. Books on chairs. Boxes of books and baskets of flowers on the floor."
Entering the small area, he encountered a "curly-haired youth" — Ralph
Hobart, Sally's "dresser and factotum." Mok explained: "He powders her,
runs her errands, helps her fill out her income tax return, combs her golden
wigs and blows up her bubbles."

Sally stepped into a deep closet, leaving the door open, and then slipped out
of her dress as Mok carefully studied his fingernails. She put on a "flowered
calico wrapper" and Ralph carefully placed a "long-haired, curly gold wig"
on her head. (Ralph was the man who was so generously sharing his
apartment with her.) As Sally left for the stage, Mok stayed put, knowing she
would return in a few minutes. When she did, he wanted to know what
people liked to ask her as she fulfilled her duties as Mistress of Conversation.
She responded:

> Most of them ask the same two questions. They ask, "Don't you get
> writer's cramp signing all those pictures? And, "How about
> signing a check for me, Sally?
>
> I've got stock answers for both of them. When they ask about the
> writer's cramp, I say, "Not at all. I'm delighted. I would be unhappy
> only if you didn't want my autograph." When they bring up the check, I
> say, "If you will sign one in the front, I'll gladly sign it on the back."

"But," the reporter probed, "don't they ask you about how it feels to dance in the
nude?" Sally paused, lit a cigarette and, looking him straight in the eye, replied:

> Nobody in the audience has EVER asked me that. The reason is
> that, no matter what attitude they may have had when they came
> in, they are literally unaware of the lack of costume after the
> performance. They are aware of nothing except the pristine purity
> of the dance itself, the classicalness of line and form.

Sally enjoyed chatting with her fans and was easily approachable. On one
occasion, a retired naval officer asked her if she remembered an episode
years before when a man had sneaked up behind her, adding that he had:
"… lifted up your dress, bit you on the butt and then took off." Sally replied:
"Yeah, I remember that." He sheepishly admitted, "Well, I'm the guy."

"You son of a bitch," she snapped. "You broke the skin when you did that."
The chastened gentleman explained that other members of the fleet had bet
him that he wouldn't do it and he had felt obliged to do whatever was
necessary to win the bet.

As anyone who knew Sally would tell you, she was a heavy cigarette
smoker, said to prefer the mentholated variety. As columnist George
Ross described it: "She talks unceasingly. She smokes incessantly — preferably cigarettes which she filches, lighted, from somebody else's hand."
Changing the subject, Ross added that, while in New York at the Diamond
Horseshoe, Sally had managed to secure better working conditions for
nightclub entertainers, even convincing Billy Rose to sign a pact with the
American Federation of Labor (AFL), making the Casa Mañana the first
closed shop cabaret in the history of Broadway. Accused of siding with
"Hollywood types" and others with left-wing sympathies, Sally brushed
such talk aside: "After all, wouldn't I look just a little too silly standing on
the barricades — with nothing on but a bubble?"

Mary Belle

As a Chicago attorney, Mary Belle Spencer was used to being in court, but
now *she* was the one in the dock. This time her appearance didn't involve
Charles Lindbergh or her personal mission to restrict the movements of Sally
Rand. Instead, she had been charged with employing a milk bottle and a
hammer to assault her youngest daughter's boyfriend, 20-year old Melvin
Draben of Chicago Heights. The young man had also been charged, but only
with the lesser offense of "disorderly conduct."

In Melvin's version of events, he had driven teen-aged Victoria home from
a Saturday night party on February 5, 1938, and had come into the house to
greet her mother and share with her his sudden realization that Victoria
was one of the nicest girls he had ever met.

Mary Belle's version was somewhat different:

> I know from Victoria herself what took place on that ride home.
> This young man refused to stop the car when he reached the house.
> Victoria screamed and screamed, but he only laughed.
>
> Then, when he did bring her home he forced his way into the
> house and actually into my bedroom. I was in pajamas and a robe.
> I told him to leave and he would not. The argument progressed
> from room to room. I seized a milk bottle to defend myself. The
> bottle broke. That was when I grabbed the hammer.

Both participants obtained release on $1,000 bond and later mutually agreed to drop the charges. Over the next few months, Mrs. Spencer managed to cool down and young Victoria's ardor for Melvin apparently cooled as well. On November 19, 1938, the 16-year old Victoria Spencer married Loren N. Hamilton, age 25, at a service that took place in the Spencer home just steps away from the scene of poor Melvin's assault only nine months earlier.[24]

Billy Rose's big gamble in staging a satire directed at the organizers of the 1939 New York Fair paid off. His Aquacade concession became one of the exposition's most successful enterprises. The star of the show was Rose's latest romantic obsession, swimmer Eleanor Holm, Gold Medalist at the 1932 Olympics. Sally had hoped to be featured at the 1939 Fair, but her chances of gaining Billy's support were severely diminished by the fact that Holm and Rose were planning to marry just as soon as they could divorce their respective spouses, Al Jarrett and Fanny Brice.

Eleanor's co-starring role in the just-released *Tarzan's Revenge* may have inspired Sally's next publicity stunt. On March 9th she announced her personal choices for the "10 best undressed women" — not implying that any of these women made a habit of parading around sans suitable attire, but only that each had the "qualifications of face and figure that make the addition of clothes totally unnecessary."

Graciously omitting herself from the list, Sally gave a nod to Billy Rose by including his current squeeze Eleanor Holm among the chosen few. She also named such well known "figures" as movie actresses Marlene Dietrich and Frances Farmer and society matron Mrs. William Rhinelander Stewart ("the most beautiful woman in New York"), as well as an assortment of other beauties — the thinly-clad ballerina Zorita, burlesque queen Ann Corio, debutante Cobina Wright, Jr., and British actresses and dancers Jesse Matthews and Adele Dixon. She even listed Princess Marina (the Duchess of Kent[25] and sister-in-law of Great Britain's King George VI).[26]

---

[24] This was a change of pace for Mrs. Spencer, as two years earlier she had opposed the marriage of her other daughter, 16-year old Mary Belle, Jr., describing her as "being too young to know what it is all about."

[25] How the Duchess happened to make Sally's list is not clear, although she was considered something of a slender Greek beauty when she married the Duke in 1934. Indeed, when she visited the United States in 1954 at the age of 47, the five-foot-six Duchess reportedly sported a figure that included measurements of "bust 36, hips 38." (How columnist Colin Frost came to know these measurements remains a mystery.)

[26] Sally surely presented an intriguing list, but what are the chances that she had actually seen any of these ladies in a state of undress? Eleanor Holm? She very well

You might think that Sally's contract with the Billy Rose show would have put her back in the chips, particularly when press reports continued to suggest she was rolling in dough. But a letter she wrote to her mother on March 5th indicated otherwise. Nettie had just arranged for a reduction on the mortgage of their Glendora property and Sally was very grateful:

> *... You know darling you are a most amazing person. Whenever a crisis happens you always summon some kind of terrific vitality and wisdom and are adequate to every situation.... I think what you have done is simply wonderful....*
>
> *You may count on the $50 a week and, God willing and helping, as much more as I can possibly squeeze out. I am having to pay back debts, many of them, and since these people gave me credit I cannot let them down, and must pay back what I honestly owe them....*
>
> *Now take it easy my sweet and before the year is out we will all be out of the rut and everything will be all right. You know how my business is. Every so often you hit a snag, and can get nowhere, and all of a sudden something good comes along; and I have an idea that ... within the next few weeks ... something very swell is going to happen to me, and I will be out in Hollywood doing a picture, and everything will be hotsy-totsy.*

By March of 1938, Adolph Hitler was making militaristic moves in Europe, announcing Germany's incorporation of Austria. While the earlier invasion of China by the Empire of Japan had attracted relatively little attention in the United States, all this changed in late December of 1937 when Japanese forces marched into China's capital city of Nanking, raping and murdering civilians and unarmed combatants. During a six-week period, from 40,000 to 300,000 people were killed. The scale and brutality of the violence were so great that many historians regard the "Rape of Nanking" as the single worst atrocity of World War II. Suddenly, people of Japanese ancestry in the United States, including Sally's maid Stella, found themselves under greater scrutiny.

---

may have. Ann Corio and Zorita? A decent chance. Mrs. Stewart? The Duchess of Kent? Not so much.

Writing from New York to her mother in Glendora on March 25th (a mere six weeks after this massacre), Sally was concerned:

> *You know that now there is a great deal of bad feeling*
> *against the Japanese people. Our nice little Japanese*
> *neighbors have been so sweet and so generous with us; I think*
> *we need to be extra kind to them since they are being the butt*
> *of much criticism. After all, the Japanese people in this*
> *country cannot be responsible for the acts and deeds of the*
> *people in Japan. All of these wars and terrible atrocities are*
> *the work of a few greedy officials who make wars and make*
> *men go to war who don't want to go to war. I don't think any*
> *man today willingly goes to war. He is forced into it with a*
> *gun in his back so he must either face the enemy or be killed*
> *by his superior officers. It is a terrible state of affairs and*
> *you know how propaganda is.*

Sally saw a parallel in the way German-Americans had been treated in World War I:

> *During the World War people were so cruel to our German*
> *citizens here in America who could not possibly help their*
> *ancestry and who could not help loving their fatherland just*
> *as we love the United States, and while they might have felt*
> *bitter against what was happening in their own country or be*
> *sympathetic with it as they would naturally, we had no right*
> *to vent our spleen against Germans in this country and to*
> *believe the terrible propaganda we were asked to believe and*
> *to treat them cruelly.*

> *The same thing is happening now with the Japanese people ...*
> *in this country. That is not fair nor right and the Japanese*
> *feel it very keenly.... Particularly in a small neighborhood like*
> *Glendora I imagine some people feel pretty strongly against*
> *them. I wrote a nice letter to Stella. I did not mention*
> *anything about the war or anything like that, but I just*
> *wanted her to know that I still love her and thought kindly of*
> *her and her nice little husband, just as a reminder.*

Little did Sally know. While it would be nearly three years before the Japanese attack on Pearl Harbor, the intentions of the Empire of Japan could no longer be ignored. A sun was rising in the West that would one day cast a shadow like no other.

CHAPTER FOURTEEN

Here Comes the Judge

A beautiful woman must expect to be more accountable for her steps, than one less attractive.

~ Samuel Richardson (1753)

Sally Rand was a heavy smoker all of her adult life. And why not? By the 1940s smoking had become the norm in our culture. A survey conducted by Gallup and the National Opinion Research Center in 1939 found that a whopping 76 percent of adult men had answered "Yes" to the question "Do you smoke?" "Yes" was also the response of 33 percent of women, a number that would grow to 50 percent within just five years. Not only was the practice of smoking nothing to be ashamed of, it was actually celebrated. Several radio shows were sponsored by tobacco companies and popular movies were full of actors and actresses who shaped their roles by their smoking styles.

Smoking knew no cultural boundaries. It was popular regardless of class, race, gender, or level of education. So, it should be no surprise that, even within the ivy-covered halls of prestigious academia, smoking held sway. For several decades, universities had been staging so-called "smokers" — special events featuring comedy skits, celebrity speakers, and other assorted entertainers. In May 1937, a promising young student at Harvard University was named chairman of the Harvard Freshman Smoker Committee. The young John Fitzgerald Kennedy distinguished himself in that office by organizing a program that included appearances by such luminaries as baseball pitcher Dizzy Dean, cowboy film actor "Fuzzy" Knight, and the "Six Lucky Boys" tumbling act. The makers of both Lucky Strike and KOOL cigarettes donated generous quantities of their products to the affair, as did the Good Humor Ice Cream Company.

Also in 1937, Dr. Raymond Pearl of Johns Hopkins University announced his finding that: "Smoking is associated with a definite impairment of longevity." *Time* magazine suggested Pearl's results would frighten tobacco manufacturers to death and "make tobacco users' flesh creep." While it would be another 25 years or so before a significant number of smokers would begin to concede any such creeping, Dr. Pearl was among the first to sound the alarm.[1]

In the following year, George A. Kuhn, Jr., a somewhat lesser light than Mr. Kennedy, assumed the chairmanship of the Harvard Freshman Smoker Committee. Lesser he may have been, but Kuhn did put together a stellar program for the May 5, 1938, freshman smoker. Foremost on the guest list was Frank "Bring 'em Back Alive" Buck, the celebrated big game hunter. Others on the bill included the Ringling Brothers' "King of Clowns," Felix Adler, and the "Texas Giant," Jack Earle, who, at 7-foot-7 inches tall, was promoted as the world's tallest man.[2] Even so, the most highly anticipated guest was a little lady who, far from being a giant, was scarcely 60 inches tall in her bare feet.

Sally Rand had agreed to fly in from Baltimore, where she was rehearsing for a play in the Spring Drama Festival. The *Harvard Crimson* announced: "Miss Rand will do neither her fan dance nor her bubble dance, but she will provide entertainment in the form of a monologue." When asked about the nature of her talk, Sally explained:

> I am going to Harvard to tell the boys to be Daniel Boones. There are still some frontiers left. While they can't hunt the buffalo, they can have their frontiers in politics and labor, where they can go out and pioneer. I am not going to Harvard with my fans and my bubbles. I am going up there to give the boys a straight from the shoulder, serious talk. You know, I once pinch hit for a college professor on a discussion of the Ethiopian situation.

When the appointed hour arrived, Sally stepped before the assembled scholars wearing a frilly taffeta dress and nervously fingering a handkerchief to deliver a speech promoted under the title "How to be Intelligent, Though Educated." Once the cheers and jeers of the 1,500 "Yardlings" who greeted her at Memorial Hall had died down, Sally thanked the young men "for recognizing me with my clothes on as I came in. This is a novel experience." The raucous gathering responded with calls of "Where's your bubble?" and "What's your phone number?" In response, Sally told them they should "stop acting like a bunch of ten-year-olds." She then proceeded to deliver a

---

[1]   Twelve years earlier, during the height of Prohibition, Dr. Pearl had published *Alcohol and Longevity*, in which he found that drinking alcohol in moderation led to greater longevity than either abstaining or drinking heavily.

[2]   According to the *Harvard Crimson*, Jack Earle was expected to display his prodigious strength by carrying two dwarfs onstage — one in each of his palms.

thoughtful lecture, emphasizing the need for ethics in labor and politics. Sally extolled the theatrical union in particular and labor in general, saying:

> Upon labor rests democracy. America is a class of laboring people. Go out and do something for them and the country. It is up to you to do it. Labor and politics are the two professions that need the most attention. They are the intellectual frontiers.

Ignoring as best she could the ongoing snide remarks and rude calls coming from the cheap seats, Sally admonished her audience:

> You've got to take something seriously someday. Somebody is going to stop "keeping you" at the end of four years. Then you're going to have to do something about it.[3]

Writing for the *Harvard Crimson* nearly five years later, Sally recalled the evening:

> They came to scoff, but they stayed to ... ask for my autograph anyway. It was the custom in that era for lady lecturers to have question and answer periods. So I had one too. What did they ask me? ... [They asked] for my telephone number, which shows that they were intelligent, if not educated....

Wednesday, August 1, 1900, was a sunny summer afternoon in the upscale community of Newport, Rhode Island. Camped out in front of the Newport Casino, a young visitor to the area was amusing himself by snapping photos of the rich and famous with his five dollar camera. When mining heiress Mrs. Theresa Oelrichs noticed him pointing the lens in her direction, the matron of "Rosecliff" mansion angrily called upon Police Officer McCormick: "Arrest that man. He has taken my picture." When the officer appeared not to hear her, Tessie dashed up the road to find her husband Hermann, a 50-year-old steamship tycoon, and advise him of her distress. The couple then pursued the impertinent

---

[3] Among the freshmen taking it all in was a local Bostonian, son of a doctor and professor at Harvard Medical School. During his matriculation at Harvard, he would become editor of the *Harvard Lampoon* and would graduate cum laude in 1941. When the United States entered the Second World War, he would join the combat medical corps, participate in the June 6, 1944, Normandy Invasion as a platoon leader, and be awarded a Bronze Star and Purple Heart. After the war he would graduate from Harvard Law School, having served as editor of the *Harvard Law Review*. One day, Elliot Richardson would be named Attorney General of the United States, a position from which he would resign in 1973 after refusing President Nixon's direct order to fire Special Watergate Prosecutor Archibald Cox.

photographer in their automobile. As they drew alongside the man, Mr. Oelrichs, a former amateur boxer, jumped from the car, exclaiming: "How dare you take a picture of my wife!" Oelrichs then grabbed the camera, threw it to the ground and began jumping up and down on it, smashing the device to pieces.

A few weeks earlier Oelrichs had been sued for assault against an intruder on his estate. Perhaps knowing this, the aggrieved young photographer wailed: "You're a fine chap to teach a fellow manners," but he otherwise offered no physical retaliation. As the Oelrichs took their leave, the chastened offender swept up the pieces into his hat and meekly retreated to a nearby saloon where he was later seen attempting to put them back together. To all within earshot, he announced his intention to sue for damages, as well as for assault.

In the early days of photography, the limits of camera mechanics required subjects to remain as still as possible. There also had to be plenty of available light. In the absence of sufficient natural light, photographers resorted to "flash" photography, both in studio and on location. The flash was achieved by using an explosive mixture of magnesium powder and potassium chlorate, ignited by hand. The startling effect on unsuspecting subjects, together with the understandable reluctance of celebrities to have their pictures taken without consent, inevitably led to clashes between would-be "candid" photographers and their reluctant subjects.

By 1905, the situation was bad enough that local governments were being implored to do something about it. On December 4, 1905, the Chicago City Council unanimously adopted a proposal by Alderman Young to draft an ordinance aimed at eliminating the "nuisance of the flashlight camera fiend." The order read:

> Whereas, the presence of the camera fiend plying his vocation whenever and wherever he pleases, making whomever he chooses his victim regardless of circumstances or surroundings is becoming a general nuisance; and

> Whereas, one of Chicago's best known and most highly esteemed citizens has recently been subjected to embarrassment and indignity by such intruders, under such painful circumstances as to make the act revolting to the heart of any man of average sensibilities; therefore

> Ordered, that the Corporation Council be directed to prepare such ordinance or amendment to the Revised Code as in his opinion will best tend to eliminate the evil herein referred to, making such

regulation particularly applicable to cases in which explosives are
used, and providing adequate penalties for violation thereof.

Despite these efforts, the situation remained unresolved. On December 13,
1909, Lyman Atwell, photojournalist for the *Chicago Record-Herald*, had been
assigned to record politicians attending the annual First Ward Democratic
Ball. Organized for the purpose of refreshing political war chests, this
notorious annual event at which pimps, prostitutes and politicians frolicked
around the ballroom at the Chicago Coliseum had become an embarrassment
to the city. All attempts by local clergy, legitimate businessmen, and reformers
to stop the event — known in some quarters as "Chicago's Rotten Tenderloin
Ball" — had failed. Ever-louder pleas of citizens to put an end to the annual
"orgy of vice" fell on deaf ears. In short, the annual ball wasn't Chicago's
proudest moment. This particular year, security at the event was especially
tight due to the recent explosion of a dynamite bomb in the vicinity.
Photographers were forbidden to attend.

Standing outside on the sidewalk, Alderman "Bathhouse" John Coughlin
was receiving guests as they exited their vehicles when he caught sight of
Atwell snapping pictures. Taking charge, Coughlin led a group that proceeded to confront and attack the cameraman and his companion, illustrator
Wyncie King. Atwell held his camera in front of his face as he tried to ward
off blows, but as he was being held by a plainclothes policeman, his camera
was soon destroyed. As he appealed to a uniformed officer for protection,
Atwell was told to "clear out of here." Meanwhile, King was knocked to the
pavement and repeatedly kicked as he lay in the gutter.

Despite Coughlin's political influence and, some say, virtual ownership of
the Harrison Street police station, some events were simply too public to
overlook. Coughlin was arrested and escorted to a jail cell. Nine days later,
the case went to trial.

According to press reports, Coughlin appeared, attired in a "faultless frock
coat, a white waistcoat, a lavender tie, patent leather shoes and illuminated by two diamond shirt studs," in front of Municipal Judge John R.
Newcomer, a Republican. The photographer testified that he and King
had been punched by Alderman Coughlin and as many as four or five of
his cohorts. The alderman's defense attorney argued that it was the
setting off of Atwell's flash powder that had created a panic in the dense
crowd. In the end, "Bathhouse John" was acquitted. All the same, the fact
that a powerful alderman had been brought to trial and forced to confront

the evidence had given political bosses throughout Chicago something to think about.[4]

Fast forward a few decades. Due in part to the enormous popularity of motion pictures during the Great Depression, advances in camera technology and the rise of celebrity worship had combined to induce photographers to use ever more aggressive tactics, especially when big money could be made by exposing celebrities in compromising situations.

Take the example of photographer Benedict Fitzgerald, Jr., a law student and employee of the *Boston Daily Record*. On April 6, 1937, as the popular crooner Rudy Vallee emerged from a theater cloakroom with showgirl Evelyn Gresham, Mr. Fitzgerald captured the pair on film. Mr. Vallee wasn't happy. Harry Paul, Rudy's publicity man, initially grappled with the photographer, snatching the photographic plate from his hand and knocking his camera to the floor. The scuffle allegedly continued through the theater lobby and out onto the sidewalk, with Vallee poking and punching Fitzgerald all the while, eventually knocking him against a taxicab. Fitzgerald brought charges.

On April 21st, dressed in an elegant gray herringbone suit, white shirt and blue tie, the debonair Vallee stood in a packed courtroom before Municipal Court Judge Daniel J. Gillen and identified himself as "Hubert Prior Vallee, orchestra leader." Protesting the charges, he argued: "It was not for myself that I resented this unwarranted intrusion. My guest that evening may not have desired to be photographed, and it was solely for her that I spoke at all."

Unconvinced, Judge Gillen fined Harry Paul $50 for assaulting the cameraman. Although the judge convicted Rudy Vallee as well, he ordered the case placed "on file," meaning that Vallee would pay no fine and have no record in the eyes of the law. Two weeks later, Vallee was said to be only a "minor factor" in the divorce suit filed by the husband of his showgirl companion.

---

[4]   Coughlin had once worked in a Turkish bath as a masseur, thereby earning the nickname "Bathhouse." With his gaudy wardrobe, raffish manners, and habit of spouting poetry, he was considered to be something of a clown. Some thought him to be slow-witted. Mayor Harrison once asked Coughlin's associate, Alderman Michael "Hinky Dink" Kenna, if Bathhouse was crazy or under the influence of drugs. Neither, Kenna said, adding: "To tell you the god's truth, Mayor, they ain't found a name for it yet."

W hile angry male celebrities have been assaulting pesky shutterbugs for more than a century, what about their fuming female counterparts? As it happens, what may be the very first case of a female celebrity assaulting a photographer involved the charismatic young woman whose name appears on the cover of this book.

By early July 1938, Sally was back in Los Angeles starting an engagement at the Paramount Theatre. And it was a little incident at the Paramount on Tuesday, July 12th, that put her right back on the front pages of newspapers from coast to coast. It happened during an early matinee that Sally had every reason to expect would be an unremarkable performance.

Hundreds of patrons had each plunked down 60 cents to see a feature film along with Sally Rand's famous bubble and fan dances performed live. Among them was a seemingly ordinary young couple — C. Ray Stanford, aged 26, and his date for the afternoon, 22-year old Hazel Drain. Stanford had made it a point to arrive early enough to get seats in the front row. There he waited, patiently cradling a camera in his lap, enjoying an unobstructed view of the stage.

> ### KING OF PAPARAZZI
>
> On June 12, 1973, actor Marlon Brando was in New York City with Dick Cavett after taping his TV show and about to enter a restaurant in Chinatown, when he noticed Ron Galella, the man widely regarded as the "King of Paparazzi." (Just a year before, Jackie Kennedy Onassis had convinced a judge to issue a court order restricting him from approaching her any closer than 50 yards.) On this day, Galella was following Marlon Brando, intent on securing some candid shots of the famously reclusive actor. Enraged by the mere sight of the man and acting without warning, Brando punched the photographer in the face, breaking his jaw and knocking out five of his teeth. Galella subsequently sued Brando for assault and battery. The case was ultimately settled for $40,000 (over $200,000 today).

Sally's fan and bubble dances proceeded without incident, or so it seemed. As the curtain came down, the audience applauded heartily and settled back in their seats, fully expecting that the only remaining entertainment would be the film *Prison Farm*, starring Lloyd Nolan. As soon as the projectionist began running the movie, everyone, including Mr. Stanford and Miss Drain, turned their attention to the flickering images on the screen.

Suddenly, Sally emerged from the wings wearing a dressing gown. Descending from the stage, she confronted Stanford in the darkened theater. Few noticed her at first. Having seen the young man in the front row with a camera, she demanded that he turn over his film. Although taken aback by the "in your face" presence of a celebrity and aware that, movie or no movie, he was probably being watched by hundreds of other eyes, Stanford was not of a mind to surrender his prize. Hoping to avoid an ugly encounter, he and his date decided it was time to leave. From that point on, things sort of got out of hand. Sally was not so easily denied, and a scuffle ensued in the aisle. What happened next depends on which version you choose to believe, but one fact is clear — Sally did manage to get the film away from Stanford and render it useless.

Thus began an odyssey in the judicial system that would carry on for the next nine months or more. Mr. Stanford and Miss Drain believed they had been unduly roughed up — indeed assaulted. Leaving the theater, they promptly engaged the services of Willedd Andrews, a prominent Hollywood attorney.[5]

Perhaps assuming Sally had deep pockets, Andrews wasted no time. On the day after the incident he announced that the couple intended to sue for civil damages. The alleged victims then followed up by marching into the office of Assistant City Attorney Don Redwine and filing a criminal complaint as well, charging Sally with assault, battery, and malicious mischief. She would now be facing both civil and criminal actions.

Addressing the press, Miss Drain declared:

> It was all very horrible. I went to the theatre with Ray and he
> started taking a couple of pictures. Next thing I knew this dancer
> was next to us. She was just like a wild woman. She grabbed at the
> camera, tore Ray's clothing and scratched me and bit my arm until
> it bled. She followed us to the cloakroom biting and scratching. In
> the fight she broke the camera and exposed the film.

In response, Sally countered:

> I never allow my picture to be taken while dancing. As I got
> through my act, I saw a man take a roll of film out of the camera. I
> put on a robe and went down where they were sitting in front row
> seats. We went up the aisle and into the cloak room and finally I
> persuaded him to expose the films. I didn't bite or scratch anyone.

On Monday, July 18th, wearing a "chic green and white summer dress and a fashionable straw hat," Sally appeared in the office of the Deputy City Attorney, where a meeting was held to determine whether a criminal complaint for "battery and malicious mischief" would be issued. The case was continued to the following Thursday, at which time both Stanford and

---

5   A year earlier, Willedd Andrews had represented evangelist Aimee Semple
     McPherson in a high profile squabble among family members, ending up as a
     defendant himself in an action for slander brought by McPherson's daughter.

Drain also filed civil suits — claiming that Sally Rand did "maliciously, unlawfully and willfully bite [and] scratch" them and tear their clothes — seeking a total of $2,622 in damages (over $42,000 today).[6]

When the assault charge came before Municipal Judge Harold Landreth, the couple insisted that Sally had chased them up the aisle and "attacked us from the rear," testifying that she had beaten and scratched them and had even bitten Miss Drain on the arm. Sally, clad in white silk slacks, told the judge that, while she "might have" grabbed Mr. Stanford by the suspenders (causing him to tear his shirt) and "might have" smashed his camera, she had not scratched anyone or bitten Miss Drain. "On account of my balloon," she explained, I must keep my fingernails clipped almost to the quick. I can't have it tearing while I'm doing my dance." How could such short nails have scratched anyone? Sally even had Dr. Hershey Goldberg standing by to confirm that Miss Drain had not been bitten.

Sally was adamant that she had a right to confiscate the camera since, as she explained, no matter how graceful a bubble dance may be in its entirety, it is bound to contain "grotesque" moments. These were the very moments, she claimed, that the cameraman had chosen to click his shutter. Finding the two accounts seriously at odds, Judge Landreth ordered the case to trial on August 18th, at which time a jury would have to sort it out.

R iding a wave of success that had been building for the past five years, Sally was in demand. Yet, her little known snub of a major Hollywood director suggests that things could have been even better.

In late June of 1938, the award-winning movie director George Cukor offered Sally a prominent role in *Zaza* playing the leader of a troupe of Paris music hall can-can dancers. At the time, things on the film set were in a state of confusion. Shooting had already begun with the so-called "Italian Marlene Dietrich" in the lead. But Isa Miranda's Italian accent was so heavy that Cukor claimed she could hardly be understood. A demanding director, Cukor didn't want to continue in a losing effort. So, after a few days of frustration, he demanded that Miranda be replaced.

Paramount's producers agreed and quickly came up with leading lady Claudette Colbert, best known at the time for her Oscar-winning per-formance opposite Clark Gable in the 1935 Best Picture *It Happened One Night*

---

6 The total included $20 for Hazel's medical bill. Her "humiliation" was valued at $500 and her general "wear and tear" at another $1,000. Ray had suffered a similar $1,000 injury, but did not claim to have been humiliated. His camera was valued at $102.70.

(the first movie to take all five major Academy Awards). Because *Zaza* had a decent budget and the cast included actors well-known at the time, Sally would certainly have been in solid company.[7]

On the face of it, this seemed like a can't-miss opportunity, a chance for Sally to jump-start her feature film career. After all, both *Zaza* and the can-can had long and colorful histories. The combination of the film's controversial subject matter and Sally's notoriety had "box office" written all over it. Originally a stage production, the story of a dancer who falls in love with a married man had been made into a movie twice before.

Drama critics had found the stage version to be well beyond inappropriate.[8] Even so, when the second silent film version emerged, few eyebrows were raised. The 1923 film had starred Gloria Swanson as "Zaza," playing opposite the same H. B. Warner whom, you might recall, Sally had encountered in the flesh while filming DeMille's *King of Kings*. So, you might think that the chance to be featured in a high-profile, big studio production would be an opportunity too good for Sally to decline. Yet she actually turned her nose up at the offer, claiming that performing the can-can would be too crude an endeavor for a true artist like herself. A syndicated columnist elicited Sally's explanation:

> People today snigger at our grandmothers who considered the can-can shocking, but grandma was right. It's essentially a brazen dance, much too brazen for my taste. The kicking and flipping up of skirts which is the essence of the can-can, and the type of undergarments the girls wear, are definitely suggestive....
>
> There is an art in my bubble dance; in the can-can merely sex appeal. The rash abandon of the can-can, from a woman's viewpoint, be it modern or Victorian, is much more embarrassing than any of the dances I do. To lead a group of Parisian can-can dancers would be detrimental to my standing both as an artist and as an exponent of the dance in its purest form.

---

[7]   Herbert Marshall was fresh off his leading role in *Angel* (opposite the actual Miss Dietrich) and Bert Lahr would soon be playing the Cowardly Lion in *The Wizard of Oz*.

[8]   When David Belasco mounted his stage production in 1899, drama critic William Winter described the title character as one of those "obtruding harlots on the stage." In his late-Victorian-Age opinion, "it would be propitious for the community if [such productions] could be played on from a fire hose and washed into the sewer where they belong." The *New York Times* review was similarly uncharitable, sermonizing that: "Nothing quite so glaringly vicious as the symbols of vice in *Zaza* have ever before been put before decent American eyes." Such was the tenor of the times.

His offer spurned, George Cukor decided to expand Claudette Colbert's role to include leadership of the can-can troupe. Filming resumed but Cukor still wasn't happy. Ultimately, *Zaza* got worked over by studio censors. Wholesale cuts were demanded, and both Colbert and Cukor felt that the picture, as released, had been ruined. Indeed, the film played to mostly negative reviews and proved to be one of Cukor's few box office failures.

Are we to believe Sally's rationale for giving George Cukor the cold shoulder? Perhaps something about submitting to the instruction of a strong-willed director was outside her comfort zone. There were whispers that Paramount balked at coughing up the salary that Sally demanded. Or, maybe her remarks should simply be taken at face value. The can-can is, in fact, rather rowdy and raucous, possibly too much so for one who thought of herself as nothing less than an artiste.

Even so, if Sally had accepted the part and ingratiated herself with Cukor and the Paramount big-wigs, the course of her future might have been dramatically altered. She often expressed the desire to return to the silver screen, yet passed on a part that could have set her on a path to a totally different life.

Who knows what other opportunities success in *Zaza* might have led to? Other films? Bigger films? Certainly, as an established movie actress, she might have found a place in television. Imagine Sally guesting on Rowan and Martin's *Laugh In* or playing the sort of naughty character roles that Betty White has taken on so successfully. Sally was still active in 1978, at a time when *Saturday Night Live* was in its 4th season. Don Pardo never said it, but, in an alternate version of our world, he might have: "And your host — Sally Raaaand." The road not taken.

Although Sally had just passed on an offer from Paramount and didn't appreciate being photographed unawares by an amateur in a movie house, this didn't mean she wasn't willing to go before the cameras. Still confident that her image rightfully belonged on the big screen, when Grand National Pictures offered her the female lead in a "Hollywood after dark" drama, Sally was ready and willing to accept the part. Filmed in the summer of 1938 and shot in six days, this would be her last feature film and the only one in which she would enjoy an above-the-title billing.

A Hollywood gossip columnist alerted the public:

> Clothes will adorn Sally Rand in the movie to be made ... for the independent producer, George Hirliman. Sally plays a woman detective in a mystery thriller titled, for the moment at least,

Murder on Sunset Boulevard. The customers will get two glimpses of the Rand underpinnings, principally in a peacock number. Always the business woman, Sally has a percentage of the picture's profits as well as her salary.

Hollywood columnist Jimmie Fidler visited the film set when the working title was *Murder on Hollywood Boulevard*. By this point in her career, Sally's casual attitude toward her body was well established. Still, Fidler was enthralled:

> The other day I managed to crash the set where her final scenes were being filmed. Sally, seemingly as unaware of the crowd on the set as if they were non-existent, wandered about in the scantiest costume ever seen outside of a nudist resort. And if her nonchalance was surprising, that of the crew was amazing. Not a man of the thirty or forty who worked on the set paid her the tribute of a glance unless it was called for by the job at hand. And I heard only one remark passed about her startling lack of clothes. Commenting on her radiant health, an electrician dryly observed that it might be due to her fondness for fresh air. Hollywood, at work, is less sex conscious than many of the would-be reformers who criticize it.

Collaborating with the Japanese dancer and choreographer Michio Ito, Sally developed a new "Dance of the Peacock" for the film. Fascinated with professional dancing from an early age, Sally shared a special bond with Ito, whose career in many ways embodied what hers might have been.[9]

By the time filming had wrapped, the film's title had been changed to *Sunset Strip Case*, accurately describing the film's Hollywood locale, while letting ticket buyers draw their own conclusions about the content. It was directed by 63-year-old Louis Gasnier, perhaps best known for his work more than 20 years earlier on the silent film series *The Perils of Pauline*.[10]

---

[9] Born into a wealthy family in Tokyo, Ito's early interest in theater led him to study singing at the Tokyo Academy of Music. He left for Europe in 1912 where he became enchanted with the performances of the famous Russian ballerina Anna Pavlova, just as the young Helen Beck had been only a few years earlier. He soon abandoned opera and pursued a career in dance. After developing a combination of eastern and western styles, he made his debut in 1914 in London, where he became acquainted with poets Ezra Pound and William Butler Yeats. He was soon the toast of Europe. Ito then made his way to the United States where, by 1919, he was teaching a systematized approach to modern dance that reflected his individual aesthetic preferences, paving the way for the famous Martha Graham.

[10] Gasnier also bore the distinction of being the gentleman who directed the 1936 cult classic *Tell Your Children*. Never heard of it? Perhaps you would recognize its more familiar alternate title — *Reefer Madness*.

Sunset Strip Case is a Hollywood murder mystery in which Sally's character — "Kathy O'Connor," nightclub entertainer and daughter of a murdered police sergeant — teams up with an assistant district attorney to bring a group of racketeers to justice. While never at risk of being nominated for any awards, the film is no more dismissible than many another low-budget picture from the period. Whatever its shortcomings, the movie survives on DVD as a unique opportunity to see and hear Sally Rand at length. She's a charmer.

With the week of filming completed, all Sally had to do was await the film's release and reap the benefits of its critical acclaim. But since nothing ever went that smoothly for her, you've got to figure there would be a bump in the road somewhere along the way. And so there was, in the form of the same "Hays Code" bunch that had insisted on trimming Sally's fan dance scene in *Boléro* five years earlier.

The Hays Code wasn't the only obstacle impeding distribution of *Sunset Strip Case*. Local censors also weighed in. Banned in Boston, the movie was approved for viewing in Pennsylvania only after a number of scenes were removed, as per the state board's "eliminations sheet." After a two-month-long tango between Grand National Pictures and the MPPDA, the Hays Office finally issued the film a certificate under the title *Sunset Murder Case*. Beyond requesting that the word "Strip" be removed from the title, Hays admonished the producers to alter the film so as not to "expose offensively" Sally Rand's breasts.

New prints were rushed into distribution and, while the title was changed in many theater billings right away, some independent theaters ignored the Hays Office altogether. Indeed, the *Sunset Strip Case* continued to play in several venues for at least a year under the original title.[11]

In any event, by January 1939, the Hays Office had done its damage and both *Sunset Murder Case* and *Zaza* were playing in competing venues around the country — with *Zaza* getting the bigger play by far. This is not surprising, considering that Oscar-winner Claudette Colbert had the substantial backing of Paramount Studios. Meanwhile, Sally's low-budget movie was handicapped by the spotty distribution of Grand National Pictures, a studio that ended up in liquidation even as the film was still making its initial rounds.

---

[11]   Posters for both the *Strip Case* and *Murder Case* versions have survived, original copies of which are reported to be hanging on the wall of an ardent (*ahem*) private collector.

Still, *Sunset* played to some modestly positive reviews, like this one, possibly furnished by the studio:

> Sally Rand ... is proving to enthusiastic audiences this week that acting is one of her talents just as definitely as is her exposition of the terpsichorean act.

Other reviews were less upbeat. Reviewer Sterling Sorensen called it as he saw it:

> Grand National Pictures, the studio presenting *Sunset Murder Case*, would have to search long and ardently before they could again find a more untutored group of actors than those assembled in this detective mystery. Miss Rand is perhaps the poorest actress seen in years of movie-going and her supporting players are mere puppets. The inanities and downright "hamminess" of the characters kept yesterday's audience constantly amused. Sally does one dance, but her movements are veiled behind a large potted palm during the number.

Sorensen's jab at the "untutored group of actors" is perhaps a little harsh. While this modest little effort may not have represented their best work, the cast did include a few actors of note. Among them, Reed Hadley, who would play the title role in *Zorro's Fighting Legion* the next year and would go on to appear in dozens of other films and television shows over the following 34 years.[12]

Much of Sally's peacock dance in the *Sunset Murder Case* DVD is, in fact, obscured by a potted palm, but the actions of the Hays Office, as well as surviving lobby cards and Sorensen's reference to "one dance" in his review, make it clear that a more explicit version (not to mention the entirety of the bubble dance) had been cut from the film before he could review it in June of 1939. The loss of the peacock dance footage is a great shame, not only for obvious reasons, but also because we are denied the chance to appreciate the full extent of Michio Ito's choreography, and are left with little more than his ballet performed by the eight young women in identical flowing gowns who introduce Sally's appearance.

---

[12] The cast also included Esther Muir (who had appeared in the Marx Brothers' *A Day At The Races*), George Douglas (who had a long career in "B" pictures and TV westerns and would play the sheriff in *Attack of the 50 Foot Woman*), and Vince Barnett (who was sometimes compared to Groucho Marx and would have roles in more than 200 films and TV shows, including the Janitor in *Dr. Goldfoot and the Bikini Machine* in 1965). Barnett can still be seen today playing "Elmo" in reruns of *Mayberry R.F.D.*

The butchered version of the peacock dance aside, Sally's solid performance of her bubble dance (as restored in the DVD) is worthy of viewing.[13] Wearing an abbreviated, diaphanous costume, she expertly maneuvers a truly huge bubble around the stage. At the end of the dance, as the lights begin to dim to darkness, Sally sort of pulls her gossamer covering to one side, revealing what we are led to imagine might be her naked body.

As Sally's August 18th trial date approached, her attorney, Milton Golden, successfully petitioned the court to have the phrases "nude dancing" and "exhibiting her nude body" stricken from the assault and battery complaint, saying: "Miss Rand's dancing is intended to be purely artistic and a description of it as 'nude dancing' is scandalous, sham and irrelevant." Golden also requested a continuance, pleading that Sally would suffer a significant financial loss unless she were permitted to leave the court's jurisdiction to fulfill her theatrical contracts in the east. Judge Landreth was agreeable. A new trial date was set for October 4, 1939.

Meanwhile, the separate civil action brought by Ray Stanford and Hazel Drain was proceeding. In answer to the young couple's suit, Sally filed court papers generally denying the charges and saying that she was merely protecting herself against the "piracy of her rights of privacy." Claiming to have been the victim of many blackmail attempts in the past, she argued that she was justified in "politely requesting" Stanford to turn over the film.

She said there were many occasions when she had been surreptitiously photographed by unscrupulous types who then tried to sell her the prints and negatives. Sally's papers stated that:

> Upon her refusal to pay large sums for such photographs, said persons had threatened to and had exhibited and sold said defamatory, vulgar, obscene and indecent pictures, all of which tended to degrade, debase and hold [her] up to popular ridicule and scorn.

Her court filing also asserted that Mr. Stanford's shots had been taken from "eccentric angles" during the bubble dance. In other words, the camera was aimed upward "from the floor of the theater at an angle which was calculated to show only" certain unmentionable parts of her body. They were surely "not intended to be photographs depicting the defendant's artistic dance interpretation," and Sally feared they could be used to further libel her.

---

[13] The entire DVD version of the film, as well as a separate video clip of the bubble dance, can be seen online at YouTube. (Just search for "Sally Rand" and "Sunset.") The dance occurs at 7:48 minutes into the DVD.

With the court's indulgence, Sally journeyed east to perform in summer stock, opening a one-week engagement on August 22nd at Connecticut's Westport Country Playhouse. Once again, she was cast as Sadie Thompson in Somerset Maugham's *Rain*.

While in that role, Sally was quite unexpectedly showcased in "The Case of the Westport Wasp" — a little drama that played out mostly within the confines of her automobile. One day, as she was being chauffeured to a matinee performance, a wasp suddenly flew in the car window and somehow stung her, as press reports styled it, on "the most celebrated callipygian curve in America." Sally's scream so startled the driver that he nearly swerved into a ditch.

Luckily, first aid was available at a cottage nearby. It was the home of Helen Boylston, the author of *Sue Barton, Student Nurse*, a series of books for young adults. Sally could hardly have stumbled upon a spot where she would have received more expert aid. Boylston had actually served as a nurse in French field hospitals in the Great War. And so, while she had no balm for wasp stings, she did take Sally into the back yard where she "applied a mud pie to the seat of the affliction."

And, since the show must go on, Sally was doubly fortunate in that her role required her to sit down only twice during the three acts of *Rain*.

On October 4th, the date set for the criminal assault and battery trial, Judge Harold Landreth and Defense Attorney Milton Golden arrived in court at the appointed hour. But as the bailiff shouted her name three separate times, the defendant was nowhere to be seen. Indeed, Sally was nearly 3,000 miles away performing in a Philadelphia theater. Her failure to appear greatly exasperated both her attorney and the judge. "My client has broken faith with me," Golden told Judge Landreth. He claimed to have advised Sally that failure to appear is not an option in a criminal proceeding.

"Humph," the judge muttered. He had previously granted Sally's personal appeal for a postponement and allowed her to leave the court's jurisdiction on the assurance that she would appear without fail. "This will affect the entire theatrical profession in the future, so far as this court is concerned," Judge Landreth grumbled, adding: "No longer will the court permit members of the profession to remain at liberty on a mere promise to appear. I am signing a bench warrant for the arrest of Miss Rand. Bail will be $2,500."

Sally's attorney assured the court that she would be back in Los Angeles on the 18th. Meanwhile, comfortably oblivious in her Philadelphia dressing room, Sally claimed to be quite surprised when word arrived that a bench warrant had been issued for her arrest. With some indignation, she said she had missed the trial only because she thought her attorney had settled the case out of court. In any event, Sally announced her plans to return to the West Coast within the next few days.

Faith

As Sally was waving her fans to the delight of audiences in Philadelphia, Faith Bacon was in Hollywood consulting an attorney. Aware that Sally was out of town and perhaps sensing that her troubles with Hazel Drain and Ray Stanford had put her in a vulnerable position, Miss Bacon chose October 11th as the perfect day to file a complaint in Superior Court asserting that Sally had "stolen" the fan dance idea from *her*. Faith's civil action sought to collect a whopping $375,000 in damages (over $6.5 million today). Potentially even more devastating, she was pursuing an injunction to prevent Sally from ever again performing the fan dance.

Faith had plenty to say on the matter:

> I'm an artist and she's a businesswoman. My dance was one of ethereal beauty. It really was. And that woman turned it into an animated French postcard.

> She's been going around the country the last few years in vaudeville using fans. And not to fan herself, either. And what happens? I come along a little later and the people who have paid to see her don't want to see me. I figure her use of my dance has netted her $1,000,000.

Faith saw herself as something of a purist when it came to nudity. She was none too complimentary about Sally's choice of attire, accusing her of wearing "invisible clothing":

> Of course the fan dance should include nothing but the fans. When I do it, I wear only talcum powder. Well, except in Kansas City. That's the one city where I have to wear a brassiere and flesh-colored pants. I always feel hampered in Kansas City.

Defending her claim of originality, Miss Bacon offered her own version of exactly how the fan dance came to be:

> I was working for Earl Carroll as a nude. I stood still on the stage, like a statue, while the lights played on me. That was on account of the law. As soon as a nude woman moved, she was indecent. So long as she stayed still, she was okay.

That didn't suit Mr. Carroll. He wanted the audiences to see me from all angles. We tried everything. I'd cover myself with the fans while dancing and as soon as I'd reach the proper position, I'd stop and hold them over my head.

We tried the idea in the *Vanities of 1930* and the show was a flop. Then it was raided on account of my dance and when I was exonerated by the grand jury, the *Vanities* was a real hit. I had to do my dance before the jury to prove it was art. When I went back to work, the foreman sent me a dozen white roses and a note saying he thought my work was lovely.

Later, I played in vaudeville. There was a comedian on the bill who had an assistant named Sally Rand. I let her hold my fans for me in the wings when I started my dance and every night she watched my performance. First thing I knew she was doing it herself. I didn't mind because I was playing on Broadway in the *Follies*.... But when I went into vaudeville a couple of years ago, I discovered exactly what she had done to me.

That woman dances the fan dance with high heels. Imagine! All she does is walk around and let the people gawk. It breaks my heart to see my art treated like that.

Ever since then, the suit alleged, Sally Rand had been presenting "inferior imitations" of Faith Bacon's original fan dance, performing an act which "deceived the public" and resulted in "grievous injury to her reputation as a high-class dancer."

On that same October 11th, blissfully unaware of Miss Bacon's suit, Sally was on her way from Philadelphia to Los Angeles to face the sour countenance of the slighted Judge Landreth in the assault and battery affair. But, blissful she was not. As always, her day was anything but boring.

Sally loved dogs, having cherished many over the years. The silky Pekingese were her favorites. Traveling by car with her longtime little companions "Snooty" and "China Boy" at her side, Sally's driver had pulled over in Speeceville, Pennsylvania, to get out and stretch his legs. Sally was napping in the back, probably assuming that her little chums were doing the same. But, somehow, the red and white China Boy jumped from an open window and took off for parts unknown. When the driver returned, he started the car and headed down the highway, unaware that he was one passenger short.

Once she awoke and realized what had happened, Sally was understandably distraught. She reported her missing dog to the Pennsylvania State Police, offering a $50 reward for his return and prevailing upon the lawmen to dispatch the little fellow's description over the state police teletype.[14]

The next day, accompanied by the now sullen little Snooty, Sally motored into Chicago, where the press corps eagerly awaited. Always a welcome visitor in the city of her previous triumphs, Sally was giving an interview in her hotel, with Snooty prowling around the room, when she received an update on his missing companion. The news was very bad.

A young bread truck driver had seen a little dog that "looked darned expensive" leap from a car window and had given chase. However, he couldn't get close enough to retrieve the little fellow and was dismayed to watch as China Boy "ran out into the highway, with several drivers swerving to avoid" him before one was unable to do so. "I can't understand it," Sally choked out in a low voice, "China Boy has been taught never to wander across highways." Calling on her friend Donald Bainbridge in Hazelton, Pennsylvania, she arranged for China Boy's body to be shipped to California so he could be buried in a Hollywood pet cemetery. Bainbridge was later quoted as saying that her little pet was "really the closest friend of Miss Rand for the past four years."

As for the outstanding bench warrant, Sally said: "I thought the assault and battery case was all cleared up. But my lawyer tells me it isn't and so I've got to go back." Moreover, as superstition informs us, bad news comes in threes.

A member of the press broke the news of Faith Bacon's lawsuit. Reacting to Faith's allegations, Sally offered a particularly adroit off-the-cuff response:

> She can't sue me for that.... I understand that a man named Americus Vespucius probably landed in America long before Columbus. But Chris gets all the credit. See what I mean? Maybe there's a reason.[15]

---

[14] Sally wasn't the only one having a bad day on the highway. The same *Harrisburg Evening News* that had reported Sally's loss on the front page also published an adjacent article relating that, some 337 miles away in Marietta, Ohio, a 42-year-old itinerant Nazarene evangelist, Rev. Joseph A. Dixon, was found tarred, feathered, and in a dazed condition on the side of the road, shortly after his wedding to 22-year-old Opal Hasley. The father of the bride, her three brothers, and her sister were among the 10 suspects arrested for kidnapping and assault.

[15] This is clever, but incorrect. While the American continents are named after Amerigo Vespucci, the Italian explorer did not land in the New World until several years after Columbus. Neither gentleman ever set foot on what is now North America.

Faith is obviously jealous of my professional standing. Why doesn't she come out from behind those fans and fight like a man? Fans or bubbles, the public has already decided which of us it likes best. I guess she must have a new press agent.

And I was fanning long before the Chicago Cubs got good at it! [16]

For Sally, the next three days motoring across the country on two-lane roadways could not have been a pleasant journey. Imagine yourself crossing the Great Plains and the Rocky Mountains, all while under the cloud of an arrest warrant, not to mention that *other* lawsuit seeking the present-day equivalent of more than six million dollars. Oh yes . . . and some random motorist has just run over your little dog.

With her concerns and frustrations mounting, Sally finally reached Los Angeles, where, speaking to the press, she was less than generous to Miss Bacon:

Absolutely ridiculous! Francis Bacon may have written Shakespeare, but Faith Bacon didn't invent anything in her dance. Cleopatra waved a fan and did a disrobing act which went over big with Julius Caesar. He may have thought it was a new one, but I'll bet it was thousands of years old then.... Faith's suing me over that dance of hers is as funny as Webster suing somebody for using words in the dictionary. And, besides, mine is refined and high art.

On the morning of October 18th, Sally and her attorney, Milton Golden, appeared before Judge Landreth to request a reduction in her bail. The chastened defendant, dressed in a "wine-colored suit and pillbox hat" crowned by a blue feather, stood tearfully before the judge, apologizing profusely. Still disgruntled, the judge turned Sally over to police matron Cheryl Goodwin, who took the petite defendant away, leaving the judge to confer with her attorney.

Goodwin later confirmed that she had placed Sally in the "bull pen" with other prisoners for 10 minutes. Sally maintained that she had actually been placed in an anteroom, not in a jail cell — an "important difference" she claimed.

---

16   The 1938 Cubs had, in fact, recently completed a highly successful season, winning the National League pennant. But, just the week before, the New York Yankees had swept them in the World Series in four games. Cubs batters had struck out (or "fanned") a total of 26 times, including 11 strikeouts against Yankee pitcher Red Ruffing in the final game at Yankee Stadium.

Although encouraged to do so by press photographers, Sally reportedly refused to pose for pictures with the "buxom blond police matron," saying: "I'll jump out a window or pose any way you want — even stand on my head — but I won't pose with a policewoman. I think she's sweet and lovely, but I won't have it." (Posed or not, photographs of the two together do exist.)

Like so many other men before him, Judge Landreth turned out to be susceptible to Sally's charms. Admitting that he wasn't as angry as he had been two weeks earlier when she had missed her scheduled court appearance, the magistrate agreed to reduce her bond from $2,500 to $1,000. Still, he admonished Sally, she absolutely *must* be in court on October 31st, adding: "I have plenty more to say, but guess I won't say it. Everything I say just seems to result in more publicity for Miss Rand."

After the hearing, Sally's attorney announced to the press that he would seek the court's permission for her to perform her fan dance for the jury in order to prove her contention that photographs taken from certain angles would be objectionable. As Sally left the courtroom, reporters called out to ask what she thought of the $375,000 suit filed by Faith Bacon. "Well, she got herself a job," Sally retorted, "and that's what she wanted."

Normally hopeful, Sally had begun her day with a certain sense of optimism that she wouldn't end up in the clink by sundown. No sooner was she out the door of the courthouse than she jumped in her car and headed north, a trip of 400 miles, to begin an engagement that very evening as part of an "old-time" vaudeville program at the Oakland Athletic Club. But the gods weren't smiling on Sally yet. Her car broke down in Fresno and she had to scramble to catch a flight on United Airlines, barely arriving in time for the show.

Never one to waste an opportunity, Sally spent part of the next day conferring with officials of the 1939 Golden Gate Exposition, scheduled to open on Treasure Island in San Francisco Bay in four months' time.

Meanwhile, in Sally's home state of Missouri, a little situation was unfolding in the State Capitol at Jefferson City. It seems that, near the entrance to those esteemed halls, visitors had long been greeted by a large framed display that typically exhibited photographs of famous Missourians — those who had made it big — or, sometimes, pictures of prize-winning Missouri livestock. Every week or so, the staff of the State Resources Museum changed the exhibit. In late October, it was announced that the display at the State Capitol would consist of "several camera studies of the comely fan dancer" and native Missourian, Sally Rand.

Not everyone was pleased. State officials received objections and the "art studies" of Miss Rand mysteriously disappeared. According to one local paper, "No one in the museum seemed to know how the pictures ... got into the [display] or who removed them." Another local columnist, noting that some unknown person had removed the pictures, leaving the cabinet bare, quipped: "Considering it was Sally being shown, a bare display was to be expected sooner or later."

W hen word got around that Sally might perform her act in the full light of an open courtroom, it generated quite a lot of excitement — or, as one columnist characterized it: "Never before in the history of Southern California jurisprudence have so many good men and true showed willingness — nay anxiety — to serve as jurymen at $3 per day."

WAR OF THE WORLDS

It is hard to overstate how big a deal the Sally Rand assault saga was. For more than a week, a dedicated press corps dutifully filed reports from the courtroom to inform a national audience transfixed by every detail of the trial's proceedings. Readers coast to coast avidly followed the trial like a soap opera via wire service reports in their local papers. The Halloween edition of a paper in Valparaiso, Indiana, placed the story on the front page, above the fold, under the headline "JURORS FLOCK TO SEE DUTY WHEN SALLY GOES TO TRIAL," right next to the bigger news of the day published under a banner headline a full nine lines tall and seven columns wide: "RADIO SKIT PANICS NATION." This, of course, was the account of Orson Welles' legendary dramatization that panicked thousands of gullible listeners into the hysterical belief that the nation was actually under attack by aliens from Mars.

On Monday morning, October 31st, Sally was present and accounted for as questioning of prospective jurors, or "voir dire," began. Sally's attorney elicited their opinions on a public figure's right to privacy, invoking the name of famed aviator Charles Lindbergh, whose infant child's kidnapping and death was still fresh in the public mind. He also called for potential jurors to disclose any prejudice they may have against entertainers dancing in "abbreviated costumes," dismissing those who expressed religious leanings. In turn, Prosecutor David Hoffman excused would-be jurors he considered too broadminded. Sally sat quietly by, dressed elegantly in a fur-trimmed jacket and hat, taking copious notes and brandishing her own single-lens reflex camera with a zoom lens. Ultimately, a jury — styled by the press as "nine elderly women and three uncomfortable males" — was selected.

The trial got underway before Judge C. A. Ballreich on Tuesday, November 1st, with presentation of the plaintiff's case. Hazel Drain, a slender young woman with regular features, wearing a light jacket and a hat topped by several feathers, took the stand first. She explained that she and her escort, Mr. Stanford, had decided to see the show at the Paramount Theater on July 12th, just five minutes before the price increase at 1:00 pm. She said it was their intention to see Miss Rand's dance and also to stay for the feature film *Prison Farm*. She testified that Stanford had his "candid camera" with him and had snapped three pictures of Sally during her fan dance and another three as she performed the bubble dance.

According to Miss Drain's account, they had tried to exit the theater shortly after the film came on the screen. "We started to leave," she said. "I saw Miss Rand come down the aisle in a robe. I shouted to Ray, 'Watch the camera!'" Sally had confronted the couple, she said, demanding that Stanford hand over his camera. He declined. "They argued," she told the jury, adding:

> They fought. They struggled up the aisle. Miss Rand tore the front of Mr. Stanford's shirt. She scratched his neck. She grabbed him by the suspenders. And all the time the rest of the audience was yelling "Down in front." So I tried to get by Miss Rand and Mr. Stanford and get an usher.

> And what happened? Miss Rand grabbed me by the bosom of my sweater and then she bit me on the arm. I cried "Ouch." I tried to break away, but my sweater wouldn't give. Later on, I pulled up my sleeve and saw a bite that was bleeding with teeth marks and it began to get black and blue.

Next, Prosecutor Hoffman entered "Exhibit A" into evidence — a long-sleeved, white, softly woven sweater that Miss Drain claimed to have worn to the theater. On the left sleeve were two large pink smears, about four inches apart: "Rouge from Miss Rand's lips," Miss Drain said. Hoffman then produced "Exhibit B," a glossy 5-by-7-inch photograph of her arm. "That's the bite, all right," she stated. "Around the edges is medicine the doctor put on me. In the middle are the teeth marks Miss Rand put on me."

Though the alleged offense had taken place three and a half months earlier, Hazel still showed faint bruise-like marks on her arm which she claimed had been inflicted by Sally's teeth. Dr. Donald Cass, represented as an expert in such matters, testified regarding Hazel's black and blue bruising.[17] Other witnesses confirmed that they had observed the bruising as well.

---

[17] Dr. Cass would later serve as President of the California Medical Association.

On cross examination, Milton Golden asked Hazel to step down from the witness stand and help him reenact exactly what she claimed had transpired (he played her as the victim and she played Sally Rand). The whole exercise was more confusing than enlightening, and Golden nearly ended up with a bite mark on his own arm before the witness was finally excused.

At that point, Hazel's companion, Mr. C. Ray Stanford was called to the stand. Handsomely attired in a suit and tie with slicked back dark hair, Stanford, introduced as "a farmer who now works in a filling station," testified that he had already taken six photos when an usher tapped him on the shoulder and asked him to desist. Stating that Sally had emerged from the wings in her dressing gown, leapt from the stage and approached him in the aisle, he said that she had snapped his suspenders, torn his shirt, banged his camera on the theater seat, and grabbed his date by her sweater. All this occurred amid cries from the paying customers of "break it up," "pipe down," and "down in front." Finally, he claimed that Sally had pursued them all the way up the aisle, clawing and scratching his neck with her sharp fingernails, and, when they reached a cloakroom off the lobby, had broken open his camera and exposed his film.

A damaged blue shirt, declared to be the one worn by Stanford on the day in question, was introduced into evidence. In an effort to diminish the potency of the evidence, Sally's attorney observed audibly that it "looked like it had just come back from the washtub."

Golden's cross examination set about to establish that Stanford had deliberately situated himself in a side section, up close, in a position where he could catch glimpses of Sally's body. Golden further argued that, although her fans may have been interposed between the dancer and the bulk of her audience, Stanford had chosen his seat with special care, hoping they would afford little barrier between her body and his camera. On the stand, while admitting he had taken some photos, the young man claimed: "... the lights were so low, I tried to shoot while she was not moving fast. She kept swishing her fans. I don't think I caught anything."

A young bank clerk who had witnessed the whole episode testified that seeing Sally's bubble dance wasn't half as exciting as watching the way she treated those folks who had annoyed her. Other witnesses from the audience agreed that it had been a very entertaining commotion, although some did grumble that they didn't get their money's worth, since the episode had detracted from their ability to enjoy the movie they had paid for.

A 1933 photo inscribed to lucky fans "Eddie and Fannie"

Arresting officers Bessie McShane and Harry Costello
pose for the camera with Sally, August 4, 1933

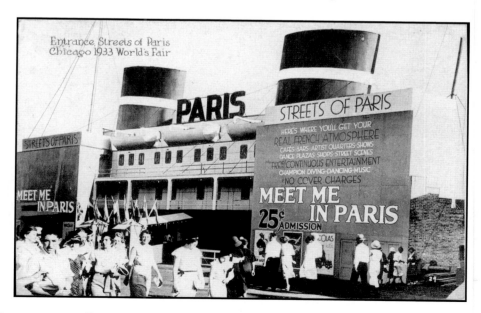

Entrance to Streets of Paris, Century of Progress Exposition, 1933

Sally with George Raft in publicity photo for *Bolero* (1934)

Sally poses with her fiancé, Charles "Chissie" Mayon

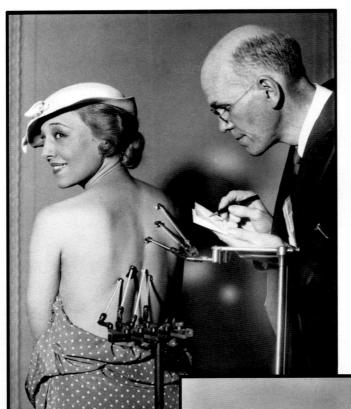

In a 1934 publicity photo, Sally bares her back for examination by Dr. Oakley Smith, founder of the Chicago College of Naprapathy

Mary Belle Spencer's daughters, Victoria and Mary Belle, Jr., as contestants in a 1934 bathing beauty contest

Iconic Sally Rand Bubble Dance photograph—
one of a series of such pictures by "Maurice Seymour"

Sally as "Leda and the Swan"

Sally always loved dogs and she was particularly partial to her little Pekingese companions

Above: Sally as "Tondaleyo" in the 1937 summer stock production of *White Cargo*

Right: Sally as Sadie Thompson in the 1935 stage production of *Rain*

Photo postcard of the exterior of Sally Rand's Ø Nude Ranch
at the 1936 Frontier Centennial in Fort Worth

Souvenir postcard from Sally's Fort Worth Nude Ranch

Faith Bacon went on tour following the Great Lakes Exposition. She appeared in Zanesville, Ohio, on October 29 and 30, 1937.

Sally Rand ads in the *Uniontown Morning Herald*, June 14, 1937 — on the same page with the "Church Announcements"

Sally addresses Harvard Class of 1941
at the annual Freshman Smoker (1938)

Sally performs the Peacock Dance in the film *Sunset Strip Case*
(released in 1938 as *Sunset Murder Case*)

Sally with Michio Ito,
possibly in San Francisco
at the Curran Theatre,
on January 15, 1939

Ray Stanford and Hazel Drain
as they file assault and battery
charges against Sally in 1938

At left: As a publicity stunt, Faith Bacon walks a fawn on Park Avenue, April 23, 1939

Above: A promotional shot of Faith Bacon in a "faun" costume to encourage her employment at the 1939 New York World's Fair

Advertisement for Sally's "Star Studded Revue"
at the Music Box in San Francisco, November 1938

1922 French magazine showing ostrich feather fans as a fashion accouterment

Lola Epp with feather fan in 1927 French magazine

Flo Ash, the "Cutest Little Nudist"

Claire Luce

Thais Giroux

Fay Baker

Ruby Bae — "Federal Fan Dancer No. 1," displays the panties that police in Minneapolis claimed she wasn't wearing

Noel Toy — The "Chinese Sally Rand"

As the day's proceedings drew to a close, Milton Golden announced that Sally would be called to the stand as her own first witness the following morning. He told reporters the camera's clicking had so upset his client that she hadn't been able to fully concentrate on where to hold her fans and bubble. Sally claimed to be distressed by the whole affair, saying: "It is tearing my heart out to have all those people staring at me. It sears my soul. All this is bad publicity."

A pack of press photographers greeted Sally as she emerged from the courtroom. Her mood suddenly elevated, she warmed to the occasion. Offering her three toy balloons and a 10-cent fan, they implored Sally to hold the items while they snapped her picture. "Just a minute boys, until I get fixed," she said, firmly grasping her girdle through her plum-colored skirt and sharply pulling it down. Noticing the surprised reaction of spectators, who apparently regarded the physically fit La Rand as someone who shouldn't require such support, Sally quipped:

> They call this the Great American Gesture. Yanking down the
> girdle, I mean. I don't really need to wear it," she assured them,
> "except to hold up my stockings. That's what I use it for. It doesn't
> make any marks on my legs like garters.

This totally irrelevant incident demonstrates just how compelling the exploits of this pint-sized woman were to a national audience constantly hungry for the latest news of her every move. The next day, the front page of the *Oakland Tribune* carried a "Stop-the-Presses!" story under the headline: "WHATTA SURPRISE! SALLY RAND WEARS GIRDLE INTO L.A. COURT."[18]

When the trial resumed on Wednesday, November 2nd, Defense Attorney Golden opened by asking the judge if he would allow Sally to demonstrate her dances in the courtroom. Looking askance, Judge Ballreich deflated the sanguine expectations of the packed house by denying the request, noting that the case was limited to the complaint of assault and battery, adding: "I fail to see what purpose could be served by Miss Rand dancing in this courtroom, either with or without clothing."

Disappointment was palpable in the court gallery. There would be no skin on display today. Quite the opposite. Sally had appeared each day wearing more clothes than anyone else in the room. On this particular day, she took

---

[18] Such insignificata is what passes as front-page "news" for those whose lives revolve around the lives of others. Just imagine how many Twitter followers Sally might have had!

the stand dressed modestly "in a blue wool dress and a Red Riding Hood cap" to begin offering her version of events.

Sally commanded the complete attention of the jury, described by one reporter as "women, mostly wearing glasses and frowns, and men looking as disinterested as possible under the circumstances." It was her testimony that when she first approached the couple in the front row she had offered to buy the film from Mr. Stanford and had pursued him only after he declined. She confessed "there was a great deal of struggle" after he refused, but stressed that the encounter had not escalated to anything like the melee being alleged.

Describing her bubble dance, Sally explained that her "costume" consisted of talcum powder and grease paint, a smile, and a wavering bubble, the orbit of which she carefully manipulated in the glow of a stage light known in the trade as "No. 37 Moonlight Blue." The dance was also performed behind a see-through gauze curtain designed to further perfect the illusion of her nudity.

Sally testified that, while performing the fan dance, she had heard the click of what seemed to be a camera in the front row. She kept watch out of the corner of her eye and noticed that the photographer only snapped a picture when her fan was moving from one vital position to another. If he had only waited until the fan was in place, it might not have been so bad, but, as it was, Sally was worried that the resulting photos would show her in a lewd and ludicrous light. After finishing her fan dance she had to immediately prepare for the bubble dance, so she had appealed to a house usher to see if someone in the front row was taking pictures with a "candid camera." He hadn't been able to find the culprit.

During her bubble dance, Sally again thought she heard clicking coming from the general vicinity of the front row, disrupting her concentration. It was particularly distracting near the end of her dance, when both she and the 42-inch bubble swung through the air as she dangled precariously by her wrists from an invisible piano wire 40 feet above the stage. She claimed it was at this point that Stanford had poked his camera around the end of the gauze curtain and snapped a photo. It wouldn't have mattered so much had his picture been taken through the translucent curtain. But, she believed, any unfiltered pictures taken from such a low "eccentric angle" could not very well have been meant to capture the beauty of the dance. Rather, Mr. Stanford's actions showed that he was trying to reveal parts of her anatomy in a most unflattering manner. "I was defenseless from that camera," she said. "Imagine!"[19]

Sally admitted that she may have grabbed Mr. Stanford's "galluses," just to get his attention, but she denied clawing or scratching his neck or tearing his shirt. Indeed, as she put it, how could she have scratched anyone, considering that she kept her nails "pared to the quick" so as not to risk breaking her bubble?

Taking off his coat, Sally's attorney cheerfully produced a tangled pair of suspenders from his pocket and began to put them on, intending to allow Sally to snap them to demonstrate just how innocent the whole affair had been. When Golden struggled with the braces, Deputy City Attorney David Hoffman stepped forward to offer his help. The sight of the prosecutor serving as a sort of valet to the defense attorney provoked so much levity in the packed courtroom that the bailiff demanded: "Let's have order here."

Sally and her attorney then thrashed about the courtroom while she clutched his suspenders with her left hand. And, since she was simultaneously holding Miss Drain's sweater with her right hand, Sally attempted to demonstrate that she couldn't very well have bitten the young woman's arm as the trio scuffled up the aisle of the theater.

Addressing the claim that she had bitten Hazel Drain, when shown the sweater with two pink smears four inches apart, Sally countered: "That's much too large to be my mouth. I do not have a mouth like a gorilla." Sally was emphatic: "I definitely did not bite Miss Drain."

To bolster her case, Sally brought out several pots containing different colored makeup creams and showed the jury how she applied them to her lips, using a brush to paint samples of each color on the back of her hand. She disputed the bite charges by pointing out that the colors she used on her lips were all semi-liquid shades of brilliant red so she could not possibly have been responsible for the pink smudge. As Sally continued her meticulous demonstration, Prosecutor Hoffman sat at his counsel table futilely seeking to match the colors in the pots with the smudges on the sweater.

---

[19] We are reminded of the epidemic of so-called "up skirt" photos in our own day. A Google search reveals many such incidents. A curious case in Osceola County, Florida, involved the 2010 arrest of a "well known evangelist" after he allegedly attached a video camera to his shoe, placing his foot in a position to record up a woman's skirt. For an outrageous example, see the YouTube video "Pervert Caught Taking Upskirt Photos at the Grocery Store!"

At one point, Golden even asked Sally to bite the sweater in evidence, which she did. The smudge that was left was red, not pink. Pressed for some alternate explanation for what were claimed to be "bite marks," Sally's attorney went so far as to suggest that during the course of the scuffle Miss Drain may have actually bitten herself.

As Sally rambled on about the nature of her dance and her right to protect herself against invasions of her privacy, the judge warned her more than once against introducing extraneous testimony: "The witness is here to tell just what happened, not to argue the case before the jury." Sally concluded her testimony by maintaining that all she did was give the young couple a "bum's rush" up the aisle to the theater manager's office, where she finally got her hands on the camera and removed the film, exposing it and rendering it useless.

Under cross-examination, Sally charged that Hazel and Ray had threatened her with a lot of bad publicity. As she recalled it, when the three adversaries reached the lobby, Miss Drain had declared emphatically: "This is going to cost you plenty!"

After Sally stepped down from the witness chair, Prosecutor David Hoffman called Miss Drain back to the stand for a single question: "Did you bite yourself?" "No, I didn't," she insisted. Proceedings were thus concluded for the day; the case was essentially ready for closing arguments and motions. Sally announced that, when it was all said and done, she intended to throw a cocktail party: "And if I win the case, I shall invite every member of the jury."

On Thursday, November 3rd, in a morning session lasting less than an hour, opposing counsel offered closing arguments.

The prosecution offered an alternative explanation as to why the plaintiffs had tried to leave the theater in such a hurry. It was not, Hoffman contended, because of any sense of guilt, but rather because they had been startled. "What would you think," he declared, "if Sally Rand came down toward you in her nightgown?" Reacting to the laughter rippling through the courtroom, he corrected himself: "Well, er, bathrobe. I don't care what she wore, would you be startled?" Concluding his rebuttal, he emphasized that Sally Rand was "a public figure" who had no right to bite customers just because they took her picture — dramatically sinking his teeth into the sleeve of Miss Drain's sweater, just in case any of the jurors had failed to appreciate the serious nature of the charge.

In *his* closing argument, Defense Attorney Milton Golden tried to portray Sally in the best light possible, saying: "[She is] just a little girl trying to earn a living at the work she knew best — and how could she do that if folks insisted on taking pictures which made her look indecent and ridiculous?" The judge then issued jury instructions and the panel retired to a private room to deliberate.

Truth be told, Sally had very little chance of prevailing. The misdemeanor of "battery" is technically very easy to commit. In his jury instructions, Judge Ballreich stressed that "if an individual's *person*, even his clothing, has been willfully and forcibly touched by another person, battery has been committed."

Still, Sally had reason to hope that the sheer force of her personal likeability, which had stood her in such good stead so many times before, would once again come to the rescue. Awaiting the verdict in the hallway, Sally's optimism may have been reinforced when she was invited by members of another jury panel to join them for lunch in the Hotel Rosslyn. Always the cheerful mixer, she accepted, saying: "I never turned down a free lunch in my life. Why should I start now?"

Lunchtime came and went. The jurors spent the better part of the day in deliberation, but returned to the courtroom at 4:00 p.m. prepared to deliver a unanimous verdict. Obviously unimpressed with Sally's explanation, they found her guilty on two counts of assault. After receiving the verdict, the judge dismissed the jury, congratulating them for being "beauty proof."

Sentencing would be on the following Monday. With the maximum penalty being a jail sentence of 180 days and a $500 fine on each count, Sally was looking at the possibility of nearly a year in a California jail. Defense Attorney Golden promptly announced his intention to file an appeal in "an effort to determine a precedent in the matter of privacy for public persons."

In the meantime, Sally was allowed to go free on $1,000 bond. Her business concluded for the day, she approached Miss Drain offering her a sweater to replace the one that was defaced, as Sally put it, not in the theater but in the witness box. Miss Drain smiled, but refused the gift.

Whatever the sentence, Sally told the press, she intended to appeal the verdict — and appeal it again, if necessary:

> I want to find out for all time how much privacy I have a right to expect. There are many conflicting opinions on this right, insofar as it affects public figures, and it's about time the issue is settled.

Four days later a new week commenced, but not in the way Sally would have preferred. Judge Ballreich denied her attorney's appeal for a new trial, pronouncing:

> There can be no privacy in that which is already public. Even if Miss Rand had been taking a bath before an audience that had paid admission, there would be no violation of her right of privacy if someone came in and took a picture. She was giving a public exhibition of herself in an artistic dance when the pictures that caused the trouble were taken. Taking a picture is not a crime.
> A person can protest against the taking of pictures, but within the law, they cannot use force.

Defense Attorney Golden vigorously disagreed. Branding Ray Stanford as a "Peeping Tom," he declared that even public figures are entitled to an appropriate right of privacy. Anticipating the worst, Sally was seen wiping wet mascara from her eyes as charcoal stained tears streamed down her cheeks. Her fears were largely alleviated, though, when Judge Ballreich fined her only $100 ($50 on each count) and, more importantly, spared her the indignity of going to jail. She promptly produced the $100 from her purse, snapped it closed and spoke to the assembled press:

> I am well enough satisfied. I think the court was very fair. Very few persons know that just grabbing a person constitutes battery.
> I didn't, but I do now. But what burns me up is that apparently I'm to have no such thing as privacy. It's the loss of that rather than the loss of $100 that hurts.

Always the sport, having wagered that she would stand on her head if the jury went against her, she did just that. A photo of Sally balanced on her head was wired to papers across the country. She followed through with the promised cocktail party as well, but the guest list may have been limited to press hawks. The jurors were not invited.[20]

As a side note, you may think it unusual for a jury in 1938 to consist of nine women and only three men. You would be right. Even though the 19th

---

[20] Over the years many other cases have involved celebrities who took umbrage at the actions of aggressive photographers and even smashed their cameras. In recent years, Sean Penn, Woody Harrelson, Alec Baldwin, and Russell Brand (among others) have been involved in aggressive confrontations with unwelcome photographers. And, contrary to what you might think, it is not always the celebrity who is held to account. Indeed, Los Angeles Defense Attorney Stephen G. Rodriguez has a webpage on the Internet touting his services in this regard: "If you are facing charges in an assault involving the paparazzi, contact our Los Angeles defense lawyers ... for a free and confidential consultation to discuss your rights."

Amendment to the U.S. Constitution had granted women the right to vote in 1920, that didn't mean that women also had the right to sit on a jury.

The campaign to secure jury rights for women in Illinois was led by Chicago attorney Grace H. Harte, who had some observations of her own about the Sally Rand "candid camera" case:

> Imagine a jury of men in Illinois finding Sally Rand guilty. In some states, especially Illinois, it has been difficult for men juries to convict a pretty woman, even of murder, but evidence shows that women jurors are not so susceptible to an Adonis on trial.
>
> Women have the courage to acquit or convict, if they believe the facts warrant. They may cry, as did the women on the jury that sent Bruno Hauptmann to the electric chair for the kidnapping of the Lindbergh baby, but they've got the courage of their convictions.

JURY RIGHTS FOR WOMEN

Some states like California were proactive on the issue. Three years before the 19th Amendment was ratified in 1920, the California Assembly passed the "Women's Jury Bill" specifically granting women the right to sit on juries. However, in 1938 many states were still denying women the right to serve, including the State of Illinois, where Sally had been such a hit at the World's Fair. It wasn't until May of 1939 that the Illinois State Legislature qualified women for jury service, even then becoming only the 25th state to do so.

Thus, the much-publicized Sally Rand assault and battery case was finally brought to an end. While a penalty had been exacted in criminal court, Sally was not yet off the hook. She had been found guilty and had paid her fine, but she had not yet seen the last of Hazel Drain and Ray Stanford. Their civil suit seeking $2,622.70 in damages was still pending and had been scheduled for trial on February 3rd, just three months hence.

No sooner had Sally begun to catch her breath than she was handed a Superior Court subpoena on November 15th demanding that she submit to a deposition the following week in response to the lawsuit filed by Faith Bacon. Whatever else was going on, Sally's attorneys were certainly piling up billable hours. Still, her life was quite tranquil compared to the lives of a community halfway around the world in Germany.

About a week before, on the evening of November 9, 1938, in an event forever infamous as "Kristallnacht," or "The Night of Broken Glass,"

Adolph Hitler's storm troops, abetted by rioting mobs, had burned and looted hundreds of Jewish synagogues, businesses, and homes all over Germany, Austria, and other areas controlled by the Nazi regime. Private properties were ransacked; shop windows were shattered; Jewish citizens were beaten, raped, arrested, and murdered — while the authorities stood by, seemingly at ease. When horrific accounts of all the mayhem appeared on the front pages of American papers the next morning, they shared space with stories on preparations for the annual observance of Armistice Day on November 11th, the day that the First World War had ended in Europe exactly 20 years before. In Alameda County, California, the *Hayward Daily Review* carried the unintentionally double-edged headline: "ILLUMINATED NIGHT PARADE IS HIGH SPOT OF LOCAL FESTIVITIES."

Faith

Sally appeared before Miss Bacon's attorney in Los Angeles on Monday, November 21st, to submit to a deposition. A portion of their colloquy illustrates Sally's disinclination to cooperate:

Attorney: How long have you been performing as a nudist?

Sally (Indignantly): As a *what*?

Attorney: As a fan dancer then.

Sally: I have never performed as a fan dancer. I am a ballet dancer.

Attorney: In your ballet dancing, do you use a fan?

Sally: I use two fans.

Attorney: And do you dance in the nude, protected only by the fans?

Sally: You come and see the dance performed and see for yourself.

The Bacon-Rand brouhaha achieved what may have been its purpose all along, that is to say, to raise the celebrity profile of Faith Bacon. Miss Bacon's career was nowhere near the level she desired. Yes, she had landed a small role in a small film — *Prison Train*, hurriedly shot and released just two weeks before she filed her suit — but she could hardly have been unaware that Sally was starring in a similarly low-budget film scheduled for release on November 11th (and already the subject of considerable buzz over its controversial title and dance sequences).[21]

---

[21] Whatever potential Faith may have had as a presence on the silver screen is totally wasted in this film. She does deliver a couple of lines, but her awkward time on screen as "Maxine" is limited to little more than 30 seconds.

In December of 1938, Sally had flown into San Francisco, reportedly loaded with baggage tipping the scales at more than 50 pounds over the maximum allowed. Four days before Christmas, she was occupied with preparations for the opening of a new Bay Area club. Taking advantage of a publicity opportunity, she was photographed hamming it up with a trio of her showgirls and Native American Indian Chief Fred Johnson ("Pun Gin Gano," member of the Concow-Maidu Tribe of northern California). He had reportedly gotten "lost in San Francisco on his way to a pow wow" and found his way instead to Sally's "paleface whoopee wigwam." At this same time, across the country in Roxbury, New York, Sally's namesake Helen Gould Shepard died in her summer home at the age of 71.

Although others commonly referred to Sally as a "stripper" or burlesque queen, she always regarded herself as nothing less than a serious artist. On January 15, 1939, she had the rare opportunity to participate in what even the media described as a highbrow event — headlining a benefit concert at the Curran Theatre in San Francisco. There, Sally would share top billing in a classical recital with Michio Ito, the acclaimed Japanese dancer and choreographer of her peacock dance. The refined event was staged for the purpose of raising funds to subsidize a San Francisco dance repertory group that Ito was slated to direct.

There would be no carnival-style barkers for *this* show. Au contraire. Sally sent out formal invitations on fancy peach-colored stationery, announcing: "You will not only be given an extraordinary opportunity to see an unusually interesting and varied program of dance, but it will prove an added inspiration to the artists."

Speaking at the apron of the stage before the curtain lifted, Sally solemnly described the purpose of the dance group, as she saw it, with the alarming winds of war in Europe and Asia in mind: "The world needs dancing now, even if only as a retreat into fantasy from the ills we suffer."

In her first number, Sally presented "an illusion of bucolic loveliness" as the "Little Shepherdess" — with staff in hand and wearing a blue ribbon in her hair— dancing to the accompaniment of Claude Debussy's "The Little Shepherd." She also performed a choreographed interpretation of the "White Peacock," music by American composer Charles Tomlinson Griffes. Next, attired in a "flowing blue chiffon dress that was diaphanous but decorous," she executed a "concert version" of her bubble dance.[22] And, finally, concluding her part in the program, Sally appeared with Mr. Ito in a performance of his famous "Persian Fantasy."

A wire service reporter offered modest praise: "Although no Pavlova, Miss Rand proved graceful and gracious in three solos and a duet with Ito," while a local music critic declared that "she was altogether captivating in the 'Persian Fantasy' with Ito, making a decidedly pretty, graceful and rhythmical dancing figurine."

The civil lawsuit's February hearing date came and went as Sally juggled a myriad of affairs. Miss Drain and Mr. Stanford persevered in a state of uncompensated humiliation while waiting for their civil case to be heard. But, once Sally had been convicted of the criminal offense of assault and battery, they felt emboldened in the pursuit of their civil claim for damages. So much so, in fact, that on March 1st, they amended their pleading to include as defendants the producers of the show, the operators of the Paramount, and several theater employees as well.

Upon further reflection (and advice from their attorney, no doubt), the pair had also came to understand that the pain and suffering Sally had inflicted was far greater than they had previously realized. Declaring that she had been "struck, beat, hit, bit, scratched and chewed," Miss Drain *now* felt that, rather than $2,622 in damages, $75,050 might be a more suitable amount to salve her wounds and relieve her shame. Mr. Stanford, similarly enlightened, sought $75,697 (the modest difference was due to the loss of his camera among other incidentals).[23]

Adding insult to injury, on this very same March 1st, Sally received the unsettling news that The Music Box, her club in San Francisco, was one of 15 area clubs to be slapped with a five-day suspension of its liquor license for selling drinks after 2 a.m. Most of the other clubs announced they

---

[22] Longtime *San Francisco Chronicle* critic Alfred Victor Frankenstein took note: "To review Sally Rand without the bubble dance would be 'Hamlet' without Hamlet ... and the *Chronicle's* coverage is nothing if not complete. Unfortunately, Miss Rand's coverage was also complete during the bubble dance last night, although her 'White Peacock' ... had partly given the customers what they came for. The bubble dance presented the lady in long gown posing and posturing with a large balloon that was a trifle hard to handle, while a piano and violin made horrible hash of real classical music."

[23] This was quite a boost from their original suit for damages equivalent to $45,000 today. In current terms, they were raising their "ask" for damages to more than $2.5 million.

would stay open and invite customers to bring their own liquor. The Music Box remained open as well, serving soda pop to its patrons.

On the same day, far across the dark fields of the republic in New York City, Billy Rose announced that he was filing suit against Sally for infringing on his exclusive right to use the name "Sally Rand's Nude Ranch." But how could Billy Rose have a greater right to use Sally's name than she herself did? Now that's a poser.

In recent months, Sally had appeared in several courtrooms, a new film, and a program of classical dance. Were there any frontiers left for the former silent film star, vaudevillian, and savior of the World's Fair to conquer? Well, she had yet to appear in wax. On March 24th, Paramount Studios reportedly approached Sally with the suggestion that her wax figure would be a nice addition to a grouping planned for a museum scene in the 1939 film *Some Like It Hot*, to be set on the Atlantic City Boardwalk and starring her old pal Bob Hope as a glib sideshow barker.[24]

While initially receptive to the idea, Sally balked when it became clear that the other figures in the group were to be Romeo and Juliet, Antony and Cleopatra, and Pierrot and Pierrette. In a telegram to the studio from San Francisco, she declined: "Those people are all dead. I wouldn't mind being in with some live ones, but I don't want to be the only live person in a bunch of deadies."

For much of the past year, Sally had been bouncing from one court to another like the little silver ball in a pinball machine. On the plus side, as Faith Bacon's star was on the rise again, her lawsuit — which, after all, may have been nothing more than a publicity stunt — quietly went away.

On March 31st, Sally filed her formal answer to the civil assault charges. All of the now familiar theories of privacy or lack thereof, and the propriety or improprieties of Sally's actions, were regurgitated. The plaintiffs were seemingly confidant that their greatly inflated demand for damages was justified since Miss Drain's humiliation had allegedly caused her to suffer a "severe nervous shock."

Sally argued that even a person who dances behind fans and bubbles should have a right to some level of privacy. Her attorney reasserted that Stanford's

---

[24]   This movie — based on "The Great Magoo," a play by Ben Hecht and Gene Fowler — also starred Shirley Ross and Gene Krupa. It has no relation to the highly-acclaimed film by the same title directed by Billy Wilder and released 20 years later.

pictures — taken from the floor at an angle calculated to crudely capture her nude image — were intended to "degrade, debase and libel her" and were certainly "not intended to be photographs depicting Miss Rand's dance."

Having wrangled over the same issues for more than eight months, Sally was keen to get on with her life. In fact, on the very day before submitting her answer to the court, she had filed papers at the State Capital in Sacramento to incorporate herself as "Sally Rand Enterprises."

Shortly thereafter, for reasons now lost in the fog of time, the civil case brought by Miss Drain and Mr. Stanford stalled and was never resumed. On January 22, 1945, at which point the litigation had been pending for more than five years, a superior court judge in Los Angeles dismissed the case, ruling that the time for trial had expired.[25]

---

[25] It may well be that Drain and Stanford got cold feet, concerned that they would be on the hook for significant legal fees in the event they did not prevail.

CHAPTER FIFTEEN

Treasure Island

I didn't create my bubble dance for nothing. I know that
what goes up must come down, but also that it's likely to
come up again if it's buoyant enough.

~ Sally Rand, 1939

L ife on the road will take a toll on anyone, even a trouper with the
stamina of a Sally Rand. And so, back in November 1938, when the
opportunity for a somewhat more permanent situation had presented itself
in San Francisco, Sally jumped at the chance to settle down for a while.
Entering into a financial arrangement with the owner of The Music Box,[1]
she was given full reign to produce and stage her own show. She began
taking steps to mount a large-scale "Star Studded Revue" featuring a cast
of 16 performers and dancers, plus herself. The headliners would be actor
and vaudevillian Alan Carney, along with Dora Maugham — that "bad,
bad woman"— a sharp-tongued comedienne who had worked with Sally
many times over the years. Among a personal staff of nine, Sally had also
installed her ex-fiancé Chissie Mayon as technical director and her mother,
Annette Kisling, as wardrobe mistress.

On opening night, patrons noticed that their shirt collars, fingernails and
teeth were glowing in the dark. The club's promotional flyer, "Music Box
Notes" (subtitled "An irrelevant nude's paper published at random") claimed
that the innovative venue was "the only night club or theater cafe in the
country equipped with the fluorescent or black lights that create such extraordinary effects in the dance numbers." As for her own appearances, Sally
performed the fan dance and the bubble dance, as well as her new "white
peacock dance" — the routine that had been created for her appearance in
the *Sunset Strip* movie.

---

[1]   A dinner theater located in the Tenderloin District, the venue is still in operation
today as the Great American Music Hall at 859 O'Farrell Street.

In December, Sally's custom-designed Christmas card called attention to a coastal rivalry between the San Francisco Bay area and metropolitan New York City. The cover illustration depicted a totally nude Sally, with legs extended, leaping across a map of the USA with an ostrich feather fan in each outstretched hand. She looks back over her left shoulder in the direction of her right toe which touches an image of the future 1939 World's Fair in New York City as her left toe points to the upcoming Golden Gate International Exposition in Frisco. Just as there had been two competing fairs in Texas three years earlier, the east and west coasts of the country were vying to host the premiere exposition of 1939.

The Golden Gate International Exposition opened on "Treasure Island" in San Francisco Bay on February 18th, and Sally Rand's Nude Ranch quickly established itself as the most popular attraction on the grounds. Press reports credited the Nude Ranch with attracting 55,449 cash customers in its first week, more than twice the draw of the next most popular concession.

All the same, after just one day of operation, square-jawed Police Captain John O'Meara announced that he had received "many complaints" from parents that minors were being allowed into the Nude Ranch and that some of the cowgirls had been intoxicated. (A follow-up investigation found no minors and concluded that everything seemed to be in order. Still, Sally had been put on notice.) Her jousting with Captain O'Meara would continue as the weeks went by. In late April, she would again attempt to assuage his concerns by having her ranch hands wear brassieres — described in the papers as looking "like they were made of tennis netting." Sally said she hoped this conciliation would "meet [their] specifications without driving people away."

Back east, the 1939 New York World's Fair, to be held on 1,200 acres at Flushing Meadows, was expected to be the grandest and most expansive fair since St. Louis's Louisiana Purchase Exposition in the year of Sally's birth. The big fair wasn't scheduled to open until April 30th and, with the acclaim of four "world fairs" already in her back pocket, Sally saw no reason why she shouldn't have a presence in New York as well. It seemed only natural that she would be invited. But, as we know, seeming does not always make it so.

Grover Whalen, Grand Poobah of the New York Fair, had declared:

> The New York World's Fair seeks to be remembered for its bold
> treatment of today's problems and for its pathfinding to the world
> of tomorrow. It is not to be the vehicle for some unclothed young
> lady to publicize herself to the world…. There may be Sally Rands

or dozens of Sally Rands. But we will not permit any dancer, nude
or otherwise, to dominate the fair. If she does, out she goes.

The director for the San Francisco event, Harris Connick, was far more
welcoming: "She's a great little business woman. We'd like to have her with
us in any capacity."

History indicated that Sally's presence would provide a major financial boost
to either expo. The Nude Ranch was already up and running on Treasure
Island, but the question remained: Where would Sally herself land? She had
a financial interest in The Music Box and was comfortably ensconced in a
penthouse apartment on the 26th floor of the Empire Hotel, so, as a "home
girl," Bay Area locals had reason to believe they had an edge.

Back in New York, another player was putting his thumb on the scales. Billy
Rose was bringing his "Aquacade" attraction to New York, an extravaganza
that would star the former Olympic swimming champion, Eleanor Holm.
He didn't care to have any competition at the box office from Sally Rand.

Even so, a different group of sponsors in New York remained boosters for
including her in some capacity or other. Responding to their encouragement,
Sally packed up pictures of her Nude Ranch girls, along with blueprints of
the Treasure Island concession, and took an overnight flight to New York to
meet with Grover Whalen on Monday, February 27th. She hoped to open a
second Nude Ranch as part of the Expo, but only on her own terms. If the
New York group would promise that her troupe wouldn't be raided,
required to put on more clothes, or otherwise harassed by the law — Okay.
In other words, take it or leave it, and "positively no brassieres."

Billy Rose was staunchly opposed. And merely keeping Sally out of town
was not severe enough for him. After her negotiations with fair officials
ended inconclusively, she prepared to return to San Francisco, but at the
airport, she was met by a process server, courtesy of Mr. Rose. He had filed a
plagiarism suit against Sally, charging that the operation of her Nude Ranch
at the Golden Gate Exposition constituted an infringement of *his* exclusive
right to operate any attraction based on his original concept. In other words,
Rose claimed that the whole idea as presented in Fort Worth had been his
alone and, consequently, he — not *she* — had the sole right to its name.

Escalating Rose's "let's poke Sally with a stick" campaign, Eleanor Holm,
whom just the year before Sally had included in her list of "10 best undressed
women," challenged Sally to a "curve-and-contour contest" to resolve a
burning question: Which of them would be the fairest attraction at the
upcoming New York World's Fair? "The tape measure will tell the bare
truth," the shapely Miss Holm had declared.

According to press reports, Eleanor had said: "This is to be a streamlined fair and Sally undoubtedly knows I can appear in daylight and don't need two 24-foot fans to hide my figure." Eleanor announced that her bathing suit maker was working off a set of measurements that included "Bust 34 inches, waist 24, hips 33, thigh 16." Although Sally's measurements were not readily available, her costume designer, Jule Lowe revealed that Sally "always has to have [her dresses] taken in at the waist. She is the dressmaker's dream."

By the first week of March, it was becoming clear that Sally probably wasn't going to be granted a spot in New York. Humorist Cal Tinney's lengthy column styled as a "letter to Grover Whalen," began: "I take my pen in hand to console you in your dark hour when it is brought more and more home to you that nobody can put on a World's fair in the United States without Sally Rand."

In the end, Sally was foreclosed from appearing at the 1939 World's Fair in New York. But, as had proven to be the case with each and every one of its recent predecessors, it wasn't long before a lack of activity at the cash registers compelled the sponsors to relax their high-minded intentions and bow to the foolish proclivities of the masses.

Faith

Also aware of the upcoming World's Fair in New York City, Faith Bacon had been plying her trade more or less out of the national spotlight. During a February 1939 booking at the Crawford House on Scollay Square in Boston where she was performing the fan dance and something she called the "Orchid Dance," an interviewer from the *Harvard Crimson* reminded her of Sally's appearance at Harvard's freshman smoker some nine months earlier. Faith reacted to the interviewer's unspoken implication:

> I would like to come to Harvard, but some of the less liberal
> minded professors might object. I would not come the way Sally
> Rand did and simply lecture. I would dance for them. I would
> dance the "L'Apres-midi d'un Faune" if they only could get me a
> symphony orchestra.

The amusements area (or "Midway") of the Golden Gate International Exposition was designated as the "Gayway" — a title not likely to be used again any time soon.[2] The Gayway covered 40 of the island's 400 acres and, along with Sally's Nude Ranch, included over 50 attractions, among them: Ripley's *Believe It or Not!*, a deep sea diving bell, Paris after Midnight, a

---

2   The name was chosen in a contest with more than 500,000 participants and fifty
     judges. The runner-up was "El Camino" and the third choice was "Fundorado."

monkey race track, the Midget Village, the ever-popular Incubator Babies, and something called "Virgins in Cellophane." Also trotted out was the famous "Stella" ("Have You Seen Stella?"), a large painting of a voluptuous reclining nude who, due to the operation of a simple mechanism behind the painting, seemed to be breathing.[3]

Sally wrote the introduction to the official program for the Nude Ranch, boasting: "We've got some mighty fine calves and white face heifers." The program's 35 photographs suggested that the gals actually were more or less nude as they played badminton, petted and fed the sheep and burros, twirled lassoes, and tossed horseshoes or basketballs. As had been the case in Fort Worth, the Nude Ranch was not a place that you could just enter and hang out. Plate glass partitions separated visitors from the 20 cowgirls, and patrons were expected to pass through a 60-foot long corridor in an orderly, if firmly focused, manner. Of course, some of the more fixated were inclined to linger. One young man recalls seeing his father and cousin emerge from the ranch cracking up with laughter. Apparently they had come across an older man, camped out on the railing, examining the girls through a pair of binoculars.[4]

Predictably, some visitors to the ranch were delighted, while others were appalled.[5] Actor Roland Young's reaction was particularly clever. After 10 minutes of watching two scantily attired "ranch hands" playing ping-pong, he turned to a friend and said: "What's the score?"

---

[3]   The original "Stella" was first shown at the Columbian Exposition in 1893. When it appeared at San Francisco's Panama-Pacific International Exposition in 1915, Stella was said to have been viewed by 750,000 patrons who paid 10 cents apiece to see her. One of the fair's top attractions, Stella raked in $75,000" (or about $1,750,000 today).

[4]   Yet another older gentleman had an interest in such goings on. In March 1939, when Sally's father retired from his job in Kansas City after 32 years as an employee of the post office department, William Beck was quoted in the press as saying that he was making plans to visit his daughter's "nude ranch" in San Francisco.

[5]   Anton LaVey's biographer tells of the time the Church of Satan's founder visited the nude ranch: "Though he was just a schoolboy, he dressed in adult-looking hats and jackets — no one questioned why he was allowed to roam about the fair alone. In Sally Rand's Nude Ranch ... he stood watching the topless cowgirls spin lariats and pitch horseshoes for at least 20 minutes before anyone showed him the door. 'I guess they thought I was a midget.' A slightly older friend pulled the same thing and got away with it, but unexpectedly spied his bare-ass Sunday School teacher among the girls. LaVey claimed that moment as his Christian disillusionment and Satanic epiphany."

When the popular columnist Ernie Pyle visited, he had nothing but praise for
Sally as a business woman, but was underwhelmed by the "ranch" itself:

> Two spielers and two pretty girls stand out on the front porch ...
> The spieler is wonderful. He goes through a 10-minute harangue.
> He gets a crowd. He says don't get the idea they are giving
> Sunday School lessons inside. He gets everybody all worked up.
> And then he throws down the bars and says, "Let's all go in." It
> costs two-bits.
>
> It's the silliest thing I've ever seen. I conducted thorough researches
> and I couldn't find a passion in a whole chuckwagon load of Sally's
> girls. Mostly they are tall and lanky and mope around as if they
> didn't know where they were.... Each girl wears cowboy boots, a
> revolver, and a scarf around her neck. That sounds pretty good, but
> of course it depends on who it is that doesn't have on any clothes.
> I can't truthfully report that there are actually any hags, crones or
> witches in the bunch; but, as somebody said, they don't need any
> glass window for protection.
>
> There isn't a show or anything. Some girls just sit on the porch
> fixing their nails. A couple of others toss a basketball.... Two are
> absent mindedly heckling a ping pong table. There's a burro tied in
> the background. Why, it was so drab I felt like taking off my shirt
> and getting in there myself. The sight of me with nothing on but
> shoes would at least scare people....

The humorous Ernie Pyle called it as he saw it, but even Sally was concerned
that some of her girls had a marked propensity toward procrastination and
sloth. Jerry Bundsen, who served as Sally's publicity agent in San Francisco,
recalled:

> Sally would get up on the balcony where the patrons couldn't see
> her or hear her and she'd yell to the girls: "Come on Nadine. Get
> over there and jump more, will you? And Helen, for God's sake,
> get up off your duff and walk over and bend down to pick the
> basketballs up." She used to stand up there like a maestro
> running an orchestra.
>
> My wife was with me one day when I went to see Sally on
> business. We were waiting by her dressing room and she opened
> the door and came out flat ass naked and said, "Come in Jerry. I
> want to talk to you about those ads." My wife almost fell over.
> After I came out of the dressing room I had to convince her it was

like being in the bedroom with your Aunt Emma getting dressed or something. You never paid attention to her at all.

Recalling that the setup for the Nude Ranch exhibit included a number of little burros, George Hubbard, who had worked at the fair, once mused about the barker outside the attraction yelling: "Come and see Sally Rand's ass!"

The World's Fair in New York was considered to be a big deal. The state had even issued special license plates that read "New York World's Fair 1939." But Californians considered the Golden Gate International Exposition to be a pretty big deal as well. Not to be outdone, the state issued its own special license plates topped with the caption: "California World's Fair 39."

As is often the case, some people didn't like it. Indeed, Patrick F. Kirby refused to display his 1939 California tags, claiming that, by affixing the plates to his automobile, not only would he be advertising the fair, but he would also be indirectly promoting Sally Rand's Nude Ranch — a circumstance he considered morally reprehensible. Kirby was promptly convicted of violating the state motor vehicle code, but he was soon vindicated when his conviction was reversed on appeal. Appellate Judge B. Rey Schauer found that the state had no more authority to require Kirby to advertise the fair "than it had to compel him to carry a banner or make speeches advertising the climate, prunes or a political party."

Faith

Sally may have been shut out in New York and Billy Rose may have been a smash with his "Aquacade" water show, but that didn't mean there wasn't still room at the fair for a nude or two.

Despite Grover Whalen's insistence that a high class enterprise like the 1939 World's Fair in New York didn't need fan dancers or anything else of that sort, a spokesman soon came forward to clarify the sponsors' policy with a bit of backtracking:

> The idea is that, while the New York fair is going to have plenty
> of amusements, these will not be permitted to submerge the arts
> and crafts. In other words, one single dancer who happens to be
> highly publicized is not going to be allowed to steal the show
> from all that is really worthwhile. There will not be any one fan
> dancer, such as Sally Rand was in Chicago. There may, however,
> be fifty fan dancers, and if one of them happens to catch the
> public fancy — well, there you are.

Responding to these words of encouragement, Faith and her publicist Lou Straus decided it was time for the "original" fan dancer to make her move. Sally had demonstrated that getting arrested for indecency produced better publicity than any promotion she could pay for, so Faith set about doing just that. Two weeks before the fair's opening, appearing with her 20 "Sun-kissed Rancherettes" at the Tower Theater in Lowell, Massachusetts, Faith had been instructed by management to cover herself well enough to remain within the constraints of the law. This she did begrudgingly — that is, until her last show.

John Daley, stage manager at the Tower Theater, claimed that Faith had "put it over" on them. He maintained that right before her final performance, she had come from her dressing room wearing a robe, as usual. Only after Faith had cast her wrap aside and stepped into the spotlight did Daley become aware that she was definitely not clad in the tights she had been ordered to wear.

Two police officers were in the audience, but neither they nor Mr. Daley felt disposed to interrupt the act, fearing they would turn the packed house into an angry mob. "She would have scratched my eyes out if I interfered with her," Daley declared, adding that he had seen several instances of Miss Bacon's temper.

After the curtain fell, Faith managed to beat it out of town and the Tower Theater suffered a two-day suspension for "allowing an indecent performance." Her act had produced the profile-raising publicity she had hoped for, just as the New York Fair was about to open its gates.

Pleased with the flap they had created in Lowell, Faith's publicist devised a plan to keep the ball rolling. Straus's strategy, based on the phrase "From the Fan Dance to the Fawn Dance," was for Faith to literally stop traffic on Park Avenue and spur the constabulary into action by parading around in a skimpy outfit while walking a fawn as though it were a pet on a leash.

But, first, Straus had to find an actual fawn. With the help of Frank "Bring 'em Back Alive" Buck, he located a woodsman in Hoosick Falls, New York, who claimed he could easily catch one in the woods and have it delivered to the Ben Hur Stables in Manhattan, a facility that regularly housed animals appearing in Broadway shows.

With Straus's plot in place, Faith Bacon emerged from her apartment on a chilly April 23rd, wearing a floor-length, translucent chiffon Grecian arrangement that left plenty of room for the exposure of her arms and legs (and even a bit more when the wind blew). Several "autumn leaves" were attached to her costume and legs in an apparent attempt to mimic the ancient Greek forest goddess known as a "faun." Crimson toenails and Grecian sandals completed the ensemble. Straus and the stableman who had brought the terrified fawn to the scene in a taxi were waiting for her, along with a cadre of press photographers and one newsreel truck.

As a crowd began to gather, Straus sent his fellow press agent, Irwin Zeltner, into a hotel lobby to call the police and report an undressed woman walking a deer at Park Avenue and 38th Street. A squad car or two finally did arrive but, sensing that the whole affair was a publicity stunt, the officers refused to cooperate. While everybody waited for something to happen, the stableman, Eddie "Fearless" Fills, was having trouble controlling the terrified fawn. As it bucked and strained against its leash, even tearing Eddie's clothing, the poor animal was thrown to the pavement several times while Fills valiantly struggled to arrange suitable photo opportunities.

Having milled around for an hour, the pack of newsmen and 100 or so onlookers was finally broken up by the police for blocking the sidewalk. Several people, along with Miss Bacon, were charged with disorderly conduct. An agent from the Society for the Prevention of Cruelty to Animals arrived to take the fawn away.

The scene at the police station was described by the *New York Times*:

> "What in the name of thunderation is this!" exclaimed Lieutenant Joseph Gross yesterday as he peered over the top of his desk in the East Thirty-fifth Street station and beheld a slim, blonde young woman attired in the flimsy costume of a Grecian dancer, flanked by a sergeant, four patrolmen, a group of photographers and reporters and four publicity men.
>
> "She wants publicity and she is under arrest," retorted Sergeant Joseph Holbert, pointing to the young woman, who was trying to look coy and indignant.
>
> "Why," interrupted the small voice of the prisoner, "I was taking my fawn for a walk up Park Avenue to my rehearsal, and they —"
>
> "You got any clothes?" interrupted Lieutenant Gross.

After responding to a few more probing questions, Faith was charged with "causing a crowd to collect." The police station colloquy ended with Lieutenant Gross observing:

> So you're a terpsichorean artist. You probably engineered the arrest for a very obvious purpose. Anyway, I think you're a nicer girl than

Sally Rand. You know, this stuff is O.K. at the World's Fair but not on Park Avenue. Five hundred dollars bail.

To cover her bail, Faith surrendered a ring supposedly worth $10,000. The charges were later dropped when she cooed to the magistrate that she was an "interpretive dancer" at the World's Fair and promised that it had never been her intention to cause a disturbance. Her ring was returned, her picture with the fawn appeared in papers across the country, and Miss Bacon advanced to a prominent position at the fair. Mission accomplished.[6]

Faith Bacon's "Afternoon of the Fawn" dance was the featured attraction at the Congress of Beauty concession, described by *LIFE Magazine* as a condensed musical show featuring Faith, Della Carroll (with her "Rose Dance"), and 45 undressed showgirls, performing in a tent that was much too hot inside.[7] One press account characterized Faith's costume as "a wisp of tulle and a huntsman's cap." Interest was so great that, several days before the fair was scheduled to open, a rehearsal of Faith's fawn dance was crashed by 500 irrepressible young men. Struggling to restrain them, guards later reported that the men were shouting: "We came to see this and we're gonna see it."

Once again following Sally's example, Faith did double duty, appearing not only at the fair, but also with her *Bare X Ranch Revue* across the Hudson River at Ben Marden's famous Riviera Club atop the Palisades cliffs in Fort Lee, New Jersey. For this engagement, Faith performed her "Gardenia Dance" (sometimes upgraded to an "Orchid Dance") that consisted mostly of the teasing removal of flowers from strategic areas. You can pretty much figure out the details.

All this activity went a long way toward revitalizing Faith Bacon's career. After the fair closed, she signed a contract to tour in a show called the *Hollywood Oomph Revue* in which she would share top billing

---

[6]   Nearly 50 years later on December 6, 1988, on Fifth Avenue between 56th and 57th Streets, a few blocks north of Faith's stunt, another enterprising publicity agent arranged for the winner of a Mikhail Gorbachev lookalike contest to emerge from a limousine, plunge into the crowd and begin shaking hands. Among those who fell for the stunt was a flamboyant real estate mogul who, along with his bodyguards, had pushed his way through the crowd to greet the "Soviet leader." Thirty years later, as President of the United States, his enthusiasm for Russian leaders would remain unabated.

[7]   Among the other headliners on the nude or near-nude menu was Rosita Royce with her "Doves of Peace" dance, wherein a covey of seven live doves carried out the task of disrobing their mistress. There was also a variation on this theme, Yvette Dare's "Dawn Dance of Bali," in which the stripping was attended to by a "strikingly colored" parrot. Even John Ringling North (of circus fame) got into the act with his "Cavalcade of the Centaurs," a widely panned horse show that paraded 16 Lady Godivas clad in "little more than their own tresses."

with "the streamlined mistress of modern melody," Rita Rio and her NBC All-Girl Orchestra.

As had happened in Fort Worth, Billy Rose's "Aquacade" swimming and diving show became the most popular entertainment attraction at the New York Fair. Along with dozens of talented bathing beauties, Rose had managed to lure Johnny "Tarzan" Weissmuller to perform a swimming duet with the show's star (and future Mrs. Rose), Eleanor Holm. One of every six visitors to the fair paid anywhere from 40 to 99 cents (from $7 to $16 today) to see the attraction.[8] Even so, many customers had a few coins left over to attend the less respectable concessions, as columnist Jack Stinnett observed:

> The entertainment zone, born under the stern announcement that there would be no nudity, has developed into the greatest presentation of undraped femininity since the Great Fire of 64 A.D. put an end to Nero's days as a producer of Roman orgies.

As for Sally Rand's absence from the fair, one entire outer wall at the front of the "Crystal Lassies" concession declared in huge letters: "The New York Fair's more than Adequate Answer to the Sally Rand Question." The show inside featured the flimsily clad "Lassies" who performed in an environment of mirrors, described on the wall as "Nine Girls Dancing Solo in Five Minute Relays Multiplied Hundreds of Times From Every Conceivable Angle . . . Daring But Beautiful."[9]

An assortment of risqué fair attractions were documented in a meticulously detailed report, compiled by Mrs. Mary Ellis, a Primitive Methodist Minister from Philadelphia well known at the time for her moral crusading. A couple of cogent excerpts convey the flavor of her report:

> The barker said "Most daring show on the Midway." One girl carried two plumes, one in each hand, one yellow, the other purple; breasts uncovered, except for tiny illumination which might have been paint, over the nipples, small illuminated shield in front over private organ, buttocks bare. Reflection in mirror under her feet showed no covering of the private organ. Navel also entirely exposed....

---

[8] The success of the Aquacade may have prompted Billy Rose to drop his plagiarism suit against Sally Rand. In any case, it was heard from no more.

[9] A low-resolution 5-minute video of the attraction is available online. At YouTube, search for "crystal lassies." Or, see the "Sun Worshippers" video (in color!) for a look at another popular nude concession at the 1939 New York World's Fair. Just search for "sun worshippers 1939" on YouTube.

The barker commented, "Boys don't chew the woodwork, leave some for the mice." He says this to those eager fellows bent on seeing everything to be seen, and insinuating their agitation. A sentence containing the word "Spiritually" is used in derision.

She described one act — the "Girl with the Red Macaw" — as wearing a breast scarf and loin cloth that were systematically removed by the macaw to reveal a "very tiny shield over sexual organ." Her report duly noted: "Appearance as though nude. Vile sexual motions of body and buttocks. Great applause."

The Reverend Ellis's entire clinically detailed report goes on for five pages, and can easily be found online.

With nothing in New York to distract her, Sally went all in at Treasure Island. Her Nude Ranch was so popular that she dubbed one of the girls, petite little Vivian Cardier, as "The Ideal Miss America" and installed her, along with a few other beauties, in a separate attraction called "Miss America." The show was described by one journalist as "a nightclub extravaganza that would do justice to a Billy Rose or Flo Ziegfeld." Other accounts suggested that the Miss America concession was little more than a "peep show" featuring only a single "dainty little morsel."

When the competing Greenwich Village "girlie" revue closed, Sally arranged to take over the premises, finance some remodeling, and produce yet a third Sally Rand show she called "Gay Paree." This new attraction (in which she was featured) also drew big crowds. Sally said of the show: "Children like fairy tales ... and when they grow up they still want make-believe. Good-looking girls, colored lighting and good music — that's my idea of a show."

Following the pattern she had established years earlier in Chicago, Sally appeared at The Music Box downtown and also at the fairgrounds. According to her, all these enterprises were making money:

> Yes, plenty. I paid off my original investment within the first three
> weeks of the fair. Since then, even with $3,000 weekly overhead,
> there has been plenty of profit. I get an average of six hours sleep
> and I spend all my waking hours at work, either directing my
> shows at the fair or at the night club. Whenever I can, I accept
> invitations to make speeches.

One such speech was delivered to a Treasure Island gathering of the Western Confectioners Association at a luncheon held on May 11th — "Candy Day" at the fair. Girls dressed in "alluring costumes" were on hand to distribute

60,000 candy bars, many of them to children under 12 who were admitted to the fairgrounds that day for only 10 cents. Rising to speak at the flower-bedecked luncheon table, Sally was described as "looking like a cross between Queen Marie and a tootsie roll."[10] She opened by teasing the assembly: "You people have been putting more and more wrappings on your products, and I've been taking more and more off mine."

Then, in a statement 50 years ahead of its time, Sally advised the confectioners to advertise the food value of candy and to print the calorie ratings on the packages. This advice was ignored for more than five decades until the 1990 Nutrition Labeling and Education Act required such labeling. Another speaker at the Candy Day luncheon, Dr. J. C. Geiger, Director of Public Health for the City and County of San Francisco, had only four months earlier pledged his support to the "maintenance of good health for millions who visit Treasure Island." Hey, public health is a good thing, of course, but everybody likes a candy bar now and again.

On May 28, 1939, with the country still mired in the Great Depression, the California Legislature was at loggerheads over the governor's budget and under pressure from a "no new taxes" movement. Sally, speaking at a luncheon meeting of members of the San Francisco Executives Association, offered a path out of the gridlock:

> Spend money! Pull the drawstring from your purses. You are all thinking of what happened yesterday. Remember, you must spend money, for only in this way will we experience the good times again which you gentlemen are always lamenting. You are more content to sit and mope and complain about how bad things are instead of getting out and doing something about them.

Sally's business acumen was attracting notice. As writer Quentin Reynolds observed:

> Sally Rand is famous because she does things with fans and bubbles. She is not famous for having one of the keenest financial minds in the United States. She is not famous for her sheer technical knowledge of lighting, scenery and dance routines. She should be.

---

[10]   This description is borne out by a photograph of Sally standing before the microphone in a vastly oversized fur coat. The reference is likely to "Queen Marie" of Romania, who had died the previous year. A granddaughter of Queen Victoria, Queen Marie was described by one biographer as "the most voluptuous queen in Europe."

As for Sally's technical expertise, Reynolds told of visiting The Music Box nightclub and listening in on a conversation between the venue's owner and host, George Riccomi, and a painter who was putting finishing touches on the front door:

"But mahogany, I said," Mr. Riccomi wailed. "Painter, please why didn't you do it mahogany?"

The painter looked up gloomily. "I started to but Miss Rand took one look and said, 'That is lousy — make it antique white instead.' I said, 'How do you make such a paint antique white?' So Miss Rand mixed the paint for me."

"What does she know about paint?" Mr. Riccomi snorted.

"Mr. Riccomi," the painter said, "I been carrying a union card twenty years and I tell you she knows more about paint than I do. And mahogany would've looked dull. That antique white is pretty, ain't it, Mr. Riccomi?"

The club's head electrician told a similar tale: "She knows as much as I do." "Who runs this place, you or Sally Rand?" Reynolds asked.

The eyes of Mr. Riccomi rolled upward ecstatically, "She fills it every night is all I know; all I know is she makes me about $2,000 a week clear, so I guess she can run it all right. The smartest woman I ever met, Sally is. What a business woman!"

How many irons can one person have in the fire? More than you might think. Besides performing in nightly shows at The Music Box and supervising the operation of her three concessions at the fair, there were several weeks in July and August when Sally also lent her name to a floor show staged at the Cal-Neva Lodge on Lake Tahoe. Billed as "The Sally Rand Glamour Girls," the show featured "12 spectacular dancing beauties in an eye-dazzling array of sparkling numbers." Each Sunday, Sally would take a break from her other engagements, fly nearly 200 miles to Reno, and appear at the lodge in person, where she would introduce the show and spend time speaking to the audience.[11]

---

[11] The Cal-Neva Lodge, called "The Castle in the Air on the Shores of Lake Tahoe," straddles the state line so that one can "dine and dance in California and play in Nevada." Frank Sinatra bought the lodge in 1960. Marilyn Monroe spent a weekend there just before her death in 1962. The resort still exists, although the present owners declared bankruptcy in 2016 and the future of a planned renovation is in doubt.

Sally's Sunday flights from San Francisco to Reno were usually piloted by celebrated aviator E. E. "Monty" Mouton, the man who, in 1920, landed at San Francisco's Marino Field carrying the first-ever batch of cross-country airmail correspondence. On one particular Sunday in 1939, their flight plan was a little different. Sally announced on Saturday, July 29th, that she would be taking control of the aircraft herself the next morning and would attempt to break the light plane record for a flight between San Francisco and Reno. At the time, the record was said to be held by Charles McKay of Fallon, Nevada — two hours, thirty-five minutes.

That Sunday morning Sally, who held a "limited private pilot's license," took off from the auto parking lot at Treasure Island in a two-passenger Luscombe 65, at 9:18 a.m., with Major Mouton as her co-pilot. (Actually, since no plane had ever before taken off from the parking area, Mouton was at the controls for the takeoff, but Sally was in control of the plane the rest of the way to Reno.)

The light all-metal monoplane flew at an altitude of 12,000 feet and averaged a speed of 100 miles per hour. At one point, Sally was forced to detour over the mountains for a short distance in order to avoid a rain storm. When the plane landed at the United Airlines airport in Reno at 11:12 a.m. on July 30th, she was greeted by a crowd of admirers who had gathered to witness the end of her record-setting flight. Sally's time of one hour, fifty-four minutes, broke McKay's record time by an impressive 41 minutes.[12] The story made headlines nationwide.

Headlines? Within weeks after the lengthy magazine article touting Sally's prowess as a businesswoman appeared on newsstands, those same stalls were selling papers with such sobering headlines as: "SALLY RAND BANKRUPT" and "SALLY RAND IS BROKE, CANNOT PAY HER DEBTS."

The news seemingly came out of nowhere — a candidate for Ripley's *Believe it or Not*. But it was true. On October 14th, under her birth name "Helen Gould Beck," Sally filed a voluntary petition for bankruptcy in federal court in San Francisco, declaring that she had liabilities of $64,631 and assets of only $8,067.[13] Her debts ranged from a promissory note for $5,025 with the Central Bank of Oakland, to a $4 debt that she owed to a costume milliner. Other debts included $739 she had borrowed on her limousine, $637 billed

---

[12] Sally's achievement also shaved four minutes off the record time of her co-pilot Monty Mouton, set in 1920 during a leg of his transcontinental airmail flight in the reverse direction, as recounted in chapter 3.

[13] Today these two figures would be just over a million dollars and something like $133,000.

for loudspeaker equipment, personal loans of nearly $3,000, and numerous smaller sums, including $25 that she owed to a Philadelphia veterinarian who had treated her dog.

At the bankruptcy hearing five weeks later, wearing a "trim dark suit, with a fluff of white chiffon at the throat, and a white feathered turban," Sally confessed to Bankruptcy Referee Burton J. Wyman and a group of none-too-happy creditors: "Oh, it's all such a mess."

She patiently explained that she had earned $74,830 from her interest in the Nude Ranch and another $100,000 from The Music Box where she had appeared nightly: "But it's all gone now. I paid good salaries to my girls. I costumed them in lavish outfits and continually changed my shows to give the customers their money's worth."

"Meanwhile," Sally elaborated, "I was paying off the mortgage on my mother's orange grove in Glendora." Producing pawn tickets to establish what had happened to her jewelry, she pressed on: "Someone a good deal wiser than myself will have to figure it out."

Hearing that Sally was in financial distress, the Kappa Sigma fraternity chapter at the University of Richmond in Virginia offered a lifeline. It seems the university had ruled that all fraternities must have a house mother, so, to the clever young gentlemen, a mutually agreeable solution seemed obvious. On November 23rd, they dispatched a poetic telegram to Sally:

> Sorry to hear of your financial bust;
> But come on down and live with us.
> We have to get a new house mother,
> And we'd rather have you than any other.

Though touched, Sally graciously declined the offer with a poem of her own:

> Thank you boys for your swell invite,
> Now that my coffers are empty quite.
> Of course, I've never been a mother,
> But I'd rather be yours than any other.

> But I must still my career pursue,
> I can't be a mother to you nor you,
> For nothing's changed, it's the old nude deal,
> I've still got my fans and my sex appeal.

> And what I'm selling is tried and trusted,
> For the public knows I'm not flat busted.

After the bankruptcy court filing, Sally addressed a Seattle businessmen's luncheon, reflecting:

> One of the reasons why I went bankrupt was that I was credited with too much business acumen. As I got deeper and deeper into business, and my reputation was built up, business men began to fear that I'd outwit them. It was better in the old days when I acted wide-eyed and helpless in business deals.

Years later, in a conversation with columnist Lloyd Shearer, she was less guarded:

> I thought I was going to mint a small fortune from the Fair at San Francisco. Instead, I was taken to the cleaners like Grant took Richmond. But that experience taught me a valuable lesson — people who become friends because you have money are no friends at all, merely fungus growths who will drop off when they can no longer feed on you.

Sally had been knocked down before, and she was nothing if not resilient. More like a peacock than a phoenix, she was still determined to rise from the ashes. Even before the bankruptcy hearings had concluded, she had put together a full blown "Star Studded Revue" and had already begun playing dates in the Pacific Northwest.

How she was able to assemble another revue so soon after her financial humiliation is suggested in a letter she wrote to gossip columnist Walter Winchell:

> *At the time of my bankruptcy, every single employee, of which there were over 100, were paid in full, and every contract kept to the letter. It took a mite of maneuvering to arrange this, the details of which I shall not go into now....*

> *... each and every employee belonged to a union — actors, musicians, stage hands, kitchen workers, waiters, etc. Should I have owed one single one of these employees belonging to these unions ... I would have been blackballed from ever playing in any theatre, or with any musicians, or with any actor, or in any cafe.*

In November of 1939, writing with unfiltered sincerity in a syndicated column published under her own byline, Sally disclosed the genesis of her financial embarrassment:

> For several years they've been billing me as a sort of ... fan-waving financier, the Nabob of Nudity. I took it big. I didn't see then that I was about to lose my shirt. Shucking off a garment or

two now and then is nothing in my young life. But losing your shirt is something else again.

It isn't the first time it happened to me. When my bank folded in 1933 it squeezed to death all the savings I had up to that time. The success I've had since, which built all that reputation as the Tycoon of Terpsichore, came during the last six years. Now I can start over again. And I will.

Some of the writers made me out a sort of combination of Hetty Green[14] and Salome. I was supposed to have thousands of acres of land and insurance annuity contracts by the bale. I was supposed to have the first nickel I ever earned, tied up in blue baby-ribbon. Well, however much of that may have been true last August, it isn't true now. No stocks, no automobiles, no annuities, not even a Rolls-Royce. Just $8,067 worth of clothes and jewels, for even a fan dancer has to have clothes for leisure moments. My creditors are trying to squeeze $64,638 out of that.

According to all the stories about me as a financial genius, I ought to be able to help them, but I can't. Where did it all go? I don't know.... So overnight I turn from an expert in "How to Make a Million" into an expert on "How to Go Bankrupt, in One Easy Lesson." And it is easy, really it is.

I've drawn $3,000,000 into the box offices during the past six years. Some have claimed I was a millionairess. I wouldn't know about that. Maybe a million has passed through my hands, but people forget the expenses that go with those big salaries. Usually the whole cost of my production and troupe came out of those big salaries. All I know is that ... I have more pawn tickets than platinum right now.

Going broke on $174,830 a year? It's easier than getting the $174,830 in the first place.

By the end of 1939, Sally had reached (or possibly even passed) the peak of her notoriety. After seven years, the fan dance was no longer a novelty. During all that time she had milked it for all it was worth — and she had not been alone.

---

14   Considered the richest woman in America and dubbed by her contemporaries as the "Witch of Wall Street," Hetty Green was an American businesswoman and financier in the Gilded Age, at a time when virtually all other major investment bankers were male.

CHAPTER SIXTEEN

Fan Dancers Galore

Almost all absurdity of conduct arises from the imitation
of those whom we cannot resemble.

~ Samuel Johnson

The 19th century British writer, clergyman, gambler, art collector, and eccentric, Charles Caleb Colton was as celebrated for his odd behavior as for his talent. Little remembered today, he is regularly cited as the author of that famous seven word quotation — "Imitation is the sincerest form of flattery."

Of course, one woman's flattery is another woman's ripoff. Frankly, anyone who introduces something new and exciting cannot be surprised when less creative admirers seek a piece of the action. Nearly every performer, every craftsman on earth owes a debt to some long-forgotten anonymous pioneer. The conception and execution of the fan dance as we know it is credited to Faith Bacon in *Earl Carroll's Vanities of 1930*. Yet, if Faith Bacon had ostrich feather fans in 1930, where did they come from? Why were they manufactured? Sally Rand is said to have bought her fans from New York supplier, Lawrence Sittenberg, for many years.[1] Who else purchased them and why?

Joseph Addison, English essayist, poet, playwright, publisher, and politician, once expounded on the use of fans to command the attention of a lover. Writing more than 300 years ago, he advised:

> Handle your fans, unfurl your fans ... flutter your fans. By the right observation of these few plain words of command, a woman ... shall be able to give her fan all the graces that can possibly enter into that little modish machine.... I need not add that a fan is either a prude or coquette, according to the nature of the person who bears it.

---

[1]   A New York City costume designer who specialized in feathered costumes, Lawrence Sittenberg is said to have made the pair of fans used by Faith Bacon for her "original fan dance" in *Earl Carroll's Vanities of 1930*. He also provided costumes and ostrich feather accessories for many other famous customers, among them, the Radio City Music Hall "Rockettes" — even for First Lady Eleanor Roosevelt.

To history detectives, the question becomes: Where, when, and by whom was the first fan dance performed? Strictly speaking, the "fan dance" can be traced to antiquity. The tomb of Egypt's King Tutankhamen (1350 BC) yielded two ostrich feather fans with gold mounts. A fresco at Herculaneum, buried by the eruption of Mount Vesuvius in 79 AD, depicts an ostrich feather fan. Various forms of the dance can be traced back for centuries in more than one Asian culture.

But all these ancient dances involved the use of relatively small, handheld fans that were incidental to a more or less classical form of elegant dance. Concealment of nudity was an unlikely element of any of these dances.[2] So, in our quest for the origin of the fan dance, let us limit ourselves to the more titillating form, performed by a solo dancer who manipulated large ostrich feather fans, intermittently concealing and exposing her possibly nude body.

Sally Rand's version of the fan dance as performed at the 1933 Century of Progress is easily the best known, but it was by no means the first. Any claim by Sally to have originated the fan dance is put to rest by the fact that Faith Bacon had previously executed the dance for a paying audience on July 1, 1930, when she stepped on the stage of the New Amsterdam Theatre as a featured performer in *Earl Carroll's Vanities of 1930*. So, is the discussion over? Or might there be an even earlier legitimate claim?[3]

Miss Bacon's claim to having originated the fan dance could well be in question if the recollections of Earl Carroll's biographer, Ken Murray, are reliable. According to him, the first fan dance may have occurred in *Earl Carroll's Vanities of 1924* in a production number called "Blue Paradise." As Carroll explained at the time: "That's where our beautiful girls will come out as peacocks. And the esthetic art of the number demands that the girls be in the absolute buff this time, not even G-strings." Murray described the number as "a very sensuous 'peacock dance,' in which each girl was to carry a huge fan and, to the strains of the music, wave it provocatively,

---

[2]   In the United States, nude or near nude dance performances (staged for an all-male clientele) can be traced back at least as far as the late 19th Century. One tantalizing report states that, in 1881, "hefty young" Labbie Maretta danced nude at the Theatre Comique in Minneapolis "while flapping a big fan." In February of that year, proprietor W.W. Brown was indicted for "maintaining a nuisance" in running the venue, the "wine rooms" of which "were nightly the scene of most disgusting orgies."

[3]   In the June 1928 issue of *Motion Picture Classic* magazine — in particular, the illustrated article "Fans Across the See" — three of the four images are of young women shielding themselves with somewhat large handheld folding fans. But the fourth photograph depicts Sally Blane (one of Loretta Young's sisters), holding two large ostrich feather fans — one in front and the other behind.

intermittently revealing glimpses of her totally nude body." He then added a few colorful details:

> As the big orchestra ... burst forth with exotic musical strains of Ravel's *Boléro*, the curtains parted, revealing a stage bathed in rainbow lights and a shimmering Biblical tableaux, followed by 108 luscious creatures strutting and gyrating around the stage, each carrying a big fan made entirely of peacock feathers and wearing a replica of the proud bird as a headdress — and *nothing* else. It was a sensation.[4]

Was Faith Bacon's suggestion to Earl Carroll in 1930 merely an iteration of an idea that he himself had conceived some six years earlier? Can we still credit Miss Bacon with creating the fan dance? The answer may yet be "yes" — but only if an essential element of the dance is the manipulation of large *ostrich feather* fans by a solo performer.[5]

B y the early 1890s, elements of what would later become the modern ostrich feather fan dance were beginning to appear in performances described, even at the time, as "fan dances." Consider this anonymous critic's opinion of illustrations depicting scenes from the 1890 edition of London's annual *Drury Lane Pantomime*:

> The sketches of scantily attired damsels who are supposed to figure in the Drury Lane Pantomime are execrable. If the young "lady" who is represented as performing "The Fan Dance" is not foully libeled in the illustration, then Mr. Sheriff Augustus Harris or his acting manager must either be exceedingly poor judges of feminine form or else the "stock" from which they selected their Christmas "fairies" must have been very limited.

A year later in March 1892, a "truly phenomenal little Spanish dancer" named Cyrene added a new dance to her repertoire at the Palace Theatre

---

4 Murray's recollection is faulty in at least one detail, as Ravel's *Boléro* didn't exist in 1924. He wrote it in 1928.

5 Sally was obviously aware of Faith Bacon's performances in the 1930 edition of *Earl Carroll's Vanities*. As described in chapter 14, she may even have been present. In an October 1933 interview, Sally (clearly attempting to claim precedence) was quoted as saying: "The fan dance I do was created in 1929, when I was attempting to invent a number which would resemble the movements of a bird. After many experiments, I decided that the fans, used as I manipulate them now, gave the best effect."

in Boston.[6] A newspaper advertisement described "Cyrene's Coquettish Fan Dance" thus:

> A fan in the hand of a Spanish woman becomes a most significant affair, and, introduced into a dance it is extremely "catching." If it conceals the piquant face for a moment, it reveals it later, brilliant and smiling. Flirting in all its phases is illustrated in this novel dance; it is not merely the graceful movement, but it is full of subtle meaning and has a language of its own.

Beginning in the late 19th century, stylish women out for an evening on the town commonly carried folding ostrich feather fans as a fashion accessory. The handles were originally of carved ivory, mother-of-pearl, or tortoiseshell, but as these fans became the ubiquitous accessory of the 1920s flapper, man-made materials like Bakelite, Celluloid, and plastic replaced the more expensive materials. Why were some of the ostrich feather fans so large? Well, over time, as is so often the case, bigger became better. And how better to show up at a formal event than with an expensive accessory designed to upstage everyone else in the room?

Of course, these fans could not have existed without the involuntary cooperation of the ostriches. In the late 19th century, ostrich feathers were in demand for all manner of fashionable uses, including headdresses and feather boas. But where to get them? This required a bit of international commerce, as the common ostrich — the largest bird in the world at eight feet tall and 350 pounds — is native only to Africa. Exports from South Africa served well enough to meet the demand in Europe, but the expense of shipping the feathers to America proved to be an issue. Perhaps some clever entrepreneur could just bring a breeding stock to the United States and proceed from there?

In 1886, Californian Edwin Cawston chartered a ship and arranged to transport 50 ostriches from South Africa to Galveston, Texas. From there, they traveled by rail to Norwalk, California, eventually being delivered to South Pasadena.[7] Of the original 50 birds, only 18 survived the journey, but this

---

6   A review in the July 9, 1892, issue of in the *Washington Post* could hardly have been more effusive: "Cyrene is little short of a marvel, and must be seen to be appreciated. She is a veritable little Celtiberian cyclone ... and when she swings one small foot at least a foot and a half above her head ... the audience goes wild."

7   While Edwin Cawston was in Cape Town, the Cape Colony government, aware of his plans, mandated an exorbitant export duty on ostriches and their eggs. In a brazen last-minute run, Cawston snuck out of South Africa with more than 50 ostriches the night before the law took effect. (How one "sneaks" 50 ostriches anywhere is left to the imagination.)

proved to be enough. In time, the Cawston Ostrich Farm was home to more than 100 birds descended from the original stock.

Besides supplying the demand for ostrich feather boas, muffs, headdresses, and fans, the farm became a popular tourist attraction.[8] Visitors could tour the grounds in an ostrich-drawn carriage, watch an ostrich gulp down a whole orange, fuss over the fluffy ostrich chicks, and even have their photos taken "riding" an ostrich. In 1933, Paramount Productions released a photo of Sally Rand doing that very thing.[9]

So ostrich feathers had become fashionable accoutrements and ostrich feather fans were readily available in the marketplace. But the question remains: When, where, and with whom did the act of *dancing* with these fans actually originate?

In France, by the early 1920s if not earlier, lavish production numbers at such famous venues as the Follies Bergère and Casino de Paris commonly featured showgirls in feathered headdresses and costumes. In a 1923 production entitled *Oh! Les Belles Filles* (The Beautiful Girls), the popular Dolly Sisters appeared in feathered costumes designed by the famous fashion designer and perfumer Jean Patou, complete with ostrich feather fans. A 1924 photograph shows dancer Edmonde Guy holding a fan that is virtually indistinguishable from the ones used by Sally Rand.

In the same year, American-born dancer Claire Luce[10] went to Paris to replace Mistinguett at the Casino de Paris. A 1926 French magazine shows Ms. Luce performing a topless "Danseuse Acrobatique," a segment of which featured her with a large peacock feather fan. She was brought back to the states by Florenz Ziegfeld to perform in his 1927 *Follies*. Wearing an ostrich feather dress, she made her stage entry riding a real live ostrich. Sliding off the giant bird's back, she performed an acrobatic dance with two huge fans.

---

[8] The Cawston Ostrich Farm continued in operation for years even after the plumage began to fade from fashion. It was finally sold at auction in 1934 to satisfy a tax claim of $142.

[9] Well, not exactly *riding*. While, early on, some may have ridden the ostriches bareback, the birds in these pictures were stuffed, as the real ones were much too unpredictable and dangerous to be mounted by an uninitiated tourist.

[10] An American stage and screen performer, Claire Luce was a contemporary of, but not related to, Claire Boothe Luce — the writer, politician, U.S. Ambassador to Italy and wife of publishing magnate Henry Luce.

These things didn't always go as planned. A Ziegfeld biography written by his niece and nephew includes the following anecdote:

> The ostrich was tall and not easily controlled; one night the bird (with Luce on board) came running onto the stage but would not slow down. It kept going all the way to the street door, heading for its stable. Since Luce could not get off, she had to skip her number that night.

Research into the matter is further confused by the dance performances of "Aleta Ray." In 1929 a New Hampshire newspaper touted the merits of an upcoming *American Beauties Revue*:

> Aleta Ray is another of the charming ladies that will appear in this revue. Aleta is a striking example of all that is lovely in womanhood. Beautiful in form as well as in face, she offers several routines of dances, including the famous Ostrich feather fan dance.

Famous? In 1929? Could this truly have been the same tantalizing dance later performed by Faith Bacon and Sally Rand? Probably not. It is highly unlikely that this early version of the "ostrich feather fan dance" became "famous" thanks to the nudity of its performer. In fact, when Aleta Ray later performed her much publicized "Fan-Dance-in-a-Church" in Milton, Massachusetts, it was not Miss Ray's reputation, but the memory of Sally Rand's performances, that attracted "a large and appreciative audience of parishioners." [11]

The congregation experienced a mixture of relief and disappointment when Miss Ray pranced onto the stage carrying two fluffy ostrich feather fans while wearing "a voluminous skirted costume." As one reporter observed: "She did not once lose a fan, and it wouldn't have mattered if she had."[12]

In any event, while ostrich feather fans had been around as a dance accoutrement for many years before Sally Rand picked up a pair in 1932, once she employed them with such dexterity and style at the Century of

---

[11] Why was a fan dancer performing for a church group? Reverend Cutbill, an ordained Congregational and Unitarian clergyman, explained: "It is one of the principles of the Unitarian creed of toleration and encouragement that people enjoy themselves. I see no harm in a classical fan dance."

[12] Even though Miss Ray's dance was not performed in the nude, there must have been some reason to characterize it as "the famous Ostrich Feather fan dance." The reference may have been inspired by another young lady. In his column of February 29, 1928, O.O. McIntyre, writing from aboard a cruise ship, mentioned that: "Claire Luce braved a rolling ship to do her ostrich fan dance at the concert this evening to rousing cheers." The difference — and you can confirm this by searching for images online — is that Miss Luce's dance costume in no way resembled a nude body.

Progress Fair, Sally became *the* fan dancer. In fact, as decades passed, she became more and more comfortable with the notion that she *was* the original fan dancer. Certainly, she made no effort to correct anyone who promoted her as such. Whatever claims and counterclaims to originality may be made, this much is certain — Sally Rand popularized this dance. She and she alone was responsible for the proliferation of imitators and the short-lived obsession with fan dancing that followed in her wake.

N o sooner had the fan dance become a sensation at the 1933 Fair than it also turned into something of a national craze, spawning an untold number of imitators trying to survive hard times. Dollars were hard to come by. Imitators were shedding their clothes and waving their fans in communities both large and small. Clubs in every city of any size featured a local fan dancer, as did many smaller towns, villages, and hamlets. Whatever small indignity may have been attached to being a poser was overcome by the opportunity to cash in on a spectacularly popular fad. To dance to the music — while the music lasted.

In 1934, Sally was quoted as saying that there were 250 fan dancers in Chicago when she left. Tall or short. Striking or homely. A bevy of otherwise unremarkable young women sought to share at least a tiny portion of Sally's spotlight.[13] To be fair, in the years before television, pretty much the only way to witness a performance by a national celebrity like Sally Rand was in the flesh. All these local and regional fan dancers at least gave their audiences the chance to see an approximation of "the real thing." Several of the young ladies actually achieved a measure of success and are worthy of further exposure ... so to speak.

Fay Baker

During a 1935 appearance in the Rathskeller in the basement of the Hotel Placer in Helena, Montana, a "little black-eyed dancer" called Fay Baker — billed as "America's Dancing Darling" with "an intriguing figure, a mop of black hair, and two very nice dimples" — described it this way:

> It all happened like this. I was walking down the street in Chicago
> a year ago last June when I bumped into Sally Rand and Faith
> Bacon. We went to lunch together. Times were bad in the show
> business and we were up a stump as to just what sort of dances we
> would feature next. We thought of a dance with fans — it was

---

13 On the first week of November 1933, at just one venue, the RKO Palace Theater in Cleveland, a show entitled *Fifty Million Frenchmen* featured "28 Fan Dancers."

something new and it might go over. We didn't know just how the
police would take it, but we were willing to try.

Miss Baker may have been able to sell such press puffery under the Big Sky
in Montana, but it is more likely that 20-year-old Mary Nebel of Watertown,
Wisconsin, got wind of the goings on at the Century of Progress Fair in the
summer of 1933 and decided to get in on the action. Adopting the stage name
"Fay Baker," she apparently did perform her version of the fan dance at the
fair, as well as at the Chicago Theatre, possibly even as a replacement for
Sally Rand in the Streets of Paris.

Why use "Fay Baker" rather than something closer to her real name like,
say, "Merry Rebel"? Well, a cynic might conclude that the similarity to
"Faith Bacon" was enough to mislead more than a few would-be patrons to
notice her placard and exclaim: "Oh, Fay Baker! That's the gal Uncle Bud
said we should see."

In any case, when the fair closed, the resourceful Miss Baker went on the
road billing herself as "The Original Fan Dancer." By December 4, 1933, she
was performing four shows a day at the Winnipeg Auditorium in Manitoba,
Canada. As the featured attraction at the "International Fur Fair" (advertised
as "The Largest Live Fur-Bearing Wild Animal Show in America"), Fay's
specialty was to sometimes perform the dance with but a single fan. When
the gig was over, she spent the rest of the month appearing as the top billed
act at several Winnipeg clubs and theaters, two of them simultaneously.
There were shows at the Uptown at 8:00 and 10:15 pm, with a 9:00 pm show
at the Roxy sandwiched in between. There was even a "Special Children's
Matinee Saturday" performance, although the management took pains to
assure that "The Fan Dance will NOT be shown at this performance."

Shortly after the first of the year, Fay announced plans to take her act into the
frozen wilds of Manitoba. She engaged a pilot to fly her some 350 miles north
of Winnipeg to the mining towns of Flin Flon and The Pas, where it was said
that fan dancing appearances had become as popular as they were in Chicago.

On January 11, 1934, after successful shows in both towns, disaster seemingly struck. A Canadian wire service reported from The Pas that:

> The barren Manitoba tundra between The Pas and Winnipegosis
> today held secret the whereabouts of fan-dancing Fay Baker of
> Watertown, Wis., who left here in a tiny cabin plane with Bill May,
> pilot for the Northwest Aeromaritime, Monday. Returning to Win-
> nipeg by air after fulfilling an engagement here, the diminutive
> dancer and her pilot are now three days overdue and are unreported.

By the next day, the press in Fay's home state of Wisconsin was reporting that a heavy snowstorm had held up the search for Fay and her pilot, who were possibly lost somewhere on vast and frozen Lake Winnipegosis. Five days passed without word of their whereabouts. Miss Baker's brother was en route from Wisconsin to join the search when, on January 15th, the banner front-page headline of the *Winnipeg Free Press* proclaimed: "MISSING DANCER AND PILOT SAFE."

Missing for several days and feared lost, both were actually alive and well. Bill May explained that he had experienced mechanical problems after taking off from The Pas and had been forced to make an emergency landing on Whiskey Jack Island, damaging the landing gear in the process. The couple had spent two days in a fisherman's shack, employing a spruce limb and fish cord to facilitate makeshift repairs to the plane. May recounted: "There were no conveniences at all. We both had eiderdowns to sleep in, but the shack would get good and cold at nights and we'd have to keep the stove supplied with wood." Besides subsisting on limited rations, the pilot observed: "The wolves were pretty thick around there, and scared her badly too."

The pair resumed their flight after an extended delay, but fog soon forced them down again at Duck Bay, where they were sheltered by local Indians. Communication with the outside world was still impossible, but the next day Miss Baker's pilot did manage to get the limping aircraft aloft and find a landing strip at Winnipegosis, an outpost of some 700 hardy souls, where phone service was available.

Following a brief hospital recuperation, the "dainty dancer" was back on stage at the Bijou Theater in Winnipeg, performing in a show advertised as: "A thrilling recital of her Arctic experiences, with actual photographs taken by her pilot and Miss Fay Baker."

Thais Giroux

Born in Butte, Montana, on July 17, 1911, Miss Giroux began dancing at the age of four. Her father was a former boxer who kept his hand in by serving as a referee and judge while employed as a sporting goods salesman. Her mother was a prominent member of Butte society. In 1928, Thais won a Girls Central High School song contest and was presented with a pearl and crystal necklace, donated by a local jeweler. The next year, at age 18, she was recognized in the local paper for "having the highest grades in a junior Christian Doctrine test."

Her talents soon came to the attention of the then-well-known adagio dance team of Betta and La Marr, at which point young Thais began her travels as an acrobatic dancer, eventually making it to New York, where in 1930 she was taken under the wing of nightclub hostess, Texas Guinan.[14] Capitalizing on Sally Rand's success and notoriety, Thais added both the fan dance and the bubble dance to her repertoire. Performing as "May Daniels" in Chicago clubs and as "Thelma Thais" in the famous Paradise Restaurant Cabaret in Manhattan, she began to fashion a nice little career for herself.

In December 1933, a seven-column newspaper headline trumpeted the imminent engagement of "THAIS, SENSATIONAL FAN DANCER" at the Majestic Theatre in Perth Amboy, New Jersey. The associated article described her "sensational act" as "even more daring than that staged at the Chicago Exposition by the celebrated dancer Sally Rand." By 1936 the beautiful and fairly well-known 24-year-old "specialty dancer" was involved in an affair with a small-time gangster, Johnny "John the Bug" Stoppelli — an ill-fated decision.[15] Their romance flickered off and on.

In the fall of 1937, Thais was offered an opportunity to join the company of a revue headed by Broadway dancer Gaby Leslie for a six-week engagement at the Municipal Theatre in Bogota, Colombia. She quickly accepted. During the Depression, the promised money was good and the prospect of a South American adventure was compelling.

The first two weeks in Colombia went off without a hitch, but, at the end of the third week, when government officials cited bogus regulations and withheld wages, the company was left in a bind. The troupe's leaders scrambled around and managed to book the show into a theater in Medellin, billing the performance as "For Men Only." Taking this to mean they were in for a racy show, many young hombres eagerly plunked down their Colombian pesos. Unfortunately, only Thais Giroux with her seductive and suggestive fan dance lived up to their expectations. Once it became clear that the other acts were pretty tame — in Miss Leslie's words, "just art" — the hissing and hooting began.

---

14 See the wonderful 1931 video featuring Texas Guinan with an unidentified, barefoot and apparently nude fan dancer (Thais?), preserved in the Historic Films Stock Footage Archive, at https://www.youtube.com/watch?v=ObiUgeCGD9A.

15 Born in New York City's "Little Italy" in 1907, as a teenager Johnny Stoppelli formed a group of young toughs who made a living off mugging and robbery. Although cleared of involvement in a pool hall murder, Stoppelli was convicted of crimes involving narcotics and guns. In short, while he successfully exploited his "bad boy" appeal to court Miss Giroux, he was wholly lacking in the character strengths one might hope for in a suitor, especially for a young woman from Montana seeking to establish herself as a legitimate performer.

As the crowd grew more agitated, even the collapse of a section of the gallery didn't deter a group of disappointed men from charging the stage and grabbing at the dresses of the dancers. With costumes in tatters, the terrified girls fled to their dressing rooms in tears. In all the commotion, the theater manager beat it out the back door, payroll in hand. Unexpectedly abandoned with limited resources in a foreign country, troupe members limped their way back to New York, booked unceremoniously in steerage.

Photos reveal Miss Giroux to have been quite a stunner. Blessed with a beautiful body and shoulder length blond hair, she may well have been the most physically attractive of all the specialty dancers of her time.

Flo Ash

In physical appearance, personality and career trajectory, Flo Ash was more similar to Sally Rand than any of her other imitators. Born circa 1911, Miss Ash was drawn to show business. She claimed to have appeared in bit parts in 41 films, including *The Half Naked Truth* (1932) and *Adorable* (1933).[16] While under contract with Columbia Pictures in 1934, she also served as a stand-in for Carole Lombard who was playing a fan dancer in the film *Lady by Choice* (a credit Flo exploited to her advantage for years to come).

Following her stint in Hollywood, Flo joined the many others hoping to cash in on the fan dance craze by securing an engagement in the Streets of Paris concession at the Chicago World's Fair. But even before the Fair closed on November 12, 1933, she was on the road, appearing at the Oriole Terrace in Joplin, Missouri: "Direct from Chicago's World's Fair" as "Hollywood's Original Sensational FAN DANCER."

In 1934 Flo toured the west and southwest, mostly as a headliner, but sometimes as a member of "The Hotcha Girls." While Sally Rand was gliding around the stage to the classical strains of Claude Debussy, Miss Ash was employing a special pair of black lace fans to perform her own version of a fan dance to the accompaniment of Ravel's *Boléro*.

An incident on February 8th led to Flo's greatest national press exposure. It happened during the second night of an engagement at the Alamo Nite Club in San Antonio, Texas, where her act had been promoted as the "Fan Dance that rocked Chicago." Midway through her show, suddenly realizing that the intermittent flashing of flesh taking place before his very

---

[16] Years later, Flo Ash had a credited role as a fan dancer in *Paris After Midnight* (1951), about the misadventures of a couple of American G.I.'s who encounter a group of sexy young women in a backstreet French hotel.

eyes was an ongoing act of criminal indecent exposure, Deputy Constable J. W. Davis dutifully rose from his seat, strode onto the dance floor, stopped the show, and placed its star under arrest. On the way to the county jail, Flo described San Antonio as a "hick town," grumbling that she had performed all over the country but had never before been arrested. After posting bail, she was back at the club in time for her 1:00 a.m. show.

A jury of "six good men and true" was duly empaneled to consider the evidence. The three prosecution witnesses, including Deputy Davis, testified that they "could see everything" when Miss Ash twirled around. The first, police reporter Walthall Littlepage, said that Miss Ash danced with a shawl and an ostrich feather fan about the size of a 10-gallon hat: "The shawl looked like silk and came down to her knees…. I couldn't see through it. But when she came out for an encore and whirled around real fast, the shawl stood out. I could see from her neck on down."

The overflow crowd in the courtroom became so noisy during the cross examination of Littlepage that Judge John Shook called for a short recess. Looking up, Defense Attorney Leonard Brown noticed a calendar behind the judge's back that displayed the image of a beautiful girl reclining in a bathing suit. Order was restored and Brown resumed his cross examination: "Isn't it a fact, Mr. Littlepage, that this dancer had on more clothes than that girl on the calendar?"

"Yes, most of the time," Littlepage conceded. In a side whisper, Judge Shook was heard to say, "I'd better get that calendar off the wall."

Testifying in her own defense, Flo declared:

> I just challenge you to come out and try to see anything from any seat in the house. It's the flash, color and action that brings the customers back. They keep coming back just to see if they really did see anything. At no time is my whole body exposed. Anyone has to have a vivid imagination to say he sees anything but the feminine form.

Brown's stirring closing argument emphasized that Miss Ash should be acquitted in the name of art and common sense. The jury deliberated for fully three minutes before reaching a similar conclusion. The verdict was greeted by a round of applause and handshaking in the courtroom, while the jurors themselves were invited to come out to the Alamo Nite Club to enjoy the show.

During a 1936 engagement in New York, the diminutive dancer adopted the moniker "Cutest Little Nudist." She toured under that billing for the next two years, when it came to her attention in October 1938 that the "brunette and just as curvesome" Miss Crystal Ames (a.k.a., "Crystal Aymes") was appearing in California under the exact same billing. Miss Ash promptly filed suit against the interloper, seeking $15,000 in damages as well as a cease and desist order. Flo was dismissive of her rival: "I'm a nude artistic dancer, while Crystal Ames — well, she's just a strip teaser." Within three weeks, a Los Angeles court ruled in favor of Miss Ash, resolving the confusion as to just exactly who was the nation's "cutest little nudist."

Like Sally, Flo traveled with several trunks and suitcases, as well as a photo gallery and a copy of the Holy Bible. According to a columnist in Hutchinson, Kansas: "... of the half dozen or so fan manipulators, Flo comes the closest to dancing with grace, rhythm and titillating artistry."

Ruby Bae

During the Depression, the profusion of fan dancers surely reflected the desire on the part of many young women to earn a few bucks, even if only by display of some slight degree of talent.

To combat rising unemployment rates and put people to work, President Roosevelt moved Congress to establish the Works Progress Administration (WPA). Besides hiring laborers for public infrastructure projects, the federal program had an arts and culture arm that offered jobless artists and performers an opportunity to become wage earners.[17] Among them was fan dancer Ruby Bae, who lost her job and became eligible for benefits after being arrested by six Minneapolis policemen for "cavorting about Coffee Dan's nightclub in the nude."

Officers claimed that she was not wearing any panties. Ruby claimed that she *was* wearing them and further announced that she had twice performed at stag parties held exclusively for police officers. "If my dance is so indecent, why didn't they arrest me then?" she inquired. Miss Bae's protest was brushed aside, she was fined $50 for disorderly conduct and the club was closed. Ruby was officially unemployed.

---

[17] Over 3.5 million jobless people (one per family) were employed under the WPA, building, repairing and improving tens of thousands of roads and highway systems, bridges, schools, hospitals, courthouses, post offices, and other government buildings. They also built thousands of cultural and recreational facilities, including museums, coliseums, community centers, and auditoriums, as well as outdoor facilities like public parks, fairgrounds, zoos, botanical gardens, playgrounds, markets, tennis courts, and swimming pools.

Soon she was rehearsing with the vaudeville unit of the Minnesota WPA and was scheduled to entertain workers at a Civilian Conservation Corps (CCC) camp. Before long, reporters got wind of the plan, and on December 13, 1935, the *Minneapolis Journal* — a newspaper actively opposed to the President's New Deal programs — ran a story revealing that there was a "stripper" in the vaudeville troupe. The exposé was accompanied by a photo of Ruby Bae, dubbed by the *Journal* as "Federal Fan Dancer No. 1." The story went national and a round of clucking began in Washington. Churches were outraged. Relief for the unemployed was one thing, but benefits for jobless fan dancers?

WPA officials at first observed that "even a fan dancer must eat." Even so, despite assurances from the Minnesota program supervisor that Miss Bae was simply auditioning for a spot in a respectable tap dancing group, Ruby was unceremoniously dumped from the program.[18] In this way, the Roosevelt administration avoided embarrassment for actively fostering taxpayer support of indecent fan dancing. The CCC camp workers, though disappointed, made do with a vaudeville troupe that included an accordion player, a juggling act, a banjoist, and a group of Scotch dialect singers.

Truth be told, the *Journal*'s story was largely false or misleading, if not an outright fabrication. Nonetheless, the so-called details were certainly amusing, if not credible. According to the report, two patrolmen and their wives had gone to the nightclub, watched two floor shows, and later claimed that Ruby had danced without a "nickel's worth of clothes on." Ruby had contradicted their version of events, asserting that she *did* have a nickel's worth of clothes on. The official expense account published by the drama division of Minnesota WPA project No. 1 settled the matter with the following entry: "Ruby Bae — fan dancer — costume $00.05."

Rosalie

Even smaller than Sally Rand, at four feet, 11 inches, Rosalie Davis showcased her act at the "Old Mexico" concession at the 1933 World's Fair in Chicago, performing her Latin version of the fan dance, featuring bright red ostrich feathers wafting to the accompaniment of Spanish rhythms. Her "eight assistant fan dancers" demonstrated just how much the fad had expanded.

---

[18] Responding to a claim that she would have endangered the morals of the young men in the CCC, Ruby quipped: "They're crazy…. I quit. In the first place, I was worried about what the CCC boys would do to the morals of a fan dancer. And then — well, I got another job."

One night, just as Rosalie completed her routine at the Little Mexico Café and stood poised with fans outstretched above her head with one knee upraised, a shot rang out. Orchestra members and patrons alike rushed for the exit or dived under the tables. After the panic had subsided, the manager and staff found what at first appeared to be a young boy in a man's suit hiding under a ringside table, revolver in hand. But, when the diminutive figure emerged, it proved to be none other than three-foot-tall Elmer Spangler, bandmaster at the Midget Village. The 23-year-old Elmer protested that Rosalie had ignored the flowers and romantic notes he had been sending to her dressing room. His unrequited love had reached such depths that he was desperate to get her attention by any means.

Oddly enough, it worked. After his release from jail, Elmer continued to patronize Rosalie's show and she made it a habit to spend a few minutes at his table. When asked if she wasn't afraid of being shot at, Rosalie replied: "No. He won't do that again. I told him I'd give him a good spanking if he did. And that I wouldn't let him brush my hair anymore."

Renee Villon

Plying her trade in Chicago in 1935, Renee Villon was sentenced to 30 days in jail for appearing "almost naked" in her "Peacock Dance." The prosecutor claimed "he had never seen a peacock with so few feathers." In a jocular mood, the judge observed: "... perhaps this is moulting season."

The following year Renee was in New York City, having wired the press in advance that she would be riding "Lady Godiva style" down Broadway and into the club where she was to appear. However, she didn't quite have Sally's talent for self-promotion. Renee barely managed to mount her steed — a white pony apparently borrowed from Central Park — and maneuver her way from the street into the club and once around the bar. Her uneasy mount became so agitated by the popping of photographers' flashbulbs that the poor animal "reared up and pawed the air." She "gallantly clung to its back and her wig," but in the end she had to abandon the stunt. The nightclub owner eventually nixed the whole idea, concerned that the pony might kick some of the customers.

Renee did manage to separate herself from the pack, modifying her act through the use of see-through black lace fans. She even created a "Gone with the Wind" dance with the help of an electric fan. But her greatest claim to fame arose from a widely reported episode that, as it turned out, had never even happened. In 1936, when reporters filed stories that Franklin D. Roosevelt, Jr., had been seen dancing with "Renee Villon" at the Paradise

Cabaret in New York, newsroom staff rushed to their morgue files to find her photograph. No sooner had the fan dancer's picture been released to the wire services, affording Renee some much-sought-after national publicity, than somebody figured out that the President's young son had actually been dancing with some other young lady of the same name.

B eyond these young beauties (and many others) who were entertaining mainstream audiences in typical American venues, there was another group of fan dancers filling niche roles and often performing before ethnic audiences.

Noel Toy

Born in San Francisco in 1918, Noel Toy was pursuing a journalism degree at the University of California, Berkeley in 1939 when she was offered a job at $35 a week posing for nude photos in the Chinese village at the Golden Gate Exposition on Treasure Island. It was there that Toy saw Sally Rand and began to get ideas for her own versions of the fan and bubble dances.

Touring the country as "the Chinese Sally Rand," Toy enjoyed moderate success into the 1940s. Perhaps her greatest triumphs were as a dancer at the Forbidden City, a popular Chinese nightclub in San Francisco, and as a featured performer at the famous Leon and Eddie's, a nightclub in New York City. By 1945, Noel Toy had married and given up her titillating dance act.

The "Sepia Sally Rand"

Several candidates vied for this title, among them:

- *Amy Spencer* — Responding to Sally's success at the 1933 Fair, orchestra leader Cab Calloway soon joined in the fan dancing craze. Describing his song "The Lady with the Fan," recorded on November 2, 1933, Calloway said: "I wrote it for the finest fan dancer the Cotton Club had ever known, Amy Spencer."[19] In 1935, still at the Cotton Club, Amy's name was added to the long list of fan dancers arrested for indecent exposure.

---

[19]   Calloway's admiration of Miss Spencer aside, he had ample opportunity to observe Miss Rand at close range, as they appeared on the same bill at the Chicago Theater in August 1933. In fact, some sources suggest that Calloway's song was inspired by that appearance. A rendition of Cab's tune featuring six "sepia" fan dancers may be seen on YouTube. It is not clear whether the redheaded Amy is among them.

- *Noma* — Like Sally, Noma also appeared at both the 1933 Chicago Fair and at a theater in downtown Chicago. In September 1933, following Sally's example, she was arrested for indecent exposure after performing at that theater. At the Wabash Avenue police station, Noma pointed out that her so-called immoral parts were actually covered with a patch of gauze, camouflaged by a flesh-colored powder. Officers booked her anyway, prompting Noma to launch into "a stiff argument on art and artless policemen," concluding: "You could not expect them to understand."

  Noma parlayed her Chicago experiences into an engagement at Harlem's Lafayette Theatre. By 1935, she had moved six and a half blocks downtown to the more prestigious Apollo Theater in Harlem to appear on the same bill with such popular performers as Pigmeat Markham, Louis Armstrong, the Nicholas Brothers, Jimmie Baskette,[20] and Stepin Fetchit.

- *Jean Idelle* — Actually billed as "the sepia Sally Rand," Miss Idelle (a.k.a. Jean Shur) studied dance at the Katherine Dunham School of Dance in New York City. She became a featured performer in Minsky's Burlesque Shows between 1950 and 1964 where she built a reputation for breaking the color barrier with her theater and nightclub performances. As recently as July 2012, she was leading a class in "The Art of Performing with Ostrich Feather Fans" at Big Al's in Las Vegas.[21]

The "Midget Sally Rand"

But, of course. Once again, there were several (you may find them yourself via a Google search). Try Mildred Dolly, Luz Villalobos, or even Stella Royale, the tiny jilted girlfriend of Elmer Spangler, the love-struck fellow who fired that gunshot in the Little Mexico Café at the 1933 World's Fair in a desperate attempt to gain the attention of fan dancer Rosalie. (Stella and Elmer both appeared as Munchkins in the *Wizard of Oz*.) A diligent Internet

---

[20] Ten years later, Baskette (né James Baskett) auditioned for a bit part in the Walt Disney feature film *Song of the South*, a partially animated movie based on the "Br'er Rabbit" stories by Joel Chandler Harris. Producers were so impressed that he was cast in the lead role as "Uncle Remus." What should have become a major film career was aborted when Baskette, suffering from diabetes, died of heart failure in 1948 at the age of 44, barely three months after becoming the first black man to earn an Academy Award for his performance.

[21] The octogenarian Miss Idelle, still living in 2017, may be seen fan dancing in videos posted on YouTube.

researcher might even come across Fifi, "the pocket-edition Sally Rand." As late as 1940, Mildred Dolly was performing at the Texas State Fair as "the only midget fan dancer in the world."

Jimmy Slater

A female impersonator in the United Kingdom, Jimmy Slater is deserving of a book of his own. He was born in 1898 in Yorkshire and, as a teenager, began performing for seaside concert parties in the years just before the First World War. He is of interest to us because of photographs, seemingly taken in the 1920s (and easily found on the Internet), that depict him dancing with ostrich feather fans. Although he was fully clothed, his act was emblematic of the sort of thing Faith Bacon may have observed during her travels in England and France in the mid-1920s. Jimmy Slater enjoyed a long career, performing in and producing revues for 40 years or more. In his later years he ran a successful costume supply business, dying in 1998 at the age of 100.

Denise Vane and Phyllis Dixey

In the 1930s, the laws in England tolerated female nudity onstage, just as in New York, so long as the young women weren't moving. At the Whitehall Theatre in London, Denise Vane adopted the same strategy in 1937 that Faith Bacon had suggested to Earl Carroll in 1930. Miss Vane laid claim to being the first fan dancer in England by mounting a performance in which her body was concealed by fans held not only by her but also by two female atten-dants. At the close of her act, as the attendants removed the fans to reveal her seemingly naked body, she would stand perfectly still, holding the pose for a tantalizingly brief period before the lights dimmed or the curtain fell.

In November 1939, Phyllis Dixey further popularized the fan dance in England when she performed what she called "Confessions of a Fan Dancer" — a dance in which she used ostrich feather fans to "give glimpses of her naked form" — at the Tivoli Theatre in Hull. Citing a breach of public decency, a police investigation ensued and an appeal was made to the Lord Chamberlain, who at the time was in charge of licensing plays and sketches. His initial reaction was to forbid the performance. With her livelihood threatened, she made a face-to-face personal plea, no doubt citing the morale of the nation during wartime.[22] The high gentleman's fears were assuaged,

---

[22] On Armistice Day in 1941, as a gesture of support for the war effort, Miss Dixey personally bought every seat in the house at the Phoenix Theatre in London and put on a show for an audience comprised exclusively of servicemen.

his approval was secured, and the show continued. Miss Dixey went on to enjoy local fame as the "Queen of Striptease" in the United Kingdom.[23]

E very fad, every craze, eventually runs its course. Flagpole sitting, coon-skin caps, hula hoops, bellbottom pants, the game of "Puff Billiards" (look it up!), "The Twist," eight-track tapes, and CB radios have mostly come and gone. "Streakers" are seldom seen. The prime time to cash in on your Cabbage Patch Doll collection may already have passed.

At the very height of the fan dancing craze, for some reason, Uniontown, Pennsylvania, was a hotbed of interest. In April 1934, local favorite Gladys Reed — "a sensational and beautiful Sally Rand of the fan dance fame" — was booked into the Baron Munchausen Room of the Summit Hotel.[24] That same month, Thais Giroux — advertised as a "challenge to Sally Rand, more gorgeous, more beautiful, more aesthetic" — was appearing each night in that same room, reportedly from "6 p.m. To 8 a.m."

But was the fad fading? Two months later, on June 25th, the "Inquiring Reporter" for the *Uniontown Daily News Standard* asked its readers: "Do you think the fan dance craze is on the wane?" Four thought it was. Max Smigelsky opined:

> Very much so and with me it was on the wane a year ago for my wife and I. After seeing Sally Rand at the Century of Progress exposition last summer, [we] visited a nightclub where an amateur fan dancing contest was the feature. Before the evening was out we had seen just 30 dancers. My admiration of them vanished with the evening.

Miss Sara Jean Townsend chipped in:

> Yes. I'm sure it is. My brother, Nat, plays the piano in the Baron Munchausen Orchestra and he says that although the fan dancers were a rage for a while their popularity seems to be on the wane. I guess folks around here have seen enough of fan dancers for a while.

---

[23] Miss Dixey's "Peek-a-Boo" show was so popular that it led to a 1978 feature film, *The One and Only Phyllis Dixey*, starring Lesley-Anne Down in the title role.

[24] The event wasn't really all that consequential, but it is fun to mention the Baron Munchausen Room.

Apparently not. About three weeks later, the Baron Munchausen Room, seemingly on a roll, ran an ad challenging Sally to a duel of sorts, offering:

> ... $1,000.00 IN CASH TO SALLY RAND if she will appear for ten
> minutes in a contest of Art, Talent and Beauty with "AMPHITRITE"
> and we will leave it up to SALLY whether Fans, Bubbles or Veils
> shall be used.

Sally didn't take the bait, although she actually was in the area, about to open a five-day engagement at the Stanley Theatre in Pittsburgh with a cast of 40. It wouldn't have been much of a contest. Sally Rand went on to become an icon and the subject of this biography, while the presumably lovely "Amphitrite" — named for the sea nymph in Greek mythology who became the wife of Poseidon, Ruler of the Ocean — is lost to history.

Even today, fan dancing is not a completely lost art. Far from it. Classes are still offered around the country at studios like the New York School of Burlesque and the Vaudezilla in Chicago. Chef and author Amber DiGiovanni continues to be available for "fan dancing" bookings.[25] And a wide selection of ostrich feather fans is still offered for sale online at Amazon.com.

By 1940, most of the second-tier fan dancers had fallen by the wayside. A devastating war was raging in Europe. Once the 1939 World's Fair had closed, there would not be another in the United States until 1962 in Seattle, Washington. The ranks had certainly been thinned, but Sally Rand and Faith Bacon soldiered on.

---

[25] Author of children's books and the cookbooks *A Passion for Food* (2006) and *Midwestern Soul Food* (2010), Miss DiGiovanni has also hosted radio talk shows and operated the Sally Rand Museum in St. Joseph, Missouri, before it closed in 2012. See her website at: www.sallyrandshows.com.

CHAPTER SEVENTEEN

A New Beginning

Afoot and lighthearted I take to the open road, healthy,
free, the world before me.
~ Walt Whitman

With bankruptcy comes a new beginning. Whatever Sally may have owed to various adversaries who were pursuing her in court — not to mention the documented sums she owed to banks, suppliers, and other creditors, all these debts were washed away by the cleansing waters of the federal judicial system.

How could such a circumstance befall the "best business woman in San Francisco"? Well, Sally had a ready answer: The management of the Golden Gate International Exposition was to blame for closing the fair more than a month ahead of schedule. Sally had just remodeled and reopened the venue housing her "Gay Paree" attraction when the whole venture suddenly folded, prompting contractors to attach her various enterprises and throw her into court. Two days later she was declaring bankruptcy. As she saw it:

> The fault with expositions is that boards of directors are not show folk.
> If expositions were run by show people they would become financial
> successes instead of the flops so many of them have been.

At any rate, Sally was soon up and running, full speed ahead. After touring the Pacific Northwest, her "Star Studded Revue" (the "Entire Production Conceived and Staged by ... Miss Sally Rand") opened on Christmas Night, 1939, at the lavish Florentine Gardens on Hollywood Boulevard in Los Angeles. Local officials were wary, as an attempt to crack down on "lewd shows" was currently under way in the city. Even so, they agreed to issue Sally's revue a permit so long as the performances would be "up to high standards" and she would remain "completely covered at all times." The dinner club's entertainment manager, Bee Carson, assured the police commission that Sally would be "well covered" and the show would be kept "clean."

If the illustrated program for the engagement is any indication, enforcement of these conditions tended to be rather lax. Both the cover and inside back cover display photos of Sally with arms extended above her head, her breasts (and pretty much everything else) fully exposed.

Despite having emerged from bankruptcy just a few weeks earlier, Sally managed to put together a large-scale production. Both the "Dinner Show" and "Supper Show" featured nine or ten completely different acts. Sally did the fan dance at one and the bubble dance at the other. The Dinner Show opened with "A Day at the Dog Show" in which nine of the "World's Most Beautiful Glamour Girls" performed, each with a different breed of trained dog. The program also featured a large cast of singers, dancers, acrobats, and comedians. A contemporary press review summarized the evening's fare:

> Smart dogs and handsome girls make up the irresistible combination
> in Sally Rand's revue. ... In an hour's time Miss Rand and her
> glamorous ladies manage to display all the fine points of any good
> musical comedy without subjecting their audience to the distraction
> of plot and dialogue. It is pretty nearly all meat and no gristle.

The new year had barely begun when Sally turned up at the Don Lee Broadcasting studios in Hollywood to make her debut on an amazing new entertainment medium — television. The experimental television station W6XAO had first broadcast a rudimentary signal as early as December 23, 1931. In March of 1933, the station telecast *The Crooked Circle*, the first motion picture ever presented on television, although only about five television receivers in the Los Angeles area actually picked up the signal. By 1939, the station claimed a viewership of 1,500 people in a few hundred homes.

Emerging from her live telecast, Sally remarked that television is the "medium for flesh and blood shows." A promising new industry was taking its first baby steps. Through a series of sales and mergers, W6XAO ultimately became KCBS, the flagship station for the CBS television network on the West Coast.

By February, Sally's revue had moved from the relatively intimate confines of the Florentine Gardens to Los Angeles' spacious and spectacular Orpheum Theatre. With up to 2,000 seats to fill, Sally continued her promotional practice of speaking to civic groups. Addressing an American Legion gathering, she offered an observation that still rings true in the overheated political climate of our own time:

> It's one thing to march to a fife and drum and it's another thing to
> have an intelligent understanding of patriotism. There's considerable

difference in being a real citizen or a mere inhabitant of this country. A citizen gets all the benefits and privileges of America and takes part in government. An inhabitant only lives here.

Sally's star was shining as bright as ever and not just in the United States. The grand "El teatro Follies Bergere" in Mexico City was interested in booking her for a multi-week engagement. This was a welcome opportunity and by the second week in March Sally had turned her attention south of the border. Needing nearly $6,000 to finance the trip (over $100,000 in today's dollars), she reportedly "mortgaged" five pairs of fans, eight hand-painted chiffon sarongs, a carton of costumes and an assortment of other items, including stage equipment. The venture was no small-scale excursion. The troupe included a large supporting cast and "two carloads of scenery" — essentially, the same "Star Studded Revue" that had played at the Florentine Gardens and the Orpheum, plus the famed magician, Señor Maldo.[1]

Sally's personal staff of ten included her former fiancé, Chissie Mayon, personal assistant Ralph Hobart, and publicist Harold Prendergast. This was in addition, of course, to her three Pekingese dogs Quani, Bo-bo and Ching-ling. Before she departed from the train station in El Paso, with no makeup and "her blonde hair rolled up in aluminum curlers under a peasant handkerchief," Sally answered the question of the day: "Why do I have Pekingese instead of Russian wolfhound? Well, you can't very well take a Russian wolfhound to bed with you in a Pullman, can you?"

Sally's revue, her performance of "El Baile Del Abanico" (the dancing fan) and, in particular, "Las Gloriosas Beldades Mundiales" (her 25 "Glorious World Beauties") were all greeted enthusiastically in Mexico City. In her spare time, Sally took a break to watch a local women's basketball team play. She also had a chance to chat and compare notes with Carmen Amaya, the Spanish gypsy flamenco dancer, who was on her way to New York City and national acclaim.

The Mexico City engagement was held over for eight weeks. As the cast, crew, and equipment were loaded back on train cars for the return to the States, Sally flew directly to San Francisco, arriving in time for yet another opening day.

---

[1] Born in Texas and raised in Mexico, the legendary Santa Barbara magician Abel Maldonado enjoyed a successful magic career touring America as "Señor Maldo." Acclaimed for his "Buried Alive!" publicity stunt, he was an esteemed nightclub magician who influenced many of today's top magicians.

On May 25, 1940, the Golden Gate Exposition opened for a second year on Treasure Island. Although Sally's own show had not been invited to participate, her "Nude Ranch" concession was back, now under new management as she had relinquished control following her bankruptcy. Billy Rose had dropped his threat to sue Sally over the right to use the name "Sally Rand's Nude Ranch," but he had also brought a version of his "Aquacade" show to Treasure Island, offering stiff competition to every other attraction. Despite having lost managerial control, Sally got into a flap with the new bosses over whether the ranch girls would continue to appear in western regalia or switch to something a little more exotic, declaring:

> The ranch ought to go Balinese this year. The girls could wear
> sarongs if the police insist on it. They could wear a few South Seas
> flowers too…. The cattle ranch idea, with scarves, holsters and
> boots, was swell for last year. But we need something new and
> different to compete with Billy Rose's Aquacade.

The concession's new operators vigorously disagreed. They liked the scarf-holster-and-boots motif just fine (although reportedly they could have been persuaded to eliminate scarves and holsters, if necessary). No longer the owner of the attraction, Sally's options were limited. She was not happy: "I'll have to see my attorneys. It's in the contract … that I can personally supervise the 1940 attraction. After all, my name is being used."

In the end, Sally was just too busy traveling the country with her new revue to pursue the matter. Yet she was too much of a ham to completely absent herself. And so, on opening day, wearing a knee-length leopard skin coat, She was on hand, along with one of "Singer's Midgets," to assist Exposition President Marshall Dill in the ribbon cutting at the "Gayway."

Faith

Faith Bacon, having gotten a boost from her appearance at the New York World's Fair, was engaged in a tour of her own. Appearing in somewhat lesser venues than Sally, she had still managed to draw decent crowds and earn an occasional spot in the news. The war in Europe was heating up. Paris had fallen to Hitler's forces on June 14, 1940. Two weeks later, Faith announced that after her current engagement in Hollywood she intended to go to New York and seek passage to England in the hope of serving as a nurse or ambulance driver. "If I can't," she added, "I'll go to Canada and proceed from there. And I'll pay my own way." Within another two weeks, the Battle of Britain had begun.

Throughout the remainder of 1940, Sally continued to tour the country, playing to enthusiastic crowds and addressing business and civic groups whenever possible. The touring company included an up and coming ballet dancer Valya (or Valia) Valentinoff, who had joined the show little suspecting that he was about to run smack dab into the troupe leader, an irrepressible force of a lady 15 years his senior.[2] During the course of the tour, the pair would appear together in such top-flight venues as the Cocoanut Grove Roof, a dinner theater atop the Park Central Hotel in New York City.

The presence of the handsome (some would say beautiful) young dancer proved a tonic for Sally. It wasn't long before they were intertwined in a manner more intimate than that of their public performances. Gossip columnists took note, one indicating that Valya was Sally's "closest fan."

Snubbed by the New York World's Fair, and with her recent bankruptcy and loss of control over the Nude Ranch still weighing on her mind, Sally saw the attentive 21-year-old Valya as a breath of fresh air — someone tossing her a romantic lifeline. She would later refer to him as "you who gave me this, my life, my heart and laughter back again."

As with all her other beaus, Sally was prone to writing lengthy, rambling letters, often including unsolicited advice. A fragment has survived from a letter she wrote to Valya, apparently in response to his complaints about not being well liked:

> ... *[The pains] you suffer cannot be hidden; you may think you hide them, but the smiling mask you put on, the strained effusion, the unctuous gratitude — all these false things are obvious. The other person doesn't stop to analyze them; other people are not interested enough in psychology and they don't care; all they know is that they just don't like you, and they are either indifferent or they are amused. They don't stop to reason why. In order to be loved, liked and admired, you must exude these same qualities ... you cannot be respected without giving respect.... Strangely enough, it all goes back to those truisms which we treat so lightly — you get just what you give!*
>
> *If I could only make a hole in your head, then get a funnel and POUR THIS FACT INTO IT! If I could get a phonograph record to repeat it to you a thousand times a day; if I could convince you*

---

2   Valya literally ran into Sally. During one of their dance numbers in August 1940, Sally was "knocked for a loop" by Valya, one columnist noting that it "was strictly accidental, but worth the price of admission."

of it in some way — you would be a phenomenal success. Dancing is not enough; artistry is not enough; technique is not enough. In order to live pleasantly in this world where society makes a place only for those who deserve it, and where we must make frequent contacts constantly, you have to be an attractive HUMAN BEING, and attractive human beings are LOVING human beings who have the greatest of charity and tolerance and admiration for the works of others....

The successful catch on quickly and apply the maxim; the vague and confused mill around and fail to see and refuse to hear and won't believe, and so fight a futile battle which must end in defeat. Don't let this be you!

Sally had a bit of a scare in late January 1941 when her "big cream-colored car" skidded off an icy highway and into a ditch near Janesville, Wisconsin. Although she admitted "it was a harrowing experience," no one was injured and, after seeking warmth in a nearby farmhouse while a wrecker was summoned, the troupe continued on its way to a successful engagement in Milwaukee. Still, she could hardly have failed to notice the chilly breeze blowing in off Lake Michigan. Suddenly, turning the wheel toward the tropics must have seemed like a very good idea, indeed.

Soon headed to Miami, Sally stopped on the way in Atlanta, Georgia, where the State Senate had adopted a special resolution inviting her to make an appearance before their august body. On February 12th, accompanied by her mother and father-in-law, she was escorted to the rostrum in the Senate chamber to make a few remarks.

Wearing a tasteful black dress, brown fur coat, and "lavender hat with a sprig of green," she addressed the assembled members and the public in the packed galleries: "There is so much seriousness to be discussed today that we all, at times, need a little relaxation and escape from reality into the world of fantasy." Sally continued: "That's what I can provide with my work. I'm glad to be here because I knew I'd meet so many of my favorite men, especially the old ones. They give you what the young ones promise."

After delivering a few more Randian observations, each one met with the usual good-natured titters and guffaws, Sally closed with the well-practiced line: "I hope you'll come out to my show this evening, so I can see more of you — and you can see more of me."

On January 20, 1936, King George V passed away at Sandringham House, the royal country home some 90 miles from London. He was succeeded by his son, who took the name King Edward VIII.

What Sally Rand was to the art of titillation, Bobby Jones was to golf. In 1930 Bobby Jones became the only golfer to ever win the "Grand Slam" top four golf tournaments in the same year — all as an amateur competitor! In 1933, while Sally was waving her fans at the Chicago Fair, Bobby was busy helping to design the Augusta National Golf Club, which would begin hosting the annual "Masters" tournament the following year.

By March 15, 1941, Bobby Jones had retired from competitive golf, King Edward VIII had long since abdicated the throne of England in order to marry divorcee Wallis Warfield Simpson ("the woman I love"), and Sally Rand had completed a sort of "grand slam" of her own, starring at several more "World's Fairs" since her triumph in Chicago. The three seemingly had little in common, yet, on this sunny Saturday in The Bahamas, they found themselves in close proximity.

Prince Edward was in Nassau because he had recently been appointed Royal Governor of the Bahama Islands. He and his twice-divorced wife, now the "Duke and Duchess of Windsor," had been delivered to the islands by a British Warship the preceding August. Noting that the former King was suspected of being a Nazi sympathizer, Prime Minister Winston Churchill had decided that Edward could do the least damage to the British war effort if he were comfortably deposited at a tropical outpost thousands of miles away from the seat of power. The Duke was none too pleased with the assignment, having called The Bahamas "a third-class British colony," but, in the grand British tradition, he had determined to keep calm and carry on.

Bobby Jones was there because, along with fellow "greatest-names-in-golf" competitors Tommy Armour, Walter Hagen, and Gene Sarazen, he had accepted the Duke's invitation to participate in a 36-hole charity match to raise money for the Bahamian Red Cross, of which the Duchess served as president. A group of star tennis players, led by Bill Tilden, Don Budge, and Alice Marble had also journeyed to Nassau to participate in exhibition matches for the same cause.

Sally Rand had come over following a club engagement in nearby Miami, where, in an item beginning with the lede: "Things for which There Is No Explanation Outside the Psychopathic Wards," columnist H. I. Phillips had remarked: "Miami, where more naked women are visible on the beaches than anywhere on Earth, is featuring Sally Rand in a night-club disrobing act! And the people are flocking to see her!"

The Islands of The Bahamas had been a destination of choice for British and American tourists since 1859 when steamship pioneer Samuel Cunard was persuaded to include Nassau as a port of call for the monthly cruise of the SS Corisca between New York and Havana. In 1900, Henry Flagler had opened The Hotel Colonial in Fort Nassau, the first beachfront hotel in the country, and had started his own steamship line to transport tourists between Florida and The Bahamas.

The tourist economy of the islands fluctuated with the world economy for the next four decades. Prospects were seriously dashed when, in 1938, the local natural sponge industry collapsed as a result of a mysterious disease. But things were looking up again by 1941 as Pan American Airlines began its first non-seaplane service between Florida and Nassau. The increased access, together with the popularity of its new "Royal" governor, spurred the Bahamas Tourist Office to stage its first "Bahamas Fair." Events surrounding the weeklong festival included a fashion show, yacht races, celebrity tennis and golf matches, and other social, sporting, and entertainment activities. The Duke and Duchess (or "David" and "Wally" as they were called by friends) couldn't have been more thrilled when, on February 21st, their dog "Pookie" took second prize in the Cairn class at the Bahamas Fair Dog Show.

What role did Sally Rand play in all of this? According to a biography of the Duchess:

> During the course of one Red Cross drive the fashionable ladies of Nassau were covered in confusion when Miss Sally Rand, the American burlesque queen, turned up and offered her services. Miss Rand was appearing in Nassau, and was eager to perform at the gala charity concert to be held that night. The Duchess was with other Red Cross committee women when the request came through. She laughed and commented: "I am playing no part in this; you must decide," and left. Sally Rand duly appeared and did her bubble dance. At the tables, Nassau society, including the Windsors, watched stonily. At the end the Duke said, "Come on. I'm not having my staff hang around here" and the party left. Next day the Duchess asked a friend in delight, "What are they saying in Nassau this morning?" Incidents like this tended to break the stuffiness of Bahamian life.

Sally's own quite different perspective is preserved in a column she wrote for the University of Wisconsin student newspaper:

> I am reminded of the time I did that command performance for the Duke and Duchess of Windsor in Nassau. There was golf the next day and the Duke with several assorted high bracket golfers played nine holes. I was fascinated, sandwiched as I was between the fabulous page-boy bob of debutante Brenda Diana Duff Frazier Junior[3] and her maw, followed by the field of bright horsey tweedy folk whose intelligent comments included such pithy and erudite phrases as "Oh, I say, good shot, old boy," [and] "That's not cricket, you know."
>
> The Duchess was perfect. From the top of her sleek, perfectly coiffed hair (topped by a tiny little skull cap, upon which she had placed two little jeweled clips containing about a gillian dollars' worth of diamonds and sapphires that exactly matched her eyes) to the tips of her wedgies (handmade, of course) with which she wore little hand-knitted blue silk socks that came to a point at the back for all the world like a miniature Robin Hood — she was the perfect person. She was prettily tanned; her blue eyes sparkled and laughed and never lost their look of utter and delightful admiration of David. Her ... bracelets were gold and diamonds and rubies and sapphires — exactly right — and you knew ... that she looked exactly right because her guy had told her she did and she had spent time and effort (we won't go into money here) in producing the effect that made him look at her that way.

As the Duke and Duchess partied on in Nassau, the citizens of London were enduring the seventh straight month of sustained bombing by Hitler's German Luftwaffe (the London "Blitz").[4] On March 19th, the city experienced its worst attack of the year to date, suffering heavy damage from incendiary bombs. But under the winter sun in The Bahamas the ongoing war in Europe

---

[3] Tagged as one of the "Poor Little Rich Girls" by the press (along with Gloria Vanderbilt, Barbara Hutton, and Doris Duke), Miss Brenda Frazier was a strikingly beautiful debutante whose celebrity alone had landed her on the cover of *LIFE Magazine* in 1938. A regular visitor to Nassau, the socialite was once pursued by eccentric billionaire Howard Hughes. Young John F. Kennedy was also said to have an interest in her. Actress Tallulah Bankhead had a different take: "That snot-nosed Frazier kid is more famous than yours truly and, God knows, I'm the most famous pussy on the planet since Cleo herself."

[4] Between early fall of 1940 and late spring of 1941 (two months after the charity event in The Bahamas), 16 British cities and towns were bombarded by aerial raids. In less than nine months, London was attacked 71 times.

was out of sight if not out of mind. The heralded match between Bobby Jones and the other famous golfers remained the topic of the day in Nassau.

And, as you might expect, the versatile Miss Rand had something to say:

> I play golf, not well, but I keep a lot of golf dates. I am a pushover for being shown how to improve my drive. I'm bright too. I only had to be gagged the first twenty times before I realized that you are supposed to be quiet when people are putting.

Miss Rand and the former King of England may or may not have exchanged face-to-face pleasantries, though the royal couple did tend to confine themselves to social interaction within their official circle. Even so, the circle is sometimes broken. At one point, Sally's press agent interrupted a golf match to ask Captain Vyvian Drury, the Duke's aide-de-camp, whether the former King would be willing to pose for a picture with the famous dancer. Revealing his British sense of humor, Drury replied: "And how would you like to have the Duke pose? With or without his trousers?"

The "Match of Champions" proceeded as scheduled. The Duchess and some 1,000 spectators followed the golfers around the course. Attired in a plaid sport jacket and yellow slacks, the Duke of Windsor served as referee, holding the pin for each shot and also deciding which golfer would shoot first. The celebrity match raised today's equivalent of $122,000 for the Red Cross and Sally Rand raised a few eyebrows.[5]

The charity concert, celebrity golf and tennis matches, fashion show and dog show had all been great successes. The hundreds of visitors who had come from South Florida by boat and by plane were in a merry mood little knowing that the Red Cross funds would soon be sorely needed to address damage from a major hurricane that would hit The Bahamas on October 6th. Barely two months later, the Empire of Japan would attack the U.S. fleet at Pearl Harbor and the country would be drawn into the Second World War. The Duke of Windsor would remain in the islands until the end of the war. On March 15, 1945, as Sally was preparing to open at the Aragon Ballroom in Chicago, four years to the day after the celebrity golf match, the Duke

---

[5]   The whole affair had been foreshadowed eight months earlier by columnist Neal O'Hara: "The Duke's appointment is very popular with the Bahamans, most of whom are Negroes. But Duke Ellington might even have been a more popular choice. With the ex-monarch reigning as the head man at Nassau, it is expected that tourist trade will be stimulated. They could get the same results, however, by appointing Sally Rand."

announced his resignation as Royal Governor of The Bahamas. A month later he and the Duchess returned to Paris, never again to reside in Great Britain.[6]

Within four days of her encounter with the royals, Sally was back on stage at the Olympia — advertised as Miami's largest, finest, and most popular theater — sharing the bill with Irish songstress Terry Lawlor, rubber-limbed comedian Gil Lamb, and Pansy the dancing horse.

Her sojourn in Miami made news on yet another front. In March of 1941, always interested in aviation, Sally reportedly enrolled at Embry-Riddle Aviation School to pursue "a course in technical plane construction." Speaking at her patriotic best, she announced that, if America were to become involved in the war, she herself would enlist in any branch of the flying service that might need her. Even if this whole thing was nothing more than another publicity stunt, Sally, a licensed pilot, *was* pictured in the press, outfitted in overalls and goggles, "learning to weld a plane's framework together."

O nce again, it was the first week in May and time for the Harvard University "Freshman Smoker." This time the Master of Ceremonies would be Ed Sullivan, the theater columnist for the *New York Daily News*, who would later host one of the all-time most popular variety programs in the history of television.[7] Since Sally was in town performing at the Latin Quarter, it was only natural that she be invited for a return appearance. She happily accepted, announcing that she would speak on the topic "What the Average College Stage Door Johnny Is Looking for when He Stage-Door-Johnnies a Burlesque House Stage Door."

Sally had been advised that she would be picked up after her show at the Latin Quarter. So, when a station wagon pulled up beside her at the appointed hour, she nodded to the nice young gentleman holding the door, and cheerfully entered the vehicle, little suspecting that these students were actually from nearby Massachusetts Institute of Technology (MIT) passing themselves off as Harvard men. She was quickly escorted to the Burton Room in the MIT dormitories where she soon recognized her error. Even so,

---

6   The title "His Royal Highness the Duke of Windsor" was created for the former King Edward the VIII after he abdicated the British throne. The title was vacated in 1972 on the death of its first and only holder.

7   Although *The Ed Sullivan Show* was very popular, TV critics were less than enchanted by Sullivan's manner. Syndicated columnist Harriet Van Horne wrote that "Sullivan got where he is not by having a personality, but by having no personality; he is the commonest common denominator." In a terse response, Sullivan wrote: "Dear Miss Van Horne: You bitch. Sincerely, Ed Sullivan."

she promptly perched on a table surrounded by students attired in bathrobes and pajamas and engaged in a quiz fest. As reported by the MIT student newspaper, "she was given a rousing, but tasteful reception." Assistant Editor S. Joseph Tankoos, a sophomore, then conferred upon the "vivacious, wise-cracking Miss Rand, the position of Associate Professor of Entertainment Engineering."

Delivering her first "lecture" in this new capacity, Sally extemporized on the subject of women, illustrating her discourse "with numerous anecdotes." The student paper reported that her "main thesis was that we should beware of girls we think are intelligent, because the chances are that all they do is just sit and listen to us spout and are in reality dumber than hell." She also warned the young MIT men to "steer clear of 'good' girls, because they are the ones who hook men fastest."

Conceding that "this is the nicest kidnapping I've ever had," Sally reluctantly advised the boys that she really did need to get back to Harvard where the school's smoker committee was no doubt becoming concerned about her whereabouts.[8] A wild ride followed, led by Miss Harriet Aldrich "in a slick two-tone coupe." The parade of 15 automobiles "overflowing with yelling, screeching Tech men" finally delivered the unruffled Miss Rand to her desired destination "like the gentlemen they were."

Rather than be further delayed, Sally submitted to being physically carried into the auditorium by John Eustin, captain of the swimming team. One can almost picture Ed Sullivan making the introduction: "And now, right here on our stage — the one, the only . . . Miss Sally *Rand!*" More conservatively dressed than her admirers preferred, Sally strode to the microphone in a floor-length gown. As she tried to begin her speech, she was met with calls of "take it off, take it off!"

Underestimating the rashness of her youthful audience, Sally called out: "I will if you will!" The episode was later described in the papers: "Almost to a man, the more than 1,000 frosh and gate crashers began to disrobe. Coats, shirts, neckties and other apparel were hurled from the balcony and orchestra to the stage."

---

8   This wasn't the first such stunt devised by those wily gentlemen of MIT. Indeed, as recently as the year before, they had intercepted Jack Benny's radio valet Eddie "Rochester" Anderson on *his* way to the Harvard smoker. Anderson actually ended up putting on a performance for them before realizing that he was in the wrong place. After the show, Anderson was asked: "How much does Mr. Benny pay you?" He responded: "Well, I'll tell you, it's roughly twenty grand, but when he smooths it out it comes to about 30 bucks."

Realizing her mistake, Sally hastily came up with another suggestion. Shouting above the din, she exclaimed: "This is something I never thought of before, but I think of it now. I've never danced a Viennese waltz with a Harvard man." Temporarily distracted from removing their pants, this invitation motivated a score of would-be dance partners to rush the stage. The first to reach her was H. Hallett Whitman, Jr., a Boston junior (and future father of Meg Whitman, former President and CEO of eBay). Hallett had barely managed a few steps before several other eager waltzers cut in.

Searching for another distraction, Sally prompted the orchestra to play "Fair Harvard." Everyone joined in. Then, realizing she still hadn't followed through on her promise to disrobe, Sally told a few stories, made some brief remarks about how thrilled she was to be there, and beat a hasty path off the stage. Soon several hundred of her devotees were pouring out of the theater onto the street, clashing with police, halting street cars and otherwise tying up traffic in Harvard Square as they raced about shouting: "We want Sally Rand without her fan." After what the press called "much scuffling," the police eventually drove the crowd back into Harvard Yard.

The next day, while entertaining three *Harvard Crimson* reporters in her dressing room between shows at the Latin Quarter, Sally cooed: "I really had fun at the Smoker this year. I didn't try to be serious this time. I just had fun. That boy who danced with me out at Harvard was pretty good." And as to whether anyone had been shocked by her stories: "Yes, there was a double entendre. Of course, I don't know anything about sex except what I read."

As if all the hubbub associated with Sally's appearance at the Freshman Smoker weren't enough, the following week the once and future Mayor of Boston, Former Governor Jim Curley, soberly weighed in during a Mother's Day address to the Cambridge Elks Club:

> It seems like blasphemy at this serious hour in our country's history for the oldest educational institution to herald to the world that it entertained a stripteaser and that the students indulged in stripping themselves.... Harvard may educate men, but it has failed to give them the moral and strong will without which no nation can endure.

Two days later, having observed Sally's performance at the Latin Quarter, City Licensing Board Chairwoman Mary E. Driscoll brought down the hammer, declaring that henceforth Sally would be banned from appearing in any Boston night spot over which the board had jurisdiction. Telling the board she was taking such drastic action because Sally had appeared in a white evening gown which she conveniently "lost" half way through the performance, Miss Driscoll also objected to some of the stories Sally had told as part of her act. Adding insult to injury, Driscoll flatly denied a request from the Latin Quarter's management that Sally be permitted to appear at a dinner show — in street clothes.

It turns out this sort of thing was standard operating procedure for Chairwoman Driscoll. Only a few days earlier, she had issued an edict closing down striptease shows in Boston nightclubs, and she had been none too charitable about the performers, declaring: "Those women don't dance. They just wiggle. And, anyway, most of them are too fat to dance."[9]

Sally wasn't happy about being "banned in Boston," protesting: "My whole career, everything I have built up for many years, is in danger, grave danger." Within a couple of years, though, Sally was more sanguine. Writing for the Harvard student newspaper, with the ongoing carnage in Europe very much on her mind, she waxed nostalgic about her Cambridge experience:

> Then there was the time I lectured at Harvard.... But hold, I was invited back again. That's really the proof of being a wanted guest, only this time I decided not to lecture. I thought it would be fun just to have a conversation with a Harvard boy or boys. It was. Then I decided it would be fun to dance a Viennese waltz with one of them.... He was six foot eight or so, and ... I, being five feet tall in my high heels, literally didn't touch the floor. The boys were delighted. Then they sang to me.
>
> I'd been giggling and having fun, and so had they. And then their voices rose in "Fair Harvard." There were a thousand of them or more. Pink faces, a sea of them ... and young. Their voices rose in unison. I thought of thousands of other young faces in Europe's war (we weren't in it then) whose voices weren't raised in song. Whose voices would never be raised in song again.
>
> All right, so I'm a ninny. I think I have never been so moved. I didn't say anything then. I couldn't explain it to them. Even if I could, it would have embarrassed them. Anyway I had a lump in my throat. They took me home. We talked, we laughed.
>
> "Goodbye, thank you. I had a wonderful time."
>
> But I never forgot. They sang "Fair Harvard" to me. Some of them will never sing anymore. But I'll remember.

---

9   Mary Driscoll was fighting the good fight as late as 1955 when she famously declared she would "move heaven and earth" to prevent Christine Jorgensen (famed for her pioneering sex change operation) from appearing at the very same Latin Quarter. Driscoll retired in 1956 after 32 years on the job. She was 76.

Sally spent the summer of 1941 traveling the country. In July she went back on the summer stock stage at the Woodstock Playhouse in New York, playing the role of Sadie Thompson once again in *Rain* and also starring as Regina Giddens in *The Little Foxes*. Other excursions took her back to her old stomping grounds in southwest Missouri to appear at the Ozark Empire District Fair in Springfield, Missouri. On September 9th, she spoke to the soldiers from Fort Leonard Wood at a training center near Rolla, Missouri, but four days later was barred from appearing at a USO dance in nearby St. Louis.

Catholic members of the USO committee had objected to Sally's appearance. W. N. Goodall, director of the service men's center, begged to differ: "She wasn't going to do a fan dance or anything like that. She was just going to make a little talk to the boys and maybe dance with some of them." But Monsignor George A. Lodes, Pastor of the Sainte Geneviève du Bois Church in Warson Woods, would hear none of it: "It makes no difference whether she was to dance or not. The fact she was to appear at the service men's center was enough for me."[10] Sally took the affront in stride, never to know that the Most Holy Reverend Lodes was standing on feet of clay.[11]

Before summer was over, she was appearing at the North Montana State Fair in Great Falls. She also found time to make a side trip to a working ranch near Red Lodge, home of the famous female rodeo trick rider Alice Greenough. The two hit it off right away.

To hear Alice talk, you might have thought it was Sally speaking, in a slightly different context:

> A cowgirl has to be able to get out there and ride just as tough a bronc as the cowboys.... You can train a girl to do trick riding and racing, but a cowgirl has to grow up in the cow country to learn the disposition of ornery broncs and critters to be any good in the rodeo arena.

---

[10] In this opinion, Monsignor Lodes was at odds with his fellow Missourian, U.S. Senator Harry S. Truman. Sally may have been denied entry to the USO dance, but she was packing them in at the 6,000-seat Fox Theatre in St. Louis. Writing to his wife Bess on September 18th, the future president reported: "I went out and took a walk last night and saw where Sally Rand was at the Fox right around the corner. Went in to see what she looked like. Her bubble dance was very nice and decent but the show was rotten, so I left and finished my walk."

[11] Twenty-five years later in 1966, Lodes gave the homily at the 25th anniversary of the ordination of Reverend Michael Owens. (Father Lodes was described as "a close friend of the jubilarian.") Ironically, a 2011 report identified the two men as "predatory priests using religious ceremony as a guise to attack young girls."

I've been smashed around a lot but fortunately I haven't any bad scars or marks to show for it. I've been trampled by broncs and hooked by bulls but always came out of it with luck on my side....

How come I never married one of the cowboys? A lot of people ask me that. It's because I know 'em too well.

As it happens, Sally was one of those gals who *didn't* know 'em all that well. But she did know that Alice had an older brother whom she had briefly encountered at the Cheyenne Frontier Days back in 1935. He too was something of a buckin' bronco rider. And, since she was in Montana, she may also have been aware of that popular song of the day by Patsy Montana, "I Want to be a Cowboy's Sweetheart."

Part Three

The Way We Were

The image of Turk Greenough giving Sally a piggy-back ride was taken at the marriage license bureau in Los Angeles on January 2, 1942.

CHAPTER EIGHTEEN

The Cowboy and the Lady

A more unlikely pair you'll never see.
~ Bobbie Goldsboro, "The Cowboy and the Lady"

On July 29, 1933, following a thrilling ride on a horse named Satan, a guy called "Turk" was declared the bucking contest champion at the annual Frontier Days rodeo in Cheyenne, Wyoming. The 27-year old cowboy would go on to win many such titles. He had ridden any number of wild horses and bulls, even broken a young filly or two. Little did he suspect that the ride of his life had yet to be corralled.

In his time, Thurkel "Turk" Greenough was the most famous of the four rodeo-riding Greenough siblings of Red Lodge, Montana (although history would eventually promote his sister Alice to the top place). There were two female rodeo riders in the Greenough family: Alice and Margie. His less famous brother Bill was also in the rodeo game. Another brother, Frank, chose to become a rancher. The fame of the four riding Greenoughs and their father, "Packsaddle" Ben Greenough, was such that they were even featured in commercial endorsements.[1]

Like many others, Greenough had gotten his first glimpse of Sally Rand in Chicago in 1933. Turk and his cowboy friend Eddie Curtis had slipped away from their wives to see her act.[2] They had waited in line for an hour to buy balcony seats, which had turned out to be disappointingly far away.

Turk got a much closer look in 1935 at the Cheyenne Frontier Days Rodeo, where Sally had been hired to entertain the crowds after the daily rodeo competition. One day after a winning ride, as Turk and his wife Helen stood by the chutes greeting his fans, a petite blonde joined the line of autograph

---

[1] The riding Greenoughs appeared together in a large display ad in the August 31, 1940, issue of *The Saturday Evening Post*. Turk also appeared in ads for Stetson hats and for Montgomery Ward saddles. After Alice won the 1940 bronco riding championship at Madison Square Garden, she too got commercial offers, including one from Chesterfield cigarettes, despite the fact that her father had forcefully forbidden her to smoke.

[2] Turk Greenough was a newlywed, having married his wife, Helen, on April 5, 1933.

seekers. If he recognized Sally, he didn't let on, but Helen knew exactly who she was. Years would pass before Turk and Sally's paths would cross again.

Meanwhile, Turk found occasional work in the movie business as a stunt rider or extra. His first film job was on the 1939 remake of *Beau Geste*, starring Ray Milland and Robert Preston along with another Montana man, Gary Cooper. Working together, Turk and Coop soon became friends,[3] leading Turk's wife to hope she and her husband might establish a permanent home in Hollywood.

By June of 1941, Helen Greenough had grown tired of the roving life and had given Turk an ultimatum: Retire from the rodeo and move with her to California or she would divorce him. Still, despite his many injuries and a rodeo career that was in decline, Turk just couldn't bring himself to quit, so Helen left and Turk went out on the summer rodeo circuit.

To promote the 1941 rodeo at the North Montana State Fair, in early August producer Leo J. Cremer had brought in Sally Rand to pump up the box office. He had gone all out for her, even bringing in a master pyrotechnician to present a fireworks show. Art Briese, who had served in that same capacity at the 1933 Chicago fair, devised a twice-life-sized set piece of Sally's silhouette for the Montana occasion. She could not have been more pleased, remarking: "I never realized how hot I was until I saw myself burning out on the infield last night."

For the rodeo parade, Cremer had Sally riding on horseback next to him, followed by Alice and Margie Greenough, with Turk bringing up the rear. Later, after riding his first bronco of the day, Turk climbed a fence to watch the next riders. To his surprise, Sally climbed up, perched beside him and began peppering him with questions. Apparently remembering her autograph request in 1935, Turk suggested that she owed him an autographed photo in return. "Alright," Sally replied, "come on over to the Rainbow Hotel at six and I'll give you one."

That evening Turk went to the hotel, looked around, and almost left when he couldn't find Sally. She managed to intercept him and promptly sent an assistant back to her room to fetch the photograph. While signing the picture, she invited Turk to come along with her and a few friends to a local nightclub. Sally wouldn't take no for an answer, so when her driver pulled up in front of the hotel in her Cadillac, Turk climbed into the back seat.

---

[3]   It was only natural that Gary Cooper would be drawn to Turk, a real cowboy. Beginning as early as 1923, Cooper had already appeared in dozens of films, in credited and uncredited roles, often playing a cowboy. He had just wrapped up work on his 1938 film release, *The Cowboy and the Lady*, with Merle Oberon.

Sally promptly jumped in after him, making a place for herself on his lap. At the club, she was predictably the center of attention. The band was playing swing tunes and, while every man there wanted to dance with her, Sally reserved her dance card only for Turk.

By all accounts, Turk was smitten. He attended all four of Sally's *Music on Wings* shows in Great Falls and even joined her in Billings, the site of her next engagement. Since Billings wasn't that far from Red Lodge, Turk invited Sally to come home with him to meet his family.

"Packsaddle Ben" liked Sally right away. So did Alice and Margie, finding her to be an independent woman much like themselves. Actually, the horse-riding Greenoughs had long resented Turk's wife because of her aversion to Montana and rodeos generally. So, when Turk eventually announced their breakup and his interest in Sally, the family approved. Returning to Billings, Sally declared that "Red Lodge is Heaven." The Red Lodge paper picked up the quote and trumpeted: "... don your white robes, citizens, and act the role. There can no longer be any question about it. This is Heaven! Sally, who looks like an angel, should know."

On September 12, 1941, Turk performed in Sally's hometown at a rodeo sponsored by the Kansas City Police Benefit Association. Sally went with him. During the visit, she also accompanied him to a gathering of "Lee Jeans" executives at the Muehlebach Hotel, as he had been invited by the Lee Company to consult in the development of a denim jeans style to be crafted especially for cowboys.

Sally sat by impatiently while little progress was made on the design. Finally interjecting herself and given the chance to demonstrate, she ripped out the pant leg seams and used a stapler to "pin" the jeans on the beaming rodeo star in a tighter cut, leaving a slight flare for his riding boots. Turk and the Lee executives were delighted with the result. Later introduced to the public in a full-page "cowboy" ad in *LIFE Magazine*, the new tighter-fitting, boot-cut "Lee Riders" quickly became Lee's most popular product.[4]

The budding romance between the rough and tumble cowpoke and the sweet and saucy fan dancer drew national coverage. In late September of 1941, after little more than a month of courtship, Sally called a press conference in Covington, Kentucky, to announce their engagement.

---

[4] Eight years later, in 1949, the company introduced Lady Lee Riders, promoting them as the best fitting jeans for the female form.

She didn't waste any time getting into take-control-of-the-relationship mode. Revealing the couple's plans to live on Turk's ranch in Red Lodge, Sally also announced that Turk would be giving up rodeo riding because "It's too dangerous":

> We'll start a new kind of dude ranch, but we will only operate it about two months each year. There won't be a singing cowboy or a guitar player on the place. We'll just have good beds, good food and good horses. And any cow hand who sings "Bury Me Not on the Lone Prairie" can pack up his bedroll and start looking for a new job.

> At other times of the year, Turk will present rodeos around the circuit, but not ride in them, and I will produce the shows at night — a kind of revue or spectacle with orchestra, then I'll work the fans one or two nights a week myself.

And, while Turk (a man of very few words) was quoted as being in agreement with her plans, the seeds of future conflict had clearly been planted.

No sooner had Sally's happy news been publicized than a slight technicality came to her attention. A story from Los Angeles was syndicated with the headline: "SALLY'S COWBOY ALREADY WED, SAYS SALLY'S COWBOY'S WIFE":

> "How can he marry that fan dancer when he's married to me?" she asked. "Turk and I were married in Red Lodge, and I went with him everywhere. We used to come out here so Turk could ride in the movies. She said she had received two letters from him, from Montana. One informed her that he was "in love with someone else."

Turk's wife felt blindsided, claiming that Sally had stolen her husband from right under her nose. Sally reacted by asserting that she had never stolen anyone from anybody and, further, that she and Turk would never have announced their engagement had they not been certain that Helen was in Reno getting a divorce.

Meanwhile, working in a Los Angeles café, Helen said that Sally had phoned her from somewhere in Ohio. "I was kind of surprised at her nerve," Helen remarked, adding "but she was sweet as pie to me on the phone":

> Helen: I don't see why you want to fool around with my husband, since he's all I've got. If you take him away from me I'll be left destitute without means of support.

Sally: Well, that's just too bad, but there is nothing to be done about it. Turk and I love each other and that's all there is to it. I'm going to marry him. He doesn't love you anymore, and when a man has stopped loving a woman it is not right that they should live together. It's not moral.

Helen: Well, if a thing like this was done to you, how would you like it?

Sally: I wouldn't like it, my dear, but what's anyone to do about it? There it is. Turk and I are really in love. He's my ideal man.

Sally confronted Helen's attorney Lewis Schaffer, asking who was paying his fees. Told that it was none of her business, Sally probed: "Well, what does Mrs. Greenough want?" Schaffer responded: "All she wants from you is that you leave her husband alone."

Alluding to Turk's charisma, the first Mrs. Greenough explained: "It's just the glamour of the rodeo business that gets 'em. These society women just get attracted to cowboys." She might be willing to give her husband a divorce, she added, "if he would make financial provisions for me."

About this time, a man claiming to be Sally's ex-husband — a certain "Mr. Cassey Gay" — popped up out of nowhere offering to assist Helen Greenough in her case. He reportedly declared that Sally had kept him and their marriage in the background many years before at a time when she was giving interviews to the effect that she was still looking for her ideal mate. As intriguing as this was, the mysterious "Mr. Gay" seems to have left the scene as abruptly as he had entered.[5]

Reporters familiar with Sally's penchant for publicity stunts wondered if the whole affair might be just another gambit to grab some headlines. But she assured them that Turk was her "perfect man" and that she had always wanted a "down-to earth, simple type like a cowboy." As for Turk's marital status, Sally said: "Naturally I'm disturbed. One doesn't commit bigamy."

We can only speculate about what truly attracted Sally to Turk Greenough. Having entertained much better offers of marriage earlier in life, her reluctance to accept them may have been driven by demands that she give up her career. This time, both intended partners eventually announced that they would continue to work in their chosen professions.

---

5   It remains unclear whether Sally was actually ever married in the mid-1920s. The name "Cassey Gay" (which was not found in a genealogical search) is certainly suspect and bears a striking resemblance to "K. C. Guy," which could easily be a play on "some guy from Kansas City."

Interviewing the couple for *The American Weekly*, Inez Robb was evidently unconvinced:

> It seemed only fair to draw a few words from Turk. "What do you admire most about Miss Rand?" I asked this strong silent man. Overcome by the necessity for words, he meditated for some time. He looked at the floor and at the ceiling. He focused an unhappy eye upon the waiter. He fidgeted in his chair. Finally, realizing that two women were hanging on his words, he spoke up. "Why, I just like everything about her," he said with earnest and Homeric simplicity.

> "See what I mean?" cried Sally triumphantly. "It'd take some guys ten thousand words to say that. But not Turk. He can sum it all up in a little sentence, and he means it." "Yeah," affirmed Turk.

While Sally was planning her wedding and making arrangements for her new home in Montana, she was stunned on December 7, 1941, — the "day that will live in infamy" — when the Empire of Japan attacked the United States Naval Base at Pearl Harbor, and the nation was abruptly forced to enter the war.

ALIEN ENEMIES

Within 24 hours of the attack on Pearl Harbor, U.S. Attorney General Francis Biddle announced that 736 Japanese nationals regarded as "dangerous to the peace and security" of the nation had been rounded up in the U.S. and Hawaii and placed in custody.

Fearing a full-scale attack on the west coast, the FBI would detain more Japanese aliens the following day. Biddle assured the public that only a few more would be arrested, adding that not all Japanese persons in the United States should be considered as enemies. Within three days, however, another 1,200 had been detained.

In March, the FBI office in Los Angeles would apprehend another 250 Japanese individuals, among them Buddhist priests, school teachers and several "house boys" in the employ of various Hollywood stars. Michio Ito — the celebrated dancer and choreographer who had previously worked with Sally — was among those accused of espionage and arrested as alien enemies.

Two days after the attack, Sally was a guest speaker at a business luncheon in Kansas City. Standing in front of an American flag, the plight of Michio Ito and her longtime Japanese maid Stella must surely have weighed on her mind. There is no record of her topic that day, but, as a conflicted patriot, Sally might very well have ventured an opinion on the matter.

By the time the pair returned to Montana, Sally had probably come to realize that Turk didn't actually have a ranch of his own. Becoming the new

Mrs. Greenough had proven more challenging than she had expected. Undeterred, Sally asked her lawyer to look into Turk's marital situation and it turned out that a state law would allow him to quietly sue for divorce as long as intent was published. So, after placing a small notice in a local paper, Turk obtained a divorce on December 19, 1941, based on the grounds of desertion and mental cruelty.

Press accounts alone offer little insight into the intimate details of their relationship. Luckily, a deeper understanding of Turk and Sally's courtship may be gleaned from surviving letters in her personal files. In one of the earliest, dated November 24, 1941 (nearly a month before his divorce), Sally had written to Turk's parents in reply to their Thanksgiving dinner invitation. Turk had just returned from a rodeo in Buffalo, New York, and Sally was in Brooklyn with her troupe, making plans for their upcoming wedding. She was also planning to renovate the house in Red Lodge where she and Turk intended to settle after years of near constant travel. In the rather long letter, Sally disclosed her hopes for the match and her apparent vision of retiring from the stage. And, while the attack on Pearl Harbor would not take place for another two weeks, she also hinted at her fears that the nation might be drawn into World War II:

> I want our new home to be substantial, [one] that will last and wear and be beautiful forever. For once we move in and settle there I don't want to ever have to move again. Turk and I are going to need help from our kinfolks because what with buying Rodeo stock and going into a new business we are not going to have very much money and labor is very high now and building materials are soaring higher still, what with defense work, etc. so I think it wise to do whatever buying we have to do now before there are none left whatsoever. And if we can save labor costs by having our kinfolks help us, we will return it "in kind"....
>
> I know that if I am not going to keep on working that we are not going to have much of an income and we will need a garden very much. Food prices soar so terribly during and after a war, and [when] I think what will happen after this War, the last one was just a picnic. We will all need gardens to help feed armies and our own selves. Also if inflation follows, the little insurance I have invested to provide for me later will not be worth very much. If we have gardens, stock, beef and pigs and are willing to expend plenty of elbow grease on them, there will never be any need to worry.... The

*one thing that recommends Piney Dell to me is the fact that
the creek runs so furiously always. We can put in a water
well and I know where I can get a small turbine from an old
theatre. It is perfectly good and would give us our own
electricity free of charge, also no fuel costs which might be
tremendous in the future.*

*I want a family, as big a one as we can feed, and the means
with which to do it for as long as we live, and they after us....
Turk and I would always be on hand if you needed us and I
like to be close by kinfolks.... Wherever I put my few small
possessions[6] at this point is where I expect to live.... I want
it to be permanent and definite and so located that neither
flood, nor drought, nor earthquake, nor landslide can affect
it, and in a place where the government can't take it over.*

Sally then laid out her plans for the wedding, including travel arrangements
from Montana to Glendora and accommodations for the Greenough family
and friends:

*Turk and I are just not going to get married without you....
We plan to have a simple church wedding with a country
barbeque on the grove afterwards with all of Turk's cowboy
friends who are out there attending. Turk wants Frank [his
brother] to be best man and Alice and Marge can be my
maids of honor.*

Just how Turk and Sally managed to buy Piney Dell is a mystery, since their
mutual assumption that the other had money turned out to be false. Sally
may have used her famous powers of persuasion to somehow convince
Piney Dell's owner, Tom Alcott, to finance the deal himself. If so, he would
come to regret the decision, as his future letters to Sally regarding non-
payment would reveal.

Once she had decided to marry, Sally knew she had to sever any remaining romantic ties with other suitors. One such "other" was her recent
dancing partner, Valya Valentinoff. Sally wrote to him on December 31st, while
staying with her future in-laws at Red Lodge, Montana. A rough draft —
with a notation in pencil, "Correspondence before fitting a wedding dress"
— has all the flavor of a classic "Dear John" missive.

---

6   In the same letter, Sally asked that the Greenoughs help with the storage of her
     considerable holdings in the way of sets and costumes: "It will be at least a 70-foot
     baggage car load." A "few small possessions," indeed!

It begins:

Valya — Dearest, Sweet name. I say it over often — like a lullaby, like the little fragment of that Chopin prélude I love so much — remember? Tendrils of sound that catch in the throat.

In five pages replete with overwrought references to dance and music and dreams of love, Sally seemed to be more captivated by her own word-smithing than considerate of the tender feelings of her ex-lover:

The world — my world — sleeps. White snow — cold, dry, bitter snow whirls in gleeful ballets under a little, bright, baleful moon....

I sit alone, in my little low log cabin, brown and earthy, a patient little peaked room, set apart from his kin, from Dad's big house and the warm, snug barn.

And in this room are my things gathered with infinite care — in a dream, in boxes and cartons, wrapped in tissue and straw — hidden but very real. All is quiet. A kind of pregnant hush — a waiting.

Once, on a red copper wire, your voice was strung like anguished prayer beads — loosed from the numbed. Over space and distance and inexorable, fixed destiny, I tried to reach you, touch you, make you know — to cradle that dark faun's head, to soothe and quiet and murmur in the dark, kind night, to hold you, make you understand my love. Yes — my love.

Love. That word you've spoken lightly, often. Sweetly, yes, and for a fleeting moment it was so, because you dignified the little mean affair by dreaming it was so — But waking brought a myriad other thoughts ... and there was no sorrowful remembrance of yester-evening, lightly spoken words of love, nor a single fleeting thought of the black despair you left behind....

I saw our love, our beautiful shining love, distilled sweetness of a thousand lovely moments. Cooing doves at dawn, a dawn we tried so hard not to see. You carrying me across a threshold at dusk, pretty dishes, summer breakfasts, Czardas music, Chopin, weaving dreams, night in the park and little ducks making sleepy noises as the city drowsed. Our fierce protection of each other against the harshness of flecked tongues that envy set in sharp staccato.

For all these gifts, these dear and precious, imperishable
gifts, my love and gratitude.... For this release, for joy, for
love, for thrill and will to work again, for Spring, for youth
you gave me, for all these I am grateful....

Out of the million years of time, the currents of mysterious
space, brought our groping hands together in this Stygian
gloom, but in the magnitude of time did not perceive that the
years between us mocked our living but this span together....

I could not bear to see our love go down, bruised and beaten
and ugly with dust. So now I hold it, shining, lovely, new,
shimmering among my other treasures. I keep them all.

My wedding day is just a few hours hence. With these vows
made in sacred, solemn troth, I give my heart, my hand, my
soul into another's keeping. Sincere and kind and quiet is
this man, my husband soon to be.

And so to you, who gave me this, my life, my heart and
laughter back again and made possible for me all this that is
to be, my undying love.

No deceit or loss is this to whom and with whom I'll share a
narrow bed. For you, who were a lover from a dream, are now
a friend, your rightful place. As friend, my love for you can
never change and bitter loss is turned to gain.

This thing I've tried to say, reduced to paper words, is for your
eyes alone and cannot rest with other paper forms, or other
paper loves.

Who knows if this letter was ever mailed. One can only imagine how such
a letter would have been received, but the sentiments Sally expressed
certainly foreclosed whatever future Valya may have anticipated.

Turk and Sally's trip to California in early 1942 was not as smooth as they
had hoped. First, their flight was grounded in Salt Lake City due to bad
weather, posing a problem. To marry in California, you had to apply for a
license three days before the ceremony. Sally called the marriage license
bureau and pleaded with city officials to keep the office open late enough for
them to reach Los Angeles. When the couple finally arrived, awaiting photographers snapped Turk as he carried Sally piggyback into the county office.
In all the rush he nearly dropped the bride-to-be when they were startled by
a process server presenting a summons to appear in court. It seems that the

first Mrs. Greenough had initiated a lawsuit against her ex-husband, seeking $100 a month in separate maintenance (nearly $1,500 today). Sally reportedly said, "I certainly wasn't expecting that kind of reception. Anyway, I don't understand why I had to be named in the suit."

The lovebirds' difficulties didn't end there. As if the couple didn't have enough financial anxiety, Turk's cowboy friends had forgotten to check the oil in Sally's car before they set out for the wedding. Consequently, they had burned up the engine on their way to California. Moreover, Sally had wanted to be married by her best friend Dorothy's husband, the Reverend Henry Scott "Heinz" Rubel, at Grace Episcopal Church in Glendora, but the local bishop had nixed that. It seems that, as a divorced person, under Episcopal canon law Turk could not be married in the church unless he was "the aggrieved party in proceedings based on infidelity." This meant the couple had to move the ceremony to the parish hall next door where it would be performed by a retired Methodist minister. (Reverend Rubel did manage to attend the wedding and deliver a prayer.) Even so, the nuptials almost didn't happen. The medical lab processing Sally and Turk's blood tests got the records mixed up and failed to provide the couple clean bills of health until moments before the ceremony.

Beyond all this, an even bigger issue loomed — one not revealed until more than 40 years later in a 1985 taped interview with Turk. At the very last minute, the bridegroom had wanted out:

> He didn't want to marry Sally; it had all been a grand idea at the time, but in the cold light of day Turk didn't want to marry Sally and he told her so. When Turk unloaded this proclamation on Sally, all hell broke loose. Sally went ballistic and began to cry. According to Turk, "She sounded like she was being murdered." Faced with all the commotion and Sally's frantic state, Turk relented.

By the time the wedding photos were taken, both bride and groom were all smiles for the camera. The wedding took place on January 6, 1942, just 18 days after Turk's divorce from Helen had become final. Press coverage was pervasive, describing the event for a curious public:

> Sally arrived at her wedding nervous and 30 minutes late, but there was no doubt about the beauty of the 37-year-old bride, fully clothed. She wore a long-sleeved, high-necked, bustled, ground-sweeping frock of white wool with pink rosebuds embroidered on it.

> Turk, 36, who can wrangle a steer and break a bronc as well as any and better than most, wore his best black cowboy suit. He made a noisy entrance, on account of his high-heeled boots.

Hoot Gibson was prominent among the well-wishers. Gwynn (Big Boy) Williams, the movie cowboy who nearly married Lupe Velez until she changed her mind, was best man. Turk's sisters, Marjorie and Alice, cowgirls both, were bridesmaids. Mrs. Jovita Rand, Sally's sister-in-law was matron of honor.

Sally spoke her "I do's" in a strong clear voice, although she had confided just moments before the Wedding March started playing: "I've never been so jittery in my life." Newsreel cameras were rolling when Sally emerged into the light of day. She had to kiss Turk seven different times before the photographers were satisfied. The ebullient new bride was heard to say: "It's a lovely day. The sun is shining, and it's the happiest day of my life."

"Happiest day"? Perhaps. But, one biographical treatment certainly painted a less than happy picture of their first night together as a married couple:

When they went to bed, Turk totally ignored Sally. Though she was deeply hurt by Turk's behavior, she made the best of it the next morning. She arose first, got dressed and prepared to leave, but not before she kissed Turk goodbye and said, "I love you, my husband."

In any case, honeymoon plans were put on hold while Sally began an engagement at the Orpheum Theater in Los Angeles and Turk left for Colorado to perform at a rodeo. Soon after that, Sally announced, the lovebirds would be retreating to "heaven" — the Heaven Ranch, that is, at Red Lodge, Montana — "a lovely, lovely place."

W inding up the rodeo in Colorado, Turk accompanied Sally as she continued her performance schedule touring the Pacific Northwest. Just weeks after the wedding, Sally had surprised the press in Idaho Falls by announcing that she was pregnant. The papers quoted her as saying: "I hope it's twin boys. But you can never be sure…. It's a little early." Years later, Turk claimed to have been surprised by the announcement too, as Sally had told him that having children was unlikely due to an operation she had as a teenager. (No further mention of this "pregnancy" has been found in either the public or private record.)

By springtime, the fields of the Puyallup Valley in Washington were spectacularly abloom with daffodils. In the Town of Puyallup, most everyone was caught up in the street parade and other festivities surrounding the annual Daffodil Festival.

Elsewhere in town things were not so auspicious. Early in March, barely three months after Pearl Harbor, President Roosevelt had ordered that tens of thousands of West Coast Japanese residents be rounded up and transported to internment camps. By then, the government program to detain suspicious aliens had expanded to include the internment of American citizens of Japanese ancestry. The Army was in the process of setting up "Camp Harmony" in Puyallup, Washington, to temporarily house more than 7,000 Japanese emigrants and their descendants from Washington and Alaska. An air of excitement pervaded the ordinarily placid community of 7,500 residents as roughly 1,000 construction workers hastily erected living quarters for the expected inflow. The camp was being constructed on the grounds of the Western Washington State Fair so, in addition to barbed wire fences and search lights, there was also a racetrack and a roller coaster.

Sally and her troupe happened to be in the area and were eager to participate in the festival. Paramount newsreel cameras were on hand as, clad in a frilly dress and wide-brimmed sunhat, Sally rode a garland-festooned horse and carriage through a field of daffodils. Later, seven of Sally's showgirls accompanied her as she cavorted through the field of flowers, wearing fewer garments and brandishing either fans or bubble. As the newsreel comes to a close, the announcer proclaims: "It's coming-out day for the daffodils, with the fairest flower of all to greet them."

Although Sally envisioned herself as being happily married, events soon sent the fledgling marriage into turmoil. Only two months after the wedding, though he was almost 37 years old and had suffered many injuries in his 17 years of rodeo riding, Turk got a draft notice from the U.S. Army. Several weeks later he was inducted and sent to Fort Lewis in Washington State on April 15th.

Three days later, Sally wrote a rambling letter from Red Lodge, Montana, to Turk's sisters, Alice and Marjorie:

> *Turk and I got home Wednesday the 8th.... Turk was working in the show and what's a cowboy without a horse as far as Joe Public is concerned, so we rented one, a kind of half trick horse, strawberry roan with red mane and tail. He looked very flashy and Turk used him to run onto the nightclub dance floor in a high lope and scare the hell out of the customers.*

> *In the meantime we had offered to us a beautiful young Palomino gelding. The color of pure gold with white mane and tail, his name is "Sungold." He is small enough for me to ride and mount easily and is a beauty, so we decided to buy him.*

*He is half Arabian and has a beautiful arched neck and fine
head with great wideness between the eyes which should
indicate good intelligence. So we carried 3600 lbs., trailer
and horses, which loaded us down....*

After some local gossip, Sally continued, mentioning a land deal that had
fallen through:

*So we haven't got a ranch and I am simply heartsick. I did so
want to get settled and get a home in which to put our things
and establish some sort of security so we would have
something when Turk got out of the Army. As it is I don't
know where to look. I know what I want but can't find it. I
wish you were here to ride around with me and see if we
could find anything.*

*I have gone ahead and bought Piney Dell, not for a home, not
for a Dude Ranch but for speculation.... It is possible that we
could do some remodeling and make Piney Dell just pay its
way which would be a good investment, as I think this will
always be saleable property. In the meantime I am still
homeless and a widow....*

With Turk having reported for military duty several days earlier, Sally
shared some private details with his sisters:

*Turk and I saddled up old Glazier and another horse and
rode up into the hills to look at the surveyor's corners on
Piney Dell and to be a little quiet amongst the beautiful
hills.... The sides of some of the hills were blue with Crocus.
We saw 50 head of deer grazing and running. It was all so
lovely and peaceful. It made our hearts ache especially that
by morning Turk would have to leave it all for God knows how
long. I know now what it means to try and hold back the
dawn, but finally 6:00 o'clock Monday morning arrived and
at 6:30 we left the ranch. Dad and Mom, Turk and I and
Jimmy. We arrived at the draft board. It was still dark and
gloomy and foggy. A few lonely figures leaned against the
brick wall. The time set for their departure was 7:15. By 7:00
o'clock many more had arrived. Singularly and in couples
and men carrying their babies and some whole families.*

*It was quite sad. We stayed in the car and waited until 8:00
o'clock.... No one could say anything. There wasn't anything to
say. One felt sort of dead and bewitched. There was a little flurry.*

A photographer had arrived and set up his little black box. For no reason at all we felt very angry toward him, possibly because we all felt much too naked emotionally to be photographed.

Two other little men arrived and bustled about with envelopes and name calling; then the herding began. We all got out of the car and Turk left us very quietly to take his place against the curb. The photographer mouthed some inane banality which resulted in stolid stares from his victims. They did remove their hats, however.

Turk didn't like removing his hat and I didn't like it either. Somehow Turk and his big hat seem to go together. It was sort of a symbol of the beginning of his regimentation. The pictures were taken, the names were called....

On that same day, Sally wrote to her mother:

I guess you heard over the radio or read in the papers Turk is gone. He is in the Army and I am heartsick. We were so happy and learned to know each other better and to live together harmoniously. It is sickening and I am miserable but I will get over it and go on just like you did and as other women have to do....

I do wish you and Ernest could see this Piney Dell I am buying. If you could see it I think you would be better able to give me an idea as to whether you think we ought to try and run it this summer. The only way I could think of running it would be for you to come up and take charge of it. There is some extensive remodeling to be done but which need not be terribly expensive. Ernest, with the help of another good carpenter and materials, could work wonders. What do you think of trying to make the trip up here? If you think you can possibly come I will arrange my route so that I could be here when you arrive.... I know both you and he could give me advice and help on this deal but I don't think you should do it at the expense of the grove.

Three days later, Sally wrote to Chicago friends William and Anne Targ about Turk's induction and, in a way, foresaw his eventual discharge:

Turk's induction came as a shock in a way because of the serious injuries he has received in his career as a Rodeo performer, including a fractured pelvis, which has never healed properly and the removal of three inches of thigh bone in his right leg. This — together with the fact that he is the sole

*support of his father and mother (both of whom are over 70
years of age), except for their very meager old age pension of
some $12.00 a month — made it seem rather improbable that he
would be called. However, he is and that is that. Quite off the
record I have been told by people who know that one of the main
reasons of his being accepted was that it is good publicity for
the Army for him to be in and for that reason they gave him no
physical examination at all. Well we shall see. Of course it
changes everything for me and dreams that were dreamed have
been put away in cotton wool for the duration....*

After apologizing for her much delayed response (blamed on her father-in-law's illness), Sally shed some light on the isolation of her recently chosen situation:

*His illness somewhat affected his memory and several
packets of mail were lost and spring house cleaning brought
them to light and in the meantime there has been no one on
the ranch who could forward. There has been no telephone,
no car and no one to drive a car if there had been one and no
communication with the outside world except by horseback
and no one well enough to make the trip by horseback.*

*We scarcely comprehend these primitive arrangements
unless we come face to face with them.*

As it happened, the couple's initial separation would be short lived. Sally and her "Lass Roundup Revue" had an upcoming theater booking in Tacoma, Washington, only nine miles from where Turk was temporarily stationed at Fort Lewis. The Army granted him leave to join her in town on April 23rd, just eight days after he had left her standing in tears as he was driven away. Interviewed by the press at their reunion, Turk (a true cowboy from the top of his hat to the tip of his boots) disclosed that he had never worn regular shoes before being issued a pair by the Army: "I always wore riding boots. Now I have to use them for bedroom slippers. Army shoes hurt my feet, but I guess I'll get used to them eventually." Sally chimed in:

Uncle Sam is really giving me the works. Turk and I have been
married but three months and along comes the draft to take him
away. And now I'm almost down to my last bubble ... and that
ain't good. But it seems my country needs both my husband and
my bubbles more than I need them. So, I'm not crying. We'll all
have to make sacrifices if we are going to win this war ... and I'm
no exception.

Intensifying her sense of separation and seclusion, aggravating and disturbing distractions seemingly never ceased in the life of Sally Rand. On the 15th of May, not quite six weeks after Turk's induction, she was back in the San Francisco bankruptcy court. Having overslept, she showed up for the hearing almost an hour late. "You just missed going to jail," Bankruptcy Referee Burton J. Wyman told her. After a final session on May 27th, newspapers across the country reported that Sally had owed her creditors $64,000 in connection with a failed night club venture back in 1939 (nearly a million dollars today). She reportedly turned over to the court her only assets — $200 worth of beads.

Turk had been deployed to the headquarters of the 2nd Cavalry Division in Fort Riley, Kansas — the place the Army sent its rodeo cowboys.[7] He soon realized that, despite his stature with the rodeo crowd, he was becoming known by the wider public as "Mr. Sally Rand." When he organized a successful military rodeo at the end of June to raise money for the Army Relief Fund, it must have been bittersweet for him that Sally was the one drawing the attention. Arriving at Fort Riley on June 18th for a two-week visit, she attracted both national and local press. The *Junction City Republic* ran a long interview under the headline, "SALLY RAND ARRIVES AND INTEREST IN RODEO LEAPS TO A NEW HIGH":

> Talk about human dynamos! Sally Rand has more pep and energy than a dozen ordinary women! She doesn't sit still a minute and she never stops talking....

> The famous fan-and-bubble dancer this morning was wearing her blond hair in two pigtails and was attired in a red, white and blue plaid shirt and the cowboy's traditional "blue jeans"....

> Miss Rand sat on the floor most of the time during her interview, and really seemed to enjoy it.... She saw a picture of her husband peeling potatoes and it nearly put her in hysterics.

Shortly after leaving the army base, Sally stopped at a Mobilgas service station and pitched about 50 broken balloons onto a stockpile of scrap rubber, keeping only two for her act. As she put it:

> I'm giving my shirt to the cause. I use this kind of language only to impress folks with the urgent necessity of contributing every article possible to the rubber collection in response to President Roosevelt's

---

7   Interestingly, Fort Riley was also where world champion boxer Joe Louis was stationed to serve in the "colored unit." The two celebrities became friends.

request, and in appreciation of the crying need for more and more
rubber to assure essential war-time transportation.

Aside from the early (and brief) reunion in Tacoma, Sally saw her husband
only twice during his wartime enlistment. Those two weeks at Fort Riley
marked one such time; the other was the following month at the 46th
annual Frontier Days event in Cheyenne, where the pair had first met seven
years earlier. Finding the publicity to be a valuable recruitment tool, the
Army granted Turk a furlough to attend the Cheyenne festivities where he
and Sally took part in the parade and other events.

One day they rode out to the Quartermaster Corps Training Center at Fort
Francis E. Warren to have lunch with the boys of Company H, Second
Regiment. Turk and Sally sat at a table with several officers later described
as having "found the food an item of only passing interest." Correspondent
Corp. Joseph E. Ray later wrote that, following the meal, Sally was properly
introduced. Responding to the welcome, she had "stepped up on her seat
and, with arms folded, delivered several well-chosen remarks":

> I don't feel out of place at all here. My father is an Army man, my
> husband Turk is, and I also have a brother who is serving. I want
> you to know that I consider it an honor to be here today and to
> play a small part in bolstering morale, which I know is a big
> problem. If I can sell more bonds as a result of the inspiration I
> have received here, I shall consider it a visit well spent.

After "thunderous applause" for Sally, the more taciturn Turk was introduced to also make a few remarks. He self-consciously proceeded to favor
his fellow soldiers "with a one-minute discourse on how he always let [his]
wife do the talking." Turk would soon complete his basic training at Ft. Riley
and would then be transferred to the newly-constructed Camp Carson in
Colorado, where it was reported that he would "break and inspect horses for
the army's remount service."

B y late summer of 1942, the war had begun to seriously impact the nation's
economy and culture. The Food Rationing Program had gone into effect,
and more restrictions were on the way. On the home front, folks found their
lives on hold. Everyone had come to understand that the country was in for a
long, uncertain period of war. Speaking at a Chamber of Commerce luncheon
in Tulsa, Oklahoma, Sally declared:

> I hope to be able to raise a family. But now, because my life stands
> still until my husband returns, I want to do something useful in the
> war effort. We, as women, are faced with the problem of bringing

children into the world and making the kind of a world that we want for them. After we win the war, our first job will be to feed the hungry world.

Sally presented herself as a true patriot with little time for those who were seemingly indifferent to the cause. Substituting for *San Francisco Call-Bulletin* columnist Marsh Maslin in 1943, she took the opportunity to vent:

> I'M BURNED UP AT: The amazing indifference of more women than you might imagine to the alarming need for nurse's aides, blood bank donors and other vital war necessities ... The disgusting beefing one hears about rationing and the lame excuses given for circumventing the rules ... Politicians in and out of the armed forces saving face for themselves and their sponsors by refusing to admit their pre-war errors ... Highly paid public relations departments feeding the public with lies ... Any leader, in labor or industry or politics, who dares to put personal desire for power above the war effort ... This is no time for picayune machinations. (I feel better!)

The more things change, the more they stay the same.

Ultimately, the rationing of foodstuffs and other essential war materials would impose significant inconvenience, if not true hardship, on the home front. Still, even in the darkest of times, the public continued to seek new forms of entertainment. The onset of the war had put the development of television on hold and had seriously curtailed the production of phonograph records. Yet, somehow the Mills Novelty Company of Chicago managed to marshal the resources to continue producing "soundies" for its new entertainment device — the "Panoram."

The first modern music videos would not appear on MTV for another 40 years, yet something very like them — the true grandparents of music videos — were enticing a national audience as early as 1940. Soundies were 16mm films (usually musical productions about three minutes in length) turned out by several production companies between 1940 and 1946. While some may have been shown in movie theaters, the primary outlet for these films was the Panoram, a sort of coin-operated film jukebox commonly found in such public places as nightclubs, taverns, soda shops, factory lounges, bus stations and pinball parlors.[8]

---

[8] Typically, a Panoram was a sturdy art-deco-style cabinet about the size of a refrigerator in which, via a clever series of mirrors, films reflected onto a 27-inch, rear-projection screen.

Both Sally Rand and Faith Bacon contracted with Official Films to appear in soundies that were produced in 1942. Sally was featured in three: *The Artist's Model*, *The Bubble Dance*, and *The Fan Dance*, none of which are particularly worthy of critical acclaim. Even so, one can only imagine how many dimes must have been slipped into the slot by hopeful viewers expecting to see something more than was ultimately delivered. Such is the story of life.

Faith

In 1942, as newlywed Sally Rand Greenough was making plans to set up housekeeping on a ranch in Montana, Faith Bacon was still in demand. Following a four-week engagement at the Latin Quarter in New York City, she literally traveled coast to coast to coast, appearing in such venues as the Olympia Theater in Miami and the Orpheum Theatre in Los Angeles. The "gorgeous, ravishing, Faith Bacon" even played for a week at the Tower Theatre in Sally's home town of Kansas City. Her soundies (*Dance of Shame* and *A Lady with Fans*) are well worth watching on YouTube.[9] In the latter film, she actually appears to be nude, but — whether she was or not — that was what kept the coins coming.

In November of 1942 while performing in Boston, Sally wrote to her mother, who was visiting with her own mother Mollie in New Mexico. Apparently, Mollie wanted to remain there, but Sally was against the idea due to her grandmother's advanced age and the lack of nearby medical services. After describing the amounts and payees of checks she was enclosing, totaling $370.24, she launched into a detailed account of her feelings about Turk and the Greenough family:

> *Turk's people are different from mine. Sometimes I think they are shockingly insensitive. There is a great deal of bitterness between the children, which is shocking to me, and I am sure grieves Mrs. Greenough greatly. Turk's Dad has been a hard man, and in his old days is stubborn and difficult, but poor old fellow, he has so many sterling qualities too, and some of his children have been a pretty bitter disappointment.... And there are many other facets to the Greenough family problems, but I cannot possibly solve their problems, nor am I curious, nor*

---

[9]   *Billboard* magazine of July 25, 1942, announced the production of a third Faith Bacon soundie, *Death of the Bird of Paradise*, but no copies appear to exist. The dance — said to consist of "Interpretive terping, with lights playing a big part" — had actually been in Miss Bacon's repertoire for several years. (Terpsichore, the goddess of dance and chorus in Greek mythology, is one of the nine Muses; her name means "delight in dancing.")

*critical. My problem is to make a home, pay for it and fix it so
that no one can ever take it away from me or Turk, or our
children. To try and make my husband as happy as I know how,
to educate him to the things he has not had the opportunity to
learn and to learn from him many sweet and beautiful things
that he knows and understands but is too inarticulate to
express.... Turk has much to learn, but then so have I. In these
last few months he has probably learned more than he ever did in
his whole life put together before.*

*What I am about to say is extremely private, a confidence
between mother and daughter in which I know that I can trust
you. Turk got himself in a jam, was AWOL, was put on trial and
has been in the guardhouse for the last two months. This was a
very bitter pill for him to take, and there were times when I was
afraid that he wasn't going to take it. He is a very willful person,
completely lacking in self-discipline; I was truly afraid he would
do some foolhardy spectacular thing and either be shot or put
away for good.... His own unfamiliarity with the theatre and his
complete disapproval of the kind of work I do in the theatre, and
his lack of trust in me, has made things very difficult. I had so
wanted to go to Montana for Christmas. Turk has written that
he could probably get out of the guardhouse by that time and
could get a furlough. However, with the press of responsibilities
being what they are I have had to forego this and will work
straight through the holidays.*

This was not the only time that Turk had landed in the guardhouse. Army
life simply did not suit him. He felt contempt for some of his superior officers
and showed it. He was transferred twice, ending up at Fort Ord, California,
for basic combat training. While there, he got a letter from Sally dated
May 10, 1943:

Dear Daddy Pie —

*Did you know I love you — madly? Well I do and I want you so
much it hurts. Honey, I hate every minute of this damn job — and
all jobs that keep me away from you. But lover, I want you all my
life — and I want our lives to be happy and I know we must have
a home and land and cattle and a place to call our own and
that's what I'm working for. I will have it, too.... Please write
and let me know what's cooking.*

Love, Daddy's Girl

According to his biographer, Turk completed his training at Fort Ord and was issued all his gear to be shipped overseas. At the last minute, however, he was pulled from the ranks by a sergeant who took away all his equipment except his fatigues and dress uniform. He didn't know what was going on until an officer told him that Congress had just passed a law exempting men over 38 years of age from combat. So Turk was again put to work peeling potatoes until the Army could find something else to do with him:

> Finally, a Colonel Holmes summoned Turk and said, "I heard you were a rodeo man. Did you get broke up? Turk allowed that he had, and the colonel ordered a series of X-rays. When the colonel examined the results, he announced, "Hell, man, you look like you've been through a war already."

Turk soon received a medical discharge and returned to Red Lodge, as did Sally, still hoping to make a success of the marriage.

In July, the two of them drove all day to Alberta, Canada, for the annual Calgary Stampede. And, although Turk had not ridden any bucking horses for the 14 months he was in the Army, he won the Championship Saddle Bronc title for 1943 — not bad for a fellow pushing 40. Although he continued to compete until 1948, this marked the final time that he would win a major rodeo title.

Soon after returning from Calgary, Sally left for a tour of Canada. Feeling despondent, she wrote Turk a letter from the train. Apparently, things were not going so well:

> *I was so unhappy and miserable when you left yesterday morning. Why oh why do we have to quarrel? Surely we can find some way of living together without quarreling. I can't stand it! When you are harsh and cross with me it simply crushes me and leaves me dead and cold. You must stop it if we are to go on together. I have told you before how it makes me feel — it simply kills my love — and I can't keep reviving it. Someday it will be completely dead.*

> *I don't ask for much — I don't care about money or glory, things like that. I just want you to be sweet and kind and reasonable and not get mad and say ugly things. You keep saying you'll try but you don't. You keep right on doing bad things. You must change, darling, so we can be happy and love each other. Please do.*

I love you with all my heart and soul and want us to be happy more than anything in the world.

Facing her fears, Sally was determined to make her marriage work and to establish a home in Montana. To this end she and Turk bought another property, Red Rim Ranch, about 30 miles from Wyola, Montana. But why Sally thought Turk would be interested in running a ranch is anyone's guess. In any case, that summer he went along with her plan, filling the ranch with livestock even though he didn't really want to be bothered with their care. And, with the war grinding on, finding hired help was practically impossible.

Despite Turk's lack of enthusiasm for ranching, Sally applied herself to the task with her usual resolve and vigor. The scope of her acquired knowledge was on display in a 1943 interview for *PM*, a New York daily paper:

> You've got to feed cattle cured hay, not green hay. A calf builds bone over the Winter, and puts on fat during the Summer. You can tell by the fat on his backside whether he's a Ready-Teddy....

> [As for the price of beef] eleven to 13½ cents a pound won't pay for freight, and there aren't any ranchers left — the draft boards. Know what we have to pay a hand? Fifty dollars a month! We used to pay $30, including food and lodgings.

The interview described Sally's typical day: "When the fan dancer is at home, on Red Rim Ranch, she says she rises at 5:30, builds a fire, makes coffee, milks a cow, makes cereal, washes dishes, skims the milk, feeds the chickens, cuts hay, does housework, and so, at 9 p.m., to bed."

On July 27th, Sally poured her heart out in a letter to their neighbors, Phil and Jessie Spears. After thanking the Spears for inviting them over for a home-cooked dinner, she got down to her real purpose, fretting about her problems running the ranch and, incidentally, exposing the headstrong will to succeed she had exhibited for most of her adult life:

> *... Turk, even though he has lived around horses and cattle and punched cattle for various ranches, has spent the greater part of his more mature life rodeoing. Furthermore, as a youngster punching cattle, as an employee of someone else, he was not particularly interested in learning things. I was tremendously surprised, for example, that he did not know the gestation period for horses, cows, sheep, or pigs. So you see, both of us must learn many things....*

Obviously, I want to give up my present work to live on the ranch with Turk. There is no question about my desire to do it. It is simply that I want to approach the problem intelligently and avoid the pitfalls and mistakes and expensive failures that are always the result of inexperience and ignorance.

You people have lived here all your lives, you have finally wrested success after years of struggle. Do help us and give us the benefit of your experience and knowledge. These are things you can't pay for, of course, but perhaps we could exchange "in kind." I mean, we could give you the use of our strong, healthy, young backs and help you as hands when you would need us, in exchange for giving us your help and advice on how to proceed with what we have with the least chance of failure and the most chance of success.

When I return from this engagement I want so much to sit down with you two and try and plan out a logical, practical, workable method of procedure. Naturally, I know that you understand that all of the above is confidential.

Sally's exploits continued to draw the attention of the press throughout 1943. On the occasion of Adolph Hitler's 54th birthday, April 20th, she was one of only seven women among the 31 celebrities whose comments were quoted by United Press:

> I would suggest a birthday trip starting with breakfast in Greece, where there is no food; a stop in Warsaw where the great music lover could listen to a concert at the famous opera house, destroyed by bombs; a birthday dinner at Lidice, Poland, with inhabitants of the village as guests [the population of Lidice was wiped out by the Nazis]; and then a return trip to Berlin in the evening for the day's climax — a fireworks display presented by the RAF and U.S. air forces.

Sally was holding her own with the likes of Bob Hope, Bing Crosby, Groucho Marx, Humphrey Bogart and Mayor Fiorello LaGuardia of New York, whose remarks regarding Herr Hitler were also solicited.

Back in Chicago and performing at the Savoy Ballroom in early May, Sally announced that she was prepared to donate a pair of her famous ostrich feather fans to the Chicago Historical Society. What more fitting spot for them, she figured, than Chicago, the site of her most celebrated appearances? And the fans would be in the company of such other artifacts as Chicago's first fire engine and a tomahawk from the Fort Dearborn Massacre. She added that her fans had earned $5,000,000 and put nine people through college.

Regrettably, when she telephoned to confirm the time of the presentation ceremony, Sally was told that the Society's board of trustees had turned down her generous offer. It seems that, after a two-hour discussion, the board had issued a statement declaring:

> The board of trustees of the Chicago Historical Society feels that
> the fans used by Miss Sally Rand at the Century of Progress ... do
> not ... have sufficient historical interest to warrant their acceptance
> by the museum.[10]

Justifiably miffed, Sally described the whole episode as a "shabby trick," while a spokesperson for the society termed the incident "regrettable." A frustrated Sally explained:

> What makes me angry is that it wasn't my idea, anyway. I'm not
> very learned about history, but a representative of the museum
> made the suggestion to me. I saw some stories in the papers but I
> didn't put them out.

An honest misunderstanding or another publicity stunt gone awry? Who knows? In any case, museum officials were not the only source of Sally's consternation. During the war, while much of our national production was diverted to wartime purposes, the government found it necessary to ration food, gasoline, and other materials — even clothing. These home front strictures on daily life had a special impact on the dancing trade.

Back in March, Sally had approached her local ration board in Glendora to seek special dispensation for her shoes. While clothing was obviously of little concern, shoes were a different matter. They were essential to her occupation. She wore out 50 pairs a year! Unimpressed, Board Chairman G.R. Rinehart had ruled that she was entitled to only three pairs, suggesting that she pool ration coupons from other family members. Sally had objected: "My family's not big enough!" Her request was ultimately bumped up to the state board — but the decision stood.

---

[10] Today the Chicago Historical Museum is home to a large collection of Sally Rand materials.

The press had quite a bit of fun with this incident at Sally's expense. Columnist Dorothy Kilgallen observed that if Sally seriously thought she was "an essential industry, then Eisenhower is visiting Africa for his health and Nimitz just felt like taking a cruise." Coming to Sally's rescue, at least in part, Mexican dancer and film star "Margo" sent her 22 pairs of dancing shoes, saying: "I will give Sally my shoes and dance barefooted. My Spanish dresses cover my shoes and as long as the war lasts I won't mind the callouses."

A Sunday supplement article describing the adverse impact of the war on specialty dancers and "striptease gals" due to shortages of body make-up, artificial eyebrow adhesive, metallic sequins and the like included this quip from Sally: "In New York, they used to have girls in the nightclubs who came out with bubbles. Now they have midgets who come out with grapes."

The article also quoted Sally as she was leaving Hollywood for another Chicago engagement:

> Sure I'm going to ride in a chair car. I couldn't get Pullman reserva-tions. But I'm not complaining. Don't forget that I've got a husband and two brothers in the Army. Let the servicemen have the Pullmans.

> Faith Bacon, who knows about fans and bubbles ... occupied a drawing room when she left recently to fill a Canadian engage-ment. But ... she had to leave two weeks in advance of the opening in order to travel in such comfort.

Sally was a patriotic booster and did her part to aid the war effort when-ever she could. Appearing in late September 1943 at the Great Hagers-town Fair in Maryland, she took part in a war bond drive that raised $50,000 (about $700,000 in today's dollars), leading other donors by example with a $500 purchase of her own. A photograph of Sally smiling and waving atop a big Army tank at Public Square was published in papers nationwide.

Even though Turk was out of the service, Sally's career demands meant that the two were still apart much of the time. This was not necessarily a bad thing, as the couple's relationship continued to show signs of strain. In mid-October, Sally indicated that she and Turk were about to be very far apart indeed, as she intended to travel overseas and entertain the troops in North Africa. Apparently she had applied to the War Department to be accepted as an "entertainer" — classification unspecified.

Initial concerns within the department and the USO over the appropriateness of an unclad damsel fanning the heated air of the Sahara were seemingly dispelled when Sally made it clear she intended to entertain the troops only as a "fully clothed trouper," explaining:

> If anyone had asked me, I would have told them that never, never, for the sake of my four brothers would I fan dance under military jurisdiction. Even if generals and colonels asked me, I wouldn't go fan dancing through military reservations. I can just hear the snide letters blue-nose mothers would write about their poor boys, not only being subjected to the horrors of war, but also to a hussy.

> It isn't that my brothers have objected. How could they? Fan dancing put them through school and bought their clothes. It's the way I feel inside. I couldn't allow the question of fan dancing to become a military matter and hurt the careers of those I love. Besides, strange as it may seem, the boys want to see me dressed.

> Maybe it sounds hammy, but I think I could give them a lift, just by being there. I can do other things beside fan dance, you know. I tell funny jokes. I can emcee. I can play the piano and sing. I've entertained with my clothes on in Army camps here, and I can do it abroad.

Celebrity visits to the troops were a recent phenomenon. Only a few months earlier, Sally's old pal Bob Hope had appeared before cheering GIs in North Africa under USO sponsorship. President Franklin D. Roosevelt and British Prime Minister Winston Churchill had conferred in Casablanca earlier in the year.[11] Maybe Sally figured that, if two old duffers like FDR and Winnie could make the arduous trip to Morocco in furtherance of the war effort, she should be able to do the same.

Alas, there would be no photographs of weary allied troops cheering Sally Rand as she waved and smiled atop a British Crusader tank in the North African desert. Instead, she chose to continue her engagement at the Folies Bergère in New York City. And, as it happened, she wasn't the only one there with a balloon act, as she would share the bill with Wally Boag, master of the "twisty and squeaky" balloon animal act.[12]

---

[11] Roosevelt and Churchill met at the Casablanca Conference, held January 14 to 24, 1943, in French Morocco. Interestingly, the movie *Casablanca*, starring Sally's former stage mate Humphrey Bogart, was released just as the conference was wrapping up. It won the Academy Award as best picture of the year.

[12] Boag actually *did* go overseas to entertain the troops. He had a command performance for the King and Queen of England in 1947. And, at the London Hippodrome, he was

By November 1, 1943, having abandoned her plan to go to North Africa, it had dawned on Sally that depending on Turk to take care of the ranch wasn't going to work out. Accordingly, she took pen in hand once again to confide in her neighbors, Phil and Jessie Spears:

> I have been more distressed than I can tell you about what is going on at Red Rim. The house was to be completely insulated, and the roof put on, and certain minor changes made in the actual construction of the house. A shed was to be built in which to put the farm machinery, with an adjoining shed for the shelter of cars and trucks. There was a month to do it in, and it could easily have been accomplished in that time, but very little happened....

> Turk is not very good at planning things, but he can carry them out once they have been decided upon, so Jesse [her secretary] did nothing but waste her time going into town every day ... and materials weren't bought, and bills weren't paid, and the cars were wrecked, and not repaired; and all together it was a very expensive and unproductive time....

> Frankly, when I think of my home, the only one I have ever known, being left without care, and with the station wagon wrecked halfway between town and the ranch, my horse running wild, the cow and calf without care — it makes me want to cry.

> I admit to being a greenhorn and know that I know very little about the things that ought to be done, but I do have horse sense, and I have tried to take care of the few things we do have, but someone has to pay the freight, and the only way I know how to do that is to keep on to the job I have.

Sally went on to thank the Spears for "taking care of things" while she was on the road, and promise that she would settle accounts with the couple when she returned home for Christmas.

By the end of 1943, Sally clearly had mounting doubts about the future of her marriage and the dream of making a home in Montana. The connection had frayed. In January, she wrote to Turk, urging him to take advantage of a friend's offer to help him improve his speaking skills. (There is no evidence

---

assisted in his "funny balloon animal" act by a 12-year-old girl, a would-be singer named Julie Andrews. In 1955, the wholesome comic was chosen by Walt Disney to perform at Disneyland's Golden Horseshoe Revue, where he delivered 40,000 performances over the next 27 years. Boag was also an early inspiration for comedian Steve Martin.

he did this, although years later Turk admitted in an interview that he should have taken Sally up on her self-improvement offers.)

Throughout 1944 both continued to pursue their respective careers. By this point, Turk had been competing in rodeos for 18 years. On October 27th, he placed third in saddle bronc riding and tied for third in the wild cow milking contest. He also entered rodeos in Boston and New York that fall and Sally showed up at both. Unfortunately, their rocky relationship was becoming even rockier, and a breakup seemed imminent. At year's end, Dorothy Kilgallen's syndicated column reported: "Cowboy Turk Greenough, Sally Rand's estranged husband, is threatening to contest her legal action — hotly — if she goes through with it."

A Sunday supplement article in early 1945 disclosed the couple's separation, even suggesting that Sally was "idling under the palms with a certain rich man." While Turk's reported reaction is suspect ("Nobody's coming between Sally and me unless it's over my dead body and then only after both my 45s are empty"), the article rings true in its description of her immense popularity:

> Right away he ran into the riptide of Sally's glamour and fame.
> When she came to the rodeo to watch him, the crowd turned their
> backs on Turk to gape at her. It happened everywhere they went,
> and on at least one occasion, Turk was politely and firmly advised
> to keep his wife away from the rodeo.

Two weeks later, gossip columnist Erskine Johnson included a curious tidbit in his "HOLLYWOOD NOTES":

> Sally Rand, the girl with the fans, and her husband, Rodeo Star Turk
> Greenough, are nearing a reconciliation. Their difference, says Sally,
> is "a mere trifle." Says she: "I don't like to wear pants. Turk insists
> that I wear them. Every time we go out he asks me, 'Sally, have you
> got your pants on?' I say 'No' and then the fight starts."

The pressure continued to build. The differences were far more than trifles. Columnist Jimmie Fidler inquired: "Wotzis about Sally Rand and her spouse feuding reportedly because he refuses to work their ranch?" Other papers divulged that Sally's income was being consumed by judgments against her. That spring and early summer, Turk spent a few months in Arizona working on David O. Selznick's film *Duel in the Sun*. Back in Montana, on June 27th he got a phone call from Sally informing him that she was filing for divorce. Sally had decided to cut her losses, both financial and personal.

The very next day the *Billings Gazette* published a syndicated article with the headline "SALLY RAND DIVORCES HER COWBOY-HUSBAND":

> Sally's real-life story of the "Cowboy and the Lady" ended Thursday when District Judge Ben Harwood granted her a divorce from Cowboy Turk Greenough, noted bronco buster from Red Lodge, Mont.

> The ink was hardly dry on her newly-won divorce papers today when fan dancer Sally Rand ... said she would go back on the stage in an effort to blot out the memory of her unsuccessful venture in married life.

Sally and Turk reached an amicable agreement and neither was angry or bitter. They agreed that neither would sue the other. All of Sally's belongings were moved out and both ranches were put up for sale. They shook hands and walked away. Summing up his wild matrimonial ride with Sally Rand, Turk would later say: "That was no marriage; that was an adventure."

In fact, Turk had never been fully committed to the coupling. He later revealed something that he never disclosed to Sally — during the war, he had been in regular contact with his former wife, Helen "Honey" Stewart, and had sent her gifts of nylons, chocolates, and perfume. He had also sent her money in 1944 when she wrote to him asking for help with medical bills.

In his unpublished biography of Turk, Michael Amundsen wrote about their post-divorce relationship that:

> Turk and Sally happily renewed their friendship without the romance. Turk describes their relationship as brother and sister, as if they had never been married. Sally would talk to Turk of old times, or would share a friendly conversation with Helen. Turk was content that his previous adventure with Sally had been resolved on friendly terms. Sally, in later interviews, would blame the divorce on Turk's problems with "paranoia." Others, writing about Sally, would hint that Turk, who never drank alcohol in his life, had a "drinking problem."

Details aside, Amundsen summed up the situation quite nicely: "Closer to the truth was the fact that they were two good people who had little in common and married each other for the wrong reasons."

While Sally's own writings indicate that she preferred to make friends of her former lovers, this pattern would not be repeated with her next husband ... nor the next.

CHAPTER NINETEEN

Sawdust and Sideshows

At the age of nine, I took a calf to a fair in Sedalia and won a prize. I've been going where the crowds are ever since.

~ Sally Rand

By the late summer of 1945, Adolph Hitler was dead, the Atomic Age had dawned, and the former Mrs. Turk Greenough was footloose, if not fancy free. The war was over. Americans were looking forward to the promise of a future long deferred. People wanted new clothes, new cars, new houses. They wanted to enjoy their newly secured freedoms. It was time to have some fun. Washing machines, television sets, and all manner of new devices and desires were suddenly within reach. Back in 1919, the end of the First World War had ushered in the age of the "flapper." Now that happy days were here once again, what new and amazing era might emerge from the fog of war?

In January 1946, Hollywood fashion designer "Renie" thought she may have captured the sense of it when she predicted the popularity of evening gowns with so-called "open air bodices."[1] According to syndicated press reports, Renie proclaimed:

> Of course, it will take a while for this to become popular. The woman who wears it for the first time will have to have a lot of courage. A lot of curves too. But I predict there will soon be nothing but transparent covering over the bosom for cocktail and evening clothes — and complete exposure in some instances.
>
> I've studied the psychology of clothes from the days people first began to wear them, and it's obvious that the female reaction to clothes after this war will be the same as in the past.... After the

---

[1] A 44-year-old costume designer for RKO pictures, Renie Conley later won an Oscar for her contributions to the 1963 film *Cleopatra*, starring Elizabeth Taylor.

last war, skirts went above the knee to expose the legs for the first time.

Reaction from her clientele was mixed, with a common sentiment being a terse "Ye, Gods!" Film star Jane Russell, well known for her frontal anatomy, observed: "Well, it might not be a bad idea. The corner wolves stopped leering at ankles when the girls started wearing knee length skirts. Maybe now I could get a little peace of mind. The only trouble is, in some cases it might be a pretty sad-looking sight."

Film actress Jane Greer agreed to pose for photographers in one of Renie's futuristic gowns (with a little added chiffon), declaring: "It might be all right for warm blooded girls, but it's pretty revolutionary. Brrrr! What we women won't do to keep in style." A rather explicit photo of Miss Greer in Renie's creation was syndicated nationwide by NEA Telephoto.[2]

Public reaction outside of Hollywood, particularly in the skin trade, was less sanguine. "Why, it's utterly disgraceful," said Gypsy Rose Lee. "I am unalterably opposed. How can girls like myself work at it when this lady wants everybody to give it away?" Fellow burlesque-house stripper, Ann Corio, concurred: "It's ridiculous. Those Hollywood dames have a lot of nerve. Most of them are faking anyway. It would make things tough for strippers, wouldn't it? I'm glad I saved my dough."

In New York City, Eunice Skelly, former Ziegfeld girl and proprietress of the Salon of Eternal Youth, declared that she was just the gal to wear an evening dress with a "window bosom," adding: "My dear, I want you to know that I think the idea is gorgeous. There isn't anything, for instance, much uglier than the average nose, yet women stick them out all over the place."

Even in New York City, this was a minority view. Famed fashion designer Adele Simpson — no slouch when it came to dresses designed to emphasize the bosom — termed the idea "just plain vulgar." And Sally? Well, she largely agreed: "It's stupid, asinine, undecorative and impractical. Even in Timothy's time in ancient Greece and Rome, women wore brassieres and blouses. I am revolted."

---

2   The exposure may have given Miss Greer's career a boost. The next year she played the lead opposite Robert Mitchum and Kirk Douglas in the film noir favorite *Out of the Past*. Later, she appeared in many television shows and series, including (*ahem*) *Twin Peaks*.

No one need have feared. Renie's vision was well ahead of its time.[3] Eighteen months later, admitting that she wasn't much of a fashion predictor, Renie was quoted as saying that her dream was a "horrible bust."

Once she and Turk Greenough had parted ways, Sally went back on the road with her "Hollywood Pin-Up Girls," crisscrossing the continent from Vancouver to New York City and back to the West Coast. Apparently not burned badly enough by her earlier financial embarrassments and bankruptcy, Sally still had visions of setting up shop in San Francisco.

Some six months after she had abandoned the fantasy of life as a Montana cowboy's wife, Sally announced in January of 1946 that she was opening her own club in the Bay area town of El Cerrito. She was quite enthusiastic about the enterprise:

> Not just a night club, really, but a different night club. There won't be any girls coming around to pester you to buy stuff — Gardenias, peanuts, cigarettes, photographs ... They'll be there if you want them, but the stuff won't be forced on you.
>
> The walls will be blue, midnight blue. There will be girls, voluptuous girls, painted on the walls. Rest rooms will be ultra-modern. I want people to be satisfied and be entertained when they come to my club. I don't want them to have to spend a lot of money. If they do, they won't come back.

When asked what the club would be called, she responded: "Sally Rand's of course." *Billboard* magazine described the Sally Rand Club as an "ultra-gorgeous nitery" — the equal of the best nightspots on either coast — "a ritzy, rich, yet comfortable room with 500 capacity." Sally's show played to overflow crowds with everyone reveling in the opening musical number "Let's Make the Boys Feel Abroad at Home." The enterprise was promoted as though Sally were the owner, or at least a partner, and all of the club's prospects seemed rosy.

---

3 Similar designs have emerged from time to time, notably Rudi Gernreich's topless monokini in 1964 and Madonna's 1992 appearance on the runway in a topless dress for Jean-Paul Gaultier's celebrity fashion show in Los Angeles. Gwyneth Paltrow caused a stir at Vanity Fair's 2002 Oscar party, wearing a see-through dress with no bra. The ultimate example may have been on June 2, 2014, when singer Rihanna stunned all observers by appearing at the Council of Fashion Designers of America Awards show at Lincoln Center in New York wearing a sparkling full-body, see-through outfit. Her fishnet gown featured over 230,000 Swarovski crystals.

Initially business was brisk, but within a few months the venue was in financial distress. All too soon, the "partnership" was declared bankrupt and, when creditors came to call, Sally pleaded that she hadn't really owned anything and had "never received a cent." She even claimed that she had to sleep where the cook and pantry man slept because, as she put it: "I didn't have any money ... I was only a servant, a sweeper-upper. I finally was told I could be a hostess. That was the kind of partner I was."

This stumble aside, no sooner did her club venture in El Cerrito fail than Sally began appearing under a similar ownership arrangement with the Club Savoy at 168 O'Farrell Street in San Francisco. And, no sooner was she fanning the breeze in her new club than the local clergy began complaining. Before long, their concerns reached City Hall and the police raided the club.

On June 25th, a detail of six police officers stood onstage in the wings and, after observing her performance, arrested Sally on charges of violating Section 311 of the Penal Code, which barred "indecent exposure, corrupting the morals of an audience, and conducting an obscene show." Sally had been around this block before. She quickly secured the services of acclaimed San Francisco criminal defense attorney J. W. "Jake" Ehrlich.[4]

The next morning, Sally arrived in court carrying a large bouquet of roses, seemingly a gift from supporters.[5] As proceedings began, Police Captain Joseph Walsh testified as to his "agony at having to watch Miss Rand reduce a full costume, garment by garment, to a mere patch over the lower torso."

Sally had, in fact, begun her performance "wrapped in ermine" while gliding down a staircase wafting her fans. Underneath she wore her standard little flowing chiffon gown, which always had a way of falling away at some point during the dance. The question of whether anything indecent had occurred revolved around what other covering may have remained. An arresting officer testified there was nothing left but Sally. She insisted there was a triangular "patch," but testified that she couldn't surrender it as evidence since it "just floated away."

---

[4]   Known for his celebrity clients, Jake Ehrlich successfully defended singer Billie Holiday, drummer Gene Krupa, industrialist Howard Hughes, actor Errol Flynn, and rapist Caryl Chessman, as well as sports figures, bigamists, madams, and 56 alleged murderers (none of whom was executed). Ehrlich's career inspired the *Perry Mason* TV series. Actor Raymond Burr is said to have spent two weeks shadowing him to better understand his mannerisms.

[5]   Sally's defense attorney Jake Ehrlich wrote in his autobiography that the roses had been "a gift of the San Francisco Chapter of the League of Decency," adding with an implied wink, "At least that was the name I wrote on the card."

Recalling his remarks to the court, Attorney Ehrlich observed that:

> It was strange that in crime-busy San Francisco (a Mafia murder
> was shaking North Beach to its wine-scented foundations) six
> police officers were required for the incarcerating of a 110-pound,
> limpid-eyed blond, unarmed except for a triangular three-inch
> patch surmounted with thirty beads.

Warming to his subject, Ehrlich added some historical context:

> Nudity is not new. The great Greek sculptor Praxiteles made use of
> it for his heroic figures. Rodin's masterpieces are exhibited before
> the public the world over. I can take any person here and show him
> more nudity among the classics than he ever saw here.... A person
> may be undressed, even nude, and not be lewd. It took six big
> policemen to arrest this lady. Look at her, Your Honor! She doesn't
> look vicious to me. I say Sally Rand is not indecent. Her dance is
> immoral only in the minds of a lot of stuffed shirts who ought to go
> to the laundry.

Then, following a familiar pattern, Ehrlich suggested to the judge:

> ... that we adjourn until tomorrow morning, at which time my
> client will perform her specialty for you. Thus instead of
> secondhand accounts and narrow-minded criticisms, we'll be
> dealing with the naked truth.

Municipal Judge Daniel R. Shoemaker, agreed to attend Sally's demonstration on her stage at the Savoy and released her, free to return to the
club. In her finale that night, Sally had a bit of fun with the police officers
seated in the packed house. When her ostrich feather fans were cast aside at
the end of her dance, Sally was revealed to be garbed in a suit of long
flannel underwear. As Ehrlich later described it: "Where the triangular
patch once forbade greater inspection of the premises, there was a small
placard. It read: Censored. S.F.P.D."

The next morning, after watching Sally's performance, Judge Shoemaker
dismissed the charges against her, pronouncing that anyone who found her
dance to be lewd and lascivious must have a perverted sense of moral values.

At age 42, Sally was beginning to tire of this sort of harassment. Repeated
financial problems and run-ins with law enforcement can take a toll on a
lady. Might there be a way to continue doing what she wanted, albeit with a
sense of security and maybe a little less personal responsibility? Sally would
soon find just such a situation in a most unlikely place — the carnival.

Carnivals encompass a little world of their own. As with many subcultures, carnies have an exclusive vernacular — colorful terms that serve as a sort of secret language intended to impart meaning only to those in the know. In carnival slang, a "top" is a tent; a "bally" is the free preview given outside a sideshow to attract a crowd. There is also the "tip," the "talker," and the "rube," among many examples.[6] And a "carnie"? Well, a carnie is much more than just someone who travels with the carnival.

With the fat lady, thin man, Tilt-a-Whirl, cotton candy, bumper cars, knock-em-over games (for some reason you can never manage to knock-em-over), flashing lights and persuasive pitch men, traveling carnivals have been around for more than 100 years. There was a time in the 1940s and early 1950s when there was no bigger deal than the coming of the carnival. The colorful lights, the thrilling rides, the sideshow "freaks" (and the exaggerated canvas paintings that portrayed them) played upon the minds of impressionable young visitors, all suggesting a way of life more exotic and yet somehow more real than their own mundane existence.

A touring carnival season usually lasted for roughly half the year, from mid-spring to mid-fall. Several big name regional operators toured the country by truck or rail, setting up in each location for only a few days before moving on. At many stops, the carnival operator shared the grounds with a state or regional fair.

Although state and local fairs operated on a thin profit margin, in one way they actually resembled their grander international cousins. The fairs' sponsors understood that agricultural, artistic, and cake baking attractions, standing alone, were unlikely to keep the turnstile turning. True, a certain number of families would make the annual pilgrimage just to see which corpulent pig had been awarded the blue ribbon or which farmer had grown the biggest pumpkin, but the price for general admission wasn't going to add up to much if nothing more compelling than Grandma's huckleberry preserves was on offer.

The real money would be generated by the midway rides, games of chance, and sideshows. To provide these amusements, local fair sponsors would contract with such traveling carnival operators as Royal American Shows, Hennies Brothers, or Al Wagner's Cavalcade of Amusements. Along with enticing attractions catering primarily to children and teenagers, most

---

6   The "talker" (never "barker") delivers the spiel to build a crowd in front of an
     attraction. The "tip" is the crowd that he gathers. If the talker is successful, he can
     "turn the tip," that is, convince onlookers to buy tickets and come inside. A "rube," of
     course, is the "townie" or "chump" who is literally taken in by the talker's bally.

carnival operators also provided so-called "girl shows" — venues where Grandpa, Dad and Uncle Earl were given a chance to see something they might otherwise never see.

On January 19th, speaking at the Michigan Showmen's Association party in Detroit, Sally disclosed that: "I expect to be one of you next season, performing under canvas." Not long afterward, she agreed that she and her troupe would join the Hennies Brothers Shows as the featured girl show attraction of the summer season.[7]

And so, beginning in 1947, the Sally Rand Show spent several seasons on the traveling carnival circuit. Why she would choose this path is really quite simple. Contracting for a season with such an operation offered several advantages, not least of which was financial stability for several months each year. That first year Sally signed on for an unprecedented sum of $60,000 ($670,000 in 2017), to be paid out of the first profits as soon as possible. She and the Hennies brothers would then split any further profits fifty-fifty. In addition, she would no longer have to arrange for individual bookings across the country.

In mid-April, Sally, her 12 chorus girls, dance director Marjorie Fielding, and producer Charles Barnes arrived in Birmingham, Alabama, to prepare for a tour of state fairs. Things got off to a rocky start. Sally and Harry Hennies locked horns over the terms of her contract and she apparently threatened to pack up her show and take a walk. Their dispute was serious enough that Harry swore out an arrest warrant against Sally on April 21st alleging that she had broken into a carnival railroad car with the intent of burglarizing "one or more wardrobe trunks." Hennies claimed Sally had "walked barefooted through the mud" and "used a crowbar" to break the lock on the train car.

Sally seemed genuinely peeved when the story of "Sally the burglar" hit the front pages. But, before the judge could gavel in a court hearing two days later, she and Hennies had patched things up. Everyone was supposedly in agreement, but when the two appeared in court to testify that the whole thing had been a misunderstanding, Assistant Solicitor Willard McCall became suspicious:

> The warrant charging burglary was sworn out Monday. Mr. Hennies admitted he gave Miss Rand permission to get the trunk. He also

---

7   The Hennies Brothers Shows had been around since at least 1934 when, described as "America's Largest Motorized Carnival," the brothers sought to cash in by touting a "World's Fair Side Show" that featured a number of Ripley's Believe-It-Or-Not subjects, including 16-year-old Price LeRoy who "pulls a large automobile with his eyelids."

admitted that, as far as he knew, she took nothing from the wagon other than her own trunk. Knowing she hadn't violated any laws, he still swore out the warrant. This action constitutes a malicious abuse of the processes of this court. It was a fictitious charge and partakes of a publicity stunt.

Obviously annoyed, Judge G. C. Boner was of a similar mind. He summarily discharged Sally and then fined Harry Hennies $50 plus court costs. Just for good measure, he sentenced Hennies to five days in jail. Flustered by the outcome, Harry appealed to the Alabama Court of Appeals and was released on $500 bond after spending nearly 24 hours in the clink. Despite these initial missteps, Sally spent the 1947 summer carnival season touring with the Hennies Brothers Shows, regularly drawing the largest crowds on the midway.

Well into the season, at the Illinois State Fair in Springfield, four teenaged girls from Ames, Iowa, abruptly quit Sally's show when one of them — a freckle-faced girl who didn't care for mascara and eyebrow pencil — refused to apply her make-up. Sally recounted:

I told her she would have to go home. The other girls said they would go too.... I paid their expense here and they showed up four hours late for rehearsal. I found them rooms in a private home and mothered them as if they were my own children.

Judy Green, aged 18, confessed that she had quit the troupe mainly because "the men whistled at us." (The girls all ended up with new job offers due to the publicity they had gotten at Sally's expense.) In any case, losing the four farm fresh fillies turned out to be the least of Sally's troubles in Springfield. Two days later, she would be caught up in an uncomfortable episode involving the fiery strip-tease dancer Georgia Sothern.

Still, the show rolled on across the hinterlands. At the Iowa State Fair in Des Moines, according to *Billboard*, Sally "played to 55,000 persons who paid $1 a head, on the same midway where Hennies Bros Shows grossed $125,000." She and Harry Hennies were apparently on their way to realizing the seemingly unreachable amounts agreed to in their contract.

When the carnival season came to an end, Sally headed south for warmer weather. A newspaper in South Florida announced in November that Sally Rand — who would be starring at a local club with eight of the "World's Most Beautiful Girls" — "will be a Florida resident from now on ... [and] has purchased a home at Key West."[8] In her new home, Sally was as busy as ever visiting patients at the Naval Hospital and appearing at an American Legion benefit for the March of Dimes. And, although it is unknown whether the two ever met, one of Sally's neighbors in Key West that winter was President Harry Truman, who retreated to his "Little White House" on a regular basis.[9]

Faith

Back in 1942, as the war against the Nazis raged on, the California-Arizona Maneuver Area (a huge desert training center) had been created at a site west of Phoenix to test equipment and train troops to operate in conditions similar to those found in North Africa. Fort Young, headquarters for the area, was under the command of Major General George S. Patton. The general and the men he trained in the desert southwest would soon distinguish themselves in North Africa and beyond, a story of great renown. But, for purposes of our story, a rather unexpected relationship was revealed in a biography of Patton's wife, written by his daughter:

> Sometimes he had cheerful things to write about, and he often sent Ma clippings and other enclosures. The best one of these was a long letter with several shiny publicity photographs of the notorious striptease artist Faith Bacon. She wrote Georgie that he was her favorite general, and that she hoped she was his favorite artiste. She wrote that, in addition to admiring him very much, she wanted him to know that he was also her cousin, and she included a photocopy of her Colonial Dames papers, which traced her ancestry to a cousin of his grandmother, Margaret Hereford Wilson.

---

[8]   Sally's 1606 square foot house at 916 Eisenhower Drive still stands. Following extensive restoration in the early 2000s, it was the recipient of the 2005 Florida Keys Foundation Preservation Award.

[9]   These were different times. One morning an Admiral came by the Little White House, and asked: "Mr. President, is there anything I can do for you?" Truman was said to have replied: "That little shit paper in New York had a story yesterday about Key West, and there was an implication there that there were some homosexuals preying on the sailors. Is there any truth to that?" And the Admiral said, "Well, we have more undesirables down here than we would like." Truman supposedly said, "Is there anything you can do about it?" The reply was, "Oh, yes sir, we can take care of that." Later that day, the Shore Patrol notified "all the joints" on Duval Street that they needed to purge their staff of "queer piano players" and the like or the establishments would be put off limits to sailors from the submarine base. On Friday afternoon, a group of fifty allegedly gay men were rounded up, put on a Greyhound bus, driven to the Miami city limits and pushed out.

Faith became interested in genealogy when she learned that she was a descendent of Peregrine White and that her great-grandfather, Henry Douglas Bacon, had been instrumental in the founding of the University of California.[10] When it came to her attention in 1945 that her great-grandfather had donated a valuable collection of pictures and other works of art to the university, Faith's curiosity was piqued. The 1887 donation had included a significant collection of marble statues, chief among them a Carrara marble reproduction of Johann Heinrich von Dannecker's famous depiction of Ariadne, riding a panther.[11] She visited the Berkeley campus hoping to see the sculptures, but was dismayed to find that, even after 58 years, the donated artworks were still in their original packing crates, stored in the basement of the women's gymnasium.

Faith was not pleased. She felt the university had not honored Henry Bacon's wishes in entrusting the pieces for public display. Her next step was to consult an attorney to draw up a demand that the university either put Ariadne and the others on display or turn over possession of the statues to her. A university spokesman had reportedly told her there was no place for them in any of the campus art collections, so she was welcome to take them. This proved to be something of a pyrrhic victory, since each of the statues weighed between eight and ten tons — not the sort of thing Faith could take home with her in the overhead compartment. It's not clear exactly what happened next, although she was said to be on the lookout for another art-loving donee who would promise to accept the pieces and do right by them.

At any rate, Faith labored on, taking engagements as the "creator of the fan dance" wherever they were offered. In 1948, following a stint at the Midnight Follies in Tijuana, Mexico (a popular retreat for Southern Californians ever since Prohibition days), she caught on with the John R. Ward Shows, a traveling carnival, signing a 30-week contract.

---

[10] Faith's research revealed that, in addition to Sir Francis Bacon and General Patton, she was also related to former President Grover Cleveland, as well as Daniel Dearborn Page, the second Mayor of St. Louis.

[11] The collection also contained a pair of nude marble nymphs preparing for their bath, as well as a piece called "The Genius of America, or the Abolition of Slavery," showing the goddess of liberty freeing a nude slave. Faith's great-grandfather had commissioned the sculpture in appreciation of President Abraham Lincoln. However, before it could be finished, Lincoln was assassinated and the sculpture was donated to the university.

Faith was pleased with the arrangement, saying:

> Personally, I am thrilled with the prospect of seeing the sun again
> and taking many deep breaths of air free from contaminated smoke
> and liquor air-laden night clubs. It's my opinion that all types and
> sizes of acts, in fact all of the show business, will sooner or later
> migrate into the outdoor traveling world.

Ralph

Sally had been married and divorced — not for the last time — and there
had been many suitors. But one of the most important men in her life, and
certainly the most devoted, was never a candidate for that role. Ralph
Hobart had known Sally since childhood, had shared his New York
apartment with her during hard times in the Twenties, and had been her
steadfast assistant for many years. More or less hers to command, he was
also a homosexual at a time when nearly every gay man in America was
deeply closeted.

Among other obligations, Ralph was charged with keeping Sally's financial
records in order — a prodigious task. On May 7, 1948, he wrote to her from
Hollywood describing his difficulty in preparing her tax return, primarily
due to duplicate entries in her records:

> NEVER have I had such a time with the tax!! I have been working
> day and night. Have been no place nor had any company. The
> number of entries necessary are at least three times any previous
> year! Even 1939 was not as voluminous.... It has been a hell of a
> job to get it done.

Adding to his misery, Ralph had also been quite ill during this period and
was very concerned about the "several possible causes":

> I had every examination known to man, so to speak, and — it is all
> from teeth. I previously had a fantastic sore throat (could not eat
> anything nor swallow and suffered agony) and then all my gums
> swelled up and suddenly I could not even see anything. I was
> worried about the previous syphilis condition, and wondered what
> else might be wrong, since I have had trouble with my eyes for
> 3 years. So, I had all these examinations. EVERYTHING! And, to make
> a long story short … the syphilis condition has not affected the spine,
> brain, nor heart, and it is doubtful if it will ever cause trouble —
> however, a course of treatment was recommended.

Hobart's dedication to Sally was nothing less than heroic. He put off attending to his teeth and other personal issues rather than fall behind on her accounts. After declaring that he was successfully getting his drinking under control, Ralph offered a glimpse into his personal life:

> I have had a friend staying with me since Easter. Remember me telling you about the Air Cadet who used to visit every weekend? That was back in 1942. I have been in touch with him ever since. He just got out of the army ... and came down here to visit.... He is going to Columbia University in N.Y. this fall, but meanwhile has a job here and is staying with me. He has been a wonderful influence and through his efforts I started going to church.... Nettie [Sally's mother] met the fellow I am writing about and thought he was very nice....
>
> So much for that — must get back to the accounts. Will contact you this coming week about the tax matters. I don't know what the answer will be, but hope for the best.... Please send money since I have to pay on the doctor bill and it takes every cent I make to live and pay for a few incidentals....

While Sally had failed to send regular payments to her unwavering assistant, she did find time to assist in a fundraising benefit sponsored by Royal American Shows for the Greater Tampa Showmen's Association. (The group sought to build a new clubhouse that would include space for the Ladies' Auxiliary.) Sally was in town appearing at the Frolics Club. Gypsy Rose Lee was also in Tampa visiting the Florida State Fair. Both ladies agreed to appear at a benefit auction that ended up raising over $5,300 (said at the time to be the largest amount ever realized at such an event). Other acts on the program included Leon Claxton's *Harlem in Havana* — the most popular jig show on the carnival circuit.

The *what*?

As we know, in the first half of the twentieth century, theaters, restaurants, and public accommodations were largely segregated. The same applied to carnival midway attractions. Even so, the operators of these businesses well understood that African-American patrons had money to spend. Just how to extract it from them was the question. Southern carnival owners came up with two ways to address the matter.

For one, they periodically designated a "Negro Day" — a day when attendance by African Americans was actively encouraged. On such days, Sally's show would often be suspended and replaced by a show featuring all black performers. Eddie Anderson, who played "Rochester" on the popular Jack Benny radio program, performed in the Sally Rand tent in 1950 and, for his two shows, drew $1,440 in paid admissions (nearly $15,000 today). Other nontheatrical events were sometimes added to the mix. Negro Day at the 1949 Louisiana State Fair in Shreveport featured stock car racing with all black drivers, as well as a high school and college football game. Negro Day at the 1950 State Fair of Texas, in Dallas, enjoyed its biggest day ever as 19,000 fans attended a football game between Wiley College and Prairie View A&M at the Cotton Bowl.[12]

The other approach was to offer so-called "Chocolate Revues" or — as they were commonly referred to by blacks and whites alike — "jig shows." Some of these shows were little more than an extension of the minstrel show tradition. Others were lavish revues, not unlike the girl shows offered elsewhere on the midway. The best known and most popular was Leon Claxton's *Harlem in Havana* — a full blown production that was just as elaborate as Sally's own show and featured dancers, comedians, and musicians who were every bit as talented. By 1949, Claxton's revue had been part of the annual Royal American Shows' traveling carnival during 15 previous seasons. It was always one of the carnival's most profitable attractions.[13]

Claxton would eventually operate his own 1,600-seat outdoor tent and *Harlem in Havana* would gross more than $150,000 per season. The show featured 21 "leggy girls" and a 10-piece orchestra.[14] As a sign of his success, when Claxton and his revue shared the program with Sally and Gypsy Rose at the 1949 benefit in Tampa, he had just purchased an $80,000 home in that city (when the average cost of new house was $7,450).

---

[12] At the State Fair of Texas, "Negro Day" more or less came to an end in 1955. It was still a feature of the Louisiana State Fair as late as 1960.

[13] While Leon Claxton was rightly called "the Tyler Perry of his time" by his granddaughter, his revue was not the only one of its kind, just the most successful. Many other touring shows offered similar attractions, among them, Jerrie Jackson's *Hep Cat Revue* (later known as the *High Steppers Revue*) and Charles A. Taylor's *Little Harlem Revue*. In the early 1940s, Sammy Green's *Hot Harlem Revue* featured an exuberant teenager named Willie Mae Thornton who, besides being a powerful singer, was also a dancer, drummer, comedienne and harmonica player. Her 1953 recording of "Hound Dog" would be covered three years later by a personable young man from Memphis who would go on to enjoy a decent singing career of his own.

[14] For a remarkable collection of photographs of the women who performed in Leon Claxton's *Harlem in Havana Revue* from 1936 to 1967, see *Brown Skin Showgirls* by Leslie Cunningham (2015).

Like his colleagues in the traveling-tent-show business, Claxton used trade publications to advertise for talent. One such ad was anything but subtle:

> WANTED! Musicians and Performers. Opening January 14th,
> thirty-two week season on old established show. Organized bands
> write.... SALARY SURE, NO LAYOFFS.... Dope fiends, booze heads
> and bums save time and stamps. Line girls send photos.

With her tent commonly located directly opposite that of *Harlem in Havana*, Sally enjoyed a cordial relationship with Claxton, even making occasional guest appearances in his revue. Neighboring shows maintained a friendly competition, each seeking to be recognized as the top-grossing attraction for Royal American Shows. At the 1948 Louisiana State Fair, midway attractions realized a 25 percent increase over the prior year, with the Rand and Claxton shows ranking numbers one and two among the top moneymakers.

W orking with the Hennies Brothers Shows in 1949, Sally was said to have earned the largest sum ever received by a single midway attraction. Even so, some might think that appearing on the midway in a traveling carnival would be quite a step down for a performer of her stature. Sally didn't see it that way at all:

> I have been asked a jillion times: "Well, how do you like it" — the
> carnival, that is. I like it. And I like being a carnie, if being a carnie
> means carnival people love and respect me as much as I do them. Of
> all the show business I know about, I can't think of any other branch
> where honor, integrity and the worth of a man's word are so
> important and valuable.

These words formed the opening paragraphs of a lengthy remembrance demonstrating Sally's insights and depth of knowledge about the operational ins and outs of carnival life. To begin with, she observed that making money during the 25-week summer season was not a given:

> ... whatever else it may be, the carnival business is a gamble! It is a
> gamble with the weather, labor, regional wealth or lack of it, crops,
> strikes and many other unforeseen and ungovernable conditions.

Carnival life wouldn't be a good fit for everyone, nor would every celebrity be successful as a midway attraction. First, she warned, it required someone with universal appeal:

> It must be remembered also that the people who visit carnival
> lots and fairs are not, on the whole, the people that one meets at
> Twenty-One and Ciro's.... [The] people who will pay a cover

charge and run up a big check at a night club or buy reserved seats in a theater won't come out on a carnival lot, get shavings in their shoes, wait for the fourth bally and sit on a hard stringer.

Producing a carnival show involved considerations not commonly found in a theater or club. Stage scenery had to fit into a 60-foot boxcar for transportation from town to town, costumes had to withstand the elements and frequent cleaning — or as Sally put it, red plush curtains and theater seats "are not going to look pretty very long ... after being dragged thru mud and rain, and after being sat on from 9 o'clock in the morning until 1 a.m." Sally understood that the cast of a girl show must be young and healthy enough to perform in as many as 20 shows a day.

She advised hiring two managers — a business manager to monitor the box office, deal with management, and generally keep patrons happy, and a stage manager to look after the technical end and keep performers and supporting crew on the same page.

The business manager couldn't be just anybody. The producer of a carnival show should expect to pay big money to get someone who really knows what he is doing. As Sally put it: "Don't fool yourself; a stooge won't do!" Such a man must:

> ... take care of you and your business, serving as your contact with the office wagon and management. He should ... watch every ticket sold, taken, torn and put in the box, make sure that every customer who comes in has a ticket, know better than to get into a beef with a drunk or a gate-crasher, how to keep ticket-sellers from short-changing customers....

> He should [know] enough to let fair officials, newspapermen and the people who should get in free get in free, even tho they don't have a pass ... and have a gimlet eye that can catch a wrong serial number on a ticket....

> He should be a diplomat with enough charm and smooth talk to get along with the advance man, the talker, the crew and all the rest of the shows on the midway. This last is important because you are liable to be next to or across from the Jig Show, the Midget Show, Hawaiian Show, Sideshow, the Funhouse, the Wild Life, the War Show or (God forbid!), the Motordrome.

After emphasizing the need for a stage manager, a publicity man, a secretary/bookkeeper and maybe even a dresser, Sally turned her attention inward:

> And now we come down to the most important item — you, yourself. If you are an introvert, or like to live in an ivory tower, if your public annoys you, or if you enjoy poor health, don't come on a carnival....

> You must autograph a jillion pictures, little dirty pieces of paper, shirts, shorts, hats, pocketbooks or anything else as many times a day as you do shows, not as a favor, not condescendingly, but gratefully and graciously....

> You've got to make coming to the carnival sound exciting, glamorous and the most absolutely amusing and wonderful thing that anybody could do. And you are not doing this as a favor to anybody. It is part of your job even tho you are doing 20 shows a day.

Beyond all this, beyond the managers, beyond the public relations, Sally called special attention to a little-known gentleman who was possibly the most important of them all — the "Boss Canvas Man":

> And who is this head canvas man? He's an artist, a prima donna, a technician, a craftsman, a weather man — and a boss. Make no mistake. He's the No. 1 guy. Without him your tent doesn't go up and it doesn't come down. Without a tent you aren't in business, and when you aren't in business you don't get paid.

> There are only a few good canvas men in the world. He has charge of several thousand square feet of living skin, which the canvas in a tent is. Strong as it looks, it is fragile and as easily hurt as a baby's backside. It's literally a skin, a living skin which lies over an intricate skeleton of hemp rope. It shrinks in the cold and the wet. It stretches in the heat. It is a dead weight of many tons. A tiny little breeze can make it buck like a bronco. A little shower can burst it from front to back like a toy balloon if it isn't properly guyed out. [When] it acts up it makes the tent poles dance like jumping jacks, and when they start to kick out they have the force of a wagon tongue being shot out of a cannon. They kill and maim.[15]

---

[15] On June 29, 1906, in Aurora, Illinois, 10,000 people were thrown into a panic during a performance of Ringling Brothers' circus when a sudden and violent wind storm wreaked havoc on the main tent. As reported the next day in the *Chicago Daily Tribune*: "Swinging quarter poles, lifted from the ground by the swaying canvas, mowed down people in scores from their seats. One man was instantly killed — a cripple, who was unable to save himself — another man died of fright as he hurried from the scene of terror with his family, and seven persons were injured, at least one of them fatally."

It is your Boss Canvas Man who knows how tight to guy it out and
when to let it loose.... He is like a doctor with his hand on a patient's
pulse, and he babies it and knows exactly what to do with it.... And
long after you are warm and snug and dry in your bed or your berth,
he and his crew — cold, wet, dirty, hungry — are pulling and
hauling and carrying by hand tons and tons of canvas and poles and
seats, stowing them away.

Sally could hardly have held her carnival companions in higher regard:

Being a carnie is a way of life. There is warmth and affection and a
cooperativeness that is unknown in any other line of show
business.... I'd like to tell you a true story.

She then related the details of an incident in East Peoria, Illinois, where, the
month before, a fire had destroyed much of her scenery and costumes, along
with a section of the tent. Walter DeVoyne, the Royal American Show's secretary, had phoned Sally saying: "Now take it easy Sally, and sit down. Your
show has just burned up." The quick thinking crew had gotten a tractor and
managed to pull the dressing room wagons, lights, sound system, seats and
other items, including a Hammond organ, to safety before the fire could
consume them. It was one o'clock in the afternoon and those assessing the
scene had predicted it would be a week or more before repairs could be
made and the show reopened.

Sally had rushed to the scene:

When I arrived, every carnie on the lot was there — black and grimy
and wet from fighting the fire. When they saw me come in, they
busied themselves and looked away — they knew how I felt and
they were too kind to look at my grief. They wasted no words of
sympathy, they lost no time with ineffectual condolences. They went
to work.... There they sat cross legged on the ground quietly and
quickly putting patient skillful stitches into a skin for the burned top.

In short, every able body pitched in. Luckily, the East Peoria stop was a still
date,[16] giving Sally time to rush into town and buy an assortment of colorful
crepe paper, rolls of ribbon and stacks of blue and white corrugated paste-
board. With "four staple guns" and "miles of scotch tape," these items were
quickly turned into decorative stage elements to conceal the smoke damage.
Like the plot from an old Mickey Rooney movie, the gang was able to borrow
a curtain from a closed movie theater and hurriedly stitch together and clean

---

[16] A "still date" is a stop at a location not associated with a fair, often meaning that
the grounds were open for business only in the evening.

some costumes. Young men from an adjoining show dragged the lights, sound system, seats, and Hammond organ back into place.

Meanwhile, Sally took "a quick French bath in some stinky toilet water." Then, as she described it: "I pinned on my best switch [and] stuck on my gee string, which had only a little ground glass and a couple of crushed benzedrines in it." Sally concluded her tale in a paragraph crammed with carnival jargon:

> Duke, the talker, called a bally, made an opening, turned the tip, Buddy played the opening fanfare, and the show was on! I looked at my watch; it was 8 p.m., sharp, the regular opening time on a still date.

Men and women thrown together by disaster had marshaled their available resources, assisted one another, and achieved the seemingly impossible. Sally couldn't have been more proud:

> As I stood in the back of the darkened tent and saw those swell kids, who only a short half hour ago were scrubbing and painting, looking glamorous and gay, dancing and singing and doing a great job, I felt a glow of pride for my profession. I looked around. Every man and woman who wasn't actually needed on their own show was there. Some of them were a bit misty eyed.... No one even dreamed we'd do a show that night, but there it was. And it didn't look make-shift either....

> I will never know how many people put their hearts and hands into getting my show ready for that night. They didn't do it for glory or personal gain. That was the day they baptized me carnie and made me one of them.

Despite the grit and grime, life with a traveling carnival clearly has an appeal not easily understood by outsiders. One of Sally's favorite little stories illustrates the attitude of her carnival companions:

> Two carnies are walking down a country road in the pouring rain. The carnival has folded, and they are walking to the next town. They're cold, wet, and bedraggled. They pass a house and look in the picture window. A father is sitting by the fire reading to his children. His wife sits by his side, smiling at him and the children. One carnie says to the other: "Look at that poor bastard. I'll bet he wishes he was in show business like us."

Sally had aspired to be a professional ballet dancer; instead, she had labored as a vaudevillian, a movie actress, and a nightclub, theater and World's Fair performer. And she was the most acclaimed fan dancer in the land. But, no less than any of these, she was also a carnie — and proud to say so.

Two days after the fire, Sally flew to her home in Key West. Something was in the works there that would become the most important thing in all her life.

Ralph

Ever loyal, Ralph Hobart continued to struggle with Sally's tax returns, chiding her about missing information he needed to complete W2 forms required for five of her employees. On February 6, 1949, Ralph wrote to Sally that he had filed a tax form for her, together with a letter informing the IRS that she was "unable to pay this at the time because of losses and not working" but that she "would take care of it at the first opportunity." There was also the matter of a past due storage bill for furniture stored at Wells Van & Storage in Alameda, a situation complicated by the fact that some of her belongings had been damaged in a warehouse fire: "Wells claims that your goods are not badly damaged with the exception of the spinet piano."

To put it mildly, Sally's payroll accounts were not in proper order, especially Ralph's own salary:

> The money situation is desperate. It has been over 7 weeks since
> you sent me money. I owe January rent and February rent is way
> past due. And rent is due on the storage room. I borrowed $25
> from Nettie to pay my December phone bill to avoid it being taken
> out. $4.75 of the $25 was for me — I have borrowed from everyone,
> but I can't go on like that. Please send me SOMETHING right away.
> All my clothes need cleaning. I haven't had a haircut for 6 weeks,
> and am embarrassed when I go to church on Sunday, because I
> can't put anything in the collection. Can't get any more groceries
> on credit, so am in a spot.

A couple of weeks after this desperate plea, Sally came through with $100 ("… can't tell you how much I appreciated it"), but things were still far from agreeable. Less than a week later, Ralph wrote:

> Things are in such a financial mess that I don't know where to
> start. This rent business is terrible. I am constantly being annoyed
> and threatened…. I also owe all my friends, tenants, grocery
> store, drug store for meals, doctor from way back in 1948, and
> worst of all … the income tax from the 1947 report which was due
> in March 1948.

Hobart's life was in chaos. His letter laid out in excruciating detail how he would be able to address his financial problems, if only Sally would send the money she owed him:

> ... you have been in arrears for so long now ... even when you pay me I will just be even ... except for about $200.00 which represents all I have saved in several years, including the $1,000.00 I received from the accident in San Francisco.... I never collected salary after I received the money for the accident and was behind before that....

> If we could only get caught up and I could get these debts paid. I have not told of all the trouble I have been through trying to do your work and no money so had to do odd jobs in order to eat.... I need it so badly, Sally, please see what you can do.... I have [not] eaten since Thursday, and so have spent $5.46 in 3 days for meals and cigarettes, and dog food! I have not one cent now. I do so hope that you are sending something this weekend. It is so difficult to do this work and be hungry and worried about eating! ...

> This time of year is so important. I need to work every minute that I can for you in order to get this work done and the more I work the more I can save you on tax. But it takes time! And I must be free to think about it and concentrate on it rather than where I can get something to eat. I am sure that you do not believe it when I tell you that I actually go hungry, pick up cigarette butts off the street in order to have a smoke, and go around in clothes looking like a bum. I would not admit this to everyone because I am ashamed of it, but I can't help it. Please send me what you can and let's get this straightened out — and at least keep it up to date.

Despite his complaints, Ralph continued to be incredibly conscientious:

> ... above all, take care of the extension on this [income] tax matter. Things are well under control and a 30 day extension will do it. Things are better under control this year than since 1946! Nothing like '48 and '47 for which I am, and am sure you are, very thankful!!!

Faith

Traveling with the John R. Ward World's Fair Shows in 1948, the *Faith Bacon Show* featured at least four other striking young women, including Rene Villon, one of the fan dancers we encountered in chapter 16. With great fanfare, Ward announced the signing of Faith Bacon at $1,800 per week, declaring his plans to build a "featured gal show" around her. The "front" for the show would be "illuminated by neon and indirect lighting and decorated with 10-foot blow-ups of the dancer."[17] The carnival show would also feature a *Beauty and the Beast* act, with Emil Van Horn reportedly wearing either a chimp costume or gorilla suit.[18]

Still a looker at age 38, Faith had been optimistic about her venture "into the outdoor traveling world," but, as it happened, the actual show lacked production values and turned out to be a bit of a dud. In fact, Ward had trouble finding a stage manager who could both punch up the show and handle the temperamental Miss Bacon. Even so, everything seemed to be going well enough until, in late May, the show reached Rockford, Illinois.

One evening in Rockford, Faith was injured onstage while performing in her usual manner— barefooted. She claimed that tacks had been scattered on her dancing platform. No stranger to the legal system, she quickly filed a lawsuit against John Ward, alleging that she had been the victim of "a campaign of terror and violence" and that Ward had deliberately scattered the tacks to provoke her into breaking her contract. Seeking $44,040 in damages — a sum intended to cover her back pay plus $38,000 to cover the remainder of her contract[19] — Faith also asked for the legal attachment of two carnival rides and a 1947 Cadillac to ensure payment of any judgment in her favor.

Ward posted bond and the carnival moved on to Sioux Falls, South Dakota — without its "featured gal." For her part, Faith elected to take two weeks of rest in a sanitarium, claiming that John Ward's "plot" to force her out of her contract had caused her to lose 13 pounds (she was down to a mere 110). In the Ward show, she was soon replaced by Zorine, "Queen of the Nudists," whom you may remember from the San Diego Exposition in 1936. Oh, and the outcome? Faith eventually lost her lawsuit against the carnival boss.

F our years earlier, in late December 1944, while General Patton and his forces were on the move in what would become known as the Battle of the Bulge, headlines back in the States had screamed: "WHOLESALE NAZI ESCAPE." In the wee hours of Christmas Eve, it seems that 12 German officers and 13 enlisted U-boat crewmen had emerged from a 178-foot-long tunnel. Painstakingly dug over a period of months, the three-foot wide passage passed under two fences, a drainage ditch and a road. So began what some described as the greatest prisoner-of-war escape of the Second World War.

---

[17] In carnival jargon, the "front" is the outside entrance and banner line for the show. On the Midway, show locations usually paid for their space by the number of front feet allotted.

[18] Five years earlier, Van Horn had been cast in the title role of *The Ape Man*, a Monogram Studios picture starring Bela Lugosi.

[19] Multiply these numbers by a factor of ten to get an idea of the values involved.

The outside world had not exactly been welcoming. It was drizzling rain and bitter cold, even by the standards of winter nights in the Arizona desert. *Arizona*? POW escapees? Curiously, yes.

Not long after the escape, most of the fugitives returned to the prisoner-of-war camp, either wandering back on their own, chilly and hungry, or upon recapture. Captain Jürgen Wattenberg, mastermind of the escape and the camp's highest-ranking officer, was the last to be apprehended, having managed to subsist in the Phoenix area while living in a cave for more than a month. Barely three months later, the war was over in Europe.

Captain Wattenberg was released and returned to Germany where he became CEO of the St. Pauli Brewery.[20]

> ### PAPAGO PARK
>
> Home to the Phoenix Zoo and the Desert Botanical Garden, Papago Park also features otherworldly sandstone formations, lagoons, bicycle paths, picnic areas, hiking trails, and the municipal baseball stadium. During World War II, this popular park where families now marvel over the giant Galapagos tortoise (and 1,400 other zoo animals) was home to the most famous prisoner-of-war camp in America, housing hundreds of German prisoners, many of whom were U-boat officers and crewmen rescued from submarines sunk in the Atlantic Ocean.

In 1946, the Arizona POW camp was converted into the Papago Park Veterans Administration Hospital — the very place where Sally Rand's own father, who had been in and out of several veterans' facilities over the previous decade, was admitted three years later. Among his regular visitors were three of Sally's half-brothers, who were also living in the Phoenix area.

D uring the first week of December 1948, jazz fans in New York City were gathering at the Clique Club, a new dinner theater at 1678 Broadway. The jazz bistro had opened with an extended engagement by Sarah Vaughan with the Buddy Rich Orchestra, as well as a trio led by blind pianist George Shearing. Opening night had attracted the usual first night crowd of local society and show business luminaries, including actor Marlon Brando. The Clique continued to book big name jazz bands into the new year, but to diminishing financial gain. By the Ides of March, the club was struggling.

---

[20] On January 5, 1985, the Papago Park Prisoner of War Camp Commission held a commemorative observance at the campsite. Jürgen Wattenberg was a special guest of honor, having made the trip from his home in Lubeck, Germany. Looking back on his time in Arizona, the 85-year-old former U-boat commander reflected on how much he had enjoyed the SPAM dinners! Wattenberg died in a Hamburg nursing home on November 27, 1995. He was 94.

Hoping for a financial boost, the management deviated from its jazz programming and engaged Sally's show for two weeks beginning March 18th.

Just five weeks earlier, Sally's brother Harold had written to advise her of their father's deteriorating condition:

> I have just received a letter from Dad which is self-explanatory.
> Needless to say it is a most distressing thing.... As I see it, he
> needs hospital care for the rest of his days.... There is no doubt in
> my mind that he is very hard to get along with and there is no
> doubt that Marie is a hellion and the boys a pretty bummy lot....
> I'm at my wits end about it and can't find any constructive
> answers.... How he has managed to hold onto his life for this
> length of time really is amazing. He has been so ill and so entirely
> miserable with that asthma.

Although her father's illness clearly weighed on her mind, knowing she was contractually committed to be in New York for a while, Sally felt he would be better off if he could stay with her. She contacted Ralph Hobart, asking him to approach a young woman who had cared for her father in the past. Now married with a 9-year-old daughter, the woman agreed to do what she could, but only on a strictly temporary basis.

On March 4th, Ralph wrote to Sally:

> She would like to take over the case, and is sure that she can get
> your father in a condition to travel in just a very short time.... I
> repeated what you told me the doctor said ... and she feels sure
> that it is just like before when she went down to Phoenix to get
> him, and he was in bed, and she had him taking walks in no time
> at all. And she could make the trip to New York with him, but the
> entire venture cannot take over a month at the most. If you think
> that something can be done about it, contact her, and she will do
> all she can.

Sally's fears somewhat quelled, she had kept on working. But Colonel Beck was neither improving nor on his way to New York. Sally had been performing at the Clique Club for only four days when word arrived of her father's passing. Suffering from severe bronchial complications, Colonel Beck had died at the veterans' hospital in Phoenix on Wednesday, March 23rd.

When Sally learned of her father's death, she asked for temporary leave from her show's $4,000-per-week contract to attend the funeral. Club operator Irving Alexander was not sympathetic, coming back with a counter offer —

that Sally finish out the week and then leave for Arizona with the understanding that she would not return to the show. Sally countered his counter
with an offer to reduce her own salary on a pro rata basis and a promise that
she would return as soon as she could. At this point, Alexander got a bit
testy, suggesting that, rather than continue to pay the other cast members in
Sally's absence, maybe they should be paid out of the bond that Sally had
posted with the American Guild of Variety Artists.

Sally was in a quandary. In her view, she had lost her father more than once
before — first when he abandoned her as a child, again when he married
Marie and started a new family.[21] This time he was gone forever. The
father-daughter relationship had always been strained and, from a distance
of 2,400 miles, Sally had to feel conflicted.

In the end, she chose to remain in New York to fulfill the remainder of her
contract at the Clique Club, presumably out of loyalty to her current "family"
— the members of her troupe.[22] Her brother, on the other hand, who was in
Los Angeles rehearsing for the annual *Friars Club Frolic*,[23] decided to drive
the 372 miles to Phoenix for the funeral.

The day after the services, Harold wrote to Sally:

> Dad looked better in death than when I last saw him. He was
> dressed very neatly in his grey suit with his hands folded and a
> look of serenity on his face. The casket was nice and it was draped
> with the flag he loved so well....

> He did not have much to leave in the way of worldly goods, but
> Marie will get the pension money. He mentioned in a previous will
> that he wanted you to have his captain's commission (the one signed
> by the president) with the provision that you have it framed....

---

[21] After marrying Sally's father, Marie gave birth to five boys — Sally's half-brothers.

[22] The nightclub's business troubles didn't end with Sally's engagement. By July, the
Clique was in such financial straits that it was forced to close. Under new management, the location reopened later in the year as a jazz club. The name? — Birdland.

[23] Harold was performing in good company. The second annual West Coast version of
the *Friars Club Frolic* featured George Jessel as emcee, assisted by Clark Gable and
Ronald Reagan. The amazing list of participating celebrities included: Jack Benny,
Edgar Bergen, Humphrey Bogart, George Burns, James Cagney, Jimmy Durante, Bob
Hope, Frank Sinatra, Gene Kelly, Harpo Marx, Vincent Price, Mickey Rooney, Jimmy
Stewart, Buster Keaton, and Spencer Tracy, among many others. Benny and Kelly
were among those appearing in drag. The 6,000 attendees who jammed into the Shrine
Auditorium raised over $300,000 for the Movie Relief Fund (about $3 million today).
It was "the largest combined venture of radio, music and motion picture industries
ever to be staged in Hollywood."

I don't know just what part of the responsibility of the funeral was yours, but I can say that it was a very beautiful and well planned one. The minister was good and the setting was beautiful. The singer was excellent as was the music. The flowers were exquisite. Dad made his final exit in a manner befitting one of his importance — OUR FATHER.

The loss of her father and her brother's account of the funeral must have led Sally to seriously reflect upon the significance of family. Indeed, in the same week, syndicated columnist Dorothy Kilgallen reported that Sally was launching a series of lectures to be delivered to women's organizations. Her intended subject: "Happy Mothers Mean Happy Babies." An unlikely subject, perhaps — especially from a single woman who had no experience as a mother. Or did she? Think back to that flight Sally made to Key West after the tent fire in East Peoria — and stay tuned.

Ralph

Seven months had passed since her father's death and Sally's finances were in even worse shape than before. Ralph had spoken to a revenue agent and promised to make a payment, but was unable to do so when Sally failed to come through. In a letter he wrote on November 4, 1949, Ralph bemoaned his situation yet again:

It looks very bad! I keep telling them things, and don't keep my word. Just like the 1948 income tax. You sent them a wire stating that you would pay $500 a week on it, but you paid nothing until September and nothing since....

I have not eaten a meal for two days. I am sure you do not understand when I tell you that I am broke, that I AM BROKE. I am not eating. It is most discouraging — you owe me this money. I go hungry — I am doing the best I can for you, Sally, and that is pretty good. The Government could step in ANY minute.... It is a serious situation!

... If publicity gets out on this, it will be difficult for you. IT CAN ALL BE AVOIDED IF you will just pay something on account and do it when you say you will.

The state of affairs was no better two weeks later when Ralph typed a four-page, single-spaced letter begging Sally for relief:

It is soooooo discouraging. Christmas coming on and no money. I want to send a few presents and should do so right away. That money you owe me is ALL that I have in the world. I do need it and can't afford to have it tied up this way. It makes you feel so insecure and uncertain....

I have never worked so hard for so long a time. Also, I promised Nettie I would come out there and go over her tax business concerning the grove.... I did not go to the beach a single day this year — worked EVERY day and Sundays, and nights — then not having any money — it was pretty tough!

N ot unlike a roller coaster on the Midway, life on the road with a traveling carnival was prone to the sudden ups and downs that can happen in any big family. A day of distress and elation in which selfless co-workers pull together to save the day after a tent show fire could easily be followed by an episode of true heartbreak. Consider Miss Rosemary "Kurt" Orban, a 26-year-old dancer in Sally's show. Back in November of 1948, she had married Roy Dean, a talker for the Royal American Show's *Midget Revue*. Only five days into their honeymoon, the couple had been on the way to visit her family when Dean awoke feeling ill in their Oklahoma City hotel room. Although his new bride had called for a doctor, Dean apparently died of a heart attack before the physician could arrive.

In 1949 the grieving widow rejoined the carnival in Harlingen, Texas, where she was sharing a room with Sally at the Madison Hotel. As the first anniversary of her husband's death drew near, Kurt was feeling depressed and asked Sally for leave to visit her family in Oklahoma. She had planned to travel by bus, but ended up accepting a ride from Thomas Gilspin, a local man who offered to take her as far as Houston.

As they made their way north, Gilspin decided to make a rest stop, pulling over onto the shoulder of the road near Refugio, Texas, at about 2:30 in the morning. Kurt got out and walked to a dimly lit service station, but found the restroom door locked.

As she returned to the car, the driver of a Continental Bus bound for Houston — possibly the very same bus that she had earlier planned to ride — had seen the car parked on the side of the road and stopped to offer assistance. At some point, backing up in the darkness, the bus accidentally struck the unseen girl. Gilspin phoned for an ambulance, helped the driver lift Miss Orban, and rode with her to the hospital. As he later told the story: "Her beautiful face was not scarred, but her legs were crushed. After they gave her blood plasma she seemed to rally, but did not regain consciousness. Then they told us she had died. The doctor said it was much better that way."

Learning of the dreadful accident that had befallen her friend and employee barely a year after the death of the young woman's husband, Sally was devastated. She called the attending physician and nurse, as well as the chief deputy sheriff and county attorney in Refugio.

She then took it upon herself to contact the family, later reflecting:

> One of the hardest jobs I ever had was breaking the news to her family. They're old. They were stunned. Kurt was their youngest child. They didn't know what to do.... Kurt supported her parents. Her father is in failing health. She was a wonderful girl.

Miss Orban was just one of eleven victims of fatal automobile accidents in the State of Texas over that Thanksgiving holiday weekend.

Ralph

As the holidays came and went, Ralph Hobart soldiered on in his position of voluntary servitude. Even the smallest crumb Sally tossed his way tended to raise his spirits. But, while things may have been looking up for Sally by March 2, 1950, it was not so for Ralph:

> Received the copies of the letters you sent to Collector Internal Revenue.... I must say the letter about the taxes was really wonderful. I think it was perfect, so straight forward and to the point. I am so glad you wrote as you did....
>
> I am in a situation now, naturally. I expected to hear from you at the end of last week and have some more money.... Worst of all, I did have a pair of slacks and a coat cleaned, rush job, so as to look presentable, and rest of things I had cleaned regularly. Now I can't get anything out so am stuck. And I sent out laundry so as not to have to take time every day to wash out a shirt in order to have more time to work, so now I have no shirts! It really is something....
>
> Sally, the situation concerning your income tax is serious! I must get to work steady on it. I have only been able to do some now and some then. The time is very short.... This year, of all times, I must do ALL I can on it so as to have it as low as possible. But, I just can't do it unless you send me some money immediately. I will have to work night and day to do it. I have to take time off for painting and odd typing jobs in order to eat. I am so far behind now it is very discouraging, but I can't help it. In all the years I have been working for you, this is the first time a situation like this has arisen, when you just sent me nothing and I had to take time off for other jobs....

Please send me SOMETHING immediately so that I can start on this
tax business. I just can't start it until I get some money to live on.
Things are in a terrible mess with me as to money — rent way
behind, the storeroom behind, phone behind — I am paying a little
now and whenever I can spare it on that phone bill, but they keep
calling and calling about it and writing. And my clothes are at the
cleaners and laundry and I can't get out anything to wear — my
shoes are all worn out, full of holes. I look like a bum. I can't go any
place because of my clothes. Please wire me just a few dollars so I
can eat and get this tax done.

Sally was not intentionally cruel to poor Ralph. It's just that she too was
strapped for cash. Working in the Miami area for the first two months of
1950, she had been able to pay her company only by borrowing from
friends, seeking advances from employers, and getting a loan on her
Lincoln Continental.

On May 2, 1950, in Montgomery, Alabama, with the taxman at her heels,
Sally began her fourth and last season on the carnival circuit. This time
she was heading up a 20-person company touring with Al Wagner's
Cavalcade of Amusements. With music and lyrics by Midge Fielding and
Charles Barnes, Sally's revue was said to have "a distinct musical comedy
atmosphere, unusual in a tented theater." The Cavalcade's 25 tented theaters
also featured Ann Perri, known as "The Jane Russell of Burlesque," plus a
minstrel show with black ventriloquist Eddie Banks. As the 1950 season
progressed, Sally was just as big a draw as in the three seasons before.

On July 4th in Madison, Wisconsin, despite competition from a band concert
and fireworks show in Vilas Park, more than 7,000 people passed through the
main gate — the biggest single day's attendance of the entire season. As usual,
Sally was operating at full throttle. During her six-day stand, she submitted to
studio interviews with four different radio stations (plus one man-on-the-
street spot), gave a lecture offering beauty tips at Hill's Department Store,
handed out awards at the district semi-pro baseball tournament, and
addressed Sigma Delta Chi, the journalism fraternity at the University of
Wisconsin. Naturally, Sally's revue "topped all shows on the midway."[24]

---

24   A local wag had a little fun at a friend's expense by placing a classified ad in the
     "Business Personals" section of the *Wisconsin State Journal*, reading: "Art Brush closed
     his shop long enough to go see Sally Rand. He can't figure why she had the fans, when
     it was Art that needed cooling off!"

Unfortunately, while poor Ralph Hobart was, in his words, working "night and day" to keep Sally's accounts in order, certain situations can defy even the most dedicated problem solver. On July 30, 1950, in Kokomo, Indiana, the taxman finally came. Wilbur Plummer of the Internal Revenue Service filed a tax lien against Sally, demanding immediate payment of $21,727.62 for unpaid taxes due, based on her income for 1947 and 1948 ($215,000 today).

Somehow, she dodged immediate consequences and Al Wagner's Cavalcade of Amusements rolled on, making stops in Ohio and Michigan on its way to the State Fair in Dallas.

Ralph

Sally was a packrat who regularly traveled with several trunks filled not only with costumes and other material for her shows, but also with an assortment of books and other items she wished to keep close at hand. In fact, her accumulation of personal possessions had multiplied to such an extent that she had to place much of it in storage facilities in various locations around the country. Her mother had written to her about the storage charges she owed to a firm in Oakland, California. In correspondence, Ralph Hobart had mentioned "another bill from the Atlantic Storage Company" as well as "that garage in Boston." Sally also owed money to the Burrelle Press Clipping Bureau, which had furnished much of the material that Ralph had helped to maintain in her voluminous scrapbooks.[25]

He referred to the albums in his letter of August 14, 1950:

> I only have the scrap books from January 1942 at the apartment ...
> I have wanted to bring those scrap books up to the apartment and
> store them here for safekeeping. I think they are very valuable
> items and, while they are safe at the storage company, they are
> inaccessible. And since the Atlantic and Pacific Storage Company
> is no longer under that operation, as soon as possible you should
> get the things out of there that you want to keep, and certainly,
> those scrap books are part of them. There has been a lot of work
> spent in keeping that up, and it is a good record of what you have
> done and where you have been, etc. But, I am up against the same
> thing here at the apartment as you are at the storage company.
> I must pay the bill!

---

[25] Twenty four of these very large and heavy scrapbooks are now in the safekeeping of Sally's son. A few others are housed in the Billy Rose Theatre Collection at the New York Public Library for the Performing Arts.

Ralph's job was especially challenging because it wasn't always clear where Sally *was*, or where she was scheduled to be. He often had to ask for clarification. Appearing at one place for three days and another for a week, she was something of a moving target when it came to knowing how to address a letter.

As Sally continued her tour with the carnival, things were no better for poor Hobart. When he wrote to her on August 14th, even the meager tools and supplies he needed to continue his efforts were in jeopardy:

> I had to take the adding machine and hock it in order to eat and finish that report. I took the report to the post office to mail and found out it would cost $1.60 to send it air mail and 80¢ regular — and I did not have that much money....

> I am now working on the 1947 [tax return] and can have it finished today, but can't mail until I can get the adding machine back and add totals....

> As I wrote you some time ago, I would have given this up long ago had it not been that something told me to keep at it, and work, and all would be well.... But, I must pay my back rent immediately, or be put out. And, if I am put out, I cannot take anything with me.... [A] climax is now here, and I must pay my rent! They are raising hell!

Not only was Ralph way behind in his rent, but his apartment landlords were getting impatient about a storage area their predecessors had always allowed him to use to store Sally's scrapbooks, tax records, and "all those photographs, which [he had] pasted up to about 1946." These, too, were at risk:

> They have been nice about it at the building, but keep asking me, "when am I going to pay, etc." — but they could just take the stuff out of there (and as far as they are concerned it is "stuff") well, I don't want to think of such a thing, and have done everything to keep them from doing it....

In addition to the strain of caretaking her belongings and the constant headache of putting Sally's accounts in order, Ralph was slavishly doing his best to address an assortment of issues raised by the State of California and a parade of creditors. He reminded Sally again of what he was dealing with, underscoring his need to get paid:

> I don't write you all the things nor tell you about them, because they are so numerous, and I take care of all of them, but they do take time, and I can't do anything else meanwhile. But I must

have money to live on while I am getting these matters straightened out, and I can get it done if I just can work steady without having to stop and wash windows or paint or type in order to get something to eat.

In 1951, with four seasons of carnival contracts behind her, Sally went back to making her own bookings. First, it was back to Boston, where she took the stage at the venerated Howard Athenaeum, affectionately known as "The Old Howard." The theater had been hosting popular entertainment for more than 100 years and everyone had played there — from Buster Keaton, Al Jolson, Sophie Tucker, and W. C. Fields to Abbott and Costello, Gypsy Rose Lee, Jackie Gleason and Jerry Lewis.

Since Sally was in Beantown, and tales of her previous appearances at Harvard were still circulating on campus, it was only natural that she would grant the boys yet another chance to share her company. So, after a 10-year hiatus, Sally agreed to appear once again at the annual Harvard Freshman Smoker. She would share top billing with radio and television comedian Morey Amsterdam and amateur talent would fill out the program (the highlight to be a "chugalug" contest to see who could down a quart of beer the fastest).

On February 23rd, the Smoker kicked off in Memorial Hall with plenty of beer drinking, smoking, and camaraderie, after which the assemblage trooped into Sanders Theatre. As with her prior appearances, everyone understood that Sally wouldn't be performing any of her famous dances. Still, many a young scholar was eager to catch a glimpse of the fabled fan dancer. The audience was delighted when she strode to the microphone and removed her ermine wrap, revealing a low-cut strapless evening gown. Once the hormone-driven applause had died down, Sally quipped: "That's as far as I go tonight."

The audience was receptive as Sally read a poem and then presented a sketch based on her interpretation of the wildly popular novelty tune "The Thing."[26] At the end of her skit, she pulled a sheaf of papers out of her bodice and proceeded to speak to the attentive freshmen on the "evils of Communism." (The U.S. had intervened in the Korean War just a few months earlier.) At first the students remained upbeat, thinking it was just

---

26 Released in October 1950, Phil Harris's recording of "The Thing" was number one on the charts for several weeks. Those of a certain age will well remember the song's tale of a man who, while walking on the beach, discovers a box with mysterious, never disclosed, contents: "I discovered a (knock, knock, knock), right before my eyes."

the set-up for another joke, but when the punchline never came, they began to get restless.

At some point, a fidgety freshman tossed a penny in Sally's direction. Without hesitation, she offered a classic retort: "Boys, there's only one animal I know who throws a scent." Most of the audience laughed heartily, but, as she gamely continued her speech, more pennies and assorted loose objects were tossed onto the stage. Sally tried to ignore the hostile shower, doing her best to speed through the remainder of her talk before hastily retreating into the wings with tears rolling down her cheeks.

The whole episode was later recalled by attendee F. Harvey Popell: "Sensing a riot in the offing, the quick-thinking emcee hurriedly had a piano rolled out, and a bespectacled young math instructor sat down and started playing and singing his own catchy, satirical compositions. He was so good that soon everyone had forgotten Sally Rand."

That entertaining young pianist was none other than Harvard mathematician and songwriter Tom Lehrer, who would go on to record several albums of diabolically clever satirical songs with such titles as: "Poisoning Pigeons in the Park," "The Vatican Rag," and his Atomic Age anthem, "We Will All Go Together When We Go." Later in his career, Lehrer acknowledged that the 1951 Freshman Smoker was his "first big gig." One source reported that he even appeared onstage a second time with Sally at the Old Howard, where he performed one of his most memorable compositions — "The Elements."

Sally would downplay the incident the next day, saying: "Why, I had a wonderful time and I hope the boys did too. That was the third time I entertained at Harvard and I certainly hope to be invited back."[27] Attendee Robert R. Rynearson,[28] a freshman from Rochester, Minnesota, was less charitable: "The guys were wrong for throwing pennies, but she was wrong, too, for giving us the kind of show we didn't want. The whole idea was that we were there for a good time, not to hear about politics." Sally's miscalculation, it seems, was that she had ignored the old adage: "You can always tell a Harvard man, but you can't tell him much."

---

[27] Adversity aside, Sally hoped to be invited to the Smoker a fourth time, but it never happened. After 1956, the tradition was discontinued due to excessive rowdiness. Dean F. Skiddy Von Stade declared the smoker "a menace to the wellbeing" of the school, and unworthy of the dignity and tradition of Harvard.

[28] Rynearson would become a highly respected, Mayo-Clinic-trained psychiatrist.

The Territory of Alaska was very much a frontier in 1951. Still more than seven years away from becoming a state, the entire territory was home to about 129,000 hardy souls, fewer than Erie, Pennsylvania, or Chattanooga, Tennessee. Greater Anchorage may have had 20,000 inhabitants on a good day, considerably less than half the number in present day Glendora, California. Early that year, a nitery called the Last Chance Club joined the American Guild of Variety Artists, becoming the first such enterprise outside the 48 states to do so. It seems that even the hardtack chewing chaps of the chilly north enjoyed being distracted by a pretty girl or two. In fact, Anchorage boasted no fewer than eight nightclubs that offered floor shows.

And so, with the summer sun blazing overhead in June of 1951, Sally Rand brought her show to the Last Chance Club for a six-week engagement, reportedly at $4,000 per week. By all accounts, Sally and her girls were just what the "sourdoughs" ordered, as the club was packed for each performance.[29]

Once she was back in the States, Sally's show played to packed houses at the 1,200-seat Palomar Theatre in Seattle. Theater critic Wil Stevens observed:

> In spite of occasionally frail supporting talent, her feathers continue to
> be solid customer bait…. The dexterity with which things disappear
> is still there, and Sally's determination to make the dance artistic
> fabulously manages to avoid the schmaltz.

On August 18th, Sally began a nine-day engagement at the Missouri State Fair in Sedalia, some 75 miles up the road from her birthplace in Hickory County. Her revue *Hi, Frenchie* was the main attraction at the "Greatest Midway on Earth." In addition to Sally and her girls, the show featured the popular baggy-pants comic, Billy "Zoot" Reed. Sally took the town by storm with her usual flurry of activities, speaking to the Jaycees on the importance of farmers and livestock and to the Optimist Club, commending its members on "the work you are doing in building youth." She even put in an appearance at the annual "Country Ham Breakfast"[30] to rub shoulders with local officials and other dignitaries, including principal speaker, U.S. Treasurer

---

[29] A few years later in 1954, Stomp Gordon, known for playing piano with his feet, sued the Last Chance Club for $5,000, claiming that he and his party (including singer Billie Holiday) were refused admission by a girl at the door who told him: "Colored people are not admitted."

[30] This was easy for her as the annual breakfast was held in Sally's tent at the fair that year.

John W. Snyder. During her brief moments of downtime and evenings off, Sally was sharing a $10,000 trailer with her Boxer watchdog, Bing, and a handsome young gentleman named Sean. We shall learn much more about him in chapter 21.

As always, Sally had her detractors, even in the "Show Me" State. Governor Forrest Smith had received "about 35 letters" protesting Sally's presence. At least one widow had advised that she no longer planned to take her three children to the Fair. On August 21st, the Governor announced that he would be on hand for the Governor's Day festivities the following afternoon. Asked by a local reporter if he intended to inspect Sally's show, the governor grinned and replied: "That's the reason I'm going tonight." A religious man who was said to own a well-thumbed Bible, Governor Smith later reported that he had seen nothing "immoral, lewd, or obscene" in Sally's show. In fact, he declared, it was "well presented." Once all the dust had settled, the State Fair drew a gate nearly a third higher than the previous year and Sally's show had outdrawn even such eagerly attended annual attractions as the baked custard pie competition.

B y the time Sally's show reached the grounds of the Kansas State Fair in September of 1951, she had been billing herself as "Her Sexcellency" for at least two years. Display ads boasted that her midway show was buttressed by "a bevy of sixteen Scandalicious Girls ... in 10 Scintillating Scenes ... and 5 Feature Acts."

The State Fair was a big deal in the host city of Hutchinson. Located pretty much smack in the middle of rural Kansas, the annual event commonly drew patrons from all around. Admission to the Sally Rand Show cost $1.00 ("Kids with Parents Free"), and souvenir booklets (which she was happy to sign) sold for 25 cents. Along with Professor Keller's trained lions, Art Spencer's "Wall of Death" motordrome, and the usual snake, Eskimo and freak shows, plus more than 30 rides, Sally's show was the main attraction.

Arriving in Hutchinson, Sally strolled into the 4-H building on the fairgrounds where she was met by a gaggle of girls. The first words out of her mouth were: "Which one of you little gals is gonna lend me a dime to make a phone call?" Thus was Sally Rand's famous personality and upbeat confidence, honed by many years of self-reliance, exhibited for all to see. State 4-H leader Glenn Busset invited her to use the phone in his office, even though he didn't recognize her until she introduced herself. Describing the event nearly 30 years later, Busset recalled: "She was painted quite a bit — you know, a carnival gal. Of course, she wasn't very young any more. She was a pleasant, attractive gal. I never did see her show though. Come to think of it, she never did offer me a free ticket."

Sally's show got off to a decent start at the Kansas State Fair, but on the second night, following one of her shows, there came a knock at her trailer door. It was Sheriff Vic Frazey announcing that he was there to attach all of her property! It seems Sally was involved in a dispute with Dallas carnival operator Ray Marsh Brydon who claimed she owed him $2,548.57 in connection with their partnership the year before at the Texas State Fair. Sally was definitely not in a cooperative mood, saying: "You can tell Ray Marsh Brydon that I'll fry in hell before he ever gets a penny."

Well, that proved to be a slight miscalculation. When the sheriff banged on the trailer door, Sally had burst out, slamming the door behind her and calling back to her secretary Anita Robertson: "Keep it locked, Nita. Don't open it for anyone until I tell you." Undeterred, the sheriff resorted to Plan B, instructing his deputies to collect whatever they could from the box office till, where they managed to scrape up several hundred dollars. A later search of Sally's trailer failed to uncover any additional cash.

It turns out that earlier in the day, while having her hair done at a local beauty parlor, Sally had overheard a conversation disclosing that attachment papers were about to be served on her at the fairgrounds. Armed with the advance warning, she had been able to squirrel away what may have been thousands of dollars in a secret hiding place. Even so, her efforts were mostly for naught. Sheriff Frazey pressed his case and, after considerable protest, Sally was forced to cough up a check for $2,021.07 to cover the rest of Brydon's claim, plus $50 in court costs.[31]

This financial hit wasn't her only vexation (with Sally it was "always something"). Kansas is conservative country, certainly no less so in the fall of 1951, so it should come as no surprise that local ministers would take a dim view of "Her Sexcellency" coming to town.

Writing for *The Christian Herald* of Hutchinson, Kansas, Pastor James R. Greer expressed it this way:

> Why the fair board would invite such a combination of scandal and
> sordid sex stimulation, calculated to attract all the "vultures" from
> one end of the state to the other, to appear as a special attraction at
> the fair, is beyond reasonable understanding....

---

[31] Actually, Sally's check was held by the court pending final resolution of the dispute and, in the end, the case was settled with Sally paying $1,600.

There are other salacious sideshows at our fair. One crier, in front
of a gleaming streamer advertises "A natural birth to be seen in
process" promising to reveal "secrets your grandmother never
knew." Other scandalous statements made over loudspeakers are
not fit to be repeated in print of any kind. If Christian people will
not work to eliminate such evils from our otherwise wonderful state
fair in our own city, I beg to ask who will?

Sally felt "hurt and deeply humiliated" by Rev. Greer's remarks:

The statements of Mr. Greer do not originate from sincere and
good intentions. [If the protests] were sincere, why then were
they not made before my appearance? I would gladly have given
a prevue of my show to a qualified group of censors or any
members of the Hutchinson Ministerial Alliance.... None of these
persons who are criticizing have seen the show. Apparently, I'm
not alone since almost 30,000 persons paid admission to see the
show, and I don't think these people are morons, or that they will
appreciate being called "vultures" by Mr. Greer because they
came to see the show.

Several other clergymen (who, like Rev. Greer, had never actually seen
Sally's show) clucked in agreement, but Virgil Miller, Secretary of the Fair,
came to Sally's defense: "Sally Rand attended the Christian church every
Sunday she was in Hutchinson. And the Wednesday night before the fair
opened, when she was busy getting her show set up, she climbed into the
truck to be driven to prayer meeting."

Years later, Miller recalled: "Sally came out to our house and had dinner
with us. We enjoyed her very much. She was a really nice lady. She could
give a talk that could hold you spellbound. She wasn't a dummy by any
means."

Sally had not only brought her fans to Kansas but also her bubble, her
peacock feathers, and even her stuffed swan. To demonstrate that she
knew her way around fairgrounds, she was photographed milking a cow.
This had become a standard stunt. In fact, in 1952, Sally would engage in
a cow milking contest with Memphis fair manager Martin Zook, saying
"My advice to Mr. Zook is to keep cool and keep his eye on the cow,
because I'm a Missouri farm girl and I know how to handle a cow."

Because she could afford to spend more on musical acts, costumes and
sets, Sally claimed there was a big difference between her show and the
"dirty little girl shows" offered at many carnivals and fairs. As she
reasoned: "... after all, if you can make people laugh by telling clean

jokes, or make them come see a dance which isn't offensive, you certainly aren't going to tell filthy jokes or do offensive dances, are you?"

The usual controversy aside, another local columnist Ernest Dewey joined the long line of journalists whose preconceptions of Sally were surprisingly shattered upon meeting the actual woman face-to-face:

> Sally Rand is the most people I ever met in one piece. She carries an assortment of personalities in her blond, curly head that she can put on and take off much faster than clothes. Meeting a cross-section of Hutchinson yesterday she demonstrated an adaptability that would make a chameleon dizzy.... She talked horses and bluegrass to a banker from Kentucky, land and farming to a real estater ... the debilitated state of manhood to the women — all with authority and bouncing conviction.
>
> When she got into a discussion of geopolitics with a plumbing contractor and a grain man it got way too foggy for me. "Where did you pick up so much political science in show business?" I asked. That stirred up quite a breeze. "Show people are citizens too," Miss Rand snapped. "If more people bothered to learn what the score is, they would be a hell of lot better off. And it wouldn't be so easy to smear out of public life the good men we do get."

Dewey did his best to question Sally about her life and her show, but had to cope with interruptions from an endless procession of well-wishers and old friends from Missouri:

> We tried earnestly to talk about art, but something or other always happened to interfere. I remember she did say: "Ah, Renoir — there was a painter! Do you know he painted fifty pictures of ladies taking a bath? His message to the world was cleanliness, I think."

After a six-day run in the Sunflower State, the Sally Rand show literally pulled up stakes on September 21st and moved on to other stops in Oklahoma and Texas.

E ach year from 1949 through 1952, Sally had performed at the State Fair of Texas in Dallas. For Lawrence Eliot Marcus, one of that city's most prominent citizens, she had created such an indelible memory during one engagement that he carried it fondly to his grave. Lawrence was the 30-something son of Herbert Marcus who, along with his aunt Carrie Neiman, had founded the eminent Dallas department store bearing their names. It is a tribute to Sally's ability to make a lasting impression that, even at age 90, "Lawrie" absolutely delighted in recalling their encounter in a department store dressing room, as reported by Alan Peppard of the *Dallas Morning News*:

> "Sally was appearing at the State Fair," Mr. Marcus told me a few years ago. "She had these fans that she would pass in front of her body in misty light, and you sat on the edge of your seat hoping you'd see some of her treasure."

> In the dressing room, she breezily showed the youngest Marcus son all of her treasure as she tried on dresses, standing naked "without her fans," he says. "It was my wildest dream come true."

In writing of carnival life, Sally had emphasized how important it was to have an experienced and competent business manager, one with "enough charm and smooth talk" to get along with anyone. During her first year on the carnival circuit, she had secured the services of just such a man, a certain Mister Finkelstein. Scion of an orthodox Jewish family, Finkelstein had previously been engaged in running three nightclubs in New York City — the 51 Club, the Mardi Gras, and the Ringside Cabaret. The two show biz professionals hit it off right away but, as a single gal touring the country with a handsome manager, Sally had put herself at risk of having a strictly business relationship evolve into something more. And that could get dicey, particularly if that handsome manager happened to be married to a well-known (and fiery-tempered) striptease artist.

CHAPTER TWENTY

When Sally Met Harry

You look like a normal person, but actually you are the
angel of death.

~ Meg Ryan as "Sally Albright" in *When Harry Met Sally*

E xactly when they met is unknown, but there is no doubt about when
the two were first linked in the media. On August 16, 1947, a press
dispatch syndicated throughout the United States and Canada described
a seemingly sordid incident in Springfield, Illinois, involving Sally, her
manager Harry, and his inconvenient wife Georgia, headlined: "SALLY
RAND ARRESTED ON DISORDERLY CHARGE."

"Harry" was Harry Finkelstein, a club manager who ran several New York
City night spots before becoming the manager of Sally's traveling show
with the Hennie's Brothers carnival. His wife — a red-haired burlesque
dancer best known by her stage name, "Georgia Sothern" — was often billed
as "The Human Dynamo" for her frenzied style of dancing and stripping
while tossing her hips in wild abandon. Born in 1909, Georgia (nee Hazel
Anderson) was raised as a child vaudeville performer. After a succession of
personal tragedies left her abandoned and forced to fend for herself, she
had launched her career as a dancer at the age of 13. With the aid of a fake
birth certificate, she was soon a featured stripper in New York's famous
Minsky's Burlesque.

What kind of a fellow was Harry? Well, whatever else he was, he was a
ladies' man. In her 1972 memoir, Miss Sothern revealed how hard she had
fallen for him:

> In my dressing room the doorman tapped on the door and pushed
> his head in. "Miss Sothern, there's a Mr. Finkelstein out here that
> wants to see ya."
>
> My heart flipped. I nodded. "Show him in."
>
> My hands shook so badly I couldn't fix my makeup. And I was
> finding it hard to breathe. He came through the door and he was the
> most beautiful sight in the world. He was wearing a dark blue suit. A

camel's hair topcoat was draped over his arm. His eyes were as blue as a summer sky. Straight black hair combed back. Six foot one or two inches of dreamboat and, I hoped, all mine.

Harry was not only considered handsome, he also appeared to be a successful businessman. When he met Georgia in the late 1930s, he and his brother Jack jointly owned a popular nightclub across from Madison Square Garden called the Ringside Bar and Cabaret. Although the exact date is unknown, Harry's marriage to Georgia (said to be her fourth) probably took place in 1937, when she would have been about 27 years old, right before Mayor LaGuardia closed New York City's burlesque houses at the end of April.

From an Orthodox Jewish family, Harry allowed three years to slip by before telling his parents about the marriage. In her memoir, Georgia recalled the mayor's crackdown on burlesque shows: "It was then that I found out my Harry was a heavy gambler. Though he was making good money at the Ringside, we would be rich one day and poor the next."

Georgia Sothern: Ecdysiast

In 1940, Georgia Sothern wrote to the popular columnist H.L. Mencken to solicit his help in improving the image of her vocation: "Strip-teasing is a formal and rhythmic disrobing of the body in public. In recent years there has been a great deal of uninformed criticism leveled against my profession. Most of it is without foundation and arises because of the unfortunate word strip-teasing, which creates the wrong connotations in the mind of the public. I feel sure that if you could coin a new and more palatable word to describe this art, the objections to it would vanish and I and my colleagues would have easier going."

Mencken rose to the occasion: "I need not tell you that I sympathize with you in your affliction, and wish that I could help you. Unfortunately, no really persuasive new name suggests itself. It might be a good idea to relate strip-teasing in some way or other to the associated zoological phenomenon of molting. Thus the word moltician comes to mind, but it must be rejected because of its likeness to mortician. A resort to the scientific name for molting, which is ecdysis, produces both ecdysist and ecdysiast." Miss Sothern immediately adopted the latter term as an apt description of her art.

By the early 1940s, the Finkelstein marriage was not going well. As Georgia later recalled:

Me and my Harry. We were beginning to have fight after fight. Maybe a part of it was that I was always living on the edge now in burlesque and always trying to dream up a new number where I would look naked and sexy but still be within the ever-tightening laws set down for us to follow.

How Harry Finkelstein came to be Sally Rand's manager is not clear. The two reportedly met in New York City in February 1947, not long after Harry and Georgia had entered into divorce proceedings and about the same time that Sally was rumored to be joining the upcoming summer carnival circuit. It may be that Harry simply had to beat it out of town ahead of his unhappy creditors and joining a traveling carnival may have seemed about as good an idea as any. In any case, no later than June of 1947, Harry found himself serving as Sally's manager on the road with the Hennies Brothers' Shows.

Georgia had performed in Harry's nightclubs in the 1940s and had previously been on the road with him. She had also appeared on Broadway in the 1942 revue *Star and Garter*, produced at The Music Box Theater by Michael Todd.[1] By the latter part of the forties, both Georgia and Sally were headliners on the carnival circuit. The two dancers were certainly aware of each other, and Sally must have known that Georgia was Harry's wife.

All of which brings us back to those "disorderly conduct" headlines. Sally and Harry were in Springfield appearing at the Illinois State Fair and things weren't going all that well. It was steaming hot, four girls had left the troupe earlier in the week, and Sally had lost her dog. On top of that, her show front had been dark for two days, either because she was ill or because she was feuding with that other "Harry" — Harry Hennies, head honcho of the carnival. The two had been at odds for some time. According to Hennies: "I took enough guff off her through the still-date season to last me a lifetime, but when she fired the boss canvasman, that was the straw that broke the dromedary's back."

In any case, on Friday night, August 15, 1947, having just flown in from a striptease engagement in Cincinnati, Georgia Sothern unexpectedly appeared at Sally's hotel room door where she heard the unmistakable sounds of her husband with Sally "laughing and talking" inside. Without knocking, she turned around and headed straight to the local police station to swear out a complaint. Georgia then led several officers back to the hotel room where they proceeded to arrest the occupants. Springfield's Police Magistrate William D. Conway later said he had issued the arrest warrants because the presence of a man in a woman's hotel room can constitute disorderly conduct.

---

[1]   A clip of Ms. Sothern's whirling, twirling, head-shaking, high-kicking dance can be seen on YouTube. Just search for "Georgia Sothern" and "Star and Garter." (Note that the end result of her frenetic "stripping" is a glittery bikini costume, not nudity.) And, yes, this was *that* Michael Todd, just eight years after his "Flame Dance" fiasco as described on page 275.

Tired of waiting for Harry and Sally to provide the information she needed for her pending divorce action, Georgia had decided to dig up some evidence on her own. She claimed she hadn't seen much of her husband since he met Sally, although she had talked to both of them by telephone several times pleading for their cooperation. "They laughed at me," she said.

Sally dismissed the whole episode as a desperate "grab for publicity" by Georgia, scoffing: "She could use some." Sally then explained that, two days earlier, she had suffered from heat exhaustion, had been forced to close her show, and was under a doctor's care. She stressed that Harry was in her hotel room only because her female secretary had left to run an errand. Finkelstein ("strictly my manager") had remained in the room to "... give me my medicine," she said. "Nothing like this has ever happened to me before. I am shocked. I'm dazed," she protested, adding: "I have nothing to hide."

On Friday night, the couple was released on a $500 bond and instructed by Magistrate Conway to return to court on Monday. When the court date rolled around, Sally's attorney requested and was granted a continuance for an indefinite term. This was tantamount to a dismissal of the case, as Sally was headed for Des Moines for the opening of the Iowa State Fair four days later. Georgia Sothern protested the extension, pointing out that she didn't know when she could return, as she had to go to New York for a leg operation.

The judge disliked postponing cases involving morals, observing: "... that's what we lack in the world today — morals and religion." However, since Sally's attorney was unavailable to proceed, he advised Georgia that the case would resume whenever she could arrange to appear.

All the negative publicity had somewhat humiliated Sally. One press report had even questioned how she could have suffered from heat exhaustion since she had been "unhampered by clothes and well equipped with fans." The *Sarasota Herald-Tribune* ran an account of the incident under the headline: "STRIP-TEASERS FIGHT OVER MAN." Shortly after the hearing, Sally called a press conference to insist that she was "just a good, clean-cut American girl" and that she had "never done anything indecent in her life." The whole business had left her feeling apprehensive:

> I will be appearing in state fairs before farm and country people ...
> who will misunderstand this distorted, trumped-up publicity....
> This sort of publicity may shock them into boycotting my shows
> and jeopardize my very income and career.

Concerned about her reputation, Sally had created a handout for the press continuing the "good girl" theme:

> All my life I have endeavored to live frankly and decently. I have meticulously conducted myself so as to never embarrass my family, my associates, nor humiliate myself. The people of America know this.

As he let everyone go, Magistrate Conway sternly advised Sally's attorney that the case against her would be heard "rain or shine" whenever a date for another hearing could be set.[2]

Despite the close call, Harry and Sally were not as cautious as they should have been. Little more than a year after the humiliating incident in Illinois, they were arrested again — this time in Arkansas — when they were stopped for speeding in the wee hours.

This unfortunate new clash with law enforcement led to yet *another* arrest several hours later, when they were again found together in the same cabin at a Fort Smith tourist court. Responding to a report of a possible morals violation, Fort Smith Assistant Police Chief V. H. Looper had corralled two other officers and, at 5:00 A.M., they knocked on the door of a room registered in the name of Harry Finkelstein at Terry's Motor Court. The press breathlessly reported the juicy details.

In an overcrowded municipal courtroom the next day, Looper testified that Harry had come to the door and opened it "about 18 inches." The officer said he had heard the bed springs creak as Harry got up from the bed and, through glass panels in the door, he had witnessed Harry leave the bed by the light of the cabin bathroom. He stated he had also seen a woman leave the same bed and hurriedly pass between himself and the light pouring from the bathroom door. Looper quoted Finkelstein as saying that the woman was his wife and that they had been married about a year.

Once Looper had gained entry to the room, Harry had taken him to a second bedroom, where he testified he had found a woman sitting on the bed. He had seen clothes, both masculine and feminine, strewn in the front bedroom and had observed that the bed in that room looked as if two persons had occupied it, while the other bedroom had appeared unused except that "Miss Rand was sitting there at the time." He further testified that Sally had warned him the officers were making a "bad mistake" and that he had better call "Mr. Murphy" — a reference to Art Murphy, Secretary of the Fort Smith Chamber of Commerce and Vice President of the Arkansas Association of Fairs.

---

2   The hearing never happened. Seven months later, Conway dismissed all charges for lack of prosecution.

Sally had been dressed in a light-colored gown "of some kind" while Harry was wearing striped sleeping pajamas. When advised that she needed to dress to be taken to police headquarters, Sally at first refused. Looper testified: "I told her if she didn't that she would come just as she was."

The other two officers then presented supporting testimony and the City of Fort Smith rested its case. Sally and Harry were represented by Defense Attorney Heartsill Ragon, Jr., son of the preeminent former Arkansas Congressman and Federal District Court Judge. Harry testified that he and Sally had eaten steaks in his room, that they had then retired to separate bedrooms, and that they were still there when he was awakened by the officers knocking at the door.

Called to the stand, motel manager E. A. Terry proved the perfect witness for the defense as he explained that it was physically impossible to see into the room through the glass door panels as Looper had claimed — they were too high. He testified that, if the cabin door were opened only 18 inches, all that could be seen from the front steps would be a few inches of the head of the bed. In addition, Terry further contended that the building's insulation plus noise from the air conditioner would have made the cabin practically soundproof — no one outside the door could have heard bed springs creaking.

After considering all the testimony, Municipal Judge Thomas Pitts ruled against the City of Fort Smith, exonerating the defendants of all charges.[3] Once again, for Sally and Harry, the record was cleared of any morals charge.

Only a couple of weeks after the incident in Fort Smith — as if there wasn't enough drama in her life — Sally flew to Key West, Florida, to conclude arrangements with an adoption attorney ... but, more about that later. Meanwhile, the triangle that was Sally, Harry and Georgia remained unresolved for several more months. On Saturday evening, January 22, 1949, Georgia was unceremoniously interrupted onstage "in the middle of a bump" and served a summons to appear regarding a claim for unpaid counsel fees. Dorothy Kilgallen's "VOICE OF BROADWAY GOSSIP IN GOTHAM" column announced: "Georgia Sothern (the stripper) and Harry Finkelstein have agreed on a

---

[3]   Even though the prominent "Mr. Murphy" was reported to have "conferred with several officials about the case," Judge Pitts was unlikely to have been biased in favor of Sally and Harry. Four years later, he fined a penny arcade operator $100 for exhibiting a film in which a woman shed her bathing suit. He halted the 30-minute film after only three minutes, declaring it too spicy for the courtroom, saying: It could "corrupt the morals of even a newspaperman."

Florida divorce." Four days after the column appeared, Georgia declared bankruptcy on February 4th, citing debts of $7,866 and assets of only $107.

Harry Finkelstein was finally available— officially. But, now, as a 45-year-old woman about to take on a major new responsibility, was Sally really in the market for a man like Harry?

Sally seemed to be contemplating a permanent relationship when she wrote to her friend Jewel on August 10, 1949:

> *No, I'm not married. In many ways I would like to be, for all of us who are unmarried, life can be very lonely, especially as one grows older.... It is difficult sometimes not to have a strong masculine arm to lean on or even a masculine chest to weep a little on....*
>
> *If I should find someone with whom I feel I could enter into such a close relationship, my first consideration of course would be "Would he be a good father?" and after that "would our experiences and our environment and background be similar enough to make it possible to live in peace and harmony without too many adjustments.... If I find that man I'm sure I'll know it ....*

It would be another year on the road before Sally and Harry would walk down the aisle. As always, there would be many challenges — another town, another hassle. On July 13, 1950, Sally was in Milwaukee fulfilling a 10-day engagement organized under the auspices of the local Professional Fire Fighters' Association. Despite being midsummer, it was only 46 degrees out in the breeze steadily blowing in off Lake Michigan.[4] Audiences were a little thin as well, but trouper that she was, Sally understood the show must go on. Back in the relative comfort of her dressing room after her show, she had the satisfaction of knowing that she had at least given her loyal audience their money's worth. And what thanks did she get?

No sooner had she begun to kick back than she was joined by a most unwelcome coterie of visitors — policewoman Geraldine Sampon and nine other members of the Milwaukee vice squad — who were there to arrest her. Sally and Harry were taken into custody and charged with permitting an indecent performance. Confronted with a badge and the declaration "you're under arrest, lady," Sally shot back: "You'll have to show me more than that. Badges are a dime a dozen." Hustled into a police car, she protested: "I've been putting that show on for 17 years. *Now* you tell me it's indecent?"

---

4 Earlier that day, Sally had made a side trip to Waukesha, Wisconsin, where she rode an elephant in the grand opening parade for the Mills Bros. Circus.

In a scenario that had become all too familiar, Sally insisted she had never performed in the nude, but declined to elaborate: "You don't ask a magician how he pulls those rabbits out of a hat, do you? Well, it's the same with me. I'm not telling you how I do it. All I'll say is that it's an illusion." Policewoman Sampon was having none of it: "She was as nude as could be. I examined her immediately after the arrest and I know." The head of the vice squad observed that Sally was "anything but cooperative," as it required three officers to muscle her into a squad car.

At the station, the 46-year-old fan dancer fell asleep in a cell while her brother Harold (traveling with the show as a performer and stage manager) leaned on troupe members to raise enough to pay for a $1,000 bond for his sister and another $500 for Harry. Police Captain Rudolph Miller expressed surprise at the arrest because he had seen part of Sally's act earlier and thought it was a "good clean show." In any case, Sally and Harry left Wisconsin relatively unscathed, as the judge released them with a warning.

The following month they would be in Ohio where readers scanning their newspapers one summer morning would be greeted by the headline: "SALLY RAND WEDS HER MANAGER." Apparently, Sally, who had written to her friend Jewel, "If I find that man I'm sure I'll know it," had come to believe that she had found "that man" right in front of her face. In any case, the pair was married in Toledo, Ohio, on August 21, 1950, after the judge waived the five-day waiting period. As characterized by the local paper:

> The empress of the ostrich-feather fans, born Helen Gould Beck in Elkton, Mo., 46 years ago, took as consort her manager, Harry Finkelstein, 40, erstwhile owner of three New York night clubs....
>
> Miss Rand was accompanied by her brother … while her publicity agent, Julian Cole, was best man.[5] She wore a simple suit of royal blue, offset by an orchid scarf, pale pink gloves and a flowered hat.
>
> Miss Rand exchanged smiles with reporters and the fast-gathering crowd which jammed the Courthouse corridors. Betraying her

---

5   Sixteen years later, Julian Cole would be hired by the Miami Dolphins to promote the new professional football franchise. Despite great success, one of his more colorful ideas was a flop. Cole proposed to install a pool in the end zone, complete with a live dolphin that would "retrieve extra-point kicks" and "leap out of the water with a flip" when the home team scored. Several candidates auditioned, but Cole would settle for nothing less than Flipper, the network TV star. Reflecting on what might happen if the team failed to score, one man commented: "Oh, come on, surely we can win one for the Flipper."

innate business sense, she eyed the crowd and murmured: "If we could only charge admission."

So, now everything was all nice and legal. And, just to put icing on the cake, a month later Sally and Harry signed a legal agreement not to sue each other. Love may be love, but business is business.

Oddly, the entry in Sally's personal diary for her wedding day reads simply: "Married Harry Finkelstein." Nothing more. Indeed, in the following days, although she found time to mention the milking of yet another cow (this time on the steps of Detroit City Hall) and had quite a lot to say in the diary about her trailer hitch, it would be another 11 weeks before she would once again make reference to Harry.

S̲ally's marriage to Harry Finkelstein is puzzling in many respects. Her surviving letters refer to a five-year relationship, so their affair had clearly commenced well before they were married. Maybe, like Georgia, Sally had been taken in by those blue eyes and that slicked-back hair? [6]

Ah, that hair.[7] That might have been it . . . or the eyes. Or maybe the marriage was just a matter of convenience. Sally was, after all, a single woman with an uncertain financial future. She and Harry had evidently been cohabiting for quite a while. They may have simply gotten tired of feeling guilty or of making excuses for occupying the same hotel room. It certainly isn't unusual for people thrown together under challenging circumstances to seek solace and stability in one another's arms.

As it turned out, matrimony did little to improve Sally and Harry's relationship. Relatively early on, Finkelstein's role as manager of her traveling show ended, and, at her suggestion, he went back to New York.

---

[6]   The slicked-back hairdo has a long and storied history, dating back over 200 years to the creation of Macassar oil. The saga involves not only the admiring glances of young maidens, but also their dismay over the soiling of their furniture. This problem was addressed by the creation of the "antimacassar" — those fancy little doily-like cloths you used to see on the backs of chairs at your grandmother's house. Sally, who could seemingly expound authoritatively on most any subject, spoke of the decline of the antimacassar in a delightful 1948 interview published in the August 24, 1948, issue of *The Minneapolis Star* (available online via www.newspapers.com).

[7]   What about Harry's hair oil? Was he sporting a dying look? Seemingly not, as the gals continued to pursue him. Considering that he looked so debonair, he may have instead been relying on Brylcreem — the "little dab'll do ya" — whose ads assured that it "leaves hair soft, healthy, manageable and shiny, without the slickness of gels … or the greasiness of pomade."

Sally wrote to Harry in mid-March of 1951, a mere seven months into their marriage:

> *At this point I have given up all hope of any kind of normal husband and wife relationship with you. Just imagine 4 years we have lived together and in that time you have never written me one line. You haven't called me but once in 2 weeks — darling I know you so well. It's a pattern that repeats itself — over and over and over again. A new cheap broad or broads. After the show — eat, drink, fuck, sleep late — no time for responsibilities to your wife … [or] the people who love you. If you could only stop kidding yourself about these affairs — and not put so much of your time and effort and charm into them — then you wouldn't neglect the important, lifetime, long-term relations that make the difference between a substantial citizen and a fly-by-night playboy.*
>
> *It's normal to want sex — and for a man, to get it — but it only takes a minute and doesn't leave a scar. And of course it's more fun if the broad thinks you're wonderful and terrific.*
>
> *But, my God, you don't have to make a career out of every whore you lay — nor bring her flowers and jewels — and wine and dine her. Why don't you be smart? Dames to lay are a dime a dozen. Finish your court at night. Call your wife, let the dame wait. Feed her, fuck her, send her home. Or get up and go home and forget about it. You got laid. What else do you want? Love? That you got from me. You want to be in love? You are — with me — only you're afraid to admit it to yourself….*
>
> *Stop telling people that our relationship is just business. Tell yourself and everybody "I adore my wife — and she loves me!" She's the sweetest, kindest, most understanding woman I know and she loves me…. And I love her. Of course, I love her. She's my wife…. She's my gal.*
>
> *If you kept saying that to people and girls and yourself, you'd see people would give you more respect, and it wouldn't queer you with your current lay. After all, what are either of you going to get out of it? Just laid, that's all. So why all the build-up? Just because a guy gets laid by a broad, does it mean he isn't in love with his wife? Take it in your stride, man. It's only a lay; don't make such a drama of it.*
>
> *The shameful part is the way you neglect your wife…. Do you think it's fun working in these joints? Lonely, harassed, dying*

a thousand deaths ... because I know what you are doing? It's agony! It's despair. I want to die when all I want is to be with my husband ... it's so little — I don't ask for a yacht, a Cadillac, diamonds, just a little nest that's home, and a guy who wants to come home to me.

You're a damn fool (and you know it). But I'm a bigger one to write like this, to beg, to plead, to care. But the day will come when I don't, and when I don't — I know me — I will look back at this and wonder what kind of spell I was under. And nothing on earth can move me — that will be that. If it's what you want, then you'll be happy. If it isn't, then you'd better do something about it — and I don't mean words. You know what you need to do. You know how twisted up your life is and your mind is. And you know what to do about it. But you won't and one day it's going to be too late. Enough of this. I'm so unhappy I'm ill. I just want to crawl away and die. And all I can do is cry and cry and nobody wants a crying woman around. So — no more — no more tears — no more letters like this, no more telling you my heart, no more pleading, no more scolding — no more. All the next moves are yours....

In time Harry became tired of the lifestyle he had fashioned for himself. In a rare mood of self-reflection he literally took pen in hand to write his first and only letter to Sally. The date is unknown, but it must have been written in 1951, sometime before December. It was an actual handwritten love letter:

I write this letter as a confession of my heart and mind. I am heart-broken and grief stricken because of our situation of which I am all to blame. I know you won't believe anything I say because of my consistent lying, cheating and my neglect to you as a husband....

Sally, this letter will contain <u>nothing but the truth</u>.

I know that I have caused you an untold amount of embarrassment, unhappiness and the most sickly and nauseating feeling in the pit of your stomach. You have suffered anguish and pain because of my behavior. Your patience and steadfast defense of me when I was wrong and bad and threw in your face cheap lousy behaviors which humiliated you and embarrassed you beyond forgiveness — but you forgave. I don't blame you for feeling the way you do toward me. I deserve it.

I don't deserve your forgiveness, pity or even a kind charitable thought. I have given you more unhappiness than any person can take. I have caused you sleepless nights — I have caused you to suffer. I have caused you not to be able to think. Everything that is bad and rotten I did to you. Why?

The women I played around with were cheap, dirty, I too felt dirty and cheap — still you forgave.

I now make a prayer — I pray for a last forgiveness — I want to be good. I want you to be proud of me. I want your respect — I want again your kindness, your thoughtfulness, and above all I pray to god that you <u>love me.</u> Sally, you are my savior, you are my strength. I worship you like a goddess. <u>I love you with all my heart</u>.

Please I beg, I pray for this last forgiveness. I want to do right. I know I could do right and be right. I want to make up all the unhappiness I have caused you. I want to make you happy. I could make you happy <u>now</u> God has shown me the light. I could feel it. I know I will be clean, honest, good. He has embraced me in this hour of need, need for you, your love, your caresses; your understanding is now the most important thing in my life.

Darling, I want to be with you always. I now feel I am a different person, the kind of person you would want me to be. I want my <u>wife</u> to be first always. I want my thoughts to be of your happiness, not mine. (I will be happy knowing you're happy). I want you to smile and laugh. We could have so much fun together. I never knew it before. I feel newly born, a complete change has taken place as I am writing this letter.

Please, Sally, give me reprieve, give me the opportunity to show you how good I can be. Give me the chance to make you happy. I promise before God you will never know an unhappy moment. Please give me this opportunity.

Inherently, I am a good boy. I have never wanted to be bad. Let us not destroy our lives. Maybe this is God's way of showing us our way. Let us be guided by his wisdom. I am God's child and he has made me good.

I love you with all my heart.

Harry

P.S. This is my first letter to you and I feel wonderful writing it. I love you.

Wow! So what did Sally do when she received this letter? She retyped it and made carbon copies! And then she sent a copy back to Harry, along with her personal notes:

> *I have laboriously typed your letter to me — so that you can have a copy of what you wrote. It is the motivation for this letter I have written to you — and I'd like you to remember what you wrote — and how you felt when you wrote it.*
> *Take this letter and go off to a secluded spot by yourself — one of the reading rooms of the Public Library would be ideal — and give yourself two hours to read and digest and decide — what you want to do. It's important to you — and me.*

Surely Sally had been moved by Harry's emotional, heartfelt missive. How could she not have been? However much of a rake he had been, the man had opened himself up to her, revealing his innermost self, possibly for the only time in his life. But Sally's mood had changed. She may still have been willing, but she would no longer be a pushover in the face of his declarations of reform. And, to clinch matters, she had learned (apparently in a phone call with Harry himself) that he was again living with his ex-wife, Georgia. No doubt, that realization diminished what might otherwise have been a more sympathetic response to his pleas for mercy.

Sally's scorching reply to Harry was 16 pages long, double-spaced. Here it is, judiciously abbreviated, but otherwise pretty much as she typed it on December 2, 1951:

> *Dear Harry,*
>
> *I am sure that this is the most difficult letter I have ever written in my life. Difficult, first, because what I write herein will affect the life of another person, you. And I feel deeply responsible for the effect that my words will have on you. – Therefore, I shall choose them carefully. This is a difficult letter, secondly, because I must search my own soul and mind and cleanse each word (and the thoughts that these words express) of bitterness, blame for yesterday's sins, my human desire to get out from under, and escape from a situation and a person who has given me pain, grief, humiliation and loss.*
>
> *What I say to you must be divested of all these emotions and must bear the harsh, white light of complete honesty. Honesty for itself alone – truth for its own sake – without a shred of any personal equation, truth not slanted at any objective, but*

truth. Not what we would like to believe, not what it's
pleasant to believe, but the truth, as it actually exists. What
then are these truths? Let's start with now!

1. *We have an adult (in years) man, making a full confession*
   of his sins and begging forgiveness of his wife, from the
   bed of another woman - !!

It doesn't make good sense, does it?

You claim extenuating circumstances —

What are these circumstances? According to you — you
have no place else to go – there is nothing else you can do. —
You must depend upon your divorced wife for food, shelter,
spending money and laundry, plus the cost of transportation
from town to town with her. No one (no woman) is going to
make this kind of expenditure without something in return,
plus the expectancy of an even greater future return.

Now what return is she getting for her money?
   1. *a bed partner*
   2. *your <u>words</u> of love*
   3. *your promises of a permanent relationship, your*
companionship, management and a mutual business
partnership which her work will bankroll and your cleverness
and experience will make successful. Yet according to your
letter you have no intention of fulfilling any of these things,
except, perhaps, the sexual exchange. Your letter pleads with
me to believe you – that you are through with lies – yet your
very life day by day, minute by minute is a lie – because while
you are accepting her food, and her bed, and her money – you
are calling me daily and writing to me of your undying love for
me – and pleading for me to give you another chance to be a
good husband and father.

So – you are lying to one of us – and all your fine and
commendable resolutions are dead before they are born.

Because honesty doesn't mean just being truthful with
one person — it means being completely honest with
everyone — and about everything.

And you know that if Georgia knew your written and
avowed intentions towards me — and us — she wouldn't
have you around for a moment. So — you are trading truth

*for a meal and a bed — integrity for a mess of potage —
dignity and honor for a cheap way of life. It's a very high
price to pay for so little.*

*What you are doing with Georgia now is exactly what you
did to me — for all the whole 5 years — and what you have
promised her and what she expects is exactly what I was led
to expect.*

*There is no point in pursuing this particular phase of this
situation further. It is repetitious.*

*Of course I don't believe you and neither does anyone else
you know — and I or they never will — until you prove by
deeds, not words, that you are <u>honest</u>.*

*As you can see, just saying it doesn't make it happen.
True, you've started in the right direction — you are
disgusted with your ways and you want to do differently —
but just <u>wanting</u> won't do it.*

*The habits of mind, and habits of mental reactions,
formulated thru years are not changed overnight.*

*About this time you are getting bored with this letter and
are saying to yourself, "O.K. — O.K., I'm an S.O.B., I know
that, I've said it already. Now what do you want me to do?
Am I coming back to you? Or shall I hold onto this deal till
something better comes along? The answer lies entirely with
you! And now you will say, "I want to be with you! etc. etc."
as per your letter to me, and your phone calls.*

*It's not that easy, Harry! This is not a matter of what <u>I</u>
<u>want</u> you to do! Nor does it concern deals, nor where your
next meal is coming from, nor a choice of women, nor who
pays your rent, nor any of the apparently expedient things.*

This concerns the <u>Man</u>, Harry Finkelstein, as he is, now!
and
*the Man, Harry Finkelstein, that you want to be! (I am
giving you credit for the sincere desire to be different.)*

*What you are now is not pleasant to look at! And you don't
want to look at it! You took a half look, just a little peek with
half shut eyes before you wrote your (only) letter to me, And
even this dim view, this little glimpse, nauseated you! Writing
the letter relieved you — it was a form of vomiting, a mental
catharsis — But it is only a temporary relief. Just vomiting is*

not going to cure you of your illness. To be well and be the man you say you want to be requires certain logical steps, taken in sequence. Whether you take these steps or not depends upon how much you want to be that other man. The decision rests with you. It is not a decision to be made lightly. It involves the hardest work you will ever do in your life. It involves struggle, bitterness and courage (all qualities you have never shown or had). It involves the use of moral muscles you have never used, and like horseback riding and ballet dancing, or any physical exercise to which your physical body is not used to, the pain is awful!...

But first you must make the decision to take the steps, and it's the most important decision <u>you</u>'ll ever make....

You must make a very thorough and complete examination of yourself (your behavior). You must, for once, really see this sick, deformed, undeveloped character in <u>all</u> its ugliness without being blinded by excuses, self-justification, self-pity or fear. This will take <u>great</u> <u>courage</u>! More courage than you've ever shown before in your whole life. Only <u>you</u> can do it. But I <u>can</u> show you the picture or reflection of the man <u>you</u> as others see you. Here it is —

A liar — I know of no one who believes you.

A thief — to take money from people or credit or their goods of merchandise, and not give them their money is the same as taking money out of their pockets.

An adulterer — a fornicator — you have no care about whom you have sexual intercourse — if you want it.

A man who lives off women.

Selfish — You care for no one but yourself.

Vain — You care more for your appearance and your clothes than you do for your soul.

Lazy and slothful — You will not do your share of an unpleasant task.

Undisciplined — and disobedient — You behave as if you were a law unto yourself, regardless of others' rights or wishes.

Cold, hard, unloving and unloved! — you do not have a single friend in all the world that would give you shelter, food, drink, money, a bed, or even affection, just for yourself alone (without they expected to be paid for it , either in money or an exchange of some material thing).

Unforgiving and unmerciful — You will hurt, humiliate little people who can't fight back for the feeling of power it gives you to be able to hurt them.

Without integrity or honor — Your <u>word</u> means nothing to you or anyone else. The mere fact that it is inconvenient or difficult to keep a promise is a sufficient reason for you to forget about it and you expect everyone else to forget about it too.

Ungrateful

Self-indulgent

Sensual

Mentally, morally and intellectually immature and undeveloped — You have never finished anything you ever started, education, marriages or business career.

You have never made a success of anything you ever started.

You refuse to do the mental work necessary to arrive at an intellectual conclusion.

You refuse to do the mental work necessary to read or study anything that would improve your mind, your philosophy, your morals.

You refuse to face or carry the obligations of a mature man — the care of wife and child — any voluntary contribution of yourself and time and effort to family, home, neighborhood, city, county, state or nation.

You do not believe that you have any obligation to any of them — or make excuses to yourself and others as to why you are unable to do so.

You are unwilling to sacrifice the sensual indulgence of the moment for the lasting and permanent rewards of the future.

You feel that you can accomplish the fulfillment of your physical and material needs and sensual desires by cunning, craft, deceitfulness, shrewdness — instead of by work, industry, thrift, and sacrificing this moment's pleasurable feelings for the future security.

You have lost the sensitivity that makes you feel shame for lies, cheating, immorality, cruelty, vanity, selfishness. You only want the shallow approbation of those around you

— regardless of their quality and when some act of yours is discovered to be less than admirable and you are held to scorn or criticism, you do not seek to make amends or work for admiration, but simply move on to a different group — a different business, a new city or community. Have you ever thought of how many people, groups and communities and businesses you can't go back to? (Unless you pay some very great indemnities and amends).

1. Not one person in your family

2. three wives and God knows how many former girlfriends

3. New York politics

4. the law business

5. the café business

6. the Carnival business

7. your former friends in Brooklyn, New York, Chicago, etc. Your sphere of new fields is narrowing down —

This is the man, Harry Finkelstein, the world sees — Not pretty, is it? Now you make your own examination — It's even uglier, isn't it? ...

In your case you have wandered so far from the truth and have gotten so lost, my advice to you, as a person whom I know and have loved and could love again is as follows:

Go to Chicago — go to a psychiatrist — get a job (with Sam Wolfe — I can fix it for you). Make your own living, live modestly, save money, go to school at night and study psychology, law and literature. Write each creditor you have, acknowledge your debt, tell them what you are doing (in part — that you are starting all over again, a new life, studying for a new career, and a new way of life — and that ultimately you will do your best to make restitution. Forget completely your old ways and old life — and start all new and fresh. Your work with the psychiatrist will open your eyes to many things and point the way for the use of your industry, talents and ability. Be faithful to a religion and acknowledge and live up to your kinship with God — whatever the religion of your choice dictates.

When you have done this you will be the man you were destined to be — the man you want to be. —

Now, about us — you and me —

All of the above concerns one individual — yourself, Harry Finkelstein, because until you have learned "To thine

own self be true, then thou canst not be false to any man"
you cannot intelligently think of yourself in relation to
anyone else. In other words, you must find yourself first —
really find out who you really are. Then you'll know what you
really want to do. — And then you can intelligently, lovingly
and wisely choose a partner, a wife, to live with you.

Maybe I am not that one. When you chose me, you did not
do so from loving, intelligent, thoughtful motives.

However, if it's me that you do want — then I have some
personal requirements that must be met. Now mind you these
personal requirements have nothing to do with your making
a success of your new life. They have only to do with us living
together for the rest of our lives as husband and wife, and as
parents of our children. Your life can be happy, wholesome
and good without your doing these things, but if we are to be
married you must do them.

They are —

1. A devout and sincere study of Christian Science,
which includes:

a. Reading the daily lesson

b. Help and instruction at least once a week from a
Christian Science practitioner — both of these things for one
year — continuously for one year

2. You change your name

3. You have plastic surgery on your nose

4. That you are sexually capable and potent with me

My reason for these four requirements are as follows:

I believe in Christian Science. I want to achieve and
attain membership in the Mother Church and in a branch
church and I desire to have class instruction with a teacher.
I would like to become a lecturer. I am studying and working
toward that end and, humbly, knowing how far short I am,
how grave are my mistakes and I know how far I have to go.
But I could not accomplish these things with my husband
being unsympathetic to Christian Science, and his help and
prayers would help me to accomplish my goal.... Further-
more, you do not subscribe nor embrace the Jewish religion.
You give it an occasional "lip service only." You do not and
never will use it as a formula for daily living. You cling to it
only because it is familiar and a habit.... I want to live my

religion every day.... God must come first, and all else will follow.

The reason I want you to change your name, and have your nose fixed, is not because I am prejudiced, for you know that I am not, but you are! You have carried the burden and the defense mechanism of sinned against, downtrodden Jew for so long — if you are to make a new life — if we are to make a new life together — this is the one burden I insist that you be rid of. Let it also be a symbol of the new man. Let it be the outward reminder of the new birth — unburdened by yesterday's old burdens and the scars they rubbed on your soul (even though they were self-inflicted). If you are in truth "born again," then let us give this new man a new name (and a new nose).

As to your sexual potency — this too must be, because I don't want any remembrance of your former humiliation because of this lack in our marriage. In other words, I don't want any hangovers of yesterday's failures. We will have only glorious todays and tomorrows.

Too long to wait? A whole year? To prove and demonstrate this new man? I have had five years demonstration of the old one, so 1 for 5 is a very good deal. Too much to ask? The nose and the religion, etc. Again we always have our choices. We are willing to do whatever is necessary to attain what we wish — if we don't do it it's because we really don't want it — we want something _more_.

And you will have to stick the year out — at school — at a job — supporting yourself — and studying Christian Science every day. I won't change my mind, and I will not discuss our relationship on any other terms. I will wait the year out, love you, help you, visit you. You may even come and work for me on your vacation. You will have to accept humbly people's distrust of you and suspicion, and by your life and your _daily_ deeds inspire in them and me the confidence your life will earn you.

It's rugged. It's a hard row you're going to have to hoe, and it's a hard decision to make. It means giving up all former vanities, being humble, speaking softly, living by a hard discipline, arising early, working hard, just barely time to eat and back to school and study, no time for nightclubs, *and cutting up jackies,[8] no time to brag, no false front, eating cheaply, living in a cheap room, wearing inexpensive clothes, keeping an account accurately of your money, owing no one, putting money in the bank, riding on streetcars and buses, learning how to study and concentrate again, and doing it all with a happy heart — opening up a closed mind to new ideas and being willing to <u>try</u> and understand — no detective stories.*

No good? — You're the doctor — Whatever you say —

And now for the practical means of this end if you decide upon the course or any part of it.
1. Sam Wolfe will give you a job — in concessions or furniture.
2. The University of Chicago has the best courses of the subjects I outlined. The tuition is not expensive. The night or day courses are the same. Rooms are obtainable near the campus, cheap.

The psychiatrist you started with is there <u>or</u> if it's a hangover and you want to start fresh with the truth, with a new one, choose the other one I recommended.

Now if you decide to also meet my other requirements for you as a husband, Dr. Thorek will do the operation — for free. The attorney will do the name change for a nominal sum I will advance. I will help you get settled and find a Christian Science practitioner for you, preferably a man, I think, and you must go on from there. If you stick it out a year, I will be waiting....

You must let me know, by letter, before I leave here what you are going to do about this new man, so that I can make arrangements in Chicago before I go to Dallas.

Always, Sally

Harry had poured his heart out to Sally, exposing his vulnerabilities in a most uncharacteristic manner, only to receive what he must have regarded as a completely unreasonable diatribe in response. Like the rest of us, Harry was both simple and complex. While he may have had a sincere desire to

---

[8] "Cutting up jackies" is carnie lingo for cutting up jackpots and also for the sort of tall tales that carnival pitchmen tell when they get together at leisure.

improve himself, the regimen Sally had demanded was well beyond any goal he might have set for himself. Understandably taken aback by her astonishing demands, it took Harry a while to regain his bearings. Eventually, he picked up the phone, called Sally and, in no uncertain terms, totally dismissed her accusations and novel suggestions.

During that conversation, Harry made no excuses for his living arrangement, but instead blamed Sally, not his admitted personal failings, for their marital troubles. Yes, he was living with his ex-wife. Yes, he had been screwing other showgirls and prostitutes on a regular basis. But even a cad, a rounder, even a cheating bastard has *feelings* and a certain sense of dignity. Harry may have been a louse, but, hey, nobody's perfect.

Around this time, Sally received a letter dated December 4, 1951, from Wendel Allen, a relative she had recently visited. He weighed in:

> I want you to know how very much I enjoyed the time that I spent with you while you were here…. You have so many of the characteristics that I admire so much in my friends and relatives. I guess it gets back to that old business "of walking with Kings and not losing the common touch." I enjoy that real old "earthy" streak in you, which you have managed to keep in spite of all your fame and glory….
>
> I wish I had … the opportunity to discuss Harry and Georgia alone with you. I am still completely flabbergasted! How any man could ever think of you and Georgia in the same breath amazes me. The girl who introduced me to Georgia told me the other day that Georgia told her that Harry had been wanting to leave you and begging her to take him back!!! Such crap! Harry wasn't worth your little finger, and I am damn glad that he is gone. Forget the whole deal — I have the feeling that both of them are getting what they deserve in each other.

It may have been sometime in the 1940s — perhaps as a result of her failed marriage with Turk — that Sally first became interested in the study of human behavior, but over the years she had become something of an armchair psychologist. If her astonishing letter to Harry was an attempt to psychoanalyze him, her lengthy response to Wendel Allen's letter incorporated a soliloquy reciting her personal aspirations, plus further "analysis" of Harry's problems:

> *I want to write and, of course, I hope that some of the books that I will write might be famous, and that I, not Sally Rand, might be famous for what I would write. I would like to be a*

Christian lecturer. I have never known a Christian Science lecturer to be "famous," but I do believe that the consecrated lives that they lead and the contributions that they make to human knowledge and to human needs is such that they will live in the ears of the people who hear them.... I would like to raise a houseful of children and to achieve a growth spiritually, intellectually and lovingly, so that their lives could be my immortality, that the things I gave them, that the knowledge I help them acquire and that the inspiration that I could give them would send them out into the world with honesty, integrity and a selfless ambition to go forth and do good....

Poor Harry. He is honestly not mentally well. He is suffering from a dreadful inferiority complex starting with the fact that he is a Jew. He has subconsciously burdened himself with all of their sorrows and miseries. He is the prejudiced one, not the Gentiles toward the Jews. As a Jew, he is prejudiced unreasonably towards Gentiles and their feelings and treatment of a Jew.... He has permitted himself forty-five years of this kind of immature, infantile self-indulgence, so that now his behavior pattern is very hard to change. What he is seeking is safety, security, adulation, petting and admiration without the mature endeavor it requires to earn adult admiration. For a male, of course, this means the admiration and adulation of inferior women. He also has a mother complex and as soon as he really respects and admires a woman, she no longer appears to him as a woman to be loved as a wife, but as a mother. He is a very confused and a very unhappy man and will continue to be until he gets himself straightened out and faces life as it is, not as he would wish it to be, or as he wants to think it is. In the meantime, I feel that I have earned the right to happiness, peace and the enjoyment of my own maturity. I am unwilling to act in the role of his mother. I want to be a wife. I also have no wish to play God, and I believe that people have to work out their own destinies, and so he must work out his....

Poor Wendel wasn't alone in becoming a repository for Sally's emotional debris. On December 14, 1951, she wrote to Sam Wolfe, the couple's long-time acquaintance in Chicago, to lament over her traumatic relationship with Harry. (While her letter employed a near stream-of-consciousness style, in consideration of the reader, paragraph breaks are included where appropriate and, believe it or not, much of the tirade is omitted.) After thanking Sam for a dinner and weighing the pros and cons of various business opportunities, Sally turned her attention to her "biggest problem," Harry Finkelstein:

> I know that your first thought in this is, "oh no, not this again," and why don't I just forget about it and give the whole thing up. Of course, this is my inclination. There is no question that I have been harassed and most unhappy with it, but as I have so frequently said, anyone can get a divorce. Marriage requires a good deal of doing and working at.
>
> Furthermore, I do not feel that I could call myself a Christian, which I try very hard to be, if I did not lend an ear to his plea as outlined in his letter. Even a condemned man is given an opportunity for a reprieve. And while, of course, there is every reason for all of us to doubt the sincerity of his plea, at the same time, if, by chance, it is a sincere one, I feel that he should be given an opportunity. I must, of course, take his words with a great many reservations, and with this in mind I have prepared a letter for him, a copy of which I am enclosing. I also enclose a copy of his letter to me, the first letter he has ever written me or the first written communication he has ever had with me during our five years of relationship.
>
> Harry has been unfaithful to me consistently throughout our relationship. He has lied to me consistently throughout our relationship. The beginning of this relationship was based on lies: 1. That he was not married. 2. That he had obtained a divorce from his wife before he met me. 3. That he was in good financial condition and immediately upon our marriage would buy a house, put it in my name and that we would live in New York. Of course, none of these things were true. They were totally untrue.
>
> During this five-year period, there has been a continuous stream of women, casual contacts with whom he has had sex relations. But over and above these, upon three different occasions he has left me and my business to be with another woman. It appears that he has been in touch with Georgia during almost the entire past year, having told her that he wanted to come back to her and they mutually made plans for

him to do so. And during last summer while he was at the hotel, he had her come on to stay with him at the hotel, at my expense, of course....

The fact that I discovered it by accident and finally confronted both of them with it and they both admitted to it — admitted is not quite the right word, but Georgia outlined the plan, and Harry by very reason of his sitting and not denying it tacitly substantiated Georgia's story of their relationship during the past year. It was at this point in New York that naturally I broke off any further relations with him at all and left him to his own devices with Georgia and whatever plans he wanted to make. He pled, he cried, he telephoned, but all the time he continued to live with Georgia....

This is a very unpleasant picture of a man, of course: a man who is afraid. Of course, you and I can both sympathize to some extent with his dilemma. He is a man who has been used to having money and good clothes and a decent place to live and sleep....

Harry needs the services of a qualified, legitimate psychiatrist very much. His difficulties started when he was very young. He was the youngest of several children. He was the youngest boy. He was his mother's pet and darling, and no matter what happened, Mama was always there to make excuses and to prove that he was the nicest little boy in the world, regardless of whatever his schoolteachers thought or whatever disciplinary measures were brought to bear.

As he grew up, no girl was ever good enough for him to date. Girls who came to the house as girlfriends of his were left in no doubt as to that fact. His first sexual experiences and remembrances are not very pleasurable or pleasant. His mother's disapproval of girls and women in general gave him a poor opinion of women. He was also very much in love with his mother and has a very strong mother fixation.

He worked in his brother's law office and just at the time when he ought to have been taking his bar exams and bringing to a successful conclusion his studies, the nightclub business started and he was in that. This was a very rich dose for a young man. The ensuing years were fraught with the usual saloon, bar and nightclub experiences, fast women, slow horses, etc., etc., a very common pattern, but an experience that he was not prepared for morally, spiritually or mentally to meet with a clear head.

His mother's death wounded him deeply and further antagonized him toward women as equals, companions, friends and wives. Because moral virtues and ethics were taken for granted in this typical Hebrew home where people went to shul, the entire family, he did not get too strong a training in the specific ethics that ought guide one's life, both personally and in business. I could continue with this analysis but I don't think it's necessary [or] actually pertinent.

Suffice it to say that in my studied opinion, psychiatry would be of great benefit. I believe that once his unfounded fears and prejudices, etc., were brought to light by an understanding, intelligent psychiatrist and viewed for what they really are, Harry could turn into an honest, hard-working, pleasant individual, well organized and well coordinated, but he must also do certain things for himself and prove to himself that he is mature enough and capable enough to do those things alone and unaided.

The plan outlined in my letter to him is the result of five years of close association with him and a very deep knowledge of him as a man and a person. You will note in reading this letter that I have laid out two plans.... If at first glance, these seem to you to be selfish and dominating, I think a closer study of them will disprove this opinion. My actual letter to Harry, I think, explains it very well, without my repeating it here....

If Harry's decision is to go forward with this plan, won't you, as his friend and mine, help him and me by giving him a job? I know that you have many concessions. I know that there must be people who oversee these things and look after them, and Harry, knowing the nightclub business, etc., would I think be a very efficient employee for you. Please do not turn a deaf ear to my request. Let's admit, as he does, that everything he has done in the past has been lousy and wrong and that his behavior to you was inexcusable, but let's also admit that his willingness to take a year and try hard for something that is good and right and constructive is a sufficient indication [that he] will do differently.

I have not received an answer from my letter to Harry, but I am hoping so much for his own sake that he will decide to start a whole new life. Half measures are never going to be of any value to him. He is the most unhappy man that I have ever known, wholly without motivation. He sleeps and stays in bed until all hours because he hasn't anything to get up for. He goes off on foolish, childish tangents because he has no real objective in life, no children, no wife, nothing that he needs to work for or wants to work for. Haircuts, shaves, manicures, and expensive clothes are his only "serious" objectives. He has never read a single book since he left school. He doesn't really love anybody, not even himself, himself least of all, because being a really bright person he doesn't want to look at himself. And so he keeps his waking hours full of nonessentials and gestures and the anesthesia of movies and detective story magazines.

If I say anything more about this, it's going to be too tedious for you even to finish, so I'm not, but I do think that you will understand all of it better after you have read my letter to Harry, and his letter to me, and if Harry does decide to do this hard and difficult thing (it is hard and difficult for a man), will you try and help us both on the job situation?

And now I have written an overlong letter. Herewith is my itinerary where ... you can find me any day and any hour. I would be very grateful to hear from you.

"Oh no, not this again" ... "too tedious" ... "overlong" — what does it say about Sally's state of mind that she would share such personal correspondence and unload such a flood of emotion on Sam Wolfe, a mere acquaintance? She had evidently constructed this letter over a period of days, as a postscript reveals Harry's reaction to her plans for his self-improvement. Apparently, Sally thought Harry would jump at the chance she was giving him. Harry's rejection notwithstanding, she wasn't quite ready to give up:

P. S.

I have received my answer from Harry, not by mail, of course, but by telephone. He was livid with anger and furious beyond telling. He completely denied everything in the letter and said that it was I who was guilty of all these unhappy faults, that he had always been honest, always made a living, never lived off anybody, that he was a man and not a child, that he did not have the patience to go to school and continue his law so that he could take his exams, that my wanting him to change his name and his nose was merely because I was embarrassed in front of people because of them. He admitted that he knew a great many people who had taken up Christian Science and found it a wonderful formula for living. However, he completely refused to give me a year.

Honestly, Sam, this is the way I feel. I did give Harry five years, and during those five years I suffered the torments of the damned, a real hell on earth, and he admits this. Now I ask him to give me just one year. One year for five years is a good deal and there isn't anything that I'm asking [him] to do which could be hurtful or harmful in any way – to the contrary, I do honestly believe it could be extremely beneficial. I don't ask him to embrace Christian Science. I only ask him to study it for a year, and if at the end of the year, after having given it daily studying and one hour a week with a teacher, he still does not want to embrace it, then I'll be satisfied. But at least he will know something about the thing in which I believe so that there will be a sympathetic rapport between us.

He was highly incensed at my even suggesting that he work for you. That he didn't need a job from Sam Wolfe, that he would find a job in New York, etc.

Of course, Sam, this is the result of his being embarrassed at his situation with you. I don't know all of it, but I know that when he talks that way, it's because he doesn't want to face something.

Sam, you have been Harry's friend. I do honestly think that you know him pretty well. Is there anything that you could do or say as his friend that would help? Of course, it means swallowing your pride too, and the natural antagonism you feel toward a person who has behaved badly, and overcoming his antagonism. The natural inclination is to say, "The hell with it. What have I got to do with this? He doesn't want to be helped, let him go to hell." That's one way to look at it. Another way to look at it is that Harry isn't honestly mentally well. He is reacting by putting up defenses, which is normal, of course, but all the things I spoke about and the reason that he is the way he is are also the reasons that he shies away from helping himself. Maybe I am not viewing it clearly. Maybe my own emotions are so involved that I'm not seeing it right. I don't know. But Sam, I would be very grateful for your own thoughts on this matter.

You are a Jew. Perhaps you understand him better than I. You have known him before I did. Perhaps you understand things that I don't. At any rate, do write and tell me what you think and if you think there is any chance of you as his friend overcoming his present state of mind and helping him on.

I have discussed this with no one, because I have no one else with whom to discuss it. You do. If I have imposed upon you and your friendship, forgive me. Where may one turn in time of trouble if not to friends?

Beyond the surprising details and insights into her personality, the sheer length of Sally's letter helps to answer another question — "What was she doing in her spare time?" And she hadn't even finished. To this very lengthy epistle, she had attached a business proposal, a little over two pages long, presenting a cosmetic line to be named for herself. The pitch was entitled: "Notes, Comments and Suggestions on the Sally Rand Cosmetic Deal."

After discussing the potential competition and suggestions for standing out in a crowded field of products, Sally's "pièce de résistance" was herself and some intriguing details about her first product:

My constant contact with the public and my observations in these contexts could be boiled down to one single question I am most asked: "What is your secret?" So taking my cue from the public themselves, I propose to have these products, the Sally Rand cosmetics, especially the first one, "My Secret" or "Sally's Secret."

I propose to start with one single item, a square four-ounce bottle containing a creamy liquid, either pale pink or pale cream color, bland in appearance, consistency and odor, only vaguely perfumed if at all. This creamy liquid is neither sticky, gelatinous nor greasy. It is absorbed very quickly into the skin without any undue amount of rubbing or massaging. It leaves scarcely any residue — only a feeling of pleasant moistness. It prepares the face for cosmetics, whether they be a pancake type which is water soluble and will not go over a greasy skin smoothly, or the most greasy type of foundation. It is also a night cream which can be worn at night without

soiling bed clothing and without giving a woman the ugly
appearance of being "greased for bed." It contains several
important ingredients but the two most important are: 1.
That ingredient which all babies have already in their skin
and which makes their skin so soft, moist and fine of texture.
2. It contains a tremendous amount of the female hormone
which is generated by nature so generously in a woman's
twenties but gradually dwindles off until the menopause, at
which point it completely disappears. This particular form of
hormone is quickly absorbed through the skin. Both of the
above ingredients and statements are scientifically accurate.
And the application of the cream does work.

Did Sally really develop her own beauty cream? She had, after all, financed the scientists who developed the balloon she used for her bubble dance. Perhaps her description was merely meant to guide the specialists who would create the product. It is worth noting that Sally proposed this cosmetic product more than 60 years ago, and in recent times the FDA has issued warnings to women not to use beauty creams with variously derived estrogens, especially for persons with a family history of breast cancer. The ingredient "which all babies have" and how it would be developed to add to a cream is anyone's guess. In any case, no actual product seems to have been developed or marketed. Why is it that she never got around to starting any of the side businesses she contemplated? Apparently, for her, there was "no business like show business."

And, while Sally thought of herself as having a certain talent for recognizing the need for psychoanalysis in others, she completely failed to recognize the irrationality of her own persistent desire to transform others into something they could never be. Understandably conflicted, her developing catharsis is laid bare in a handwritten letter to Harry she composed sometime after his phone call:

Between El Paso & Los Angeles at 16,000 feet:

Seeing you standing alone gave me such a terrible sense of
loss and loneliness. My heart is broken — to see you so alone
— especially at the holidays. I can't stop crying.

It gives me such a sense of inadequacy and failure to know
that I have spent almost 5 years with you and still have
never gotten near enough to you to spend one warm family
Christmas. Is it that the day has no holy meaning for you and
therefore you feel no special tenderness for it? I wanted this

*to be a Happy Christmas so much — I need to be a little
happy — my heart is so empty, and I'm so utterly miserable
about everything.*

*How can I be happy when I know you're alone and sad and
confused? Christmas means sharing and giving happiness and
I have given none to you — whom I love most. It's a lie. And
I've been a failure to you, and then I say to myself, [why]
should I be so miserable over him? He didn't care or grieve
about me when he left me alone, nor does he understand my
loneliness.*

*Why should I grieve for his unhappiness when he willingly and
knowingly cut my heart out and laughed at me when he saw me
bleeding and dying a thousand deaths — in bitter agony —
flowers for a whore — being naked with Fay — all on a
Valentine's Day — tra la — don't talk about it, you say. Stop
rehearsing it, you say. I would pay any price if I could erase it
from my memory.*

*Why do you find fault with yourself for sending him back to
New York, I say to myself. Why indeed? That was his choice.
That's where he went. He ran off, like a thief in the night,
lying — I'll be back tomorrow and we'll go into New York
together. That was all — he just disappeared and went
straight to another woman's bed — don't tell me you had to
— it's a lie.*

*All you had to do was bullshit me — make love to me (it takes
so little to convince me of what I want to believe). But that
wasn't what you wanted. You wanted Georgia and you got
her. And now you find you really don't know what you want.
You think you want me but you are unwilling to do a single
thing I want you to do. I want you to be a Godly man — in
other words a Good man, with reverence for God — and his ten
commandments, with respect and love [for] your fellow men,
with respect and fidelity to your wife, to be pure in heart, to be
honest and unselfish.*

*You say you left my letter in your bag — you know you didn't
... for Georgia to find and read? Why won't you ever tell me
truth? Why?*

Harry, I shall never write you another letter till you answer this one. I have given you my plan, which you refuse. Now you outline a plan you want to follow in writing, beginning now.

What do you want to do next? Write me this plan.

I am willing to sacrifice personal desires....

I want this to be a happy letter — and the more I write, the more I cry. So I'll stop.

Awareness of the tension between Harry and Sally was not confined to their immediate circle. In mid-December 1951, at the very time that this exchange of letters and calls was taking place, Dorothy Kilgallen's syndicated column "On Broadway" was announcing: "Stripper Georgia Sothern and her ex-husband Harry Finkelstein will try it again after a separation of more than five years." Harry may have been torn, but — while other arms reached out to him — like an old sweet song, Georgia was on his mind.

The comings and goings of Harry Finkelstein would never again rise to a level of importance worthy of coverage by the press. And, although he and Sally would remain legally married, it would be early 1954, more than two years later, before anything more about him would appear in Sally's surviving correspondence.

Having rejected Sally's self-improvement plan, Harry seems to have found himself in emotional disarray, perhaps kicked out by Georgia and likely suffering financially as well. Simply put, Harry had also had enough. He was looking for an opportunity to exit the situation on whatever terms might be available.

Both Sally and Harry wanted out, but, if Harry was to go, Sally insisted that his path to freedom be achieved by way of an annulment. Unlike divorce, annulment is generally retroactive — technically, an annulled marriage is considered to have been invalid from the beginning — almost as if the nuptials had never taken place.

In the 1950's, grounds for divorce and other domestic proceedings were often agreed to among the parties with a wink and a nod, while the courts commonly approved these arrangements without looking too closely into their legitimacy. Under the law, impotence is a potential basis for annulment — simply put, if a man is physically unable to consummate a sexual relationship, his spouse may seek relief in court. This is the very ground on which Sally chose to press her case.

Considering Harry's extramarital escapades and reputation, it's laughable to maintain that he might actually have been impotent (although later in their turbulent relationship he apparently had become unable to "perform" with Sally). In any case, Harry agreed to play along as long as Sally would make it worth his while. After all, a guy can't be expected to admit to impotence unless the coin of the realm is applied to soothe the pain.

For legal reasons, the annulment proceedings were culminated in South Carolina, and Sally was quite satisfied with the arrangement, writing to her attorney there:

> *I am pleased to secure the decree of annulment.*
>
> *I have paid you in full the money you asked for to successfully complete the entire transaction, i.e., $300 for which I have receipts....*
>
> *I told you the day of my first visit ... that Mr. Finkelstein would not admit to being sexually impotent (albeit it's the truth) unless he got paid. Courts view such procedure as collusion.*
>
> *In order to start this action for annulment, you had to get Mr. Finkelstein's signature to a defendant's consent to judgment as prayed for, otherwise all he had to do was to deny that he was sexually impotent. There is no possible way of proving him a liar. This is one instance where the only witness there is the male concerned, unless he had been castrated, in which case the surgeon's testimony would be accepted. Neither doctor nor psychiatrists, depositions, even if they could be obtained, would constitute proof, because, as is well known, the impotency for which he consulted them may have been temporary.*
>
> *This annulment procedure was predicated upon having three documents signed by Mr. Finkelstein. These 3 documents are:*
> *(1) The consent of judgment prayed for.*
> *(2) A general release.*
> *(3) A power of attorney to me for any alleged community property.*

Mr. Finkelstein agreed to sign these three documents for the sum of $500. But, before he would sign anything, he had to be paid.[9]

Writing to Abe Berman, her personal attorney back in Glendora (who may have played a role in the proceedings), Sally expressed her relief: "You're an angel as always. Thank God the Finkelstein deal is over."

So, Harry was gone, receding from Sally's consciousness like an unwelcome hitchhiker in the rearview mirror. In later years, when she occasionally reflected on the men she had been married to, Harry's name would not even be mentioned.

---

[9]   This payment would amount to around $4,600 nowadays.

CHAPTER TWENTY-ONE

And Baby Makes Two

I know it's corny but I have been in an I-love-everybody mood
since I first took Sean Orion Rand home. He's the best thing
that ever happened to me, and my luck hasn't been too bad,
remember?

~ Sally Rand

Back in 1929, perhaps in an attempt to cool his ardor, Sally advised Jack
Crosby that she was unable to have children of her own. Disappointed,
but not dissuaded, on October 28, 1929 (the day before the Wall Street crash),
Crosby wrote to her in his typically overwrought manner:

> Sally dear, I would give my very life if by doing so it would make
> it possible for you to have children. Since the fact that you can't
> have them can't be altered, there is nothing I can do and nothing
> you can do. Now to look at it differently.... Did you ever think that
> we might adopt a pretty little curly haired baby — one with blue
> eyes like yours? I'd love to if it would make you happy.... You
> would grow to love it as your own.

Jack had planted a seed in Sally's mind that would germinate for nearly
20 years, as she became a figure of national prominence, too busy perhaps
to consider following through on his suggestion.

It is true that Sally was unable to conceive a child, probably the consequence
of an earlier Mexican abortion. Also, as a middle-aged and single traveling
carnival attraction in mid-century America, she would not have been a particularly good candidate for the services of an adoption agency.

Still, she had desperately wanted to be someone's mother — to love and be
loved in return. Years later, one of her former showgirls, Holly Knox, wrote
of a young girl from Tallahassee, pregnant out of wedlock, who had sought
Sally's assistance. The father was said to be a married man and the girl's
family had turned her away. Sally had supposedly offered to support the
girl in exchange for the adoption of her baby — a story that, considering
the circumstances, is believable enough.

Believable, perhaps ... but not true. What *is* true is that Sally was not above putting pressure on one of her girls in order to get her way. The case of Lorie Barnes is instructive. Sally had known Lorie and her parents, since 1933 in Chicago when Lorie was a toddler. Lorie's mother, Marjorie "Midge" Fielding, was a director and choreographer, while her father Charles "Charlie" Barnes, worked as a stage manager, singer, emcee, and bit writer for Jackie Gleason among others — both in vaudeville and the theater. Lorie says that her mother choreographed Sally's fan and bubble dances.

Since her parents had worked for Sally off and on over the years, it wasn't surprising that Lorie, too, had gone to work for Sally in 1946 when she was just 16 years old. It was then that Sally had come up with the stage name "Lori Jon." As Lorie recalled:

> I think she realized — and she was right — that my mom was a very good choreographer, but not so good as a mother.... Sally kind of took over with me when we went to California. She got me a phony birth certificate and introduced me in the El Cerrito club and then in San Francisco. I was in every single number — dancing and singing. My dad was stage manager and he also sang in some of it and Mom was the choreographer. So it was kind of a family thing.

And how was Sally as an employer? According to Lorie, she was "very firm. She knew what she wanted. And she usually managed to get it. She was strong-willed. She treated me like I was her daughter. She could be sweet and motherly but also bossy, very bossy."

Lorie and her father stayed with Sally at the San Francisco club for most of a year, but then went back east where Lorie married her first husband, John Delaney, also a dancer. The birth of a son soon followed and, when the infant was barely four weeks old, Lorie and John joined Sally's carnival train:

> Paul was born in 1948, so that was when John and I went with Royal American Shows — the big carnival with Sally. We were a dance team and I was singing production numbers as well as doing my solo and dancing with John — 10 shows a day.

Baby Paul attracted a lot of attention from the troupe, not least from Sally herself, who became so obsessed with the child that she cadged, cajoled, threatened and begged Lorie to let her adopt him. It got so bad that at one point Lorie and Sally actually got into a brawl:

> She was the only one I ever hit (except one of my husbands), but she called me terrible names, really a gutter mouth. She called me a

whore. I slapped her. She tore into me. I don't know what happened. I think I just took off. I kneed her. Next thing I knew, I just ran. It's the only time I've ever had a fight with anyone but one of my husbands.

Lorie finally left the show, taking the baby with her. Her father put them on a train to Springfield, Massachusetts, where her mother ran a dancing school. By the time she went to work for Sally again in 1949, Sally had found herself another more compliant young mother, and Lorie had found herself another husband.

Lorie remembers this story of how Sally finally did adopt a child:

The mother was one of her showgirls from California, I think. I never met the girl. But Sally learned of her pregnancy and she knew the father and he was apparently good — she looked up the family and she apparently liked what she heard. The girl didn't want the child; neither did the father, so Sally sent her away to her home. I'm not sure if it was Key West, but I think so. She had a home somewhere in Florida.

Lorie's account is similar to Holly Knox's version and close enough to the truth that it may simply reflect the tale Sally preferred to tell members of her troupe. The reality is this: A baby boy — who would come to be known as "Sean Orion Rand" — was born at 11 p.m. on August 1, 1948, at Galey Memorial Hospital in Key West, Florida.

Sally had arranged to adopt Sean even before he was born, but it wasn't until October that the adoption became public. She announced the news in Jackson, Mississippi, where she was performing at the state fair midway, telling the press that she had "made plans to adopt the boy some time ago" but had chosen to leave him "where he could receive full hospital care."

The two-month-old infant made his public debut before reporters on October 12th, as Sean "peered over the edge of his blue bassinet and gurgled at a trio who thought it was just going to be a routine interview" with Sally. The beaming mother revealed: "He's not being named for anyone. It's just a good Irish name for John." (It is likely that Sally was aware of the Irish meaning — God's gracious gift.)

According to press accounts, the baby was: "living with its adopted mother in Sally's circus wagon," an accommodation that the public was assured contained "nearly all the comforts of a kitchenette apartment." Sally reported that she had also taken steps to ensure that the trailer was "air conditioned and cork lined for his health's sake and comfort."

In a letter typed on October 15th, Sally declared:

> *As concerns my adopted son Shean:*[1] *he is two months old, has blue eyes, red hair, weighs 12 lbs., 13 ounces. He is healthy, handsome and happy. He is legally adopted by me, with all due processes of the law. No other statistics are pertinent. (Where, when, under what name, or any other details or circumstances are not pertinent.) To probe and pry into these matters can only be detrimental to the child's future.*
>
> *I retain each and every one of my legal rights to privacy, both now and in the future, and I will zealously defend these rights especially as they concern my son.*

Readers of *Billboard* magazine were met with a surprising twist: "The child, born August 1, was the second adopted by Miss Rand during a recent visit to Florida. The first, a girl, died the week after birth." (No further details of this intriguing disclosure were reported.) [2]

National interest in Sally's baby may not have risen to British royalty level, but the press *was* on the case and, coast to coast and beyond, the public remained curious about the details. If nothing else, this new development knocked the unwelcome "morals charges" stories off the front pages. After all, Sean's unveiling occurred only three weeks after Harry and Sally's embarrassing motel room incident in Ft. Smith, Arkansas.

More than five months later, under the headline "FAN DANCING SALLY RAND BRINGS HER MYSTERY BABY TO MILWAUKEE," a long article about Sean, complete with a photo of Sally and her baby, began:

> Sally Rand, who parlayed a few feathers and some rubber balloons into a fortune, not once but several times, is busily engaged in trying to repeat the stunt. This time she intends to hang onto the fortune, because she now has a child to support. It is a handsome, blue-eyed mystery boy, aged 7 months.

The article continued:

> Sally, who has always been ready to talk about anything from the art of dance to how to handle a wolf, from economics to proper

---

1   Sally wrote "Shean" (pronounced "Shawn") in her diary as late as 1952.

2   The infant girl who, according to *Billboard,* "died the week after birth" may have been the child that Lorie Barnes remembered. Sean Rand confirmed the event: "She was actually going to adopt a little girl, but the little girl died just prior to the adoption. Mother had a pair of little patent leather shoes with little rhinestones on them. They were around when I was a kid. I'd see them and pick them up and she'd say, 'Those were for your little sister.'"

body paint, is not talking about her baby. All she will say is that she adopted the infant the day it was born and she doesn't want anyone speculating about its parents or the place of its birth.

Reporters never did uncover the full story of Sean's parentage and adoption, and Sally was in no mood to enlighten them. Decades later, the only thing we know for certain is that Sean's birth mother was Imogene Younger Hepler, a 20-year-old housewife married to Electrician 3rd Class George Hepler who was stationed at the naval base in Key West, Florida.

Beyond this, Sally told her son that the young mother had agreed to give up the infant for adoption because the baby's biological father had been killed on a ship stationed at the Key West naval base when the main gun accidentally backfired. This unknown man's best friend — 23-year-old George Hepler — had stepped up to marry Imogene and given the newborn his name. The original birth certificate shows the "Full Name of Child" as: Robert Hepler.[3]

How did Sally happen to become a party to all this? As a property owner and frequent visitor to Key West, she was well known and well connected among the populace of some 20,000 "conchs." In the 1940s, she commonly performed on the patio at the Havana Madrid, a nightclub frequented by sailors from the base.[4] Naturally, Sally was a big favorite among both the rank and the file.[5]

In short, Sally — a woman on a mission to adopt — was well positioned to know who was involved with whom on the island of Key West and who might be both pregnant and vulnerable to her appeals.

Issues regarding Sean's birth certificate remained unresolved for years. When he reached the age of five, Sally wrote to County Solicitor Allan Cleare, Jr., in Key West to straighten things out and express her displeasure with respect to the document that Cleare had previously furnished.

---

[3] George and Imogene Hepler were married on March 6, 1948, in Piggott, Arkansas, some 43 miles northwest of Caruthersville, Missouri, where the two resided, having known each other there since childhood. Shortly after the ceremony, they relocated to Key West, roughly five months before Sean was born.

[4] Although Sally's was a solo act, when performing at the Havana Madrid, she occasionally partnered with an 8-foot python named "Henry."

[5] An oft repeated Key West tale asserts that she once came to the aid of an attractive young ensign who had apparently spent time with her late into the night, overslept, and missed the sailing of his ship the next morning. Consigned to the brig, the young officer escaped court martial only after Sally pled his case with the Admiral, a personal friend, saying: "He's the best ensign in the entire U.S. Navy."

The letter, dated October 3, 1953, read:

> *Baby's Birth Certificate:*
>
> *I finally received it. It had been buried in a drawer at home when my uncle went to the hospital.*
>
> *It's time for Sean to go to school — Did you look at this birth certificate before you sent it?*
>
> *My son's name is — SEAN ORION RAND*
>
> *This birth certificate is for a child named "Robert Hepler."*
>
> *I know no such child — The school authorities would know no such child — and Sean would be lost and miserable if he was anyone else but Sean Orion Rand....*
>
> *One of the promises that you made me was that his birth certificate would be in my name. Now what are we going to do?...*
>
> *Remember, I took care of all this adoption deal before Sean was born. Remember the day in your office when the father and mother both signed — I was there — remember — I paid all the hospital and doctors, etc., and left it to you to obtain his proper birth certificate.*
>
> *There was no doubt of my adoption of him — even tho I did not get to Key West to pick him up till September — I paid his mother's doctor and hospital bills.[6] His doctor bill for circumcision; his hospital bill for every day he was in the hospital — till I picked him up. So there was no reason for the misinformation to go to the Bureau of Vital Statistics....*
>
> *P.S. I had Sean christened in the Episcopal Church. His christening certificate reads — Sean Orion Rand.*

Sean's birth parents may have had misgivings about signing the adoption papers and may even have thought that the act of filing the birth certificate themselves would undo the adoption. Indeed, there is evidence that Sean's birth mother later went to some lengths to locate, if not retrieve, him.[7]

---

[6]   Actually, Sally did not take custody of Sean until October. It is most likely that she flew to Key West after the closing of the Alabama State Fair in Birmingham, on Sunday the 10th, returning with Sean the next day in time to begin her appearances at the Mississippi State Fair in Jackson on October 11th.

[7]   All of Sean Rand's recollections in this chapter of his life with his mother are transcribed from in-person interviews of Sean conducted by Bonnie Egan in September 2012, plus follow-up telephone conversations and correspondence.

Asked if he had ever met his biological mother, Sean replied:

> No, other than it was reported she wanted me back and my mother
> had me hide out with her friends a few times. Ruth Wible was one
> and another was Sunny Nivens, a former showgirl who lived in New
> York. They were two people who told me stories about how my
> mother came to them and gave them a bunch of money and said
> "Take him, go here and don't open the door — even to the police."
> I was hiding out. I stayed with Sunny when I was in New York in
> '63, lived there when my mother left — went to some place out of
> New York.... Ruth had the same kind of story.

Sean mostly stayed in Glendora during the school year and traveled with his
mother only in the summer. And, when she was home, Sally loved to cook,
doing "some fancy gourmet-type cooking." As he remembers it:

> My mother was a very good cook — she just didn't have the time
> to do that much. But when she'd be home with me, she'd cook all
> kinds of different things. I remember for breakfast, she'd make
> what she called "Surprise Pancakes." You'd get a sausage in one, a
> blob of peanut butter in another, a strawberry maybe — she'd
> make these up for me when I was a little kid.

On holidays in Glendora, Sally would usually prepare the meals, but Sean
remembers that "she couldn't eat any kind of a bird. It didn't matter if it was
chicken or turkey, she couldn't eat it." She explained that this went back to
when she was a girl and had a pet chicken. In rural Missouri, everyone had
chickens that ended up on the dinner table. As Sean recalled, the experience
had a lasting effect on her:

> Every time she'd even take a bite of chicken, she'd gag so she just
> quit. She couldn't eat any kind of bird. So Thanksgiving never
> involved turkey for her. She was big on things like Crown Roast....
> We'd still have turkey for everybody else.

Besides her culinary skills, Sally was an artist and much more:

> She loved to read. She'd been a pilot early on. She was accomplished
> in all these different areas. And she was good with horses. She knew
> how to ride from the time she was small. She got me interested in
> horses. Of course, when I grew up, there was Gene Autry and Roy
> Rogers and Hopalong Cassidy. So, as a kid, I had some horses out at
> the ranch in Vegas and at the ranch here in Glendora. She was
> talented in so many ways. I got into lots of things because of her.

As the son of the famous Sally Rand, Sean naturally ran into celebrities: "... because we were around everybody — you name it — just about any personality you can imagine — I met them." Very few made much of an impression on the young boy, but he *was* enamored of cowboys.

Sean was thrilled to meet Roy Rogers and Hopalong Cassidy:

> Bill Boyd was a real good friend of hers. They both worked for DeMille. She told me a great story there. William Boyd lived right next door to her in the bungalow and one morning she got up early and she saw him being lowered down on a rope from the second or third story of a building, coming out of the home of an actress by the name of Pola Negri. And he had broken his leg. My mother confronted him. She said that was an odd way to come out of a place. Nobody else saw him because it was so early in the morning, but she saw him. He didn't answer. She said his face got really beet red and he took off to wherever he was going to get his leg fixed.
>
> That was in the '30s [actually the '20s], I guess. And then in the '50s we saw him at the state fair. Of course, I was a kid growing up with all the cowboy shows, so he was Hopalong Cassidy to me. And she said, "No, his name is Bill Boyd. I know him, I've known him forever." She took me to meet him.
>
> He was happy to see her. He picked me up and sat me up on Topper — I have pictures of me sitting on the horse, and she's standing next to the horse doing their publicity.[8] And, at the end of that conversation, she goes, "Bill, it's been 30 years. Tell me how you broke your leg." His face got beet red again. He picked me up, handed me over to her, and just rode off into the sunset — he just took off. Later she said, "I never did get an answer out of him."

There were temptations for Sean as well. One was the lure of her balloons:

> I'd take an old vacuum cleaner and hook it up in reverse, and I'd blow these balloons up, and they would get huge. And the kids in the neighborhood were like, "Wow, you've got a big one." She was probably out of town when I found a balloon with one of my pals. I remember blowing it up — we kids took it outside and started bouncing it and got it going and it shot way up in the air. It went way up over a church steeple — probably a good 35 to 40 feet in the air. It went up and over and came down on a street and then a

---

8   The photograph of Sally, Hoppy and Sean (reproduced in this book) was taken at the Cotton Bowl in Dallas, Texas, on October 10, 1952.

cop caught us and he wanted to know if that was my balloon. I said "Yeah" and he said, "You're going to cause a major accident. That thing is going to come down and give a driver a heart attack." So he asked us to deflate it and take it back. Of course, we did.

During Sally's 11 years at the Silver Slipper in Las Vegas, Sean went to school in Glendora. Except for his 6th grade year, he lived with Sally in the summers, spending a lot of time backstage:

> I was involved with the performances there at the Slipper for years. Growing up, she had always taken me and walked me around backstage and she'd show me things, saying, "This is a prop, this is a prop — and she'd say, "You don't touch anything, nothing. Everything is in a place for a reason and you don't touch it. That's an unwritten rule of show business." She made that very clear to me as a kid. I'm sure she knew kids would just pick up anything.

While Sally had been thrilled to meet the Duke and Duchess of Windsor in Nassau, it was an encounter with an even higher order of royalty — the "King" himself — that Sean well remembers:

> I believe it was about 1957 or so — I just remember being there and all of a sudden a buzz started. Everybody was jumping, moving around — and I'm thinking, "What's wrong with all these people?" Then I heard, "Elvis is coming! Elvis is coming! He's almost here!" And I'm thinking, "Who's *Elvis*?" Anyway, he comes through the door and all these showgirls and people backstage were all around him. [9]

> He walks in. I'm standing there. He walks up to me, pats me on the head, and says, "I understand you're Sean. I'm looking for your mother." So we went back where she was and they had a conversation. And what he came down there for was to ask her permission to date one of the girls in her show. I remember her saying, "Elvis, this is a free world. I don't own these girls. They just work here in the show. Whatever you want, it's up to you." So he dated this redheaded girl for a while and she ended up getting leukemia and dying. That was my interaction with Elvis.

---

[9] Billed as "The Atomic Powered Singer" (in recognition of the nearby Nevada nuclear testing grounds), Elvis Presley made his Las Vegas debut in the Venus Room of the New Frontier Hotel on April 23, 1956 — the beginning of a two-week engagement. While popular with teens, his act received a "cool reception" from the Vegas crowd. It would be another 13 years before he would once again perform on a Las Vegas stage.

Sean saw the Silver Slipper shows so often he learned them by heart:

> As I traveled around the country, I'd be backstage and I'd listen to
> the performance. I could just sit there and, when these comedians
> would go on to tell their jokes, I could tell them along with them. I
> could be sitting backstage and repeat [the jokes] before they said
> them — I'd heard them so many times.

His mother's post-performance talks were a big part of her popularity:

> At the Slipper, they would perform usually about three shows a
> night. Her part of the show was about five minutes. Then the talk
> that she always gave afterwards — she varied it a little bit but for
> the most part she had it down — she'd change real quick and she'd
> come out — she'd be in a nice big gown, come out on stage, greet
> her audience then and talk to them. One of her classic lines was:
> "It's nice being here. This is one of the places where it's risky to
> talk about the weather. The only weather they're interested in is
> 'Whether you will or whether you won't.'"

After her talk, Sally would personally greet her fans:

> She would sit at a table and people would line up for hours to
> meet her.[10] She had these little cards for autographs and people
> would say, "Sign it this way?" "Can you sign one more?" "Can
> you sign it to my aunt and uncle?"

> It used to just amaze me how people would just wait and wait and
> wait for an autograph and then would get so flustered, they'd walk
> off and leave very expensive pens. As a kid, I never had to buy a
> pen. My mother had boxes of them — she'd have all the top-name
> makers of pens. People would just walk away and leave them. A
> few times over the years people wanted me to sign a picture of her
> for them and I thought, "That's odd." "Just sign it with her name,"
> they'd say. Once or twice I signed "for my mother, Sally Rand."

Sally always traveled with her sewing machine. She was a gifted seamstress
and could whip up or patch a showgirl's costume on short notice. But she

---

10 To many, Sally's act may have seemed fanciful, if not frivolous, but she was dead
serious about her craft and work ethic. Because her dance lasted only a few minutes,
she commonly spoke to the audience after the show, sometimes even joining fans at
their tables: "Inevitably, the first gal in the audience I speak to says: 'What's your
secret?' The secret? It's a state of mind. It's hereditary. It's geographical. It's
discipline, constancy, order.'"

also used her considerable skills on her son's behalf. Sean remembered one Halloween costume in particular:

> One time I was a black cat. She made the costume for me for second grade. She put a very long tail on it. I didn't want the tail dangling behind me because I knew people would step on it, so I jerked the tail off. She said, "What kind of cat is that without a tail?" I said it was a bobcat, even though it was black. I can't remember many other costumes except the cowboys, but they would get pretty elaborate — way, way more than you could buy at the store.

Sally loved it that Sean was basically unimpressed with most of the VIPs he met. As he recalled, his mother "got a big kick out of the time we were somewhere and I said to her, 'Why can't we just go home and get around some normal people?' I always thought the show people were crazy."

Sean made an exception for cowboys when he was little, and then, when he was a bit older, it was baseball players:

> She started saying, "I was never anybody with my son until one day we were talking and I mentioned Casey Stengel." And I said, "*You* know Casey Stengel?" and she said, "Yes, we came from the same home town — born in Kansas City, Missouri." And she went on to explain that his name wasn't really Casey; his name came from Kansas City — K.C. Stengel — his real name was Charles, but fans gave him that name and it just turned into Casey. So she said, "I became *somebody* in his eyes when I said I knew Casey Stengel."

Sean's first big experience with baseball was every boy's dream:

> Mother was always a Yankees fan and, in 1963, I went to New York with her. She knew the public relations man for the Yankees — his name was Jackie Farrell — and I stayed with him when she had to leave. He lived over in New Jersey and we'd go to the park every day and go down in the dugout and out on the field with the players of that time, like Mickey Mantle and Roger Maris. When she came back, he set it up for her to give a talk at the Old-Timers' Banquet at Toots Shor's, so we went to that.
>
> It was kind of an exclusive thing. Jackie Farrell told me my mother was the first woman who had ever attended an Old-Timers' Banquet. They had approved it because she was from their time period. Of course, she sat up at the front table with DiMaggio and Berra and some of the other players. Maris, I think, was up there. Anyway, she gave a talk and I sat at one of the tables with some of

the old-time players like Bob Feller and Dom DiMaggio — some like that — Frankie Frisch, Bill Terry — they were all famous New York guys and they all autographed a baseball for me.

She just talked in general about how long she's been in New York — arriving there when she was, like, fifteen or sixteen. She didn't have any way to support herself, so she hung around and watched rich people eat. She told me: "Rich people get a sandwich and eat half and leave the other half. Then they'd get up from the table and that's when I'd run and get my food." She took speech lessons and did some dancing. It was obviously rough times.

Like many kids my age, Mickey Mantle was my idol. So I got to meet him. With Farrell, I got to meet the whole team. I came back to her and I said, "Well, I met Mickey Mantle and you met Mickey Mantle. What do you think?" And she said, "He's all right." I said, "What do you mean 'he's all right?' He's not your favorite?" She said, "No." So I said, "Well, who do you like?" And she said, "I like Yogi. He's a better personality. I like everything about him." She said, "He's the real deal" — that's what she thought. She liked him and she liked Roger Maris.

I remember going into the dugout with Jackie Farrell. He left me there because he had to go do some things. It was before the game started and there was nobody else in the dugout. I was just sitting there on the bench and, all of a sudden, here comes Tony Kubek and he sits down — I mean, the whole bench was empty — and he sat right next to me. He could sit down anywhere. The place was empty.

I'm 15 years old and he has his glove on and he takes it off and slaps it on my knee and takes his hand out and leaves the glove on my knee. And I just sit there. I don't even touch it or do anything, and Kubek says, "Have you ever touched a major league glove?" And I said, "No," and he said, "Well, pick it up." So I picked it up. About that time some other players started coming in. It was just before a game.

I remember Whitey Ford coming in, and Berra, and the bench just filled up. And the manager came in and started to talk to the team. Here I am a freshman year baseball player, and I'm thinking: "Now I'm going to be in real trouble. They're starting to go over the game and the signals and I'm here and they're going to think I'm a spy and I'm going to get shot. They're going to think I'm going to go out and tell the other team." That's what's going through my mind.

About that time, Farrell comes back looking for me and he says, "Hey Sean, c'mon let's go" and I just flew out of there. We went up to the announcer's booth and this guy came around with little cubes of ice cream that had little wrappers around them and said, "You want one of these?" so I reached over and took one. All of a sudden this guy sitting next to me leans around and he looks at me and says, "I'm old Diz. You're a kid, aren't you? Kids and ice cream go together." And then he swept a whole bunch of them off the tray onto my plate. That was Dizzy Dean.

Sally took pains to treat her teenaged son to awesome baseball experiences:

When I was in high school, I played baseball for the local team. One day my mother asked me and a couple of my baseball friends if we wanted to go to a game out at Dodger Stadium. And we said, "Sure!" So she made arrangements.

We got seats right on top of the dugout. She flagged a pitcher down to give Casey a note. So the ballplayer goes down and all of a sudden Stengel runs out of the dugout and runs out toward the first-base line and turns around looking into the crowd, seeing if he can spot her. Then when he did, she went down and they talked there at the rail. Later, he took us out to the Brown Derby Restaurant. For my friends and me, it was a treat to sit there and listen to Casey Stengel tell us stories.

The summer before his senior year in high school, Sally got Sean his first job. Helen and Fenton Mangam ran a Chicago area resort — Mangam's Chateau — a popular supper club at the time. As Sean recalled:

It was out in the suburbs of Chicago in a place called Lyons, Illinois. It's very built up now, but we're talking in the '60s — it sat in the middle of a cornfield. Helen Mangam had a very exclusive clientele, so she gave me a job as a busboy in the nightclub. I was trained by some of the waiters for a while and then all of a sudden Mrs. Mangam called me into her very nice home that was attached to the theater. She gave me instruction on how to set a table, how to do everything, where to position myself, everything like that — very high-end.

She and my mother were very good friends from their time in vaudeville. She took me back in and said, "I think I've got him wired right so he'll know how to do it now." I worked there all summer and then I bought a car. That was part of my deal — to work and earn money so I could buy a car. I bought a '65 Mustang for $1,200. Then I drove it from Chicago back out here.

Every year, I'd come back to high school from an interesting
summer. I would travel around with her to the different places —
wherever she was playing. That summer, my mother took me to
see Al Capone's grave. I was interested in seeing it because when
I was working at Mangam's Chateau some gangsters came in
there. The waiters would tell me, "The gangsters are going to be
in tonight. Don't hang around the tables, just pour the water, do
this, that. Don't listen to any conversations" — stuff like that.

I remember one night the Chicago Bears came in — Mike Ditka and
some of the other players. They got kind of rowdy and they actually
pulled the bar off the wall — pulled it loose from the wall. Helen
Mangam came down and she got in Ditka's face and said, "Mike,
you get up here now and put my bar back." He did whatever she
wanted him to do. She got them to put everything back — smoothed
out. That was probably the most action I saw in the place.[11]

Sean had only recently gotten his driver's license. In his time off from
work, he liked to hop in his Mustang and visit towns in the Chicago area,
like St. Charles, some 42 miles west of Chicago, where his mother was
starring in a show with Margaret O'Brien at the Pheasant Run Playhouse.
On September 7, 1966, Miss O'Brien and Sally opened a 19-day engagement
there in *Love from a Stranger*, a 1936 play based on an Agatha Christie short
story. An interview of the unlikely pair went something like this:

"What are we doing in the same play? Well maybe I'm not being
discrete," said Miss Rand, but we both understand it thoroughly.
Margaret here is a wonderful actress and I sell tickets."

"My age? I'm 29," said Margaret, in a voice barely above a whisper.

"I'm 62," boomed Sally, "and I brag about it."

"I was once asked to read the Gettysburg Address before General
Marshall, General Eisenhower, and Admiral Nimitz," said Margaret.

"I knew General Pershing," said Sally.

"I met President Truman and I once got spanked for sliding down
the bannisters at the White House when Franklin Roosevelt was
there," said Margaret.

"I once fell asleep on Theodore Roosevelt's lap," countered Sally.

---

[11] Starting in 1944, Mangam's Chateau featured big shows in the style of the 1930s and '40s,
continuing such entertainment into the 1970s. It employed the last regular chorus line in
the Chicago area. The venue closed in 1976 and the building was destroyed by fire in 1979.

When on the road without Sean, Sally did her best to stay in touch with him. Her letters were usually several pages long and full of pleas to study, help around the house and yard, spend time with his grandmother, and "please, please" write more about what was going on in his life.

She wrote to him from Pheasant Run on September 22, 1966, just after he had driven home from Illinois in his new white Mustang, peppering him with questions. She expressed her hopes for him while proposing a schedule he should follow and waxing sentimental about the meaning and importance of "home," before launching into what she felt Sean should contribute as he approached adulthood:

> Sean has been a "little boy" till now and we all served him so he would grow tall and strong and self-sufficient.
>
> Now, all the love, and food and vitamins and good diet and good doctors and care and watching and nursing and laundry and books and planning and praying have resulted in you — our tall, strong, beautiful man.
>
> Still a little wobbly like a young colt, not really sure about many things, but pretending (in a loud voice) to be....
>
> Beds have to be made every day, dishes washed, teeth washed, body bathed, clean clothes — and grass, weeds, flowers, leaves, puppies, babies, all grow every day — also boys into men....
>
> Make this contribution lovingly, cheerfully, faithfully. It is a priceless contribution to Home.
>
> Please believe me — a million dollars will never make you as happy as working for something and/or someone you love — and I think you are beginning to understand this now. So I will give you $10.00 a week allowance for gas, dates, and misc. so you will have time to study, and keep up on your athletics program without too much sweat.
>
> In return for which I expect (1) Good grades (2) lawn, hedge, roses, gardening patio well done all the time (3) Tender Loving Care for Mom (4) a letter a week to me typed with news, plus your report cards (I saw none last year) (5) regular dental appointments kept (6) regular doctor appointments for anti-tetanus booster, polio and complete physical. This is simply assuming adult responsibility. O.K.?

Remember darling, you are not doing these things for $10.00 a week.
You are doing them with and for love — and starting to assume
your adult male responsibility to home and family and society.

Indeed, Sean well remembers how loving his mother was, and how hard
she tried to be the best mother she could be:

> She would tell me that she was 44 years older than me, that she
> was old enough to be the parent of my friend's mom and dad. She
> would tell me, "The devil will never tempt you beyond what you
> can withstand. If Jesus is with you, who can be against you?"

Nearly a year later on September 14, 1967, Sally wrote again, with a handwritten note at the top: "This is not a lecture." Then followed a seven-page,
single-spaced, typewritten homily revealing her parenting style and her deep
devotion to her teenage son, in which Sally made detailed observations about
the difficulties — for both a 63-year-old parent and a 19-year-old child — of
transitioning to adulthood, concluding with:

> *You really are growing up when you understand that parents*
> *have felt just the way you do. I don't really ever want to make*
> *decisions for you, and I don't think I ever really have tried,*
> *though at times I have felt very strongly. I have said how I felt,*
> *but I haven't tried to force you to feel that way. I have tried to*
> *place seeds in your mind and have set certain examples for you*
> *— especially as concerns ethics, fundamental honesty, respect*
> *for other people's possessions, courtesy to others, a belief in God*
> *— but, in attempting to teach you these things which I want you*
> *to hold and have forever, I have tried not to just give them lip*
> *service, but to act upon them as well, and hoped that you would*
> *be discerning enough to see that behavior in this fashion works*
> *out to well-being, happiness, and good.*
>
> *I do understand that pushing out of the nest and breaking the*
> *umbilical cord and trying wings on journeys that haven't yet*
> *been taken is difficult. It's a difficult time for the young, who are*
> *going through it; but have a little compassion for we adults too,*
> *because it's also hard on us because we love you so much.*
>
> *You are my dearest beloved. Every day of your life has been a*
> *happy and rewarding experience for me, and seeing you grow*
> *and mature is very stimulating and deeply rewarding. I have*
> *complete confidence in your intelligence, character and*
> *goodness, and if I prod you a little sometimes, it's only*
> *because I want you to be aware of it, too.*

Not quite 30 months later on March 27, 1970, the 21-year-old Sean and his high school sweetheart Linda Schessler would be married in Glendora. But, before he could get a marriage license, he had to meet with a judge to finally resolve the issue of his birth certificate. Apparently, Sally was anxious about it. As Sean explained:

> I went down to the courthouse in Pomona, California, to meet with a judge. My mother was with me but she waited in another room. The judge said, "This is a private conversation between you and me. You're 21 years old and you can say and do whatever you want. It's legal now. You don't need to be beholding to anybody. You can change your name."
>
> He went through the whole thing. "Just let me know right now what you want to do. Just tell me who you are." And we'd go back and forth. And I said, "I don't care what you say, I'm not accepting it." He said, "Well, we'll be here all day. You're stubborn, you're not going to give in and I'm just telling you what the legalities are — this is who you are." And he said, "Who do you want to be?" I said, "Who I am." He went through all these different names over the years since I'd been with her. "You don't have to keep these names."[12] And I said, "I'm Sean Rand — that's who I am." I went back out and she was all worried I'd say I was somebody else, but I said, "I'm the same guy that went in."

And so the issue was resolved. Sean finally had a birth certificate stating that his mother was "Helen Gould Beck d/b/a Sally Rand." She was listed as the sole parent. All other records were wiped out. Sean never met his birth mother and never wanted to discuss it again, telling the judge: "Button your lip, throw the key away."[13]

Sean and Linda settled down to establish a home, attending local events with Sally whenever possible. When Linda became pregnant with Shawna, their first child, Sally proudly began billing herself as a grandmother.[14]

---

[12] Apparently, Sean could have chosen to go by the name Robert Hepler (his birth name) or Robert or Sean Lalla, Sean Beck, Sean Kisling, or possibly even the ethnically incongruous "Sean Finkelstein."

[13] Efforts were made to secure Imogene (Hepler) Gibson's version of the details surrounding Sean's adoption, but she and her family have chosen not to reply.

[14] Sally had two other grandchildren — a grandson named Gregory, and a granddaughter named Lindsey whom she never met.

In a 2012 interview, Sean was asked: "What did you like most about her?" He was quick to answer: "Well, obviously, the caring part of being a mother. She would do anything and everything to help you and better you." He especially remembered something Sally often said:

> She asked me "Who do you know that's had more experience in the world than me? You're not going to run into anybody who's had as many experiences as I've had." She said "Use me. Read me like a book." She would teach me all these little things that would guide you — get you through life. She would just say "you can rely on me and whenever you're in doubt you can ask questions. Never be afraid to ask questions; that's how you learn."

As far as Sean is concerned, "Helen Gould Beck d/b/a Sally Rand" is all the mother he ever wanted or needed. He knew he was loved. One memory stands out for him:

> She told me right from birth that I was adopted — went through the whole thing. She said, "Other people have babies and they get what they get." And then she told me, "You're special because you were chosen." She did all kinds of things so I wouldn't feel inferior because I was adopted.

> One time— it must have been in the early '70s — I was taking her to the airport to drop her off and when I came back to the car after taking her to the plane, I saw a paper bag there and I opened it up. There was a little poem, printed on a little scroll of felt-like material, and it had little psychedelic flowers. It said:

>> Not flesh of my flesh, Nor bone of my bone,
>> But still miraculously my own.
>> Never forget for a single minute,
>> You didn't grow under my heart –
>> But in it.

> She got out of the car and never said a word to me. After she left and I got back in the car, I thought she had forgotten something, so I opened the bag. I read the scroll and I knew she meant to leave it for me.

CHAPTER TWENTY-TWO

Sally in Lallaland

The trouble with some women is they get all excited
about nothing — and then they marry him.
~ Cher

By 1952 Jack Benny had come a long way since appearing with Faith
Bacon in *Earl Carroll's Vanities of 1930*. He was now the star of the most
popular program on network radio. Among the many running gags on *The
Jack Benny Program* was one about a song Jack had written, "When you say I
beg your pardon, then I'll come back to you." The gag reached its zenith on
the March 2nd broadcast when it was sung by the all-star guest vocal group
of Frank Sinatra, George Burns, Groucho Marx and Danny Kaye. That same
program featured a segment with this repartee between Jack, Dennis Day,
and Phil Harris:

Jack: Now, Dennis stop being silly and answer me. Are you
        having a good time?

Dennis: I'll say. Friday night I went to the Chi Chi and saw Sally
        Rand. I never laughed so hard in all my life.

(*pause*)

Jack: (*to Don Wilson*) You know, Don, the weather here has
        been so beautiful today, I think I may . . .

Phil: (*interrupting*) Wait a minute, wait a minute. Hold it. Let's
        go back here a minute. Look, uh . . .

Jack: Hmm?

Phil: Didn't you listen to what this kid just said?

Jack: I listened to it, heard it and ignored it.

Phil: Well, I ain't gonna ignore it. Dennis, you went to the Chi
        Chi and saw Sally Rand's act?

Dennis: Uh-huh.

Phil: *The* Sally Rand?

Dennis: Uh-huh.

Phil: And when you finally saw Sally Rand's act, you laughed?

Dennis: Yeah — I was sittin' up so close those fans tickled.

The "Friday night" Dennis Day referred to was Friday, February 29, 1952, when Sally Rand and her "Star Studded Revue" opened a four-week engagement before a "standing-room only crowd" at the Chi Chi Starlite Room in Palm Springs. Her supporting cast included the "amusing dancing comedian" Willie Shore (an old acquaintance from her Chicago days), as well as comic violinist Edith Dahl. The club's impresario, Irwin Schuman, was taking a risk by also booking such striptease artists as Gypsy Rose Lee, Tempest Storm, and Lili St. Cyr. (In fact, Schuman had once paid a fine of $500 after Sally allegedly performed her fan dance in the nude.)

The extended gig at the Starlite Room was just what Sally was looking for. At age 48, though still quite beautiful, she was no longer a young woman, and fewer, longer engagements meant less travel, less wear and tear, and, presumably, fewer hassles. So, while she would continue to travel, appearing in clubs and theaters and at state fairs in the U.S., Canada and even the Territory of Hawaii, her fortunes were mostly back in her own hands, not in those of a carnival operator or personal manager.

Faith

"Slowly she raises her eyes and looks at you, you, and even you — and says ... nothing." So was gossip columnist Walter Winchell quoted in an advertisement touting an appearance by the dancer he had called "the most mysterious beauty of all." The date was February 21, 1952, and the venue was the Park Burlesque in Youngstown, Ohio. Faith Bacon — billed as the "world's most sensational dancer, star of 7 Broadway hits and 3 World's Fairs" — was engaged for the "first time ever to play a burlesque theatre."

Sally may no longer have been a young woman, but neither was her closest rival. Even so, after nearly 20 years of playing second feather to Sally Rand, Faith was still in demand, at least on the burlesque theater circuit. Still, that summer, Faith reportedly suffered a nervous breakdown, spending two months in the hospital.

By September, she found refuge at the home of a former lover, wealthy book and art collector, Thomas Edward Hanley. Her access to him had been somewhat restricted since his marriage to the former Tullah Innes on Christmas Day of 1948, yet Edward and Tullah had welcomed her into their home.

Thin and listless, Faith was put up in a studio above the couple's garage, to which Edward had ready access. One might presume that his wife would be jealous of any attention he paid to Faith, but Tullah was extremely liberal about her own sexuality and seemed to pity the barbiturate-addicted Faith more than envy her. Over a period of weeks, Faith rested, gained some weight, and got back to a semblance of her former self.

Through her own agent, Tullah managed to arrange some new bookings for Faith, beginning with an appearance in Buffalo, New York. But it didn't go well. According to Tullah: "Agents feared her … Faith does not keep her jobs, is unreliable, is often drugged while on stage, and nonchalantly removes all her garments. The clubs fear being closed for obscene exhibition."

R eviewing Sally's October 1952 engagement at the Texas State Fair, *Billboard* magazine observed: "Despite all the tub thumping being given the Sally Rand show and the Parisian Follies revue, Dick Best's Four-Legged Girl, Betty Lou Williams, is making a surprisingly strong bid for top honors among the money-getting shows."

This was a time when "freak shows" were not yet regarded as politically incorrect. The youngest of twelve children, Betty Lou Williams was born in Albany, Georgia on January 10, 1932, with a parasitic sibling. (Most of Betty Lou's not-fully-formed twin was embedded in her abdomen, but the undeveloped legs protruded into view from her side.) From the age of one, she had been on display as the "four-legged girl." Her show made big money at the 1934 Chicago World's Fair, where she was featured in Robert Ripley's "Odditorium," just a short walk from Sally's show at the Italian Village.

Although drawing big crowds, Sally's tax issues had become so severe that on October 6th the IRS filed a lien against her for unpaid taxes of $17,064.45. The next day, Midway operator Ray Marsh Brydon advanced $2,500 to avoid attachment of her show properties.[1] A week later on "Negro Day," Sally lent her tent to Leon Claxton and made appearances in all 12 performances of his *Harlem in Havana*, to what *Billboard* described as "tremendous business."

O n December 28, 1952, Sally was the "mystery challenger" on *What's My Line*, the popular television program with host John Charles Daly and panelists Dorothy Kilgallen, Bennett Cerf, Arlene Francis, and Robert Q. Lewis. When the blindfolded Bennett Cerf asked: "Are you a lady?" — Sally

---

[1]   One columnist observed: "Sally, the fan dancer, is in trouble with the Bureau of Internal Revenue, obviously for taking off too much."

responded coyly: "Well . . . a lady you said? Well, that has been questioned upon occasion, but I'm of the feminine gender." Sally's appearance was nothing short of a total delight. In truth, you should put down this book right now, go straight to your computer, and watch the segment on YouTube.[2]

On New Year's Eve, playing a long way from home at the Holiday Theater on Broadway, she wrote in her diary: "This is the last hour of the year. I will never spend another one away from my baby and mother." And even though 25 years had passed since the young Navy pilot had declared his love for her, Sally wistfully included the notations "Jimmie" and "1927."

In 1953, Sally crisscrossed the continent, logging many miles — from her week in February at the Beaver Club in Montreal, Quebec, to her summer stint at the "49th State Fair" in Honolulu. The Hawaii trip took place in the midst of serious upheaval in her life. In a letter to her Key West, Florida, attorney, Allan Cleare, she wrote:

> *At long last — I have just returned from the Pacific.*
>
> *Seven members of my family were lost in a plane crash in Alaska — my mother has been with the bereaved family. My uncle, left at home to take care of the mail and things, had a heart attack, and is still hospitalized. My secretary [Anita Robertson] had to be sent home from the Pacific with T.B. — and is now in a sanitarium in Lawton, Oklahoma.*
>
> *Therefore, my life and my affairs are in a mess at the moment.*

Sally continued to speak at business luncheons and also to stir up controversy, particularly among members of the Catholic hierarchy. In September, Bishop Joseph Willging called upon good Catholics to boycott the Colorado State Fair in Pueblo because of Sally's allegedly "lewd" show (which he acknowledged he had never seen). Fair manager William Kittle and several Catholic girls in the show protested his protest, but the good bishop was unmoved. A baton-twirling performance by children from the Sacred Heart Orphanage was canceled simply because the venue was too close to Sally's revue.

Back in Glendora to celebrate the holidays with her family, Sally met a much younger man named Frederick J. Lalla, a Los Angeles area plastering contractor whom she quickly sized up as a possible new love interest. Telling one reporter that she had met him at a church service around

---

[2] Four years later (March 12, 1957), Sally appeared as "Helen Beck" on *To Tell the Truth*.

Christmastime of 1953, she didn't say whether Fred had disclosed that he was married with three children. Yes, he was a married man, but this circumstance had never proved much of an obstacle in the past. At the time, Sally was 50 years old and Fred was 30.

Fred's first letter to Sally — dated January 8, 1954, and written on her personal stationary — indicates how far their relationship had come in a short time. Fred was separated from his wife, Mae, and was apparently living at Sally's home in Glendora while she was on the road. He wrote that he had been trying to sell a house but had failed because the realtor had turned out to be a "jerk," telling Sally that he had been forced to restrain himself "from breaking this guy up." He repeated over and over how much he loved her, starting with:

> I love you, Honey. I know that's not such a good way to start a
> letter but, that's the way I felt when I set down to write this
> letter.... All the plans I am making for us are just about complete.
> All they need are a few finishing touches, which only you can do.

After another declaration of undying love, he signed off with his somewhat incongruous pet name:

> Remember Pop's is waiting home for you. Until that day My Love,
> may God bless you & protect you, for I love you with all my heart
> & passions. And I will until the end of time. Your Pop's

He even added a "poem" of sorts, beginning:

> As I am writing this Letter, I am so alone & so blue
> I know it's because, I am thinking of you.
> The wonderful thing's, we both seem to create,
> I know it's because, you're my perfect mate.

(The reader will be spared anything further.)

Two weeks later, Fred wrote again, beginning with how blue he was, how he was missing his darling, and continuing:

> Baby, if only you were here now I'd say some real juicy things to you
> like, kissing your neck, and around your nipples and such wonder-
> ful nipples, ohhhh. I'd squeeze you oh so very tight, my Love, I'd
> take your beautiful face into my hands and kiss you so tenderly, so
> juicy, and I might even stroke your round bottom so gently, by that
> time my Love, we'd be out of this world, and into one of our own
> special. Eh???? Gotta stop talking like this Baby, you know???

A couple of weeks later, in a letter obviously written in response to concerns Sally had about the disparity in their ages, Fred reassured her: "The difference in our ages like you said is all on our side." Apart from finding it an asset that Sally "knows her own mind, excepts [*sic*] the facts truthfully and honestly, and knows right from wrong," Fred expressed relief that he didn't "have to worry about [Sally] chasing men and taking [someone] out every nite." Confessing he was comfortable with the fact that she knew "how to make a man happy," he gushed: "I am so at ease when I am with you ... when young girls haven't the slightest idea what even makes the world go around." He went on to express his frustrations with his wife, Mae:

> I've been going through this hassle practically since we were married. Honey believe me, I've layed [*sic*] awake at nites trying to figure out how just plain how to make my wife happy & satisfied, how to make her understand the Beautiful Love and Companionship, we should enjoy. But as I now realize, she was just too young. Our ages? Baby I'd never have it any other way. I'd never marry a young gal again.

Looking for a way out of his marriage, Fred had developed a plan to prove that Mae was cheating on him:

> Baby I've been watching, even had a witness with me, no dice as yet. Just hugging — I guess they do their screwing in the car. I've contacted the Welfare Board — they said to just phone when the things go on and they would come right out to witness. Yes, my Darling, I am working on this. You know how badly I want the children. But, if worse comes to worse, and I don't get them, Honey, I can't just crawl in a hole and die....

Sally may have been infatuated with Fred, but she was also fully aware of his shortcomings and the conflicts he felt as a result of leaving his family. On February 27, 1954, she wrote two letters to him from Lowell, Massachusetts, apparently intended to occupy the same envelope. The letters were handwritten, so it is not known whether they were typed and sent, edited and sent, or even sent at all. Both drafts say "7 AM" at the top:

> *We have just finished our long talk — $60.00 dollars' worth.*

> *The tension has been mounting every day since I spoke to you in the booth at Lowell.... I have had this awful <u>premonition</u> that something awful was going to happen. I started to call you a dozen times last week and didn't. I was too cowardly to face unpleasantness and I feared to hear things I didn't want to hear. And as long as I didn't really know, I could be happy — except*

I felt so uneasy. Finally, I had to call. I couldn't stand it any longer. But being so uneasy, I couldn't write <u>coherently</u> either.

So now we've talked. It really wasn't much of a talk. You are not a very <u>articulate</u> person at best. Actually, you just vaguely answered questions, and you answered me very reluctantly. None of the above is a "beef" nor am I criticizing you. I'm just commenting on "our talk." I knew no more after I finished talking with you than I did before. My premonitions and uneasiness about your sentiments for me, and the seriousness and sureness of your plans for our future, were verified — that's all. I don't know what's happened, how you feel, what you have been doing or expect to do.

But there's one thing I do know — <u>indubitably</u> — No one — not you, nor me, nor anyone can have their cake and eat it too.

Also, no man can serve two masters.

Also, there is no compromise between right and wrong. You can't fool God even if you kid yourself along.

Either your marriage with Mae is a Holy Sacrament fulfilled with honor and dignity — or it isn't. Either it is a human relationship you wish to continue — or it isn't. It's just that simple and this must be decided upon, by you, once and for all, irrevocably, before you have the right to even think of loving anyone else, let alone involving someone else in what must be a heartbreaking experience.[3]

It is dishonorable, dishonest and degrading — and belittles the depth and sincerity of all your emotions to vacillate back and forth. It just isn't something you change your mind about. What I mean is — Once you have reached a point of decision — and this decision concerns the very roots of your being, your life and four (five) other people's lives.

---

[3] Distressed over the situation with Fred's wife (whom she disparaged as "this strange ... boyish bitch — you lie beside"), Sally had a habit of scribbling notes on a legal pad before making what she knew would be an emotional phone call. A barely legible example follows: "Hi — it's me — you know [how] drunk I am, and have to be to call you — to importune — to scathe & rake you — warm & close & naked — beside that little bag you call your wife. Wife is it? Is it a woman? Our son (he's such a beautiful young male) has greater chest than this wench — and isn't this the nightmare that you screamed and wrestled in our bed? You have her now. Enjoy it — if you can.... Are you bewitched?"

Now, you may ask, why were certain words oddly underlined? In her second letter, Sally added a bit of instruction for Fred:

> *Each word I write and underline with "red" I want you to look up in the dictionary, and write the dictionary definition of the word that applies to the way I have used it. I am not being "smarty pants" or superior but I find it difficult to express myself adequately in the limited and immature vocabulary you employ. I shall also send you a list of words that you have misspelled in your letters. Study them for I shall ask questions and I expect you to have the right answers. It is incredible to me that you have been exposed to a 7th Grade Grammer [sic] School education and spell so poorly, [are] so inarticulate and have so limited a vocabulary. We are down to fundamentals now, my love; being merely emotionally stirred about each other will not produce, for us, a happy life together, nor lasting happiness.*

Sally pointed out that, since she had only completed half of her sophomore year in high school, he actually had more education than she did, adding:

> *If I can do it, you can do it. One of my marriages was wrecked because my husband felt inferior to me for lack of education. I don't want to be married to a man who feels that I can top him at anything. Furthermore, I need a complete intellectual companionship with the guy I sleep with. This presumes a similarity of intellectual development which has nothing to do with age, but has to do with growth, mental alertness and a continuing, never-ending mental and intellectual curiosity and hunger. If you and I do get married, make up your mind (it's one of the conditions) I am going to high school and college and you are going right along with me. And not only keep up with me, top me!*

> *There are more kinds of adultery than just laying someone else. If I married you, and enjoyed you as a bedmate, and let you assume responsibility of me and my son, and then had to seek elsewhere for my intellectual companionship (I don't mean in another person) in books, music, religion, etc. pretending and deceiving you meanwhile that our partnership was complete, in my opinion I would be as guilty of deceiving you as if I laid with another man.*

> *Thinking and analyzing is one of the things that people hate to do the most. It requires self-discipline and concentration,*

which most people hate with a passion. They would much rather daydream and smugly resign themselves to their unfair Fate. All in the world that you have to do to be a success is first, think, [get] the accurate facts, achieve a premise, analyze the contributing factors, arrive at a conclusion and then, dammit, get off your lazy ass and act.

Lalla, I'm not saying you are lazy. To the contrary, I think you keep busy as hell and try hard and are sincere. But just being physically busy isn't the same — ditch diggers and garbage collectors work like bastards, but the rewards of their labors are not very spiritually rewarding. And not very financially rewarding. The work they do is honest and respectable and I'm all for it if that's as far as they can mentally reach, but if they daydream of being executives, writers, lawyers, or doctors, and then don't do anything about it, I have no patience with their "beef" with what life hands them.

I don't propose to let "life" hand me anything — I am going to research, prod, dig and achieve out of life what I want, it's all there. All I have to do is pitch in and get it. If a garbage collector dreams of being a great atomic physicist he can use the money he earns to continue his education — night school, extension courses, home study.

Sally then went on to detail all the subjects a garbage collector would need to study, plus all the things he would have to sacrifice, to achieve his goals, concluding: "So it's just a matter of what you really want." Reminiscent of her attempts to get Turk to improve himself (and Carl Schlaet's prodding of her 25 years earlier), Sally couldn't resist some none-too-subtle chiding:

You have available at this moment a typewriter & 3 books that will teach you typewriting if you will practice the exercises they tell you. Ten-year-old children learn to be expert typists so why can't you? There are 5 books on grammer [sic] for adults, and 3 on increasing your vocabulary. You haven't even looked at them — the books in my house are sufficient to give anyone a good education — you live with them every day. But for all you know of them they might as well be on the bookstore shelf. You've never even explored them.

You want to be a singer? You love music. You want to play the guitar?

Read and study "Good American Speech" by Margaret
Prendergast McLean. You have to speak well enough to be
understood before you can sing. You have to understand the
box your voice comes out of before you can produce it! It's all
there. You only have to remember 8 different notes on the piano
to read music – and you can't sing unless you can read music.
You want to play the guitar, you have to know those 8 notes.

The piano is there. I showed you the 8 notes (I'll make a chart
for you again — it's enclosed) — learn them — you have to
learn them first. Do it! Stop dreaming about it.

It might interest you to know that Nettie played the guitar.
She traded her guitar for my brother's baby carriage.

Looking back over communications between Sally and her three husbands,
it is impossible to ignore the inarticulate and immature nature of Fred's
letters, not to mention Harry Finkelstein's many shortcomings, and Turk
Greenough's disinterest in expressing himself verbally. One can hardly
fail to be struck by how intellectually vacuous each of the men Sally chose
to marry seemed to be compared to her suitors of earlier days. Indeed,
each of her husbands seems an odd choice for a woman who was so
proud of her own hard-won language skills, morals, and work ethic.

The antagonistic tone Sally sometimes struck in writing to these men —
chiding and didactic (and sometimes mean-spirited) — comes through loud
and clear. What's the explanation? Maybe she could only feel fully comfortable when she could see herself as the superior partner in her relationships
— always the teacher, never the student. If true, this may have sown the
seeds of their ultimate failure.

Even so, Sally could be more mellow, less judgmental, from thousands of
miles away on the road. Consider this March 8th letter to Fred, sent from a
club in Corning, New York, that she had handwritten to her "Darling Pops"
on the back of several table order blanks for "Taylor's, the Finest Name in
Wines and Champagnes":

I love you — I wish I had other ways to say it — I mean it so
deeply and these words anyone can say. You see why I can't
stand these goodbyes and off and on — it tears me to pieces.

I want to be married to you, and sleep in our own big bed, and
do things together. There are so many things I want to do with
you — dance, swim, read, talk, play music, go to Hawaii, raise
Sean and sleep and love and eat breakfast — and live.

Dearest, your letter, the one you left for me, is the dearest and most deeply cherished of my possessions — How I adore you for writing it.... Thank you dearest for my beautiful engagement ring. I will wear it round my neck till you are free and I can wear it on my finger with dignity.

Dearest Love, don't worry about the drinking business. I never drank as much in my whole life as I did the days you were here —just because I was excited and happy. But you and I both know that Lalla's girl and Lalla's future wife could never be a one to drink too much or get tight — and neither could Sean's mommy. So put your mind at ease and your heart at rest — it will never happen.

Also, as to the language and four letter words, I know how totally unbecoming the bad language is, and I apologize for acquiring such an ugly habit — there is no excuse for it and I'm very wrong. So I shall cease this ugly bad habit and there will be no more of it....

All my love

Your Mrs. Pops

Or this one, written a couple of days later on stationery from The Baron Steuben Hotel:

The breakfast will be up any minute now — and I wish you were too — (up that is) Joke! You see how crazy I am in the morning? Hi, Ho, I love you. And if you were here, I'd give you a tight hug, a big kiss, and a savage scrunch-turnover, put my cold fanny next to your warm tummy & go back to sleep. ... One of the reasons I want you to type accurately and fast is so you can help me write my book — this way we can do it together instead of me spending hours away from you.

Faith

On March 1, 1954, as things were heating up for Fred and Sally in Glendora, a woman named Frances Verdier was found by her friend, a female musician, lying unconscious on the floor of her Hammond, Indiana, dance studio. Firemen administered oxygen and the young woman was later revived. Treated at St. Margaret's Hospital for an overdose of sleeping pills, she was released the following day.

This would all be unremarkable save for the fact that "Frances Verdier" was actually the "former fan dancer Faith Bacon, who now operates a ballet studio." She told investigators that she had accidentally taken too many of the pills prescribed for her chronic insomnia.

While Sally was on her way to a successful run in Las Vegas, Faith seemed to be headed in the opposite direction. The date is unknown, but at some point after this incident she married Sanford Dickinson, a film "music consultant" 23 years her senior.[4] Some suggested that she married him only to counter persistent rumors that she was a lesbian.

B y May 1954, Sally was in Las Vegas performing at the Silver Slipper. There followed a record-breaking 32 weeks at the Last Frontier Hotel. As her career was flourishing, the outgoing Miss Rand was becoming acquainted with a long roster of celebrated performers. On one occasion she filled in for Forrest Duke, writer of the popular "Visiting Fireman" column in the *Las Vegas Review-Journal*, offering her book and local entertainment recommendations. Excerpts provide a taste of what her life in Vegas must have been like:

> As a rule when any of my friends are in the hospital I get them a copy of "Fun in Bed." A book designed to keep one cheerful and in possession of his sense of humor, despite hospital routine. I shall now abandon "Fun in Bed," (Book-wise that is) for Ernie Kovacs' "Zoomar." By far the most hilarious tome I've read for many a moon. The Detroit Times has this to say of it and I quote, "Good fun. Not good clean fun, mind you — but good fun...."

> Last night Jan Rubini, one of this country's better violinists and his son Michel, a fabulous concert pianist, came backstage to visit with me after seeing the Slipper show.[5] Such nostalgia! Jan, a concert violinist ... back in those dear dead days when theatres had 60-piece orchestras and Fanchon and Marco ... made television spectaculars look like dancing school recitals. Jan and Michel are just returning from a concert tour with Michel accompanying his famous Dad. What a fabulous boy! Tall, dark and handsome.

---

4   Dickinson was the music consultant on such Z-grade films as Ed Wood's cult classic *Glen or Glenda*, as well as *Merry Maids of the Gay Way* and *'B' Girl Rhapsody*.

5   Michel Rubini, a professional classical pianist and composer, had a hand in composing soundtrack music for many movies and television shows in the 1980s and 1990s, including *The Hunger* with Catherine Deneuve and two episodes of the HBO *Tales from the Crypt* series. He was a producer, conductor and arranger for Motown Records and also toured with such stars as Ray Charles, Sonny and Cher, and Barbra Streisand.

Seventeenish and a positive genius on the ivorys. I asked him to play for me. We went out into the darkened showroom between shows. He played Debussy, and the obscure Chopin E Minor Nocturne Opus 17, and thence into a Rock & Roll boogie beat and wound up with some way-out-yonder modern jazz.

Two little dancers rehearsing on the stage crept down the stairs to sit chin on hand, enchanted. The cocktail waitress forgot to set up the room and silently listened in the front row. A couple of shills and a dealer or two, hearing the strange music, stopped in and stood transfixed. A proud father and a completely charmed Fan Dancer comprised the balance of this strangest of all audiences....

To the Sands to hear Sinatra.... One reads a lot of razzle dazzle stories ... of why he behaves like Frank Sinatra. It's my private opinion that most of this drivel is so much malarkey, paid for by the word. As far as I'm concerned he sings a helluva song, doesn't sit in his wardrobe (no wrinkles in his trousers), and gives a completely perfect performance.... In my opinion there is only room in the theatre for this kind of perfection. Maybe I'm naive but I still believe that when John Public pays his admission and buys a ticket he has a right to see a perfect performance by professionals.

I have met Mr. Sinatra ... casually a couple of times, as people who are in the same profession do. He has no reason to remember me particularly or to go out of his way to be cordial or hospitable. Several nights later I went to the Sands for breakfast with a couple of members of the Slipper cast. Mr. Sinatra was hosting a small group of friends in the lounge. It was very gracious of him to ask us to join him and his friends....

That pretty doll with dimples, Candy Barr, was in tonight. We're so glad this lovely one is out of the hospital[6] and back to work at the Largo in Los Angeles....

I stay here for months for much less money than I get other places. Frankly, I get lonesome for show business and for contacts with other actors.... In Las Vegas, sooner or later every actor I've ever known and worked with (if they are still alive) is bound to show up....

---

[6] The beautiful exotic dancer had been hospitalized as a result of a ruptured tubal pregnancy. About this time she also began a relationship with mobster Mickey Cohen, one of a group of men who contributed to the dark side of Las Vegas's reputation.

The first time I played in Las Vegas was in 1942 (maybe it was
41).... In the spring of 1954 I came up to visit ... my old friend
Eddie Fox and talked myself into a job at the Slipper where I stayed
for almost a year. I have been honored by being asked back nearly
once a year since then and look what's happened ... Las Vegas has
grown from a neon lit country town to a real metropolis and has
stolen New York's thunder to become the mecca of show business.

Besides moonlighting as a columnist in 1954, Sally was also hosting *Let's
Visit*, a half-hour show on KLAS-TV — the only television station in Las
Vegas — featuring Sally's interviews with celebrities plus her commentary
on books, music and the home.[7] You might think that all of this would have
finally given her a long-sought and well-earned sense of security, but it was
slow in coming.

Sally's diary entries during the month of May expose the roller coaster ride
she was on with the much younger (and still married) Fred Lalla:

May 9:   This is one of the worst days I've ever had — Mother's Day
           — a farce — my own baby not here.

May 24:   1st TV show with [Xavier] Cugat and Abby Lane....
           Turned out well. He's gone. I don't believe it.

May 25:   Didn't want to come home but he just might be here —
           but no. This is too horrible ... the numbness of shock is
           over and I hurt too much.

May 26:   Another day, no Lalla. No word, can't sleep. This is too
           horrible. He called.

May 28:   Pappa came home this morning — nothing matters, he's here.

May 29:   This is a good day — the best day we've ever had. We lived.

By 1954, TV had supplanted radio as America's favorite home entertainment. The Tournament of Roses Parade was the subject of the first
national color television broadcast in January of that year. Staring transfixed
before the television screen had become so common that many viewers were
leaving the traditional family dinner table to camp out in front of their sets
and consume a Swanson "TV dinner" on a collapsible table while watching
such popular programs as *I Love Lucy*, *The Jackie Gleason Show*, and *You Bet
Your Life* with Groucho Marx. On April 12th, a little known band calling

---

7   Three years earlier, Sally had tried her hand at the innovative medium, working with
     KPRC-TV in Houston, Texas.

themselves "Bill Haley and his Comets" recorded a catchy tune titled "Rock Around the Clock." In 1955, the wildly creative rhythm and blues singer Chuck Berry would record "Maybellene," and the world of popular music would be changed forever. A paradigm-shifting revolution in popular culture was taking the country by storm.

Into this mix would come a brash new gossip and exposé magazine called *Confidential*, "the most terrifying force ever to hit Hollywood." Tossing aside prior norms of journalistic restraint, the uninhibited publication's logo promised that the magazine: "Tells the Facts and Names the Names." First published in December 1952, within a few years the scandal sheet would claim a monthly circulation of more than 4 million readers. The magazine's success was so pronounced it would soon spawn more than a dozen imitators with such titles as *Uncensored, Hush-Hush, The Lowdown* and *On the QT*.

Considering the nature of the life she had been leading, Sally could hardly have expected to escape the attention of such rags. In the June 1956 issue of *Whisper* (*Confidential's* sister publication), an article titled "SALLY RAND AND HER LALLA-POP" detailed her efforts to demonstrate that Fred's estranged wife was something less than a paragon of virtue. According to regular contributor Sam Schaeffer, Sally was very keen to help Fred obtain custody of his three children.

Having learned that Fred's wife was having a fling with a co-worker at the Los Angeles box factory where she worked, Sally had hired private investigators to surveil them. On the night of July 1, 1954, the detectives had followed Mrs. Lalla and her companion back to her residence on Crestmoore Place in Glendale and observed them entering her home, later noting that "the California sun was high the next morning before the pair emerged." The next two evenings, Mae's behavior was similarly documented.

On the 4th of July, concealed in a strategic spot, Fred himself observed the couple through binoculars. They were "swinging in the kid's swing in the backyard and kissing like young lovers." He waited. At 3:30 in the morning, he entered the home along with a photographer and a pair of private investigators to confront his wife and her lover. Finding this behavior to be somewhat ironic from a man who was "cozy" with Sally Rand in Las Vegas, Mae ran into the bedroom and returned with a gun. Waving it around, she picked up the phone and called the police, demanding that they "come and arrest the whole pack."

Once on the scene, the officers confirmed that Fred, as the legal owner of the house, had a right to be there. Declining to make any arrests, the officers did advise the two "gumshoes" and photographer to depart the premises for the general good of the neighborhood, which they proceeded to do, leaving behind "a mess of flashbulbs on the living room rug."

At barely 30, Mae Lalla was young enough to be Sally's daughter. She was described in the press as "a shapely brunette and mother of three children ranging in age from two to nine." On July 8th, just four days after she had been more or less ambushed by Fred and company in their home, Mae obtained an interlocutory decree of divorce in the State of California. The court also denied Fred custody of the children and, according to Schaeffer, Sally was so upset by the denial that she refused to hand over the $900 balance of the $1,200 she had originally offered the private investigators.

In any case, Sally's professional life had settled down somewhat, and she was once again ready for her personal life to do the same.

O n August 12, 1954, between performances at the Last Frontier Hotel in Las Vegas, Sally and Fred Lalla were married in the hotel chapel. Both parties listed their ages on the marriage license as "over 21." The previous day had been momentous for each of them: Fred had obtained his own divorce in Las Vegas, while in Los Angeles Sally was being served a summons relating to a 14-year-old debt that had grown to $8,000 (about $70,000 today).

The upshot of Fred's divorce was less agreeable than he had hoped. The legal standing of his quickie Nevada divorce meant that it would be almost 11 months before Sally's marriage to Fred would be recognized in California. On the same day that the nuptials were announced in all the papers, Mae was quoted in a news interview threatening to charge Fred with bigamy if he failed to pay her court-ordered alimony and child support or made any effort to take their children: "I won't seek a bigamy complaint against Freddie Boy unless he tries to take our three babies away from me."

Mae charged that Fred had been living with Sally for some time (which he denied). Sally asked Mae if the children could come to Las Vegas to visit their father. Mae rejected her plea: "I thought that was a lot of nerve," she scoffed, "and I didn't allow it." As for the happy couple's "honeymoon"? Just as she had done with Turk Greenough, Sally repaired directly to her dressing room after the ceremony to get ready for her evening performance.

Once again, Sally had trod the bridal path, ever optimistic that marital bliss was within her reach. Among the congratulatory missives was a telegram from her longtime lawyer, Abe Berman: "DEAR SALLY: CONGRATULATIONS. I HOPE THIS IS IT. YOU DESERVE SOME HAPPINESS. LOVE ABE"

A mere four days into her new marriage, Sally and her show were on their way to Casper, Wyoming, for a five-day engagement at the Central Wyoming Fair and Rodeo. Typical of her struggles, the truck hauling her stage and props from Las Vegas was destroyed by a fire en route to the venue. According to *Billboard* magazine, despite the adversity, somehow "a new layout was improvised ... and the show opened on time to strong business." The Wyoming event broke all previous attendance records and the gross take was up by 22 percent over the year before.

Back home in Vegas, the newlyweds resumed a life of marital harmony. Well, sort of. Less than two weeks after the wedding, Sally's diary included such entries as:

> August 24: Lalla home in time for dinner — brought presents of glass and dishes — tired and angry.
>
> August 26: Lalla in a tantrum this morning.

By September 18th, things were looking more hopeful. Sally wrote in her diary: "This day a wonderful day in God's heart. All is well. We love and are loved.... Pray we'll always be as one."

Three days later Fred and Sally wrote a joint letter to his parents. The hand-written draft reveals their tenuous hopes for the future (with echoes of Sally's prior attempts to make a family with Turk's parents and siblings). Fred commenced:

> I have started this letter a thousand times.... Honest to God, we couldn't be any happier, for the first time, I have found true Godly spirit, in Love and God's ways.... Sure, Mom and Dad, I miss my children, sometimes I believe I can't stand it. But when I look to God for help and understanding, he's always there.... I am so grateful to him for giving me my wife Sally, threw [*sic*] her I find true contentment & happiness, such a wonderful wife, I could ever dream of.... Folks, the reason I haven't written sooner is because we wanted to find out if Sally was going to be held over again, also look around to kinda see how things would shape up. Well first off they signed Sally up again so we know we are going to be here for some time, in fact, we are going to make our home here.

Sally's new husband then included what may have been a bid to secure financial help from Mom and Dad Lalla, suggesting to his father that they go into business together because "building houses here looks real great." (Sally was looking into all kinds of business opportunities, taking Fred around to look at property.)

After sharing that he had been doing plastering work for $30 a day, Fred offered insight into their financial struggles a mere six weeks into their marriage:

> As you probably know, Sally works 7 nights a week, with no days off. I feel so sorry for her — poor kid hasn't had a day off since May 1. And to make it worse, Uncle Sam has held her wages since 7 weeks ago. So as you can tell it gets a little narrow at times on just my pay, trying to feed the other family in Los Angeles, too.

He signed his part of the letter, "Your kids, Sally and Fred." (At the time, Sally was a 50-year-old woman, so Fred's parents may not have been much older themselves.) Sally kept the ball rolling, adding over four pages in her familiar scrawl to outline her ambitious business plans for the family:

> *May I join Fred in extending an equally enthusiastic desire for you to come and be with us? I know you will love Nevada; Las Vegas is "Fabulous." Because the town is expanding so rapidly, the business opportunities are wonderful. There are really 4 lots available so we could build a house for you and a house for us — and an income building on the two center lots — the income from which would more than pay out the entire 4 lots, all the buildings and the taxes. You and Fred could then continue to build and sell for profit — or build and rent for income.*

> *I always like to have more than one thing going for me, so you could have the book bindery right at home. The lots are 165 x 150 — a separate workshop — or studio — Fred has his plastering. I can take an occasional dancing engagement and have a dancing school and costume shop.*

> *Sean is now 6 years old and in the first grade. I adopted him when he was 8 days old. It is especially necessary for an adopted child to feel the security of a permanent home and family — and the sure knowledge of his parents' love and nearness. For this reason, I must be home with him from now on — and must plan accordingly. Of course, on summer vacations we can all take to the road in our trailers like gypsys — and play the Middle West Fairs — and get home in time for school.*

> *I am so grateful to have Fred for a husband and father for Sean. I could not have dreamed that I could be so blessed.*

She then went on to bluntly discuss Fred's ex-wife, Mae:

> *I could not be happy, or live with myself, if being so was at*
> *the expense of someone else's happiness, home, and security,*
> *and depriving three little children of their father. Fred's*
> *marriage to Mae was destined for tragedy long before Fred*
> *even knew her. Mae's sad and sordid premarital experiences*
> *gave her an abnormal feeling of fear, disgust, hate and guilt*
> *for sex under any circumstances — together with a grim and*
> *vicious subconscious determination to make any and all men*
> *suffer, as punishment. Any normal impulse of love and*
> *warmth and natural sexual impulse was frozen by her early*
> *disgust.*

Since she had yet to meet Mae, Sally's depiction of her attitudes toward sex and men could only have come from Fred:

> *Mae really feels that "all men are alike. Since they are going to*
> *try to do it to you, do it to them first. Use them, get all you can,*
> *give nothing in return, use sex as a decoy, put out the honey to*
> *catch the flies. Promise everything, give nothing, now you can*
> *make them squirm and hurt. Get your revenge for all the*
> *things they did to you and all the other women in the world."*
> *The words of the marriage didn't — couldn't — change this*
> *hurt girl's attitude.*

Sally's fantasy of becoming a "stay-at-home mom" never really came to fruition. According to Sean:

> Actually in the 2nd grade, I went to school in Vegas, Glendora,
> Chicago, and Tampa, Florida, and then she got a tutoring permit
> and she tutored me. I did all that in the 2nd grade and then in the
> 3rd and 4th grade I was back in Glendora with my grandmother —
> they had a battle. She'd say that's no place for a kid — out on the
> road. So they brought me back out here and I went to a local
> military school in Glendora. In 3rd grade, 4th grade, 5th grade, and
> in the 6th grade, my mother took me back up to Vegas.

While she may have enjoyed a successful run in Las Vegas, Sally was once again in financial distress. Just a few weeks before the wedding, to satisfy an IRS claim of about $10,000 in unpaid taxes, two pieces of property she had bought in Key West, Florida, were auctioned off on the courthouse steps.

Maintenance of this property, purchased as an investment, had been problematic for Sally, as revealed in a letter to her Key West attorney some nine months earlier:

> *As concerns the North Beach house —*
>
> *What am I paying taxes for — if not for police and fire protection? How is it that a person's home can be entered and used by bums and tramps — and the police permit it?*
>
> *If the city should choose to tear my house down, I would sue them to the highest courts — for criminal negligence in not protecting my property, and for daring to destroy that which is mine —*
>
> *The house was [locked], boarded up, nailed, and otherwise protected — I have receipts from you and the carpenters — for this work….*

Sally advised her attorney that she would soon be flying to Key West ("I will bring the money with me for the taxes") to fix everything. She claimed she had bought "aluminum weather-board siding" and other supplies that she was arranging to have trucked in by carpenters who would then handle any needed repairs.

Whether or not any repairs were ever made on her Key West properties, Sally soon suffered another major blow. On October 13th, barely two months after her wedding, the newly minted Mrs. Frederick J. Lalla, was filing for bankruptcy in the United States District Court in Las Vegas.

"Wait a minute," you might say. "I thought Sally had already gone bankrupt." To be sure, Sally *had* filed for bankruptcy in San Francisco nearly 15 years to the day earlier. However, under the federal bankruptcy code, sufficient time had elapsed that she could once again seek to have her debts discharged. This time, the bulk of her $2,047,380 liability (over $18 million today) was attributable to a lawsuit brought against her by an Illinois corporation. In filing for bankruptcy protection, "Mrs. Lalla" claimed to have current assets in the amount of only $950 in cash, $750 in clothing and furniture, a $100 pony (for her son), and four used fans valued at $425. The details of her actual financial situation are unclear, but less than three weeks later a bankruptcy referee reportedly ruled that Sally was, in fact, bankrupt.

S tumbling blocks aside, the honeymoon afterglow continued for a while as evidenced by the affectionate letters between husband and wife that stretched into February 1955. Fred's poorly spelled, ungrammatical letters contained very little news but were full of expressions like "dearest beloved,"

Sally Rand in her dressing room with pictures of
Valya Valentinoff (note that the inscription reads:
"To my darling 'Helen' — I give all my love, Valya")

A photograph of Turk Greenough lassoing his little Sally —
part of a publicity campaign in the fall of 1941
announcing the couple's engagement

Turk and Sally's wedding day, January 6, 1942

Turk and Sally had been married for only 74 days when he was inducted into the Army and assigned to the Cavalry Division

Sally's "front" at the State Fair of Texas, Dallas (1951)

A scene from Leon Claxton's "Harlem in Havana,"
a show that toured state fairs from the 1930s to the 1960s

Sally marries Harry Finkelstein
in Toledo, Ohio on August 21, 1950

Harry and Sally at police headquarters after their arrest in
July 1950 for staging an indecent performance in Milwaukee

One-year-old son Sean with Sally and family boxer "Bing," said to be the brother of "Mazelaine Brandy," the reigning "Best in Show" winner of the Westminster Dog Show

Portrait of Sally with schoolboy Sean. Happy times!

William "Hopalong Cassidy" Boyd with Sally and
four-year-old Sean at the State Fair of Texas, October 1952

In August 1957 at the Missouri State Fair in Sedalia, Sally poses in a Christian Dior gown with a porcine companion — notice that both gals are adorned in a sparkly tiara and earrings — proving that there is no business like "sow business"

Sally marries
Fred Lalla
in Las Vegas,
in August 1954

Mae Lalla at age 30

Fred and Sally in a pose
that speaks for itself

Sally poses in her hotel room during a stint in 1963 when she replaced Ann Corio in the Off-Broadway production of *This Was Burlesque*

At age 67, Sally demonstrates that the miniskirt isn't just for young girls

In 1965, Sally celebrates her 61st birthday, performing in the Chantilly Lounge at Mangam's Chateau in suburban Chicago

Sally with her dear friend and assistant, Anita Robertson (1949)

Lorie "Lori Jon" Barnes and her husband John Delaney with the Royal American Shows

"Sunny Van" — Grace Hedenkamp (Vaudeville, 1931)

After decades of dancing with her fans and bubbles,
Sally began billing herself as "Her Sexellency."
Was she, in truth, an artiste or a sex symbol?
Well, a picture is wotth a thousand words.

Sally playfully poses on her dressing table. Who says a 66-year old gal can't be sexy?

Sally and a stuffed toy prize ride a Ferris wheel in 1963 with the owner of Royal American Shows, Carl J. Sedlmayer, Jr.

A few months before her death in 1979, Sally proudly poses in her "tent" minidress at the YWCA's third annual "Mr. Glendora" Pageant, standing with Fred Baumann, the 1978 title winner

Sally and her best friend Dorothy Rubel stand at the grand piano during a soirée in the Tin Palace at "Rubelia" in Glendora, California

Sally celebrates her 70th birthday with Charles Pierce at the Dorothy Chandler Pavilion in Los Angeles

Your fan
Vanda Lust

Ken/Kate
Marlowe

Sally relaxing with other performers from the
Man's Country Music Hall, Chicago 1975

At age 71, leggy Sally appears at a Seattle nightclub in December of 1975, still waving the ostrich fans that had served her so well for the prior 43 years

Sally poses with Barbara Hanks from *Sugar Babies* (June 1979)

"I'm the luckiest man in the universe," and "feeling so blue, missing you." He'd been gardening, looking for but not finding any plastering work, going to church, and praying to God to keep his beloved wife safe. He also kept a diary for most of the month while Sally was away — a diary he apparently expected Sally to see, as all of the entries are about missing her, "lighting their candle," feeling blue.

While Fred's letters commonly consisted of little more than "I love you" repeated over and over, Sally's were filled with excuses punctuated with pleas for him to take care of obligations at home. One letter, written on March 25, 1955, a couple of weeks before her return to the Los Angeles area, began:

> *Dearest Angel Puss,*
>
> *How is my sick baby? Your letters are so wonderful. They say so much more.... I open at Larry Potter's [Supper Club in North Hollywood] April 8th — they talk of having me stay over here 3 days more — that would include my birthday. I don't know yet, but one thing I do know — from the minute I arrive until I leave I must work on taxes without distraction or interruption. I may get Anita to come out and type for me. I will try to get Ralph. I am preparing you so it won't be a big surprise.*
>
> *Darling, it must be done or I'll go to jail.*

She urged Fred to move furniture to the garage, strip the paint off a chest of drawers, and complete other chores: "The floors need scrubbing and waxing, the windows washed, the bookcases and books dusted...." She also wanted him to go with her to Los Angeles to "fix up" the house where he and Mae had lived. Did Fred have a housekeeping allowance to hire help? He sure could have used one.

Less than a year after marrying Fred, Sally started up a correspondence with his ex-wife. Mae had apparently relented and was allowing the children to visit their father. Sally clearly felt the need to reassure Mae. In a letter written on June 16, 1955, she was frank and forthright:

> *Mae and Fred have definitely and for all time dissolved their partnership. Each must and will go his and her separate ways.... And now that the daily friction of living together is over, you can learn to know each other from a different standpoint — and really like each other and be friends because there is still one piece of business this partnership started that must be completed together.... Only you two people (with God's help) can*

*save these three sweet innocent children from misery, lifelong
unhappiness and a life of failure and despair....*

*The thing they need to make them good, happy, successful,
normal well-educated, well-adjusted people, strong and self-
reliant, able to face life happily as it is ... only you two people
can give them ... and that thing is they must know for sure you
both love them.*

Sally offered a measure of support, remarking that Mae had been *so young*
when she had married:

*When you start at sixteen, you are still growing and, at 16
your opinions and likes and dislikes are not yet formed.*[8] *As
you grew in these 12 years you grew in different directions,
instead of together. This is not anyone's fault....*

*But this doesn't change in any way the status of the children.
No matter what other partners the parents may choose or have
chosen later, the irrevocable fact remains that these two, Mae
and Fred, are the loving parents of these three children. All of
this means, Mae, that you and Fred should make decisions
about the children privately between yourselves without
anyone else sticking their noses in — unless you care to include
us. I know by this time you and the children know that there is
no intention or desire on my part to usurp you, nor take your
place, nor compete for their affections. To the contrary, I know
that their future happiness lies in loving their mother deeply
and knowing that she loves them above all others.*

Sally had given considerable thought to the situation faced by children of
divorced parents. She had often described how *she* had felt rejected by her
own father. Clearly worried that Fred's daughter, Sharon, was especially
distressed about her parents' divorce, Sally filled her letter with armchair
psychology and speculation about what can become of children who don't
have stable homes.

---

[8]   Mae's claim to have been "only 16" when she married Fred is not supported by the
evidence. The marriage license issued to Mae Bodfield and Fred Lalla lists her date of
birth as July 30, 1924, which would have made her 19 at the time. However, this date
may have been falsified to avoid parental consent requirements in California. A later
marriage license shows her birthdate as July 30, 1926, which corresponds to data in
the 1940 census. The truth appears to be that Mae Bodfield was actually 17 years, two
months, and five days old on the day that she became Mrs. Fred Lalla.

She also expressed concern about Mae herself:

> *Now this page is between me and thee — destroy it after you read it. It's been 1 year and 6 months and you've had two steady fellows. I know you felt the 1st one was nice and good and honest and kind and look what a chicken s--t he turned out to be — just wouldn't stand up when the going got rough. This is not your fault, nor does it show that you are a bad picker — not at all. Any man can deceive any woman. How can we know that he's lying? Only time and his actions can prove that he is what he says.... Why don't you give yourself a chance to have some fun, some nice friends, and don't tie yourself down. You were married for 12 years to one guy. Now be free for a little while.... You're young and lovely and you have plenty of time to marry and you could, just by accident, fall in love with a rich fellow — it's possible.*
>
> *Now ... let me thank you for the pleasure of enjoying Stevie.... He is an angel and good as pie and loves his mommy so much — and his daddy — and is so full of love he has some left over for me too — and Sharon and his brother Mike. God bless him. We talk about Mommy every day and when I say "I love you" Stevie says "and my mommy too?" And I say yes, I love your mommy. She's so pretty and sweet and he says "my mommy is pretty." I am grateful to you for letting us enjoy him for this time and, of course, it makes a new man of Fred. I've never seen him so happy. Thanks.*

Sally apparently wrote to Mae Lalla quite often, mainly about the children. Determined to get their mother involved in their lives (and to obtain her permission for whatever plans she had in mind), Sally sometimes enclosed paper and a stamped addressed envelope to make it easy for Mae to respond. She went out of her way to be kind and reassuring:

> *Dear Mae, we do not want Stevie to be "weaned" away from you — God forbid — no love, nor money, nor advantage that we could ever give him, could ever make up for the loss of his mother and his love for her. By loss, I mean being away from you too long.... Honey, I know and understand this so well. Remember I have a little boy of my own, and I have to be away from him to make a living for him.... I have suffered the tortures of the damned because my mother has selfishly wanted him to love her best and has not done for me what I am doing for you. Please believe me....*

*Now stop worrying and fretting. We love you. Be sweet, stay
sweet and good as you are. This is God's beautiful day.*

One can only marvel over what Mae's reaction must have been to the unsolicited "advice" she was getting from the very woman she regarded as
having broken up her family and stolen her husband.

Faith

Fast forward to Chicago on September 16, 1956. No longer fresh-faced and
girlish, Faith Bacon was pounding the pavement, hoping to find work as a
dancer. Her most recent booking had been over the Labor Day weekend in a
small nightclub in suburban Chicago, and she had needed to rent a pair of
fans for the engagement. Residing at the Alan Hotel, she was sharing a dingy
room-without-bath with grocery clerk and close friend Ruth Bishop.[9]

Beginning to despair of ever reviving her career, Faith simply couldn't find
employment, not even on Chicago's Skid Row. Miss Bishop later reported
that Faith had seemed particularly depressed:

> Faith wanted to be in the spotlight again. She came to Chicago
> three weeks ago from Erie, Pa., living on an allowance from her
> folks. She was broke and couldn't get a job.

Telling Ruth that she "would have taken any kind of work in show business,"
Faith had muttered: "If I can't do any better here, I'll go back to Erie and my
fans. Maybe they'll use me with my old equipment." Miss Bishop elaborated:
"We argued at dinner. We argued afterwards, as we watched television. She
fell asleep for a while and when she awakened, I asked: 'Are you leaving me,
or not?'" Faith then bolted from the room.

Half an hour later, Ruth found her in a hall bathroom. The door was locked.
Faith's roommate continued: "I knocked. She didn't answer at first. I knocked
again. I heard a moan. I broke in. Faith seemed dazed, almost in a stupor.
I took her arm." The two women returned to their room and Ruth declared:
"Faith, if you're determined to go home, finish packing your bag." Faith
jerked away, running out the door and down a few steps to a landing between
the third and fourth floors. Ruth followed.

Shortly after midnight on September 26th, as the two women continued to
quarrel in the stairwell, Faith suddenly dashed toward an open window.
Ruth tried to stop her, but Faith broke away and plunged through the
casement, landing below on the roof of a tavern next door to the hotel.

---

[9]   According to Tullah Hanley, Faith was sharing her hotel room with a "butch" lesbian.

"I grabbed her," Miss Bishop added, "but her dress tore from my hands as she fell."

Faith was rushed to Grant Hospital, unconscious but still alive. Early editions of the next day's papers referred to the incident as a "failed suicide attempt." A press photo showed police and firemen carrying her broken body from the scene on a stretcher. Later editions reported the tragic truth. Emergency surgery had failed to revive her.

Despite the best efforts of medical staff over several hours, Faith died without ever regaining consciousness. The cause of death was said to have been a fractured skull, perforated lung, and internal injuries. A hospital spokesman addressed the press: "She was really pretty, still slender and not a bit hard looking as you might expect. The doctors who tried to save her left in tears."

Miss Bishop despaired: "We had been arguing for six hours about her plan to return to Erie. She had been told her folks would cut off her allowance if she didn't come. I couldn't hold her," she sobbed, "Faith was so beautiful. So lovely."

At age 46, Faith Bacon — "the originator of the fan dance" — had left a meager estate of miscellaneous clothing, a white metal ring, a train ticket to Erie, Pennsylvania, and 85 cents. Among her effects was a pair of rented fans.

Faith's trials were over, but for most everyone else the world continued to turn. It took 13 innings, but, as Chicago civil servants were transporting Frances Yvonne Bacon's body to the morgue on the afternoon of September 26, 1956, the underdog Chicago Cubs were eking out a win over the St. Louis Cardinals at nearby Wrigley Field. Someone in the bar beneath the roof that had broken Miss Bacon's fall dropped a nickel in the juke box and punched the buttons for the biggest hit of the year — "Heartbreak Hotel" sung by some young fellow from Memphis, Tennessee.[10] In the waning months of the year, a new generation of blond beauties was coming to the fore, eclipsing the likes of Faith Bacon and Sally Rand. Three in particular were grabbing the attention of the nation's young filmgoers: Marilyn Monroe in *Bus Stop*, Jayne Mansfield in *The Girl Can't Help It*, and Carroll Baker in *Baby Doll*.

In June of 1958, Fred Lalla was arrested for failure to pay child support, placed on probation and ordered to pay Mae $120 a month through the Probation Department. However, since the three children continued to live

---

[10]   Just 17 days earlier, Elvis had made his first appearance on the Ed Sullivan television show.

with Fred and Sally much of the time (and the probation officer didn't see much need for Fred to report), the order went largely unenforced.

As Sally's career rolled along in Las Vegas and elsewhere, Fred's troubles with Mae did the same. In fact, by the summer of 1960, the marital strain was so great that Fred and Sally's relationship reached an impasse. On the 16th of August, the media reported that Sally Rand had been granted a decree of divorce from Fred J. Lalla the day before. Sally cited "cruelty" as grounds for the split, a claim that was uncontested. Many newspapers around the country carried the item on the front page.

While details are unclear, Sally and Fred maintained a close relationship and apparently continued to live together in Las Vegas despite their divorce. A piece published in *Parade* magazine five months after their marriage ended described Sally and Fred as "still the closest of friends." The article even suggested that a reunion was possible: "... reconciliation may be imminent. Sally, for example, continues to look after Lalla's son, Michael, by his previous marriage."

The next year, on May 25, 1962, Fred was again arrested for failure to keep up his child support payments. This time, though divorced, Sally and Fred quickly hired a lawyer to jointly petition the court to restore Fred to probationary supervision rather than put him in jail.

Papers filed with the County of Los Angeles Municipal Court offer insights into what had been going on in their messy relationship. Dr. Rudolph G. Novick had testified in an affidavit that Fred had been under his psychiatric care during the spring and summer of 1956 and that the "domestic difficulties of his previous marriage constituted a significant element of the problem." Fred's deposition told of the ongoing "mental and emotional difficulties" for which he had received treatment in 1959 and 1960 and which, more importantly, had prevented him from working full time.

In an 11-page affidavit, Sally testified to incident after incident where, even before she and Fred had moved into their own house in Glendora, Mae would unceremoniously dump the three Lalla children on them and later appear without notice to pick them up:

> I observed my husband, Mr. Lalla, during the entire period of our marriage try to conscientiously and lovingly take care of his three children.

> Throughout this time, I personally observed a complete and shocking lack of parental responsibility on the part of their mother, Mae.

These children were shuttled back and forth between Los Angeles, Las Vegas, their grandmother's, their aunts and uncles, and their mother's various apartments and homes without the slightest regard for their school attendance or change of schools.

Their clothing, new and otherwise, and equipment, including the new bicycles we bought them, were left scattered from place to place and never picked up again for their use....

[The] children were dropped on our doorsteps in Las Vegas and Glendora at any hour of the night, sleepy and frightened, accompanied by Mae, always under the influence of alcohol with a succession of different boyfriends. We never knew when they were coming or how long they would stay or where we were to take or send them, nor Mae's whereabouts.

Mae had threatened to call the police if Fred and Sally didn't do as she instructed. Once she had even directed them to take the children over to stay with her mother and, unaware that they were coming, Mae's mother had refused to take them in. The tales of mistreatment, threats, and demands for money went on and on.

Sally insisted that "A great deal of money, time, effort and evidence was put forth to change the status of the custody ruling," but the deck was stacked against them. Some of their evidence had been excluded. And Fred's attorney had warned that the judge "was notorious for refusing custody to fathers and any further efforts would be futile, if not dangerous."

Sally's affidavit then chronicled the personal and financial damage that Fred had suffered since his divorce from Mae in July 1954:

He had lost his wife, his children, his home and his business. His once flourishing contracting business came to an end precipitously and finally the day the divorce court ordered him to quit the premises of his home and take nothing with him but his personal clothing; he was cut off from the lifeline of his business, the telephone, and his business listing in the yellow pages of the Los Angeles business telephone directory. This same order put a Sheriff's padlock on the yard in which his equipment was kept (plaster and cement mixers, scaffolding, etc.).

These losses had "left him a broken man without will or incentive," Sally declared, adding: "I knew all this but I loved him deeply. I felt that knowing he was loved, mothering, time and psychotherapy could free him of the nightmare of being inadequate.

And so, Sally had paid all child support payments to Mae until April of 1957 when Fred got a job with the City of Covina — a job that Sally claimed "used neither his talent, craft nor brains":

> [The job] paid him $144.00 twice a month. Deduct $120.00 a month [for] child care and the balance hardly covers his cost of transportation from Glendora to Covina, his lunches and laundry of his work clothes.

All of this turmoil had led to Fred's mental breakdown. And Sally had become profoundly upset as well. The extent of her distress was so great that her affidavit included a surprisingly harsh take on her own mother's involvement:

> [Fred's] condition was further seriously aggravated by my aged and senile mother whose greed for my economic support and whose vanity and vicarious status depended upon being "Sally Rand's mother." She hated him passionately and senselessly. She never missed an opportunity to downgrade him and gossip viciously about him to the extent that she seriously disturbed his standing in the community — with our church — and with our credit rating. She destroyed his opportunity of becoming a councilman of our small town, Glendora.[11]

Sally's affidavit continued, beseeching the court's compassion:

> [On] April 11, 1960, Mr. Lalla quit his job with the City of Covina. He was desperately ill, night sweats so severe that the bed had to be changed several times a night, crying in his troubled sleep ending in hysteria; nightmares in which he fought and struggled, constant migraine headaches so severe his eyes would be swollen almost shut and the veins in his temples swollen and extended until the throbbing was visible to the eye. He demonstrated all the symptoms of stomach ulcers, violent pain [in] the solar plexus, gnawing hunger, vomiting, unable to eat and lost weight from 160 to 130 pounds.
>
> I was his wife — and he needed my care. I had to work in Las Vegas. Dr. Miller told him I was not safe to leave alone — I had suicidal tendencies — so he came to Las Vegas to keep me from killing myself, and to be cared for by me when he was so ill.
>
> I feel that these separate circumstances deserve the consideration of the Court.

---

[11] According to a local press report, Lalla was "disqualified for running for the Glendora City Council because of an irregularity in his petition."

Sally maintained that Mae had actually been provided *more* than the required $120 a month and that Fred should never have been put on probation in the first place. She claimed he had not been represented by counsel and should never have been advised to plead guilty, concluding:

> He was much too ill to know what he was doing and was under sedation a good part of the time. And, at the time, I didn't know enough of the details of the probation to do anything about it.

Well, at least this was the story Sally chose to include in her affidavit. A later, more entertaining account of her attraction to Fred and her decision to sustain their connection despite her mother's objections emerged from an unpublished interview. In the face of her mother's warnings of impending doom, Sally had married her "lusty Italian" because, as she confessed: "I just couldn't help myself, he was so damn sexy."

Ultimately, Sally had to admit that Nettie had Fred pegged from the outset:

> He wouldn't go out to work at all. I guess he thought it was beneath the husband of Sally Rand. No amount of ranting and raving would help. I guess he thought his best work could be done in bed.

The same interview included an account (likely exaggerated) of Sally's response to Fred's aversion to employment:

> About this time, Sally hit upon what she thought was a brilliant idea. She would just quit work, retire, become a devoted wife and mother. She paid off all her husband's charge accounts and told everyone not to give him any more credit, then sat back to wait him out: "Things just went from bad to worse. First they cut off the gas and electricity. I was determined not to let any of it get to me. Mother would sneak in a little food and milk for Sean once in a while. Can you imagine, there I was, sitting in that ... house cooking over an open fire in the fireplace."

Fred finally went out and got a job as a garbage collector. Sally was delighted:

> I think he thought it would embarrass me. I couldn't have been happier. He was finally contributing. I even called a press conference to let everyone know.[12]

---

[12] Years later Sally still enjoyed telling this story. In a 1974 letter, she revealed herself as a farsighted environmentalist and early adopter of recycling: "One of my dearest and nicest husbands was a garbage collector (very highly paid work, by the way). This often leads to one's own business of 'junk yard' salvage, recycling or whatever name you give it — for society has so long been conditioned to the expendability of

While it is hard to imagine that the Sally Rand we have come to know was ever suicidal, she certainly experienced more than her share of stressful situations. During the years she spent with Fred Lalla struggling with his problems, she was also beset by the sort of obstacles that had always plagued her appearances on the road.

Once, during a 1957 booking at the Gayety Theater in Baltimore, she was robbed and assaulted by an intruder at 6:30 in the morning. Less than a week after her home on the opposite coast in Glendora had been burglarized for "$290 in loot," Sally was in her dressing room packing when a "shoeless Negro" burst in "brandishing a fire ax" and demanded $50. When she implored that she had no money, the barefoot bandit had punched her in the mouth and searched the room, finding her wallet which contained $524. Possibly feeling guilty about socking a middle-aged woman, the man had taken only $114 before fleeing the scene. A porter saw the thief running through the theater and chased him out into the street, where he disappeared. The papers reported: "Miss Rand was treated for a slight laceration of her upper lip and released."[13]

Sally's son Sean never really got to know Turk Greenough or Harry Finkelstein, but he did have a fairly close relationship with Fred Lalla. Although he spent a few summers in Las Vegas, the only time Sean was there for an entire year was when he was in the 6th grade. However, he also spent time with Fred in Glendora. As Sean recalled, "Lalla was the only one I knew because she was married to him for eight years during the time I was around, so when she'd be on the road, I'd stay with him."

One of Sean's memories of Fred is particularly vivid:

> He was nice to me. He actually saved my life one time when the car door flew open and he reached out and grabbed my leg while I was flying out the door.... She was 15 years older than him [actually 20]. He was a plastering contractor and had been a professional boxer. He was obviously very good with his fists, and I guess women in general found him pretty attractive. He was easily swayed by women.

'things,' fortunes are put in the 'garbage' every day. The wise, with perspicacity ... collect the things that the careless throw away, to be re-used, which conserves our planet's resources, helps save the atmosphere and ecology of our planet, and makes income for the collector (what a gabby old broad)."

[13] Not every experience in Baltimore had been so traumatic. In November 1950, Sally had tossed out the official game ball at a Baltimore Bullets professional basketball game one day and at the Colts football game the next.

He also remembered Sally's faithful associate, Ralph Hobart:

> He died when I was pretty young. Lalla didn't like him. I just
> remember as a kid that he'd get mad because Ralph Hobart was a
> gay man. My mother and Ralph were friends from when they were
> kids so she gave him a job; and all those years he traveled with her,
> and he put these beautiful big scrapbooks together with all the
> newspaper clippings and things like that…. Ralph was nice to me,
> but Lalla was always making fun of him.

Sally loved having Sean with her in Las Vegas. She could hardly have been
more proud of him. She understood how implausible it was that she had
been able to adopt him in the first place. But more than once she had also
dreamed of having a daughter, one she could dote upon, and introduce to
the wonderful world of dance. Despite the circumstances of her life having
precluded that dream from becoming reality, she reasoned, "Well, there are
plenty of men who benefit from instruction in ballet, so why not my son?"

As Sean recalls:

> I remember in Vegas, probably about '61 or '62, my mother had a
> friend come out and she stayed at our house. She was a famous
> ballerina. Her name was Madame Ella Daganova and my mother
> just thought the world of her — she had taught my mother.[14]

> Here I am, wanting to go outside and play with other kids, and my
> mother is scheduling ballet lessons for me. She always wanted me to
> go into the dance — from a young age bouncing in the crib and she
> thought "Oh, this kid's going to be a dancer." And growing up, I had
> the body, shape, legs and everything. I had all the right makeup and
> everything, but I didn't have any desire to do that. So mother put me
> with this lady and she started teaching me and I would just get bored
> and give them all a hard time. So she sits me down and I say "I can't
> do this" and she says "Why?" I said "Because this is for girls." She
> said "No" and went on and on and I said "No, this is a sissy sport."

Madame may have been discouraged, but she was not deterred. Realizing that
Sean shared the same interests as every other young boy, she took another

---

[14] Madame Ella Daganova had been a member of Anna Pavlova's company, both in
London and in the United States. According to Eleanor Fairchild Cadwallader in her
2005 book *A Pot for Every Lid*, Sally had backed Daganova financially when she
opened a Manhattan dance studio in the 1930s. Five-time Tony-award-winning
choreographer Jerome Robbins (*West Side Story*, *Gypsy*, etc.) once swept her floors
in return for ballet lessons.

tack, describing to him how she had not only trained many members of the military, but had also given ballet lessons to such famous athletes as Joe DiMaggio. Sean remembers her stories of "Joltin' Joe" and other he-men:

> He came to me in New York and, you know, he was known as the most graceful player, could run like a gazelle. He took ballet from me for years. During World War II, the United States Army contacted me to give training to the Airborne Rangers. After the war many of these men came back and told me that I saved their lives.

Sean then understood:

> Because they were dropped behind enemy lines ... they had to be very graceful and quiet and they had to do it in combat boots.... So, then I started taking ballet and I felt a little bit better about it.... And, of course, Lalla would come by and tease her and call her "Queenie" and all kinds of stuff.[15]

Just how long Sally continued to maintain some sort of relationship with Fred Lalla is unclear. Although the two were granted a divorce in 1960, a handwritten draft of a letter from Sally to Fred composed nearly four years later suggests they were entangled in each other's lives well beyond their official split. Their bond was finally broken when Fred's behavior became so intolerable that Sally reached the end of her patience. On June 8th, writing from New York City where the 1964 World's Fair was in progress, the 60-year-old Sally unloaded on poor Fred (apparently in response to his unwelcome platitudes):

> *It's a pity, and stupid of me to make maudlin phone calls — it's terribly expensive. Like I've always said, the cost of F--- is too high, but when the cost of not doing it gets expensive, that's too much....*
>
> *What a pompous, rationalizing moron you are! These qualities are so neatly hidden within a physical exterior that an accident of birth made to look beautiful, gentle and human. That pleasant facade completely camouflages the sadistic cruelty, viciousness, lack of morals, ethics, and wanton*

---

[15] Over the years Madame Daganova had apparently become more self-confident and outgoing. In a letter to Valya Valentinoff written more than 20 years earlier, Sally had remarked on some facets of her personality, describing "poor old Ella" as being "eccentric and shy beyond belief: Her cold, indifferent manner is a dreadful shyness and inferiority complex.... Love her for what she is, and God knows she is a great teacher."

destructiveness. Only a moron could deceive himself into believing the mindless clichés he spouts are deathless quotes of wisdom and insight, an oracle.

"Live each day." Do you call what you're doing living? At least I move, travel, dream of the stars, and strive for them. I have the capacity to love, grieve, feel remorse, know right from wrong, and try not to make the same mistakes again. These are emotions you know only as words, and you're not sure of all the words.

"You're getting old, and don't like it, and you're frightened." What infinite wisdom and perspicacity — oh great prophet! Christ! It took you forty years to figure this out? Idiot! Of course, I'm "old, and don't like it, and I'm frightened." But not for the reasons you think.

I like being my age because it has taken this long for me to learn the things I wanted to know. I don't like being this close to death, because it doesn't give me the time I would like to have to do all the things I want to do yet, more for physical reasons than mental ones.

It is very frightening to observe how society in general, and children in particular, treat old people who are alone. They are relegated to oblivion — and forcibly put into "homes" and institutions — without regard to their will, privacy or possessions. Economic status has little to do with it; the more money involved, the more likely to be declared incompetent!

Older people who are married, who have partners who love each other, present a united front; they help each other and are able to retain a normal life. I looked forward to this kind of life replete with serenity, dignity, love and happiness. I made a tremendous investment of money, effort and love — and sacrifices you wouldn't understand.

You were my loved one and loved me. You would be my companion and share all the pleasures of security, serenity, peace and happiness. We'd never be alone. I'd have a strong male protector. I would be cherished, not thrust aside as useless and in the way.

I earned the right to have this by the service I rendered you, when you hit bottom, by consistent and constant loving care and concern. Anything you wanted and needed to achieve emotional healing and equanimity — whatever time and *money you needed to learn what you wanted to know to give you status [and] security. I was unaware of the fact that you rejected the opportunities, and made no use of them — the doctor in Chicago, the lessons, the long months of idleness after our marriage — while you became "adjusted."*

The bad temper, insane and unwarranted jealousies, bad manners, social embarrassments, grimy little affairs, horrible predicaments in which you involved me — being witness to sights no wife should see — the heartbreak, the rejection, the disappointment, the disillusionment.

I never weakened. I held on to my dream, to my loved one. He will wake up. He will be well. He will see.

God damn it, I earned the right not to be alone. You and you alone took it from me — stole it — exactly as if you had taken money from my purse. You stole my time, the only time I had left. You stole my love, that I can give to no one else, my money, that I can never earn again — and the pleasure of my child, who needed me, and whom I needed. He's grown now, no longer have I a little boy. I could never stay home and be with him because of you. And now it's too late, and I have nothing.

Thus do the destroyers and jackals prey on the unprotected and unsuspecting. I know all your answers, and all your defenses, and there is no truth in them — as there is no truth in you. So I grieve over those wasted years, nor do I castigate myself for so doing. Grief is a normal reaction to loss — one would have to be insensible not to. You do not grieve, because you have never lost anything. You have to love something to know when you've lost it.

I also know that nothing I say moves you because you're a thing — you feel nothing — nothing save lust, and a weak pleasure at another's pain. You don't even understand what I'm saying, but it's good therapy for me.

When, emotionally, one hits bottom and for that suspended time (however long or short it is) we go through all the motions, making appropriate gestures, genuflecting properly, and nodding at the right times, unmotivated, without will or purpose — a kind of somnambulant Saraband. No one notices. We are conditioned to the familiar and reassuring sounds of our daily dialogue (written by lunatics).

In years to come, Sally would say of Fred Lalla: "He was wonderful in bed, but I couldn't get him to do anything else — like work."

Back in 1924, a movie magazine had called attention to Sally's film roles as a "comedy vamp" — a girl with a talent for "luring men ... from the straight and narrow." And, whether by circumstance or design, for three vulnerable married men, Sally had done just that. She had enchanted Turk Greenough and beguiled Harry Finkelstein. She had cast such a spell over Fred Lalla that he left his wife in order to marry a woman old enough to be his mother.

Sally's issues with each of her husbands were of the sort commonly addressed by columns like "Ask Ann Landers." Such advice-givers have been around for decades, if not centuries. Back in the 1930s, one of the more popular advice columnists of her day was Caroline Chatfield. On May 8, 1937, her column addressed the choices that certain women make:

> ... there's one [type of] marriage that always materializes according
> to predictions of the onlookers: It is the marriage of a clever, capable
> girl to the no-account who can't keep a job because he won't work.
> For some reason, either by his design or because Mother Nature
> leads him to his opposite, he usually fastens on a hard-working girl
> who makes her living. And when he has woven his spell around her
> she's blind to all the earmarks that show him to be a four-flusher and
> a ne'er-do-well.

> Proverbially, he is a lady-killer with a weakness for the bottle,
> flashy clothes and speedy cars.... His hat sits at a rakish angle and
> when he struts down the street admiring himself in the mirrors,
> one would take him for a successful businessman....

> Either he's going into a new job or coming out of one to remain idle
> while he waits for something to turn up that is commensurate with
> his talents, in line with his taste, suitable salary attached. During the
> interims, he sponges on his family, borrows from his friends, asks
> credit of the merchants and lets his girlfriend buy his dinners and his
> movie tickets. He's adept at telling fairy stories, which he must half
> believe, or he couldn't appear so plausible.... The gullible girl in love
> with him is completely befuddled by his fine appearance, his
> polished manners, his lofty sentiments and his fair promises....

> So she marries him, mothers him, pays his debts, advances funds,
> feeds him, clothes him, pays the piper for the two of them to
> dance.... Yet as the months roll by and the bills roll up, as

expenses increase and he's still waiting for something to turn up,
she begins to recoil from him....

She must admit that all his pretty talk was bunk, all his polish
veneer. As a suitor he was swell. As a husband he's a sell-out.

This is the marriage that turns out exactly as the onlookers predicted.
Everybody knows the inevitable result but the poor girl herself.

Caroline Chatfield's column certainly hit the nail on the head. The only thing
is, it wasn't actually *her* advice; Chatfield had been taking a break that day. In
her place, the syndicate had secured the services of a celebrated performer
who was more than happy to fill in for her. The true but uncredited author
was, of course, none other than Sally Rand.

Appearing at the Earle Theatre in the New York City Borough of Queens,
Sally had accepted an invitation to fill in for the syndicated advice columnist.
Published in the *New York Daily News* under the headline "SALLY RAND'S
LOVE THEORIES" more than four years before Sally's first acknowledged
marriage, the column offered observations on the prospects of marital bliss
from a single gal who had pretty much everything going her way. It is
nothing short of astonishing that Sally so literally foretold the details of her
own future circumstances by so many years.

So the last of Sally's marriages had come to an end. Turk Greenough,
Harry Finkelstein, and Fred Lalla all had something in common: They
were all good looking, happy-go-lucky men who lived in the moment. And,
like so many other women, both before and since, Sally had firmly believed
that she could take such a man, whip him into shape, and somehow reform
him into a responsible, dependable husband. Such efforts nearly always fail.

Some of the suitors from her youth, those she had taken a pass on, actually
were such men, but they had not been malleable. Instead, they had been fully
formed men who on some level might have equaled or surpassed Sally's own
intelligence and abilities. They were *too* constant, *too* reliable. They were not
challenging, not exciting enough. They didn't make the blood run hot. The
allure of the "bad boy" will be with us always. But such men, whatever their
raw appeal, are irredeemable. Sally Rand was one smart cookie. She knew a
lot about a lot. But this one simple truth, this enduring fact of nature, she
either didn't know or didn't want to know.

CHAPTER TWENTY-THREE

The Sixties

Wouldn't it be wonderful to find the moment when I
stopped being an old bag and became an American
tradition?

~ Sally Rand

A featured headliner at the big resort hotels on the Las Vegas strip
in the mid-to-late fifties, Sally enjoyed extended runs at both the
Last Frontier Hotel and the adjacent Silver Slipper. She had other irons in
the fire as well. In an interview with film columnist Bob Thomas at the
hotel pool, Sally revealed that she had been taking college courses in her
spare time:

> It took some doing, because I never graduated from high school.
> But I was allowed to take some courses through the University of
> California ... physics, math, chemistry and psychology. And I'm
> proud to say that I had a 95 average.

She also claimed to have been offered a job by the American Cyanamid
Company in Azusa (near Glendora), at a not inconsiderable salary of $800 a
month (or about $84,000 a year these days). Sadly for the chemical industry,
tax problems and other expenses led Sally to stick with the more lucrative
show business gigs.

While her dances had changed very little over the years, Sally was always in
the market for something new to reinvigorate her act. A recently developed
garment called "Panti-Legs" was just such a product. When this early version
of "pantyhose" entered the mass market around 1959, she immediately saw
its potential to heighten the illusion of nudity. There was just one hitch — the
darned things had seams up the back.

Taking it upon herself to remedy the situation, she wrote to the manufacturer, North Carolina's Glen Raven Mills, telling them: "Your Panti-Legs
are the greatest thing I've ever had!" However, as a woman with years of
experience in costume design, she also suggested that they would be even
better without the seams. After receiving Sally's comments — and, not

incidentally, shortly after the introduction of the mini-skirt — it wasn't long before the company took the hint and retooled its production line. "Seamless pantyhose" soon took the hosiery business by storm.

In 1961, as baby boomers were becoming adults and ushering in the counter-culture "Age of Aquarius," Sally Rand was persevering. She may have been getting older, but she was in no way ready to accept it. The youthful 56-year-old summed up her attitude in an interview with Lloyd Shearer published in *Parade* magazine as a feature article:

> Why should any woman feel old at 50 merely because society expects it? So many of us are cowards to conformity. Why can't a woman radiate sex appeal at any age? The answer is she can. I think I'm living proof of that.

> Off-stage, men regard me as matronly, a nice, pleasant, intelligent woman. But on-stage, whirling and twirling my fans, I become an object of secret thoughts. And being able to do this does wonders for me. It's a kind of therapy. And I only hope I can keep it up forever.

Thoroughly impressed, Shearer had opened his article by gushing: "Sally Rand is incredible." He later clarified his complex reaction:

> From talking to her you get an idea of what the real Sally Rand is like. She is intellectual, bedeviled and eloquent....

> Her big personal problem, of course, is that she wants to be wanted and loved for her mind. But the men she meets and the men she married — well, let me put it this way, in my opinion they are not particularly interested in philosophy, psychology or physics. To them, Sally Rand spells eternal sex.

As we have learned, soon after rising to stardom as a fan dancer, Sally had discovered her talent for public speaking. And, after nearly 30 years in the entertainment world, she continued to value oratory as a means of promoting her appearances.

Her speeches commonly went well beyond self-promotion. In late February of 1962, in the middle of the Cold War, she was invited to speak to the Phoenix Exchange Club, sharing the platform with Dr. Arthur Lee, "historian and expert on the life of George Washington." In her part of the program, Sally addressed somewhat more current issues, urging club members "to speak out against the evil influences which threaten our country today" and proclaiming: "We do not really have a democracy today in the United States." After declaring that she still believed our form of government to be better than any other kind of government, she added: "I don't honestly believe that our ideology and communism can exist on the same planet."

As she was making these remarks, President John F. Kennedy was barely into the second year of his only term. He and Soviet Chairman Nikita Khrushchev had exchanged several confrontational messages in recent days. The Cuban Missile Crisis was just eight months in the future. Sally may have been a mere exotic dancer, appearing in Phoenix at the Carnival Room in a light-hearted (some would say frivolous) show, but she also had her eye on the big picture.

F requently flying between engagements, Sally was always at risk of losing part or all of her luggage, which typically consisted of several (if not many) separate pieces. In a letter written to Valerie Huff on March 10, 1962, from the Old South Club in Hot Springs, Arkansas, Sally described a particularly harrowing experience.[1] She had just flown from Los Angeles to Hot Springs (changing planes in Dallas) and all had not gone well:

> *I got off the plane in Dallas with the help of the agent, having in mind the large basket with the music in it, the makeup box, and the fans. The agent was entrusted with the large basket and the fans (I thought).[2] I ... dragged my weary bones and aching bottom (where I fell down) for miles through the subterranean passages of the Dallas Airport, over crossways, up ramps, down escalators with the agent bringing up the rear. Having finally arrived at the ... waiting room, I collapsed on their decorative and violently pink chairs. The agent deposited the luggage at my feet and fled. After a few moments of complete collapse, I decided I had better get a skycap to check what I was carrying, and check in with Trans-Texas for the last leg of the flight to Hot Springs. Imagine my horror when I discovered there were no fans.*

---

[1] A longtime friend from California, Miss Huff was a vaudeville dancer and Broadway performer in the 1930s.

[2] Sally regularly transported her fans in a round four-foot-long case, woven of native black walnut strips by a friend in West Virginia. When questioned by airport personnel about the case, she would reply: "Don't worry, it's just my pet snakes."

I bolted to the [airlines] desk ... to have them contact the plane I had just flown in on. Too late! It had taken off for Memphis and Idlewild [in New York]. The lethargic, blasé, and very busy young man ... to whom I wept my plight [assured] me the fans would be taken off at Memphis and flown back to Hot Springs by morning.

All seemed too good to be true, and there was a nagging suspicion in the back of my mind that maybe I hadn't even gotten on the plane with them in L.A.... I barely made the Trans-Texas flight....

Shaken and desperate, I went directly to rehearsal.... I can't think when I have been so miserable. I finally bought $20 worth of quarters (and subsequently $20 more) and started calling Dallas, L.A., Memphis, and Idlewild. Remember by this time it's six o'clock in New York, and everyone whose business it would be to take care of such matters as this had left their respective offices. Finally some poor soul traveled the miles between airport and hanger and found the fans, neatly hidden behind the back seat where the cleaners had missed them.

So now, my problem is from Idlewild to Hot Springs. Obviously, I wouldn't have them for Monday night; but I was afraid the vague young man who had them in his hands would relegate them to the lost and found department where they might go through channels for months; so it cost me $13 to have him put a note on the fans with the name and address, put the fans on the desk of the man whose business it was to take care of such things, obtain this man's residence number on Long Island, reach him and explain about sending them back here. In the meantime, time is flying. The show is at 8:30. I am sleepy. I can hardly keep my eyes open, and I know somewhere, somehow I've got to get something to use for fans. In Hot Springs, Arkansas!

It was really the first time I ever wanted to really give the whole thing up, take a hot bath, go to bed, and have a good cry. Unfortunately, I am not economically able to afford this luxury; so I decided to get a cab and canvass the main street for florist shops which might conceivably prepare something with wires and tufts of net that I could use in lieu of my traditional props....

Believe me, I left no stone unturned. I went to every florist shop, all of whom viewed the entire matter as a huge joke and, I am sure, firmly believed I was quite mad. None was willing to even attempt anything that I suggested. The best I could do was an already made funeral wreath. All I could think of was a classic story about a tramp who stole a girl's clothes while she was bathing and stayed on the bank to enjoy her chagrin. All she could find to cover her nudity while she bawled him out was an old rusty dish pan she found at the bottom of the river. Covering herself with this, she wound up by saying, "and furthermore, you know what I think." To which he replied, "Yes, you think that dish pan has a bottom in it." Obviously, funeral wreaths wouldn't do!

Department stores, furniture stores, art and gift shops, auction houses, all were firm in their conviction that, not only did they not have fans or fireplace fans, but they had never even heard of them. By this time, all the stores were closing; and the cab driver was getting pretty nervous. He said there was one more little art shop, but he was sure it wouldn't have them. When we got there the doors were locked, but the lady was still in the shop.... I knocked on the door and asked. She finally let me in when I told her who I am.... I left the shop cheerfully grateful with two fireplace fans, my baggage to unpack, hair to do, and makeup to put on....

Arriving at the club at 7:30, and, God help me, shaking like a leaf, thoroughly convinced that this was the end of a long, if not illustrious, career — I did it! So help me, I don't think anyone in the audience knew the difference. They were fans, weren't they, and I am a fan dancer. So? One of the waitresses who was here last year asked me if I didn't use a different kind of fan last year. That's all.

Sally was in town for an extended engagement and, while she was commonly in hot water with members of the religious community, it seems that she was not at odds with the Catholic hierarchy in Hot Springs. In fact, on Sunday, April 1st, near the end of her several weeks' stay, she was among the celebrity entertainers and bandleaders who performed at The Vapors Club (a swank supper club and gambling casino) for an elaborate "Wild Duck Dinner" staged to benefit the construction of a new St. Michael's School at the Good Shepherd Home of Hot Springs. She provided her services for free.[3]

A cross town from the Old South Club, George Gray, the band instructor for Ramble Elementary School, had been looking forward to Sally's engagement with great anticipation. One of his most prized possessions was a program from the 1933 fair in Chicago where the popular Wayne King Orchestra had performed one of Gray's compositions at the famous Aragon Ballroom.

In 1957, as a grade school music teacher, Gray had been impressed by the talent of one of his 10-year-old students and had encouraged him to take up the saxophone: "He liked the idea, but didn't have a sax of his own, so I lent him mine." By 1962, the 16-year-old was a standout in the Hot Springs High School band. Gray recalled: "Billy had excellent pitch and rhythm ... and he worked hard, but you could always tell he had his mind on other things. He enjoyed playing music, but he enjoyed the debating team even more."

At the time, Gray was leading a local band of his own which had been engaged to back up Sally Rand during her extended stay at the Old South. One evening, he invited his star student to sit in with the band — the only gig he would ever have as a professional musician. And so it was that an Arkansas teenager with a big future ahead of him once sat in with the band at a Hot Springs nightclub to accompany the legendary fan dancer. His name? William Jefferson Clinton.

O n December 18, 1903, back when Annette Beck was in her fifth month of pregnancy, papers around the country had broken the astonishing news that, on the previous day, two brothers from Dayton, Ohio, operating on a beach near Kitty Hawk, North Carolina, had achieved the first successful flight of a powered aircraft. A dispatch from Norfolk, Virginia, reported the feat: "The machine has no balloon attachment, but gets its force from propellers worked by a small engine." Less than four months later, Annette Beck would give birth to Helen Gould Beck, whose life would parallel the further development of powered flight.

---

[3]   Besides the free entertainment provided by Sally, singer Johnny Desmond, and others, the food and most everything else was donated, including the wild ducks furnished by Wag's Game Reserve. *The Guardian*, official publication of the Catholic Diocese of Little Rock, also provided free publicity.

In fact, as "Billie Beck," Helen would be piloting a single-engine biplane before she was out of her teens, and, over the years, she would become an avid flying enthusiast at a time when aircraft would play a greater and greater role in the outcome of two world wars and postwar life.

On April 9, 1959, just five days after Sally's 55th birthday, the National Aeronautics and Space Administration (NASA) announced the selection of seven military pilots to become the original Mercury 7 Astronauts. A little over two years later, on May 5, 1961, Alan Shepard, Jr. would become the first of the group to be launched into space.

Speaking to a joint session of Congress three weeks later, President Kennedy famously proclaimed: "I believe that this nation should commit itself to achieving the goal, before this decade is out, of landing a man on the Moon and returning him safely to the Earth." Less than nine months later, John Glenn would be the first American to orbit our planet. An instant national hero, he was celebrated in a ticker-tape parade in New York City reminiscent of the one held for Charles Lindbergh when he returned from his solo flight across the Atlantic 35 years earlier.

In response to the President's aspiration and Glenn's achievement, in September of 1961, NASA announced plans to establish a "Manned Spacecraft Center" (MSC) southeast of Houston on undeveloped land donated by Rice University. Construction began in the spring of 1962 on what is today the Lyndon B. Johnson Space Center.

On the Fourth of July 1962, special ceremonies were staged to welcome the astronauts who were moving their families to Houston. After a downtown parade with a motorcade of 36 convertibles, the seven men were introduced at the Sam Houston Coliseum, each wearing a suit and tie, as well as a Western-style Stetson hat. The Harris County sheriff handed out tin badges designating the group as "space deputies."

As the astronauts walked to the platform, a high school band struck up *Dixie*, followed by *The Eyes of Texas*. Local dignitaries spoke, the national anthem was played, and an invocation was given by Rev. J. Thomas Bagby, minister at St. Martin's Episcopal Church, where George H.W. and Barbara Bush were members.

The solemn ceremonies were followed by a traditional Texas barbeque and entertainment organized by the Chamber of Commerce. Actor Gene Barry (who had recently starred in three seasons of the popular TV Western *Bat Masterson*) served as master of ceremonies. Performing in front of a large banner proclaiming "Welcome MSC," Mr. Barry demonstrated his prowess dancing the Twist with the young daughter of a local official.

Then, to the astonishment of many in the hall, an unexpected guest was announced. The band began to play, and none other than Sally Rand stepped to the microphone, delivered a few remarks, and proceeded to perform the fan dance to the strains of her trademark "Clair de Lune." It isn't clear whether she had been formally invited to participate or had simply taken note of the event and volunteered her services (one source described her as a "surprise entertainer").[4] As usual, some considered Sally's contribution to be inappropriate, if not bizarre. After all, the celebration honoring the Mercury 7 was held on Independence Day in the middle of the afternoon with many young children in attendance.

In his 1979 book *The Right Stuff*, which tells the story of the Project Mercury astronauts, Tom Wolfe described Sally as a past-her-prime dancer who had "winked and minced about and took off a little here and covered a little there and shook her ancient haunches at the seven single-combat warriors." In his view: "It was quite electrifying. It was quite beyond sex, show business, and either the sins or rigors of the flesh." In Wolfe's mind, the decision to include Sally in the festivities as she "shook her fanny in an utterly baffling blessing over it all," was incomprehensible.[5]

Others in attendance were delighted — not least of whom, Sally herself.

In early August of 1962, Sally addressed the annual "Ladies' Night" program of the Brazoria County Bar Association in Texas. After discussing what she perceived to be an unfortunate shortage of competent counsel,[6] she pivoted to shed a little light on the personalities of show people and their fear of rejection:

> None of us have real talent. We went into the theater because we were emotionally disturbed. We used applause as a substitute for the warmth and affection we lacked elsewhere. If we succeed, it is usually by accident. All of us are rejected people. We are not completely normal.

---

4   Sally was in town at the time, appearing in a production of the musical comedy *Gypsy*. Although not cast in a leading role, she did play "Tessie Tura," the larger-than-life, uninhibited trouper who sings one of more memorable numbers in the show — "You Gotta Have a Gimmick."

5   In the film version of *The Right Stuff*, actress Peggy Davis rather inaccurately depicted Sally's appearance in Houston. Some filmgoers view the episode as a symbolic fabrication, but Sally actually *was* there.

6   Sally said: "It is with dismay that I frequently see lawyers with wrinkled, untidy, unkempt clothing approach the bar of justice with casual disregard for the dignity of the court."

We don't always tell the truth, as you see the truth, but often it's the truth as we see it. But if we can give you one moment of beauty and charm, of entertainment and pleasure, we have discharged our obligation.

Sally told the assembled barristers that as a child she had always considered herself to be unattractive, and that her father, whom she had adored, had gone overseas to World War I and hadn't come back: "He wasn't killed. He just found someone he liked in Paris and didn't come back." Sally confessed that she had "never completely recovered from that."

In the summer of 1963, 20th Century Fox released *The Stripper*, a movie starring Joanne Woodward in the role of a young woman who, after a failed movie career, becomes a vaudeville dancer, breaks up with a boy-friend, and ends up performing in a Kansas City strip club. A collection of balloons serves to shield her body from the gaze of the movie audience. In the 1960s, strip clubs were experiencing something of a renaissance. Every big city and even some middle-sized towns had one or two and, of course, local church groups and police departments were alert to the threat. Plyers of the trade well understood that a crackdown on stripping and go-go dancing would threaten the livelihood of a significant number of young women. A polishing of the public image was in order.

On November 13th in Los Angeles, at the sixth annual convention of the Exotique Dancers League of North America, the organization announced at a luncheon meeting that it would be incorporating itself in an attempt to "improve the image of the strip-tease as an art form" and add "prestige and dignity" to the league's image. The group's festivities included the naming of "1963's 10 best undressed" — a list of ladies that counted among its members not only strippers Lili St. Cyr, Ann Corio, Jennie Lee, Rita Atlanta, Tempest Storm, Tinker Bell and Virginia Bell, but also non-stripper and 59-year-old Sally Rand.[7]

Nine days after this event, President John F. Kennedy was riding in an open-car motorcade in Dallas, Texas, when he was assassinated by former U.S. Marine and Soviet defector Lee Harvey Oswald, firing a high-powered rifle from a sixth floor window of the Texas School Book Depository. Two days later, while being ushered out of Dallas police headquarters, Oswald himself

---

[7] Entertainment for the event included a fashion show of the "latest stripper styles" modeled by Lavender Hill, Crazylegs Griffin and Linda Doll. In addition, actress Mamie Van Doren was made an honorary league member.

was shot and mortally wounded by Dallas nightclub owner Jack Ruby as seen by millions on live television.

Ruby had been proprietor of the Theater Lounge, a strip club that, along with his Carousel Club, was one of several Dallas burlesque venues.[8] A recurrent visitor to Dallas, Sally had worked for Ruby on occasion and, like many others, she had a low opinion of the gentleman. Her son Sean remembers his mother's reaction to the killing of Oswald:

> That goes to figure. Jack Ruby is just as big a sleazeball as Al Capone
> ever was. I worked for Ruby many times over the years. He was a no-
> good guy. He's dying and he's just trying to go out of the world a hero.

Over the years, Ruby had befriended many Dallas police officers, allegedly providing them with free booze and prostitutes. He was a familiar figure with easy access to police headquarters. As Sally had suggested, Ruby was in poor health. He died three years later at Parkland Hospital, the same facility in which Kennedy and Oswald had each been pronounced dead.

Sally continued to occupy the spotlight throughout 1964. On Sunday, April 12th, she hosted and narrated a color television program entitled *Carny*, an NBC News special devoted to this poorly documented billion-dollar-a-year branch of show business. Considered by some to be an ugly stepsister of the entertainment industry, carnivals were "terribly important" to Sally, who explained her early attraction:

> I've been going to state and county fairs since I was a girl. As a
> child back in Sedalia, Missouri, we'd always go to the fair. I'd take
> my fat little calf or my pig. My fat little calf won a red ribbon
> once. Years later, I played that same fair as the star attraction.

> All this began back in the feudal days. You had to gather crowds to
> sell your goods. Nothing has really changed since then. We're still
> gathering crowds at agricultural, state and pumpkin fairs so the
> farmers can meet, look over animals, win prizes and have a little fun.

> Over 500 shows go out every May and the receipts from them are
> greater than the combined gates of baseball, football and basket-
> ball. The farmer is the key to the carny. We're still playing for him at
> the state fair. If the farmer goes the carny goes.

---

[8] A bachelor who shared his Dallas apartment with a man named George Senator,
Jack Ruby apparently never hit on the strippers at his clubs. He did, however, enjoy
the companionship of several dachshunds, and he was known to refer to one in
particular (named "Sheba") as his "wife."

You pick up important pieces of information traveling with the carny. For instance, I first learned about "mouseries" when I had to take care of two South American pythons.[9] Natasha, the snake charmer, got a live one and took off leaving me with the snakes. I'm living in Key West, trying to keep the pythons in mouse food. Up comes a hurricane, the pythons get loose and the house is about to fall apart in the storm. I tell you, I should write a book.

L ate in August 1964, Sally set up shop at the 1,400-seat Globe Theatre on the Boardwalk in Atlantic City, an engagement that coincided with the convening of the Democratic National Convention at Boardwalk Hall some 15 blocks down the street. Around town a mixed bag of entertainers was being offered up for those delegates and visitors who wanted to fill their time with something a bit more exciting than the nomination of incumbent President Lyndon B. Johnson to face Republican Senator Barry Goldwater in the upcoming general election. Eddie Fisher was appearing at the 500 Club, Mickey Rooney and Milton Berle (whose wife was a member of the California delegation) were holding forth at the Steel Pier, and Dick Gregory was playing at Basin Street East.

As politicians were gathering at Boardwalk Hall, Sally was being escorted to the convention floor by Atlantic City radio personality Pinky Kravitz, who considered the assignment a boost for his ego.[10] Spotting Senator Hubert Humphrey in the crowd, she called out: "Hubie baby, Sally's here!" LBJ's rumored pick to share the democratic ticket as candidate for vice president exclaimed: "Hey guys, Sally's here!" At this point, she turned to Pinky, said "Thank you, sonny," and stepped away, leaving the deflated young man standing alone, thinking: "All of a sudden, I had been ten feet tall and I went down to one foot off the floor."

Sally's show was doing decent business at the city's only burlesque theater but, frankly, delegates could have seen more bare skin on display by simply walking across the street to the beach where all manner of young girls were disporting themselves in the skimpy new two-piece bathing suits described by the media as having a bottom piece that "starts down much lower than it used to do. As for the top one, well, they would have raided the old Howard Theater in Boston if the girls had worn them there."

---

[9]   Mouseries are places where mice are bred and raised in captivity, either as show mice or as food for other animals. Show mice?

[10]   Often called "Mr. Atlantic City," Pinky Kravitz hosted "Pinky's Corner" for 57 consecutive years on WOND (1400 AM), the leading news-talk station in southern New Jersey. On October 31, 2015, Kravitz died at the age of 88.

While the Globe's paying customers seemed to think Sally's legs were still well worth seeing, the theater itself was on its last legs. Urban planners believed it was time for the aging theater to meet the wrecking ball. Addressing the Atlantic City Junior Chamber of Commerce, Sally protested: "Why would they want to do that to such a beautiful theater?" Sadly, her pleas and those of others fell on deaf ears, as the old Globe Theatre was closed not long thereafter.

The Democratic convention adjourned on August 27th. No sooner had all the political placards, cigarette butts, drink cups, banners, and confetti been cleared away than, three nights later, a predominantly young and mostly female crowd of 18,000 jammed into the hall to scream excitedly at a concert presented by a quartet of mop-haired British rock-and-rollers who earlier that same year had caused quite a stir on the Ed Sullivan television show. Next up at the convention hall? The Miss America Pageant.

Dick Gregory? Bikinis? The Beatles? Clearly, a cultural breeze was blowing. Just eight months earlier, a controversial new singer named Bob Dylan had released "The Times They Are A-Changin'" — the classic tune on the time-honored album of the same name. With so many new trends in vogue and so many cutting edge entertainers making names for themselves, could Sally Rand remain relevant? After all, she had been snubbed by the organizers of the 1964 World's Fair at age 60, and she wasn't getting any younger.

True enough, but Sally hardly seemed to notice. Besides, she was still in demand. On the 17th of September, fresh from Atlantic City, she appeared on the popular CBS-TV program *House Party* hosted by Art Linkletter. Then, in early 1965, she shared guest honors with the two-foot-taller professional basketball star Wilt Chamberlain on *That Regis Philbin Show*, where she related the story of how she had saved the 1933 World's Fair. And it wasn't all just nostalgia. Sally had one more police raid and arrest to look forward to.

B y the summer of 1965, you might think that the 61-year-old Sally Rand would no longer have to worry about being arrested for indecent exposure. The country had become so tolerant of nudity that it was popping up in big budget motion pictures. Even the revered Dr. Martin Luther King, Jr., had submitted to an interview for *Playboy* magazine that year. But on July 9th in Omaha, Nebraska, Sally Rand had managed to get through only a single performance of a nine-day engagement at Mickey's No. 1 Club before being arrested by the vice squad. Both she and club owner, George F. Earl, were booked at the Central Police Station and released on $300 bond each. The arresting officer, Vern Prescher, considered Miss Rand's act to be, as he put it, beyond the "bounds of propriety."

This case was a little different from Sally's previous arrests, in that she may actually have been dancing in the nude this time. Prescher testified that Sally had first appeared in a white gown, carrying two large ostrich feather fans, and dancing in a slow tempo to recorded organ music. He said that, after about one minute, he looked away for a moment and then the gown was gone, and her body was exposed to the audience for about six minutes.

A second vice squad officer, Sgt. John Quist, testified that when he talked to Sally after the show she told him that she typically made a new under-the-gown costume for every show, but because someone had borrowed her scissors she had been unable to make the costume that day. She claimed she had not danced "in the nude" in any case because she was wearing "shoes and fans and other intimate articles" that she didn't wish "to discuss in public."

The municipal ordinance under which Sally was charged read:

> It shall be unlawful for any person to appear in any inn, tavern, theater, street, alley or other public place in the City of Omaha, or upon the private property of another, in a state of nudity, or in a dress not belonging to his or her sex, or in an indecent or lewd dress, or to make any indecent exposure of his or her person, or be guilty of any lewd or indecent act or behavior.

Beyond the question of whether or not Sally had actually appeared "in a state of nudity," her attorney, Thomas Kelley, challenged the constitutionality of the municipal ordinance, arguing that the law was too vague and general. Kelley contended that the prohibition against any person from wearing the apparel of a person of the opposite sex in public would criminalize a teenage girl for wearing jeans and a boy's shirt. Allowing the prosecutor time to respond to this argument, the judge continued Sally's case until August 24th, more than six weeks after the alleged offense.

After that subsequent hearing, Judge Eugene A. Leahy held the Omaha ordinance to be unconstitutional on a technical point.[11] He dismissed all charges against Sally and the club manager, saying:

> I'm not making any decision on the morality or immorality of the act put on by Miss Rand. I sincerely feel that these laws must be

---

[11] Sally's defense attorney successfully argued that restricting people from wearing clothes of the opposite sex "makes the doing of an innocent act a crime." In another case decided that week, a different Nebraska judge remarked that members of a football team could be arrested for undressing in front of each other in the locker room. Since the court held certain applications of the law to be unconstitutional, the entire provision was found to be invalid.

cleared up by the Legal Department. I'm sick and tired of trying to interpret these laws for them.

Predictably, Judge Leahy's decision wasn't popular with everyone. A representative of the Legion of Decency in Cincinnati, Ohio, wrote of the judgment: "Your knowledge of the obscenity laws is abysmally ignorant." Apparently this sort of criticism didn't have much impact on the electorate, as four years later the judge was elected mayor of Omaha.[12]

In the mid-to-late sixties, while the country was embroiled in a brutal war half a world away, Sally just kept moving forward. In 1966, she performed at the "Fan Ball" at New York's Hotel Plaza — a benefit for the Children's Cancer Fund. In 1967, she was featured in the touring company of *Anatomy of Burlesque*, demonstrating the "Charleston" as well as performing her famous fan and bubble dances.[13] Headlined by Joey Faye, "veteran of the baggy-pants school of comedy," the nostalgic program offered "old-time burlesque in a series of sketches, blackouts, comedy, song and dance" and provided audiences a couple of hours' respite from the turmoil in the world outside the theater. When asked if she planned to entertain the troops in Vietnam, Sally demurred: "I don't want to get involved in anything controversial."

On May 8, 1967, Sally began a limited engagement at The Body Shop at 8250 Sunset Strip in Los Angeles,[14] with a show billed on the marquee as "Sally Rand and her Nudie Revue." By this time, she had devised a new way to make her grand entrance. Two chorus girls would come out in pink chiffon formal dresses, wearing pink shoes and carrying large ostrich feather fans. After waltzing around the stage for a bit, they would come together at the center of the stage with the fans between them, forming a sort of swinging saloon door arrangement. Sally would then approach from the rear of the stage, push the fans aside and emerge to eager applause.

---

[12] Eugene "Gene" Leahy served as Omaha's mayor from 1969 until 1973. His colorful antics, such as wearing a bunny suit when attending charitable occasions, endeared him to many. He was also known for reading the Sunday comics on a local television station. Gene Leahy Mall in Downtown Omaha is named in honor of him.

[13] According to a feature article in the *Miami News*, at age 63, Sally was still expertly wielding her two large fans (each fan weighed 7 pounds with 21 separate ribs, up to 52 inches long) and her huge translucent bubble which was five-feet in diameter — as tall as Sally.

[14] The Body Shop ("the only all-nude gentlemen's club on the Sunset Strip") is still in operation at this location. It is open to adults seven days a week until 4 a.m. for the all-day admission price of $10, plus a two-drink minimum (non-alcoholic).

As Sally always wanted to look her best for the opening night, she had arranged for an old acquaintance, celebrated hairdresser Kenneth Marlowe, to style her hair. Marlowe was not your ordinary hairdresser. His 1964 autobiography recounted in shocking-for-the-time detail his adventures as a female impersonator. It even included the story of how, as a young man in the fifties, he had successfully auditioned for a position at the Club My-O-My in New Orleans by performing a Sally Rand fan dance.

To say the very least, the 40-year-old Marlowe had led an unconventional life.[15] His book's dust jacket gives us an inkling:

> As an unwanted child, Kenneth Marlowe turned to sex and it became the key to his life, opening myriad dismal doors until he was able to find himself.

> Kept by a Sugar Daddy as a teenager, he went on to become a star-stripper in gaudy Calumet City, and a hairdresser in a New Orleans cathouse. After the Kefauver Investigations, he was drafted and raped by fourteen men in his barracks — and enjoyed it! He studied for the missionary, owned a theatrical telephone answering service and operated his own male Call House in Hollywood. And between these and other escapades, worked in every kind of hair salon and resort until he reached the top as the personal hair stylist of the world's most celebrated women.

Marlowe arrived at The Body Shop to do Sally's hair around four o'clock in the afternoon. It was only a few hours before showtime and Sally was busy adjusting the blue lights and checking on the music for her show when one of her featured "fan holders" called in sick. She came away from the phone "cussing like a sailor." But then she had an idea:

> She lifted Ken's trouser legs and said, "Are your legs still as good looking as they used to be?" Sally pulled Ken's hair back and said, "I've got a blond wig that will look great on you. Get upstairs and get your legs shaved. I'll be up in a few minutes to make you up." Sally called to her assistant and told her to get up there and alter that dress so it would fit Ken.

> "But Sally," Ken yelled, "what will I do for tits?"

> "Oh, hell, take off your socks," she replied.

---

15 Marlowe, as "queen of a beehive of pretty little homosexual slaves" was reputed to have offered certain "services" to an "exclusive Hollywood clientele."

Ken paused a second time and yelled back, "But I'm not as young as I was when I was on stage years ago."

"With these blue lights, nobody will notice. Hell, I'm 63, honey, and I'm still taking off my clothes. Don't worry about it."

The impersonation went off without a hitch and, apparently, no one was the wiser. As a Marlowe biographer recalled:

Ken stayed in the act for five nights. Salary was never mentioned. Eventually, the newspapers got wind of the story and reported that one of the chorus girls was a man. Sally told Ken that she could not afford to have that kind of publicity. Besides the other girl was well now.

Ken Marlowe enjoyed himself immensely and did his best to wrangle a permanent position in the show. But the club owner wouldn't hear of it: "This is an all girl show." Although disappointed, Marlowe did come away from the experience with a rare distinction — he is the only person that Sally ever personally taught to perform the fan dance.

In July 1968, Sally returned to Fort Worth and the Casa Mañana, the site of her earlier success and the place where she had created the "Nude Ranch." At 64, she was exactly twice as old as she was when Billy Rose first brought her there for the Texas Centennial in 1936. This time she was in town as a featured performer in *A Funny Thing Happened on the Way to the Forum*.[16] Sally's performance was well received. According to the local press, "she got herself an ovation from the packed house."

A young man named Jay Wallace was serving as her personal assistant during the engagement. He marveled at Sally's lack of self-consciousness:

There were so many times and so many stories and so many things that happened to Sally. I shall never forget. Well, you know what it's like to walk into a restaurant here with a star. And Sally was just unique. We were at the Pancake House late and she had never had one of those Dutch Babies, you know one of those

---

16   According to Jack Sheridan's local review of the play: "When the show opened on Broadway a few years back there was no female character billed as 'Fantabula.' There is now — and how! Casa Mañana, in a stroke of genius, engaged a durable lady who has made the fan dance all her own institution, put her six-minute spot in the show, and called her 'Fantabula' — Sally Rand."

things they fold over and do a whole production on.[17] She saw them making one on another table and said, "That's what I want." So we ordered it for her. She ate it down to the bare plate. You know the wonderful way she ate, with such relish and gusto. And she took the spoon and was lapping up every bit of the sauce and syrup that was left and then finally picked up the plate and was licking it — and everyone was looking — but who else in the world could get away with that but Sally.

The two weeks Wallace spent with Sally as her assistant, or quite literally her "body man," were like none other in his life.[18]

This was also the year that Sally began to get serious about writing her life story. An incurable pack rat, she had accumulated a huge trove of photographs, correspondence, press clippings, and memorabilia over the decades, and she knew that these materials, along with her exceptional memory, could easily serve as source material for a definitive autobiography.

Knowing that her friend Gypsy Rose Lee had published her own autobiography some 10 years earlier, Sally wrote to her on June 26, 1968, seeking her advice:

> *I am now in the midst of the "book." There are so many things I wanted to ask you about, publishers, advances, publicity and all the things that go along with a book....*
>
> *I know what a busy gal you are, but do you think you could tell me something by letter?... Harper and Row, World, Putnam's and Rand McNally have all contacted me about it. Whom should I choose?*

After adding a page and a half of questions about literary agents, royalties, and photographs, she apologized for asking so many questions.

Miss Lee replied to Sally's entreaty a week later, writing:

> Am working like a dog right now — one project after another. But I will certainly answer your letter in length when the horizon is clearer.
>
> So glad you have finally decided to start the book.

---

[17] A "Dutch Baby" pancake is a sort of cross between an omelet or crepe and a popover. The recipe for this brunch favorite with a light, puffy crust and a tender, custard-like middle can easily be found online.

[18] More of Jay Wallace's experiences with Sally are revealed in chapter 25.

Around this same time, Sally wrote to her friend, Chet Hagan, the NBC news producer who four years earlier had produced the *Carny* TV special. He responded with advice on hiring an agent and obtaining a publisher's advance and royalties. He suggested that she send him an outline, including a sample chapter or two: "You can be assured that I will treat it with tender loving care and I would think that interest will be high."

Hagan's letter also included a tantalizing reference to a project that was never developed but, apparently, might have been: "Re the TV series — still very interested, of course, and am trying to line up financing." Ten months later, another letter hinted at what may have been in the works: "The talk show thing ain't dead, but TV is a crazy business and I've decided to let it rest for a couple of weeks and then pitch a whole new series of contacts."

Talks about "the book" dragged on for a year; several publishers either contacted Sally or were contacted by her. Some confusion arose in the correspondence, since there were two proposed publications being discussed simultaneously — the less significant handbook "Here's How" and Sally's actual memoirs.[19] By late April of 1969, Sally's longtime personal attorney Abe Berman had drawn up a contract that was under review by John Greenya, president of Writing, Incorporated, in Washington, DC. After some disagreement over the terms, Berman advised Sally:

> A very important book will be written on the life of Sally Rand.
> Do you want to tie yourself down to Writing, Incorporated and give them 20% even though the book may be placed by some other agent either in Hollywood or New York?

Resigned to the breakdown in negotiations, Greenya wrote to Sally:

> As usual, life refuses to be simple. I thought Abe understood our agreement, but I guess I was wrong.... I wish my attorney took as good care of me as Berman does of you. I see why you so value him.

In the end, all the presentations, contacts, and haggling over terms came to nothing. Neither manuscript was ever published.

Taking note of the ever-increasing dominance of television and looking back nostalgically on the arc of her career, in a surviving fragment of her memoirs (written in 1969), Sally lamented the passing of an era with characteristic insight, recalling that there were once "elaborate motion

---

[19] An outline of Sally's "Here's How" has survived. It would have been an interesting read, as evidenced by the excerpts in chapter 25.

picture houses all over the United States that augmented their pictures ...
with fabulous stage shows": [20]

> They had maybe thirty girls in line and sixteen showgirls and
> singers and dancers and novelty acts and goodness knows what.
> There were several tremendous companies producing these
> shows that ran in over three hundred theaters, fifty-two weeks a
> year ... that gave employment to thousands of actors, dancers,
> choreographers, musicians, etc.

> With the inception of television, people stayed glued to the boob-
> tube and nobody went to the theater. And so, theaters grew darker
> and darker and the first thing to go were the stage shows and
> finally pictures themselves — why leave your home, why go out
> and pay admission to a theater when you can see ... the finest talent
> in the whole world on television.... There is a generation, which
> has never seen a live stage show.

While Sally could still secure bookings in a few major venues like Miami
Beach, she also had to take whatever was available elsewhere to make ends
meet, as evidenced by her September 1969 tour in Iowa. Stops there included
not only East Dubuque, Iowa City, and two weeks at Sastos Lounge in Des
Moines (where "Living Legend" James Brown was appearing just down the
way), but also a six-day engagement at the Pussy Cat Lounge in Oelwein.[21]
As an "Extra Added Attraction," Sally's show included appearances by Edna
Brown,[22] "The Swingin'est Gal in Town," and "the fabulous" organist
Henry Roddeger. The local press noted that Sally was no longer just a fan
dancer but also a "scholar, lecturer, and raconteur."

---

[20] In 1930, weekly attendance at the movies was estimated at 80 million people, or about
65 percent of the U.S. population. By 2000, attendance had fallen to only 27.3 million
people, a mere 9.7 percent of the U.S. population (MPAA, U.S. Statistical Abstract).

[21] Truth be told, Oelwein, Iowa, may not have been the cultural backwater you might
presume. Sally's act at the Pussy Cat Lounge was competing with a film at the
Oelwein Drive-In Theatre, *Naked Angels*, that a local newspaper ad described as
"Mad Dogs from Hell! Hunting down their prey with a quarter-ton of hot steel
between their legs!"

[22] A singer from Michigan, Edna Brown enlivened her act with off-color jokes between
songs. She joined Sally in 1966, touring with her for 10 years before returning home
to Michigan. Crowned Ms. Senior Michigan in 1991, Edna Brown spent her
remaining years entertaining seniors.

At 65 Sally understood her situation all too well. As she "took a deep drag on her cigarette," she told local columnist Donald Kaul:

> In the days when I was making so much money, I had expected that, at this stage in my career, I would be working mainly in the theater. Unfortunately, what I did to make all that money precludes anyone from taking me seriously. People hear my name and say: "Sally Rand. My God! Is she still alive?"

Sally's appeal had long outlived her early critics' predictions of its likely demise. This durability had been forecast 34 years earlier by author Stanley Walker: "It appears probable that she will remain popular until withered by age, or until the yearning apple-knockers of the provinces cease their moony worship of alabaster torsos."

Kaul himself observed that Sally had "a vulnerable quality, a kind of inde-structible innocence" that "manifests itself in the candor with which she looks at herself." As Sally told him:

> I wish I'd lived a profound life; been able to produce great and wonderful things to advance the state of man.

> But I haven't. Not many people's lives are very profound. And perhaps those whose lives we look upon as profound don't realize it themselves.

> If I didn't do this, what would I do? I'm not exactly the needlepoint type.

> And I have a hell of a long time yet to go.

For most of Sally's life, she and her mother had enjoyed a close relation-ship. Annette had been a member of Sally's traveling staff off and on for many years. At one point, she even had personalized stationary made to order with the name "Annette Rand" at the top.

As she celebrated her 65th birthday in Miami Beach on April 4, 1969, Sally wrote to her "Dearest Mother," who was by then quite frail and confined to her home in Glendora:

> *This is my birthday. An incredible sixty five years ago you gave me my life.*

> *When they put me in your arms, what prayers did you tiredly whisper in gratitude for safe deliverance from that fearful travail and for the child that you had borne?*

Did you, as I did, look in awe and wonder at the tiny human creature that God and love had created and given the miracle of life? Did you examine the minuscule pink feet, dream of all the steps and myriad paths they would take, and ardently wish that they would all be bright and happy ones? And the small starfish hands and say "Oh, God, let these hands be kind and gentle, and because it is my baby please, graceful and pretty, too?...

Dear Mother, I do thank you for my life... for wise and honest counsel in my stubborn and tempestuous teens, for compassion and silence when I made irreparable mistakes, for your joy, pleasure, and pride in my success, for the then and now, and all the tomorrows and birthdays, all my gratitude and love.

Nettie was now nearly 88 years old and no longer able to fully care for herself. Sally had found it necessary to engage the services of a cousin, 33-year-old June McAda, as a live-in caretaker. At the time, her husband Harold was serving in Vietnam and, in addition to three young children who were living with her in Glendora, June also had an older son with severe mental retardation who was living in an institution in Austin, Texas. Writing to Sally four days later, she reported on Nettie's deteriorating condition and delivered some unsettling news:

She seems to tire so easily these days and complains so of being drunk. I believe her eye sight is worse, since you have been gone. She has several good days and then for a day or so she is in the bed most of the day....

Gee, my Harold may come home the end of May. We don't know where we are going but probably Texas. Harold wants to be near our son, Rodney.... I am wondering if you have someone in mind to come and stay with Aunt Net when I have to leave.

Sally would have to find someone else to look after her mother. Upset at the prospect, she wrote to June, none too subtly indicating her distress:

... I am terribly sorry to have to think of you leaving, because of course, there is no way of replacing you. No matter at what price, one can never buy love ... and certainly you have given mother that.

Now what I am about to say has nothing to do with my feeling about you taking care of mother, because after your husband comes back from Vietnam, even if you stay in Glendora, I would not expect you nor want you to spend time away from your house and family. However, I do think it is the greatest mistake for you to make so drastic a move clear to Texas just to be near Rodney. I don't care how much advance he seems to be making in learning skills; you must face up to the fact that this child's brain is not all there…. Rodney has no understanding, nor can he have, of his prior life with you or your relationship to him. They have established for him a simple, disciplined daily routine to which he has become accustomed and I am sure that the attendant nurses and teachers in that institution, as well as the doctors who recommended it for him, will tell you that your presence near him or with him can only be a disturbing factor….

I just have to believe, June, that … you … will move near Rodney only to be hurt again and again by seeing with your own eyes his pitiable condition. This suffering that you will undergo … is self-flagellation, a kind of masochism, like punishing yourselves for having produced such a child. As if there was some guilt attached to you because he is retarded. For God's sake, June, stop dreaming. This child's condition is not your fault, nor Harold's fault, nor anyone's fault. Who are we to question God and God's infinite wisdom?… Thank God that Rodney is infinitely better and happier than with the family. You have seen and experienced the truth of this. Now take the first step. Let loose of it. Release it. He is in God's hands. …

… Perhaps you think that I am overly zealous about this because it means you can no longer take care of Mom, but this is not true. I will say no more about it, ever, but I wish you would think about it seriously.

Sally's exhortations were in vain. All the same, she did find a replacement caretaker within a few weeks, signing an employment agreement with Jerry H. Gardiner to serve as a live-in nurse and companion to her mother. Beyond assisting Mrs. Kisling with her medications, meals, transportation and the like, the custodial contract specified that Gardiner's job responsibilities would include laundry, grocery shopping and helping Sally's mother with bedroom and bath functions, adding:

You will be expected to keep the rest of the house in reasonably good order, with the exception of my son's room, which he cares for himself, and my quarters, which are not to be disturbed, and see that the outer door is kept locked at all times.

By the following year in the summer of 1970, Annette Kisling was in further decline — so much so that Sally was shocked into the realization that the end might be near. On the night of August 8th, she composed this heartfelt letter to her "Dearest Mom," written in pencil on a yellow legal pad:

Angel Darling

Please read this — and understand it — and if you can't, ask Sean to read it to you — it's very intimate and personal —

Please, Please, don't go — Stay with me — I need you so — There is no use for anything without you — no meaning — What's the use of dancing — if not for you — every night I see your face out there — being proud of me — like tonight the audience stood up and cheered — and all I thought of was you — and how proud you would have been — and all my smiles, and all my bows were to you and for you — It's no use — no good if you're not here — The garden, the flowers the roses — all for you — The pretty house and gold furniture, and cups and saucers — and beautiful China, just for you, to see your pretty face smile and glow with pleasure and pride because they're yours —

To fix the house and make things nice — just for you —

What use is any of it — if there is no you?

Oh mamma, you're so strong — you can do anything — if you want to — you always have and you still can —

Just try — Please try — hold back that old man — don't let him in — Live — Be you

You can do it — We've got it made Mom — This is a wonderful job — a great show — and the critics and audiences love me — read the good write ups — we're in Gravy now — Oh stay with me — don't go now — I have nothing to live for but you.

Sean doesn't need me — He doesn't even like me — He doesn't want our home — or like it.

But We do.

Stay with me darling so we can enjoy it together – I'm getting the Book done — and I'll get a lot of money for it.

So I can stay home —

Hang on Mamma —

Hang on —

Please tell me you will — Please tell me you understand this letter.

I love you —

Sally

Exactly five months later on January 8, 1971, Mary Annette Kisling died in Glendora, California, at 89 years of age. Perhaps more than most, she had been that rock for her daughter that mothers so often are. With her passing went nearly seven decades of intimate experiences that, while still possible for Sally to recall, could never again be shared.

CHAPTER TWENTY-FOUR

Girls Just Want to Have Fun

Oh, such shenanigans!
~ Anita Robertson to Sally, 1948

W hile Sally seemed to charm every red-blooded male within her orbit, her charismatic powers were not limited to members of the opposite sex. Chorus girls and other members of her troupe commonly responded to her as if she were their mother, mentor, valued colleague, or dear friend. Their stories and correspondence suggest what life may have been like for a woman on the road with Sally Rand.

Lorie Barnes

Daughter of choreographer Marjorie Fielding and stage manager, singer, and emcee Charles Barnes, Lorie was born on the 10th of June in 1930. The family had first crossed paths with Sally at the 1933 Chicago World's Fair when Lorie was only three years old, but, since both of her parents ended up working for Sally off and on over the years, she came to know Sally and her company quite well.

In 1943, the 13-year-old found herself enchanted by a handsome young dancer in Sally's troupe — Johnny Delaney. An attraction had been sparked, but it was wartime and Johnny soon left to enter the Navy. When the war was over they reconnected, marrying in 1946. Lorie was 18 years old and a new mother when she and Johnny rejoined Sally as a dance team with the Royal American Shows' traveling carnival in 1948.[1] Singing and performing solo dances as well, Lorie soon became a valuable member of Sally's troupe. She described the rigors of doing "like ten shows a day" at the carnival:

> I went down to a skeleton and John — who was about 6'1",
> 180 pounds — went down to about 145 pounds. It was tough. We
> ate pretty well, but we were just sweating it off. It was hot under
> that tent. We were under the lights and it was hot to begin with.

---

[1] The tale of how Lorie Barnes acquired the stage name "Lori Jon" and was pressured by Sally to give up her baby Paul for adoption was told in chapter 21.

Lorie recalled appearing alongside Sally in the fan dance:

> She was nude — no body stocking — but she wore flesh-colored patches over her nipples and her pubic hair. That was all. They looked like flesh; they were specially made. We had bikini-type costumes with silver sequins, very brief — little bras that were like little cups with strings around. We were covered — somewhat. I had some body back then, let me tell you….

> On the show train, John and I had a stateroom. There was just enough space for one person on top and a double bunk on the bottom that we slept in. Friends had built a little crib up top that swung open and we kept Paul in that. And we had a little Coca-Cola icebox that we kept his formula in. We had to trudge 48 cars down to get a chef to boil his bottles every other day. We didn't have plastic bottles or paper diapers. When we came to town, we would find a Laundromat and wash what we had — we had a big bag full of diapers.

> We'd eat on the train when we were en route. But when we got there, there was something called a cook tent and the chef would be cooking there. Or if we had any time off (we'd have a few hours in the evening maybe), we would go into town (but not often). I left the show when we were in Alberta, Canada, because of a terrible fight John and I had. It got pretty bad. John had a bad temper. And we were under terrible strain.

Confirming rumors that Sally had been intimately involved with her father, Lorie recalled:

> She had a crush on my Dad…. Sally was a free soul. Sally did what she wanted, but she was very critical of other people doing it. She was a bit of a hypocrite. I think it all started because she kept him as her stage manager. I think maybe it was going on because mother was a horrible flirt. I'd almost classify Mom as a nymphomaniac. She was after everything in pants….

> The last time I worked for Sally was in 1949. I was married to my second husband, but John was in the show. She opened [in "Sally Rand and her Fan-Tale Revue"] at the Maryland Theater in Baltimore. Dad was still working for her, so I went down and did that show….

> It was so funny. Sally was a complete study in opposites. She could be such a lady when she wanted to — in interviews and when she wanted to present herself that way — but, if you were alone in her dressing room … she could use the most vile language, like a truck driver.

Anita Robertson

Born in 1913, a redhead from Oklahoma, Anita Louise Robertson, was a single gal in her early twenties when she went to work for Sally. In the same way that Ralph Hobart was Sally's fully dedicated "major domo," Anita Robertson was her equally dedicated secretary and traveling companion. The two worked and traveled together off and on from the late 1930s to the early 1950s. They often shared close quarters, as at the Kansas State Fair in 1951, where as you may recall the two conspired to keep the local sheriff from confiscating Sally's cache of cash. The trailer they shared was jammed with costumes, publicity material, extra closets, and a spare bed for three-year-old Sean.

Little exists in the public record on the nature of Anita's personal relationship with Sally, but a series of letters that she wrote in November of 1948, shortly after Sally had adopted Sean, clearly indicates the level of affection that Anita felt for her boss.

At the time, Sally was performing at the Frolics Club in Tampa, appearing at a fundraiser with Gypsy Rose Lee and receiving plaintive letters from Ralph Hobart begging her for funds. On November 6th, from her home in Lawton, Oklahoma, Anita composed a handwritten letter to her "Dearest Sally":

> Hi honey. So I 'spose you're in warm & sunny Florida — me, I had to get into bed with the Prune to get warm. What's the Prune? Well, it's a very poor substitute for you, I can tell you for sure — not half as nice a bedfellow — but it does warm my feet. They're getting toasted right now and it's very pleasant — but I'd much rather share my bed with you. How's about it? Come on, crawl in baby.

After a page and a half detailing her work around the house and her struggles in looking after a "lively little 4 year old," Anita closed with:

> Sally dear, I'm so sleepy, guess I'll have to say goodnight again. But I'll be with you in my dreams, dearly beloved. You are the very sweetest one and I adore you. Hurry and bring your darling Shean & your own precious self to visit me, won't you please? Thank you again, angel, for your lovely letter and thank you for loving me & for letting me love you — oh how I do.

Three days later, in a manner reminiscent of Sally's persistent suitor Jack Crosby twenty years earlier, Anita took pen in hand once more:

> Here I am in bed with the Prune again. Why can't it be you instead? Hurry and make time fly until you are here with me darling. It won't be too much longer, will it sweet? ...

I love you so much precious, you surely must feel it. And oh how
proud & thrilled & gratefully happy it makes me to be your "dearly
beloved friend." Thank you Sally sweet. I'm about to wear your letter
to shreds reading & re-reading it. How's about writing me another to
share the wear and tear? Sure enough baby, I'd be so pleased to hear
from you again — not only for the sake of hearing from you, though
that is reason enough to cause me joy certainly — but you know how
interested I am in your plans and activities ... I'm thinking good
thoughts for you & loving you every minute my dearly beloved.

Back in the 1930s, Anita's sister Babs had been one of Sally's showgirls. In
another letter, Anita recalled a number of amusing episodes that Babs had
kept a record of:

I practically had hysterics at some of the cute things Babs wrote —
for instance, the lingering odor from a mule act of the previous
week in a theatre at Zanesville; and the hilarious fun on stage
during the last show on closing night with extra flourishes of
truckin' added to the finale; the time the ballet was cut but
somebody forgot to notify the dancers and they suddenly found
themselves standing bewilderedly on stage with no music and here
you came down the steps with your fans for your number saying
"shoo, scat, scram!"; the time that Edith Goode took the fantastic
notion that she would learn to play a hot trumpet & lead her own
band & whenever she'd hit a high note she'd stand up & bump[2]...

Anita remembered several pranks Sally had played on the girls:

There was the time we all had done five or six shows & were at the
slap-happy stage when in breezed fresh-as-a-daisy you &
mischievously informed the girls that they would all have to shave
for the 3 A.M. show to be performed in the nude for the Elks; the
time that Nell Kelly proudly bragged that she had cleaned her
dressing room for the first time in years and you simply couldn't
bear it until she had gone on for her number, then you & Ralphie &
the others really tore it up — but good — messing up her makeup
shelf, tossing her coat & things from her trunk all around,

---

[2]   This brings to mind the lyrics of "You Gotta Get a Gimmick" by Stephen Sondheim, a
       song in the 1959 Broadway musical *Gypsy*, based on the life of Gypsy Rose Lee. The
       show-stopping tune, delivered by "Miss Mazzeppa," concludes with:

       If you wanna bump it,
       Bump it with a trumpet
       Get yourself a gimmick
       And you too can be a star.

emptying all the wastepaper baskets on the floor, then watching
the fit Nell threw when she returned to find it; and another stunt
pulled on Nell, decorating her dressing room as a dive with a red
light & signs outside the door quoting hours & prices, then
inquiring of her "How's business?" — Oh such shenanigans!

Anita continued, describing a bit of on-stage tomfoolery:

Then there was the time everybody got to telling jokes on stage
trying to break each other up — Peggy Anne's verse — "Chigger, my
lad, Chigger, my buck, come out to the garden, and I'll give you a —
flower" — and Babs' question to Jackie "What's the difference between
a rich man & a poor man?" to which Jackie's answer was "I don't
know." The next time they maneuvered near enough each other for
speech — so Babs says "A rich man has a canopy over his bed & a
poor man has one under his," which drew a blank stare from Jackie
until somewhat later in the number Babs looked across stage to see
Jackie suddenly start bouncing up & down with laughter…. Such
goings on with that Randy Dandy Bunch! They were really a grand
gang, weren't they?

She concluded her letter with expressions of concern that Sally was working
too hard and appreciation for her financial help, closing with:

Never, never can I repay you for being so good to me, for loving
me & letting me love you, for being such a dear, sweet, wonderful
person, for your own lovely beautiful self. I'm so very grateful for
you Sally, for your friendship and your love. And I truly do
worship you, dear.

Thank you again, my darling, for talking to me on the phone
tonight. Don't forget the suggestion about my coming to meet you
& driving back with you. Let's work something out, hmm? I mean,
if you want me to, if I could help you any. For me, every minute I'm
with you I'm in heaven…. Hug that precious Shean[3] for me — I'm
sending enough love for you both. Goodnight kisses to you sweet.

---

[3] Sally had recently sent Anita several newspaper clippings announcing her adoption of
baby "Shean." In this same letter Anita inquired: "What would you say to my sending
one to Joan Crawford? Had a letter from her shortly after I returned from my week
with you[;] … I want to tell her about my wonderful visit with you & the happy plans
for the future. I have had a couple of the snapshots we took finished to send her — the
one of you & me together and the precious one of you, lovely you, alone in your
finale gown — the Dior one."

Anita had a habit of clipping out little poems and quotes (both poignant and amusing) and taping them in the margins of her letters, among them:

> There was a young lady named Banker,
> Who slept while the ship was at anchor.
> She woke in dismay
> When she heard the mate say,
> "Now hoist up the topsheet and spanker."

She would also hand copy and insert more thoughtful lines from published works, such as these from *To an Adored One* by Julia A. French:

> My adoration runs through little themes
> And falls a breathless poem at your feet.

In the last of her letters to Sally that November, Anita revealed the same insecurities that so often characterized the letters from Sally's suitors in the 1920s:

> You're a very special person, you know, certainly in my book ...
> I'm sure no one could love you as much as I do. I hope, Sally, you
> don't think I'm crowding you, writing you as often as I have &
> telephoning you. I don't mean to, dear, but maybe my enthusiasm
> is too much — you did say "keep writing" though, didn't you, so
> I hope I'm not wearing out my welcome by overdoing it.... Do
> hope you don't think me a nuisance. Try to love me in spite of it,
> won't you sweet? I'm just counting the days till I see you.... Wish
> I could get a nice big letter from you in tomorrow's mail — well, I
> can dream, can't I? And I think that's just what I'll do right now
> since it's past midnight. I 'spose your night is only just beginning
> there at the night club. Well, I'll join you in my dreams & let's
> make a sure 'nough good night of it. It's bound to be wonderful if
> I'm with you, beloved Sally.

Anita had health problems that often kept her at home in Lawton when she would much rather have been on the road. Sally did find a way to keep Anita in the loop by sometimes sending her the lengthy letters that she had handwritten to others so that Anita could type and mail them out.

Sunny Van

Born in 1909, Grace Van Hedenkamp was one of three daughters of Mr. and Mrs. William Van Hedenkamp of Philadelphia. She and her sister, Meta, had gravitated to show business, following in the footsteps of their aunt Emma Marion, a renowned dancer. Fresh out of high school, the petite Grace picked up the nickname "Sunny" because of her golden blond "bob" hairstyle. A trained ballerina, Sunny's professional career advanced rapidly as she spent two seasons with the Metropolitan Opera Company, even dancing a solo in *Petrushka*.

Still teenagers in September of 1924, Sunny and Meta were performing in the chorus of the musical comedy *Dear Sir* at the Forrest Theatre in Philadelphia when disaster struck. Rehearsing a scene that required her to dive into a large wooden water tank, Meta was gravely injured when she miscalculated her leap and struck her head on the edge of the tank, breaking her neck. Sunny witnessed the accident.

Devastated by the death of her sister, Sunny nevertheless persevered in her chosen profession, ultimately landing a spot with the Albertina Rasch[4] dance group and later appearing in several Broadway productions alongside such stars as Ruby Keeler, Marie Dressler, and Eddie Cantor. Not just a member of the chorus, Sunny commonly secured speaking parts and solo dances, including such specialty numbers as the popular "snake hips" dance.

By 1931, Sunny had met and fallen under the spell of Mischa Markoff, a Russian "Gypsy" dancer nine years her senior who was master of ceremonies and principal entertainer at the Russian Art Cabaret on 2nd Avenue in Manhattan. The couple subsequently married.

At some point, Sunny joined Sally's traveling show and they soon became fast friends. The two had a lot in common. Both were trained ballerinas, both petite charmers with outgoing personalities, and each knew how to use her effervescence and bat her eyelashes to advance herself.

While Sally and Sunny may have been friends, their relationship was always that of employer and employee. Over the years, as Sally developed into a savvy business woman, Sunny remained quite immature, even as a middle-aged married woman. It was a shattering blow to her when Mischa died early in 1955, leaving her a widow and understandably distraught.

Sally reacted to Mischa's death with compassion, offering to fly her old friend from New York City to Denver to join Sally's tour as a paid assistant. Sunny agreed to come, but the arrangement turned sour within a matter of weeks. From Sally's perspective, her rescue efforts had fallen flat. Sunny spent most of her time in Denver drowning her sorrows at the bar and doing very little work. She ultimately returned to New York.

---

4   Vienna-born, Mme. Albertina Rasch was a prominent ballet instructor and choreographer who opened her own New York dance studio in 1923 and formed a troupe that appeared in many Broadway productions, including the Ziegfeld *Follies* and George White's *Scandals*.

Even so, back in Glendora, Sally reached out to Sunny once again. This time she paid for Sunny to fly to California to stay with her and Fred Lalla, her husband of only eight months. No job or payment was involved, but it was understood that Sunny would lend a hand around the house. Apparently, she liked the "moving in" idea all right, but the "helping out" part? Not so much. Sunny ended up moving out to stay with a woman friend she called "Poops."

Frustrated and embittered by what she saw as her friend's self-indulgence and irresponsible behavior, Sally grabbed a pen and legal pad to spew out a diatribe of more than 33 pages! In an apparent attempt at an intervention, she recited their recent experiences in excruciating detail.[5]

Referring to her offer to let Sunny move in with her and Fred in exchange for help with the housework, Sally recalled:

> ... *You laughed and said, and I quote "I never even cooked for myself — my Misha did all my cooking. Anyway I'll stay here [at Poops' house] for a while. I just love it...."*

> *If you could have come up here and been content ... to have helped me get this hard mean job done, by putting your hand to whatever you could do to be useful — cheerfully and happily — we could have managed beautifully ... but I knew that life would be hell, I would get mad and nothing would get done....*

> *It's time for you to grow up. Sunny, you are no longer Misha's "little girl." Your private world of being a perpetual little girl ended with Misha. Face it. It was fun. We'd all like to do it — be pampered and babied and waited on and indulged. You had it. You have it no longer, nor are you going to have it again, for no matter whom you marry, they are not going to hold still for a "quart-a-day, bloated, middle-aged little girl."*

> *Face it, there is nothing unlovely [or] sad about being middle-aged, except when [people] make themselves the object of ridicule and objects to be pitied and laughed at because they are living in an unreal world of their own making.... Wake up, yesterday is gone, it is not here, you cannot change this no matter how hard you try, nor how you close your eyes, nor how drunk you get, nor how long you stay drunk. For God's sake (and yours) discard the poke bonnets, the Mary Jane flats, the*

---

5   A major portion of this overlong handwritten draft has survived. It is unclear whether the letter was ever typed and/or sent after Sally had a chance to consider her words in the cold light of day.

little girl clothes, the baby talk, the baby superstitions and the little girl whims and whimsies and your fierce determination to accept no mature responsibilities.

Here are the facts —
You are fifty (or near about)
Fat
Bloated
Under the influence of whisky 24 hours a day

You have no money — no home — no job — and in your present state, no prospects for marriage (Bill is too smart to marry you as you are). You have no education that would make you useful at a job that requires brains (except dancing). You do not look well enough to get a job dancing.... Your appearance is bad because you are fat — and bloated and look like a drinker — your clothes are in bad taste because they don't fit your age or your body.

Sally felt she had sincerely reached out to her grieving friend by offering her work and attempting to redirect her thoughts to the future. Sunny would have been a sort of all-around assistant, helping out in the dressing room and also serving as the unseen hand pulling Sally's gown away from behind the curtain at the climax of the fan dance. She believed she was being quite magnanimous in extending a hand to Sunny:

I can get a girl to pull my fan dress, keep my dressing room cleaned up, my makeup table straight and make my quick change for a maximum of $1 a show.... I don't have to send clear to New York to get a girl. For $50 a week, room and board & traveling, I can get an expert stenographer & bookkeeper — [one who] goes to the theater and helps me with my changes too. So why did I send for you? Real simple.

You are my friend. I love you. You had suffered a deep and irreparable loss; you were grieved and lonely and confused, and frightened. How can I best help my friend who is troubled? ... My whole object in bringing you to be with me in Denver was to be of help and comfort and service to you in time of trouble — and how did it work out?

Not very well. Sally ended up paying for Sunny to come from New York to Denver by train (after she had refused to fly). She had arrived the day before the end of a three-week engagement and had cost, as Sally grumbled: "an extra expensive fare from Chicago to Denver and back to Chicago again — for what? — to pull my fan dress off four times?" The troupe then left for

Milwaukee. Once there, Sunny did so little work that other members of the staff were griping about it. After a two-week stay, they moved on to Detroit for another two weeks. It was at this point that Sunny abruptly announced she wanted to go back to New York, where acquaintances at a residential hotel called the Whitby had planned a posthumous birthday get-together in remembrance of her late husband.[6]

Sally was exasperated, imploring Sunny:

> *At least go to Atlanta with me and get me open, then go to New York if you must. But no — you are still determined to live in your dream, still a ... pathetic little girl, forlorn and playing birthday party with a dead husband, for all the Whitby to comment on. The Whitby is just a building — made of stone and mortar, full of would be, has been, half-assed, mediocre actors and such. It isn't a way of life. It isn't the world. The opinion of the people living there doesn't mean anything. Or is it that you're afraid to face life....*

> *Are you afraid to give up what to you is a little throne — in a tawdry little world called the Whitby? The questionable distinction of being the oldest resident, the arbiter and last word on modes and manners at the Whitby — what one does and doesn't do at the Whitby with everyone watching with bated breath to see what the sad little girl widow of the glamourous Russian does, will do, has done — the most important conversation piece since "Bubbles Goldberg" slashed her wrists with her lover's false teeth on Passover. Ridiculous. You've lost your perspective. Thousands, millions, billions of people never heard of the Whitby. Wake up, take off your glasses, this is 1955 ... you're free, the world is your oyster. You can do anything you want to. Misha is gone. He isn't coming back.*

---

[6]   Originally a residential hotel, the property is now a co-op. As reported in the *New York Times* on December 29, 2014: "Since it opened in 1924, the Whitby, a stout beige building with 217 units on 45th Street just west of Eighth Avenue, has attracted artists, performers, writers and stagehands. In fact, it was the first residential building in the city created especially for them, not least because performers were often shunned for their odd hours, odd lifestyles and, most of all, odd bank accounts.... Among the stars who came to reside at the Whitby were Doris Day, Betty Gable, Clarence Derwent, Diane Ladd and Wallace Shawn, as well as Al Capone, though legend says it was the showgirls, not the amenities, that drew him there."

Ever willing to suggest measures others might take to improve themselves, Sally then proceeded to outline how Sunny might rescue herself, if she could only bring herself to do it:

> ... *work* <u>*hard*</u> *at being a really loving, kind, adult human being ... [rather] than just existing here pickled in alcohol like an unborn in a bottle at a side show. Wake up — get ahold of yourself — do something for somebody (besides pouring them a drink). You've got to earn a living for yourself and you might be lucky enough to be able to help somebody else.*

Sally went on to propose that Sunny might raise her self-esteem by doing such things as helping "all the Korean children ... dying every day for lack of simple care" or pursuing a course that would allow her to work as a practical nurse or dental technician:

> *Be of service to those for whom you work, take your respon- sibility as an adult seriously. You want to teach dancing? O.K. Get a job and save some money till you can have your own studio and be successful. The hell with this hand-to-mouth, insecure, fear-ridden, live-in-one-room, scrounging, chinchy existence. This is too high a price to pay for the whining of being a perpetual little girl — refusing responsibilities ... of being an efficient, effective, successful adult in a competitive world.*

From Sally's perspective, the letter was a valiant effort to force her friend to face reality and find her way to a new life. But it was also an unsparing indictment of Sunny's behavior. Sally just couldn't get past how thoughtless Sunny had been, especially in light of her own bounteous generosity:

> *Come closing night in Detroit, we shopped, got separated, I came back, took you to dinner and before I could finish, you excused yourself, went upstairs, got your bags and left for New York. You left me with all the packing to do, tickets and transportation to arrange as well, publicity, unpacking, rehearsal, dressing room, lights, music, etc. to do alone — to say nothing of the fact that Sunday was my birthday, to be spent alone.... And you're the one who said, "Please don't leave me alone in Detroit to take a train when you fly to Atlanta." Sunny, Sunny, what selfishness!*

After Sunny Markoff's disappearing act to attend festivities at the Whitby, Sally had to complete her 10-day engagement in Atlanta on her own and then scramble back to California, where she had been booked to open at Larry Potter's Supper Club in Hollywood.

Despite everything, Sally took pity on her friend yet again, paying for Sunny to come to California and once more serve as her dressing room assistant. She even renewed her offer of free room and board at her home in Glendora. While Sunny did agree to Sally's proposal and did fly to California, she didn't manage to show up until the very last minute. Sally was fuming:

> So now I am to open at Larry Potter's the day after I close in Atlanta. I can barely make it. It's a Hollywood opening and important. My dresses should be taken out to be pressed. My switches need rolling. My dressing room arranged, my makeup and stuff put out, my clothes unpacked. I have to rehearse my music for lights, do a thousand things — and, God help me, here is Miss Markoff, who has taken a trip to California at my expense to take my dress off 2 times a nite and zip a zipper twice a nite, for 2 weeks — arrives like a star — 20 minutes before showtime. I was so damned mad I could have wept. How could you — on an opening nite? Were you trying to prove to Poopie that you weren't my maid and didn't have to be there? Look Sunny — if you were my manager — you'd have been there at noon — my agent — at 1 o'clock — my secretary at 2 o'clock — my friend — at 4 o'clock at least.
>
> All you proved was that you were irresponsible, not efficient, disinterested, excess baggage just along for the ride.

It was perhaps the last straw for Sally when she learned that Sunny had called her husband, crying, claiming that Sally "owed her $400." She was beyond exasperation:

> You're out of your mind girl…. I gave you an "out" if it was getting too much at Poop's … to come up here, but you didn't want to do housework while I did bookkeeping. So, why bring you and spend my time waiting on you. As it is Lalla does the simple cooking and dishwashing — we don't make the bed and we're happy — but with 2 women in the house and no housekeeping and cooking — he'd blow his stack — and I wouldn't blame him. He's sacrificing $30 a day to stay home and not work to help me. As for owing you — Sunny you spend a minimum of $5 a day on whiskey & mixer. So all you could have left is $15 a week…. You received $110.00 cash at Larry Potter's — I was only there two weeks.

Was this amazing letter ever sent or was Sally simply "venting"? We'll never know.

Hilda Vincent

A successful stand-up comic at a time when she was one of the very few females in the business, Hilda was best known in the 1960s and '70s, when she played comedy clubs, major New York hotels, and even the Playboy Club in Boston. In October 1969, she appeared on the David Frost television show the same night as Tiny Tim, his fiancée Vicki Budinger, actress Dyan Cannon and singer Paul Anka. After relocating to California, she appeared in TV specials with Richard Pryor, conducted seminars on comedy, and even spent a year performing on cruise ships.

Hilda's humor was commonly self-deprecating and often included clever little jokes with surprising twists. Among her favorites were:

> My girlfriend was determined to meet a man. She kept going away for "singles weekends" to the Catskills, made 25 round trips by bus. She ended up marrying the bus driver.

> I'm not a self-destructive person, but after I broke up with my boyfriend I didn't care anymore. I ate a piece of unwashed fruit.

> I agree with Women's Lib. I don't want men opening doors for me. The last time a man opened a door for me, we were going 50 miles an hour.

Hilda met Sally in January of 1973 when both were appearing in *A Night at the Palace*, a vaudeville revival show, at the 878-seat Civic Theatre in Chicago. The bill included a number of old-time troupers, including Beatrice Kay, Fifi D'Orsay, the Ink Spots, the De Castro Sisters and the Marquis Chimps.[7] Hilda found working with the chimpanzees to be "a lot of trouble":

> The trainer would get drunk once in a while and then one of the chimps would take advantage of him. He smoked a cigarette, he ran into the audience. They could be dangerous, you know. I would go on before them and I was always afraid of those chimps.

Sally took to Hilda right away, saying: "I like you because you're clean too," meaning that her comedy didn't depend on off-color material. Several months after their Chicago gig, Sally called Hilda from California and invited her to go on the road with her to Florida. Hilda quickly agreed, figuring it

---

[7] A variety act, the Marquis Chimps were a trio of trained chimpanzees dressed as humans. In addition to doing live theater, they appeared on several popular television shows in the 1960s, including Ed Sullivan's *Toast of the Town*. For one season they even starred in their own series, *The Hathaways* on ABC (considered by at least one critic to be "possibly the worst series ever to air on network TV").

had to be a lot better than spending a cold winter in Manhattan, performing mostly for free in Greenwich Village.

Sally was well into her 70th year when her Florida tour kicked off with a three-week engagement at the Desert Inn in Daytona Beach. The two ladies had a fine time together. Sally described Hilda as a "lovely woman" and a "sharp dresser, who adds a lot" to the act. Interviewed for this book, Miss Vincent offered several observations:

> I used to put her body makeup on her. She was a natural blond. Her skin was very light and doesn't look so good on stage....

> She was married three times ... but she told me that she never married anyone who was her equal. I don't know about her education, but I know she was very curious and very bright. And she was a nice woman. She also liked to help people....

> She used to use a very thin piece of silk that she could only get in the millinery district in New York. She couldn't find it in California.... So she said, "Would you buy this for me?" and I said "Certainly." It was a small thing and she pasted it on the triangle in front and in the back, then took a little strap and put it in the crack of her butt. You're nude, but you're not really nude....

> She was kind and she wasn't so self-centered. That's one of the things I liked about her. The world didn't revolve around her.

Sally called again in 1979, asking Hilda to join her show once more, this time for an engagement in Galveston, Texas. As Hilda recalled:

> She said, "I just want to know if you can come?" and I said "Yeah," but then she died. So she was working to the last minute. When you think of a 75-year-old woman taking her clothes off, it's really amazing. She had a very tight behind. I know because I was putting the stuff on her. Obviously she exercised and danced. And as far as her face is concerned, she put on makeup. She had long blond hair. She didn't look twenty, but she didn't look her age, body-wise. Her face is another story....

> Nobody does what she does. I've seen strippers — some of them her friends — but nobody does what she does. She was unique in the sense that she could hold an audience like that. I mean, you really looked. You never saw anything like it. I imagine in her young days she must have been really terrific. But she did it with nothing — blue light and "Clair de Lune."

CHAPTER TWENTY-FIVE

Her Sexellency

What in heaven's name is strange about a grandmother
dancing nude? I'll bet lots of grandmothers do it.
~ Sally Rand

On June 19, 1964, in the North Beach section of San Francisco, a grand
piano was hydraulically lowered from the ceiling of the Condor Club.
Atop that piano, go-go dancer Carol Doda made her first appearance as a
topless dancer, wearing a "monokini" swimsuit created by famed designer
Rudi Gernreich.[1] With enthusiastic support from attendees of the 1964
Republican National Convention, her act quickly became a "must see."

With the arrival of Miss Doda and her pneumatic look, alongside the debut
of Bob Guccione's *Penthouse* magazine, a new era of sexually explicit entertainment was ushered in. Sally Rand's relatively tame feathers-and-bubble
show was no longer all that naughty. The risqué Carol Doda was just 26 years
old; Sally Rand was 60.[2]

Sally never considered herself to be in competition with striptease artists,
topless dancers, porn stars, or any other kind of explicit or exploitative
performer. No one can deny that Sally was a tease. But a stripper? Never.

She didn't think much of naturists either. Interviewed at the Paramount
Theatre in Brooklyn in March of 1934, Sally disclosed that she had been
offered "a big sum" to endorse a group of west coast nudists:

> "The offer shocked me," she said. "I knew that if I endorsed it, a lot
> of fat old men would join the cult just to see me without fans. It

---

[1] An Austrian-born Jewish refugee who fled Hitler to find freedom, Rudi Gernreich
ultimately became an American fashion designer with an award-winning career in
trend-setting fashion design spanning the early 1950s through the 1980s. Like Sally,
Gernreich abhorred the idea that the body was essentially shameful. He introduced
the modern androgynous unisex style, including body-hugging clothes based on
leotards and tights.

[2] On June 19, 2014, at the still-operating Condor Club, the Internet talk show
"Speakeasily" celebrated the 50th anniversary of Miss Doda's first topless dance.
Carol Doda died on December 9, 2015. She was 78.

made me sick that my lovely dance should be confused with such things. All the nudists I ever saw had scratches all over their rear ends where they had been sitting on thorns."

In point of fact, Sally actually was a professionally trained dancer, as she had always claimed. Even so, no serious work about Sally Rand would be complete without ample coverage of her sexuality.

Indeed, at some point Sally had begun referring to herself in promotional material, newspaper ads, and even in her letterhead as "Her Sexellency."[3] And, let's be honest, a lady doesn't bill herself as "Her Sexellency" unless she intends to attract an audience whose interest in the art of the dance might include at least a small component of the prurient. So, while it is not the purpose of this book to pander to anyone's salacious curiosity, an appreciation of Sally's personal views on the role of sensuality, obscenity, and the human body is essential to an understanding of her life.

Sally Rand was a highly intelligent, uninhibited, red-blooded woman with normal hormonal urges and plenty of opportunities to give them full expression. Over the course of a career spanning nearly six decades, she found many occasions to state, or even demonstrate, her views on human sexuality and related matters. Shall we explore a few?

As an employer of young girls (many of whom had a limited grasp on the ways of the world), Sally felt she had to be ever vigilant regarding their wellbeing, lest heartbreak, abuse, scandal or worse bring problems that she just plain didn't need. Back in 1949, her show at the Clique Club in New York City had been promoted by a syndicated photo feature on what was said to be Sally's new booklet "How to be a Good Girl in a Big City" — a mimeographed compilation of rules and guidelines meant to instruct her showgirls on the art of avoiding "wolves" and their wily ways. Distilling into a few pages what Sally had learned in her years of observation, both personal and detached, of the American "genus homo," the gist of her handbook's guidance was:

> "Discretion." That's the word for my advice. I don't expect miracles
> nor am I worried about the birds and bees. Let the mamma birds
> and bees worry. I just want my kids to know that the sweet guy

---

3   Exactly when Sally adopted this moniker is not clear, but references in the press
     can be found as early as 1949. Her show was promoted as "Sexhilarating" and
     "Scandalicious" as early as 1941. Publicity for a 1951 appearance at the Club Gay
     Haven in Dearborn, Michigan, added "Girlorious."

who says he wants nothing but friendship may try to knock out
their teeth if that's all he gets.

If chapter titles are any indication, the booklet must have offered some pretty
useful advice: "So He Wants to Be a Brother to You," "How to Drink Like a
Lady," "My Wife Doesn't Understand Me," "Even If He Really Has Etchings,"
"Roomers Start Rumors," "I'm No Prude But ..." and "Third Finger Left
Hand." As Sally had explained to the press:

> I want to impress on these kids — and this goes for any small town
> kid — that standards are the same all over. The Broadway crowd
> only pretends things are different here. Some saps believe them. I
> say it like this: "What's wrong in Bohunk is wrong on Broadway."
> If you think of it like that, it's easy to spot the wolf crawling up
> behind a camouflage of champagne and orchids.

For decades, the question of what, if anything, Sally wore behind her fans
and bubbles has both fascinated and confounded students of the subject.
The speculation has varied over the years from "nothing at all," to a sort of
body paste, to some arrangement of "invisible" coverings. Perhaps Sally
herself offered the most complete description of her "costume" in a deposition she had given in Canton, Ohio, on December 3, 1951.

After the first night of a three-night engagement at the Casablanca Club,
investigators for the Ohio Liquor Control Board had issued a citation against
the club owner claiming that Sally's show had violated a regulation against
"lewd shows" and demanding that she wear more clothes or be at risk of
additional citations. Although not directly charged, Sally worried that press
accounts connecting her show with the term "lewd performance" could well
pose a threat to her livelihood and even jeopardize the continued custody of
her adopted infant son. She filed a formal declaration seeking relief from the
board and offered to show them her costume:

> I asked them to come back to the dressing room and see for
> themselves what I wore. They said no, that they didn't want to come
> back to the dressing room, that there were other girls back there, so I
> brought from the dressing room and presented for their inspection
> the costume which I wore, always have worn, and which they could
> easily see had been worn by me during my performance.

> There was a bright white table lamp on the table. I showed them a
> G-string, two pairs of panties, and a brassiere. I described to them
> that these garments were held to my body by liquid adhesive (a
> special preparation used in plastic surgery which adheres tightly

to the skin and to bandages of cloth). I described to them that the brassiere could not be seen because there was no strap or rubber across my back to hold it on, that it was pasted on. I described to them that the panties were held close to my body in the same way, to avoid the rubber cutting into my flesh and making an indentation. I held the panties over my hand under the bright white light and showed them that there were three layers of material and that it was impossible to see my hand through the material or to see the cracks of my fingers through the material. I did this with both pants and brassiere. I further showed them the G-string made of seven layers of material, which I always wear pasted over the pubic area to avoid any possibility of being able to see a shadow or the darkness of the pubic hair. I showed them that it was impossible to see through this G-string even when it was placed over black.

To ease the liquor board's concerns, Sally also took additional measures to make her stage costume "more obvious" for the remaining two nights of her contract.[4]

As Sally revealed 20 years later, things had changed quite a bit by 1971:

I used to wear a chalk white thick body make up all over me. It helped me with the strict (and sometimes stupid) censorship I had to meet and solve in times past. Like I was a statue, sculptural, an impersonal art object, etc., I hated it. It ruined my clothes, was sticky and miserably uncomfortable, and hard to remove. So I stopped using it ... when I had won my court cases and proved legally, to the satisfaction of censors and vice squads, that I wasn't a hussy, my performance wasn't lewd, and wouldn't corrupt the morals of the public and the young, and that I would not and could not be intimidated, that I would fight, and take it to the highest courts to prove my point and my right to perform my dance. And that, above all, I would NOT "pay off."

Yet another take on this theme was shared by Dr. Charles W. Keller, who, as a student at Northwestern University in 1959, happened to visit with Sally during a club appearance in Chicago. He observed: "Her only adornments besides the fans were her high-heeled shoes, a wide diamond choker necklace, matching bracelets on both wrists and both ankles." He ventured to

---

4   Sally's engagement at the Casablanca Club was immediately preceded by popular
     sob-singer Johnnie Ray. The week after her show closed, the entertainment was
     supplied by an up-and-coming young singer, 25-year-old Tony Bennett.

ask: "In your show your body looks so young and perfect. There is not a dimple or a wrinkle. How do you keep your body in such perfect shape?"

Sally then leaned forward with a big smile and pulled the wide elasticized diamond necklace away from her neck to reveal a seam. She showed him the same seam on both wrists and on both ankles, disclosing:

> I have a total body stocking made for me by the Hanes Hosiery Company. I always keep a dozen on hand at all times in case one gets a run. It takes two girls to get me in the stocking for my show every night. My girls get every body part in place, push and shove and smooth out all the wrinkles. They essentially shape me! And the wide diamond bands hide the body hose seams.

Within three years after topless dancer Carol Doda had "enhanced" her breasts from a bra size of 34B to a somewhat overstated 44DD (insured for $1.5 million by Lloyds of London), interest in breast augmentation had spread to an audience well beyond that of patients seeking reconstructive surgery. "Big bazooms" were "in."[5]

Mrs. Elise Kline, an acquaintance in Glendora, had apparently sought guidance on the subject, as evidenced by Sally's advice to her in a letter dated September 8, 1967:

> *The doctor's name is Leslie Orleans on Wilshire Boulevard. You can find the address in the L.A. telephone book. Be sure to tell him that Angel Ray recommended you to him....*

> *You may remember the girl, Angel Ray, by far the prettiest girl in the show that you saw at the Body Shop with by far the best figure. She told me that her bosoms looked like two aspirins on an ironing board before the injections. She has a six-year old daughter, though at the present moment she is only 22 years old and, as you know, pregnancy and conception changes the entire structure of the female mammary glands. Now she has indubitably the most beautiful pair of boobs I have ever seen....*[6]

---

[5] Cosmetic breast implant surgery dates to as early as 1895, but it wasn't until the mid-twentieth century that the availability of silicone injections and implants began to create a demand for the procedure.

[6] Angel Ray appeared as the "Girl in Tub" in Russ Meyer's 1970 "softcore" film, the melodramatic musical parody *Beyond the Valley of the Dolls*. She also played the "Young Girl" in Meyers' *Cherry, Harry & Racquel* released the same year.

Since it was you who mentioned this to me and I know that there
are some psychological reasons why you want it so much, I give
you this information, though frankly, knowing you are as loved
as you are by a devoted husband and, in my opinion, the prettiest
woman in Glendora, I don't see why you need it, but if you want it
here it is.

Sally had very firm views on the subject of breast enhancement. She used
as her jumping off point the famous painting by François Clouet of Diane
de Poitiers in her bath "displaying what is conceded to be probably the
most beautiful pair of boobs in the world." Writing to NBC producer Chet
Hagan on April 11, 1969, Sally described how she intended to treat the
subject in a forthcoming little booklet on health, diet, mind and body, which
she had tentatively titled "Here's How":

I go through the whole bit on boobs, honestly and frankly, like
if you're under 30, to exercise the pectorals, which hold up the
mammary glands. I did it accidently, by doing a trapeze act
with the Ringling Brothers Circus when I was 16, but it won't
do much good after you're 30. I think there is too much focus
on them in our time, but then, I've never had the problem of
not having any.

I go on to say what can be done — inserts, which look beautiful,
but no man will ever touch them twice. It really turns a male off.
Silicone injections, even though the American Medical
Association frowns on it, are still the most effective method at
$50.00 a shot. What to do if you have the fried egg variety and if
yours are the gourd type, pendulously on your abdomen. There is
only one way to go for this and you may do it guiltlessly —
surgery, which snips out all the excess pendulousness and
replaces the areola and nipple in the right spot. This kind of
surgery is advisable because this kind of pendulous breast is
very cancer prone. This type of surgery, followed by a couple of
silicone shots, and you're back in business.

Sally said she planned to donate her share of the royalties from the book to "a
foundation for geriatric research," and then segued into her views regarding
the dignity of the aged:

I view with great emotional trauma the vast group of the
aging [who] ... worst of all ... are by way of "golden age" being
put away in homes and made into vegetables, whose lives in a
vegetable state are extended to the longest possible period for

the sake of the money the homes receive. I have personally encountered it in my own family and I am appalled that heartless children and grandchildren can condemn their parents to this kind of living and what I have said above is true of the most expensive [homes]....

They are sedated, strapped down (the strappings are concealed, of course, under fancy nighties, etc.) and diapered. It is much easier to take an old lady's diaper off her and profusely wash her, than it is to wheedle her out of bed into a wheel chair and to the bathroom. They take their teeth, their hearing aids and their glasses from them so they can't talk, they can't hear and can't eat. They feed them a kind of Pablum and poke it into their mouths like baby birds. Let me tell you, it removes every shred of human dignity not to be able to wipe your own ass and feed yourself.

The surviving outline for Sally's little "Here's How" booklet provides an intriguing example of just the sort of things she hoped to address:

In discussing ridding oneself of old guilt (specifically, love or perish), you must learn to love yourself, or you can't love anyone else.

I discuss the prurient Victorian era with which we are still hung-over — sex, masturbation, perspiration, bathing, being naked, being born by way of the vagina, voiding the bladder, and bowel movements were taboo. The fact that babies kept on being born and the purpose for which outhouses were built was ignored, except for the compilation of vital statistics and the ultimate consumption of mail order catalogs. It is incredible that a whole society could be so deluded. I'll never really know, because Freud and psychiatry were still bad words, but [it] would be interesting to know ... how many red-blooded American boys found themselves to be sexually impotent men ... because they felt guilty about masturbation or [how many] warm and sensual women became suicides, nuns, insane, frigid and barren trying to expiate their guilt? And God knows, we must have been the most constipated culture in history. We took such pains to keep anyone from knowing we ... uh ... defecated.

No wonder the lid's blown off. No wonder the pendulum has swung so far to the other side and is stuck there. No wonder

our society is full of impotent men, sexually promiscuous
women, the weirdest sex deviations, and an unbelievable
population of homosexuals. We still can't be rid of Victoria,
damn her!

Come on, now, are you going to let yourself get hung up on
this? Feeling guilty — "I'm no good — I'm not fit to be loved —
I had hot pants when I was 14 — I necked and went too far
when I was a teenager — I did a little way-out experimenting
with sex, etc., etc., etc." Well, let me tell you, you're not alone!
We all have, and we all did, and doesn't everybody? Now stop
it! You're a big girl. What happened yesterday is done. You
can't change it. Forget it. Everybody else has, probably.

Over the years, Sally had developed a pronounced nonchalance about being nude in informal situations. Whether the accidental observer was the Governor of Florida visiting her dressing room at Casa Mañana or the son of a Nieman-Marcus founder standing goggle-eyed as she changed clothes in the family's famous Dallas department store, it mattered not to her. Indeed, there is no evidence that Sally was ever embarrassed about being nude in the presence of others.[7] On the contrary, she seemed perfectly comfortable in the company of fully clothed visitors in her hotel room or dressing room while she herself was stark naked. By all accounts, Sally didn't seem to notice when a guest was surprised or shocked. She may even have enjoyed a bit of perverse pleasure from contributing to the visitor's discomfort.

Sally's lack of reserve was definitely on display in Fort Worth when she returned to the Casa Mañana in July of 1968 to appear as "Fantabula" in the Tony Award-winning Stephen Sondheim musical *A Funny Thing Happened on the Way to the Forum*. Jay Wallace, whose mother was also in the show, had been employed to serve as Sally's personal assistant during the two-week engagement. On his first day on the job, he was bowled over by the nature of their first encounter:

Sally did not come in until Friday or Saturday before the show because she had nothing to do except go on and do her dance. But she had come in and I literally flew in from California just

---

7   As early as 1935, Sally expressed a rather casual attitude about nudity: "There should be nothing unfamiliar about the place in which we live and since we live in our bodies for all our days, surely there is nothing grotesque or fantastic about them unless we make it so."

minutes before dress rehearsal. I walked in the back door and
they said, "She's waiting for you." I was scared to death. I walked
in the room and she turned around. She was stark naked. It meant
nothing to her.

We were introduced, she turned around and handed me a bottle
and said, "You take the back, I'll take the front." And my only
thought was, "Oh my God, my mother's out there in dress
rehearsal and this woman and my mother are the same age, and
I'm putting makeup all over her body." And of course that was
another thing. Sally and Mother were very good friends. Their
lives were totally different but Mother accepted her and her way
of life and it was wonderful.

This was but the beginning of Wallace's exposure to the singularity of Sally
Rand. As he later recalled the days that followed:

Then that night at the end of the rehearsal — this was back when
Casa Mañana was still giving big cars to the stars — she had a
Lincoln Continental. So she turned to me and said: "You take
these keys and pick me up at 10:00," you know how she talked.
She was almost demanding, but in a very kind way, and you had
to know her. And the better I knew her, the more I understood
that. She said, "You drive this car for me for the next two weeks. I
don't know where I'm going or what I'm going to do. I know I
have an interview at 10:00 in the morning."

Well, I met her at 10:00 the next morning. They had her in the
Presidential suite at the Worth Hotel, which was grand. I called
her from here and told her I was leaving and she said, "I'm getting
ready to get in the tub, so I'll unlock the door and you just come
on in." So, when I arrived the door was ajar and I walked into this
huge living room and was aware that she was in the bedroom area
somewhere. I called out and she said that she was in the
bathroom. I walked in and she was sitting in the tub. She said
"Here," and handed me the douche bag and said, "Hold this while
I douche." Again, I'm thinking, "My God, what am I doing here?"
But she couldn't find a nail to hang it on to get it high enough.

But you know, this wonderful little woman with no hair at that
point and sitting there in the tub ... and for the next two weeks
it was just one fun thing after another. And by the time the
two weeks was over, I was really hooked. I just loved every
minute of it.

A registered Republican, Sally Rand was politically conservative and a patriotic volunteer during World War II. She never would have called herself a feminist.[8] Philosophically, though, and in her personal behavior, especially with regard to sex and the human body, she was unabashedly radical for the times.

Sally's success in vaudeville and Hollywood was undoubtedly due more to the force of her irrepressible personality than to the magnitude of her talent. When the stock market crashed in 1929 and the Great Depression tightened its grip on the American economy, she had needed to use every resource at her disposal to make ends meet. While many young women had resorted to prostitution during the Depression, it is highly unlikely that Sally, even at her most desperate, would ever have given a thought to turning in that direction. Rather than seek the comfort of a john's hotel room, she would have slept on a park bench. Still, necessity is the mother of invention.

If Sally had not been down on her luck in 1932, would she ever have conceived of dancing in a way that appeared to expose her nude body to the public? Perhaps not — and surely not had she been able to realize her dream of becoming a classical ballet dancer. Still, while she had maintained a reservoir of religious morality, Sally was no saint. She freely engaged in sexual liaisons outside of marriage. Commonly expressing herself in a very explicit manner, she was no stranger to vulgarity. Former employee Holly Knox wrote about a luncheon that she and Sally had attended at the University of Oklahoma, expressing surprise and relief that her boss had been a model of decorum in her discourse — not the "potty mouth" that she was accustomed to hearing at work.

Sally definitely had a facility, if not a propensity, for swearing like a sailor. She even had a few choice retorts she reserved for dealing with hecklers in the audience. Fellow entertainer, Chuck Mitchell,[9] who sometimes served as Sally's emcee and driver, liked to recall one of her old stand-bys, which she occasionally deployed when dealing with an unruly female: "An acrobat can do a cunning stunt, but you my dear are a — need I go further?"

Clearly, when it came to passion, Sally was a liberated woman. At a time when even the suggestion of divorce was largely frowned upon, she had

---

8   Late in life, Sally was quoted as saying: "I could never become a women's libber. I've enjoyed being a girl too much. I have enjoyed all the prerogatives that go with it, like having your cigarette lit and having doors opened for you and things like that. I think it's great being a sex symbol. Isn't that what we were made for?"

9   Chuck Mitchell is best remembered for his role as the title character in the 1982 cult classic film *Porky's*.

resorted to the proceeding more than once. Sally was 38 years old when she married rodeo star Turk Greenough. At the time, she fancied herself retiring from fan dancing and settling down as a Montana rancher's housewife. But, all too soon the couple found her large ego and his laid-back style to be incompatible. Sally's other marriages were similarly doomed. Having shed both Harry Finkelstein and Fred Lalla, she would never marry again. But, even in her later years, Sally hinted that she occasionally enjoyed private time with certain gentlemen from a select group of old friends.

In an era when women were commonly told "don't worry your pretty little head about it," Sally was not in the least reluctant to express her opinions and expound on subjects both mundane and profound. Approaching her 70th birthday, she shared with columnist Earl Wilson how she felt about the explicit performances of certain striptease dancers:

> When you stick a naked body out in those dreadful white lights, you destroy all the illusion. But then this girl's entire pubic hair area is shown and it's not even well groomed ... it's still parted from last night's orgy ... well, that's hardly appetizing.

> And they all have fried-egg boobs and dirty toenails and bare feet. Who could be sexually titillated by anybody with dirty toenails?

> What else can they do besides showing their vaginas? One of them said to me, "I bend over and have sparklers out of my ass." And that's what she did. She twinkled her rectum.[10]

When Wilson inquired: "What about those gals who can pick up things with their vagina?" Sally replied:

> Snappers! Girls with snappers are very good in bed, especially toward the end of the sex act. Acrobats are very good snappers because they have great muscle control, and since I'm an acrobat....

How Sally Rand (or Earl Wilson for that matter) came to be familiar with such performances is not clear. At any rate, it's not the sort of entertainment that one encounters every day.[11]

---

[10] Earl Wilson reported Sally's blunt observations about the explicit performances of some striptease dancers in his book *Show Business Laid Bare*. On March 5, 1975, Sally wrote to Wilson: "Oh, what a dirty old man you are! What an exercise in how to write the world's dirtiest book, 'Tsking' and protesting all the way! A very funny, funny book — and indubitably the dirtiest I've ever read. Of course porno isn't my bag."

[11] There is little published expert discussion of this "talent." Serious students of the subject might want to research the career of flautist (and "Ping Pong Queen"), Michelle Pradia.

Sally seemed to be turned off by the prevailing state of affairs, but she also understood that trends come and go, remarking at a 1975 press conference in Louisville, Kentucky:

> If an act gets raunchy, it burns itself out in a hurry. But the
> pendulum swings, it'll come back. When I started dancing, Victoria
> and her slimy philosophy still hung over us. Now it's swayed too
> far the other way.

Never mind the coarser variety, Sally had little truck with strippers in general. She certainly did not regard them as "sexy." In fact, she was known to disparage women who plied the trade. In a 1965 interview she openly demeaned them:

> Many strippers are emotionally disturbed people. In their past
> you'll find, almost invariably, a distorted father image. The father
> was an alcoholic. Or he was mean to the mother. Or he wouldn't
> work. Or there may have been a succession of "uncles." The result
> is that many of the girls develop a great hostility toward men. By
> stripping and flaunting their bodies, they are getting even with
> their fathers. To these girls, it's a look-but-mustn't-touch situation.
> They conceive this to be the ultimate punishment for men.

Disdain for the stripper's craft aside, as her own star began to fade, Sally sometimes had to accept bookings in less than agreeable venues just to get a paycheck. On March 18, 1976, the nearly 72-year-old fan dancer wrote to booking agent Don Di Carlo to complain:

> An agent just outside Washington, D.C., was working on some
> bookings for me in Iowa. I had to ask to be excused from playing
> them because they had "strips" on the same bill who showed pubic
> hair — but as a concession to me would not "spread" — revolting! I
> do not wish to work in places where there are other strips — but
> often have to, to work.

So, just what and who *did* Sally consider to be sexy? In a 1964 interview, she addressed the subject from a cultural viewpoint:

> They vary with age and geographic location. The Ubangis work
> very hard stretching lips because it's considered so attractive. To
> us, sheer black Bikini panties are sexy. To the Japanese a kimono
> cut low in the back has the same effect. They think we're very
> primitive.

> I'll tell you who I think is the most girl-girl. Simone Signoret. I
> saw her in the movie "Seventh Heaven," and in one scene she

wore little cotton panties. It was the sexiest thing I'd seen and it made those girls strutting around in beaded G-strings look like nothing.

Oh, yes, I want to mention the actress Luise Rainer.[12] Oh, she had it. She was the most womanly-woman....

Cleavage is the big thing nowadays. Why girls are even painting shadows down their fronts and have you seen these bras made with golf balls?

Toward the end of her career, again and again reporters asked the now-elderly Sally about the propriety of carrying on with her famous dance. Her typical response has come down to us as one of her more famous quotes: "What in heaven's name is strange about a grandmother dancing nude? I'll bet lots of grandmothers do it."

Sally Rand was one of a kind. For practically all of her professional life she was a single woman operating in a man's world, subject to the mores, rules, customs and strictures established over untold centuries by those in author-ity — men. In a 1974 essay she titled "The Weaker Sex," Sally addressed the gender issue:

Women are hardier than men. True from moment of conception all through life. Women live longer than men, according to insurance statistics. About 5 years longer.

True, women have more aches and pains. But that's because of her extremely complex physical makeup, and these painful symptoms — headaches, backaches, tiredness — in no way interfere with the ability to throw fits and survive serious illness.

Truth of the matter is — man is stronger in just one way — muscular strength. Women recognize this and can always utilize their sex appeal to trap a man into the backbreaking work they want done. Maybe that's the reason they live longer than men.

Sally was nothing if not resilient. Maybe that's why she not only persevered but regularly prevailed, despite the relentless headwinds of discrimination. For most of her adult life, she was literally up to her neck in the struggle between free expression and censorship. Without fail, she had insisted that

---

[12] A German-American actress known primarily for her films in the 1930s, Luise Rainer was the first to win back-to-back Oscars as "best actress" (1936/1937). She died in 2014 at the age of 104.

nudity was natural, that her dances were art. Others were adamant that her only possible motivation was to titillate, to exploit the weakness of the flesh for personal gain.

Way back in 1934, Sally's Japanese maid Stella had described her employer's situation quite succinctly: "Two classes of people coming to see dance, the one looking for risqué and no find; the others not looking for art and have got."

Were Sally's performances primarily about art or were they mostly about sex? Art or sex? Sex or art? This is a distinction without a difference. The biological imperative of sex is the urgent desire to immortalize one's self. Art is the same.

Part Four

From Here to Eternity

This image of the mature Sally in a trench coat and trilby hat is from a series of similar studio portraits from Sally's files and was probably taken in California, circa 1972-1978.

CHAPTER TWENTY-SIX

The Toast of Glendora

Do you know the definition of a "smart ass"? It's one
that can sit on an ice cream cone and tell the flavor!
~ Sally, in a letter to Dorothy Rubel (1976)

For most of the past 50 years, home had been wherever Sally could find a
hook to hang her hat on. But, during all those decades on the road, there
actually *was* a place where the home fires were burning, a residence Sally
kept in a southern California community called Glendora.

The connection between Chicago, the site of Sally's greatest success, and the
community of Glendora dates to the earliest days of the California town's
founding. In 1885, George D. Whitcomb, the wealthy founder of the
Whitcomb Locomotive Company in Chicago, seeking a healthier climate,
moved his wife and family to southern California where he purchased a
parcel of 200 acres that now comprises the heart of the town. It was
Whitcomb who created the name "Glendora," combining "Glen" (for the
narrow valley at the north end of present day Glendora Avenue) with his
wife Leadora's nickname, "Dora."

Bordering the Angeles National Forest in the foothills of the San Gabriel
Mountains, Glendora today is a city of 52,000 residents located 23 miles east
of downtown Los Angeles. The famous U.S. Route 66 is its primary east-west
thoroughfare. Despite the town's predominantly conservative politics, the
notorious Sally Rand remains its most famous former resident. A special
section of the Glendora Historical Society Museum is devoted to her career.
But how did she land there in the first place?

In 1988, one of her former chorus girls wrote that Sally had taken a room
"in a family home" in Glendora because "it was close to the Azusa area,
where many early silent films were shot on location." She added that Sally
had been charmed by Glendora and had written "increasingly enticing
letters about it to her mother, urging her to come to California." Sometime in
the mid-1920s, Sally's mother accepted the invitation, traveling from Kansas

City to visit her famous Hollywood daughter.[1] It proved to be a life-changing decision for both women.

Details are sketchy, but, as Sean recalls it, Sally had arranged to take her mother to a theater in Pasadena for a blind date with a citrus grove owner from Glendora named Ernest Gordon Kisling. They were two 40-something singles on a blind date — possibly an unusual circumstance at the time — but it couldn't have gone better. Sean's grandmother Annette ended up marrying Ernest on March 10, 1929, and taking up residence at his home in Glendora. Sally's vagabond days were over. For the next half century, Glendora would be her home.

While we're at it, we may as well dispel a recurrent Glendora myth — the assertion that Sally once lived in a Frank Lloyd Wright house. The truth is that Sally's home in Glendora was a relatively modest edifice of no particular architectural significance.

As for the origin of this persistent story, in 1954, architect Foster Rhodes Jackson (a student of Wright) had built an ultramodern model home for display at the fifth annual California Living Show. Situated inside the Los Angeles' Pan-Pacific Auditorium, the eight-room home was promoted as having been "built for Sally Rand," who was engaged by the builder to fly in from Las Vegas and make personal appearances at the home show. (Attendees could pick up an illustrated brochure for "The Sally Rand Home," complete with architectural drawings and details about the furnishings.)

After the show closed, the model home was moved to a location near the southwest corner of Valley Center and Sierra Madre Avenues in Glendora, where it remained open to the public for an indefinite period. Proceeds from admission fees were donated to charity.

Sally's connection to this residence seems to have been solely for promotional purposes. There is no compelling evidence that she ever owned the house or lived in it. And even if she did, it was not a "Frank Lloyd Wright" house.

Eventually, Sally, her mother, her brother, and from time to time other members of her extended family all found themselves living in Glendora. And, perhaps just as important to Sally, the person who came to be

---

[1]   Exactly when Sally's mother visited the Glendora area for the first time is unclear. An undated society notice preserved in one of Sally's early scrapbooks noted that Nettie was on her way to Hollywood to stay with her daughter. Based on adjacent press clippings, this trip likely occurred in late autumn of 1925. In any case, by early 1927, Sally and her mother were making a permanent home in Glendora.

her dearest and closest friend would also make her way to "the Pride of the Foothills." Her name was Dorothy Deuel Rubel.

During vaudeville's heyday in the mid-1920s, Dorothy Deuel and her sister Eleanor were enjoying successful careers performing as "The Deuel Sisters" — a song and dance act that included such uncommon maneuvers as synchronized cartwheels.[2] When Irving Berlin took note of their act and booked them in his revues, the sisters soon found themselves performing alongside such distinguished company as Fannie Brice, Jack Benny and Paul Whiteman. According to Sean, his mother and Dorothy had "met each other in New York as chorus girls."

Despite enthusiastic audiences and rising prospects, the Deuel sisters' public careers came to a halt when each decided that being a wife and mother offered a more attractive future than the roller coaster ride guaranteed by pursuing a life in show business. In the mid-1920s, while starring with her sister on Broadway as a headline dancer in *Music Box Revue*, Dorothy met Harry (Heinz) Rubel at "The Little Church Around the Corner" where both were members of the Episcopal Actors' Guild.[3] Heinz was also an Episcopal minister who, in addition to his higher calling, was writing skits for vaudeville and musical numbers for Broadway performers.[4] Finding themselves in love, the pair were married on December 28, 1927.

Dorothy's transition from Broadway celebrity to domesticity was not without consequence. She was quoted by the press as admitting that "the adjustment from a paycheck of $1,000 a week to $100 a month when we married was quite a shock, but everything worked out for the best." In 1936, after a few more years of city life, the couple moved from New York to Glendora, where Dorothy renewed her acquaintance with Sally Rand. The two quickly became fast friends.

---

[2]   The Deuel Sisters act was promoted by New York vaudeville agent Lew Golder, the same man who was managing Fred and Adele Astaire.

[3]   A New York City landmark founded in 1848, this Episcopal parish church is located between Madison and Fifth Avenues in Manhattan. The story is told that, at a time when actors were viewed as social outcasts, the rector for a nearby church refused to perform funeral services for an actor named George Holland, proffering, "I believe there is a little church around the corner where they do that sort of thing." Thus began the church's tie with theater people that has continued for more than a century.

[4]   Rubel also wrote songs and scripts for Joe Penner, whom some may remember as the "Wanna Buy a Duck?" man.

After her mother died in January of 1971 and for much of the rest of her life, Sally came to depend more and more on her friend Dorothy. In addition to running her own real estate agency in Glendora, Dorothy served as Sally's unofficial home-front manager, taking care of the sort of things that Ralph Hobart had once handled for her. Correspondence between the two women often contained lists of tasks to be done — home repairs, bills to be paid — things that, while typically mundane, still demanded someone's attention.

Writing from Galveston, Texas, on April 11, 1975, just after celebrating her 71st birthday there, Sally implored Dorothy to attend to such disparate matters as arranging for repair of a damaged ermine coat, picking up packages, and securing general maintenance for her apartments. Regarding issues affecting one of her apartments, Dorothy had apparently suggested that Fred Lalla might take care of needed repairs to a balcony and window.[5] Sally disagreed:

> *Lalla doesn't know shit from Shinola about mildew and dampness in walls. He's just a good plasterer. I can tell you now what needs to be done. The earth on north and south has to be dug out down below the foundation level. The walls dried inside and out, by artificial means if necessary. Then waterproofed inside and out…. The little space under the side window on the N.E. corner of Apt. 2 gets clogged up and holds water and dams. Unfortunately I am no longer physically able to do that much digging anymore. I'll have Sean come out and poison the bamboo on the east side of the Apts, so it can be dug up when I get home. And we'll go from there.*

After reassuring Dorothy that her health was OK, Sally also observed: "This sea level altitude seems to aggravate my breathing difficulty, damn it."

With Sally about to leave for Skull's Rainbow Room in Nashville a few days later, Dorothy wrote to let her know that the apartment's balcony and walls had been taken care of for $150 and that roof repairs had been completed as well: "I think it looks good. It was fortunate that it got [repaired] on the day it did. Yesterday we had a cloudburst and hail — for about 30 minutes."

Dorothy's efforts were largely uncompensated, although Sally did find a way to share the wealth with her friend from time to time. In a letter to

---

[5]   Even though the two had been divorced for 15 years, clearly, Fred Lalla was still in the picture.

Dorothy's son Michael, written a little over a year after his mother's death, Sally disclosed:

> *The services she rendered me through the years in re: the apartments and blue house rentals, for which she ... would not take any compensation, were invaluable, making it possible for me to survive. Without her, I would now be homeless, with nothing to show for a life's work....*

> *Through those years, when I'd have a T.V. show or royalties or income over and above the weekly, poorly-paid nightclub jobs, I shared these extra windfalls with Dorothy — never showing them on tax accounts. It was strictly between we two — very private, loving, gifts of love. Recounting them, even to you, makes me very uncomfortable....*

> *She was dear to me and I loved her more than any other person in the world — but I was only one whose life was touched by her and made richer, better, more beautiful.*

> *I cannot bear it that you think I took advantage of her economically or owed her money. Truly, this is not so.*

Sally may have been the city's most famous celebrity, but there was (and still is) a unique and extraordinary thing in Glendora that attracted as much if not more attention than Sally herself — a man-made fortress like no other.

Called "Rubelia," it was the brainchild of Dorothy's son, Michael. In 1959, Michael Clarke Rubel acquired a defunct citrus orchard, warehouse, and packing operation situated on two and a half acres in Glendora. He called the property "Rubel Pharm" and took up residence in the huge packing house, claiming one of the large refrigerator chambers as his personal bedroom.

Over the years, Michael improved the existing buildings and constructed fanciful new ones of his own design, chief among them a personal "castle" fashioned from tons of concrete, salvaged river rock, telephone poles and whatever other suitable material came to hand. With no actual construction plans, over a period of two decades while local building and zoning officials sort of looked the other way, a five-story building with a vintage clock tower gradually rose from the earth, becoming the centerpiece of a complex that came to be known as Rubelia.[6] The creator's eccentricities are fully in evidence, with various odds and ends — wine bottles, a toaster, the occasional piece of silverware and even a golf club — protruding from the stonework walls.

The pharm's grounds include a number of outbuildings, a large water tank (converted into a swimming pool for family use), a Santa Fe Railroad caboose (renovated into a guest house), a separate tiny "house" for Michael made entirely of empty bottles bound together with mortar, and a "cemetery" filled with headstones mostly salvaged from the discards of a local stonemason. With prodigious help from hundreds of family members, friends and fans, work on the castle and grounds of Rubelia continued for 28 years before Michael's untimely death in 2007.[7]

Once Dorothy Rubel joined her son at Rubel Pharm, she transformed the citrus packing house into an offbeat but welcoming home. The huge 118-by-24-foot main living area was singularly suited to holding large social gatherings. Dubbed "the Tin Palace," the premises welcomed a wide variety of characters over the years, with Dorothy and Michael serving as hosts. The Rubel's unconventional creation charmed and astonished such luminaries as Dwight Eisenhower, Bob Hope, Jack Benny, Edward G. Robinson, and Alfred Hitchcock — even Henry Kissinger and Prince Phillip, the husband of Queen Elizabeth.

Some of the parties at Rubelia were said to have entertained as many as 1,500 guests. Whenever she was in town, Sally Rand never missed one of Dorothy's extravagant soirées. And, while she sometimes performed at the Tin Palace, there were many other partygoers who were nearly as quirky. Dorothy would commonly invite such performers as the Tammy Shanter Caledonian Pipe Band[8] or a random exotic dancer from Thailand. Dorothy

---

6   A working restored tower clock manufactured in 1911 by the Seth Thomas Clock Company crowns the 74-foot-high tower. (If you are really lucky, your tour of Rubelia will include a visit to see the inner workings of the clock.)

7   The story of Rubel Pharm is worthy of a book of its own and, fortunately, there are two: *Every Town Needs a Castle* by Dwayne Hunn, Xlibris (2010) and *One Man's Dream: The Spirit of the Rubel Castle* by David C. Traversi, Strange Publications (2003) [of particular interest is the cover illustration rendered by none other than "Sally"]. The property is now administered by the Glendora Historical Society. Tours may be arranged through the society, during which you might encounter some of the artists who make their home in apartments on the premises. Check out pictures of "Rubel's Castle" at Google Images.

8   Members of the band were Scottish bagpipers from Tammy Shanter, a "fish & chips" café in Duarte, midway between Pasadena and Glendora.

herself would ofttimes stand beside the huge grand piano and sing nostalgic tunes from her days in Broadway revues.

Among the Pharm's more unusual shindigs was the party thrown upon the occasion of Scott Rubel's passage from single to double digits. As he remembers it:

> I saw my first stripper dance when I was ten years old…. I may be the youngest kid to have Sally Rand dance at his birthday party. Honestly I don't know how it all came about, except that she was my grandmother's good friend. There she was in all her ostrich-fan glory, kicking up her legs, singing happy birthday to me at the end of my first decade. Heck, she was a star, sort of like Marilyn Monroe. Made me feel like J.F.K., except she was 65 and I was ten.
>
> There I was sitting on the Oriental Carpet with a few friends, awestruck quiet for the first time in six years. We were all wearing masks (my birthday happens to fall on Halloween) but under those masks every one of us had our mouths hanging open. When Mrs. Rand finally came down off the back of that flatbed truck I was so traumatized I could barely look at Lauren, the one girl I had invited over to anything, ever. Sure it was a unique experience, one that most kids won't have, but I advise normal birthday parties. It took a while for Lauren to speak to me at school again.[9]

As the grandson of her best friend, young Scott's activities were of special interest to Sally, and she was not the least bit reluctant to offer her guidance. Writing to him on March 3, 1973, at his college-prep boarding school near Santa Barbara, Sally opened with: "I've known you (and loved you) all your life." Over four typed pages she then proceeded to give him a heavy dose of unsolicited advice on such matters as how to choose a salutation for a letter, the importance of getting enough sleep, and, most emphatically, how to make the best use of his time:

> *"Just fooling around," horsing with the fellows, dilatory time wasting … is stupid.*
>
> *That which you hate most, do first — quickly, cheerfully, efficiently. This saves time for you to do that which you enjoy. Never again will your mind be as receptive and retentive as it*

---

[9] This story is excerpted from Scott Rubel's recollections posted at: www.theshriek.net/castle_memories.html. Your author is deeply grateful to Scott for the personal tour of the fabulous Rubelia.

is now, so use this time for maximum learning skills to be called on later.

Above all, the habits you acquire now are setting your "life style" for all the rest of your life. You control the making of "your habits." Stop being slovenly.

She then went on at length about the importance of oxygen in the blood, poisonous toxins, and the demands of a young man's growing body, skeleton, and organs, as well as the proper scheduling of his daily activities:

Discipline yourself to make better use of your 24 hours.

Immediately deduct 8 hours off the top (let the 8 include showers, teeth washing, prayers, and lights out). This leaves 16 hours. Deduct 2 hours for meals and B.M. — 14 left.

5 hours classroom — 5 hours equal study; you can't learn spit without equal study time. 6 hours left for your assigned school maintenance duties, personal correspondence and "recreation" (?).

Make out a schedule and keep it.

The most difficult part of this whole "time use" schedule is the decision you make on "FIRST THINGS FIRST"!

So what's first? — Health.

Without health, you're dead. Damn it, I don't care what's expected of you ... It's your life, your time (and it's limited), and regardless of "expected" pressures and your own inclinations to sloth (all humans have the temptation of sloth, but discipline overcomes it), do your thing! With efficiency, accuracy and good humor....

So O.K. — I'm a yacky old broad and write letters too long — O.K., I admit it. ONLY I kept and still have my father's long, wordy letters. Part of my hostility to them and him was — he was always so damn RIGHT!

Anyway, I've said it, and I'm glad.

As an adult, Scott Rubel admitted the unusual nature of Sally's letter, but also observed that maybe he should have paid more attention to her advice.

Over the years, Sally was quite generous to her employees, as well as to her friends and family, often to a fault. She commonly provided financial assistance, even when her own situation was none too stable. She was also known to reach out in a more personal way. A notable example occurred in Glendora when, at age 71, Sally offered refuge in her home to an abused woman. As she recounted in a letter to Dorothy Rubel, dated September 17, 1975:

> In answer to your question, "Is Troy fearful?" I would call that a miracle of understatement! She has sustained two terrible beatings in the last couple of years from the men in her life, one with whom she lived for several years, rich, affluent and a hopeless alcoholic. The other a moving picture producer, director. My opinion is he hoped to use her to attain financial backing. When the chips were down, down to the bottom of the barrel, and the nitty gritty — in frustration, anger, sadism, who knows what, he almost killed her — left terrible scars on her face — and damaged one kidney irreparably. She is ill, frightened and broke.... A girlfriend of hers was married to a rich, affluent, influential bisexual man who used his married status and his wife as a front for his male relationships, orgies, et al.... The orgies, pot parties (and worse) in the home finally became unbearable, especially when she was forced into participation, ran out and off, no coat, no money and walked to Troy's. Could you refuse her? Troy couldn't, which is one of the reasons she is at my house.... She is fearful and suspicious of everything and everyone, except, maybe me....
>
> I'm the calm one, I have nothing to fear, but then I haven't experienced the cruelty of an insane husband, the rejection, the lack of means to make a living, the beatings, the ill health, the fear of tomorrow. When I'm around she calms down, and is almost normal. My house and my presence represents total safety — a calm and harmonious atmosphere, peace in the midst of the storm — probably the only safety and peace she's known since her parents were killed in an accident when she was 10 — and her grandmother died when she was 16.

Although Sally was one of the most independent and resourceful women of her time, she was never reluctant to ask for assistance. When in Glendora, she commonly called on a friend or acquaintance to drive her somewhere or to help with a household chore. As described by Steve Quillen, who was staying with Sally in 1974 helping to sort through her files in preparation for writing (or assisting Sally in writing) the long-promised story of her life:[10]

> She could be anything she needed to be. She could go instantly
> from being Sally Rand with the fans to this little old lady from
> Glendora who needed help, and could you give her a ride home or
> could you help her with this, or could you help her with her
> baggage, or whatever she needed. If she could only transfer that
> ability to the stage, she could probably be one of the World's great
> stage actresses. If there was nobody around, Sally could always
> manage to do it, but she could also usually manage to find
> somebody to do it for her.

The story is told of an occasion when a neighborhood youth was called upon to help Sally retrieve some boxes from the attic of her home.[11] Imagine his mixed emotions when, while holding the ladder for his elder, the young gentleman happened to look up toward the attic access opening only to observe that his celebrated neighbor had apparently overlooked the donning of an undergarment that day.

---

[10]   Among Quillen's notes were these observations:
- She has books everywhere. Half of the hallway is taken up by floor to ceiling bookcases. She has a wide and diverse area of interest.... Seems to have a real love of science fiction.
- We have a charge account at the local neighborhood market, two blocks away. Only buy food for one day at a time. No place to store more. Mostly frozen foods and snacks. Have two-burner hot plate and toaster oven for heating. An old under-the-counter refrigerator. There is no sink.
- Sally eats at any hour, whenever she gets hungry, i.e., two or three in the morning.... Starts the day with cup of instant coffee, glass of Tang and Dexedrine. Then back to bed to wait for capsule to begin to take effect.
- We wash dishes in bathtub or bathroom sink once a week or if we need some particular pan or dish.

[11]   Sally's attic was full of millenary goods, costumes, furniture, boxes and more boxes.

Like many of her show business colleagues, Sally loved nothing more than being the center of attention. As she once revealed in a letter to Dorothy Rubel:

> *Of course the applause, praise, cherishing, flowers and*
> *friends, old and new, coming to visit is a great ego trip — I*
> *realize that. But don't we all need some of this? (Some of us*
> *more than others — like me)*

During her later years in Glendora, Sally seldom passed up a chance to serve as the "Mistress of Ceremonies" — presiding over parties, parades, and special ceremonies of every nature. In January of 1975, when John Fields, then a high school junior, was staging his show *Fields' Follies* at Glendora High School, Sally was more than willing to take control of the whole production, passing on her decades' worth of show business tips to the enthusiastic coed performers.[12] The show played to a packed house at the Citrus College Auditorium (now the Haugh Performing Arts Center), raising thousands of dollars for the 1975 Junior Class Prom.[13]

A few years later, Dorothy Rubel wrote *Sisters*, a show about her own brief vaudeville career performing as half of a song-and-dance team with her sister Eleanor. When she presented it at the Glendora Woman's Club, Sally was thrilled to assist with the costumes and production. Then, when the local YWCA sponsored the second annual "Mr. Glendora Pageant" in April of 1978, Sally was happy to step in as the Mistress of Ceremonies, even arranging for her friends and performing companions, the comic impersonator and singer Chuck Mitchell and tap dancer Gene Bell,[14] to appear as "special guest star entertainers." Color photographs from the occasion confirm that the 74-year-old Sally still had the legs of a far younger woman.

---

[12] *Fields' Follies* was first produced in 1973 and then again in 1974-75, when a more elaborate version was mounted starring Sally Rand. This later version also starred Lucianne Buchanan, Miss California of 1974, who became first runner-up for the 1975 Miss America title.

[13] John Fields continues to be a prominent citizen of Glendora. In July 2007, he donated his "Rodgers Trio" Theater Organ to the Glendora Historical Society. The instrument had originally been installed in Madison Square Garden before it was moved into the Tin Palace at Rubelia. On the evening of August 6, 2007, John treated a select gathering to an amazing concert the likes of which the old packing house had never heard.

[14] Gene Bell began performing when he was 10, tap-dancing outside the Palace Theater while his sister provided accompaniment with a comb and a slip of paper. Nationally known, he appeared in major venues such as the Hollywood Bowl, the Kennedy Center, Madison Square Garden and Harlem's Apollo Theater, opening for stars like Josephine Baker, Red Skelton, Don Rickles, and Wayne Newton.

Dorothy Rubel was far more than a close and generous friend. She and Sally had both been born in 1904 and they had shared many memories from their early careers in vaudeville. Their relationship had flourished over the years that they were neighbors and chums in Glendora. But, most of all, they were kindred spirits. Dorothy was an intelligent, kind, and caring confidante, perhaps the only person in Sally's life with whom she could be open without reserve. When Dorothy became ill and died on August 1, 1977, she was only 72. Sally was devastated. After taking a few days to gather her thoughts, she wrote to Dorothy's son Christopher:

Dear Christopher:

To you whose mother she was, my deepest sympathy for the irrevocable loss of one so precious and very special.

I cannot imagine life without her — she was mother, sister, dearest and closest friend. A friend is someone who knows all about you and loves you anyway. She was my business manager and social arbiter. With her impeccable taste and education she edited and advised on what I wrote and wore, and all things. She was my teacher and my advisor. I never made a decision without her. She admonished me, peremptorily, with vigor, when I had or was about to behave badly or without taste. She was my constant example of elegance in all things. She forgave me lovingly (and laughingly, sometimes). She gave me praise, for which we show business hams have such urgent need and hunger. It was she with whom I could "laugh all my laughter, and cry all my tears."

She was my most beloved.

Within a few weeks of writing this letter, Sally herself was taken ill. She was hospitalized in Detroit for "an undisclosed illness." Hospital officials declined to discuss her case but, in an unintended pun, reported that she was "in fair condition."

Glendora's interest in its most famous citizen continues to this day. On May 29, 2011, the Glendora Historical Society held a special public meeting to honor and reminisce about Sally. Among those in attendance was a would-be biographer who had flown in from the East Coast to read from his nascent manuscript and speak of his plans.

CHAPTER TWENTY-SEVEN

A Gay Old Time

The tragedy of old age is not that one is old, but that one is young.

~ Oscar Wilde, *The Picture of Dorian Gray*

B y the 1970s, Sally's act had fully transitioned from a daring exhibition into a comfortable nostalgia act. Interviews from the time tended to focus more on her past than on her present.[1] In December of 1971, she opened in *The Big Show of 1928* at the Huntington Hartford Theater in Hollywood. A retrospective vaudeville revue featuring Cab Calloway, Louis Jordan, and the Ink Spots, the show was described as "reminiscent of a more care-free time before wars and depressions, when the Charleston and Black Bottom dances were sweeping the country." Following a two-week engagement, the revue hit the road for a tour of the United States and Canada. The cast of performers varied from city to city and, by the time the troupe reached Toronto, Rudy Vallee was being billed as the show's co-star.

The show evolved to such an extent that, when it opened at the Felt Forum (the huge theater at Madison Square Garden in New York City), it had been repackaged as *The Big Show of 1936*, featuring Jackie "The Kid" Coogan, among others, with Alan Jones as master of ceremonies.

Older audiences brushed off critical reviews and flocked to performances, even at the John F. Kennedy Center in Washington. The show rolled on, moving back across the country in August to San Francisco, where it would be the premiere revue at the newly reopened 2,000-seat Orpheum Theatre. A columnist in the city trumpeted Sally's return to the Bay Area:

> She is shapely, supple and bouncy in body and saucy and effervescent in spirit.... Miss Rand said she is convinced that her style of dancing, with pink fans in a soft blue light, is far more meaningful than staring at "a stark naked broad standing flat-footed on a stage. Like

---

[1] During a 1971 engagement in Chicago, Sally sat down for an interview with Studs Terkel. You can listen to a five-minute excerpt at http://conversations.studsterkel.org/htimes.php.

sex itself, nudity is more exciting, more turning on, when there is mystique and illusion about it."

In a minidress, Miss Rand displayed a superbly conditioned figure with legs to turn a girl watcher's head.

On opening night, a receptive audience arrived at the Orpheum in vintage automobiles, attired in period costume. A reviewer for the *Stanford Daily*, a student-run paper, singled out Sally as one of the highlights of the evening. Overall, though, he felt the show missed the mark:

> While the show may appeal to the nostalgiacs, it's difficult for anyone who hasn't seen the original to evaluate it on anything but a performance level or as a museum piece. The show does provide some clues as to why Vaudeville died.[2]

In June of 1973, Sally accepted an invitation to perform at the annual Phoenix House Benefit in New York City, a fundraiser for its drug and alcohol rehabilitation programs to be held at the legendary Roseland Ballroom on 52nd Street in Manhattan. The theme of the event was "The Golden Olden Days of Burlexque."[3] The festivities included drag queens, nude models with colorfully painted bodies, and a bevy of famous performers and patrons that included Paul Newman, Joanne Woodward, Rhonda Fleming, Lainie Kazan, and Shelly Winters, as well as Alice Cooper and Alexis Smith (both in drag), evangelist Marjoe Gortner, and Andy Warhol accompanied by his bare-bottomed underground star Gerri Miller. Even Georgia Sothern was on the guest list. Sally's performance was said to have gotten the biggest hand of the evening from the assemblage of 1,200 benefactors.

Sally's experience at the Phoenix House Benefit seems to have set her on a sort of "gender bender" path. While her older followers from 40 years back may have been dying off, it had become clear that there was a whole new potential audience out there among a group of alternative-lifestyle fans to whom she might become a sort of icon.

---

[2] A glimpse of *The Big Show of 1936*, including interview footage of Sally and Jackie Coogan (both smoking cigarettes), may be seen at https://diva.sfsu.edu/collections/ sfbatv/bundles/189623. The KPIX video appears to be unedited raw footage, but it *is* in color and includes a brief look at the 68-year-old Sally performing the fan dance.

[3] This is not a typo; they did spell the word "Burlesque" with an "X" in advertising materials.

While gay "baths" have been around for decades, if not centuries, by 1970 they had begun to appear in major metropolitan areas as more or less acceptable commercial enterprises. In 1972, Chuck Renslow renovated a building on North Clark Street in Chicago and opened the "Man's Country" bathhouse. He transformed the second floor into a music hall that regularly presented local talent and would occasionally feature an act like Wayland Flowers and his puppet "Madame." By early 1974, however, the club was seeking to raise its profile by engaging bigger-name entertainment. After initially considering famous stripper Tempest Storm, club manager Gary Chichester opted to invite Sally Rand instead.

According to Chichester, Sally wasn't all that receptive to the idea at first, as she had recently become apprehensive about appearing in the wrong kind of club. As the story goes, she had been booked in Lexington, Kentucky, for an engagement at a place she had been told was called the Gold Mule. However, when she arrived at the venue, she discovered it was actually a sleazy dive called the Brass Ass. Not wanting to repeat that experience, she arranged for trusted friends from Chicago to inspect Man's Country before she would agree to appear there. After the "elderly couple" had visited the premises covertly, they gave Sally a thumbs-up, and even reported that the music hall had a ceiling high enough to accommodate her bubble dance.

Sally was booked at the bathhouse for a 45-minute show but, since her dance required only a fraction of that time, she filled the balance with a Q & A session. She had so many show business anecdotes that there was no trouble keeping the towel-clad crowd spellbound. When asked how she felt about playing to a room full of homosexuals, Sally quipped: "I don't know about that, because I haven't seen you fellows having sex. All I know is that there's a room full of half-naked men and they're all admiring and paying attention to me, and at my age what more could I ask for?"

Chichester could hardly have been more pleased: "It was absolutely amazing. People just loved it and Sally Rand turned out to be one of the most fabulous and fascinating people I've ever met. I have to say they loved her. They really loved her." She was the first real star to play at Man's Country and her appearance helped to legitimize the venue with its neighbors. As one elderly woman put it: "Well, if Sally Rand can appear there, it can't be all bad."

By 1974, Sally's one-time hairdresser, Kenneth Marlowe, had relocated to San Francisco and, at age 47, the female impersonator had begun to get serious about his vision of becoming "Katherine Marlowe." After a consultation at the Stanford Medical Center, he was advised that the surgical procedure he sought was going to cost $8,000, none of which would be covered by insurance. The price was beyond his means, but, together with his friend Richard Nelson, Marlowe came up with a plan to raise the money. They would rent a hall, throw a grand party, and invite enough paying attendees to raise a major portion of the required sum. The gala would include such an alluring assortment of entertainers — two bands, a magic act, fire jugglers, even a talking dog act — that the affair would become a must-be-there event for the alternative-life-style crowd in the Bay area. Nelson recalls Marlowe exclaiming with his usual flamboyance:

> Nelson! You've got it. That's a great idea. I'll sell tickets at five dollars apiece. We'll have a bar and — hey, wait a minute. I was a hairdresser to the stars, remember? I'll call and arrange for someone to come up to headline the show.... I can see it now, Nelson. I'll call it: THE BALL TO END ALL BALLS!"

Of course, that "someone" was Sally Rand. Whether or not Marlowe knew of her turns at Man's Country, he felt confident she would agree to appear. After all, Sally owed him for coming to her rescue at The Body Shop seven years earlier. Besides, the occasion could be combined with a celebration of her birthday. Marlowe arranged for a local bakery to make a huge round cake adorned with 70 candles. Asked what she thought of the whole sex-change affair, Sally responded: "If a girl wants to be a girl, she ought to be a girl."

The grand gala took place on March 29, 1974. Steve Quillen, who was working with Sally at the time, recalled her role in making the occasion a triumph:

> Now, when we did that Ken Marlowe benefit up there, Ken booked her on to a morning talk show in San Francisco to pull in people.... In San Francisco, he had rented California Hall. They had a 22-piece big band orchestra — music of the thirties and forties — they had a dance marathon, a jitterbug contest, and they had all kinds of things — and Sally was going to dance. And you've never seen such a mish-mash of people coming for different reasons. There were hippies, there were the drug addicts, there were the street people, there were drag queens, there were little old ladies with their blue hair and their furs and their baldheaded husbands who remembered Sally. He was pulling from all sections of San Francisco.
>
> It was a great success. It was a wonderful evening. He had rented old vintage cars and had klieg lights outside and he arrived in semi-drag with two white Russian Wolf Hounds. Sally arrived in a Duesenberg convertible, and it was just — it was wonderful!

As Sally ended her dance, she was astonished to find herself surrounded by 70 young men, each holding a lighted candle. The reported 900 partygoers raised enough cash for Marlowe to call the Stanford Medical Center the following week and schedule an appointment. Preliminary surgery was performed and, after four weeks of recovery, "Kate" was soon eager for the next step — a breast enhancement procedure. As Nelson recalled: "To raise money for the big event referred to as 'Tittie Day,' Kate auctioned off the furniture at a local night club."

S ally's 70th birthday party in San Francisco was but the first of such cele-brations. One week after the Ken/Kate Marlowe gala, and apparently still in a transgender mood, Sally observed the occasion once again, this time opposite the celebrated female impersonator Charles Pierce in a one-night-only appearance at the Los Angeles Music Center's illustrious Dorothy Chandler Pavilion. Twenty-two years younger than Sally, Pierce was known for his spot-on impersonations of such Hollywood stars as Bette Davis, Mae West, Tallulah Bankhead, and Carol Channing.[4]

Sally met with Pierce at the apartment of producer Stephen Papich, where they agreed that she would perform both the fan and bubble dance. She insisted that the bubble dance be staged as the finale and that there be a scrim across the front of the stage to create a "dream like quality." She also informed Papich that she wanted $2,500 for the show, to be paid in advance.

For the bubble dance, the plan was for Sally to make a grand entrance, flying through the air like Peter Pan. As usual, she was concerned that everything connected with her appearance be "just so." As Steve Quillen recounted events leading up to the scheduled performance:

> The night we went over to the Dorothy Chandler for rehearsal, it
> was the first time the crew people were there doing the rigging ...
> and they were sitting at the flying mechanism ... and in walks this
> little 70-year-old lady, not quite five feet tall, in her little Glendora
> shirtwaist dress and her little overcoat and she sits down with her
> shoulder bag and she starts talking to these guys — these big, huge
> six-and-a-half-foot guys that are backstage working crews, and she
> knows all the proper terminology for all the lighting, for all the
> rigging, for all the ropes, for all the cleats and everything ... and
> within five minutes she had all their respect.... They rehearsed
> once, they flew her once and she told them what kind of
> adjustments she needed made to the rigging.

---

[4]   A couple of years earlier, Channing had reportedly gone backstage to see Pierce after
his show at Gold Street in San Francisco and declared in her signature husky voice,
"Cheee-yarles: you do me better than I do!"

The night of the performance we got there two hours early and she sat backstage and played a couple of hands of Poker with the guys and later she said that she was just ensuring that she was going to have a good performance. She said, "Those guys are going to be flying me and it's going to make the difference as to whether I look mediocre or whether I look great.... If they're doing it for a friend, they're going to make me look great...."

When the big night arrived, Sally was exuberant. She told Quillen: "It's the greatest moment of my life to play this place. It's sort of a final acceptance by L.A. society." But before her "greatest moment" could materialize, she got into a dispute with Papich over the advance payment and whether use of the scrim would be limited to the finale as she wished. Papich felt that either Pierce should be able to use it as well or a portion of the cost should be deducted from her compensation. Sally was miffed, delicately remarking to Quillen: "That motherfucker is ruining the greatest night of my life."

In any event, the show came off without a hitch, with Sally getting two standing ovations. After the show, a reviewer for *The Los Angeles Times* heaped praise on Sally. Finding her to be "in beautiful physical shape" and "the epitome of graceful, tasteful burlesque," he declared:

> In an era when sex symbols tend to be silicone and hard-nosed hype, it was nice to see that sex kittens from the old school have very little of either. Miss Rand simply entered with her plumes (or giant bubble) and did her number.... It's nice to report that she hasn't joined the modern world.

And, there was yet *another* 70th birthday party for Sally, this one arranged by actress Beatrice Kay, an old vaudeville pal who had toured with Sally in *The Big Show of 1936*. Afterward, Sally wrote a thank-you note to Miss Kay, expressing her delight at all the attention she had gotten:

> *What a birthday this, my 70th, April 3rd. Dinner with my son and daughter-in-law, announcement that I will be a grandmother in November. April 6th, after 55 years in show business my most exciting night in the theatre. A performance at our posh Los Angeles Music Center, in the Dorothy Chandler Pavilion. A packed 3,000 seat house, standing ovation, WOW! What a ball to do at 70 what one did at 17! Really, more than that you can't ask.*

Despite all the accolades and the anticipation of becoming a grandmother, sadly, financial matters continued to intrude. The tax man was never very far from the door. In a letter to a creditor dated October 23, 1974, Sally pled:

> *Please be patient! The minute I hit home — I have the income tax people who will descend upon me like vultures — and I have to get books and receipts for them — horribly time consuming; then, the new baby expected November 17th and I will have to help care for mother and child.*

Sure enough, on November 15th, Sean's wife Linda gave birth to a baby girl to be named Shawna Michelle Rand. Someone you've been reading about for many chapters now was totally delighted.

In the spring of 1975, during an engagement at Buddy Kirk's Steak House in Galveston, Texas — one of her favorite venues — Sally celebrated her 71st birthday. Buddy and his wife Jean went all out to make the celebration a memorable occasion, even bringing out a huge cake decorated with hot pink icing and 71 sugar roses. Photos confirm that the cake was actually taller than the guest of honor. Sally responded to all the fuss with one of her most famous quips: "New fans but the same old fanny."

Telegrams, phone calls, and tape recorded greetings poured in from a wide range of celebrities, including: Vincent Price, Helen Hayes, George Burns, Rudy Vallee, Bob Hope, Milton Berle, George Raft, Chicago Mayor Richard Daley and even President Gerald Ford. Sally responded with a fistful of thank-you notes, including this one to former St. Louis Cardinals' baseball star, Stan (The Man) Musial:

> *Thank you for autographing the baseball for my 71st birthday.*
>
> *The first time I became a heroine to my son he was a little boy and found a photo of me and Babe Ruth, taken in Hollywood in the 20's.... Now I've got to be the most glamorous grandmother in the world with an official birthday greeting from the Cardinals — and an autographed baseball from Stan the Man and Lou Brock.*

Clearly touched by the turnout at the reservations-only party, in her brief remarks to the more than 200 well-wishers, Sally observed:

> I think you only retire from what you don't like — and God knows I like this. I'm not sure I have youth. I have good health. I love living. I should hate to have to die, dammit. When you love living, you try to take care of the equipment. Take your vitamins. Be happy. That's the whole bit.

On July 30, 1975, Jimmy Hoffa, former head of the powerful Teamsters Union, arrived at the Machus Red Fox restaurant in the Detroit suburb of Bloomfield Township. He was there for a meeting with organized crime figure Anthony Giacalone and union leader Anthony Provenzano. Hoffa was observed waiting in his 1974 Pontiac Grand Ville, which was subsequently found unlocked and abandoned in the restaurant parking lot. A truck driver later claimed to have witnessed Hoffa seated behind the unknown driver of a Mercury Marquis Brougham as it pulled out of the parking lot. In any event, Hoffa was never seen again. Seven years would pass before he would be declared legally dead. The mystery of his disappearance has been the subject of popular speculation ever since.

As her son Sean recalled, Sally had her own take on the union leader's fate:

> "You know, you met Jimmy Hoffa." And I said, "I did?" She said, "Yeah, remember back in the '60s we were on a boat in Minnesota cruising with the lieutenant governor. The Twist was a big dance at the time and I was dancing with a guy doing the Twist — that was Hoffa. We have pictures of it." I said, "That was Hoffa, huh?" He was just another guy on the boat to me. She said, "This is what happened to Hoffa. They'll never find him. They put him in a vat of lye. There's nothing left — no toenails, no fingernails, no teeth — nothing. Everything's gone."
>
> I don't know that anybody actually told her that happened. I think it was just, with all her experiences over the years being around the mobsters, she knew what they do.

Now in her eighth decade, Sally still felt the lure of the legitimate stage. In late January of 1976 she began a four-week engagement in *Night Watch*, a "whodunit" at the Pheasant Run Playhouse in St. Charles, Illinois. She was cast in a featured role opposite Jack Kelly (perhaps best remembered as brother "Bart" to James Garner's "Bret" in the ABC television series *Maverick*). A local critic observed that Sally's performance as psychiatrist Dr. Tracey Lake was "excellent": "Though tiny in structure, the 'lady of the fans' is large in dramatic talent."

And Sally was by no means ready to slow down. She kept an active schedule throughout the 1970s, augmenting her usual shows with charity events and taking advantage of whatever new opportunities came her way. One such occasion showcased yet another of Sally's little known talents — oil painting. In May of 1975, ensconced in booth number 79, she displayed and offered for sale several of her paintings in the "Fine Arts" section at the Pomona Antiques and

Art Show held at the Los Angeles County Fairgrounds. According to Sean, Sally purposely didn't sign her paintings, explaining: "If I put my name on anything, I'm going to get judged because of my name." She did sign them ("in tiny little red letters") once they were back home.

On May 29, 1976, she participated in the Bicentennial Galaxy Ball, a benefit in Fort Worth for the Texas Association for Mental Health (sponsors said "we wanted to get their attention"). Eight days later, she was in Kansas City serving as auctioneer at the "Strip the Folly," a fundraiser for the restoration of the Folly Theater. Several G-strings, a parrot cage, and a "genuine red velvet swing" were among the burlesque memorabilia sold. In September, Sally returned to Kansas City to attend MidAmeriCon, the 34th World Science Fiction Convention, as the special guest — front row, reserved seat — of her old classmate, the convention's "Guest of Honor," Robert Heinlein.[5] She even served as a judge for the masquerade costume contest.

Besides appearing with the touring company of *A Funny Thing Happened on the Way to the Forum*, Sally made "homecoming" appearances both at the 50th reunion of her class at Columbia College (formerly Christian College) and in her birthplace of Elkton, Missouri, where a reported crowd of 60,000 turned out to greet her. Commenting on the notoriety of Sally's chosen profession, local coffee shop owner Elaine Payne observed:

> She kind of drawed attention because nothing like that had ever happened in this area. Didn't bother me a bit and it still doesn't bother me. You know, everybody does his own thing. That's the way I've always felt.

In late August of 1977 she was performing at the Royal Ascot Supper Club in the Detroit suburb of Lincoln Park. Newspapers reported that not only were the gentlemen in her audience applauding her show but "the ladies don't seem put off by the flaunting of her septuagenarian figure." As Sally saw it: "It gives them great hope. If I can do it, so can they." However, at age 73, the question would soon become: Could she, in fact, still do it? After her second show on Saturday night, September 3rd, Sally complained of respiratory trouble. She was admitted to Henry Ford Hospital in Detroit.

When reached by phone three days later, she declined to discuss her condition, but acknowledged: "I'm having difficulty breathing. I can't talk if I

---

5   Heinlein's lifelong crush on Sally found expression in some of the characters in his science fiction stories. In particular, in the original published version of "Let There Be Light," the character Mary Lou Martin had a "Figure like a strip dancer, lots of corn-colored hair, nice complexion, and great big soft blue eyes."

can't breathe." After 17 days of what was reported as "convalescence for a lung ailment," she resumed the final two weeks of her supper club engagement. For a heavy smoker less stubborn than Sally, the episode might have served as a wake-up call. Instead, it proved a portent of things to come.

Sally had always considered her Christian faith to be an important part of her persona — in word at least, if not always in deed.[6] Most of her life she had been a member of one Protestant congregation or another. So, in the summer of 1978, it came as a bit of a surprise when, at the urging of her son, she converted to Mormonism, becoming a member of the Church of Jesus Christ of Latter-day Saints. She later described the experience: "The biggest thrill of my life was when Sean baptized me."

Wholeheartedly applying herself to her new faith, Sally devoured *The Book of Mormon* and developed an ability to speak with authority about such matters as the mysterious golden tablets and the "miracle of the seagulls."

As 1978 drew to a close, disparate sects of Christian faith were very much in the news: Spencer W. Kimball, President of the Church of Jesus Christ of Latter-day Saints, received a revelation allowing him to make the Mormon priesthood available to African-American men; within the space of 10 weeks, three different men held the position of Bishop of Rome, leader of the worldwide Catholic Church; the evangelical former Governor of Georgia, Jimmy Carter, was winding up his second year as President of the United States; and, on November 18th, in Jonestown, Guyana, Rev. Jim Jones led his People's Temple congregation in the mass murder and suicide of 909 of its members. Oh, and a quasi-religious film starring Warren Beatty and Julie Christie — one of the biggest motion pictures of the year — was about to be nominated for nine Academy Awards: *Heaven Can Wait*.

Sally was now 74 years old. Her old friend Joan Crawford had died the previous year. Gypsy Rose Lee had died eight years earlier. Recent months had seen the passing of Norman Rockwell, Hubert Humphrey, Edgar Bergen, Bing Crosby, Charlie Chaplin, Groucho Marx, and even Elvis Presley. Most of her other contemporaries were long retired, if not deceased.

Sally was not the retiring kind.

---

6   Sally's spirituality had not always been demonstrated even "in word." In the late sixties, the controversial radio talk show host Joe Pyne had asked: "Are you religious?" To which she responded: "Not really." Sally explained that she was an Episcopalian but had studied many religions.

CHAPTER TWENTY-EIGHT

The Last Dance

I'll tell you something. I shall be here at the turn of the
century. I will have a glass of pink champagne, dance a
Vienna Waltz with a nice young man and sleep late the
next morning. After that, I don't give a damn.
~ Sally Rand 1973

As Sally unsuspectingly entered the last year of her life, she showed little sign of slowing down. Although she gloried in her recent conversion to Mormonism, its strictures had little impact on her desire to perform.

In a September 10, 1978, letter to Steve and Helen Vaughn, Sally revealed that she had jumped into her new faith with both feet:

Now, I have become a member of the Mormon Church! With my son and family. It has been a profound and joyous experience; though I would not have believed it, myself, a year ago.

Wanting to be of use, Sally asked her old "carnie" pals for their help in locating the popcorn and cotton candy machines she needed for an up-coming church bazaar ("I'll need sacks and/or boxes too."):

Anyway, I'll be very grateful if you can help me with this project — help me be a "big shot" in my new church. I don't imagine there will be more than a hundred or so people attending. The L.D.S. don't advertise (or I'd have "papered" the area)....

Best for your life in your new home. I'd like to give you a "house present" — something nostalgic, memorabilia from my career or R.A.S., come by and pick out something. How about a 24-sheet — how many people have a 24-sheet in their house?[1]

---

[1]   A "one-sheet" — an eye-catching poster measuring 27 by 41 inches — is often found at the entry or in the lobby of a movie theater. The less common "three-sheet" is 41 by 81 inches (equal to three one-sheets, stacked vertically). Ordinarily, you would need a billboard to accommodate a "24-sheet." ("R.A.S." refers to Royal American Shows.)

Speaking of 24-sheets, back in 1971 Sally had told Chuck Thurston of the *Detroit Free Press*:

> I once mentioned 24-sheets to a night club owner and he said "We will have them, I'll take care of all that." I thought, "Some high class joint, they have their own 24-sheets." The afternoon I arrived, the proprietor proudly presented me with 24 clean white bed sheets! Being of ribald mind, I wondered if he thought I'd take tricks between shows.

For Sally, converting to Mormonism had also meant terminating her longtime association with Grace Episcopal Church where her late friend Dorothy Rubel's son Christopher served as pastor. Her relationship with the Rubel family had been strained since Dorothy's death the year before, a state of affairs largely due to financial misunderstandings and the resulting bruised feelings, all mixed up with their mutual grief. Christopher, in particular, was troubled by the tensions that had erupted between Sally and his brother Michael. Writing to her on September 10th, Christopher had observed:

> Your pain since Dorothy's death has been with me in one form or another. I knew you were leaving the church long before you wrote the letter ... I knew you didn't like anything that was going on and all the overwhelming turns of events during this past year or so.[2] It has been one hell of a time for you, and for many of us. Our lives are turned upside down.
>
> One thing that is a positive note in this whole thing is that you and Sean have found a way to become close again. I'm sure he has needed you as much as you have needed him and his family. The whole family process of aging ... and the alienation that goes on is brutal, it seems to me. This whole life seems to push us more and more into ourselves for our resources because we find less and less through the presence of others.
>
> You are part of my life, somehow.... I have always and still do admire you for your ability to roll with the punches and come up on your feet. God cares less which way you worship Him. I will

---

2   Sally had often prevailed upon young Christopher to serve as her driver. On one such occasion, she had asked him to drive two of her showgirls out of state. Not in a position to comply, he had begged off as diplomatically as possible. After the girls were tragically killed in an automobile accident on the trip, Sally had lashed out at him, suggesting that they would still be alive if only he had not been so selfish.

miss you at Grace, but think of you as being fully filled in the community of the Mormons.... Much love through the pain ...

Dorothy's daughter Dorchen was also caught up in the emotional turmoil, writing to Sally:

> It is sad that so many things were said that month that cannot be undone. So many things left unsaid. Mother loved your adventures and lived show business and a glamourous life through you. I'm sure you gave her much pleasure and much dear, dear, friendship. I know she truly loved you.

Months before, producer Chet Hagan had written to Sally on May 6th, broaching once again the subject of a possible film about her life.[3] In her belated response, the 74-year-old Sally playfully observed that the proposed film might be called *How to Take Off Your Pants and Be a Success — Without Trying*. After revealing her preferred choice to play the lead role, she disclosed a persistent anxiety, no doubt dating back to the perceived abandonment by her father many decades earlier:

> *There was a company out here, at M.G.M. — wildly enthusiastic about doing a T.V. story on SR — right now — yesterday, etc. — then it piddled out.... One of the conditions of that contract ... (and one I would have to have with you, should I decide to do it) was my O.K. on the person who was to play Sally Rand as a young woman. My choice was, and still is, would you believe, Sandy Duncan.*

> *Why? Because: She is a really good, well trained dancer.... Her appearance, her face, is essentially very plain. I was a painfully plain, child, teenager and young woman. I cannot tell you how totally enchanted and bewitched I was, to discover what make up — curly wigs and hair pieces could do to make one "pretty." "PRETTY." To be pretty, that most cherished dream, and Sandy can be very "pretty" and "gussied up," and that's what I did. Put it on and off like a*

---

3   Hagan had approached Sally nine months earlier, informing her that the Cates Brothers Company (producers of the *Fame* television series, as well as several David Copperfield TV specials) was "interested in doing a made-for-TV movie on that aspect of your life revolving around the Chicago World's Fair." The producers offered Sally a $5,000 option up front, plus another $25,000 for use of her name and personal recollections. They also brought up "publishing rights" on her book, telling her: "I know that you are determined to write every word yourself and I can appreciate that."

uniform — always dreaming of being loved by a man, for the inside me, and my crazy, plain little face. It never happened — but I could dream, couldn't I?

Ponder then on the phenomena of the most publicized Sex Symbol, the most wanted Theatrical attraction of that time, suffering and agonizing with an obsessive fear of rejection! The recipient of bushels of orchids, fabulous gifts, poems of praise, more newspaper coverage than Mrs. Roosevelt — swathed in mink and ermine, squired by dozens of attractive eligible beaux — racked by the fear of rejection.

F orty-five years after her first triumphant appearance there, Sally returned to the Chicago Theatre on September 24th to perform her famous fan dance at a fundraiser organized by the Chicago Area Theatre Organ Enthusiasts, a group that had recently restored the auditorium's huge pipe organ. Live shows had become a rarity by this time, and it was hoped that the Sally Rand show might reverse the fortunes of the playhouse.[4]

Two days earlier, having accepted an invitation from Chicago's American Academy of Art, Sally served as a model for a life drawing class. Dressed in a pair of gold mules and pink panty hose, she stood in front of a black back-ground and presented several five-minute poses while arranging her two pink ostrich feather fans in a series of typically seductive poses. Two rows of some 35 to 40 students sat in a semicircle facing her with their easels and sketch pads. A spotlight on the ceiling illuminated the makeshift stage. Several photographers and two television crews covered the event, prompting Sally to quip: "I'll have to call my son in Los Angeles and tell him to turn on the television and watch his naked mother in an art class."

J ohn Walter III, whose grandfather had started a small newspaper in London on January 1, 1785, that would later become known around the world simply as *The Times*, once famously wrote: "How frequently the last time comes and we do not know." And, little did Sally know it, but, nearly 200 years later, as the sun would come up on *another* New Year's Day, she was about to experience her own series of events, each for the last time.

---

4   After further decline, the venue was closed on September 19, 1985. Happily, however, a restoration effort did save the building from demolition and a refurbished Chicago Theatre reopened on September 10, 1986, with a gala performance by Frank Sinatra. The iconic venue remains open to this day.

A few weeks into the new year, Sally performed for an audience of 2,500 at a "gala evening of vaudeville nostalgia" held in the old Loew's State Theatre in Syracuse, New York — the same stage where 45 years earlier her show had been cancelled due to pressure from local clergymen. She shared the stage with fellow stage veterans Henny Youngman and Alan Jones, as well as a trained dog show — the Burger Animal Review — billed as "the first and only performing Afghans in the world." Newswriter Winston Collins was in the packed house to document the entire evening's proceedings:

> After Alan Jones had belted out his final encore, the master of ceremonies came out and shouted to the audience, "Wait till you see what's coming next. The sexsational Sally Rand, who's still dancing with only the benefit of two fans." Whistles and wolf cries from randy males reverberated throughout the ornate theatre. Obviously they'd never seen the Rand in action.

> The stage was bathed in deep blue lights, a pianist began Chopin's Waltz in C Sharp Minor and a black curtain was drawn to reveal Sally Rand holding two large ostrich feather fans. Dressed in a gossamer gown, she slowly descended a five-step staircase and wafted gracefully back and forth across the stage, her fans undulating. Two minutes later the gown mysteriously vanished and her only attire was her blond wig, her gold shoes with stiletto heels, and her pink fans. The fans were in constant motion as she lithely turned and twirled. Her body hair had been shaved. Although she showed more of her breasts than her friend Gypsy Rose Lee ever did, Sally Rand's eight minute dance was more sensual than sexy, more ballet than burlesque. After a dramatic backbend, she ascended the staircase and, fans extended, finished with the full frontal pose that always reminded stripper Ann Corio of the statue of Winged Victory.

> "It's all an illusion," says Miss Rand of her moonlight-romance performance. "If that's destroyed it would just be tacky and raunchy, and I'd stop doing it." To make sure illusion was maintained, Miss Rand had sent precise instructions to the Syracuse stage manager. Still, not everything was right. "Two overhead lights were on," she says, "and someone left that goddamn microphone on the stage. I used to just sweep the thing into the orchestra pit with my fan. I didn't care that it cost $400."

Emerging for a curtain call dressed in a baby-doll silver robe edged with pink feathers, Sally recognized the volunteers who helped save the classic theater. She then urged everyone to do their part in saving these grand old theaters, just as she had done in Chicago and elsewhere.

After the show, Sally retired along with Winston Collins to a gathering in a comfortable middle-class home where she continued to emote for an audience of 10 admirers. Sally loved to talk and it wasn't unusual for her to hold court. Collins' account of the mid-winter, late-night colloquy continued:

"Let's face it," she said, cadging a drag off a cigarette, "it's pretty bizarre for a 74-year-old broad to dance naked" ....

She nestles into the corner of the living room sofa and becomes what she likes to be: the center of attention. Her tiny body (5 feet, 98 pounds) is clad in a silver minidress riding high on her nude-shade pantyhose. A blonde hairpiece of moderate proportions doesn't hide the thin scars of a facelift. She dangles a stiletto-heeled shoe on her toe; she smells of Aliage cologne; and she talks.

"A comeback? Comeback from *where?* I've worked 40 weeks a year for more than 40 years. But I haven't worked that much the last two years." In 1977 viral pneumonia sent her to the hospital and now she has chronic asthma. "Until these last two years I'd been a tractor. But when you're not getting enough oxygen to breathe, it's murder. I hate it."

When she's nesting in a living room sofa sipping beet borscht and yogurt, illusion submits to reality. Sally Rand's a dolled-up grand-mother who'll be 75 on April 3. But she looks after herself — a health food diet, no booze, vigorous and regular exercise, a surgical lift here and there. She detests being slowed down, not having things under control, and her ultimate horror is not being able to perform. "I'd be devastated if I couldn't do it anymore!" It isn't money that makes Sally Rand dance; real estate investments in California have made her financially comfortable. She carries on because she's always carried on, a little trouper with a big ego. "Performers are egoists. It's a fault, but that's what we need to keep going."

Sally may have been slowing down, but she was keeping busy in other ways:

"I live by myself in a large house that used to be full of kinfolk," she says. There she sews clothes for her extensive doll collection, plays the harp (which she took up in 1956), makes grape jelly and tends her garden.

Holding forth for Collins and the others until 4:00 in the morning, Sally carried on with spirited accounts of her days and ways:

When I was a child, I climbed into the cemetery and took ribbons off graves to make clothes for my dolls. My mother found out and said "God never tempts you beyond your will." I knew then I had it made. I've done a lot of things in my life that might not be considered proper. But I've never been tempted beyond my will.

Winston Collins' wide-ranging article was published in a weekend supplement carried by 21 newspapers across Canada. The issue also included a separate illustrated article devoted to the history of the striptease.

Predictably, the publication generated controversy. Seven Canadian newspapers declined to include the supplement, finding the content to be in poor taste: "We have a responsibility to our subscribers that anything we deliver to their households is suitable for family consumption." The decision provoked an outcry as described in a front page article accompanied by a photo of people heaving large stacks of the weekly insert captioned "Copies of Weekend Magazine Destined for the Dump."

Readers who *did* receive the supplement were quick to respond to the content — some pro, but mostly con:

- Gretta S. Betts of Moncton, New Brunswick, declared: "The content was unfit to place in the homes of our people. I read only an excerpt and felt I needed a bath."

- Mrs. Robert Cripps of that same community protested: "If anyone wants to see pornography, read filth, four letter words, see evil glorified and decent standards ridiculed, he or she has access to endless trash at the magazine racks. However, for those of us who choose not to feed such to our own minds, and are trying desperately to protect the purity of lovely teenaged daughters, it is the last straw when we have to censor the newspaper."

- A.R. Scammell of St. Johns, Newfoundland said: "*Weekend* has lately been feeding its long suffering readers a steady fare of women parading as sex objects.... While I own to being as appreciative as the next healthy male of the curves and planes of Venus unadorned, too concentrated a diet of vibrating mammary glands and cigarette puffing vaginas is taking the edge off my libido."

- Mr. J. Bowes of Lethbridge, Alberta, offered a different perspective: "I found nothing offensive in the *Weekend* article about Sally Rand and her fellow strippers, but the one in the following week's edition entitled 'Bloody Thursday,' complete with a picture of a bullet-ridden corpse, was offensive. It probably did more harm to young minds than an article about pathetic and obviously aged strippers."

Sally continued to believe she would someday find time to write her memoirs. On March 26th she wrote to New York literary agent Rodney Pelter to advise him that she was reviewing his proposal to be her exclusive agent, saying: "Your constant and consistent enthusiasm cheers me. I am sorry that I can't leap up with the material you want, but I do have it and I'm getting closer to it."[5]

In May, Sally traveled to Albuquerque and Santa Fe, New Mexico, to make what were reportedly her final public performances. Sally's stage show at the Albuquerque Convention Center was billed alongside a "recreational living show" offering "two million dollars' worth" of home furnishings. Adult tickets were $1.50 and children under 12 were admitted free. Artist, costumer and present-day blogger "Guenevere" recalls being taken by her grandparents to see Sally's act:

> I had been told that the key to Sally's act was that she was naked, but she kept these giant fans moving in a way that allowed only the tiniest glimpses of her body.... In her prime, she was very, very famous and many people my grandparents' age recalled her as a strong erotic influence of the times.

> This day, at the not-at-all glamorous convention center, Sally was 75 years old. I can't remember where the music came from, but as she danced I could see that she was wearing a full, nude-colored body stocking. She still had bleached blonde hair, and wore the same makeup she'd worn her entire life to perform. The fans were huge, lovely ostrich feathers that gently molted here and there.

> I recall being moderately horrified. I couldn't decide if the body stocking were a good thing ... or if Sally Rand was cheating us out of the true spectacle. She was not able, as she was when younger, to really keep the fans going fast enough to disguise her body, and I could see flabby arms and wrinkly hands that contrasted oddly with the smoothness of the body stocking.

Even as a 10-year-old, Guenevere was struck by how frail Sally had seemed:

> Once her performance was finished, she came back out, and ... she grabbed the mike stand and laboriously dragged it closer to

---

  Two years earlier, Pelter had served as Andy Warhol's literary agent for his memoir, *The Philosophy of Andy Warhol: From A to B and Back Again*.

herself, and then she thanked everyone for coming. Except, she was breathless, and had to pause between every one or two words.... She sounded so weak, and sick, and I felt shocked that she would perform in this condition.

And yet, despite her fragile condition, by her own account Sally had had a wonderful time in Albuquerque. Describing her visit in a letter written on May 3rd to Bishop Paul Doxey Donaldson in Glendora, she expressed her growing enthusiasm for her recently adopted Mormon faith:

> *I had such a happy and rewarding experience in Albuquerque. One of the ladies from the Indian School Chapel ... took me to the Sacrament meeting, presented me with a beautiful book I didn't have, "Faith Precedes the Miracle," by our prophet, Spencer W. Kimball, and brought a large number of her group to see my show and gave me a wonderful tour of the city. It was delightful.*

> *This morning Mr. Don Nelson from Radio Station KSL in Salt Lake City called long distance to interview me for broadcasts which he will use in the next couple of days ... He, too, is an L.D.S....*

> *Gosh, it's nice to be a Mormon!*

As the summer of 1979 approached, it had been 46 years since that night in May when Sally made her Lady Godiva ride into Millicent Hearst's prestigious dinner, opening the door for her triumph at the Chicago World's Fair. Her fan dance had been a sensation and the ripple effects had buoyed her for many years. But Sally's time had passed. A small army of sexy young performers were commanding public attention.

In 1971, a 30-year old singer from Murcia, Spain, who called herself "Charo" was headlining shows in Las Vegas, and was reportedly being paid as much as Frank Sinatra, Ray Charles or Dean Martin.[6] In the early 1970s, the flamboyant young Cher was generating as much or more controversy as anyone around, exposing various parts of her anatomy in gorgeous, revealing costumes created by famed designer Bob Mackie. In 1976, Farrah Fawcett was playing the role of Jill Munroe in the made-for-TV movie *Charlie's Angels,* and untold numbers of young men were taping her poster to their bedroom walls, resplendent in her red swimsuit and megawatt smile.[7] And,

---

[6]   On June 1, 1971, both Sally and Charo (María Rosario Mercedes Pilar Martínez Molina Baeza by birth) were guests on *The Merv Griffin Show*, a show that ran for over two decades and hosted many important cultural, political, and musical icons.

[7]   The iconic poster of Ms. Fawcett has been recognized as the best-selling poster in history.

in 1978, a young actor named John Travolta, fresh from his career-making role in *Saturday Night Fever*, stood by while a talented and fresh-faced young beauty from Australia named Olivia Newton-John was introducing herself to starstruck American audiences in the movie musical *Grease*.

There was little room in such company for a 75-year-old fan dancer. Still, there was one last memorable appearance in Sally's future. She may not have had any further bookings, but she couldn't very well pass up a chance to see herself portrayed on the stage in a saucy homage to the burlesque era.

One of four Broadway productions to be nominated for the Tony Award as the Best Musical of 1980, *Sugar Babies* starred Mickey Rooney and Ann Miller. The production is of interest to us because of the sixth scene in Act One: "Feathered Fantasy (Salute to Sally Rand)."[8] Although the award for best musical went to *Evita*, *Sugar Babies* collected eight nominations and the show ultimately ran for nearly three years — 1,208 performances.

B efore opening on Broadway, *Sugar Babies* previewed in June of 1979 at the palatial Pantages Theatre, a Hollywood Art Deco landmark and one of Los Angeles' leading venues for live theater. Publicist Jasper Vance, taking note of the tribute to Sally Rand, mulled over the promotional possibilities and decided to invite Sally herself to do a publicity shoot with Barbara Hanks, the young dancer portraying her in the show. Sally quickly agreed to come to the theater on opening night. As Vance recalled the meeting:

> Well, she came to this thing and I was standing in the lobby of the Pantages and Mr. Blackwell was there with me, and he said, "Good God, who is that apparition?"[9] And it was Sally and she had on a pair of scarecrow yellow pantyhose, some sort of strap kind of shoes and a mini-dress, with this boa feather trim around the bottom, and I said: "Well, if my thoughts are right, and I haven't seen her for a number of years, that's Sally Rand." He said, "My God, I cannot believe this. You're not going to get her on the stage," and I said "No, but we have all these people ..." and she did look a bit strange, because the mini had been long gone and her

---

8   The music to the song "Sally" was written by Jimmy McHugh, the famous composer of such standards as "When My Sugar Walks Down the Street," "I'm in the Mood for Love," "I Can't Give You Anything But Love," "Exactly Like You," and "Diga Diga Do."

9   "Mr. Blackwell" was a celebrated fashion critic, writer, and television personality, best known for his annual "Ten Worst Dressed Women List." He was the author of two books, *Mr. Blackwell: 30 Years of Fashion Fiascos* and an autobiography, *From Rags to Bitches*.

legs were sort of so-so, but the yellow pantyhose — it was such an electric kind of yellow that you could not miss this lady....

She came in and a lot of people didn't recognize her.... I introduced myself and I explained ... "We'll introduce you from the audience if that's alright," and she said "Fine. I'd be very happy to. I'm having a little trouble with the asthma, but I'd be very happy to come backstage."

Sally did go backstage where it was hoped that she could pose for a usable set of publicity photos. As it turned out, the photo session wasn't very productive, so Vance optimistically arranged for another get-together, this time at the Brown Derby restaurant:

And we did photos with her, Ann Miller, and Mickey Rooney. And then Rita Hayworth came out — she was a guest that evening — and she was really kind of wasted ... in fact she walked up to me, because I looked like Orson Welles, and said "I'm really alright, Orson. I'm really air tight, really I am," and I said, "Rita, I know you are," and she said, "Really." Oh, it was so pathetic ... and I said, "We've got to get a photo of the two of them together" and we did.

More photos were taken but Vance concluded that he couldn't "do anything with these things because she's standing there in that goddamn tent dress and she looked terrible." Two attempts to memorialize the Sally Rand tribute on film had fallen flat. Perhaps a third time would be the charm. Vance called Sally and once again he prevailed upon her to come to the theater:

So she came down and that time she was dressed in a — it was very strange — it was like *uhh*, it wasn't that tent thing. It was something else. It was also a short kind of thing, and after the performance we go backstage — she was introduced that night again from the audience — and the people in the audience had been very respectful, a very large audience, she wasn't a has-been. So we go backstage ... and there were a lot of celebrity-type people back there.

Well, we were standing in the wings of the Pantages and I had a photographer there and I said to him: "Now look, *this* time I've got ... the lady who's playing Sally Rand. I've got the real Sally Rand, and Sally has brought her own set of fans tonight. Don't give me this little lady from Glendora. I've got to have the *real* Sally Rand." He said, "Whatever you want, just line her up and I'll do it." I said, "Sally, can you just hold the fans around you?" and she said, "Alright, I'll get ready." Well, with that she pulled this dress off and she was in a pair of nude-colored pantyhose, naked to the waist. And I thought, "Oh my God," I didn't know she was going to get *that* ready…. I said something dumb like, "Are you sure you're not in a draft?" and she said, "Oh, I've done this for years, don't worry…."

And I was standing there and my assistant — the one who goofed the first time — he was standing there, the photographer was standing there. There were all these people who had come backstage to see other people, and I thought, "Jesus God, I've got Sally Rand naked in the wings of the Pantages, what the hell was I going to do?" So she said to this big guy that came with her, "Give me the fans." And they were in long boxes and she pulled them out, and I'm thinking, "Oh, God, please put one around you," because the people are all just rubbernecking and she stood there and all of a sudden she picked the fans up and I said, "My God, you've got a lovely bosom," and she said, "You would too if you had the muscle training I've had," and her breasts just came right up! …

I stood there and watched her that night go from the Glendora matron into Sally Rand. It was the reverse of the first time I met her because she stood there and all at once she did this (lifts arms) and the bust came up into place and she looked like she was 30 years old…. The minute she pulled those fans up … it was like God gave her suspenders and everything just came right back to where it belonged. And she was lovely. She was really lovely. And she put them behind her and in just a matter of seconds she was *the* Sally Rand…. That is the one thing that I think I'll probably remember all my life, that she went from being a grandmother from Glendora, and she turned into this showgirl. And she could still be a showgirl at her advanced age.

And I've got to tell you this in all honesty, she looked better than the lady that was playing her, because the lady who was playing her didn't have — Sally had very full bosoms, a really full bosom — and the woman that was playing her didn't. But what we did, we got the two of them side by side…. Those photos were just superb, absolutely superb…. I took them down to AP and UPI. They both ran them.

Sally just loved the whole affair, sending "thank you" letters to Mickey Rooney, Ann Miller, Jasper Vance, and at least four others, including this one to Barbara Hanks:

> *I was deeply touched by the "Tribute." Deeply grateful to the powers that be … And all your dancing teachers, the blood, sweat, and tears you put in through the years to be the good dancer that you are. It doesn't happen by accident, and it ain't easy!*
>
> *Thank you, thank you, thank you.*

Soon after the Los Angeles opening of *Sugar Babies,* newspapers published a United Press photo of Sally and Miss Hanks showing both ladies in high heels, wrapped in ostrich feather fans and looking quite ecstatic. Being portrayed by another performer in a big-time musical production would mark Sally Rand's transition from celebrity to living legend.[10]

By the end of July, Sally had become painfully aware that her deteriorating condition was severely limiting her activities. On July 30th she wrote to Doreen Ellsworth, a leader in the local L.D.S. church, declaring that "This has been one of the happiest years of my life, because I belong to our Mormon Church." But, considering her current state of health, even with her dogged optimism, she also had misgivings:

> *We who have spent our lives in more or less worldly pursuits, like show business and such ... discover one day, we've been labouring under some pretty giddy delusions of grandeur! For shame! And "self-righteousness" is one of its ugliest symptoms! And I was so guilty of this.... Thank you for bringing me back to reality....*

> *I would rather be at Sunday School and sacrament meeting than any place on earth — and the Pioneers' picknick, and the relief society meeting.... Please know that ... if I'm not there, it's because I am physically unable to crawl to it. Either the quality of my "lung trouble" or the air quality has worsened. But I am NOT resigning myself to it. My physician and lung specialist, Dr. "Roberta," has some new thoughts on the lung thing, and we will work on it.... I shall be well! I know it!...*

> *As long as I stay in the air conditioned, air filtered house I manage pretty well.... It's getting out in the smog and being on my feet too long that gets to me.*

In late July, Sally sat down with Hollywood reporter Bob Thomas at her home in Glendora for what was probably her final interview. Reflecting on her career, she mused:

> I can't imagine doing anything else. I am a very natural person and I know that I am always "on." I'd rather perform and hear the

---

10 Despite the flesh being weak, Sally's spirit was still willing. In a letter written on June 16th to *Sugar Babies* producer Harry Rigby, she suggested: "Maybe you'll send out another company — you might lose one of your stars and need another name (I would do just a cameo appearance with the fan)?"

applause than do anything else. People ask me, "What the hell are you doing it for?" Well, it's a lot better than doing needlepoint on the patio.

Thomas had last interviewed Sally some 15 years earlier. When he arrived for the 1979 interview, he was taken aback. His impression was that the years had not been kind to her: "Could that toothless little old lady in the faded nightgown really be Sally Rand?" After inviting him in, Sally said she would be a little delayed and went into the kitchen of "the comfortable, heavily furnished bungalow," where she was showing two teenage boys how to string yarn on bent coat-hangers to make poodle toys for the church bazaar.

When the boys left, Sally excused herself for a few more minutes. As Thomas related, "she returned transformed. Smartly dressed in a blue and white suit, she seemed decades younger than her years." Even so, he had the audacity to inquire about possible facelifts.

Sally's response was frank:

> Certainly. More than once. It's no more complicated than keeping my hair blonde — which isn't hard to do because it's practically white. I'm due for another lift, but I want to wait until I can have a bridge made. A few of my teeth were loosened in an accident and I had to have them removed. The legs are still good.

Thomas agreed, noting: "She demonstrated their limberness by touching the floor straight-legged. When not performing, she visits a nearby ballet school or practices at her home barre."

As always, Sally was candid:

> I've saved a few dollars. I've got the apartments in back and a few certificates. I can't afford a yacht, but I once owned a Rolls Royce station wagon. Pretty jazzy, huh? I used to have picnics on the tailgate. That impressed my snooty friends.

> How long since I've had a beau? I'll equivocate on that one and say not since 1964. In the interim, every so often I go to the islands or some romantic place and I meet with an old friend with whom I have been in love. It's best when it happens that way; no questions, no argument, no recrimination.

> I think it's a good rule never to go to bed with anyone you don't love. It's better to have someone who knows all about you and

still loves you.[11] [Today's promiscuity] is like taking a shower with a raincoat on.

Sally admitted to Thomas that her old friends were "dying off like flies." While she told him that her son and his family lived close by and she "delights in their company," he also reported that "her house, once filled with visitors, is now empty most of the time." She was apparently planning to hit the road again just as soon as she had some dental work done, declaring cheerfully as she ended the interview: "As long as it's fun and I get paid, I'll keep doing it."[12]

Two weeks to the day after publication of the Bob Thomas interview, on Thursday, August 23, 1979, Sally checked herself into Foothill Presbyterian Hospital in Glendora, suffering from congestive heart failure and cardiogenic shock. Her prognosis was guarded. By the 29th, she was moved into the intensive care unit in critical condition.

Seemingly unaware of the seriousness of her situation, Sally had often attributed her bouts of weakness and shortness of breath to asthma, the symptoms of which can mimic the signs of heart failure. Her actual diagnosis? Sally had suffered a *second* heart attack. The first had been a silent attack two years earlier when she was hospitalized for three weeks in Detroit. This new insult to her system, combined with her persistent respiratory issues, had led to a 70 percent reduction in her heart's ability to function normally. Little wonder that these serious conditions had finally caught up with her after another two years of pursuing a strenuous lifestyle.

---

[11] While it is unknown exactly who Sally was referring to, a good candidate might be Texas columnist Christie Mitchell. He had known Sally for more than 30 years and had praised her effusively whenever she came to Galveston for one of her many shows at Buddy Kirk's Steak House. This is sheer speculation, but it is based on hints in her letters ("one of my favorite beaus, whom I dated 'a while ago' ... a brilliant mind and a great newspaperman"), as well as on clues in Mitchell's columns, including one entitled "A HOT LETTER FROM SALLY RAND." He also fondly remembered the time Sally visited his restaurant in Galveston and swam with the famous 350-pound "Pete the Talking Porpoise."

[12] On August 7th, Sally wrote to the booking agent for the Landmark Theatre in Syracuse, New York, confirming the availability of performers she had recommended for a special benefit show to be held on November 24th. Besides herself and an "old, old really heart friend" Martha Raye, the show was to include Rudy Vallee: "He's a hell of good name and draw, but God he does such a bad act. If he would just stick to singing and leave out his terrible jokes he would be great." When this program failed to materialize, it was replaced by "Bubbling Brown Sugar," a celebration of the golden age of Harlem, complete with "Zoot-suit hepcats" and the music of Duke Ellington and Cab Calloway.

Despite her severely weakened condition, Sally wanted to be discharged from the hospital and taken to her home a relatively short distance away. Her doctors advised the family that this would not be possible, as she would most likely not survive the transport.

News of Sally's illness rapidly spread, and fans from coast to coast responded with alarm. The dozens of callers to the hospital included a wide range of the concerned, from the Associated Press and ABC News to many of her old friends and acquaintances. An anonymous hospital staff member dutifully compiled a log of names, phone numbers, messages, and notations. Among them:

August 29:

Misty (her "adopted" daughter) ...

Estelle Winwood would like a call if any serious change

Toni Ranch & Darlene: "Love her very much" ... Evansville, Ind

Erwin Gelsey: "Give her my love" (He's 80 years old)

Olga (from Bob Hope's office): "Hope wanted to send flowers; will send a wire or a note instead"

Benjamin Bronstein, Orlando, Fla, was with her in the World's Fair in Chicago. Very concerned, sends his love.

Winnie Davis, Woodstock, NY: "You're always in my thoughts. Get Well. Love, Winnie." (She sent a wire to the wrong hospital).

August 30:

Lulu Moore called, Tampa, Fla: "Tell her I love her."

Barbara Hanks (with Sugar Babies)

Speed Cosboon: "If any blood is needed or anything he can do to help, don't hesitate to call."

Bob Hope did send a telegram: "Dear Sally, I hear you're interred for a moment and I hope you improve rapidly. My warm regards." Martha Raye's wire arrived on the same day: "Hang in there doll. My prayers are with you."

On August 31, 1979, Sally Rand drew a final breath, her doctor observing: "How she lasted eight days is beyond me." She was 75 years young.

Epilogue

All stories, if continued far enough, end in death, and he is no true-story teller who would keep that from you.
~ Ernest Hemingway, Death in the Afternoon

R eports of Sally's real estate investments and other financial resources proved to be exaggerated. The truth is she was strapped for cash more often than not. She had continued performing almost until the end, in part because she still had bills to pay. After her death and an inquiry into the status of her hospital bill, the family was told that an anonymous party had stepped forward to pay the outstanding balance of $10,000.[1] The identity of the benefactor was a mystery.

Years later, after a "Sally Rand" event at which her son Sean had spoken, he was approached by a woman who had worked at the hospital in Glendora at the time of his mother's death. According to Sean, she had disclosed:

> "I wasn't supposed to talk about this, but I will now because all the parties are gone." She told me they got this call ... and this person said "Give me the bill — whatever it costs. I'll send you a check for it." She said they wanted to remain anonymous.... A lot of people thought Sinatra did it ... but it turned out to be Sammy Davis, Jr.

This revelation had jogged Sean's memory:

> I remember, back in the '60s when that song "Mr. Bojangles" came out, one day she said, "Mr. Bojangles, you know who that is, right?" And I said, "I don't know who Mr. Bojangles is." And she told me, "His real name is Bill Robinson and he was the greatest dancer of all time. He taught Sammy Davis, Jr. to dance and he was a good friend of Sammy's father. Back in the days of vaudeville, I was friends with Sammy, Sr. and Bill Robinson. They were very, very poor and I was fortunate." So she gave a lot of money to them, helped them out. By the time she died in 1979, $10,000 was probably like a penny to

---

[1] The bill would be over $66,000 today, based on medical cost inflation from 1979 to 2015.

Sammy Davis, Jr. I guess he thought, "She did a lot for me in the early years and this is my time to pay her back."

Sally and Sammy had renewed their acquaintance during their tenure as Las Vegas performers. He had never forgotten her support and generosity, not only for his father, but also for Gene Bell, whom he regarded as the best tap dancer in the world.

During her long career, Sally had often been influenced by or touched the lives of others. We have met quite a few of them along the way, each one the central figure in a story of their own.

THE PRODUCERS

Cecil B. DeMille

In his 1959 autobiography, DeMille recalled encountering a certain new talent during his early days in silent films:

> For my first picture made at the DeMille Studio, *The Road to Yesterday* ... Vera Reynolds portrayed a very modern miss, and among her flapper friends ... was a pretty youngster who was later to receive more revealing fame, Sally Rand. That later fame, I fear, has given the public an extremely erroneous idea of Sally Rand. She is an intelligent and serious-minded person; I still hear from her occasionally, and her letters are always thoughtful and wise.

DeMille went on to become a prolific film producer and director, perhaps best known for *The Greatest Show on Earth*, winner of the Oscar for the Best Motion Picture of 1952, and for the religious epics *The King of Kings* (1927), *Samson and Delilah* (1949), and *The Ten Commandments* (1956), his last and most lucrative film.

On the evening of January 20, 1959, fearing that DeMille might have a serious heart ailment, his personal physician advised him to go to the hospital. DeMille is reported to have replied: "No, I think I'll be going to the morgue instead." He died at home the next day at the age of 77.

Earl Carroll

The young producer who had first brought Faith Bacon and her "original" fan dance to prominence in his *Vanities of 1930* continued to mount his extravagant revues on Broadway until 1940. In 1938, he opened the Earl Carroll Theater in Hollywood, a huge supper club/theater presenting such showgirls as Yvonne De Carlo and the young Mamie Van Doren on an amazing stage.[2] The 1945 Hollywood film *Earl Carroll's Vanities* was nominated for an Oscar in the Best Music category.

Like Sally, Carroll had maintained a lifelong fascination with aviation, serving as a U.S. Army Air Force pilot in the First World War. On June 17, 1948, accompanied by his girlfriend Beryl Wallace,[3] he boarded United Airlines flight 624 from San Diego to New York City. Unfortunately, the flight crew had missed a written notice warning them to wear oxygen masks during flights to protect against potential hazard from discharge of carbon dioxide into the pilot's cabin. Approaching LaGuardia airport, the four-engine DC-6 crashed at full speed into a wooded hillside near Mt. Carmel, Pennsylvania, killing all 43 persons aboard. The entire crew had been asphyxiated before impact. Earl Carroll was 57 years old.

The ashes of Mr. Carroll and Miss Wallace were buried in the same crypt at the Forest Lawn Cemetery in Glendale, California, in the company of such contemporaries as William Boyd, George Burns, Walt Disney, Casey Stengel, and Humphrey Bogart.

Appropriate for an internationally famous "purveyor of pulchritude," Carroll's headstone features a life-sized statue of a nude "Winged Hope" — cast in bronze 37 years before by German sculptor Adolph Weinman and purchased for $50,000 by the executors of Carroll's estate.

Billy Rose

The brilliant impresario Billy Rose had enhanced (and also collided with) Sally's career on more than one occasion. By bringing her to the Fort Worth Frontier Centennial in 1936, he had provided a launching pad for much of her future success — whether or not he was due any credit for the creation of the "Nude Ranch" concept.

By 1939, the diminutive producer was operating the Diamond Horseshoe, a popular New York nightclub in the basement of the Paramount Hotel near Times Square. In that same year, Gene Kelly was recommended as a choreographer to help Rose develop his cabaret-style shows. Billy objected to Kelly, saying he wanted someone who could choreograph "tits and asses,"

---

[2] A thousand patrons could be seated in the club's terraced cabaret. With a 60-foot-wide double revolving platform, an under-stage elevator, a revolving staircase, a rainmaking machine, and swings to lower showgirls from the ceiling, the stage apparatus was so technologically advanced it has not been duplicated in another American theater.

[3] Beryl was also the beautiful face at the club's entrance in the form of an iconic 24-foot sign in zeon (a more colorful, more flexible version of neon). Although the original sign was destroyed, a copy is on display at Universal City in Los Angeles.

not some "soft-soap from a crazy Armenian."[4] Ultimately, Kelly did get the job — an important boost for his budding career.

Divorced by Fanny Brice, Rose married his Aquacade star, Olympic swimmer Eleanor Holm, in 1939. Their union lasted until 1954. The couple's explosive breakup began in July 1951 when a young actress was found in Billy's private apartment, having attempted suicide. Although Eleanor managed to get over this humiliation, the collapse of their relationship accelerated in October when she found yet another woman in Billy's apartment and locked him out of their townhouse. After a torrent of affidavits, charges and countercharges were exchanged, Mrs. Rose filed a separation suit in 1952. Billy countered by filing for divorce. The divorce was finally granted in 1954, with Eleanor receiving a large settlement in monthly alimony, plus a lump sum of $200,000 ($1.7 million today).

The press actively followed the case, dubbing the messy and volatile divorce trial "The War of the Roses" — an apt description for the personal drama that spawned the 1989 movie directed by Danny DeVito and starring Michael Douglas and Kathleen Turner. Rose was married thrice more, twice to the same woman.

In 1943, he produced the innovative musical *Carmen Jones* with an all-black cast and lyrics and book by Oscar Hammerstein II. Rose had taken a chance on the show, but his production was a hit. From 1959 until his death, he was the owner-operator of the Billy Rose Theater, home to the original 1962 production of *Who's Afraid of Virginia Woolf?*

William Samuel Rosenberg died of pneumonia on February 10, 1966, in Montego Bay, Jamaica, where he maintained a winter home. He left an estate worth an estimated $42 million, all of it going to the Billy Rose Foundation, which to this day operates in support of the fine and performing arts.

In recognition of his lesser known accomplishments as a lyricist, Billy Rose was inducted into the Songwriters Hall of Fame in 1970. He is given full or partial credit for dozens of songs, including such tunes as "It's Only a Paper Moon," "Without a Song," Anything Goes," and "Me and My Shadow" — not to mention "I Found a Million Dollar Baby," "Barney Google" and "Does the Spearmint Lose Its Flavor on the Bedpost Overnight?"

---

4   Gene Kelly was Irish, not "Armenian"; however, at the time, he was appearing on Broadway in *The Time of Your Life*, the Pulitzer Prize winning play by Armenian-American William Saroyan.

THE SUITORS

Carl Schlaet

Having courted, cajoled, and pleaded with her beyond exasperation, even progressing so far as to nail down a possible wedding date, oil man Carl Schlaet eventually abandoned his pursuit of Sally Rand. On October 25, 1932, just as Sally was first deploying her fans at the Paramount Club in Chicago, he was marrying the former Mrs. Ada Johnson Held, the ex-wife of famous "Flapper Girl" illustrator John Held, Jr. The marriage to Ada didn't last. Sometime after 1934, Carl married Sandra Johnson.

As the decades passed, Sally kept in touch with Carl, even meeting him on occasion. During a three week period in March and April of 1952, while Carl was living with Sandra and their 15-year old daughter Dolly, he visited Sally in Palm Springs and again in Los Angeles, where he made a deposit in her Glendora bank account to help her with the payment of back taxes.

In 1953, Carl became seriously ill and Sally discovered that he was being treated in the Harkness Pavilion at New York Presbyterian Hospital only a few miles from where she was staying at the Warwick Hotel. Having finally put the Harry Finkelstein "horror show" behind her, she desperately wanted to see Carl, but knew it could be awkward while his wife Sandy was at his bedside. Realizing she loved him in a way that transcended momentary passion, Sally wrote to him on April 10th:

> I reached Dr. Stansfield, who apprised me of... your whereabouts — also that Sandy is at the Ambassador and that all visitors must be cleared through her. I then called Dr. Southworth and explained our long friendship, also that it was probably not a very propitious time to try and explain me to Sandy, since I'd never met her.... You know that I would not complicate a situation in any way - nor do, nor say, nor wish to do anything that would hurt or disturb anyone....
>
> Of course, I want to see you so much ... if you feel that I should not come, then I will write to you in care of Dr. Southworth and he could give you my letters at his discretion.

Sally suggested to Carl that he should send any letters to her in care of her attorney, Abe Berman, since: "I know it would cause comment for you to address letters to me." She added: "You will no doubt want to destroy this letter, so I will put Mr. Berman's address on a separate sheet of paper."

Three days later, with no word from Carl, Sally typed a very detailed, single-spaced, three-page letter to Carl's physician, Dr. Hamilton Southworth. Enclosing copies of her letters to Carl, she advised the doctor of her concerns:

If there is any part that you think he should not read, take the scissors and snip it out ... especially that part about my knowing his condition.

Does he know the truth about his condition?

This is the information I have.... Exploratory surgery determined a cancer of the esophagus and extending in the large vein leading to the aorta.

The condition was considered inoperable and he is presently having X-ray or radium treatments to arrest the condition.

Correct?

Sally was torn between behaving appropriately or giving in to a compulsive desire to insert herself into the situation. To her credit, after having typed 11 paragraphs of advice and personal observations to Dr. Southworth ("I've poured out my heart to you, a complete stranger"), Sally concluded: "Sometimes people just want to be left alone."

Five days later, Carl Schlaet wrote to Sally from the hospital in a beautiful and steady hand:

Dear Sally —

I do appreciate the thoughtful consideration prompting your letters and calls, but if you want to help me, and I know you do, please do not try to communicate with me at any time or in any way until you hear from me to the contrary. I'm not strong enough to go into all the reasons & I'm sure our friendship is strong enough so that you'll accept my request without hurt feelings.

Thanks for the photos. They're especially good of your mother and boy.

Best of luck to you now and always,

Carl

Less than six weeks later, on May 27, 1953, Carl Schlaet died at the age of 58.

Jack Crosby

Sally's one-time dance partner — who in 1928 had professed to his "dear little wench ... I do love you and I hope we can always be together" — had figured out by October 1930 that it wasn't going to happen. Crosby went on to enjoy a successful career as a dancer and choreographer. By the late 1930s, he was Samuel Goldwyn's dance director.[5]

On Valentine's Day of 1944, Jack married former Ziegfeld showgirl and actress Poppy Wilde, a celebrated dark-haired beauty whose Hollywood credits included very small parts in a number of films starring such luminaries as James Cagney, Bob Hope, and The Three Stooges. Poppy's early life had been anything but glamorous. She had lost her father, a railroad worker, to a freak accident. Although her mother had struggled to raise Poppy and her siblings alone, her efforts were in vain. Poppy was ultimately put up for adoption and adopted by a wealthy railroad executive from Salt Lake City, Utah. When her talent was spotted by a movie producer, her adoptive father had taken the 15-year-old girl to California to help her launch her show business career.

Jack and Poppy led a fun-filled life with the Hollywood crowd. Their son Dennis Crosby remembered the couple entertaining a lot, "square dancing every Thursday night at Lucille Ball and Desi Arnaz's house, Fred Astaire stopping by, and television star Captain Midnight playing poker with his father." Years later, the pair moved to Coeur d'Alene, Idaho, where Jack enjoyed the life of an outdoorsman.

Jack Crosby died in 1979, the same year as Sally.

Jimmie Thach

Writing in 1929 on stationery bearing the letterhead of the U.S. Navy Aircraft Squadrons, Battle Fleet, John S. "Jimmie" Thach had confided to Sally: "Why can't I tell you how much I really worship you? Sally, I know it will always be this way." Eventually, however, he turned his attention to Madalyn Jones, a senior at San Diego State College majoring in music and education. The pair were married in December 1931.[6] Before settling down, Jimmie had

---

5   Jack Crosby's Hollywood choreography credits in the 1940s include DeMille's *Unconquered* with Gary Cooper and Paulette Goddard and *Whistle Stop* with Ava Gardner and George Raft.

6   According to Thatch's biographer, Madalyn Jones was "intelligent, articulate, and cultured" and "brought all the desirable attributes to the marriage necessary to complement and further Jimmie's Navy career."

enjoyed hobnobbing with the celebrities he had met in Hollywood, even appearing on screen as a stunt pilot.[7]

Thach spent the 1930s serving as a Navy test pilot and instructor, becoming known as an expert in aerial gunnery. In the early 1940s, he took command of Navy Fighter Squadron Three (VF-3), also known as the "Felix the Cat Squadron," where he developed a fighter combat tactic known as the "Thach Weave" to counter Japanese fighter planes with tactics designed to enable our pilots to outsmart the enemy.

In the early days of World War II, Thach's squadron was assigned to the *USS Yorktown* which lost 141 men when it was sunk in the Battle of Midway on the 7th of June 1942. Three days before, on the morning of June 4th, while leading a six-plane sortie escorting a strike from the *Yorktown*, Lt. Commander Thach had come upon the main Japanese carrier fleet. Immediately attacked by 15 to 20 Japanese fighters, Thach and his group made use of the "weave" maneuver to shoot down a number of Japanese Zeros.

After the Battle of Midway, Thach became a highly respected combat flight instructor. When the Japanese resorted to their infamous "Kamikaze" suicide attacks, he devised a strategy called the "Big Blue Blanket" to protect aircraft carriers and troopships. At the close of the war in Europe, Commander Thach returned to the Pacific as the operations officer to Vice Admiral John McCain's fast carrier task force. (Yes, this is the father of Senator and former presidential candidate John McCain of Arizona.) On September 2, 1945, Thach was present at the formal surrender of the Japanese aboard the *USS Missouri* in Tokyo Bay.

Promoted to captain after the war, Thach was given command of the escort carrier *USS Sicily* during the Korean conflict, leading an operation to capture a Soviet MIG-15 fighter jet for intelligence study. He was made rear admiral in 1955. In recognition of his contributions to anti-submarine warfare during the Cold War, his image graced the cover of the September 1, 1958, edition of *Time* magazine. In 1967, Admiral Thach completed his 44-year military career as the Commander-in-Chief of U.S. Naval Forces in Europe.

Admiral John S. "Jimmie" Thach died in Coronado, California, on April 15, 1981. On March 17, 1984, the guided missile frigate *USS Thach* was commissioned in his honor. His love letters to Sally Rand remain to this day in her personal filing cabinet.

---

[7] Piloting a Curtiss F8C-4 "Helldiver," Jimmie Thach flew dozens of hours as a stunt pilot, producing footage that was used as background in the MGM film *Hell Divers*, starring Clark Gable.

Charles "Chissie" Mayon

Sally broke off her engagement to Mayon sometime in 1935. In October 1936, Walter Winchell reported that the two had reconciled and, as late as November 1937, Sally was still denying that they were secretly married.

During the 1940s, Mayon had a low-profile career in the movies, appearing in 11 films, all but one in an uncredited role. Chissie and Sally's brother Harold played together in at least three films, notably as blackface minstrels in Paramount's *Dixie*. This 1943 film starring Bing Crosby and Dorothy Lamour was a loose biopic about the man who wrote the famous song. On October 15, 1943, Chissie married actress Irene Crosby, an attractive young blonde who later served as a stand-in for Marilyn Monroe in such films as *Gentlemen Prefer Blondes*.

Twenty-five years later, on October 26, 1968, a sixty-four-year-old man named "Charles Mayon" (whose birth date matches that of our "Chissie") was arrested in San Diego, California, on suspicion of smuggling marijuana into the country from Mexico. Charles Howard Mayon died on January 11, 1972, and is buried in Forest Lawn Cemetery in Glendale, California.

Valya Valentinoff (Paul Valentine)

When Sally cut loose her handsome young love interest Valya Valentinoff, choosing instead to marry rodeo rider Turk Greenough, the 6'3" ballet dancer went on to enjoy a wide-ranging career. In addition to performing as a featured dancer in both the Detroit and St. Louis municipal opera companies, he took a turn as a professional boxer. According to gossip columnist Hedda Hopper, Valya (sparring under the name "Bill Wolf") had "knocked out three adversaries in as many prize fights." In the mid-1940s, he had two small roles in the hit Broadway musical *Follow the Girls* — a show about a burlesque stripper named "Bubbles LaMarr" and her hapless admirer, a sailor named "Goofy Gale." Valya shared the stage with 28-year old comedian Jackie Gleason playing the part of Goofy.

In mid-1946, Valentinoff adopted the screen name "Paul Valentine."[8] In August of that year he married striptease artist Lili St. Cyr, becoming the

---

[8] Valentinoff had several name changes. At age 14 he changed his name from William Wolf Daixel when he joined the Ballets Russe and the director Léonide Massine dubbed him "Vladimir Valentinoff." He was billed as "Valia," "Valya," or "Val" before becoming "Paul Valentine" in Hollywood.

third of her six husbands.[9] He is credited with creating her famous bathtub routine. Nevertheless, when the couple divorced in 1949, he complained: "Everybody in the country could see more of her than I did." In June of 1950, Paul took up singing, sharing the bill with Bobby Short at Jim Dolan's Café Gala on the Sunset Strip in Hollywood. *Billboard* magazine reported that "his pipes are trained and pleasing and his stage manner shows that he has worked hard to switch from terp to song."

As Paul Valentine, he appeared in more than a dozen movies including the 1947 film noir classic *Out of the Past*, starring Robert Mitchum and Jane Greer. He was also in *Love Happy* (1949) with the Marx Brothers and Marilyn Monroe, *True Confessions* (1981) with Robert De Niro, Robert Duvall and Charles Durning, and even *Pennies from Heaven* (1981), with Steve Martin and Bernadette Peters.

In 1952, Valentinoff married Flaveen Sultana Ali Khan, daughter of an Iranian businessman. When he died in 2006 at the age of 86, their marriage had endured for more than 50 years.

THE FAN DANCERS

Perhaps someday someone will write a book about the other fan dancers. Until then, the fate of several is worthy of mention.

Fay Baker

After her ordeal in the wilds of Northern Canada, Mary Amelia Nebel of Watertown, Wisconsin, continued performing her fan dance in and around Winnipeg and Calgary, Alberta, under her stage name "Fay Baker."

In early 1934, during an official inquiry into her immigration status in Canada, Miss Nebel conveniently met and married Constable J. H. Leslie, a handsome member of the Royal Canadian Mounted Police with whom she was barely acquainted. It didn't last. Only weeks after the furtive nuptials, Fay obtained a legal separation, announcing that she planned to return to California to secure a divorce. Poor John Leslie was discharged from the R.C.M.P. for sneaking off without permission in order to marry. Eight days later, Leslie filed a petition for annulment, claiming that, while they

---

[9] During the mid-1940s, Valya Valentinoff was romantically linked with both Carmen Miranda, the Brazilian singer, dancer, and actress known for her fruit bowl hats, and Beverley Michaels, a chorus girl from Billy Rose's Diamond Horseshoe, who was later featured in such Hollywood films as *Wicked Woman*, *Betrayed Women*, and *Blonde Bait*.

had indeed been married on March 31st, the couple had separated only a few hours later.

An annulment was granted on June 28th and, by August, the once-again-single fan dancer departed the Canadian provinces for Hollywood where she was hoping to break into the movie business. It didn't happen. Fay continued to tour the western United States through 1935, even adding a version of the bubble dance to her act. Her 1935 summer tour included three months of engagements in Mexico.

On January 12, 1936, then-25-year-old Mary Nebel married 31-year-old M. Aubrey Freeman in Longview, Texas. Following this happy occasion, "Fay Baker" — who had once passed herself off as the "original fan dancer" — passed into history and was heard of no more.

Thais Giroux

By early 1938, her "South American nightmare" a few months behind her, Miss Thais Giroux was living at the Berkshire Hotel in Chicago, performing wherever available bookings led her. But, on April 18th, having returned to New York and staying in a room at the Hotel Lincoln, the talented dancer from Montana spent the day unsuccessfully searching for a job.

Owing $46.90 in back rent on her hotel room, the discouraged young woman passed the evening in Greenwich Village, bar hopping with a girlfriend from the Paradise Cabaret where she had performed two years earlier. As the evening wore on, the girls hooked up with Thais's sometime boyfriend, Johnny "John the Bug" Stoppelli. After a night of heavy drinking, Johnny took Thais back to her hotel room. The two talked about hard times, their old romance and the sorry state of her career. At some point Thais disrobed. Apparently, the conversation grew rather heated and the level of frustration elevated. The next day, a syndicated news service reported: "With a bitter goodbye to Broadway, a beautiful, blonde dancer plunged nude today from her fifth floor room in a mid-town hotel."

Thais was rushed to Bellevue Hospital, but it was clear that nothing could be done for her. She died two hours later of a fractured skull and other injuries, her death ruled a suicide.

Under police grilling, Stoppelli told officers that Miss Giroux had suddenly cried: "I'm sick and tired of it all. Goodbye, so long, it's all over." Pressed for details, he insisted that he had only left the room for a few minutes, thinking that she was just joking: "I was coming out of the bathroom when she did it. She just waved her hand, yelled 'goodbye' and then she went out the window." He also offered that he had a wife and family. Apparently satisfied, the police released him.

The following year in Butte, Montana, Thais's father, widower Ray Giroux, married Katherine Wellcome, a member of a prominent pioneer family. Fifteen months later, the sporting goods salesman and his wife brought new-born twins into the world. The mother and babies had a particularly difficult time with the delivery, remaining in the hospital for an extended period. After finally returning home, Mrs. Giroux spent a week of exhaustive effort struggling to care for the twins, but she could not successfully nurse them.

Unable to cope with the enormity of his personal situation, shortly after midnight on October 17, 1940, Giroux entered the couple's bedroom with a .22 caliber revolver and fatally shot his wife in the head, before putting bullets into the heads of their 17-day-old twin babies as they lay in their cribs. Turning the gun on himself, he then aimed a final shot into his own brain. Giroux lingered until the next day, telling authorities in an interval of consciousness: "There is nothing to tell. I'm just cracked and crazy and shot the wife and kids." Friends said he had been moody since the death of his daughter who, they said, had gone to New York to "dance her way to hell."

Flo Ash

The fan-dancing career of Hollywood bit player and Sally Rand look-alike Flo Ash extended well beyond those of Sally's other would-be rivals. By 1944, she had become smitten with Pietro Gentile, the "Latin Troubadour," and the two formed the nucleus of a touring act. There was just one problem: Flo was already married to an aircraft worker named Bruce Wilson.

Hoping for a future with Pietro, Flo filed for divorce, claiming that the travails of her marriage to Wilson were ruining her professional career. As she explained to the press:

> I worked all night and came home completely exhausted. Then I
> had to get up at 6 a.m. and cook my husband's breakfast. And I got
> nothing but abuse from him for all my trouble.

Her explanation was "corroborated by" Gentile, who was ostensibly there to offer his support.

Within a few weeks of her divorce from Bruce Wilson, Flo and Pietro tied their own matrimonial knot on Valentine's Day— but the tie was not to last. On November 5, 1947, Flo was once again in divorce court, splitting from Gentile after complaining to the judge in Los Angeles that he continually belittled her art and called it "degrading." Moreover, she said, he had always resented her for getting top billing in their act.

Flo continued to perform as the "Cutest Little Nudist" for several years. In 1951, she appeared with Tempest Storm in the schlock-grade motion picture *Paris After Midnight*, playing a fan dancer who "flashes the audience with her fabulous feathery fans." Her last reported booking was in 1953 at the Crystal Inn in Bakersfield, California, in an act featuring her "copyrighted Mirror Dance" on a revolving stage.

Renee Villon

Remembered primarily as the "Renee Villon" who had been misidentified on front pages across the country — the one who had *not* been seen dancing with the son of President Franklin D. Roosevelt — Miss Villon continued plying her fan dancing trade well beyond the tenure of most other Sally Rand pretenders. Said to have "danced before the royalty of Europe," in August 1942, Renee opened as the featured dancer at Harry Finkelstein's Club 51 in New York City. She continued to perform in one capacity or another at least into 1948 when she was a member of the Faith Bacon Show in the John R. Ward carnival.

Noel Toy

In 1945, "The Chinese Sally Rand" married Carleton Young, an American character actor who appeared in scores of movies and television shows.[10] At her husband's request, Noel Toy traded her fan dancing career for acting, appearing in as many as 20 films and TV shows, often as a stereotypical Asian in an uncredited role. You can see her on YouTube, as well as in reruns of *M*A*S*H* appearing in four episodes as a character called "Mama San." She ultimately tired of being typecast as "the ornamental Oriental" and took up a career in real estate. Noel Toy Young died on Christmas Eve 2003 at the age of 84.

---

[10]   While most of his acting career consisted of hundreds of roles in television, Carleton Young's film career spanned a spectrum from 1935 to 1962, including roles in *Reefer Madness* (1936), *The Flying Leathernecks* (1951) and *The Day the Earth Stood Still* (1951). One of his last significant movie parts was as newspaper editor Maxwell Scott in *The Man Who Shot Liberty Valance* (1962), the movie in which he delivered the famous line: "This is the West, sir. When the legend becomes fact, print the legend." He and Noel Toy had been married for nearly 50 years when Young died in 1994.

THE BIT PLAYERS

Manuel Herrick

The eccentric congressman who had gained national attention with his efforts to outlaw beauty contests failed in his 1922 bid for reelection. During the second year of his only term in Congress, he had actively pursued a longtime interest in aviation, even styling himself as an "aerial daredevil." He was also in the news for having been "jilted" by Ethelyn Chrane, his congressional stenographer, who claimed that he had concealed his violent temper from her until after he had won her heart.

The rejected suitor was not pleased. In a $50,000 lawsuit against his fiancée for breach of promise, his pleadings revealed intimacies of a most personal nature, including the allegation that she:

> … had been sitting upon plaintiff's lap, hugging and kissing him
> from 7 p.m. to 11 p.m., and defendant finally became so passionate
> that she removed her pajamas and invited plaintiff to have sexual
> intercourse with her. Plaintiff refused to go any further than to kiss
> her, on the grounds that he and the defendant were not married….
> The defendant had, in the meantime, laid down upon some mail
> sacks that were in the room and undertook to argue the matter
> with the plaintiff, saying, "You played with me until you got me
> passionate, so come and FINISH THE JOB NOW."

In a formal answer to Herrick's suit, Miss Chrane alleged that, when she had refused to go along with his "libel plot" against certain newspapers, the congressman had "threatened her, cursed her and declared that he would injure certain of her relatives." Although she was found guilty of breach of promise, it was a pyrrhic victory since Herrick was awarded damages in the amount of one cent.

Rejected by the voters, Herrick returned to Oklahoma where he tried, and again failed, to regain his congressional seat. He persisted in this effort every two years, finally giving up after the 1930 election. As the Dust Bowl descended upon the prairies, he joined the thousands of other "Okies" who left the state to seek a better situation in California.

By 1933, while Sally was fanning her way to fame at the Chicago World's Fair, Herrick was trying his hand at gold mining in northern California. For many years he lived more or less as a hermit in a small cabin in Quincy, the county seat of Plumas County. In a vain attempt to return to Congress,

Herrick ran once more in 1948, this time receiving only 85 votes in the California Republican primary.

On January 11, 1952, nearly blind and in the company of another elderly man, Herrick set out in knee-deep snow to walk the few miles to his cabin on a bitter cold day. During the trek the two men were caught in a blizzard and became separated. Apparently losing his way, Herrick died of exposure. His body was not found for seven weeks. Former congressman Manuel Herrick was 75 years old and never married.

Judge Joseph B. David

A respected Superior Court Judge in Cook County, Illinois, Joseph Bradley David had presided over Mary Belle Spencer's failed attempt to remove Sally's "lewd and lascivious dances and exhibitions" from the Streets of Paris at the 1933 Chicago World's Fair. Judge David was 69 when the 29-year-old fan dancer appeared before him.

No sooner had he dismissed the charges against Sally than Judge David found himself in the spotlight again, presiding over the sensational case of Dr. Alice Wynekoop, who had been charged with murdering her daughter-in-law in an attempt to benefit her philandering son.[11]

Four years after making his famous remark in 1933 that some people would "put pants on a horse," the controversial Judge David issued a ruling meant to keep Chicago from becoming "a second Reno," declaring that states like Nevada "that ask for only six weeks' residence for the filing of a suit for divorce should be kicked out of the union."

On September 28, 1937, Judge David collapsed with a heart ailment and was hospitalized under an oxygen tent. The 74-year-old jurist lingered for nearly five months, dying at his son's home on February 17, 1938. That same day, Sally Rand was in court filing suit in Scott County, Iowa, to recover $350 owed to her for an appearance in Davenport.

Dr. Milton W. Hamilton

Remember the history professor from Albright College in Reading, Pennsylvania, who was invited to give a lecture on Mussolini's invasion of Ethiopia? By ungraciously backing out at the last minute rather than share the program with Sally Rand, he simultaneously embarrassed himself and

---

[11] It would be worth your while to look up this bizarre case. Although the 62-year-old physician was convicted of murder, she was spared the death penalty and served just 14 years for her crime.

gave her an opportunity to delight everyone with her own remarkable knowledge of the subject.

Once he had recovered from his temporary status as a local laughingstock, Dr. Hamilton went on to have a distinguished career as an authority on New York's colonial history. In June 1936, the year after his near encounter with Sally, the bespeckled young professor received a Ph.D. from Columbia University and published his first book, *The Country Printer*, a study of early printers, editors, and publishers. In 1949, he was named senior historian in the New York State Education Department's Division of Archives and History. Dr. Hamilton died on February 26, 1989, at age 87.

SUPPORTING ROLES

Michio Ito

In 1941, within hours of the attack at Pearl Harbor, the Japanese dancer and choreographer who had worked so closely with Sally in making the film *Sunset Strip Case*, and had performed with her at a 1939 benefit concert in San Francisco, was taken into custody as an enemy alien. Following their involuntary transfer to an internment camp, Ito and his wife were repatriated to Japan in 1943 as part of a prisoner exchange. They never returned to the United States.

Soon after the war, the American Occupation Administration hired Ito as the dance director of the Ernie Pyle Theatre in Tokyo, a clear indication that no one seriously believed him to be an enemy agent. Years later, he was commissioned to choreograph the opening and closing ceremonies for the Tokyo Olympics of 1964, but his plan for a performance intended to highlight the spirit of harmony between the winners and losers of the war would never materialize. Michio Ito died suddenly on November 6, 1961, at the age of 69. An obituary described him as "a man who pursued beautiful dreams all his life."[12]

Georgia Sothern

After divorcing Harry Finkelstein in 1949, the fiery stripper rebounded with a career that went on to match Sally's in longevity. Having started out as a child vaudeville performer, Georgia Sothern continued performing until her retirement at age 67. In 1973, Sally and Georgia were photographed together at the annual Phoenix House Benefit held at the Roseland Ballroom in New

---

[12] A 22-minute documentary film *Michio Ito: Pioneering Dancer-Choreographer* was released in 2013. The film's trailer can be viewed on YouTube.

York City. By this time, Georgia had married husband number six, a lawyer, John J. Diamond, to whom she dedicated her 1972 autobiography, *Georgia: My Life in Burlesque*. The couple remained married until her death from cancer on October 14, 1981, at the age of 72.

Anita Robertson

In her later years, poor health forced Sally's longtime secretary, bookkeeper and adoring traveling companion to return to her hometown of Lawton, Oklahoma, still dreaming of being on the road with Sally. Anita Louise Robertson was twice admitted to Lawton Memorial Hospital in January of 1971. Fighting a lengthy illness, she died on February 19, 1974, at a Lawton nursing home, just one week shy of her 61st birthday. She never married.

Learning of Anita's death, Sally's childhood friend, actress Joan Crawford, wrote to her: "I am so sorry to hear about Anita Robertson…. She wrote such gentle and beautiful letters to me." In a letter to Anita's sister, Babs Shankman, Sally lamented:

> *Death, grief, and loss cause unusual reactions in me.*
> *I instinctively feel "don't look now maybe it will go away," as*
> *if by not actually acknowledging it, it won't have to be so.*
> *That is exactly what happened when you called me about*
> *Anita. I just couldn't acknowledge the fact that there never*
> *ever was going to be Anita again.*

Sally visited Lawton in September of 1975 to dedicate the "Sally Rand Room" in Anita's former home at 713 C Street, which was being turned into the Robertson House, a gourmet restaurant.

Marjorie "Lori Jon" Barnes O'Brien

"Lori Jon" — the young woman touring with Sally in the 1940s who had rebuffed Sally's efforts to adopt her infant son — retired to an apartment in New York City, but now lives in Virginia. By a coincidence almost too amazing to believe, her son Paul now lives in a Greenwich Village apartment located in the same building as that of your author's collaborator, Bonnie Egan.[13]

---

[13] Videos of the octogenarian Lorie dancing in her apartment are posted on YouTube (search for the terms: Grandma Dance Lorie O'Brien).

Featured Players

Mary Belle Spencer

On August 5, 1937, as Sally was toiling away in New England summer stock theater, her 1933 World's Fair nemesis, the prominent Chicago attorney and mother of the well-publicized "do-as-we-please girls," was in court filing for divorce from her husband, Chicago Heights physician Dr. Richard Vance Spencer. Making her case to the press, Mary Belle declared:

> The Spencer ship of matrimony has plunged to Davey Jones' locker. This will be the most unusual domestic suit ever filed in the United States and maybe even in Europe.... I am doing this for my two daughters, not for myself. I want to protect their future. Dr. Spencer's only contribution to our married life was one baby carriage. I am the biggest fool of all time and I'm going to get up and make fun of myself in public.

Although the Spencers were separated for several months, the divorce never did go through. Eleven months later on July 11, 1938, Dr. Spencer died at the home of his elder daughter Mary Belle, Jr. and her husband Edward Wright.

When Mary Belle belatedly learned of her husband's death, she rushed to her daughter's home. Discovering that the body was at the "wrong" funeral home, she arranged to have it moved, but when she came back to collect her deceased husband's personal belongings, Mary Belle, Jr. and her husband Edward blocked their mother from entering their home. Fuming over the change in their arrangements, the couple had called the police, who apprehended the humiliated matriarch and took her to the station. Mrs. Spencer was released in time to complete the funeral arrangements. Although still infuriated, she said about her daughter: "Mary Belle may come if she pleases. All is forgiven for not telling me about his death."

Four years later, on July 1, 1942, after suffering an illness lasting several months, Mary Belle Spencer died at St. Luke's hospital in Chicago. She was only 59. Her younger daughter Victoria died in 1982 at the age of 60. Mary Belle "Junior" died the following year, at age 63.

Faith Bacon

On September 26, 1956, despondent and nearly penniless, Faith Bacon had thrown herself from a hotel window in Chicago at the age of 47. Oddly, although Faith's death had followed a quarrel culminating in a threat to leave her roommate and go back to her family in Pennsylvania, authorities were unable to locate any relatives in the Erie area. Eventually, Miss Bacon's body was claimed by the American Guild of Variety Artists, which arranged a pauper's funeral for her.

Once described by Florenz Ziegfeld as the "most beautiful woman in the world," Faith Bacon Dickinson was buried in Wunder's Cemetery in Chicago. Tullah Hanley's husband Edward Hanley erected a white marble headstone, paying in advance for ten years of maintenance and upkeep for Faith's grave.

Thomas Edward Hanley was a renowned collector of important manuscripts, books and art, much of which is now on display in museums and galleries around the country. Tullah had kept a large number of research notes about Faith, intending to write her story under the title *The Biography of a Nude Dancer*. After her husband's death, Tullah found a hidden drawer in his desk with a trove of "ardent, sex-toned letters" dated after Faith's visit to the Hanley home — letters that Faith had written to Edward expressing her desire to be in his arms again, to relive, as Faith put it, the "beautiful sexual joys we had together in your studio, where I long to return, and to love you again, and be always by your side."

Ralph Hobart

Like Sally, her faithful bookkeeper, "official makeup man," and self-professed "male maid" had been born in Missouri (she in Elkton and he in Kansas City). Ralph Richard Hobart was barely two months older than Sally and was her schoolmate, close friend and off-and-on assistant for most of his life. Ralph died September 1, 1956, in Los Angeles, and is buried in the Hollywood Forever Cemetery. He was 52 years old.

Mary Annette Beck Kisling

A strikingly attractive woman in her own right, Sally's mother died on January 8, 1971, at the age of 89. Mother and daughter had been as close as any two strong-willed women likely ever are. Traveling with Sally's show in the early years, "Nettie" had been totally enamored of her daughter's career. Nothing had pleased her more than to tell anyone who would listen that she was Sally's mother. Although she had strongly disapproved of all three of Sally's husbands, their personal mother-daughter bond remained solid until the end.

Sally spent hours personally preparing her mother for the funeral, saying:

> It was a gruesome thing to have to do and I didn't enjoy it, but I
> wanted her to be so pretty. I wanted everything to be perfect
> because I knew she'd want it that way. The people at the funeral

home kept asking me when I'd be through. I just told them to go on about their business and leave us alone. When I was finished I'd let them know. It was the last chance I had to talk with her. You should have seen her. She was so beautiful.

Nettie's husband, Ernest G. Kisling, had preceded her in death by nearly a decade. The two were married for 32 years. Widowed at the age of 80, in her grief Annette had lamented: "Who will want to make love to me now?"

Harold Rand

Sally's brother was born on April 16, 1908, four years and a few days after Sally. As she attained professional success, Harold Lawton Beck and concern for his career in show business were never far from her mind. Indeed, he often traveled as a member of Sally's show, as a song-and-dance man and as a stage manager.

An aspiring songwriter, Harold penned a number of published works — "Don't You Feel That Way," "Double Crossed," "Teasin'," and "Two Heads Together Are Better Than One" — but none you are likely to recognize. Harold also had a modest career as a movie actor. As "Hal Rand" he appeared in more than 20 films in uncredited roles, ranging from a dancer in *King of Burlesque* (1936), a song-and-dance man in *The Perils of Pauline* (1947) with Betty Hutton, a party guest in *The Great Gatsby* (1949), and a desk clerk in the musical *Aaron Slick From Punkin Crick* (1952) with Dinah Shore and Alan Young (of *Mr. Ed* fame) to a club patron in *Kiss Them For Me* (1957) with Cary Grant and Jayne Mansfield.

In 1936, Harold married Jovita Jordan and they became the parents of a son named Dennis. In concert with many of his contemporaries, Harold took a break from his show business career to serve as a corporal in the Army in World War II. By 1974, he was living in the San Fernando Valley of Los Angeles County with his second wife. According to Sally's son, his uncle had health issues, among them a tendency for his lungs to fill up with fluid. On June 16, 1974, while eating dinner at home, Harold fell forward into his plate and died. He was 66 years old. The grave of Harold L. Beck is located in Oakdale Memorial Park in Glendora.

THE HUSBANDS

Turk Greenough

After he and Sally divorced in 1945, Turk resumed his activities on the rodeo circuit. In the course of his travels, he attracted several "rodeo groupies" and even a girlfriend or two, but none of the relationships were all that serious. The truth is, the whole Sally Rand experience had been a fanciful interlude and he was drawn to constancy. Less than a year after his divorce, Turk and his former wife Helen were quietly remarried in Yuma, Arizona.

Between rodeo appearances, Turk performed as a stunt man in several films, including *Angel and the Badman* (1947). He became friends with the leading man John Wayne and established other valuable contacts in Hollywood. He had hoped to carry on in the entertainment world, but a grueling rodeo schedule had taken its toll on his already battered body. And so, in 1948, he decided to hang up his spurs at age 43.

Turk and Helen moved to Las Vegas and settled in with Helen's niece Shirley, a sort of "adopted" daughter. There, he enjoyed a 25-year second career as a casino security guard, mostly at the Sahara Hotel. In this capacity he interacted with many famous celebrities, even running into Sally from time to time.

Turk's wife was none too happy with these encounters. She had loathed Sally for many years, but, over time, the two had managed to patch things up. Sally had assured Helen that she and Turk had broken up years ago when he realized that he loved Helen more. On one occasion, when Sean was six or seven, Sally had introduced him to Turk, saying: "Sean, this is Turk. We were married once, and now we're friends."

Turk was forced to fully retire in 1977 and, on the first of August of that year, after 39 years of marriage (including the years before Sally), Helen died from a brain tumor at the age of 66.

In 1983, Turk and his two sisters, Alice and Margie, were inducted into the Rodeo Hall of Fame in Oklahoma City, the first time a family group had been inducted together. Other recognition followed, including a series of limited edition bronze castings and the 1989 documentary film *Take Willy with Ya* (*The Ridin' Greenoughs*).

In 1995, after suffering a series of strokes and heart attacks, Thurkel "Turk" Greenough died on May 30th, a mere three months shy of his 90th birthday.

Harry Finkelstein

Harry and Georgia Sothern (nee Hazel Anderson) may have remarried, since she was being referred to in the press as "Mrs. Hazel Finkelstein" as late as 1956. Beyond this, an extensive search has turned up absolutely no mention of Harry after he and Sally parted ways. He seems to have fallen off the face of the earth. Perhaps he changed his name.

Fred Lalla

When he last saw Fred Lalla in 1979, Sally's son was debating whether or not to honor Fred's request to be a pallbearer at his mother's funeral. One of Sally's longtime lady friends intervened, saying: "Unh-uh, no way. He should not be any part of that." Fred persisted, asking to ride in the family car, but Sean turned him down. As he recalled:

> Then he got to the funeral and when the services were over as he was walking by the casket, he reached out and grabbed one of the roses and a thorn stuck him. He leaned over and said: "There, I got stuck. I knew she would stick me in the end."

Frederic J. Lalla died 15 years later on May 11, 1994, in Riverside, California. He was 70 years old.

THE LEGACY

In 1984, five years after Sally's passing, at the 57th annual pageant in Atlantic City, a beautiful 20-year-old named Vanessa Williams became the first African-American woman to be crowned as Miss America. When *Penthouse* magazine's publisher Bob Guccione announced his intention to publish photographs of Miss Williams assuming several nude poses (including simulated sex with another woman), all hell broke loose. In the midst of the ensuing media frenzy and threats by sponsors to pull out of the next year's pageant, Miss Williams bowed to pressure by pageant officials, called a press conference, and resigned from the position on July 23, 1984.[14]

---

[14] Vanessa Williams' career survived all the brouhaha as she went on to become a successful singer, actress, fashion model, and producer. From 2006 to 2012, she was featured in all four seasons of the ABC television series *Ugly Betty* and in seasons 7 and 8 of *Desperate Housewives*. On September 13, 2015, she was welcomed back to Atlantic City and invited to serve as a judge for the Miss America contest, where she received a formal apology from Sam Haskell, executive chairman of the pageant, for her treatment decades before.

The clash between conflicting views of morality continues unabated. In May of 2015, after an eight-month investigation, a police task force arrested more than half a dozen women at Lipstick, a "gentleman's club" in Lafayette, Louisiana — most for engaging in "exotic dancing" without a permit — and charged them with obscenity for allegedly exposing their nipples to under-cover officers. This, more than 80 years after a *Chicago Tribune* editorial on October 11, 1933, had addressed "The Puzzle of Sally":

> Miss Sally Rand, a disturbing element in this community ever since the fair opened, has been sentenced to a year in jail for representing a century of progress in the exposition of the human body. A jury found her guilty of nudity and the judge decided that the expiation to society would require a year in the calaboose. Pending further legal proceedings Miss Rand continues to entertain or dismay the city. There are at least two opinions.
>
> Sally's ups and downs this summer, those of the fans included, would have been the glory of any press agent, but the brightest of them never could have kept up with her. She has crashed the front page by the simplest of expedients which she herself described as taking her pants off, thereby exposing not so much herself as the confusion of the human mind. It is betrayed in the utmost perplexity. It doesn't know whether the human body, certainly no strange phenomenon in the world, is innately noble or innately vile....
>
> Sally makes a professional success on one side of the fence and is sentenced to jail on the other. Thousands pay their money to see what the fans allow them to believe they see and 12 men in a jury say the young lady is a menace to the sober minds of the community.

Sally Rand has secured her place as an American popular culture icon. Given the longevity of her fan dancing career — working 40 weeks a year for more than 40 years — her public exposure may well be unrivaled. It has been claimed that she was seen in person by more people than any other performer in history.[15]

On June 27, 2004, a stellar event was held at Town Hall in midtown Manhattan to celebrate the 100th anniversary of Sally's birth. (The benefit — *Fans! A Sally Rand Centennial Celebration* — also served as a fundraiser for Animal Haven to support its activities on behalf of abandoned cats and dogs.) Participants included film critic Rex Reed and Broadway stars Bebe

---

[15] Similar claims have been made on behalf of Bob Hope, Billy Graham, Pope John Paul II, and the Rolling Stones.

Neuwirth and Marge Champion, among many others. The noted ballerina Deborah Wingert performed a ballet solo in the style of Anna Pavlova. Broadway musical performer and choreographer Caitlin Carter did a fan dance and Barbara Bruno took a turn with her version of the bubble dance.[16] Injecting some humor, four chorus girls stripped their way out of full-body chicken suits. Music was provided by the campy Lounge-O-Leers.

In August 2009, *Fandance: The Legend of Sally Rand* — a musical tribute written and directed by Misty Rowe — made its debut on the stage of the Big Bear Lake Performing Arts Center in California.[17] The following spring the show moved east for a five-week run at the Downtown Cabaret Theatre in Bridgeport, Connecticut, amid anticipation that a spot on Broadway might be in its future. Regrettably, critics failed to give the show the boost it needed to advance.

S ally's funeral was held at 9:00 a.m. on Tuesday, September 4, 1979, at the Church of Jesus Christ of Latter-day Saints in Glendora. A spokeswoman suggested that donations be made in Sally's name to the City of Hope National Medical Center in Duarte, California. A reported 150 relatives, friends, and admirers attended the public service. Praising "Sister Rand," Mormon Church Elder Gary Heck was quoted as saying: "I guess the highlight of her life was the day she walked into the waters of baptism."

Sally is buried in Oakdale Memorial Park in Glendora, California, in Section Elm Lawn, Lot 34, Grave 10. A simple plaque reads:

Helen Gould Beck
"Sally Rand"
1904 – 1979

---

[16]   The former dancer Barbara Bruno has written an unproduced film script, mini-series and multimedia musical based on Sally's career. More recently she has been an NFL analyst and commentator as well as an independent film producer.

[17]   Misty Rowe, an actress, writer, director and choreographer (perhaps best known for her 19 years on the television series *Hee Haw*) had previously delighted Bridgeport audiences in *Always...Patsy Cline*, a big hit for the Downtown Cabaret Theatre several seasons earlier. Growing up and as a young woman, Miss Rowe had known and fallen under Sally's spell when they both lived in Glendora, California. She is almost certainly the "Misty" who, on August 29, 1979, left the "adopted daughter" message for Sally during her final hospitalization.

Afterword

In some ways, Sally Rand's life was much the same as yours and mine — a series of major and minor struggles, each of which must be addressed in some fashion or another just to make it from one day to the next. Hers was a life of hopes, dreams, and fears — and, most of all, of compromises — all the while seeking financial security and the love if not the approval of others. For most of her life, Sally was a single woman with outsized responsibilities, living in a society that was largely resistant to her aspirations. Yet, she overcame.

You might ask: "Why her?" What was it, really, that separated Sally Rand from her competitors? Any number of other fan dancers might have captured the public fancy. Was it just good fortune? Right place, right time? It is undeniable that luck — the convergence of preparation and opportunity — played a role in her success. But, there was something more.

Much like the fan dance itself, the answer is both simple and elusive. Was she an exceptionally talented dancer? No. Was she a truly stunning physical beauty? "Cute" would be closer to the truth. Yet, like Mistinguett, Ethel Merman, Bette Midler and others who could be named, she commanded attention by the sheer force of her personality. Sally Rand was an imp, a brat, a coquette, a vixen, a tease. She was gracious, stubborn, charming, sharp-tongued, generous, stingy, a savvy business woman, a holy terror, and a determined young woman to the end. Still, there was something more.

How to describe it? The source of Sally's appeal was never so much her objective beauty as her charisma. When Clara Bow starred in the 1927 silent film entitled *It*, she was forever after known as "The It girl." At the time, "It" was said to be "that quality possessed by some which draws all others with its magnetic force." Call it what you will, Sally had it in abundance. Even in later life, on stage or off, she never lost that girlish, just-beyond-your-grasp appeal that, while difficult to describe, is unmistakable to anyone who confronts it in the flesh.

Whatever else she was, Sally was a whirlwind of activity. She was constantly moving from place to place, hauling trunks full of costumes and Lord knows what else, struggling to make payroll for her troupe, being interviewed, auditioning and rehearsing new girls for her show, adjusting stage lighting, giving speeches, falling in and out of love, fighting off charges of indecency, writing startlingly long letters, and dodging the tax man, all the while doing it, as often as not, as a single woman. She was indefatigable. Just imagine, by the close of her travels with seasonal carnivals in 1952, she had maintained this pace day after day and month after month for 20 years and had just as many still to go.

Sally Rand was barely five feet tall, but she was larger than life — a self-made woman — in turns beloved and scorned, praised and chastised, cheered and reviled. A public figure, she was recognized by millions in an era long before the dawn of mass media. Sally shared herself with us in a manner and for a period of years never likely to be duplicated. But, deep inside, she remained the vulnerable little girl who had been rejected by her father and never fully recovered. As the years passed by, her uninhibited public persona masked a lifelong insecurity.

We think we saw it all, but how much did we really see? No sooner did we glimpse the woman beneath the fan than our view was obstructed yet again. Some would swear they had seen everything, but, like every one of us, Sally had hidden more than she revealed.

Acknowledgments

A book as large and comprehensive as this one could never have come to be without significant contributions from both primary and secondary sources. Sally's son, Sean Rand, was easily the most important primary source. He has faithfully maintained his mother's voluminous files and scrapbooks over the decades. Had your author not been granted access to her personal correspondence, photographs, and other materials, this biography would have been little more than a slender shadow of itself. Gratitude for Mr. Rand's exceptional generosity is beyond my ability to adequately express.

Portions of Sally's story, particularly from the period before 1923, are largely based on the generally unattributed newspaper clippings found in her earliest scrapbooks — items lovingly and diligently clipped and pasted into place by her faithful assistant Ralph Hobart.

With respect to secondary sources, several archival resources were of particular value: www.newspapers.com, www.newspaperarchives.com, the Sally Rand papers collection at the Chicago History Museum, the Sally Rand collection at the Billy Rose Theatre Division of the New York City Public Library, and the Turk Greenough papers preserved in the Carbon County Historical Society Museum in Red Lodge, Montana. Quotations not otherwise attributed in the text or source notes, were likely derived from one or more of these sources.

Photographs reproduced in this book were provided by Sean Rand or are from the personal collection of the author. Mr. Rand's quoted recollections are from extensive interviews conducted and transcribed by Bonnie Egan, who spent many hours laboriously combing through the seemingly unending contents of Sally's file cabinets and scrapbooks. Simply put, this book would not exist without her tireless efforts.

Ms. Egan's other interviews and contacts also produced valued contributions from Lorrie Barnes O'Brien, Paul Delaney, and Hilda Vincent, among others, each of whom is due many thanks for shared recollections. Many thanks also go out to Steve Quillen, Aslan Heidorn, and Jay Wallace for material from their undeveloped biographical effort from the early 1980s, which came into my possession by a circuitous route. Thanks also to Melodie Ramone for permission to use the quote from her *After Forever Ends* as the epigraph at the top of the Prologue.

Special appreciation is owed to Kay Waters, the former President of the Glendora Historical Society, and the other members of the Society who warmly provided their support. Each of you (Hello, Rexine and Zelda!) is aware of the nature of your contribution. Many other residents of Glendora generously contributed their time and recollections, foremost among them, Scott Rubel and his father Christopher Rubel. In connection with Bonnie's several trips to Glendora, special mention must also be made of the valuable assistance supplied by her brother Patrick Egan and her sister Barrie Egan.

Extra special thanks are extended to Erica Landmann who, after attending the May 31, 2011, meeting of the Glendora Historical Society's tribute to Sally Rand, was motivated to encourage Mr. Rand to offer his cooperation in what has proven to be a long and rewarding journey.

Thanks are also due to Susan Carey, Nancy and Bob Henning, Margie Wright, and Bethany Lowe, each of whom has graciously read portions of the unfinished manuscript and offered valuable observations and encouragement. Bob Holladay and Vic and Sandee Vickers, all of Sentry Press, are certainly due commendation for granting free rein to a first-time author of advancing age and for making his dream a reality.

Last, but certainly not least, the English language is beggared to describe the extent of the assistance and support of the author's wife, Sharon, who, over a period of years, has sacrificed untold hours editing and otherwise polishing the manuscript into what is a far more presentable product than it otherwise would have been. Any remaining errors of substance, structure, spelling, or grammar are due solely to the oversight or obstinacy of the author. And, one more thing — it would be an unforgivable omission were I not to declare my boundless affection for our precious little Louie, the most adorable miniature long-haired dachshund on Earth, who has kept me relatively calm during the ups and downs of these past eight years.

Source Notes

Whenever a newspaper article is cited as a source, such as a syndicated item that may have appeared in many papers, I have endeavored to cite a source that can be found online. Source note citations to the Steve Quillen papers reference material in the author's files from an aborted effort in the early 1980s by Steve Quillen and Aslan Heidorn to prepare a biography of Sally. Quotations from Sally's correspondence and other original writings, except where otherwise noted, are extracted from copies in her personal files. In a few instances, editorial license was exercised with respect to punctuation, spelling, and grammar. Certain uncredited material from 1950 and 1952 is from Miss Rand's personal diaries.

PROLOGUE

4-13   Two drafts of William Beck's letter to Rosa Steward exist. One includes the account of Joe Kelly's beating and is 10 typed pages, single-spaced. The shorter, presumably final version is 14 pages, double-spaced. The Prologue text is excerpted from both drafts and condensed.

CHAPTER ONE: IN THE BEGINNING

18   The account of Sally's grandfather Grove dying of pneumonia after crossing the Pomme de Terre River in winter is from a three-page document in Sally's files, headed: "Quoting from pages 11 & 12 of Goldiann's biography" — a source otherwise unknown.

18-19   According to Mrs. L. D. Ames, "The Missouri Play-Party," Vol. 24, Num. 93, *Journal of American Folklore* (1911): "In the neighborhood where I was born and reared, the play-party was the common form of amusement at the gatherings of young people of the best class.... These play-parties were really dances. The players did not dance, however, to the music of instruments, but kept time with various steps to their own singing.... The better class of people in the country did not believe in dancing. Regular dances, where the music was furnished by a 'fiddler,' were held, for the most part, only in the homes of the rough element. They were generally accompanied by card-playing, and frequently by drunkenness and fighting. The better class ranked dancing, in the moral scale, along with gambling and fishing on Sunday. It was not good form, and was tabooed on grounds of respectability."

19   Sally's account of her parents' early life in Springfield, Missouri, is from a letter published in *The Springfield News-Leader*, September 20, 1970.

21   Sally's remarks to Studs Terkel about the world at the time of her birth are from an interview of Sally in his book *Hard Times: An Oral History of the Great Depression*, Pantheon Books (1970). Audio is available online from: studsterkel.matrix.msu.edu/htimes.php (no "www"). To listen to the brief conversation, scan the page for the "Sally" link.

22   Two-year old Helen's visit with her mother to see her "Aunt Lucy" in the hospital was described in an article by Lucy Newton Wilson, circa 1954, styled as a submission to the popular "My Most Unforgettable Character" feature in *Reader's Digest* magazine.

22   Sally wrote this childhood reminiscence for an article entitled "My Life," as published in the March 1938 issue of *The National Police Gazette*.

23   Sally's radio interview was documented in Mary Margaret McBride's *Out of the Air: The Most Radio-Active Woman in America*, Doubleday & Co., Inc. (1960).

25 Joseph Ireland's account of Madame Hutin's performance is mentioned in *Players of a Century* by H.P. Phelps (1890) and elsewhere. For an extended rant on the subject, Google "Madame Hutin" and "Bowery" and select the result that leads to *The Quarterly Christian Spectator*.

25 Sources describing Mme. Hutin's performance and the audience reaction include *Striptease: The Untold History of the Girlie Show* by Rachel Shteir, Oxford University Press (2004).

25 For more about Morse, see *Lightning Man: The Accursed Life of Samuel F. B. Morse*, by Kenneth Silverman, Da Capo Press (2004).

30 The description of "Macaronies" is from *The Origins of English Words: A Discursive Dictionary of Indo-European Roots* by Joseph T. Shipley, Johns Hopkins University Press (1984).

32 Teddy Roosevelt's speech on Memorial Day, May 30, 1916, is worth reading, particularly passages on the equal responsibilities of the wealthy and the working man. See: http://www.theodore-roosevelt.com/images/research/txtspeeches/671.pdf

32-33 Billy Sunday's diatribe on his detractors is from *The Gazette Globe* (Kansas City, Kansas) and the *Mexico Weekly Ledger* (Missouri), May 1 & 4, 1916, respectively. For his sermon on dancing and card playing, see *The Baltimore Sun* (Maryland), April 1, 1916.

CHAPTER TWO: COMING OF AGE

38 The apocryphal story of Helen Beck running away to join a carnival is from *Sally Rand: From Film to Fans* by Holly Knox, Maverick Publications (1988).

61 Footnote 8: The description of Helen as the "bathing suit girl from the *Follies*" is from *The Kansas City Journal-Post* (Missouri), December 14, 1924.

62 Details about Walt Disney's early life in Kansas City are based, in part, on information in *Walt Disney: The Triumph of the American Imagination*, by Neal Gabler, Alfred A. Knopf (2007).

64 The description of the excitement surrounding the arrival of the Ringling Brothers and Barnum and Bailey Circus is from *The Kansas City Times* (Missouri), September 13, 1920.

65 Sally's advice on breast enhancement is from a letter she wrote to Chet Hagan on April 11, 1969.

65-66 The story of Sally's relationship with Casey Stengel is from *Sports Illustrated*, April 7, 1969.

CHAPTER THREE: LADIES AND GENTS: MISS BILLIE BECK

71 The "Duke Duchme" date is described in the *Milwaukee Journal* (Wisconsin), July 20, 1935.

71-72 Details of Billie's 1921 New York ventures are sketchy, but the *Hutchinson Gazette* (Kansas), September 24, 1922, cited her understudy role and reported that she "had her fling in Little Old New York as a model at Mexines and Resenwevera," and "modeled for Clair and for Lucille." A likely spelling error, "Resenwevera" may be Reisenweber's Café (birthplace of the modern cabaret?) and "Lucille" may be New York fashion icon "Lucile" (Lady Duff Gordon).

74 Manuel Herrick's comment that women were more concerned with their looks than their homes is from *The Hutchinson News* (Kansas), August 13, 1921.

75-76 For Manuel Herrick's volatile reaction to his "perceived enemies" ("Let the slur writers rave"), see *The Washington Herald* (D.C.), August 25, 1921.

76 Congressional reaction to Manuel Herrick's proposal to outlaw beauty contests was described in the *Racine Journal-News* (Wisconsin), September 7, 1921.

78 Sally's observations regarding the time she posed as a life study model at the Art Institute of Chicago are from an interview conducted by columnist Kathleen Nichols in 1933.

79 Details of the encounter between Billie Beck and Lew Leslie are from the article "I'LL SHOW THEM NOW!" by Jerry Lane, *Screen Book* magazine, March 1934.

79-80 Sally's comments about meeting with Lew Leslie and gaining the lead role in the café revue *The Cabinet of Terpsichore* are from her 1933 interview with Kathleen Nichols.

80-81 Information on show business entrepreneur Nils Granlund is from *Nils Thor Granlund: Show Business Entrepreneur and America's First Radio Star* by Larry J. Hoefling, McFarland (2010).

81 For the item on William Seabury choosing girls for his revue *Frivolics*, see *The Capitol Times* (Madison, Wisconsin), September 27, 1923.

81-82 The review of William Seabury's production of *Frivolics* at the Hamilton Theatre in New York City is from the *New York Clipper*, July 11, 1923.

85-86 Alice Paul's comments on the defeat of female candidates in the 1922 general election are from the *Chicago Tribune*, November 10, 1922.

CHAPTER FOUR: MAKING A SPLASH IN HOLLYWOOD

93   For Billie Beck's specialty dance in *The Lady Barber*, see *The Reel Journal*, January 5, 1924.

95-96   The "one source" of how Cecil B. DeMille changed Billie Beck's name is: *Sally Rand: From Film to Fans* by Holly Knox, Maverick Publications (1988).

96   Al Allen's 1976 interview of Sally regarding the origin of her name is from the *Oakland Tribune* (California), July 1, 1976.

97   The description of a "party girl" is from *Picture Play* magazine, July 1925.

97   Footnote 12: The report of Sally's Charleston dance contest wins at the Cocoanut Grove is from the *Culver City News* (California), September 2, 1925.

98   Sally's article illustrating the steps for doing the Charleston ("HERE'S HOW YOU DO IT") is from the *Los Angeles Examiner*, July 12, 1925.

101   The YWCA war on beauty contests is described in *The New York Times*, April 18 & 20, 1924.

102   Kathryn Ray's opening number in the 1924 *Vanities* is described in Ken Murray's biography, *The Body Merchant: The Story of Earl Carroll*, Ward Ritchie Press (1976).

110-111   The account of "casting couch" practices at the comedy studios is from "THE MORALS OF HOLLYWOOD AND THE ARBUCKLE CASE," *The Dearborn Independent*, December 10, 1921.

111   The suggestion that DeMille may have "propositioned" Sally is reportedly from the *Chicago Daily News*, August 10, 1926, as cited by Rachel Shteir in *Striptease: The Untold History of the Girlie Show*, Oxford University Press (2004).

112   Sally's attraction to a "Pan boy" is recounted in "WHAT SORT OF MAN APPEALS TO ME?" in the *News Sunday Magazine Section* of *The Miami News*, March 15, 1925. Also see Patricia Merivale's *Pan the Goat-God: His Myth in Modern Times*, Harvard University Press (1969).

113   The "trussed chickens" review of Faith Bacon's role in the Shubert brothers' production of *Artists and Models* is from the *New York Evening Post*, July 3, 1925.

117   The paper in which Colonel Beck had seen the picture of his daughter "toe-writing" was Hearst's *New York Evening Journal*, October 15, 1925.

120-121   The "puff piece" promoting Sally with her new Essex ("HER ONLY LOVER HER AUTO — SO SHE DECLARES") is from *The Los Angeles Times*, February 14, 1926.

121   The news that Sally would be driving a trainload of new washing machines into the local train yard is from the *Riverside Enterprise* (California), October 2, 1926. Photos are posted at the USC Digital Library website at: http://usclibstore.usc.edu/keyword/0603;women/i-w3jJPXg

129   The tale of DeMille's constraints on cast and crew for *The King of Kings* is from Jon Solomon's *The Ancient World in the Cinema (Revised & Expanded Ed.)*, Yale University Press (2001).

129-130   Sally's relationship with H. B. Warner is recounted in Peter Hay's *Movie Anecdotes*, Oxford University Press (1990).

CHAPTER FIVE: THE VAUDEVILLE YEARS

133   The Eddie Cantor/Sally Rand encounter is mentioned in Shana Alexander's memoir *Happy Days: My Mother, My Father, My Sister & Me*, Doubleday (1995). (Shana's father, Milton Ager, composed the music for "Ain't She Sweet.")

133-134   Sally's confrontation with her brother Harold over his skipping school to give tennis lessons to young "beauties" is from Bonnie Egan's interview of Sean Rand in October of 2014.

143   Milton Berle's assessment of Broadway producer Earl Carroll is from *The Body Merchant: The Story of Earl Carroll* by Ken Murray, Ward Ritchie Press (1976).

143   "Requirements" for choosing show girls were set forth in the program for the *Vanities of 1930*.

143   The "more provocative example" of Earl Carroll's pursuit of "flawless femininity" is from *The Body Merchant: The Story of Earl Carroll*.

145   Faith Bacon's idea for Earl Carroll to permissibly include more nudity in his shows is from Kaspar Monahan's interview for *The Pittsburgh Press*, February 26, 1934. Also see "THE 'TOUCH-ME-NOT' FAN DANCER ..." in a King Features Sunday supplement, July 26, 1936.

145-146   Faith Bacon's costume mishap on opening night in *Earl Carroll's Vanities* is from *The Body Merchant: The Story of Earl Carroll*.

149   Jack Benny's reported memory of Faith Bacon and his role in the 1930 production of *Earl Carroll's Vanities* is from drama critic Jack Gaver's syndicated column, February 1963.

150-152   Details of the Hammerstein-Haskell-Rand ruckus are sometimes at odds. The account presented is based on an article from *Variety* magazine, August 1930, as well as other press reports.

155-156   The description of the "entertainment" presented at the "Fête Charrette" benefit held at Chicago's Drake Hotel is from *Time* magazine, October 10, 1932.

156   Data on Chicago unemployment in the early 1930s is from the online *Encyclopedia of Chicago*. Go to: www.encyclopedia.chicagohistory.org and look for the "Great Depression" entry.

CHAPTER SIX: THE SUITORS

158   For the early days of Texaco, see: http://www.fundinguniverse.com/ company-histories/ texaco-inc-history/. The story of the 40 American employees of Cortez Oil held for ransom in Mexico was widely covered. See *The Topeka State Journal* (Kansas), June 27, 1922.

158   Footnote 2: Carl Schlaet's athletic exploits at Yale in the 1915-16 swimming season were reported in many papers. See *The Philadelphia Inquirer* (Pennsylvania) and *The New York Times*, March 18, 1916; also see the *St. Louis Star and Times* (Missouri), April 4, 1916. For an amazing performance by Duke Kahanamoku, Hawaiian hero and master of swimming and surfing, see the *Hartford Courant* (Connecticut), April 12, 1916.

159   Footnote 3: For the story of Neville Penrose and his proposals to repeal the Texas poll tax and to enact an anti-lynching law, see *The Odessa American* (Texas), January 8, 1953.

160   For more on Ma Ferguson, the first female governor of Texas, see the website of the Texas State Historical Association at: https://tshaonline.org/handbook/online/articles/ffe06 .

163   Footnote 6: The claim by Walter Winchell that Sally's supposed "first husband" was a man named "Cassey Gay" may be found in *The Cincinnati Enquirer* (Ohio), October 28, 1941.

165   Jack Crosby's experiences as a young man in Ogden, Utah, were reported in the *Oakland Tribune* (California), June 14, 1928. For the favorable notice of Crosby's musical theater role in Gershwin's *Oh, Kay*, see *The Los Angeles Times*, August 17, 1927.

167   For a hometown review of "the Crosby boys" playing with Sally Rand in the Fanchon and Marco revue *Sally from Hollywood*, see *The Ogden Standard-Examiner* (Utah), July 29, 1928.

168   For Sally's general discussion of military training, her father's military experiences, and her views on stage marriages, see the *Oakland Tribune*, June 14, 1928.

168-169   Sally's "ideal man" is from an interview published in *Screen Secrets* magazine, February 1928.

174   *The Second Mrs. Kong* is a two-act opera with music by Sir Harrison Birtwhistle and libretto by Russell Hoban. It was first produced in England in 1994.

174   For notice of Naval Orders assigning Ensign J.S. Thach to "Battleship Division, Battle Fleet," see *The Los Angeles Times*, April 24, 1928.

176   For an item on the "Three Life Boys" performing with Sally in a colorful Vaudeville act, see *The Morning Call* (Allentown, Pennsylvania), April 17, 1931.

CHAPTER SEVEN: THE NIGHTTIME RIDE OF SALLY RAND

179   The Polar Bear Club picture of Sally in a one-piece swimsuit enduring Lake Michigan's icy waters can be seen in the *Moorhead Daily News* (Minnesota), October 18, 1932.

179   Sally's 1972 interview with John Wheeler (she was "touched by the poor selling apples") is from *The Daily Times-News* (Burlington, North Carolina), July 13, 1972.

180   Sally's memories of the Depression are from "The Fan Dancer," an article by Winston Collins, published in the *Weekend Magazine* and distributed throughout Canada on February 3, 1979. See *The Ottawa Journal* (Ontario) of that date.

180   How Sally got a job at the Paramount Club ("All my uncles are stagehands") is recounted by Studs Terkel in *Hard Times: An Oral History of the Great Depression*, Pantheon Books (1970).

181   Sally described the bird-movement inspiration for her fan dance in a syndicated interview with feature columnist Dorothy Roe for NEA Service, published in October 1933.

181-182   How Sally created a "costume" for her debut fan dance at the Paramount is from Studs Terkel's *Hard Times* interview (a story amplified in the Steve Quillen papers).

184   Sally's inspiration to appear as Lady Godiva was related in her interview with John Wheeler as published in *The Daily Times-News* (Burlington, North Carolina), July 13, 1972.

184-186   The story of planning for the 1927 Beaux Arts Ball is from the online archives of the *Chicago Tribune*. Benjamin Marshall's remarks were in the *Chicago Tribune*, November 14, 1927.

186 Lady Godiva's botched appearance at the 1927 Beaux Arts Ball was reported by several contemporary news sources. Besides the *Chicago Daily Tribune* ("GODIVA GOES TO ARTS BALL..."), November 26, 1927, an extensive account with pictures ("AND WHEN THE LOVELIEST LADY GODIVA GLIDED IN!") may be found in a Sunday supplement for the *Ogden Standard-Examiner* (Utah), January 1, 1928. And for those dedicated trivia buffs who read every source note, no matter how lengthy: Miss Hightower was the wife of Melvyn Edouard Hesselberg, better known as the future two-time Oscar winning actor Melvyn Douglas.

187 "Hefty" Sally's approach to Andrew Rebori, as described by Chicago bureau columnist W.A.S. Douglas, is from *The Baltimore Sun*, August 13, 1933.

187-188 Hotelier Ernest Stevens' financial and legal troubles and the repercussions for Stevens and his son John were reported in the *American Bar Association Journal*, April 9, 2010.

188-189 Jack Stanley Morris's annulment was reported in *The Los Angeles Times*, December 31, 1932. The story of his unreciprocated pursuit of Faith Bacon and her "kindly but frigid lecture" is from a King Features Sunday supplement, April 28, 1935 ("2-ACT FLOP...").

190 The story of Al Quodbach and the shooting incident at the Café Granada is from *The Last Mogul: Lew Wasserman, MCA, and the Hidden History of Hollywood* by Dennis McDougal, Crown Publishers (1998).

191 The story of Cati Mount's reaction to Sally's horse was syndicated nationally. See the *Tallahassee Democrat*, November 30, 1932, and *Time* magazine, June 29, 1936.

191-192 The story of Sally at the Beaux Arts Ball was widely covered. See a highly-illustrated account in the *American Weekly* Sunday supplement in the *San Antonio Light*, September 24, 1933.

CHAPTER EIGHT: CRASHING THE PARTY

196-197 Sally's experience with masseur and trainer Doc Field in Miami was reported in Tony Weitzel's column in the *Naples Daily News* (Florida), September 14, 1975.

197 Paul Harrison's syndicated observations about table-to-table telephone calls at the Monte Carlo and Faith Bacon "hiding behind a few beads" are from "IN NEW YORK," March 1933.

199 The story of the Chicago elite at Mrs. Hearst's Milk Fund Dinner is from *The 1933 Chicago World's Fair: A Century of Progress* by Cheryl R. Ganz, University of Illinois Press (2008). See the syndicated column by John Wheeler in *The Baltimore Sun* (Maryland), July 20, 1972.

199-200 Sally spoke of crashing the Milk Fund Dinner as part of an oral interview she gave to Studs Terkel for his book *Hard Times: An Oral History of the Great Depression*, Pantheon Books (1970). Also see *The Philadelphia Inquirer* (Pennsylvania), May 17, 1970, page 125. To listen, go online to: studsterkel.matrix.msu.edu/htimes.php and search for the link to "Sally".

CHAPTER NINE: THE NUDE DEAL

205 Footnote 2: The Sky-Ride's connection to *Amos and Andy* is from *Chicago's 1933-34 World's Fair: A Century of Progress* by Bill Cotter, Arcadia Publishing (2015).

209 Sally's indoor performances at the Café de la Paix were described in a syndicated article by Sam Knott. See the *Manitowoc Herald-Times* (Wisconsin), July 19, 1933.

210-211 Footnote 8: The suggestion that Mary Belle Spencer was duped by Ben Serkowitch into filing a petition to enjoin "lewd and lascivious dances" at the Streets of Paris is from *The Family Circle*, July 7, 1939. The idea was corroborated in *The National Police Gazette*, July 1947.

215-217 For a complete and compelling debunking of the "Little Egypt" myth, see *Looking for Little Egypt* by Donna Carlton, IDD Books (1995).

219 For the story of Rev. Philip Yarrow's censure of Sally Rand, see the article by syndicated correspondent Bruce Grant in *The Dispatch* (Moline, Illinois), July 30, 1933.

220 The account of William Randolph Hearst signing the 1933 Fair's "large gold guestbook" is from Carl Kane's column in the *Cedar Rapids Tribune* (Iowa), December 17, 1953.

221 The promotional sheet touting "hundreds of fan dancers" at the Fair is from the "World's Fair Edition" of *Chicago Bright Spots*, July 31, 1933.

CHAPTER TEN: THE MOST FAMOUS WOMAN IN AMERICA

227 George Burns' recollections of the Chicago World's Fair in the 1930s are from *100 Years, 100 Stories* by George Burns, G.P. Putnam's Sons (1996).

229   For the more risqué attractions at the Chicago Fair, with Sally at the Old Manhattan Garden, see "THE WORLD'S FAIR SEXATIONAL," *East St. Louis Journal* (Illinois), October 1, 1933.

230-231   For Sally's widely reported battle with club manager Sam Balkin (whom she claimed had given her a black eye), see *The Morning Herald* (Uniontown, Pennsylvania), September 20, 1933.

231-235   Sally's trial and conviction for "performing an obscene and indecent dance in a public place" was reported by Virginia Gardner. See the *Chicago Sunday Tribune*, September 24, 1933.

235   Footnote 7: Reverend Savidge's remarks are from the *Omaha Bee*, September 25, 1933. After his death, the *Omaha World-Herald* (Nebraska) described him as an "Omaha institution."

236   Radio editor Norman Siegel's mixed assessment of Sally ("She's a nice-looking person dressed up....") is from the *Cleveland Press* (Ohio), October 2, 1933.

236-237   Alois Knapp's comments on nudity were published in many papers on October 19-20, 1933.

237   Sally's "none too charitable" observations on the subject of nudity are from an unattributed article in *The Sandusky Register* (Ohio), December 31, 1933.

239   The notion that Sally sheathed her "shapely chassis" with a "bit of gauze" is from *The Los Angeles Times*, October 7, 1933. The "spoiler alert" techniques that Sally employed to get ready for a stage performance were described in *The Bridgeport Herald* (Connecticut).

239   For Aimee Semple McPherson's widely covered faked kidnapping, see "EVANGELIST IS CHARGED WITH FAKING STORY" in *The Oneonta Star* (New York), September 18, 1926.

240   For Aimee's comments about her turn on the Broadway stage, see *The Los Angeles Times*, September 1, 1933, and the *Star-Gazette* (Elmira, New York), September 26, 1933. The misquoted biblical passage seems to be a mashup of Old and New Testament text — the "broad ways" text in Jeremiah 5:1 and the "Wedding Banquet" verse in Mathew 22:9 or Luke 14:23.

240-241   McPherson's Broadway appearance was described by Morris Markey in *The New Yorker*, September 30, 1933. The "freak draw" remark is from *Variety* magazine, September 26, 1933.

241-242   For Commissioner Sidney Levine's censure of Sally's act, see *The Brooklyn Daily Eagle* (New York), October 11, 1933 and the *Reading Times* (Pennsylvania), October 12, 1933.

242   For reports of Sally in "long flannel underwear" or "bloomers," see *The Greenville News* (South Carolina) and *The Lubbock Morning Avalanche* (Texas), October 12 & 13, 1933, respectively.

242   Footnote 12: The adjacent articles about Sally's attire and the banning of "Negro jazz" in Germany are in the *Nevada State Journal* (Reno), October 12, 1933.

243-244   The heartland pastor's eyewitness account ("I Saw Sally Rand Dance") was by Rev. Fred Smith of the First Congregational Church for *The American Spectator*, November 1933.

244   For articles on Faith Bacon's hit-and-run accident, see *The Akron Beacon* (Ohio) and *The Philadelphia Inquirer* (Pennsylvania), November 6 & 7, 1933, respectively.

244   Syndicated columnist John T. Thompson interviewed Sally about filling in for Aimee. See the *Dunkirk Evening Observer* (New York) or *The Sheboygan Press* (Wisconsin), October 27, 1933.

245   Sally discussed her hoped-for future in movies in an interview with movie reviewer Irene Thirer for *The New Movie Magazine,* February 1934. For the portrayal of Stella Onizuka, Sally's "quaint Japanese maid," see *The Amarillo Globe-Times* (Texas), December 28, 1933.

246   Sidney Skolsky's story of Sally's first day of filming on the set of *Bolero* was in his Hollywood gossip column "Tintypes"; George Raft's related quote was from a *San Francisco Call-Bulletin* column by the fictive "Tom Peeping" (dates unknown).

247   For the story of Sally's refusal to pose for photographers with her legs crossed ("Why it would be immodest"), see *The Pittsburgh Press* (Pennsylvania), November 16, 1933.

247-248   Max Baer's disruption of Sally's fan dance for reporters in her San Francisco hotel room is from a syndicated story by Ronald Wagoner. See the *News-Journal* (Mansfield, Ohio), June 20, 1934.

248   Don O'Malley's description of the Manhattan "fan dancing craze" is from the *Daily News* (Huntington, Pennsylvania), November 2, 1933.

249   Grace Kingsley was the L.A. critic who praised Faith Bacon's performance in *The Century of Progress Revue* (see *The Los Angeles Times*, April 20, 1934).

249   For "would-be" Sally Rands in 1933, see: "Sally Rend" in *The Daily Times* (Davenport, Iowa), August 29; "Sally Randall" in *The Courier News* (Blytheville, Arkansas), November 18; *Streets of Paris* with Al Trace in *The Edwardsville Intelligencer* (Edwardsville, Illinois), December 4; and "Sally De Rand" in *The Sunday News and Tribune* (Jefferson City, Missouri), December 31.

250   Sally's explanation for her decision to leave Hollywood to return to vaudeville is from the *Hartford Courant* (Connecticut), January 22, 1934.

250-251   Sally's engagement to Charles "Chissie" Mayon became public when his hospitalization was widely reported. See *The News-Herald* (Franklin, Pennsylvania), January 30, 1934. The announcement of his recovery is from the *Ogden Standard-Examiner* (Utah), February 7, 1934.

252-254   While the wire services may have missed the tale of Sally's encounter with an Iowa haystack, the *Omaha World-Herald* reported the story on February 23, 1934 ("SALLY HERE BY AUTO, PLANE FORCED DOWN"). Sally's telegram is from the same issue.

253-254   Bishop Rummel's attempts to block Sally's show are from the *Omaha World-Herald*, February 22, 1934. Ward Calvert's opposing view is from the same paper, February 25, 1934.

255-256   Movie critic Keene Abbott's effusive review of Sally and her "Bevy of Beauties" is from the *Omaha World-Herald*, February 24, 1934. The same issue had an item about Omaha Police Chief Allen's thoughts on the show, as well as an editorial on Sally and censorship.

256   Bishop Rummel's conclusion that the "public exhibition of nudity" violates "objective moral standards" is from the *Omaha World-Herald*, February 25, 1934.

CHAPTER ELEVEN: THE SECOND TIME AROUND

258   The idea that stage lights were so dim it would be "impossible to see the other members of your party, much less Miss Rand" is from James Aswell's syndicated column of March 15, 1934.

258   Owner John McMahon's reported letter to Sally claiming that the Streets of Paris would be "clean this year" is from the *Waterloo Sunday Courier* (Iowa), April 1, 1934. The prediction that attractions would "avoid the shocking" is from *The New York Times*, May 20, 1934.

258-259   Sally Rand's vital contribution to the prosperity of the Chicago Fairs was declared by syndicated columnist Westbrook Pegler. See *The Muncie Evening Press* (Indiana), February 12, 1937.

259   Bruce Grant's syndicated column on all the "goings-on and comings-off" at the 1934 Fair was published in *The Morning Call* (Allentown, Pennsylvania), July 9, 1934.

260   Bishop Duffy's dire warning to Catholics that they should avoid performances by "the Rand woman" is from *The Catholic Advance* (Wichita, Kansas), July 7, 1934.

261   Sally's protestation that her show had not been cancelled by the Loew's State Theatre in Syracuse is from the *Democrat and Chronicle* (Rochester, New York), June 22, 1934. Joseph Imburgio's comments on her show ("it's a wow") are from *Time* magazine, July 2, 1934.

261   Max Baer's failed attempt to meet with Sally at the Park Central Hotel in New York ("I'll smack him with a hairbrush") was reported in the *Oakland Tribune* (California), June 23, 1934.

262-264   For the story of the "nudely weds" at the 1934 Fair, see *The Ogden Standard-Examiner* (Utah) and *The Times* (Shreveport, Louisiana), June 29 & 30, 1934, respectively. For the couple's arrest and sentencing, see *The Times* (Munster, Indiana), July 13, 1934.

265   Louie Greenberg's claim that the Chicago mob "owned Sally Rand" is from *The Last Mogul* by Dennis McDougal, Crown Publishing (1998).

266   For Sally's relations with the Oak Rubber Company (manufacturer of her balloons) see http://thomasriddle.net/cah/articles/history_of_chamber_commerce_in_ravenna_by_max_riddle.html

267   The eyewitness who described Sally's bubble dance at the 1934 Fair was John S. Van Gilder, Tennessee businessman, magic enthusiast, and Rotarian, writing for the *Knoxville Journal* (Tennessee), July 25, 1934. Bubble dance film footage can be found online at *YouTube*.

270   Footnote 10: Douglas Flamming discussed use of the term "the Race" to indicate African Americans and their culture in the introduction to his book *Bound for Freedom: Black Los Angeles in Jim Crow America*, University of California Press (2005).

271-272   The story of Sally's acceptance of the invitation to appear at the NAACP benefit is from *The Chicago Defender*, August 4, 1934. For a promotional article touting Sally's appearance at the benefit (and Faith Bacon's rebuff since "only so many persons can be used in a four-hour show"), see the *Pittsburgh Courier* (Pennsylvania), August 4, 1934.

272-273   The story of the breakfast meeting of the naprapaths' Post Mortem Club is from *The San Bernardino County Sun* (California), August 3, 1934.

274   An item in the August 13, 1934, issue of *Time* magazine asserted that the medical community had "supreme contempt for the medical theories of 'Dr.' Oakley Smith."

274-275   Praise for Faith Bacon's show at the "Hollywood-at-the-Fair" concession is from an article on World's Fair nightlife in the *Dixon Evening Telegraph* (Illinois), August 9, 1934.

276   The account of Sally stealing the show at the NAACP benefit is from *The Chicago Defender*, August 11, 1934.

277-279   Everett Holles's interview of Mary Belle Spencer is from the *San Bernardino County Sun*, September 1, 1934. Also see the *Montana Butte Standard*, August 31, 1934.

279-280   Sally's engagement to Chissie Mayon was widely reported. See the *Detroit Free Press* (Michigan), January 30, 1934, and *The Sheboygan Press* (Wisconsin), September 12, 1934.

280-281   For the offer made by the Young Men's Business Club of Granby, Missouri, to "buy Sally Rand," see *The Dispatch* (Moline, Illinois), August 18, 1934.

281   For the closing of the 1934 World's Fair and the aftermath, see the *Xenia Daily Gazette* (Ohio), October 31, 1934, and the *Kingsport Times* (Tennessee), November 1, 1934.

281-282   For Sally's conviction in Chicago for performing an "obscene and indecent dance in a public place," see *The Salt Lake City Tribune* (Utah), September 24, 1933. For the verdict's reversal on appeal, see *The Indianapolis Star* (Indiana), November 20, 1934. For Sally's reaction, see *The Tampa Tribune* (Florida), November 22, 1934.

282-283   Syndicated columnist James Aswell said Sally was "packing them in" at the Paradise Club; see the *Star-Gazette* (Elmira, New York), December 4 & 8, 1934. Also see the *Detroit Free Press* (Michigan), December 6, 1934, for Ed Sullivan's remark about Sally's "No Cover Charge" sign.

283-284   The story about Dr. Dafoe at the Paradise Club and his observation about Sally's posterior was recounted in *Winchell Exclusive* by Walter Winchell, Prentice Hall (1975).

284-285   The Lindbergh trial was covered nationally. For Mary Belle Spencer's jury tampering effort, see the *Chicago Tribune* and the *Pampa Daily News* (Texas), both from December 24, 1934.

CHAPTER TWELVE: SALLY SALLIES FORTH

287-289   Sally's talk before the Sales Executives Club of New York was covered in "SALLY RAND HOLDS DANCE A BUSINESS," *The New York Times*, February 12, 1935. The speech's content is similar to Sally's article "BUBBLES BECOME BIG BUSINESS," *American Review of Reviews*, April 1935.

290-291   Press agent Max Elser's proposal that the corset industry conduct an ad campaign based on the word "Callipygian" is from Stanley Walker's book *City Editor*, Frederick A. Stokes Company (1934). Sculptor Bryant Baker's opinion that the ideal woman must be "judged from the back" was widely covered. See the *News-Journal* (Wilmington, Delaware), May 29, 1934.

291-292   "Sensation" (a girdle by Nemo Flex) was advertised in *The Reading Times* (Pennsylvania), April 12, 1935. Ads in the *Wisconsin State Journal* (Madison), July 8, 1934, offered shopping tips by "Arlene" on how a Pouff [girdle] could give one a "beautiful rear profile." Similar ads were in the *Journal* on June 17 and November 11, 1934. "Absolute flatness" was promoted in *The Daily News* (Frederick, Maryland), April 25, 1934. For the "Miss Cooper" campaign, see *The Sydney Morning Herald* (New South Wales, Australia), February 28, 1935.

292   For the committee's search to find the "perfect callipygian," see the *Nevada State Journal* (Reno), November 14, 1934. For the contest (with Sally in "14 pounds of clothes"), see *The News-Herald* (Franklin, Pennsylvania), February 12, 1935.

292-293   Footnote 3: For the photo of Miss Hoffman draped in a banner, plus another of Sally with three other finalists, see the *Steubenville Herald-Star*, February 9, 1935. For a picture of Sally measuring the winning contestant, see the *Decatur Herald*, February 5, 1935.

293   For a colorful account of Sally's wardrobe malfunction before judges of the callipygian contest, see Theon Wright's "FAN MY B-B-BROW" in *The Pittsburgh Press* (Pennsylvania), February 3, 1935. Another account was circulated in Paul Harrison's syndicated column "IN NEW YORK".

294   The article on Ralph Hobart is from *The Reading Times*, April 12, 1935.

295-296   Sally's role in presenting Kohana's dance recital at the Guild Theater in New York City is described in Stanley Walker's *Mrs. Astor's Horse*, Blue Ribbon Books, Inc. (1935).

297   Sally's visit to the Illinois State Legislature was described in the *Decatur Herald*, June 30, 1935.

298-299   For Sally's Wisconsin court appearance to defend her advance man Raymond Roger for displaying "obscene posters," see *The Sheboygan Press* (Wisconsin), July 8, 1935.

299   Sally's Capitol Theater appearance in Manitowoc, Wisconsin, was covered in the *Manitowoc Herald-Times*, July 11, 1935. The local bridge club's presence was covered two days later.

299-300   For Sally's Frontier Days costume, see "Exhibits" at: www.oldwestmuseum.org. For the reaction of Bishop McGovern, see Corryne Drake's "A Look Back in Time: Naughty no-nos" online at the *Star-Tribune*, July 26, 2010 [reissued from the *Casper Tribune-Herald* (Wyoming), July 17, 1935].

300   For Turk Greenough's depiction as a "red-haired … bronc peeler," see the *Oakland Tribune* (California), July 26, 1935.

300-301 Sally talked about loneliness, her lack of women friends and her "ideal man" in an interview for *True Confessions* magazine, July 1935.

301-303 Sally discussed her "new daring dance" in an interview with Art Arthur. See *The Brooklyn Daily Eagle* (New York), January 3, 1935, and *The Sheboygan Press*, August 6, 1935.

304 The positive review of Sally's performance in *Rain* is from "Sally's Sadie Proves the Fans Concealed an Actress," *Newsweek* magazine, September 7, 1935.

305 For Sally's decision to continue to perform her fan dance rather than switch to dramatic acting, see *The Daily Herald* (Provo, Utah) and *The Pittsburgh Press*, September 5 & 15, 1935.

305 George Ross was the reviewer who quoted a fan gushing over Sally's "swellest performance" as Amy in *They Knew What They Wanted* (see *The Pittsburgh Press*, August 2, 1937).

306 Written with his daughter Carla Malden, Karl Malden's memoir *When Do I Start?* as published by Simon & Schuster (1997) includes his searing account of working with Sally in *Little Foxes*.

306-307 Sally's radio debut on NBC's WJR was promoted in *The Winnipeg Tribune* (Manitoba, Canada), September 10, 1935. For her failure to appear and Nils Granlund's collapse, see *The Pittsburgh Press*, September 12, 1935.

307 For the debate over the banning of *Tobacco Road* and Sally's reaction, see *The Nebraska State Journal* (Lincoln), May 21, 1939. *The Press Democrat* (Santa Rosa, California), November 13, 1935, wryly observed: "Anyone sickened by a show usually declines to return for another performance. Sally is among the few who persist in being 'sickened.' "

309 Footnote 11: For articles related to Rev. McKitchen's banning of Sally's bubble dance, see *The Lowell Sun* (Massachusetts), October 15, 1935, and *Motion Picture Daily*, October 18, 1935.

310 The item on Sally's luncheon speech for the Kiwanis Club in Ottawa is from the *Ottawa Journal* (Ontario, Canada), November 9, 1935.

310 The window-breaking incident at Freiman's Department Store was described by Mrs. A. McLewin in a letter to *The Ottawa Journal*, March 24, 1979. Also see Lawrence Freiman's *Don't Fall Off the Rocking Horse: An Autobiography*, McClelland and Stewart (1978).

311-313 Both Sally's speech and the trained dog act were well received by Exchange Club members in Reading, Pennsylvania. For the story, see *The Reading Times*, November 20 & 21, 1935.

313-314 For more on "Big Jim" Colosimo and the colorful characters in his life, see Arthur J. Bilek's *The First Vice Lord: Big Jim Colosimo and the Ladies of the Levee*, Cumberland House (2008), or visit the "Chicago Crime Scenes Project" at www.chicagocrimescenes.blogspot.com .

314 Faith Bacon was interviewed by an unknown "cub reporter" for the June 1936 issue of *The Spotlight*, a monthly magazine published in Chicago for "the world of music and entertainment."

314 See the *Tallahassee Democrat*, March 5, 1936, for more on Sally's brief stop in Florida's capital.

316-317 For Sally's dust up with Zoro Garden nudists, see *The Philadelphia Inquirer* (Pennsylvania) and the *Daily Capital Journal* (Salem, Oregon), April 12 & 13, 1936. For the item from the Zoro Gardens brochure, see *San Diego's Balboa Park* by David Marshall, Arcadia Publishing (2007).

318-319 For items on the 1936 fan dancers' convention, see the *Harrisburg Telegraph* (Pennsylvania) and *The Salt Lake Tribune* (Utah), April 10 & 22, 1936. A short silent video is posted at www.criticalpast.com (search for "fan dancers' convention").

319 Sally's encounters with slingshots and bee stings were extensively publicized. See the *Medford Mail Tribune* (Oregon) and the *Bluefield Daily Telegraph* (West Virginia), April 16, 1936.

319 For the Rosita Royce advertisement, see *The Salt Lake Tribune*, April 20, 1936.

319-320 Among other sources, details of the casting of Calamity Jane for *The Plainsman* are from Wood Soanes' "CURTAIN CALLS" column in the *Oakland Tribune*, May 21, 1936.

CHAPTER THIRTEEN: THE NUDE RANCH AND BEYOND

322-324 Accounts of the Fort Worth Expo — including Carter's exchange with reporters ("when smut actually *was* popular") — are from *Amon: the Texan who Played Cowboy for America* (Rev. Ed.) by Jerry Flemmons, Texas Tech University Press (1998) and *Billy Rose Presents ... Casa Mañana* by Jan Jones, TCU Press (1999).

323 Details on the Casa Mañana café-theater at the Fort Worth Frontier Centennial are from *Billy Rose Presents ... Casa Mañana*.

324 Reviews of Billy Rose's revue at the Texas Frontier Centennial are from *Billy Rose Presents .... Casa Mañana* and "Makin' Whoopee" by Jerry Flemmons in *D Magazine*, April 1978 (available online at: https://www.dmagazine.com/publications/d-magazine/1978/april/makin-whoopee/).

326-327   The story of George Lester seeing Sally's Nude Ranch from atop the Ferris wheel is posted online at: www.texasescapes.com/Texas1930s/FortWorthFrontierCentennial1936.htm .

327   For accounts of the jealousy and outrage felt by the Fort Worth clergy, see "Makin' Whoopee" by Jerry Flemmons in *D Magazine*, April 1978.

327   Tarleton State University history professor Dr. T. Lindsay Baker wrote a column for the local newspaper in Thurber, Texas. He authored the "She's everywhere" quote.

327   *Fort Worth Press* columnist Jack Gordon extolled Sally's many virtues, calling her "an amazingly brilliant woman" in *Billy Rose Presents ... Casa Mañana*.

328-329   Footnote 6: The story of Sally inviting a reporter into her dressing room while she lay naked reading the Bible is from an article by Jerry Flemmons' in *D Magazine*, April 1978.

329-330   The magazine article attributed to Faith Bacon (as told to Lee Mortimer) — "Professional Nude" — was published in *Real Screen Fun*, October 1936.

330-331   Faith Bacon's aversion to men was recounted in *Love of Art and Art of Love: Tullah Hanley's Autobiography*, Piper Publishing (1975).

331-332   The details of Faith Bacon's onstage accident and its aftermath are from a syndicated column by Phil Newsom. See *The Times* (Munster, Indiana), February 25, 1937.

332-333   The story of Sally's battle in the lighting booth is from an unattributed El Paso newspaper clipping dated December 14, 1936, found in one of Sally's scrapbooks.

334   Bishop Schremb's distress at seeing Sally riding in an open car in Cleveland's St. Patrick's Day parade ("I am deeply humiliated") was widely covered. See *Time Magazine*, March 29, 1937.

335   For an ad for *The King's Scandals* at the Oriental Theatre, see page 18 of the *Chicago Tribune*, March 1, 1937. (For the show in Davenport, Iowa, see the *Quad-City Times*, April 22, 1937.)

335-336   Victoria Spencer's brief role as a fan dancer in *The King's Scandals* was reported in *The Hutchinson News* (Kansas), March 1, 1937.

338   Stories related to the Great Lakes Exposition and, in particular, Herman Pirchner's engagement of Faith Bacon to appear on the S.S. Moses Cleaveland may be found online at: http://clevelandmagazine.com/in-the-cle/sex-celebrity-carnival-charm

339   For the anecdote about the governors of Florida and Ohio celebrating "Florida Week" at the Cleveland Exposition, see the *Fort Myers News-Press* (Florida), September 5, 1937.

341   The Cleveland "Torso Murders" were extensively covered (thousands of articles appeared in the U.S., U.K. and Canada). Several books were published. See the website for the Cleveland Police Museum: www.clevelandpolicemuseum.org/collections/torso-murders/.

342   Footnote 18: New York restrictions on publicists were described in *Publicity Stunt! Great Staged Events that Made the News* by Candice Jacobson Fuhrman, Chronicle Books (1989).

345   For Sally's Uniontown, Pennsylvania, arrest, see the *Altoona Tribune* (Pennsylvania). Also see the front page of the *Deadwood Pioneer-Times* (South Dakota), June 17, 1937.

346   For George Ross's column on Sally's foray into summer stock ("SALLY RAND WANTS TO FORSAKE FANS AND TRY STAGE EMOTIONS"), see the *Tallahassee Democrat* (Florida), July 7, 1937.

347   Footnote 22: Popularized by Hedy Lamarr, the catch phrase "I am Tondelayo!" served a generation of female impersonators according to film critic Pauline Kael's book *5001 Nights at the Movies*, Holt, Rinehart and Winston (1982). For Harold W. Cohen's review of the film, see the *Pittsburgh Post-Gazette* (Pennsylvania), August 24, 1937.

347-348   Theresa Wright's comment about Sally in *White Cargo* is from Yvonne Shafer's *Performing O'Neill: Conversations with Actors & Directors*, St. Martin's Press (2000).

348-349   Sally's views on why she didn't need a man in her life ("A man is so biological ...") are paraphrased from an interview she gave the *New York World-Telegram* in September 1937.

349   The account of Faith Bacon and her comedian friends being robbed in Memphis by two "brigands" is from the *Fresno Bee* (California), November 19, 1937.

349-350   For Walter Winchell's specious claim that Sally had a "lovely home in Westport," see his column in the *Muncie Evening Press* (Indiana), January 31, 1938. George Ross's similarly false assertion that she lived "at an expensive midtown hotel" and owned "a country home on Long Island" is from his column in *The Pittsburgh Press* (Pennsylvania), April 29, 1938.

351   James J. Kennedy's review of *Let's Play Fair* ("LION ABOUT TOWN") is from the Columbia University student newspaper, the *Columbia Daily Spectator* (New York City), March 8, 1938.

353-354   The story of Mary Belle Spencer's arrest for assaulting Melvin Draben with a "milk bottle and a hammer" is from *The Daily Reporter* (Greenfield, Indiana), February 8, 1938.

354   Sally's choices for the "10 best undressed women" were named and described in an article, with photos, as published in the *Muncie Evening Press* (Indiana), March 21, 1938.

354   Footnote 25: The column in which Colin Frost listed the Duchess of Kent's measurements ("bust 36, hips 38") is from the *Argus-Leader* (Sioux Falls, South Dakota), August 19, 1954.

CHAPTER FOURTEEN: HERE COMES THE JUDGE

357-359   Sally's appearances at the Harvard Freshman Smoker were reported in *The Harvard Crimson*, May 2-6, 1938, and February 10, 1943.

362   Footnote 4: The story about Alderman John "Bathhouse" Coughlin is from Chicago historian and blogger Troy Taylor. (See: www.prairieghosts.com/graft.html)

363-365   Sally's widely publicized encounter with Roy Stanford and Hazel Drain and their initial appearance before Judge Landreth was syndicated in stories appearing July 14-15, 1938.

365   Removal of Isa Miranda from her starring role led to an international incident when Mussolini threatened to boycott Paramount films for firing her. J. D. Spiro reported her experience in *Screen and Radio Weekly*, a Sunday supplement to *The Detroit Free Press*, July 10, 1938. For more on the "Italian Marlene Dietrich," search for "Isa Miranda" at www.revolvy.com.

366   For Sally's rejection of Cukor's offer to play a can-can dancer in *Zaza*, see the syndicated column by Charles G. Sampas in the *Lowell Sun* (Massachusetts), July 21, 1938.

367-368   Harrison Carroll's syndicated column describing Sally's role (and wardrobe) in *Murder on Sunset Boulevard* is from *The Bristol Daily Courier* (Pennsylvania), August 8, 1938.

368   Hollywood columnist Jimmie Fidler's description of Sally's nonchalance and the crew's indifference to her scanty costume is from *The Chronicle-Telegram* (Elyria, Ohio), August 19, 1938.

370   Sterling Sorensen's review of *Sunset Murder Case* blasting Sally as "the poorest actress" was published in the afternoon edition of *The Capital Times* (Madison, Wisconsin), June 8, 1939.

373-374   For Faith Bacon's claims that she created the fan dance and once let Sally "hold my fans," see her interview with syndicated columnist Frederick C. Othman as published in the *Pittsburgh Press* (Pennsylvania), October 11, 1938. For Faith's accusations that Sally had "deceived the public" and that her dance was an "inferior imitation," see *The St. Louis Star and Times* (Missouri), October 11, 1938, and *The Salt Lake Tribune* (Utah), November 16, 1938.

374-375   Footnote 14: The Speeceville, Pennsylvania, incident involving the death of Sally's dog was reported in *The Evening News* (Harrisburg), October 12, 1938, next to an item about a traveling evangelist who was "tarred and feathered." Details are from the next day's paper.

375   For Sally's reaction to Faith Bacon's charge that Sally had stolen the fan dance idea from her, see *The Pittsburgh Press* and *The Morning News* (Wilmington, Delaware), October 13, 1938.

376   Sally's complaint to L.A. reporters about Faith Bacon is from the *American Weekly*, a Sunday supplement in *The Tennessean* (Nashville), November 27, 1938.

376-377   Sally's second court appearance in L.A. (after her prior failure to appear), her brush with police matron Cheryl Goodwin, and her take on the Faith Bacon lawsuit were covered by *The Courier-Journal* (Louisville, Kentucky), the *Press and Sun-Bulletin* (Binghamton, New York), and the *Jefferson City Post-Tribune* (Missouri), October 18, 1938.

377-378   The *Joplin Globe* announced the display of Sally's pictures at the state capitol in Missouri on October 23, 1938. When they mysteriously disappeared, stories appeared in the *Joplin Globe* and the *Jefferson City Post-Tribune* on October 25th. Volmer Friedheim's column about the incident ("SOMETHING ABOUT NOTHING") was in the *Globe* on October 30th.

378   The willingness of "so many good men and true ... to serve as jurymen at $3 per day" in Sally's "candid camera" trial is from Frederick C. Othman's "JURORS FLOCK TO SEE DUTY WHEN SALLY GOES TO TRIAL." See *The Vidette-Messenger* (Valparaiso, Indiana), October 31, 1938. The sidebar on Orson Welles' *War of the Worlds* radio drama comes from the same issue.

379-381   The widely covered Stanford/Drain case went to trial on November 1, 1938. Many sources contributed to this story. In particular, see Bill Henry's columns in *The Los Angeles Times* and Frederick C. Othman's columns in *The News-Herald* (Franklin, Pennsylvania), *The Sheboygan Press* (Wisconsin) and the *Oakland Tribune* (California), November 1-4, 1938. For Sally's interplay with reporters, see Othman's column in the *Oakland Tribune* ("WHATTA SURPRISE! ....") and see the Madison *Wisconsin State Journal*, both November 2, 1938.

381-384   On the second day of trial, the question of whether Sally would display her dance was resolved and Sally described her struggle. See *The Ogden Standard-Examiner* (Utah), November 2, 1938.

384-385   For the closing arguments presented on day three (when the case went to the jury), see the *Philadelphia Inquirer* (Pennsylvania) and the *Nevada State Journal* (Reno), November 3, 1938.

386   It is apt, if somewhat ironic, that Sally's defense attorney should brand Ray Stanford as a "Peeping Tom"— the character in the Lady Godiva story.

385-386   For the verdict, see the *Chicago Tribune*, November 4, 1938. For the sentence and Sally's reaction, see the *Oakland Tribune*, November 8, 1938.

387   The arguments of Chicago attorney Grace Harte in favor of allowing women to serve on juries can be found in *The Lima News* (Ohio), May 12, 1939.

388   Sally's deposition in response to Faith Bacon's lawsuit was well covered in the press. See the *San Bernardino Daily Sun* (California), November 22, 1938.

389   For the story of Chief Fred Johnson being photographed with Sally and "her showgirls," see the *Oakland Tribune* and *The San Bernardino County Sun*, December 5 & 11, 1938.

389-390   Sally's San Francisco benefit concert with Michio Ito was reported in *The Daily Courier* (Connellsville, Pennsylvania), January 13, 1939, and the *Oakland Tribune* and *Daily Independent* (Murphysboro, Illinois), both January 16, 1939.

390   The account of the revival of the Drain/Stanford lawsuit (upping the ante to a total of $150,747 in damages sought) is from *The San Bernardino County Sun*, March 1, 1939.

391   Sally's nixing the idea of being included as a wax figure in a scene from the 1939 Bob Hope movie *Some Like It Hot* is from *The Pittsburgh Press*, March 29, 1939.

391-392   For Sally's reaction to the revived civil assault case, see the *Ogden Standard-Examiner*, April 2, 1939, and the *Corsicana Daily Sun* (Texas), April 1, 1939.

392   For the dismissal of the Drain-Stanford case, see *The Los Angeles Times*, January 23, 1945.

Chapter Fifteen: Treasure Island

393   For more on Dora Maugham, see *The Pittsburgh Post-Gazette* (Pennsylvania), February 26, 1934. For the announcement of Sally's revue at The Music Box, see *Variety*, December 1938.

394   Find articles on Sally's Treasure Island Nude Ranch in *The San Bernardino County Sun* (California) and the *Hartford Courant* (Connecticut), March 1, 1939. For the story of Sally putting "brassieres" on her "ranch hands," see the *Oakland Tribune* (California) and *The Ogden Standard-Examiner* (Utah), April 28, 1939.

394-395   For the conflicting reactions of fair directors Grover Whalen and Harris Connick to giving Sally a spot at the fair, see *The San Bernardino County Sun*, January 15, 1939.

395-396   For Eleanor Holm's "curve-and-contour contest" challenge, see *The Ottawa Journal* (Ontario, Canada), April 9, 1939, and *The Los Angeles Times*, March 9, 1939. Humorist Cal Tinney's "MAN OF THE WEEK" column is from the *Ogden Standard-Examiner*, March 5, 1939.

396   Faith Bacon's comment that she "would like to come to Harvard" to "dance for them" with a symphony orchestra is from *The Harvard Crimson*, February 25, 1939.

397   Roland Young's jest while watching Sally's nude ranch hands play pingpong is from Harold W. Cohen's "HOLLYWOOD" column in the *Pittsburgh Post-Gazette*, August 16, 1939.

397   Footnote 5: Anton LaVey's boyhood visit to the nude ranch is from *The Secret Life of a Satanist: The Authorized Biography of Anton Szandor LaVey* by Blanche Barton, Feral House (1992).

398   Ernie Pyle's comments about Sally's nude ranch are from his column "THE RAMBLING REPORTER" as published in the *El Paso Herald-Post* (Texas), May 25, 1939.

398-399   Recollections of Jerry Bundsen and George Hubbard are from *The San Francisco Fair: Treasure Island · 1939-1940*, by Patricia F. Carpenter and Paul Totah, Scottwall Associates (1989).

399   For Judge Schauer's comments on the case involving the display of "California World's Fair 39" license plates, see *The Brooklyn Daily Eagle* (New York), February 25, 1940.

400   Faith Bacon's engagement at the Tower Theater in Massachusetts was announced in *The Lowell Sun*, April 12, 1939. Her last-minute costume switch and the resulting suspension of the theater's license were reported in the *Sun*, April 26 and May 3, 1939.

400-402   Some details of Faith's fawn episode are from a Leo Straus story in *Argosy* magazine, November 1957. Others are from *The New York Times*, April 24, 1939.

402   Footnote 6: For the 1988 stunt involving a Gorbachev lookalike and a real estate mogul, see *The New York Times*, December 7, 1988.

402-403 Faith Bacon's fawn dance and the Congress of Beauty concession are from *LIFE Magazine*, May 1 & 8, 1939. For the syndicated account of nudity at the 1939 Fair and Faith Bacon's "wisp of tulle" costume, see *The Hutchinson News-Herald* (Kansas), June 11, 1939. Walter Winchell's column mentioning Faith's *Bare X Ranch Revue* was published from March 31 to April 6, 1939. For notice of the *Oomph Revue*, see *The Evening Review* (Liverpool, Ohio), December 15, 1939.

403 The excerpt from Jack Stinnett's syndicated column on the entertainment zone's profusion of "undraped femininity" is from *The Daily Mail* (Hagerstown, Maryland), June 23, 1939.

403-404 Rev. Mary H. Ellis's report "on things seen and heard" at the New York World's Fair is available online at: www.exhibitions.nypl.org/biblion/worldsfair/story/story-burlesque.

404 Stories about Sally's concessions at Treasure Island are from the feature article "BANG! WENT SALLY'S BUBBLE — AND SHE'S BROKE" in *American Weekly*, the weekend magazine in *The Minneapolis Star* (Minnesota), December 3, 1939.

404 Sally's comments concerning the profitability of her various enterprises are from a syndicated column by Roger Johnson. See *The Eugene Guard* (Oregon), June 21, 1939.

404-405 Sally's Treasure Island speech at the Western Confectioners Association luncheon was described in *The Coast* magazine, June 1939.

405 Sally's speech at the San Francisco Executives Association luncheon was covered by Roger Johnson in the *Santa Cruz Evening News* (California), June 22, 1939.

405-406 Quentin Reynolds' article on Sally's "business acumen" was in *Collier's* magazine, August 26, 1939. For her bankruptcy, see *The Palm Beach Post* (Florida), October 15 & November 5, 1939.

406 Sally's ad promoting her engagement at the Cal-Neva Lodge on the shores of Lake Tahoe is from the *Nevada State Journal* (Reno), July 22, 1939.

407 For Sally's record-breaking flight, see the *Nevada State Journal*, July 31, 1939. (For a photo of Sally with her plane and co-pilot, see *The Minneapolis Star*, August 3, 1939.) Sally's speed record did not last long. A few weeks later, with better weather, Ted Morrill and Vic Williams of Reno beat her flight time by four minutes (see the *Nevada State Journal*, August 25, 1939).

407-408 For stories of Sally's bankruptcy, see *The Philadelphia Inquirer* (Pennsylvania), October 15, 1939, and *The Capital Times* (Madison, Wisconsin), November 22, 1939. Her appearance before Burton J. Wyman is from *The Ogden Standard-Examiner*, November 21, 1939.

408 The poetic frat house invitation and Sally's reply were publicized before her show in Eugene, Oregon. See *The Eugene Guard* ("SALLY FOR HOUSEMOTHER ..."), November 29, 1939.

409 The excerpt from Sally's speech on bankruptcy at a Seattle businessmen's luncheon is from a full-page, illustrated article titled "'BANG!' WENT SALLY'S BUBBLE — AND SHE'S BROKE," in *The Minneapolis Star*, December 3, 1939.

409 Sally's comments to Lloyd Shearer about her financial misfortunes are from his article "THE INDESTRUCTIBLE SALLY RAND" in *Parade* magazine, January 29, 1961.

409-410 For Sally's syndicated column about her bankruptcy as a "nabob of nudity" — "HOW TO GO BROKE ON $174,830 A YEAR" — see *The Palm Beach Post*, December 1, 1939.

CHAPTER SIXTEEN: FAN DANCERS GALORE

411 For more on Lawrence Sittenberg's influence on the fan dance, see the six-page essay in *My Ears Are Bent* by Joseph Mitchell, Sheridan House (1938). The article announcing Joseph Addison's upcoming lecture on "The Passions of the Fan" is from *The Spectator*, June 27, 1711.

412-413 Ken Murray's recollections are from his book, *The Body Merchant: The Story of Earl Carroll,* Ward Ritchie Press (1976).

413 Footnote 5: Sally's inspiration for the fan dance was reported in a widely distributed biographical article. See *The Tallahassee Democrat* (Florida), October 19, 1933.

413 The critique of magazine sketches in the *Drury Lane Pantomime* is from *The Primrose League Gazette* (London, England), February 14, 1891.

413-414 For items on Cyrene, see these papers from Philadelphia, Pennsylvania: *The Philadelphia Inquirer*, April 10, 15 & 17, 1892, and *The Times*, April 24, 1892.

414-415 The story of Edwin Cawston sneaking ostriches out of Cape Town is from local historian Rick Thomas's *South Pasadena's Ostrich Farm,* Arcadia Publishing (2007).

415 The amusing tale of Claire Luce and the runaway ostrich is told in *The Ziegfeld Touch: The Life and Times of Florenz Ziegfeld, Jr.* by Richard and Paulette Ziegfeld, Harry N. Abrams, Inc. (1993). According to the authors, "After the show, the ostrich was sold for $991.11."

415-416   The New Hampshire critique of the *American Beauties Revue* with Aleta Ray is from *The Portsmouth Herald*, September 11, 1929. Her "fan-dance-in-a-church" was reported in the *Daily Illini* (student newspaper for the University of Illinois), the *Medicine Hat News* (Alberta, Canada), and the *Mason City Globe-Gazette* (Iowa), all on January 19, 1935.

416   Footnote 11: Rev. Cutbill's comments are from the *Fitchburg Sentinel* (Massachusetts), January 17, 1935.

416   Footnote 12: For O.O. McIntyre's description of Claire Luce performing a fan dance on a "rolling ship," see *The Miami News* (Florida), February 29, 1928.

417-419   The story of Fay Baker in Helena, Montana, and her account of the origin of the fan dance is from *The Helena Daily Independent*, February 6, 1935. For her ordeal in Manitoba, Canada, see the *Lethbridge Herald*, January 11, 1934, and the *Winnipeg Free Press*, January 15, 1934.

419-420   Thais Giroux's story comes from several sources. See the *Montana Standard* (Butte), December 14, 1928, and the *Great Falls Tribune* (Montana), April 20, 1938. Also see the front page story from the *Mount Carmel Item* (Pennsylvania), April 19, 1938.

421-422   Flo Ash's acquittal for indecent exposure was covered in the *Laredo Times*, February 18, 1934. (See San Antonio's *Express and News*, March 9, 1963, for an article on her defense attorney Leonard Brown.) Her damage suit against Crystal Ames ("CUTEST NUDIST SUES CLAIMANT OF TITLE") is from the *Oakland Tribune* (California), October 20, 1938. Her positive review is from *The Hutchinson News* (Kansas), February 20, 1935.

425   For Jack Diamond's column about Renee Villon ("CAMERA-SHY WHITE HORSE SPOILS LADY GODIVA STUNT"), see *The Pittsburgh Press* (Pennsylvania), May 20, 1936. The story of Franklin Roosevelt, Jr. and the press mix-up of the two Miss Villons is from a King Features Sunday supplement to the *Star Tribune* (Minneapolis, Minnesota), May 17, 1936.

426   For the story of Noel Toy ("the Chinese Sally Rand"), see her obituary in *The Tallahassee Democrat*, January 24, 2004.

426-427   Regarding "the Sepia Sally Rand": Besides Amy Spencer, Sally was also credited as the inspiration for Cab Calloway's "The Lady with a Fan"; see *The Pittsburgh Courier* (Pennsylvania), November 4, 1933. For an article showcasing Noma's return to Harlem, see *The Pittsburgh Courier*, November 18, 1933. For more on Jean Idelle (a.k.a. Shur) fan dancing in her 80s, see *Newsday* magazine online (www.newsday.com/lifestyle/retirement/coram-great-grandma-revisits-burlesque-1.5897570).

430   For a newspaper ad offering Sally $1,000 in cash to join in a "contest of art, talent, and beauty" with "AMPHITRITE," see *The Morning Herald* (Uniontown, Pennsylvania), July 19, 1934.

CHAPTER SEVENTEEN: A NEW BEGINNING

431   For Sally's act at the Florentine Gardens, see the *Titusville Herald* (Pennsylvania) and *Escanaba Daily Press* (Michigan), December 20, 1939 (see *The Los Angeles Times*, January 4, 1940, for ad).

432   Sally's television debut at station W6XAO in Hollywood, California, was reported in the *Long Beach Independent* (California), January 16, 1940.

432-433   Sally's engagement at the Orpheum Theatre in L.A. was described in *The Los Angeles Times*, February 15 & 22, 1940.

433   For Sally's excursion to Mexico City ("SALLY WILL WAVE PEACOCK PLUME SOUTH OF THE BORDER"), see the *El Paso Herald-Post* (Texas), March 11, 1940. The story of how she hocked her fans to get there is from *The Los Angeles Times*, February 29, 1940. Her return home was reported in the *Taylor Daily Press* (Texas), May 28, 1940.

434   The debate over Sally's "Nude Ranch" at the Golden Gate Exposition ("SALLY RAND'S VERBAL FIREWORKS …") is from the *Oakland Tribune* (California), May 23, 1940. For the fair's opening, including Sally's role in the ribbon cutting, see the *Tribune* from May 26, 1940.

434   For Faith Bacon's announcement that she hoped to serve in the war as a nurse or ambulance driver, see the *Petaluma Argus-Courier* (California), July 2, 1940.

435   Footnote 2: The account of Sally's being "knocked for a loop" by Valentinoff is from the *Olean Times-Herald* (New York), August 20, 1940.

435   For Dorothy Kilgallen's "VOICE OF BROADWAY" column describing dancer Valya Valentinoff as Sally's "closest fan," see *The News-Herald* (Franklin, Pennsylvania), July 14, 1941.

436   Sally's auto crash on an icy road in Janesville, Wisconsin, was reported in "NOTHING TO MAR SALLY" from the *Wisconsin State Journal* (Madison), January 23, 1941.

436 The Georgia Legislature's special resolution honoring Sally was covered in the *Ogden Standard-Examiner* (Utah), February 13, 1941. See "SALLY VISITS STATE SENATE."

437 The Duke of Windsor's reported reaction to his appointment as Governor of The Bahamas is from Michael Bloch's *The Duke of Windsor's War*, Coward-McCann (1983).

437 For columnist H. I. Phillips' remark about Sally's club engagement in Miami ("... people are flocking to see her!"), see the *Arizona Republic* (Phoenix), March 7, 1941.

438-439 Sally's presence at the Duchess of Windsor's charity concert in Nassau is from Geoffrey Bocca's *The Woman who Would Be Queen*, Rinehart & Company (1954). Sally's perspective is from a column she wrote in the summer of 1950 for the University of Wisconsin's *Daily Cardinal*.

440 The anecdote about Sally's press agent asking the Duke of Windsor's aide-de-camp whether the Duke would pose for a picture with Sally is from *LIFE Magazine*, June 9, 1941.

440 Many papers covered the Nassau "Match of Champions," including the *Tallahassee Democrat* (Florida), March 6, 1941.

440 Footnote 5: The comment about the Duke as "the head man at Nassau" is from "NEAL O'HARA SAYS..." — a column in the *Altoona Tribune* (Pennsylvania), July 18, 1940.

441-442 Sally's playful abduction by a group of young MIT men ("DOUBLE SNATCH BY TECH ...") was covered by the student newspaper *The Tech*, May 9, 1941.

442-444 Sally's account of her experience at the Harvard Freshman Smoker in 1941 is from the *Harvard Crimson*, February 10, 1943.

443-444 Sally's banning from Boston night spots and her reaction was covered in *The Wilkes-Barre Record* (Pennsylvania) and the *Fitchburg Sentinel* (Massachusetts), both May 17, 1941.

445 For the story of Monsignor Lodes barring Sally from a USO dance in St. Louis, Missouri, see *The Times* (Shreveport, Louisiana), September 13, 1941.

445 Footnote 10: President Truman's reaction to Sally's show is from the Truman papers at the Harry S. Truman Library and Museum (searchable at www.trumanlibrary.org).

445 Footnote 11: The 2011 report on predatory priests is from "Thy Child's Face" — a website sponsored by Michael Wegs, an investigative blogger focusing on "the sexual violence inflicted on children by predatory Roman Catholic priests."

445-446 Alice Greenough's interview with syndicated columnist Robert Geiger ("A CANDID TALK WITH A COWGIRL") is from the *Portsmouth Daily Times* (Ohio), October 23, 1939.

CHAPTER EIGHTEEN: THE COWBOY AND THE LADY

447-449 Sally's meeting with Turk Greenough at the North Montana State Fair is from an unpublished book by Michael Amundsen, *Broncs, Broadway and B Westerns* (1993). For her appearance at the fair and a photo of her standing by her fireworks display with Art Briese, see pages 1 & 5 of *The Great Falls Tribune* (Montana), August 8, 1941. For a picture of Sally in her cowgirl regalia, see James M. Reich's *Billings (Postcard History Series)*, Arcadia Publishing (2009). For Sally leading the rodeo parade, see the *Great Falls Tribune*, August 6, 1941.

449 Sally's visit with Turk's family was reported in the *Great Falls Tribune*, August 17, 1941.

449-450 Sally and Turk's engagement was well covered. For early banns, see the *Montana Standard* (Butte) and *The Sandusky Register* (Ohio), October 1, 1941. Helen Greenough's reaction is from *The Brooklyn Daily Eagle* (New York) and the *Oakland Tribune* (California), October 3, 1941. Inez Robb wrote extensive columns: "SALLY RAND ... COWHAND'S BRIDE" in *The Courier-Journal* (Louisville, Kentucky), October 10, 1941, "AN OLD COW HAND" in the *St. Louis Post-Dispatch* (Missouri), October 15, 1941, and "THAT COW HAND SWEETHEART ...." in the *American Weekly* magazine, supplement in *The Tennessean* (Nashville), November 2, 1941.

450-451 The account of Sally's phone call with Helen Greenough is from a clipping in Sally's scrapbooks, apparently published in New York on January 4, 1942.

452 The interview of Sally and Turk is from Inez Robb's "THAT COW HAND SWEETHEART ...."

452 Details in the sidebar on the roundup and arrest of Japanese individuals in the U.S. and Hawaii after Pearl Harbor are from reports in *The St. Louis Star and Times* (Missouri), December 8, 1941, and *The Los Angeles Times* (California), March 14, 1942.

456-458 For Sally and Turk's wedding, see: *The Abilene Reporter-News* (Texas), the *Berkeley Daily Gazette* (California) and the *Evening Observer* (Dunkirk, New York), January 5, 6 & 7, in turn.

457 Excerpts from the 1985 interview of Turk Greenough are from Tom Ringley's *When the Whistle Blows: The Turk Greenough Story*, Pronghorn Press (2008).

458   The quote about Turk and Sally's first night together as a married couple is from an unpublished book by Michael Amundsen, *Broncs, Broadway and B Westerns* (1993). Sally's claim that she might be pregnant is from *The Post-Register* (Idaho Falls), February 19, 1942.

458-459   A 45-second video of Sally at the Puyallup Daffodil Festival is posted under "502798071" on the Videos page at www.gettyimages.com. For details on the relocation center ("Camp Harmony"), see: www.historylink.org/File/8748 or look up "Puyallup (detention facility)" at "Densho Encyclopedia" — a website on the history of Japanese Americans in WWII.

463   Sally's tardy arrival to her bankruptcy hearing was reported in *The Press Democrat* (Santa Rosa, California), May 16, 1942. The story of her $64,000 bankruptcy debt and her surrendered assets ("$200 worth of beads") is from the *Oakland Tribune*, May 28, 1942.

463-464   The story of Sally's visit to Fort Riley, Kansas, is from William Allen White's "OUR DEMO-CRATIC ARMY" in *The Anniston Star* (Alabama), August 6, 1942. Also see the *Montana Standard*, April 25, 1942, and *The Emporia Gazette* (Kansas), June 22, 1942.

464-465   Sally's desire to "raise a family" and "do something useful in the war effort" was reported in the *Tulsa Tribune* (Oklahoma), September 18, 1942.

465-466   For a demonstration of the Panoram and its inner workings and to view some "soundies," search for "Panoram soundies" on YouTube. Add "Sally Rand" or "Faith Bacon" for their films.

467-468   Turk's unhappy experiences in the Army and his medical discharge were documented in Tom Ringley's *When the Whistle Blows: The Turk Greenough Story*.

469   Sally's acquired knowledge of ranching was on display in an interview she gave to Peggy Wright of the New York City daily paper *PM* on an undetermined date in 1943.

470   The sarcastic column on birthday "wishes" sent by the press to Adolph Hitler — including Sally's featured response — was in *The Mason City Globe-Gazette* (Iowa), April 20, 1943.

470-471   For Sally's widely covered clash with the Chicago Historical Society over the donation of her fans, see the *Chicago Tribune* and *The Ottawa Journal* (Ontario, Canada), October 12, 1943.

471-472   The story of the war's impact on specialty dancers ("SORRY PLIGHT OF THE RATION-STRICKEN SIRENS") is from the *American Weekly* in the *San Antonio Light* (Texas), June 6, 1943. Sally's personal dispute with the local ration board over her dancing shoes (and her "rescue" by the Spanish dancer Margo) got broad press coverage. See *The Courier-Journal* (Louisville, Kentucky), March 13, 1943, and *The Nebraska State Journal* (Lincoln), March 14, 1943.

472   Sally's generous support of the bond drive in Hagerstown, Maryland, was reported by the local paper *The Daily Mail*, September 23, 1943.

472-473   Sally's plan to go to North Africa as a USO entertainer for the troops, and her response to the War Department's rejection, is from the *Piqua Daily Call* (Ohio), October 21, 1943.

473-474   Footnote 12: For the story of Disneyland comic Wally Boag and Julie Andrews, see the comedian's obituary from *The Los Angeles Times*, June 7, 2011.

475   For Dorothy Kilgallen's comment about Turk and Sally's estrangement, see the *Times Herald* (Olean, New York), December 28, 1944. The feature story on their separation ("TOO MUCH FAME FOR TURK'S GAL, SAL") is from the *American Weekly* in the *San Antonio Light*, February 11, 1945. Erskine Johnson's hint that they might reconcile is from the Dunkirk *Evening Observer*, February 22, 1945. Jimmie Fidler's query about their feud is from his column in *The St. Louis Star and Times* (Missouri), March 12, 1945.

476   News of Sally and Turk's divorce is from *The Billings Gazette* (Montana), June 28, 1945, and the *Daily Journal-Gazette* (Mattoon, Illinois), June 29, 1945. The description of their amicable divorce agreement is from Tom Ringley's biography *When the Whistle Blows: The Turk Greenough Story*. The couple's post-divorce friendship was described by Michael Amundsen in his 1993 unpublished book, *Broncs, Broadway and B Westerns*.

CHAPTER NINETEEN: SAWDUST AND SIDESHOWS

477-478   The bosom-baring styles of designer Renie were debated in "EVENING GOWNS ARE MORE DARING" from the *Camden News* (Arkansas), January 31, 1946. For more, including Eunice Skelly's reaction, see "TO WEAR OR NOT TOO BARE ..." in *The Pittsburgh Press* (Pennsylvania), February 1, 1946. A photo of Jane Greer modeling a Renie gown was posted in the *Daily Register* (Harrisburg, Illinois), February 4, 1946. For reaction from Gypsy Rose Lee and Ann Corio, see *The Rhinelander Daily News* (Wisconsin), February 6, 1946. Renie's admission that her idea was a "horrible bust" is from *The Daily Herald* (Provo, Utah), July 2, 1947.

479-480   For Sally's El Cerrito nightclub venture, see *Billboard* magazine, March 16, 1946. For the club's bankruptcy and ensuing lawsuits, see the *Oakland Tribune* (California) August 25, 1946.

480-481   Jake Ehrlich's courtroom argument is reconstructed from Ehrlich's autobiography, *A Life in My Hands*, G.P. Putnam's Sons (1965) and from *Never Plead Guilty: The Story of Jake Ehrlich* by John Wesley Noble and Bernard Averbuch, as published by Farrar, Straus & Cudahy (1955).

483   Footnote 7: The history of Hennies Midway attractions is from *The Daily Plainsman* (Huron, South Dakota), September 6, 1934

483-484   For the story of Harry Hennies falsely accusing Sally of attempted burglary, see *The Philadelphia Inquirer* (Pennsylvania), April 22, 1947, and the *News-Press* (Fort Myers, Florida), April 25, 1947. For Hennies' penalty for abusing court processes, see *The Waco News-Tribune* (Texas) and *The Courier-Journal* (Louisville, Kentucky), both April 25, 1947.

484   For the story of the four Iowa girls who quit Sally's show in Illinois, see *The Morning News* (Wilmington, Delaware) and *The Des Moines Register* (Iowa), both August 12, 1947.

484   Statistics on the reception of Sally's show at the Iowa State Fair are from the column "FAIR CHRONOLOGY" in *Billboard* magazine, January 3, 1948.

484-485   The announcement that Sally had purchased a home in Key West and would soon become a Florida resident is from *The Miami News* (Florida), November 14, 1947.

485   Footnote 9: The story of President Truman at the "Little White House" seeking to eliminate "undesirables" from "preying on" Key West sailors is from an oral history interview with *New York Daily News* reporter Frank Holeman. See "Truman Papers" at: www.trumanlibrary.org.

485   Faith Bacon's letter to General Patton is found in *The Button Box: A Daughter's Loving Memoir of Mrs. George S. Patton* by Ruth Ellen Patton Totten, University of Missouri (2005).

485-486   For the dilemma over what to do with Henry Bacon's donated sculptures, see "FAITH BACON'S 9-TON NUDES" by Edward S. Sullivan, *American Weekly* Sunday supplement, July 8, 1945.

488-489   Information on the attendance and proceeds earned on Negro Day at the 1950 State Fair of Texas is from *Billboard* magazine, October 28, 1950.

489-490   Leon Claxton's traveling show *Harlem in Havana* is described in a memorial tribute to Claxton in *Jet* magazine, November 30, 1967.

489   Footnote 13: The comparison of Leon Claxton to Tyler Perry is from an article by Paul Guzzo originally published February 8, 2015, and posted on www.TBO.com — an online publication of the *Tampa Bay Times* (Florida).

490   The reference to Sally in *Harlem in Havana* is from her personal diary, October 13, 1952.

490-494   Sally's account of her years with traveling carnivals is from a draft in her personal files.

494   Sally's tale of two carnies walking down the road in the rain is told in *Life Upon the Wicked Stage: A Sociological Study of Entertainers* by Jacqueline Boles, iUniverse (2010).

496-497   The description of the "front" for Faith Bacon's "featured gal show" with John R. Ward's World's Fair Shows in 1948 is from *Billboard* magazine, March 13, 1948.

497   For Faith Bacon's lawsuit over "scattered tacks" and the aftermath, see Illinois papers *The Pantagraph* (Bloomington), June 6, 1948, and *The Decatur Herald* (Decatur), June 9, 1948.

497-498   For the escape of German POWs from the Arizona desert camp, see the *Arizona Republic* (Phoenix), December 25, 1944, the *Reno Gazette-Journal* (Nevada) and *The Vernon Daily Record* (Texas), both January 30, 1945, and *The New York Times*, December 4, 1995. Or, see: www.historynet.com/the-not-so-great-escape-german-pows-in-the-us-during-wwii.htm

500   Footnote 23: The story of the star-studded show at the Shrine Auditorium in Hollywood to raise money for the Movie Relief Fund is from *Billboard* magazine, April 23, 1949.

501   The item in Dorothy Kilgallen's "VOICE OF BROADWAY" column about Sally launching a lecture series is from *The Record-Argus* (Greenville, Pennsylvania), March 24, 1949.

502-503   For Rosemary "Kurt" Orban's fatal bus accident near Refugio, Texas, see the *Valley Morning Star* (Harlingen, Texas) and *The Monitor* (McAllen, Texas), both November 27, 1949.

504-505   For Al Wagner's Cavalcade of Amusements (with Sally's revue) see the *Akron Beacon Journal* (Ohio), July 26, 1950, and *Greater Show World*, Vol. XXXIII, No. 9, September 1950. The IRS tax lien filed against Sally for unpaid taxes due on her income from 1947 & 1948 was reported by Verle E. Ludwig for the *Kokomo Tribune* (Indiana), July 27 & 28, 1950.

507-508   Sally's appearance at the Harvard Smoker was reported in *The Pittsburgh Press*, February 24, 1951. Her reaction to the penny tossing episode is from the *Ogden Standard-Examiner* (Utah), February 25, 1951. Her later turn with Tom Lehrer at the Old Howard was mentioned in Gerald Nachman's *Seriously Funny: The Rebel Comedians of the 1950s and 1960s*, Pantheon (2003).

509   Footnote 29: The story of Stomp Gordon's Jim Crow lawsuit against the Last Chance Club in Anchorage, Alaska, was reported in *Jet* magazine, September 30, 1954.

509   Wil Stevens' observation about Sally's show at Seattle's Palomar Theatre is from *Billboard* magazine, July 28, 1951.

509   Sally's speaking appearances while she was performing at the Missouri State Fair were covered by the *Sedalia Democrat* (Missouri), August 21 & 22, 1951. Items in the *Mexico Ledger* (Missouri) described Governor Forrest Smith's plans to attend Sally's show (despite protests) and conveyed the governor's approval of the show, August 21 & 23, 1951.

510   For a display ad billing Sally as "Her Sexellency" while she was performing at the Kansas State Fair, see *The Hutchinson News-Herald* (Kansas), September 16, 1951.

510-511   Midway attractions at the Kansas State Fair were described in *The Hutchinson News-Herald* on September 14, 1951. Decades later, an article describing state 4-H director Glenn Busset's introduction to Sally at the 4-H building appeared in *The Hutchinson News*, September 13, 1980. At Busset's retirement, another article was published in *The Salina Journal* on April 5, 1981.

511   For the story of Sally's $2,548.57 dispute with Dallas carnival operator Ray Marsh Braydon, see *The Hutchinson News-Herald*, September 20, 1951.

512   Recollections of Virgil Miller, Secretary of the 1951 Kansas State Fair, are from an interview conducted decades later and published in *The Hutchinson News*, September 6, 1987.

512-513   For Paul Murphy's lengthy column about Sally's adventures at the Kansas State Fair, see *The Hutchinson News-Herald* on September 9, 1951. Sally's cow-milking quote is from *The Tennessean* (Nashville), September 21, 1952. Ernest Dewey's article was published in that paper the next day.

513-514   Lawrence Marcus's department store dressing room encounter with Sally ("MANY STORIES TALL") was recounted by Alan Peppard in the *Dallas Morning News* (Texas), September 10, 2007. Blogger Michael N. Marcus (no relation) posted the story online the next day as "Neiman Marcus Opens for Business" in his blog "For the First Time."

514   Sally's case for hiring an experienced and competent business manager is from a draft on carnival life in her personal files.

CHAPTER TWENTY: WHEN SALLY MET HARRY

515   The 1947 arrest of Sally Rand and Harry Finkelstein for disorderly conduct was reported in the *Ottawa Journal* (Ontario, Canada), August 16, 1947.

515-516   Georgia Sothern's story of her early passion for Harry Finkelstein is from her memoir *Georgia: My Life in Burlesque*, New American Library/Signet (1972).

516   H.L. Mencken's response to Ms. Sothern's letter (the sidebar on the origin of "ecdysiast") is from a syndicated column by George H. Beale. See *The Pittsburgh Press*, April 19, 1990.

517   Sally's feud with Harry Hennies ("IT LOOKS LIKE SALLY AND HARRY HAVE REACHED THE W.K. IMPASSE") was reported in *Billboard* magazine, August 23, 1947.

517-519   Sally's "disorderly conduct" incident in Springfield was widely covered. See "STRIP-TEASERS FIGHT OVER MAN" in the *Sarasota Herald-Tribune* (Florida) and "FAN DANCER SALLY NABBED IN HOTEL...." from *The Pittsburgh Press* (Pennsylvania), August 17, 1947. Her post-hearing press conference (offering reporters a "good girl" defense) and Magistrate Conway's comments are from *The Galveston Daily News* (Texas), *The Belvidere Daily Republican* (Illinois) and the *Logansport Pharos-Tribune* (Indiana), August 19 & 20, 1947.

519-520   Details of the Fort Smith tourist court incident are from a clipping in Sally Rand's personal scrapbooks of a news item from the *Fort Smith Times Record*, September 24, 1948. Also see the *Statesville Daily Record* (North Carolina), September 23, 1948.

520-521   Georgia's mid-act summons is from the *Long Beach Independent* (California), January 23, 1949. For Dorothy Kilgallen's column, see *The Pittsburgh Post-Gazette*, January 31, 1949. Georgia's bankruptcy was reported in the *St. Louis Star and Times* (Missouri), February 3, 1949.

521-522   Sally's Milwaukee arrest was well covered. See *The Journal News* (White Plains, New York) and the *Traverse City Record-Eagle* (Michigan), both July 14, 1950. Also see the *Chicago Tribune*, July 14, 1950, and *The Republic* (Columbus, Indiana), July 15, 1950.

522   Sally and Harry's courthouse marriage in Toledo, Ohio, was covered worldwide. See the *Toledo Blade*, August 22, 1950. Also see the *Palm Beach Post* (Florida) and Australia papers the *Daily News* (Perth) and the *Morning Herald and Miner's Advocate* (Newcastle), August 23, 1950. *Billboard* magazine published a small notice of the union, September 2, 1950.

522   Footnote 5: Julian Cole's idea for using a live dolphin to promote Miami Dolphins' football scores was described by Tom C. Brody for *Sports Illustrated*, August 8, 1966.

546   For Dorothy Kilgallen's widely published "ON BROADWAY" item revealing that Harry and Georgia would "try it again," see the *Pittsburgh Post-Gazette*, December 13, 1951.

546-547   Details of the dissolution of Sally's marriage to Harry Finkelstein are from a February 9, 1954, letter from Sally to Marshall Bridges, the attorney who handled the annulment.

CHAPTER TWENTY-ONE: AND BABY MAKES TWO

549   For the Holly Knox version of how Sally happened to adopt a baby, see *Sally Rand: From Film to Fans* by Holly Knox, Maverick Publications (1988). For yet another version, see *Behind the Burly Q* by Leslie Zemeckis, Skyhorse Publishing (2013).

550-551   Lorie Barnes' recollections are from interviews conducted by Bonnie Egan in 2012 and 2013.

551-552   Sean Rand's public debut in Jackson, Mississippi, was reported coast to coast and beyond. See Jackson's *Clarion-Ledger*, October 13, 1948, *The Honolulu Star-Advertiser* (Hawaii), October 14, 1948, *The Winnipeg Tribune* (Manitoba, Canada), October 21, 1948, and *Billboard* magazine, October 23, 1948. The *Billboard* article also asserted that Sally had previously adopted a baby girl who had died a week after birth.

552-553   The lengthy article about Sean ("FAN DANCING SALLY RAND BRINGS HER MYSTERY BABY TO MILWAUKEE") was published on March 31, 1949, in the *Milwaukee Journal* (Wisconsin).

553   The story of Sean's biological father's accidental death is from Bonnie Egan's interview of Sean.

553   Sally's Key West adventures with the Navy are described in *Key West: Conch Smiles* by Jeane Porter, Mancorp Publishing (1999).

554   The Certificate of Birth for "Robert Hepler" was filed with the Monroe County Registrar on August 16, 1948, as certified by the Florida Bureau of Vital Statistics on August 30th.

555-562   Sean Rand's recollections are from a series of interviews conducted in 2012 by Bonnie Egan.

557   Footnote 9: For the story of Elvis's 1956 appearance as "The Atomic Powered Singer" at the Venus Room of the Frontier Hotel, see *The Los Angeles Times*, August 5, 2007.

562   For Glenna Syse's column "ODD PAIR PAIRED," describing an informal Chicago "interview" of Sally Rand and Margaret O'Brien, see *The Pittsburgh Press*, September 7, 1966.

566   The poem Sally left for Sean was "The Answer" by Fleur Conkling Heyliger (commonly called "The Adoption Poem"), as published in the April 5, 1952 edition of the *Saturday Evening Post*.

CHAPTER TWENTY-TWO: SALLY IN LALLALAND

568   The debut of Sally's revue at the Chi Chi Starlite Room was announced in *The Desert Sun* (Palm Springs, California), February 21, 1952.

568   Faith Bacon's appearance at the Park Burlesque in Youngstown, Ohio, was advertised in *The Salem News* (Salem, Ohio), February 21, 1952.

568-569   Faith Bacon's episode in 1952 involving Edward and Tullah Hanley are from Tullah's autobiography *Love of Art & Art of Love*, Piper Publishing (1975).

569   The review of Sally's engagement at the Texas State Fair (referencing Betty Lou Williams, "the four-legged girl") is from *Billboard* magazine, October 18 & 25, 1952.

569   Footnote 1: The witty quip about Sally's taxes is from Erskine Johnson's syndicated column. See *The Rhinelander Daily News* (Wisconsin), August 15, 1950.

570   Sally's clash with Bishop Joseph Willging was reported in the *Albuquerque Journal* (New Mexico), September 8, 1953.

577-578   Faith Bacon's rescue from an "accidental" overdose of sleeping pills was reported in *The Republic* (Columbus, Indiana), March 3, 1954.

580   Sally's work with TV stations KLAS and KPRC is documented in the Sally Rand Papers at the Chicago History Museum, Biographical/Historical Note and Box 35, Folders 2-11.

581   For information on *Confidential* magazine and publisher Robert Harrison ("the King of Leer"), see "Confidential's Reign Of Terror" by Neal Gabler in *Vanity Fair*, April 1, 2003.

582   Stories on the Lalla divorce, Sally and Fred's marriage, and Mae Lalla's threat to charge Fred with bigamy were widely reported. See *The Los Angeles Times*, August 13, 1954. Also see *The Bakersfield Californian* and the *Nevada State Journal* (Reno), both August 14, 1954.

583   The destruction by fire of Sally's truck carrying her stage and props was reported in the "Fairs-Expositions" section of *Billboard* magazine, September 11, 1954.

585-586   For reports of the auctioning of Sally's Key West lots to pay off a $10,000 tax lien, see *The Sandusky Register* (Ohio), July 2, 1954, and the *Tallahassee Democrat* (Florida), July 6, 1954.

586   Sally's second bankruptcy was widely covered, publicized coast to coast for two weeks. For an early article, see the *Reno Gazette-Journal* (Nevada), October 14, 1954.

590   Footnote 9: Ms. Hanley's remark that, when she died, Faith Bacon was sharing her room with "a 'butch' lesbian" is from Tullah's memoir *Love of Art & Art of Love*.

590-591   Faith Bacon's last hours in Chicago were well publicized. In Indiana, see *The Times* (Hammond and Munster), September 26-27, 1956, and the *Anderson Herald*, September 30, 1956.

592   The Lalla divorce was covered in *The Miami News* (Florida) and *The Reno Gazette-Journal*, August 16 & 20, 1960, respectively. For Sally and Fred's post-divorce friendship, see *Parade* magazine in the *Independent Press-Telegram* (Long Beach, California), January 29, 1961.

594   Footnote 11: Fred Lalla's disqualification for election to the Covina City Council was reported in the *Independent Star-News* (Pasadena, California), March 2, 1958.

595   The 1981 interview describing Fred Lalla's aversion to work is from the Steve Quillen papers.

596   The account of Sally's robbery by an intruder (a "shoeless Negro") while she was working at the Gayety Theatre in Baltimore is from *The Baltimore Sun* (Maryland), May 27, 1957. For the burglary of Sally's home in Glendora, see the *Covina Argus* (California), May 23, 1957.

601   The movie magazine calling Sally a "comedy vamp" was *The Reel Journal*, January 5, 1924.

601-602   Sally's uncredited essay on the pitfalls of marriage (as she filled in for advice columnist Carolyn Chatfield) is from the *Daily Press* (Newport News, Virginia), May 8, 1937.

CHAPTER TWENTY-THREE: THE SIXTIES

603   The chapter's epigraph ("Wouldn't it be wonderful to find the moment …?") is from Donald Kaul's interview of Sally; see *The Des Moines Register* (Iowa), September 14, 1969.

603   Sally's poolside interview with Bob Thomas was widely reported. See the *Lima News* (Ohio), July 14, 1958, and the *Arizona Republic* (Phoenix), July 16, 1958.

603-604   The story of Sally's influence on pantyhose is from *The People's Almanac Presents The 20th Century: History with the Boring Parts Left Out* by David Wallechinsky, Overlook Press (1999). For an online excerpt, see: www.vice.com/en_us/article/4wag4b/peoples-lists-v15n4 .

604   Sally's remarks about a woman's sex appeal in her 50s are from "THE INDESTRUCTIBLE SALLY RAND," Lloyd Shearer's interview for *Parade* magazine. See the *Independent Star-News* (Pasadena, California), January 29, 1961.

604-605   Sally's speech to the Phoenix Exchange Club is from the *Arizona Republic*, February 22, 1962.

608   The story of future President Bill Clinton backing up Sally's Hot Springs show is from an article about George Gray in *The Indianapolis Star* (Indiana), February 16, 1993, pages D1 and D2.

609-610   Photographic evidence of Sally's appearance in Houston to welcome the seven Mercury astronauts is in the July 11, 1962, issue of NASA's *Space News Roundup* (vol. 1, No. 19).

610-611   Sally's remarks to the Brazoria County Bar Association about the emotional needs of entertainers ("WE'RE ALL REJECTED PEOPLE") are from *Brazosport Facts* (Texas), August 7, 1962.

611   The report of the luncheon meeting of the Exotique Dancers League of North America is from *The Los Angeles Times* and *The Akron Beacon Journal* (Ohio), November 13 & 14, 1963.

612-613   Sally's comments on carnival life are from the *Santa Cruz Sentinel* (California), March 15, 1964, and the *Asbury Park Press* (New Jersey), April 11, 1964.

613   For performers in town during the 1964 Democratic Convention, see the *Pittsburgh Post-Gazette* (Pennsylvania), August 24, 1964. On November 23, 2013, local writer Steven Lemongello wrote about Pinky Kravitz escorting Sally to the convention floor. See: www.pressofatlanticcity.com .

613   For Jim Becker's syndicated column about the girls in skimpy bathing suits on Atlantic City beaches competing with Sally's act, see the *Hartford Courant* (Connecticut), August 25, 1964. (He also quipped that her show would be followed by a "more sedate group" — the Beatles.)

614   For Sally's appearances on shows hosted by Art Linkletter and Regis Philbin, see *The Pensacola News* (Florida), September 5, 1964, and the *Tucson Daily Citizen* (Arizona), January 29, 1965. For an item on the Beatles' show flanked by the Democratic National Convention and the Miss America Pageant, see the *Courier-Post* (Camden, New Jersey), August 29, 1964.

614-616   For Sally's indecent exposure arrest at age 61, see the *Omaha World-Herald* (Nebraska), July 10, 12 & 17, August 31, and September 26, 1965. Also see the *Janesville Daily Gazette* (Wisconsin), July 10, the *Arizona Republic*, July 11, and *The Lincoln Star* (Nebraska), September 1, 1965.

616   For Sally's appearance with Joey Faye in *Anatomy of Burlesque*, see the *Fort Lauderdale News* (Florida), July 22 and August 24, 1967, and the *Hartford Courant*, July 30, 1967. Her comment about Vietnam is from *Miami Herald* (Florida), August 20, 1967.

616   Footnote 13: For measurements of Sally's fans, see the *Desert Sun* (Palm Beach, California), February 8, 1964, and Bella Kelly's column in *The Miami News*, August 24, 1967.

617-618   Stories of Sally and Kenneth Marlowe are from his autobiography, *Mr. Madam: Confessions of a Male Madam*, Sherbourne Press (1964) and from *Call Me Kate: The Story of Katherine Marlowe, a Transexual*, a biography by "Nelson" published by Writers Club Press (1999).

618   For the notice and review of Sally's Fort Worth appearance in *A Funny Thing Happened on the Way to the Forum* see the *Lubbock-Avalanche-Journal* (Texas), July 14 & 21, 1968.

618-619   The anecdote of Sally relishing a "Dutch Baby" pancake is from Jay Wallace's recollections in the Steve Quillen papers.

622   Sally's enduring popularity was predicted by Stanley Walker in his book, *Mrs. Astor's Horse*, Blue Ribbon Books (1935).

622   Sally waxed eloquent about her life at age 65 in an interview with columnist Donald Kaul. See "MISS RAND IS FINE, THANK YOU" in *The Des Moines Register*, September 14, 1969.

CHAPTER TWENTY-FOUR: GIRLS JUST WANT TO HAVE FUN

632-633   For the early career of "Sunny Van" Hedenkamp, her sister Meta, and her husband Mischa Markoff, see *The Brooklyn Daily Eagle* (New York), November 18, 1931.

639   Comedian Hilda Vincent's appearance on *The David Frost Show* was in TV listings nationwide. She was twice featured in "My Favorite Jokes," a column for *Parade Magazine*. For her jokes, see the *Albuquerque Journal* (New Mexico), October 3, 1971, or June 17, 1973.

CHAPTER TWENTY-FIVE: HER SEXELLENCY

641, 645   For Carol Doda's story, see *The Los Angeles Times*, November 12, 2015.

641-642   Sally's denunciation of nudists in 1934 was reported in Joseph Mitchell's *My Ears Are Bent*, Sheridan House (1934). Also see *The Pittsburgh Press* (Pennsylvania), March 11, 1934.

642-643   The story of Sally's 1949 booklet "How to be a Good Girl in a Big City" was widely covered. See Robert Musel's column in the *Waukesha Daily Freeman* (Wisconsin), March 22, 1949.

643-644   For articles on Sally's run-in with the liquor board in Canton, Ohio, see Ohio papers: *The Akron Beacon*, December 3, 1951, and *The Tribune* (Coshocton), December 5, 1951.

645-646   For more on the topic of cosmetic breast implant surgery, see *Breasts: A Natural and Unnatural History* by Florence Williams, W.W. Norton & Co. (1994).

648   Footnote 7: Sally's casual attitude about nudity is from a draft in her files for an article she wrote for the Canadian magazine *City Lights* (circa 1935).

650   Footnote 8: Sally's comments about her attitude toward the Women's Liberation Movement are from an interview with Al Allen. See the *Oakland Tribune* (California), July 1, 1976.

651   Sally's observations on the explicit performances of striptease dancers (and "snappers") are from *Show Business Laid Bare* by Earl Wilson, G.P. Putnam's Sons (1974).

652   The press conference with Sally in Louisville, Kentucky ("If an act gets raunchy ...") led to a charming column by Billy Reed in *The Courier-Journal*, April 23, 1975.

652   An interview with Robert McMorris published in the *Omaha World-Herald* on July 12, 1965, included Sally's remarks about strippers being "emotionally disturbed people."

652-653   Sally's notions about what constitutes sexual attractiveness are from an interview she gave to columnist Charles Witbeck. See the *Asbury Park Press* (New Jersey), April 12, 1964.

653   "The Weaker Sex" is an unpublished essay from the collection of Sally's papers in the possession of her son, Sean Rand.

654   For the observations of Sally's Japanese maid Stella describing the "two classes of people coming to see" Sally's act, see *The Salt Lake Tribune* (Utah), February 25, 1934.

CHAPTER TWENTY-SIX: THE TOAST OF GLENDORA

655   The chapter's epigraph is of unknown origin, but it may have come from female impersonator Charles Pierce, who appeared with Sally in 1974 and was known to use the line in a sendup of a Tallulah Bankhead-Bette Davis feud.

655-656 The notion that Sally chose to move to Glendora because it was near Azuza is from *Sally Rand: From Film to Fans* by Holly Knox, Maverick Publications (1988).

656   The 1954 California Living Show with the "Sally Rand Home" was advertised throughout the state. See the *Long Beach Independent* (California), August 12, 1954.

664   Footnotes 10 and 11: The quoted material in these footnotes, as well as in the relevant text, is from the Steve Quillen papers.

665   Footnote 12: Gene Bell's story is from his obituary in the *Los Angeles Times*, June 29, 1995.

CHAPTER TWENTY-SEVEN: A GAY OLD TIME

667   For articles on *The Big Show of 1928*, see *The San Bernardino County Sun* (California), December 3, 1971, *The Los Angeles Times* (California), December 29, 1971, and *The Morning News* (Wilmington, Delaware), January 26, 1972.

667-668 The critique of *The Big Show of 1936* at Felt Forum is from Dan Dietz's *Off Broadway Musicals, 1910-2007*, McFarland & Co., Inc. (2009). Leif Erickson's review of Sally's "shapely, supple and bouncy" act is from *The Los Angeles Times*, August 1, 1972. Andy Israel's column calling the show a "museum piece" is from *The Stanford Daily*, August 4, 1972.

668   An ad for the Phoenix House Benefit ("Golden, Olden Days ...") was published in *The New York Times*, May 27, 1973. For Earl Wilson's comment about seeing Sally at the benefit, see his column "Wilson's Last Night" in *The Daily Reporter* (Dover, Ohio), June 7, 1973.

669-670 The episode at Man's Country, a gay bathhouse in Chicago, is from *Leatherman: The Legend of Chuck Renslow* by Tracy Baim & Owen Keehnen, CreateSpace Independent Publishing (2011).

670-671 The story of the fundraiser for Ken Marlowe's surgery is recounted in *Call Me Kate: The Story of Katherine Marlowe, a Transexual*, a biography by "Nelson," Writers Club Press (1999).

671-672 Sally's birthday party at the Dorothy Chandler Pavilion was widely publicized. See the *Evening Herald* (Shenandoah, Pennsylvania) and the *Springfield Leader and Press* (Missouri), both April 6, 1974. For Alan Cartnal's review of the Sally Rand-Charles Pierce Show at the pavilion, see *The Los Angeles Times*, April 9, 1974.

673   Sally's "same old fanny" quip appeared in an item about her 71st birthday bash from *The Galveston Daily News* (Texas), April 5, 1975. The wisecrack was also in an Earl Wilson column ("BEST LAUGHS OF THE FIRST HALF OF 1975") from the same paper on July 13, 1975.

673   Sally's remarks to guests at her 71st birthday party at Buddy Kirk's Steak House in Galveston, Texas, were widely reported. See the *Arizona Republic* (Phoenix), April 3, 1975.

674   The review of Sally's stage role as psychiatrist Tracey Lake in the murder mystery *Night Watch* is from *The Daily Chronicle* (DeKalb, Illinois), January 30, 1976.

674-675 For an item on the auction of burlesque memorabilia at the Folly Theater in Kansas City, Missouri, see *The Kansas City Times*, May 28, 1976.

675   The part Sally played in the 1976 Bicentennial Galaxy Ball was covered in the *Denton Record-Chronicle* (Texas), May 28, 1976. Search for "Sally Rand" at www.like2do.com for an online account of Sally's role in MidAmeriCon — the 34th World Science Fiction Convention.

675   For Sally's 1976 visit to Columbia College (Christian College) to celebrate her 50th reunion, see: *Friends: Special Sesquicentennial Issue (The Gates of Change, 1851- 2001)*, online at: www.ccis.edu (search for "sesquicentennial"). For images and descriptions of Sally's school and classmates, see pages 17-27. There is even a tribute to the imposing Luella St. Clair Moss.

675   Sally's performances at Detroit's Royal Ascot Supper Club at the age of 73 produced a well-reported reaction from older women. See the *Detroit Free Press* (Michigan), August 22, 1977.

675   In the fall of 1977, Sally's "convalescence for a lung ailment" in the Henry Ford Hospital in Detroit was extensively covered. See *The Journal News* (White Plains, New York), September 7, 1977, and *The Orlando Sentinel* (Florida), September 21, 1977.

676 Winston Collins described Sally's late-life baptism in "The Fan Dancer," written for *Weekend Magazine*, as circulated in Canada. See the *Winnipeg Free Press* (Manitoba), February 3, 1979.

Chapter Twenty-eight: The Last Dance

679-680 For Sally's choice of Sandy Duncan to play her in a TV biopic, see *The Corpus Christi Caller-Times* (Texas), October 6, 1975. (Connie Stevens and Shirley MacLaine were her other choices.)

680 For an item on Sally's performance at the Chicago Theater fundraiser for Chicago Area Theatre Organ Enthusiasts, see the *Chicago Tribune*, September 25, 1978.

680 For Sally posing at the age of 74 for art students at Chicago's American Academy of Art, see Laura Green's *Chicago Sun-Times* column in the *St Louis Post-Dispatch*, September 24, 1978.

680 The poem by John Walter III was inspired by his son's untimely death at the age of 25 (John Walter IV fell through the ice at Bearwood Lake while trying to rescue his brothers). The sad story may be found online at: www.arborfieldhistory.org.uk/families_john_walter_4.htm

680-683 Winston Collins wrote of Sally's "gala evening" at Loew's State Theatre (including her late-night confab) in "The Fan Dancer," published on February 3, 1979, in the *Weekend Magazine* as distributed in Canada. See the *Winnipeg Free Press* or *The Ottawa Journal* (Ontario).

683 For the controversy over the Winston Collins' article and the associated "Fifty Years of Striptease" by Bill Gladstone which led many Canadian papers to dump the *Weekend Magazine* supplement, see *The Lethbridge Herald* (Alberta), February 2 and 5, 1979.

684 Sally's New Mexico performance at age 75 was described by Guenevere McMahon in her blogpost on January 25, 2014. (See: https://artfullydressed.wordpress.com/2014/01/25/aging-when-your-body-is-your-commodity/) Also see "SALLY: AN AMERICAN CLASSIC RETURNS" from the *Albuquerque Journal*, April 20, 1979.

686-688 Jasper Vance's account of his photo shoots in June of 1979 is from a transcription of Vance's interview in the Steve Quillen papers. A picture of Sally posing with Barbara Hanks and looking "quite ecstatic" may be seen in *The Salina Journal* (Kansas), June 19, 1979.

689-690 For Sally's extensively covered home interview with Hollywood reporter Bob Thomas a month before her death, see *The St. Louis Dispatch*, August 6, 1979.

691 Footnote 11: For the Christie Mitchell column titled "A HOT LETTER FROM SALLY RAND," see the *Galveston Daily News,* May 5, 1975.

Epilogue

694 DeMille's recollection of his early days in silent films is from *The Autobiography of Cecil B. DeMille*, as edited by Donald Hayne, Prentice-Hall (1959).

695 Footnotes 2 & 3: The amazing stage and iconic neon sign at the Earl Carroll Theater in Hollywood are described on a website dedicated to the producer (www.earlcarrollgirls.com).

695-696 Billy Rose's consideration of Gene Kelly as a candidate for choreographer was described in *Gene Kelly: A Life of Dance and Dreams* by Alvin Yedkoff, Billboard Books (2001).

696 For Billy Rose's widely covered relationship with Eleanor Holm, see *The Orlando Sentinel* (Florida), July 25, 1954.

699 Erica Curless's article on Poppy Wilde ("POPPY LIVES ON IN MOVIES AND IN FAMILY'S HEART") is from *The Spokesman-Review* (Washington State and northern Idaho), September 9, 2000.

699-700 Jimmie Thatch's personal and military history is from *Thach Weave: The Life of Jimmie Thach* by Steve Ewing, Naval Institute Press (2004).

701 Hedda Hopper's item about boxer "Bill Wolf" is from *The Los Angeles Times*, January 8, 1949.

702-703 Fay Baker's marriage to Royal Canadian Mountie John Leslie (and subsequent annulment) was covered in a series of Canadian articles in 1934 in *The Winnipeg Tribune* (Manitoba), April 24 & 25, May 3, and June 29 and in *The Ottawa Journal* (Ontario), May 11.

703-704 For the death of Thais Giroux, see *The Escanaba Daily Press* (Michigan) and the *Chicago Tribune*, both April 20, 1938, and the *Muncie Evening Press* (Indiana), April 25, 1938.

704 The story of Ray Giroux's murder-suicide lunacy after his daughter's death is from the *Montana Standard* (Butte), October 18, 1940. Also see these Montana papers: *The Independent Record* (Helena), *Montana Standard*, and *Great Falls Tribune*, October 19, 22, and 26, 1940.

704-705   Flo Ash's divorce, marriage, and subsequent divorce were widely covered. For her divorce from Wilson, see *The Los Angeles Times* and *Lansing State Journal* (Michigan), January 26, 1944, and the *Nevada State Journal* (Reno), January 27, 1944. For her marriage and divorce from Gentile, see the *Kingsport Times* (Tennessee), November 6, 1947. Flo's appearance (and mirror dance) at the Crystal Inn in 1953 was promoted in *The Bakersfield Californian*, February 26, 1953.

705   The item on Renee Villon's dancing "before the royalty of Europe" and advertising her appearance at the New 51 Club is from *The Brooklyn Daily Eagle* (New York), August 7, 1942.

705   For Noel Toy styled as the "ornamental Oriental," see Dorothy Kilgallen's column in the *Star-Gazette* (Elmira, New York), December 9, 1941. Toy's marriage to Carleton Young was announced in *The Los Angeles Times*, December 20, 1945. Her real estate career was recognized in that paper on May 3, 1992.

705   Footnote 10: The quote by Carleton Young's character in the classic James Stewart/John Wayne movie *The Man Who Shot Liberty Valence* can be seen on YouTube.

706-707   Legal proceedings between Manuel Herrick and Ethelyn Chrane are from *The Okie Jesus Congressman* by Gene Aldrich, Times-Journal Publishing (1974). California reports on the search for Herrick's body (and its recovery) are from the *Indian Valley Record*, February 14 & March 6, 1952, respectively. For detailed accounts (and tidbits on his life), see the *Feather River Bulletin* from February and March 1952 at: www.newspapers.com.

707   From November 1933 through 1934, thousands of stories were printed on Dr. Alice Wynekoop, her son Earle, and her murdered daughter-in-law Rheta. For her confession, see *The Piqua Daily Call* (Ohio), November 24, 1933; for the verdict, see the *Chicago Tribune*, March 7, 1934.

707   For Judge David's attempts to keep Chicago from becoming "a second Reno" and details on his death, see *The Evening Courier* (Champaign, Illinois), February 18, 1938.

707-708   Prof. Milton W. Hamilton's PhD was awarded in June 1936; see the *Reading Times* (Pennsylvania), May 22 and June 6, 1936. For his naming as Senior Historian, see *The Ithaca Journal* (New York), June 1, 1950. For his obituary, see *The New York Times*, February 28, 1989.

708   Michio Ito's arrest was reported in *The Independent Record*, December 18, 1941. For his obituary, see *The Honolulu Advertiser* (Hawaii), November 8, 1961.

708-709   Georgia Sothern was well remembered after her death. See the *Democrat and Chronicle* (Rochester, New York), October 19, 1981.

709   Sally's memorial benefit in Lawton, Oklahoma, for her former secretary, Anita Robertson, was reported by Bill Crawford in *The Lawton Constitution*, September 16, 1975. For Miss Robertson's death notice, see the paper's issue from February 19, 1974.

710   Stories about Mary Belle Spencer's divorce from Dr. Richard Spencer and the tumult surrounding his death and funeral were widely published. See *The San Antonio Light* (Texas), August 6, 1937, and *The Oshkosh Northwestern* (Wisconsin), July 12, 1938.

710-711   Details of Faith Bacon's relationship with Edward and Tullah Hanley are from *Love of Art and Art of Love* by Tullah Hanley, Piper Publishing Inc. (1975).

711   For an article about Ralph Hobart (Sally's "Major-Domo" and childhood friend), see *The Reading Times*, April 12, 1935.

713   Information about Turk Greenough and his sisters is from Turk's biography, *When the Whistle Blows: The Turk Greenough Story*, by Tom Ringley, Pronghorn Press (2008).

AFTERWORD

717   For the story of the turn-of-the-century French superstar Mistinguett, see *The Mistinguett Legend* by David Bret, St. Martin's Press (1991).

717   For the life of Ethel Merman, the Broadway diva and entertainer extraordinaire, see *Ethel Merman: A Life* by Brian Kellow, Penguin Books, reprint edition (2008).

717   For a personal memoir by The Divine Miss M (a "kind of last hurrah"), see *A View from A Broad* by Bette Midler, Simon & Schuster (2014).

717   English romance novelist and screenwriter Elinor Glyn defined the term "It Girl" — as applied to Clara Bow and other charismatic figures — in the February 1927 issue of *Cosmopolitan*.

Selected Bibliography

MAGAZINE ARTICLES

"$380,000 Suits for Sally – Can't Wear One of 'Em," *American Weekly* (November 27, 1938).

"A Fan Dancer Talks," *True Confessions* (July 1935): 28-29, 89.

"'BANG!' Went Sally's Bubble – And She's Broke," *American Weekly* (December 3, 1939).

Collins, Winston, "The Fan Dancer," *Weekend Magazine* (February 3, 1979).

"Failed When She Wore Clothes, Succeeds When She Doesn't," *American Weekly* (September 24, 1933).

Flemmons, Jerry, "Makin' Whoopee," *D Magazine* (April 1978).

Holden, Stan, "America's Oldest Stripper," *Cabaret* (December 1955): 10-14, 46-47.

Rand, Sally, "Bubbles Become Big Business," *American Review of Reviews* (April 1935).

Schaeffer, Sam, "Sally Rand and Her Lalla-Pop," *Whisper* (June 1956): 8-9, 49-50.

Shteir, Rachel, "Material Girl," *Chicago* (October 2004): 103-105, 140, 150-154.

"Sorry Plight of the Ration-Stricken Sirens," *American Weekly* (June 6, 1943).

Straus, Lou, "Faun in the Afternoon," *Argosy* (November 1957): 26-27, 70-73.

Sullivan, Edward S., "Faith Bacon's 9-Ton Nudes," *American Weekly*, July 8, 1945.

BOOKS

Carlton, Donna, *Looking For Little Egypt*, Bloomington, IN: IDD Books, 1995.

Cotter, Bill, *Chicago's 1933-34 World's Fair: A Century of Progress*, Arcadia Publishing, 2015

Flemmons, Jerry, *Amon: The Texan Who Played Cowboy for America*, Texas Tech University Press, 1998.

Ganz, Cheryl R., *The 1933 Chicago World's Fair: A Century of Progress*, University of Illinois Press, 2008.

Hoefling, Larry J., *Nils Thor Granlund: Show Business Entrepreneur and America's First Radio Star*, Jefferson, NC: McFarland & Company, Inc., 2010

Jones, Jan, *Billy Rose Presents: Casa Manana*, Fort Worth: Texas Christian University Press, 1999.

Kinney, William Howland, *Chicago Jazz: A Cultural History, 1904-1930*, New York: Oxford University Press, 1993

Knox, Holly, *Sally Rand: From Film to Fans*, Bend, OR: Maverick Publications, 1988.

Marlowe, Kenneth, *Mr. Madam: Confessions of a Male Madam*, Los Angeles: Sherbourne Press, 1964.

Murray, Ken, *The Body Merchant: The Story of Earl Carroll*, Pasadena: Ward Ritchie Press, 1976.

Nelson, Richard, *Call Me Kate: The Story of Katherine Marlowe, a Transexual*, San Jose: Writers Club Press, 1999.

Price, Ryan Lee, *Stories of Old Glendora*, History Press, 2012.

Ringley, Tom, *When the Whistle Blows — The Turk Greenough Story*, Pronghorn Press, 2008.

Shteir, Rachel, *Striptease: The Untold History of the Girlie Show*, Oxford: Oxford University Press, 2004.

Sothern, Georgia, *Georgia: My Life in Burlesque*, New American Library/Signet, 1972.

Stencell, A.W., *Girl Show: Into the Canvas of Bump and Grind*, Canada: ECW Press, 1999.

Terkel, Studs, *Hard Times: An Oral History of the Great Depression*, New York: Pantheon Press, 1970.

Traversi, David C., *One Man's Dream: The Spirit of the Rubel Castle*, Strange Publications, 2003.

Walker, Stanley, *Mrs. Astor's Horse*, New York: Blue Ribbon Books, Inc., 1935.

Zemeckis, Leslie, *Behind the Burly Q: The Story of Burlesque in America*, Skyhorse Publishing, 2013.

Ziegfeld, Richard, *The Ziegfeld Touch: The Life and Times of Florenz Ziegfeld, Jr.*, Harry N. Abrams, Inc., 1993.

Index

Between the 1920s and the 1950s, Sally compiled
dozens of oversized scrapbooks filled with news
clippings and other material documenting her career

The 1933 "Century of Progress" was not the first World's Fair to be held in Chicago. In the summer of 1893, the "Columbian Exposition" had enchanted more than 25 million attendees with its "White City" and abundance of enticing attractions. On "Chicago Day" alone, more than 750,000 had visited the grounds — a record at the time.

On July 3, 1893, just as festivities at the Columbian Exposition were reaching full swing, Missouri Governor William J. Stone was issuing a pardon to young William F. Beck, who for eighteen months had been serving time in the Missouri State Penitentiary for the murder of Thomas Mashburn.

Meanwhile, as the 19-year-old Beck was about to begin life anew, never imagining he would one day father the star-touched little girl known to us as Sally Rand, the celebrated band master John Philip Sousa was holding forth at the Columbian Exposition, delighting his audience with a rendition of the most popular tune of the day:

> After the ball is over,
> After the break of morn,
> After the dancers' leaving,
> After the stars are gone,
>
> Many a heart is aching –
> If you could read them all.
> Many the hopes that have vanished
> After the ball.